THE

ART OF C

MA

PLAIN ai

Which far excels any Thing

CONTAINING,

I. A Liſt of the various Kinds of Meat, Poultry, Fiſh, Vegetables, and Fruit, in Seaſon, in every Month of the Year.
II. Directions for Marketting.
III. How to Roaſt and Boil to Perfection.
IV. Sauces for all plain Diſhes.
V. Made Diſhes.
VI. To dreſs Poultry, Game, &c.
VII. How expenſive a French Cook's Sauce is.
VIII. To make a Number of pretty little Diſhes for Suppers, or Side or Corner Diſhes.
IX. To dreſs Turtle, Mock-turtle, &c.
X. To dreſs Fiſh.
XI. Sauces for Fiſh.
XII. Of Soups and Broths.
XIII. Of Puddings and Pies.
XIV. For a Lent Dinner; a Number of good Diſhes, which may be made uſe of at any other Time.
XV. Directions for the Sick.
XVI. For Captains of Ships; how to make all uſeful Diſhes for a Voyage; and ſetting out a Table on board.
XVII. Of Hog's Puddings, Sauſages, &c.
XVIII. To pot, make Hams, &c.
XIX. Of Pickling.
XX. Of making Cakes, &c.
XXI. Of Cheeſecakes, Creams, Jellies, Whipt Syllabubs.
XXII. Of Made Wines, Brewing, Baking, French Bread, Muffins, Cheeſe, &c.
XXIII. Jarring Cherries, Preſerves, &c.
XXIV. To make Anchovies, Vermicelli, Catchup, Vinegar, and to keep Artichokes, French Beans, &c.
XXV. Of Diſtilling.
XXVI. Directions for Carving.
XXVII. Uſeful and valuable Family Receipts.
XXVIII. Receipts for Perfumery, &c.

IN WHICH ARE INCLUDED,

One Hundred and Fifty new and uſeful RECEIPTS, not inſerted in any former Edition.

WITH A COPIOUS INDEX.

By Mrs. GLASSE.

A NEW EDITION,
With all the MODERN IMPROVEMENTS:
And alſo the ORDER of a BILL of FARE for each Month; the Diſhes arranged on the Table in the moſt faſhionable Style.

LONDON:
Printed for T. Longman, B. Law, J. Johnſon, G. G. and J. Robinſon, H. Gardner, T. Payne, F. and C. Rivington, J. Sewell, W. Richardſon, W. Lane, W. Lowndes, G. and T. Wilkie, W. Nicoll, W. Fox, Ogilvy and Speare, J. Debrett, J. Scatcherd, Vernor and Hood, Clarke and Son, J. Nunn, J. Barker, B. Croſby, Cadell and Davies, and E. Newbery.

1796.

TO THE

READER.

I Believe I have attempted a branch of Cookery, which nobody has yet thought worth their while to write upon: but as I have both ſeen, and found by experience, that the generality of ſervants are greatly wanting in that point, therefore I have taken upon me to inſtruct them in the beſt manner I am capable; and, I dare ſay, that every ſervant who can but read, will be capable of making a tolerable good cook, and thoſe who have the leaſt notion of Cookery cannot miſs of being very good ones.

If I have not wrote in the high polite ſtyle, I hope I ſhall be forgiven; for my intention is to inſtruct the lower ſort, and therefore muſt treat them in their own way. For example, when I bid them lard a fowl, if I ſhould bid them lard with large lardoons, they would not know what I meant; but when I ſay they muſt lard with little pieces of bacon, they know what I mean. So in many other things in Cookery, the great cooks have ſuch a high way of expreſſing themſelves, that the poor girls are at a loſs to know what they mean: and in all Receipt Books yet printed, there are ſuch an odd jumble of things as would quite ſpoil a good diſh; and indeed ſome things ſo extravagant, that it would be almoſt a ſhame to make uſe of them, when a diſh can be made full as good, or better, without them. For example: when you entertain ten or twelve people, you ſhall uſe for a cullis, a leg of veal and a ham; which, with the other ingredients, makes it very expenſive, and all this only to mix with other ſauce. And again, the eſſence of ham for ſauce to one diſh; when I will prove it, for about three ſhillings I will make as *rich and high a ſauce as all that will be, when done. For example:*

Take a large deep ſtew-pan, half a pound of ham, fat and lean together, cut the fat and lay it over the bottom of the pan; then take a pound of veal, cut it into thin ſlices, beat it well with the back of a knife, lay it all over the ham; then have ſix-penny-worth of the coarſe lean part of the beef cut thin, and well beat, lay a layer of it all over, with ſome carrot, then the lean of the ham cut thin and laid over that; then cut two onions and ſtrew over, a bundle of ſweet herbs, four or five blades of mace, ſix or ſeven cloves, a ſpoonful of all-ſpice or Jamaica pepper, half a nutmeg beat, a pigeon beat all to pieces, lay that all over, half an ounce of truffles and morels, then the reſt of your beef, a good cruſt of bread toaſted very brown and dry on both ſides: you may add an old cock beat to pieces; cover it cloſe, and let it ſtand over a ſlow fire two or three minutes, then pour on boiling water enough to fill the pan, cover it cloſe, and let it ſtew till it is as rich as you would have it, and then ſtrain off all that ſauce. Put all your ingredients together again, fill the pan with boiling water, put in a freſh onion, a blade of mace, and a piece of carrot; cover it cloſe, and let it ſtew till it is as ſtrong as you want it. This will be full as good as the eſſence of ham for all ſorts of fowls, or indeed moſt made diſhes, mixed with a glaſs of wine, and two or three ſpoonfuls of catchup. When your firſt gravy is cool, ſkim off all the fat, and keep it for uſe.——*This falls far ſhort of the expence of a leg of veal and ham, and anſwers every purpoſe you want.*

If you go to market, the ingredients will not come to above half a crown; or for about eighteen-pence you may make as much good gravy as will ſerve twenty people.

Take twelve-penny-worth of coarſe lean beef, which will be ſix or ſeven pounds, cut it all to pieces, flour it well; take a quarter of a pound of good butter, put it into a little pot or large deep ſtew-pan, and put in your beef: keep ſtirring it, and when it begins to look a little brown, pour in a pint of boiling water; ſtir it all together, put in a large onion, a bundle of ſweet herbs, two or three blades of mace, five or ſix cloves, a ſpoonful of all-ſpice, a cruſt of bread toaſted, and a piece of carrot; then pour in four or five quarts of water, ſtir all together, cover cloſe, and let it ſtew till it is as rich as you would have it; when enough, ſtrain it off, mix it with two or three ſpoonfuls of catchup, and half a pint of white wine; then put all the ingredients together again, and put in two quarts of boiling water, cover it cloſe, and let it boil till there is about a pint; ſtrain it off well, add it to the firſt, and give it a boil together. This will make a great deal of good rich gravy.

You may leave out the wine, according to what uſe you want it for; ſo that really one might have a genteel entertainment for the price the ſauce of one diſh comes to; but if gentlemen will have French *cooks, they muſt pay for* French *tricks.*

A Frenchman *in his own country will dreſs a fine dinner of twenty diſhes, and all genteel and pretty, for the expence he will put an* Engliſh *lord to for dreſſing one diſh. But then there is the little petty profit. I have heard of a cook that uſed ſix pounds of butter to fry twelve eggs; when every body knows (that underſtands cooking) that half a pound is full enough, or more than need be uſed: but then it would not be* French. *So much is the blind folly of this age, that they would rather be impoſed on by a* French *booby, than give encouragement to a good* Engliſh *cook!*

I doubt I ſhall not gain the eſteem of thoſe gentlemen; however, let that be as it will, it little concerns me; but ſhould I be ſo happy as to gain the good opinion of my own ſex, I deſire no more; that will be a full recompence for all my trouble: and I only beg the favour of every lady to read my Book *throughout before they cenſure me, and then I flatter myſelf I ſhall have their approbation.*

I ſhall not take upon me to meddle in the phyſical way farther than two receipts, which will be of uſe to the public in general, one is for the bite of a mad dog; and the other, if a man ſhould be near where the plague is, he ſhall be in no danger; which, if made uſe of, will be found of very great ſervice to thoſe who go abroad.

Nor ſhall I take upon me to direct a lady in the œconomy of her family; for every miſtreſs does, or at leaſt ought to know, what is moſt proper to be done there; therefore I ſhall not fill my Book *with a deal of nonſenſe of that kind, which I am very well aſſured none will have regard to.*

I have indeed given ſome of my diſhes French *names to diſtinguiſh them, becauſe they are known by thoſe names: and where there is a great variety of diſhes, and a large table to cover, ſo there muſt be a variety of names for them; and it matters not whether they be called by a* French, Dutch, *or* Engliſh *name, ſo they are good, and done with as little expence as the diſh will allow of.*

I ſhall ſay no more, only hope my Book *will anſwer the ends I intend it for; which is to improve the ſervants, and ſave the ladies a great deal of trouble.*

PREFACE

TO THE

PRESENT EDITION.

NOTWITHSTANDING the vast number of books on the subject of Cookery, which are every day presented to the public, Mrs. GLASSE's Work has continued to maintain a decided preference: The reason of this must be obvious to every one on comparison, when they observe that, in point of quantity, her Book exceeds every one in print, by at least one half, and in point of usefulness, beyond all comparison; insomuch that many persons who have been induced for the sake of novelty, or by the sound of a name, to try other publications, have on experiment laid them on the shelf, and returned to their old director, as more easy, comprehensible, and useful.

But, as there is a fashion in Cookery, as well as every thing else; and it is as well to know nothing, as not to know the most modern improvements in the art, this edition has been undertaken to give all the additional information which can be communicated; and so to improve the established receipts, as to make them of general use, and entitle them to increased approbation: For this purpose, upwards of one hundred and fifty new Receipts are given in this Book, all of them useful, and highly genteel and ornamental.

That some few of these have been taken from other publications, the Editor does not pretend to deny; but the greater part are original, collected and improved during a service of eighteen years in the most respectable families: If those taken for this edition from other printed books were to be restored, it would only diminish the size of the volume by a very few pages; but if all they have borrowed from our book, and put into theirs, in a worse form, were to be taken away, many a large and high-priced publication would shrink to a bulk no greater than a child's spelling book.

In this edition, the greatest care has been taken to unite elegance with œconomy, and to enable the Housekeeper to make a fashionable appearance at as small an expence as possible; an object highly desireable in all classes of life, as unnecessary profusion is a mark of folly rather than generosity.

Great pains have also been taken to arrange the subjects, so as to introduce one by another, and to enable people to find what they want without much difficulty; and the care bestowed on the Index and table of Contents, will render it easy to find whatever is wanted in a moment's search.

CONTENTS.

CHAP. I.

Containing a Liſt of the various Kinds of MEAT, POULTRY, FISH, VEGETABLES, *and* FRUIT, *in Seaſon, in every Month of the Year.*

CHAP. II.

Directions for Marketting.

CHAP. III.

Roaſting, Boiling, &c.

To

CHAP. IV.

Sauces for all the Dishes mentioned in the foregoing Chapter.

CHAP.

CHAP. V.

Made Dishes.

CHAP. VI.

To dress Poultry, Game, &c.

To

CHAP.

CHAP. VII.

Shewing how expensive a French Cook's Sauce is.

CHAP. VIII.

Pretty little Dishes.

CHAP. IX.

Turtle, Mock Turtle, &c.

CHAP. X.

Fish.

CHAP. XI.

Sauces for Fish.

CHAP. XII.

Soups and Broths.

CHAP. XIII.

Puddings, Pies, &c. which are not included in the Lent Chapter, on account of their being made with Meat, Suet, &c.

CHAP. XIV.

For Lent, or a Fast Dinner, a Number of good Dishes, which may be made use of for a Table at any other Time.

Almond

CHAP. XV.

Directions for the Sick.

CHAP. XVI.

For Captains of Ships.

CHAP. XVII.

Hogs' Puddings and Saufages.

CHAP. XVIII.

To Pot, make Hams, &c.

CHAP. XIX.

Pickling.

CHAP. XX.

Of making Cakes, &c.

CHAP. XXI.

Of Cheesecakes, Creams, Jellies, Whipt Syllabubs, &c.

CHAP.

CHAP. XXII.

Of Made-Wines; Brewing; Baking French Bread and Muffins; Cheese, &c.

CHAP. XXIII.

Jarring Cherries, Preserves, &c.

To

CHAP. XXIV.

To make Anchovies, Vermicelli, Catchup, Vinegar; and to keep Artichokes, French Beans, &c.

CHAP. XXV.

Distilling.

CHAP. XXVI.

NECESSARY DIRECTIONS *whereby the Reader may easily attain the* ART OF CARVING.

CHAP. XXVII.

Useful and valuable Family Receipts.

CHAP. XXVIII.

Receipts for Perfumery, &c.

An

The ORDER *of a* MODERN BILL *of* FARE, *for each Month, in the* MANNER *the* DISHES *are to be placed upon the* TABLE.

JANUARY.

FIRST COURSE.

	Cheſnut Soup.	
Small Leg of Houſe Lamb.	Petit Patties.	Boiled Chickens.
Chicken and Veal Pie.	Cod's Head.	Tongue.
Rabbits ſmothered with Onions.	Raiſolds.	Porcupine Beef.
	Vermicelli Soup.	

SECOND COURSE.

	Roaſt Turkey.	
Marinated Smelts.	Tartlets.	Mince Pies.
Roaſt Sweetbreads.	Stands of Jellies.	Larks.
Almond Tort.	Maids of Honour.	Lobſters.
	Woodcocks.	

THIRD COURSE.

	Morels.	
Artichoke Bottoms.	Dutch Beef ſcraped.	Macaroni.
Cuſtards.	Cut Paſtry.	Black Caps.
Scolloped Oyſters.	Potted Chars.	Stewed Celery.
	Rabbit Fricaſſeed.	

FE-

FEBRUARY.

FIRST COURSE.

	Peas Soup.	
Curry.	Chicken Patty.	Veal Blanquets.
Small Ham.	Salmon and Smelts.	Chickens.
Pork Cutlets Sauce Robert.	Oyſter Patties.	Harrico.
	Soup Santè.	

SECOND COURSE.

	Wild Fowl.	
Cardoons.	Diſh of Jelly.	Stewed Pippins.
Scolloped Oyſters.	Epergne.	Ragout Mele.
Comport Pears.	Caromel.	Artichoke Bottoms.
	Hare.	

THIRD COURSE.

	Two Woodcocks.	
Craw-fiſh.	Aſparagus.	Preſerved Cherries.
Pigs' Ears.	Crocant.	Lamb Chops larded.
Blanched Almonds and Raiſins.	Muſhrooms.	Prawns.
	Larks à la Surpriſe.	

MARCH.

MARCH.

FIRST COURSE.

Soup à la Reine.

Beef Olives.	Almond Pudding.	Fillet of Pork.
Boiled Turkey.	Stewed Carp or Tench.	Small Ham.
Veal Collops.	Beaf Steak Pie.	Calves' Ears forced.

Gravy Soup.

SECOND COURSE.

A Poulard larded and roaſted.

Aſparagus.	Blanc-mange.	Prawns.
Ragooed Sweetbreads.	A Trifle.	Fricaſſee of Rabbits.
Craw-fiſh.	Cheeſecakes.	Fricaſſee of Muſhrooms.

Tame Pigeons roaſted.

THIRD COURSE.

Ox Palates ſhivered.

Tartlets.	Potted Larks.	Stewed Pippins.
Cardoons.	Jellies.	Spaniſh Peas.
Black Caps.	Potted Partridge.	Almond Cheeſecakes.

Cocks'-Combs.

APRIL.

FIRST COURSE.

Crimp Cod and Smelts.

Chickens.	Marrow Pudding.	Cutlets à la Maintenon.
Breaſt of Veal in Rolio.	Spring Soup.	Beef Tremblant.
Lambs' Tails à la Baſhemel.	Pigeon Pie.	Tongue.
	Roaſt Beef.	

SECOND COURSE.

Ducklings.

Aſparagus.	Tartlets.	Black Caps.
Roaſt Sweetbreads.	Jellies and Syllabubs.	Oyſter Loaves.
Stewed Pears.	Tanſey.	Muſhrooms.
	Ribs of Lamb.	

THIRD COURSE.

Petit Pigeons.

Muſhrooms.	French Plums.	Piſtachio Nuts.
Marinated Smelts.	Sweetmeats.	Oyſter Loaves.
Blanched Almonds.	Raiſins.	Artichoke Bottoms.

Calves' Ears à la Braiſe.

MAY.

FIRST COURSE.

	Calvert's Salmon broiled with Smelts round.	
Rabbits with Onions.	Veal Olives.	Collared Mutton.
Pigeon Pie raiſed.	Vermicelli Soup.	Macaroni Tort.
Patties.	Ox Palates.	Matelot of Tame Duck.
	Chine of Lamb.	

SECOND COURSE.

	Fricaſſeed Chickens.	
Aſparagus.	Cuſtards.	Cocks' Combs.
Green Gooſeberry Tarts.	Epergne.	Green Apricot Tarts.
Lamb Cutlets.	Blanc-mange.	Stewed Celery.
	Green Gooſe.	

THIRD COURSE.

	Lambs' Sweetbreads.	
Stewed Lettuce.	Rheniſh Cream.	Raſpberry Puffs.
Lobſters ragooed.	Compoſt of Green Apricots.	Buttered Crab.
Lemon Cakes.	Orange Jelly.	French Beans.
	Ragout of fat Livers.	

JUNE.

FIRST COURSE.

	Green Peas Soup.	
Chickens.	Haunch of Venison.	Harrico.
Lamb Pie.	Turbot.	Ham.
Veal Cutlets.	Neck of Venison.	Orange Pudding.
	Lobster Soup.	

SECOND COURSE.

	Turkey Poults.	
Peas.	Apricot Puffs.	Lobsters.
Fricassee of Lamb.	Half Moon.	Roasted Sweetbreads.
Pickled Sturgeon.	Cherry Tart.	Artichokes.
	Roasted Rabbits.	

THIRD COURSE.

	Sweetbreads à la Blanche.	
Fillets of Soals.	Potted Wheat Ears.	Ratafia Cream.
Peas.	Green Gooseberry Tart.	Forced Artichokes.
Preserved Oranges.	Potted Ruff.	Matelot of Eels.
	Lambs' Tails à la Braise.	

JULY.

JULY.

FIRST COURSE.

	Mackerel, &c.	
Breaſt of Veal à la Braiſe.	Tongue and Turnips.	Pulpeton.
Veniſon Paſty.	Herb Soup.	Neck of Veniſon.
Chickens.	Boiled Gooſe and ſtewed red Cabbage.	Mutton Cutlets.
	Trout boiled.	

SECOND COURSE.

	Roaſt Turkey.	
Stewed Peas.	Apricot Tart.	Blanc-mange.
Sweetbreads.	Jellies.	Fricaſſee of Rabbits.
Cuſtards.	Green Codlin Tart.	Blaized Pippins.
	Roaſt Pigeons.	

THIRD COURSE.

	Fricaſſee of Rabbits.	
Apricots.	Pains à la Ducheſſe.	Forced Cucumbers.
Crawfiſh ragooed.	Morello Cherry Tart.	Lobſters à la Braiſe.
Jeruſalem Artichokes.	Apricot Puffs.	Green Gage Plums.
	Lamb Stones.	

AUGUST.

FIRST COURSE.

Fillets of Pigeons.	Stewed Soals.	Turkey à la Daube.
French Patty.	Ham.	Petit Patties.
Chickens.	Crawfish Soup.	Rosard of Beef Palates.
	Fillet of Veal.	
	Whitings.	

SECOND COURSE.

Macaroni.	Roast Ducks.	Fillets of Soals.
Cheesecakes.	Tartlet.	Apple Pie.
Matelot of Eels.	Jellies.	Fricassee of Sweetbreads.
	Orange Puffs.	
	Leveret.	

THIRD COURSE.

Stewed Peas.	Wheat Ears.	Crawfish.
Apricot Tart.	Potted Lampreys.	Cut Pastry.
Prawns.	Fruit.	Blanched Celery.
	Scraped Beef.	
	Ruffs and Rees.	

SEP-

SEPTEMBER.

FIRST COURSE.

Diſh of Fiſh.

Chickens.	Stewed Giblets.	Veal Collops.
Pigeon Pie.	Gravy Soup.	Almond Tort.
Harrico of Mutton.	Partridge panes.	Ham.

Roaſt Beef.

SECOND COURSE.

Wild Fowls.

Peas.	Damſon Tarts.	Ragooed Lobſters.
Sweetbreads.	Crocant.	Fried Piths.
Crawfiſh.	Maids of Honour.	Fried Artichokes.

Ducks.

THIRD COURSE.

Ragooed Palates.

Comport of Biſcuits.	Tartlets.	Fruit in Jelly.
Green Truffles.	Epergne.	Cardoons.
Blanc-mange.	Cheeſecakes.	Ratafia Drops.

Calves' Ears à la Braiſe.

OC-

OCTOBER.

FIRST COURSE.

Cod and Oyster Sauce.

Jugged Hare.	Neck of Veal à la Braise.	Small Puddings.
French Patty.	Almond Soup.	Stewed Pigeons.
Chickens.	Tongue.	Torrent de Veau.

Fillet of Beef, &c.

SECOND COURSE.

Pheasant.

Stewed Pears.	Apple Tarts.	Mushrooms:
Roast Lobsters.	Jellies.	Oyster Loaves.
White Fricassee.	Custards.	Pippins.

Turkey.

THIRD COURSE.

Sweetbread à la Braise.

Fried Artichokes.	Potted Eels.	Pigs' Ears.
Almond Cheesecakes.	Fruit.	Apricot Puffs.
Amulet.	Potted Lobsters.	Forced Celery.

Larks.

NO-

NOVEMBER.

FIRST COURSE.

	Diſh of Fiſh.	
Veal Cutlets.	Roaſted Turkey.	Ox Palates.
Two Chickens and Broccoli.	Vermicelli Soup.	Gammon of Bacon.
Beef Collops.	French Pye.	Harrico.
	Chine of Pork.	

SECOND COURSE.

	Woodcocks.	
Sheeps' Rumps.	Apple Puffs.	Diſh of Jelly.
Oyſter Loaves.	Crocant.	Ragooed Lobſters.
Blanc-mange.	Lemon Tort.	Lambs' Ears.
	Hare.	

THIRD COURSE.

	Petit Patties.	
Stewed Pears.	Potted Chars.	Fried Oyſters.
Gallantine.	Ice Cream.	Collared Eel.
Fillets of Whitings.	Potted Crawfiſh.	Pippins.
	Lambs' Ears à la Braiſe.	

DECEMBER.

FIRST COURSE.

	Cod's Head.	
Chickens.	Stewed Beef.	Fricando of Veal.
Almond Puddings.	Soup Santé.	Calves' Feet Pie.
Very ſmall Fillet of Pork, with ſharp Sauce.	Currey.	Tongue.
	Chine of Lamb.	

SECOND COURSE.

	Wild Fowls.	
Lambs' Fry.	Orange Puffs.	Sturgeon.
Gallantine.	Jellies.	Savoury Cake.
Prawns.	Tartlets.	Muſhrooms.
	Partridges.	

THIRD COURSE.

	Ragooed Palates.	
Savoy Cakes.	Dutch Beef ſcraped.	China Oranges.
Lambs' Tails.	Half Moon.	Calves' Burs.
Jargonel Pears.	Potted Larks.	Lemon Biſcuits.
	Fricaſſee of Crawfiſh.	

N. B. In your firſt Courſe always obſerve to ſend up all Kinds of Garden Stuff ſuitable to your Meat, &c. in different Diſhes, on a Water-diſh filled with hot Water on the Side-Table; and all your Sauce in Boats or Baſons, to anſwer one another at the Corners.

THE

ART of COOKERY

MADE

PLAIN AND EASY.

CHAP. I.

Containing a List of the various Kinds of MEAT, POULTRY, FISH, VEGETABLES, *and* FRUIT, *in Season in every* MONTH *of the* YEAR.

BEFORE any instructions are given for dressing and preparing a dinner, it is certainly necessary to inform the reader what is to be had; for that reason I have, in this edition, altered the order observed in former ones, by treating of this subject first, which has been always hitherto placed at the end, or in the middle of books, so as to escape attention, or be difficult to find. The following list is greatly enlarged and improved.

JANUARY.

MEAT. Beef, mutton, veal, house-lamb, pork, doe-venison. —N. B. The three first articles, being in season all the year, will not be repeated in the future months.

POULTRY and GAME. Pheasant, partridge, hares, rabbits, woodcocks, snipes; hen-turkeys, capons, pullets, fowls, chickens, tame pigeons; and all sorts of wild fowl.

FISH. Carp, tench, perch, lampreys, eels, crawfish, cod, soles, flounders, plaice, turbot, thornback, skate, sturgeon, smelts, whitings, lobsters, crabs, prawns, oysters, dorey, brill, gudgeons, cockles, muscles, sprats, &c.

VEGETABLES. Cabbage, savoys, coleworts, sprouts, brocoli purple and white, cauliflowers (by art) and artichokes in sand, spinage, cardoons, beets, turnips, potatoes, carrots, parsnips, parsley, endive, lettuces, cresses, mustard, radish, rape,

 sorrel,

ſorrel, celery, chervil, tarragon, cucumbers in hot-houſes, mint, thyme, ſavory, pot-marjoram, ſage, hyſſop, ſkirrets, ſalſifie, ſcorzonera. *To be had though not in ſeaſon,* Jeruſalem artichokes, aſparagus, muſhrooms.

FRUIT. Nuts, almonds, ſervices, grapes, medlars, golden-pippins, and various other fine eating and boiling apples, bergamot, bon-chretien and other pears, foreign grapes, and oranges.

FEBRUARY.

MEAT. Houſe-lamb and pork.

POULTRY and GAME. Pheaſants, partridges, hares, tame rabbits, woodcocks, ſnipes, turkeys, pullets with eggs, capons, chickens, tame and wild pigeons, and all ſorts of wild fowl, (which in this month begin to decline.)

FISH. Cod, ſoles, turbot, carp, tench, ſturgeon, thornback, flounders, plaice, ſmelts, whitings, ſkate, perch, eels, lampreys, gollin, ſprats, dorey, hollebet, anchovy, lobſters, crabs, prawns, oyſters, crawfiſh.

VEGETABLES. Cabbage, ſavoys, ſprouts, coleworts, brocoli purple and white, lettuces, endive, celery, onions, leeks, garlick, ſhalots, rocambole, cardoons, beets, ſorrel, chervil, chardbeets, parſley, creſſes, muſtard, rape, tarragon, burnet, tanſey, mint, thyme, marjoram, ſavory, turnips, carrots, potatoes, parſnips; *alſo may be had* forced radiſhes, cucumbers, aſparagus, kidney beans, ſalſifie, ſcorzonera, ſkirret, and Jeruſalem artichokes.

FRUIT. Golden and Dutch pippins, with various other kinds of apples, winter bon-chretien pear, winter maſk and winter Norwich, &c. &c. grapes, and oranges.

MARCH.

MEAT. Houſe-lamb and pork.

POULTRY. Turkeys, fowls, pullets, capons, chickens, ducklings, tame rabbits, pigeons.

FISH. Turbot, thornback, ſkate, carp, tench, mullets, eels, whitings, ſoles, flounders, plaice, bream, barbel, mackerel, dace, bleak, roach, crabs, prawns, lobſters, crawfiſh, and oyſters.

VEGETABLES. Carrots, potatoes, turnips, parſnips, Jeruſalem artichokes, garlick, onions, ſhalots, coleworts, borecole, cabbages, ſavoys, ſpinage, brocoli, beets, cardoons, parſley, fennel, celery, endive, tanſey, muſhrooms, lettuces, chives, creſſes, muſtard, rape, radiſhes, turnips, tarragon, mint, burnet, thyme, winter-ſavory, pot-marjoram, cucumbers, and kidney-beans.

FRUIT. Golden pippins, rennetings, loves pearmain, and john-apples, the latter bon-chretien and double-bloſſom pear, oranges, and forced ſtrawberries.

April.

Meat. Graſs-lamb.

Poultry. Pullets, ſpring fowls, chickens, pigeons, ducklings, young geeſe, turkey poults, wild rabbits, leverets.

Fish. Mullets, carp, tench, ſoles, turbot, chub, trout, crawfiſh, ſalmon, ſkate, ſmelts, herrings, crabs, lobſters, prawns; oyſters, lamprey or lampor eels, and mackerel.

Vegetables. Sprouts, coleworts, brocoli, ſpinage, aſparagus, young radiſhes, parſley, chervil; Dutch brown lettuce, and creſſes, young onions, celery, endive, ſorrel, burnet, tarragon; all ſorts of ſmall ſalad, and early kidney-beans.

Fruit. Forced cherries, green apricots, and gooſeberries for tarts, pippins, Weſtbury apple, ruſſeting, gilliflower; the latter bon-chretien, oak pear, and oranges.

May.

Meat. Buck veniſon, and graſs lamb.

Poultry. The ſame as in April.

Fish. Salmon, carp, tench, eels, trout, chub, ſoles, turbot, herrings, lobſters, crawfiſh, crabs, prawns, ſmelts.

Vegetables. Lettuces, creſſes, muſtard, all ſorts of ſmall ſallad herbs, early potatoes, carrots, turnips, radiſhes, early cabbages, cauliflowers, artichokes, ſpinage, parſley, ſorrel, aſparagus, peas, beans, kidney-beans, cucumbers, thyme, ſavory and all other ſweet herbs, purſlane, fennel, mint, and balm. Now is the proper time to diſtil herbs, which are in their greateſt perfection.

Fruit. May cherries, May dukes, apples, pears, ſtrawberries, melons, green apricots, gooſeberries, currants for tarts; and oranges.

June.

Meat. The ſame as in May.

Poultry. Ducklings, green geeſe, turkey-poults, fowls, pullets, chickens, plovers, wheat-ears, leverets, rabbits.

Fish. Turbot, trout, tench, pike, eels, ſalmon, ſoles, mullets, mackerel, herrings, ſmelts, ſkate, chub, grigs, lobſters, crawfiſh, prawns, ſturgeon; this fiſh is commonly found in the Northern ſeas, but now and then we find them in our great rivers, the Thames, the Severn, and the Tyne. This fiſh is of a very large ſize, and will ſometimes meaſure eighteen feet in length. They are much eſteemed when freſh, cut in pieces, roaſted, baked or pickled, for cold treats. The caviare is eſteemed a dainty, which is the ſpawn of this fiſh.

Vegetables. Beans, peas, carrots, turnips, potatoes, parſnips, rape, creſſes, and all other ſmall ſallading, Batterſea and

Dutch cabbage, cauliflowers, artichokes, radiſhes, onions, cucumbers, ſpinage, purſlane, parſley; all ſorts of pot-herbs, borage, burnet, and endive.

FRUIT. Green gooſeberries, ſtrawberries, ſome raſpberries, currants white and black; duke cherries, red hearts, the Flemiſh and carnation cherries, codlins, jannatings, the maſculine apricot, pears, and oranges.

JULY.

MEAT. The ſame.

POULTRY. The ſame; with young partridges, pheaſants, and wild ducks, called flappers or moulters.

FISH. Cod haddocks, mullets, mackerel, herrings, ſoles, plaice, flounders, ſkate, thornback, ſalmon, carp, tench, pike, eels, lobſters, prawns, ſhrimps, crawfiſh, and ſturgeon.

VEGETABLES. Carrots, turnips, potatoes, cabbages, ſprouts, artichokes, celery, radiſhes, endive, onions, garlick, finocha, chervil, ſorrel, purſlane, lettuce, creſſes, and all ſorts of ſallad-herbs, rocombole, ſcorzonera, ſalſifie, muſhrooms, cauliflowers, mint, balm, thyme, and all other pot-herbs, peaſe of various kinds, beans, kidney-beans, cucumbers.

FRUIT. Muſk-melons, wood-ſtrawberries, currants, gooſeberries, raſpberries, red and white jannatings, and ſeveral early apples and pears, morella and other cherries, peaches, nectarines, apricots, plumbs, figs, and grapes. Walnuts in high ſeaſon to pickle, and rock ſamphire. The fruit yet laſting of laſt year, is the deuxans, winter ruſſeting, and ſome oranges.

AUGUST.

MEAT. The ſame.

POULTRY. Green geeſe, turkey-poults, ducklings, pullets, fowls, chickens, leverets, rabbits, pigeons, young pheaſants, wild ducks, wheat-ears, plovers.

FISH. Cod, haddock, plaice, ſkate, flounders, thornback, mullets, mackerel, eels, herrings, pike and carp, trout, turbot, ſoles, grigs, ſalmon, ſturgeon, chub, lobſters, crabs, crawfiſh, prawns, oyſters, and ſhrimps.

VEGETABLES. Beans and peaſe of ſome kinds, cabbages, ſprouts, cauliflowers, artichokes, cabbage-lettuce, beets, carrots, potatoes, turnips, kidney-beans, all ſorts of kitchen herbs, radiſhes, horſe-radiſh, cucumbers, creſſes and ſmall ſallad, onions, garlick, ſhalots, rocomboles, muſhrooms, celery, endive, finocha, cucumbers for pickling.

FRUIT. Gooſeberries, raſpberries, currants, figs, mulberries, filberts, apples; bergamot, Windſor and other pears; Bourdeaux and other peaches, nectarines, plumbs, cluſter, muſcadine, and Cornelian grapes, melons, and pine-apples.

SEPTEMBER.

September.

Meat. Graſs-lamb, pork, buck-veniſon.

Poultry. Geeſe, turkies, pullets, fowls, chickens, ducks, teal, pigeons, larks, hares, rabbits, pheaſants, partridges.

Fish. Cod, haddock, flounders, herrings, plaice, thornbacks, ſkate, carp, tench, ſoles, ſmelts, ſalmon, pike, gudgeons, chub, trout, ſturgeon, lobſters, crabs, prawns, ſhrimps, oyſters, &c.

Vegetables. Carrots, turnips, potatoes, garden and ſome kidney-beans, rounceval peas, artichokes, radiſhes, cauliflowers, cabbage-lettuce, ſmall ſallad, chervil, onions, garlick, ſhalots, and leeks; tarragon, burnet, celery, endive, muſhrooms, ſkirrets; beets, ſcorzonera, ſalſifie, cardoons, horſe-radiſh, rocombole, cabbage and ſprouts, ſavoys.

Fruit. Peaches, grapes, figs, pears, plumbs, walnuts, filberts, nectarines, morella cherries, melons, pine-apples, almonds, quinces.

October.

Meat. Pork, doe-veniſon.

Poultry. Turkies, geeſe, pullets, fowls, chickens, pigeons, rabbits, wild ducks, teal, widgeons, woodcocks, ſnipes, dottrels, larks, hares, pheaſants, partridges.

Fish. Cod, haddock, ling, mullet, dories, holobert, herrings, ſprats, barbel, ſoles, flounders, plaice, dabs, eels, chars, pike, tench and ſea-tench, oyſters and ſcollops, thornback, gudgeons, ſalmon-trout, brill, perch, cockles, muſcles.—N. B. Skate maids are black, and thornback maids white; grey baſs come with the mullet; there are two ſorts of mullets, the ſea-mullet and river-mullet, both equally good.

Vegetables. Some cauliflowers, artichokes, beans, peas, cucumbers; alſo July-ſown kidney-beans, turnips, carrots, parſnips, potatoes, ſkirrets, ſcorzonera, beets, onions, garlick, ſhalots, rocombole, chardoons, creſſes, chervil, muſtard, radiſh, rape, ſpinage, lettuce ſmall and cabbaged, burnet, tarragon, blanched celery and endive, cabbages and ſprouts.

Fruit. Late peaches and plumbs, grapes and figs, mulberries, filberts and walnuts; bullace, pines, and great variety of pears and apples, medlars, ſervices, quinces, hazle-nuts.

November.

Meat. Houſe-lamb, and doe-veniſon.

Poultry. Geeſe, turkies, fowls, chickens, pullets, pigeons, woodcocks, ſnipes, larks, wild ducks, teal, widgeon, hares, rabbits, dottrels, partridges, pheaſants.

Fish. The ſame as laſt month.

VEGETABLES. Cauliflowers in the green-houſe, and ſome artichokes, carrots, parſnips, turnips, beets, ſkirrets, ſcorzonera, horſe-radiſh, potatoes, onions, garlick, ſhalots, rocombole, celery, parſley, ſorrel, thyme, ſavory, ſweet-marjoram, dry and clary cabbages and their ſprouts, ſavoy cabbage, ſpinage, late cucumbers, hot-herbs on the hot-bed, burnet, cabbage, lettuce, endive, blanched Jeruſalem artichokes; and all ſorts of pot-herbs.

FRUIT. Bullace, medlars, walnuts, hazel-nuts, cheſnuts, pears, apples, ſervices, grapes, oranges.

DECEMBER.

MEAT. Houſe-lamb, pork, doe-veniſon,

POULTRY. The ſame as laſt month.

FISH. Turbot, ſturgeon, gurnets, dorees, holoberts, barbel, ſmelts, cod, codlings, ſoles, carp, gudgeons, eels, perch, anchovy, perriwinkles, cockles, muſcles, oyſters, brill, and ſcollop.

VEGETABLES. Many ſorts of cabbages and ſavoys, ſpinage, and ſome cauliflowers in the conſervatory, and artichokes in the ſand, roots as in laſt month, ſmall ſallading on hot-beds, alſo mint, tarragon, and cabbage-lettuce under glaſſes, chervil, celery, and endive blanched; ſage, thyme, ſavory, beet-leaves, tops of young beets, parſley, ſorrel, ſpinage, leeks and ſweet-marjoram, marigold flowers, and mint dried; aſparagus on the hot-bed, and cucumbers on the plants ſown in July and Auguſt; onions, garlick, ſhalots, and rocombole.

FRUIT. Apples, pears, medlars, cheſnuts, walnuts, ſervices, grapes, hazel-nuts, and oranges.

CHAP. II.

DIRECTIONS FOR MARKETING; *containing the Names of all the Joints of every Beaſt; and Inſtructions how to chuſe all Kinds of Butcher's Meat, Poultry, Fiſh, Butter, Eggs, and Cheeſe.*

OF BUTCHER'S MEAT.—*Pieces in a Bullock.*

THE head, tongue, palate; the entrails are the ſweetbreads, kidneys, ſkirts, and tripe; there is the double, the roll, and the reed tripe.

The Fore-Quarter.

FIRST is the haunch, which includes the clod, marrow-bone, ſkin, and the ſticking piece, that is, the neck end; the next is the leg of mutton piece, which has part of the bladebone; then the

chuck,

chuck, the briſket, the fore ribs, and middle rib, which is called the chuck rib.

The Hind-Quarter.

FIRST ſirloin and rump, the thin and thick flank, the veiny-piece, then the iſch-bone, or chuck-bone, buttock, and leg.

IN A SHEEP.

THE head and pluck; which includes the liver, lights, heart, ſweetbreads, and melt.

The Fore-Quarter.

THE neck, breaſt, and ſhoulder.

The Hind Quarter.

THE leg and loin. The two loins together is called a chine or ſaddle of mutton, which is a fine joint when it is the little fat mutton.

IN A CALF.

THE head and inwards are the pluck; which contains the heart, liver, lights, nut, and melt, and what they call the ſkirts, (which eat finely broiled,) the throat-ſweetbread, and the wind-pipe-ſweetbread, which is the fineſt.

The fore-quarter is the ſhoulder, neck, and breaſt.

The hind quarter is the leg, which contains the knuckle and fillet, then the loin.

IN A LAMB.

THE head and pluck, that is, the liver, lights, heart, nut, and melt. Then there is the fry, which is the ſweetbreads, lamb-ſtones, and ſkirts, with ſome of the liver.

The fore-quarter is the ſhoulder, neck, and breaſt together.

The hind-quarter is the leg and loin.

IN A HOG.

THE head and inwards; and that is the haſlet, which is the liver and crow, kidney and ſkirts. It is mixed with a great deal of ſage and ſweet herbs, pepper, ſalt, and ſpice, ſo rolled in the caul and roaſted; then there are the chitterlins and the guts, which are cleaned for ſauſages.

The fore-quarter is the fore-loin and ſpring; if a large hog, you may cut a ſpare-rib off.

The hind-quarter only leg and loin.

A BACON HOG.

THIS is cut different, becauſe of making hams, bacon, and pickled pork. Here you have fine ſpare-ribs, chines, and griſ-kins, and fat for hog's-lard. The liver and crow is much admired fried with bacon; the feet and ears are both equally good foufed.

To choofe Beef.

If it be true ox-beef, it will have an open grain, and the fat, if young, of a crumbling, or oily fmoothnefs, except it be the brifket and neck pieces, with fuch others as are very fibrous. The colour of the lean fhould be of a pleafant carnation red, the fat rather inclining to white than yellow, (which feldom proves good,) and the fuet of a fine white.

Cow-beef is of a clofer grain, the fat whiter, the bones lefs, and the lean of a paler colour. If it be young and tender, the dent you make with your finger by preffing it, will, in a little time, rife again.

Bull beef is of a more dufky red, a clofer grain, and firmer than either of the former; harder to be indented with your finger, and rifing again fooner. The fat is very grofs and fibrous, and of a ftrong rank fcent. If it be old it will be fo very tough, that if you pinch it you will fcarce make any impreffion in it. If it be frefh, it will be of a lively frefh colour; but if ftale, of a dark dufky colour, and very clammy. If it be bruifed, the part affected will look of a more dufky or blackifh colour than the reft.

Mutton and Lamb.

Take fome of the flefh between your fingers and pinch it; if it feels tender, and foon returns to its former place, it is young; but if it wrinkles, and remains fo, it is old. The fat will alfo, eafily feparate from the lean, if it be young; but if old, it will adhere more firmly, and be very clammy and fibrous. If it be ram mutton, the fat will be fpongy, the grain clofe, the lean rough, and of a deep red, and when dented by your finger will not rife again. If the fheep had the rot, the flefh will be palifh, the fat a faint white, inclining to yellow; the meat will be loofe at the bone, and, if you fqueeze it hard, fome drops of water, refembling a dew or fweat, will appear on the furface. [If it be a fore-quarter, obferve the vein in the neck, for if it look ruddy, or of an azure colour, it is frefh; but if yellowifh, it is near tainting, and if green, it is already fo. As for the hind-quarter, fmell under the kidney, and feel whether the knuckle be ftiff or limber; for if you find a faint or ill fcent in the former, or an unufual limbernefs in the latter, it is ftale.] The fentences included in crotchets, will likewife be the marks for choofing lamb; and for choofing a lamb's head, mind the eyes; if they be funk or wrinkled, it is ftale; if plump and lively, it is new and fweet.

Veal.

OBSERVE the vein in the ſhoulder; for if it be of a bright red, or looks blue, it is newly killed; but if greeniſh, yellowiſh, or blackiſh, or more clammy, ſoft, and limber than uſual, it is ſtale. Alſo, if it has any green ſpots about it, it is either tainting, or already tainted. If it be wrapped in wet cloths, it is apt to be muſty; therefore always obſerve to ſmell to it. The loin taints firſt under the kidney, and the fleſh, when ſtale, will be ſoft and ſlimy. The neck and breaſt are firſt tainted at the upper end, and when ſo, will have a duſky, yellowiſh, or greeniſh appearance, and the ſweetbread on the breaſt will be clammy. The leg, if newly killed, will be ſtiff in the joint; but if ſtale, limber, and the fleſh clammy, intermixed with green or yellowiſh ſpecks. The fleſh of a bull-calf is firmer grained and redder than that of a cow-calf, and the fat more curdled. In chooſing the head, obſerve the ſame directions as above given for that of the lamb.

Pork.

PINCH the lean between your fingers; if it breaks, and feels ſoft and oily, or if you can eaſily nip the ſkin with your nails, or if the fat be ſoft and oily, it is young; but if the lean be rough, the fat very ſpongy, and the ſkin ſtubborn, it is old. If it be a boar, or a hog gelded at full growth, the fleſh will feel harder and rougher than uſual, the ſkin thicker, the fat hard and fibrous, the lean of a duſky red, and of a rank ſcent. To know if it be freſh or ſtale, try the legs and hands at the bone, which comes out in the middle of the fleſhy part, by putting in your finger; for as it firſt taints in thoſe places, you may eaſily diſcover it by ſmelling to your finger; alſo the ſkin will be clammy and ſweaty when ſtale, but ſmooth and cool when freſh.

Brawn.

THE beſt method of knowing whether brawn be young or old, is by the extraordinary or moderate thickneſs of the rind, and the hardneſs or ſoftneſs of it; for the thick and hard is old, but the moderate and ſoft is young. If the rind and fat be remarkably tender, it is not boar brawn, but barrow or ſow.

Dried Hams and Bacon.

TAKE a ſharp-pointed knife, run it into the middle of the ham, on the inſide, under the bone, draw it out quickly and ſmell to it; if its flavour be fine and reliſhing, and the knife little daubed, the ham is ſweet and good; but if, on the contrary, the knife be greatly daubed, has a rank ſmell, and a hogoo

goo iſſues from the vent, it is tainted. Or you may cut off a piece at one end to look on the meat; if it appear white and be well ſcented, it is good; but if yellowiſh, or of a ruſty colour, not well ſcented, it either is tainted or ruſty, or at leaſt will ſoon be ſo. A gammon of bacon may be tried in the ſame manner, and be ſure to obſerve that the fleſh ſticks cloſe to the bones, and the fat and lean to each other; for if it does not, the hog was not ſound. Take care alſo that the extreme part of the fat near the rind be white, for if that be of a darkiſh or dirty colour, and the lean pale and ſoft, with ſome ſtreaks of yellow, it is ruſty, or will ſoon be ſo.

Veniſon.

TRY the haunches, ſhoulders, and fleſhy parts of the ſides with your knife, in the ſame manner as before directed for ham, and in proportion to the ſweet or rank ſmell it is new or ſtale. With relation to the other parts, obſerve the colour of the meat; for if it be ſtale or tainted, it will be of a black colour, intermixed with yellowiſh or greeniſh ſpecks. If it be old, the fleſh will be tough and hard, the fat contracted, the hoofs large and broad, and the heel horny and much worn.

OF POULTRY.

To know if a Capon be a true one or not, or whether it be young or old, new or ſtale.

IF a capon be young, his ſpurs will be ſhort and blunt, and his legs ſmooth: if a true capon, it will have a fat vein on the ſide of the breaſt, a thick belly and rump, and its comb will be ſhort and pale. If it be new, it will have a cloſe hard vent; but if ſtale, an open looſe vent.

To chooſe a Cock or Hen Turkey, Turkey-Poults, &c.

IF the ſpurs of a turkey-cock are ſhort, and his legs black and ſmooth, he is young; but if his ſpurs be long, and his legs pale and rough, he is old. If long killed, his eyes will be ſunk into his head, and his feet feel very dry; but if freſh, his feet will be limber, and his eyes lively. For the hen, obſerve the ſame ſigns. If ſhe be with egg, ſhe will have an open vent; but if not, a cloſe, hard vent. The ſame ſigns will ſerve to diſcover the newneſs or ſtaleneſs of turkey-poults; and, with reſpect to their age, you cannot be deceived.

A Cock, Hen, &c.

IF a cock be young, his ſpurs will be ſhort and dubbed; (be ſure to obſerve that they are not pared or ſcraped to deceive you;)

you;) but if ſharp and ſtanding out, he is old. If his vent be hard and cloſe, it is a ſign of his being newly killed; but if he be ſtale, his vent will be open. The ſame ſigns will diſcover whether a hen be new or ſtale; and if old, her legs and comb will be rough; but if young, ſmooth.

To know if Chickens are new or ſtale.

If they are pulled dry, they will be ſtiff when new; but when ſtale, they will be limber, and their vents green. If they are ſcalded, or pulled wet, rub the breaſt with your thumb or finger, and if they are rough and ſtiff, they are new; but if ſmooth and ſlippery, ſtale.

To chooſe a Gooſe, Wild-Gooſe, and Bran-Gooſe.

If the bill and foot be red, and the body full of hairs, ſhe is old; but if the bill be yellowiſh, and the body has but few hairs, ſhe is young. If new, her feet will be limber; but if ſtale, dry. Underſtand the ſame of a wild-gooſe, and bran-gooſe.

Wild and tame Ducks.

These fowls are hard and thick on the belly, when fat, but thin and lean, when poor; limber-footed when new; but dry-footed when ſtale. A wild duck may be diſtinguiſhed from a tame one, by its foot being ſmaller and reddiſh.

Buſtard.

Observe the ſame rules in chooſing this curious fowl, as thoſe already given for the turkey.

The Shuffler, Godwits, Marle, Knots, Gulls, Ruffs, Dotters, and Wheat-Ears.

These birds, when new, are limber-footed; when ſtale, dry-footed: when fat, they have a fat rump; when lean, a cloſe and hard one; when young, their legs are ſmooth; when old, rough.

Pheaſant Cock and Hen.

The ſpurs of the pheaſant cock, when young, are ſhort and dubbed; but long and ſharp when old; when new, he has a firm vent, when ſtale, an open and flabby one. The pheaſant hen, when young, has ſmooth legs, and her fleſh is of a fine and curious grain; but when old, her legs are rough, and her fleſh hairy when pulled. If ſhe be with egg, her vent will be open; if not, cloſe. The ſame ſigns, as to newneſs or ſtaleneſs, are to be obſerved as were before given for the cock.

Heath

Heath and Pheasant Poults.

THE feet of these, when new, are limber, and their vents white and stiff; but when stale, are dry-footed, their vents green, and if you touch it hard, will peel.

Heath Cock and Hen.

THE newness or staleness of these are known by the same signs as the foregoing; but when young, their legs and bills are smooth; when old, both are rough.

Woodcock and Snipe.

THESE fowls are limber-footed when new; when stale, dry-footed: if fat, thick and hard; but if their noses are snotty, and their throats moorish and muddy, they are bad. A snipe, particularly, if fat, has a fat vein in the side under the wing, and in the vent feels thick.

Partridge Cock or Hen.

THESE fowls, when young, have black bills, and yellowish legs; when old, white bills and blueish legs; when new, a fast vent; when stale, a green and open one, which will peel with a touch; if they had fed lately on green wheat, and their crops be full, smell to their mouths, lest their crops be tainted.

Doves or Pigeons, Plovers, &c.

THE turtle-dove is distinguished by a blueish ring round its neck, the other parts being almost white. The stock-dove exceeds both the wood-pigeon and ring-dove in bigness. The dove-house pigeons are red-legged when old: if new and fat, limber-footed, and feel full in the vent; but when stale, their vents are green and flabby.

After the same manner you may choose the grey and green plover, fieldfare, thrush, mavis, lark, blackbird, &c.

Teal and Widgeon.

THESE, when new, are limber-footed; when stale, dry-footed; thick and hard on the belly, if fat; but thin and soft, if lean.

Hare.

IF the claws of a hare are blunt and rugged, and the clift in her lip spread much, she is old; but the opposite, if young: if new and fresh killed, the flesh will be white and stiff; if stale, limber and blackish in many places. If the hare be young, the ears will tear like a sheet of brown paper; if old, they are dry and tough.

Leveret.

Leveret.

THE newneſs or ſtaleneſs may be known by the ſame ſigns as the hare; but in order to diſcover if it be a real leveret, feel near the foot on its fore leg; if you find there a knob or ſmall bone, it is a true leveret; but if not, a hare.

A Rabbit.

IF a rabbit be old, the claws will be very long and rough, and grey hairs intermixed with the wool; but if young, the claws and wool ſmooth; if ſtale, it will be limber, and the fleſh will look blueiſh, having a kind of ſlime upon it; but if freſh, it will be ſtiff, and the fleſh white and dry.

OF FISH.

To chooſe Salmon, Trout, Carp, Tench, Pike, Graylings, Barbel, Chub, Whiting, Smelt, Ruff, Eel, Shad, &c.

THE newneſs or ſtaleneſs of theſe fiſh is known by the colour of their gills, their being hard or eaſy to be opened, the ſtanding out or ſinking of their eyes, their fins being ſtiff or limber, and by ſmelling to their gills. Eels taken in running water are better than thoſe taken in ponds; of theſe, the ſilver ones are moſt eſteemed.

Turbot.

IF this fiſh be plump and thick, and its belly of a cream colour, it is good; but if thin, and of a blueiſh white on the belly, not ſo.

Soals.

IF theſe are thick and ſtiff, and of a cream colour on the belly, they will ſpend firm; but if thin, limber, and their bellies of a blueiſh white, they will eat very looſe.

Plaice and Flounders.

WHEN theſe fiſh are new, they are ſtiff, and the eyes look lively and ſtand out; but when ſtale, the contrary. The beſt plaice are blueiſh on the belly; but flounders of a cream colour.

Cod and Codling.

CHOOSE thoſe which are thick towards the head, and their fleſh, when cut, very white.

Freſh Herrings and Mackerel.

IF theſe are new, their gills will be of a lively ſhining redneſs, their eyes ſharp and full, and the fiſh ſtiff; but if ſtale, their

their gills will look dusky and faded, their eyes dull and sunk down, and their tails limber.

Pickled Salmon.

THE scales of this fish, when new and good, are stiff and shining, the flesh oily to the touch, and parts in fleaks without crumbling; but the opposite, when bad.

Pickled and Red Herrings.

TAKE the former, and open the back to the bone; if it be white, or of a bright red, and the flesh white, oily, and fleaky, they are good. If the latter smell well, be of a good gloss, and part well from the bone, they are also good.

Dried Ling.

THE best sort of dried ling is that which is thickest in the pole, and the flesh of the brightest yellow.

Pickled Sturgeon.

THE veins and gristle of the fish, when good, are of a blue colour, the flesh white, the skin limber, the fat underneath of a pleasant scent, and you may cut it without its crumbling.

Lobsters.

IF a lobster be new, it has a pleasant scent at that part of the tail which joins to the body, and the tail will, when opened, fall smart, like a spring; but when stale, it has a rank scent, and the tail limber and flagging. If it be spent, a white scurf will issue from the mouth and roots of the small legs. If it be full, the tail, about the middle, will be full of hard reddish skinned meat, which you may discover by thrusting a knife between the joints, on the bend of the tail. The heaviest are best, if there be no water in them. The cock is generally smaller than the hen, of a deeper red when boiled, has no spawn or seed under its tail, and the uppermost fins within its tail are stiff and hard.

Crab fish, great and small.

WHEN they are stale, their shells will be of a dusky red colour, the joints of their claws limber; they are loose, and may be turned any way with the finger, and from under their throat will issue an ill smell; but if otherwise, they are good.

Prawns and Shrimps.

IF they are hard and stiff, of a pleasant scent, and their tails turn strongly inward, they are new; but if they are limber, their

their colour faded, of a faint smell, and feel slimy, they are stale.

The seasons for eating all the above-mentioned articles may be seen in the foregoing chapter.

OF BUTTER, EGGS, AND CHEESE.

To choose Butter and Eggs.

WHEN you buy butter, taste it yourself at a venture, and do not trust to the taste they give you, lest you be deceived by a well-tasted and scented piece artfully placed in the lump. Salt butter is better scented than tasted, by putting a knife into it, and putting it immediately to your nose; but, if it be a cask, it may be purposely packed, therefore trust not to the top alone, but unhoop it to the middle, thrusting your knife between the staves of the cask, and then you cannot be deceived.

When you buy eggs, put the great end to your tongue; if it feels warm, it is new; but if cold, it is stale; and according to the heat or coldness of it, the egg is newer or staler. Or take the egg, hold it up against the sun or a candle; if the white appears clear and fair, and the yolk round, it is good; but if muddy or cloudy, and the yolk broken, it is bad. Or take the egg, and put it into a pan of cold water; the fresher it is, the sooner it will sink to the bottom; but if it be rotten, or addled, it will swim on the surface of the water. The best way to keep them is in bran or meal; though some place their small ends downwards in fine wood-ashes. But for longer keeping, burying them in salt will preserve them almost in any climate.

Cheese.

CHEESE is to be chosen by its moist and smooth coat; if old cheese be rough-coated, rugged or dry at top, beware of little worms or mites; if it be over-full of holes, moist or spungy, is subject to maggots. If any soft or perished place appear on the outside, try how deep it goes, for the greater part may be hid within.

CHAP. III.

OF ROASTING, BOILING, &c.

THAT professed cooks will find fault with me for touching upon a branch of Cookery which they never thought worth their notice, is what I expect: however, this I know, it is the most necessary part of it; and few servants there are that know how to roast and boil to perfection.

I do

I do not pretend to teach professed cooks, but my design is to instruct the ignorant and unlearned (which will likewise be of great use in all private families), and in so plain and full a manner, that the most illiterate and ignorant person, who can but read, will know how to do every thing in Cookery well.

Rules to be observed in roasting Meat, Poultry, and Game.

I shall first begin with roast of all sorts, and must desire the cook to order her fire according to what she is to dress; if any thing very little or thin, then a pretty little brisk fire, that it may be done quick and nice; if a very large joint, then be sure a good fire be laid to cake. Let it be clear at the bottom: and when your meat is half done, move the dripping-pan and spit a little from the fire, and stir up a good brisk fire; for according to the goodness of your fire, your meat will be done sooner or later. Take great care the spit be very clean; and be sure to clean it with nothing but sand and water. Wash it clean, and wipe it with a dry cloth; for oil, brick-dust, and such things, will spoil your meat.

BEEF.

To roast a piece of beef about ten pounds will take an hour and a half, at a good fire. Twenty pounds weight will take three hours, if it be a thick piece; but if it be a thin piece of twenty pounds weight, two hours and a half will do it; and so on according to the weight of your meat, more or less. Observe, in frosty weather your beef will take half an hour longer.

Be sure to paper the top, and baste it well all the time it is roasting, and throw a handful of salt on it. When you see the smoak draw to the fire, it is near enough; then take off the paper, baste it well, and drudge it with a little flour to make a fine froth: take up your meat, and garnish your dish with nothing but horse-radish.

Never salt your roast meat before you lay it to the fire, for that draws out all the gravy. If you would keep it a few days before you dress it, dry it very well with a clean cloth, then flour it all over, and hang it where the air will come to it; but be sure always to mind that there is no dampness about it; if there is, you must dry it well with a cloth.

MUTTON.

A leg of mutton of six pounds will take an hour at a quick fire; if frosty weather, an hour and a quarter; nine pounds, an hour and a half; a leg of twelve pounds will take two hours; if frosty, two hours and a half; a large saddle of mutton will take three hours, because of papering it; a small saddle will take an hour and a half, and ſo on, according to the ſize; a breaſt will take half an hour at a quick fire; a neck, if large, an hour; if very ſmall, little better than half an hour; a ſhoulder much about the ſame time as a leg.

In roaſting of mutton, the loin, the chine, or ſaddle, muſt have the ſkin raiſed and ſkewered on, and, when near done, take off the ſkin, baſte and flour it to froth it up. All other ſorts of mutton muſt be roaſted with a quick, clear fire, without the ſkin being raiſed, or paper put on. You ſhould always obſerve to baſte your meat as ſoon as you lay it down to roaſt, ſprinkle ſome ſalt on, and, when near done, dredge it with a little flour to froth it up. Garniſh with horſe-radiſh.

LAMB.

If a large fore-quarter, an hour and a half; if a ſmall one, an hour. The outſide muſt be papered, baſted with good butter, and you muſt have a very quick fire. If a leg, about three quarters of an hour; a neck, a breaſt, or ſhoulder, three quarters of an hour; if very ſmall, half an hour will do. Theſe laſt-mentioned joints are not to be papered, or have the ſkin raiſed, but to be dreſſed like mutton, and garniſhed with creſſes or ſmall ſallading.

VEAL.

As to veal, you muſt be careful to roaſt it of a fine brown; if a large joint, a very good fire; if a ſmall joint, a pretty little briſk fire; if a fillet or loin, be ſure to paper the fat, that you loſe as little of that as poſſible. Lay it ſome diſtance from the fire till it is ſoaked, then lay it near the fire. When you lay it down, baſte it well with good butter; and when it is near enough, baſte it again, and dredge it with a little flour. The breaſt you muſt roaſt with the caul on, till it is enough; and ſkewer the ſweetbread on the backſide of the breaſt. When it is nigh enough, take off the caul, baſte it, and dredge it with a little flour. To every pound allow a quarter of an hour's roaſting.

PORK.

Pork muſt be well done, or it is apt to ſurfeit. To every pound allow a quarter of an hour: for example, a joint of twelve pounds weight, three hours, and ſo on; if it be a thin piece of that weight, two hours will roaſt it. When you roaſt a loin, take a ſharp pen-knife and cut the ſkin a-croſs, to make the crackling eat the better. The chine muſt be cut, and ſo muſt all pork that has the rind on. Roaſt a leg of pork thus: take a knife, as above, and ſcore it; ſtuff the knuckle part with ſage and onion, chopped fine with pepper and ſalt: or cut

 a hole

a hole under the twiſt, and put the ſage, &c. there, and ſkewer it up with a ſkewer. Roaſt it criſp, becauſe moſt people like the rind criſp, which they call crackling. Make ſome good apple-ſauce, and ſend up in a boat; then have a little drawn gravy to put in the diſh. This they call a mock gooſe. The ſpring or hand of pork, if very young, roaſted like a pig, eats very well; or take the ſpring, and cut off the ſhank or knuckle, and ſprinkle ſage and onion over it, and roll it round, and tie it with a ſtring, and roaſt it two hours, otherwiſe it is better boiled. The ſparerib ſhould be baſted with a little bit of butter, a very little duſt of flour, and ſome ſage ſhred ſmall: but we never make any ſauce to it but apple-ſauce. The beſt way to dreſs pork griſkins is to roaſt them, baſte them with a little butter and ſage, and a little pepper and ſalt. Few eat any thing with theſe but muſtard.

To kill a Pig and prepare it for roaſting.

STICK your pig juſt above the breaſt-bone, run your knife to the heart, when it is dead put it in cold water for a few minutes, then rub it over with a little roſin beat exceeding fine, or its own blood, put your pig into a pail of ſcalding water half a minute, take it out, lay it on a clean table, pull off the hair as quick as poſſible, if it does not come clean off put it in again, when you have got it all clean off waſh it in warm water, then in two or three cold waters, for fear the roſin ſhould taſte; take off the four feet at the firſt joint, make a ſlit down the belly, take out all the entrails, put the liver, heart, and lights to the pettitoes, waſh it well out of cold water, dry it exceedingly well with a cloth.

To roaſt a Pig.

SPIT your pig and lay it to the fire, which muſt be briſker at the ends than in the middle, or hang a flat iron in the middle of the grate. Before you lay your pig down, take a little ſage ſhred ſmall, a piece of butter as big as a walnut, and a little pepper and ſalt, and a cruſt of bread; put them into the pig, and ſew it up with coarſe thread; then flour it all over very well, and keep flouring it till the eyes drop out, or you find the crackling hard. Be ſure to ſave all the gravy that comes out of it, which you muſt do by ſetting baſons or pans under the pig in the dripping-pan, as ſoon as you find the gravy begins to run. If juſt killed, let it roaſt an hour; if killed the day before, an hour and a quarter; if a very large one, an hour and a half. But the beſt way to judge, is when the eyes drop out, and the ſkin is grown very hard. When it is enough, ſtir the fire up briſk; take a coarſe cloth, with a good lump of butter in in it, and rub the pig all over till the crackling is quite crisp, and then take it up. Lay it in your dish, and with a sharp knife cut off the head, and then cut the pig in two, before you draw out the spit. Cut the ears off the head and lay at each end, and cut the under jaw in two and lay on each side: melt some good butter, take the gravy you saved and put it into it, boil it, and pour it into the dish with the brains bruised fine, and the sage mixed all together, and then send it to table.

Another way to roast a Pig.

CHOP some sage and onion very fine, a few crumbs of bread, a little butter, pepper, and salt rolled up together, put it into the belly, and sew it up before you lay down the pig: rub it all over with sweet oil; when it is done, take a dry cloth and wipe it, then take it into a dish, cut it up, and send it to table with the sauce as above.

To roast the Hind-quarter of Pig lamb-fashion.

AT the time of the year when house-lamb is very dear, take the hind-quarter of a large roasting pig, take off the skin and roast it, and it will eat like lamb with mint-sauce, or with a sallad, or Seville orange. Half an hour will roast it.

To bake a Pig.

LAY it in a dish, flour it all over well, and rub it over with butter; butter the dish you lay it in, and put it into the oven. When it is enough, draw it out of the oven's mouth, and rub it over with a buttery cloth; then put it into the oven again till it is dry; take it out, and lay it in a dish: cut it up, take a little veal gravy, and take off the fat in the dish it was baked in, and there will be some good gravy at the bottom; put that to it, with a little piece of butter rolled in flour; boil it up, and put it into the dish, with the brains and sage in the belly. Some love a pig brought whole to table; then you are only to put what sauce you like into the dish.

To roast Venison.

TAKE a haunch of venison and spit it; take four sheets of paper well buttered, put two on the haunch; then make a paste with some flour, a little butter and water; roll it out half as big as your haunch, and put it over the fat part, then put the other two sheets of paper on, and tie them with some pack-thread; lay it to a brisk fire, and baste it well all the time of roasting; if a large haunch of twenty-four pounds, it will take three hours and an half, except it is a very large fire, then three hours will do; smaller in proportion. When it is near done, take off the paper and paſte, duſt it well with flour, and baſte it with butter; when it is a light brown, diſh it up with brown gravy.

To dreſs a Haunch of Mutton.

HANG it up for a fortnight, and dreſs it as directed for a haunch of veniſon.

To dreſs Mutton veniſon-faſhion.

TAKE the largeſt and fatteſt leg of mutton you can get, cut out like a haunch of veniſon, as ſoon as it is killed, while it is warm, it will eat the tenderer; take out the bloody vein, pour over it a bottle of red wine, turn it in the wine four or five times a day, for five days, then dry it exceeding well with a clean cloth, hang it up in the air, with the thick end uppermoſt, for five days, dry it night and morning to keep it from growing muſty. When you roaſt it, cover it with paper and paſte as you do veniſon. Serve it up with veniſon ſauce. It will take four hours roaſting. A fine fat neck may be done the ſame way.

To keep Veniſon or Hares ſweet; or to make them freſh when they ſtink.

IF your veniſon be very ſweet, only dry it with a cloth, and hang it where the air comes. If you would keep it any time, dry it very well with clean cloths, rub it all over with ground pepper, and hang it in an airy place, and it will keep a great while. If it ſtinks, or is muſty, take ſome lukewarm water, and waſh it clean; then take ſome freſh milk and water of the ſame warmth, and waſh it again; then dry it in clean cloths very well, and rub it all over with ground pepper, and hang it in an airy place. When you roaſt it, you need only wipe it with a clean cloth, and paper it as before-mentioned. Never do any thing elſe to veniſon, for all other things ſpoil it and take away the fine flavour, and this preſerves it better than any thing you can do. A hare you may manage juſt the ſame way.

To roaſt a Tongue and Udder.

PARBOIL them firſt for two hours, then roaſt them, ſtick eight or ten cloves about them; baſte them with butter, and have ſome gravy and galintine ſauce, made thus: take a few bread crumbs, and boil in a little water, beat it up, then put in a gill of red-wine, ſome ſugar to ſweeten it; put it in a baſon or boat.

To roaſt Geeſe, Turkies, &c.

WHEN you roaſt a gooſe, turkey, or fowls of any ſort, take care to ſinge them with a piece of white paper, and baſte them with

with butter; dredge them with a little flour, and ſprinkle a little ſalt on; and when the ſmoak begins to draw to the fire, and they look plump, baſte them again, and dredge them with a little flour, and take them up.

As to geeſe and ducks, you ſhould have ſage and onion ſhred fine, with pepper and ſalt put into the belly, with gravy in the diſh; or ſome like ſage and onion and gravy mixed together. Put only pepper and ſalt into wild ducks, eaſterlings, wigeon, teal, and all other ſorts of wild fowl. A middling turkey will take an hour to roaſt; a very large one, an hour and a quarter; a ſmall one, three quarters of an hour. You muſt paper the breaſt till it is near done enough, then take the paper off and froth it up. Your fire muſt be very good. The ſame time does for a gooſe.

To roaſt a Fowl pheaſant-faſhion.

IF you ſhould have but one pheaſant, and want two in a diſh, take a large full-grown fowl, keep the head on, and truſs it juſt as you do a pheaſant; lard it with bacon, but do not lard the pheaſant, and nobody will know it.

To roaſt a Fowl.

ROAST a large fowl three quarters of an hour; a middling one, half an hour; very ſmall chickens, twenty minutes. Your fire muſt be very quick and clear when you lay them down.

To roaſt Pigeons.

TAKE ſome parſley ſhred fine, a piece of butter as big as a nutmeg, a little pepper and ſalt; tie the neck end tight: tie a ſtring round the legs and rump, and faſten the other end to the top of the chimney-piece; baſte them with butter, and when they are enough, lay them in the diſh, and they will ſwim with gravy. You may put them on a little ſpit, and then tie both ends cloſe. Twenty minutes will roaſt them..

To roaſt Partridges.

LET them be nicely roaſted, but not too much; baſte them gently with a little butter, and dredge with flour, ſprinkle a little ſalt on, and froth them nicely up; have good gravy in the diſh, with bread-ſauce in a boat, made thus: take about a handful or two of crumbs of bread, put in a pint of milk or more, a ſmall whole onion, a little whole white pepper, a little ſalt, and a bit of butter, boil it all well up; then take the onion out, and beat it well with a ſpoon; or take poivrade-ſauce in a boat, made thus: chop four ſhalots fine, a gill of good gravy, and a ſpoonful of vinegar, a little pepper and ſalt; boil them up one minute, then put it in a boat. Twenty minutes is enough to roaſt them.

To roaſt Larks.

PUT a ſmall bird-ſpit through them, and tie them on another; all the time they are roaſting keep baſting them very gently with butter, and ſprinkle crumbs of bread on them till they are almoſt done; then let them brown before you take them up.

The beſt way of making crumbs of bread is to take the crumb of a ſtale loaf, rub it through a fine cullender, and put into a little butter in a ſtew-pan; melt it, put in your crumbs of bread, and keep them ſtirring till they are of a light brown; put them on a ſieve to drain a few minutes; lay your larks in a diſh, and the crumbs all round, almoſt as high as the larks, with plain butter in a cup, and ſome gravy in another. Twenty minutes will roaſt them.

To roaſt Woodcocks and Snipes.

PUT them on a little bird-ſpit, and tie them on another, and put them down to roaſt; take a round of a threepenny loaf, and toaſt it brown and butter it; then lay it in a diſh under the birds; baſte them with a little butter; take the trail out before you ſpit them, and put into a ſmall ſtew-pan, with a little gravy; ſimmer it gently over the fire for five or ſix minutes; add a little melted butter to it, put it over your toaſt in the diſh, and when your woodcocks are roaſted put them on the toaſt, and ſet it over a lamp or chafing diſh for three minutes, and ſend them to table.

Another Way.

PLUCK them, but do not draw them, put them on a ſmall ſpit, duſt and baſte them well with butter, toaſt a few ſlices of a penny loaf, put them on a clean plate, and ſet it under the birds while they are roaſting; if the fire be good they will take about ten minutes roaſting; when you draw them, lay them upon the toaſts on the diſh, pour melted butter round them, and ſerve them up.

To roaſt a Hare.

TAKE your hare when it is caſed, truſs it in this manner, bring the two hind-legs up to its ſides, pull the fore-legs back, put your ſkewer firſt into the hind-leg, then into the fore-leg, and thruſt it through the body; put the fore leg on, and then the hind-leg, and a ſkewer through the top of the ſhoulders and back part of the head, which will hold the head up. Make a pudding thus: take a quarter of a pound of beef-ſuet, as much crumb of bread, a handful of parſley chopped fine, ſome ſweet herbs of all ſorts, ſuch as baſil, marjoram, winter-ſavory, and a little thyme chopped very fine, a little nutmeg grated, ſome lemon-

lemon-peel cut fine, pepper and ſalt, chop the liver fine, and put in with an egg, mix it up, and put it into the belly, and ſew or ſkewer it up; then ſpit it and lay it to the fire, which muſt be a good quick one. Put three half pints of good milk in your dripping-pan, baſte your hare with it till reduced to half a gill, then duſt and baſte it well with butter; if it be a large one, it will take an hour and a half roaſting, and require a little more milk.

To roaſt Rabbits.

BASTE them with good butter, and dredge them with a little flour. Half an hour will do them, at a very quick, clear fire; and if they are very ſmall, twenty minutes will do them. Take the liver, with a little bunch of parſley, and boil them, and then chop them very fine together; melt ſome good butter, and put half the liver and parſley into the butter; pour it into the diſh, and garniſh the diſh with the other half. Let your rabbits be done of a fine light brown; or put the ſauce in a boat.

To roaſt a Rabbit hare-faſhion.

LARD a rabbit with bacon; roaſt it as you do a hare, with a ſtuffing in the belly, and it eats very well. But then you muſt make gravy-ſauce; but if you do not lard it, white ſauce, made thus: take a little veal broth, boil it up with a little flour and butter, to thicken it, then add a gill of cream; keep it ſtirring one way till it is ſmooth, then put it in a boat or in the diſh.

N. B. If your fire is not very quick and clear when you lay your poultry or game down to roaſt, it will not eat near ſo ſweet, or look ſo beautiful to the eye.

To keep Meat hot.

THE beſt way to keep meat, poultry, or game hot, if it be done before your company is ready, is to ſet the diſh over a pan of boiling water; cover the diſh with a deep cover, ſo as not to touch the meat, and throw a cloth over all. Thus you may keep your meat hot a long time, and it is better than over-roaſting and ſpoiling the meat. The ſteam of the water keeps the meat hot, and does not draw the gravy out, or draw it up; whereas if you ſet a diſh of meat any time over a chafing-diſh of coals, it will dry up all the gravy and ſpoil the meat.

BROILING.

General Directions concerning Broiling.

As to mutton and pork ſteaks, you muſt keep them turning quick on the gridiron, and have your diſh ready over a chafing-diſh of hot coals, and carry them to table covered hot, and only a few at a time. When you broil fowls or pigeons, always take care your fire is clear; and never baſte any thing on the gridiron, for it only makes it ſmoked and burnt.

To broil Beef Steaks.

FIRST have a very clear briſk fire; let your gridiron be very clean; put it on the fire, and take a chafing-diſh with a few hot coals out of the fire. Put the diſh on it which is to lay your ſteaks on, then take fine rump ſteaks about half an inch thick; put a little pepper and ſalt on them, lay them on the gridiron, and (if you like it) take a ſhalot or two, or a fine onion, and cut it fine; put it into your diſh. Keep turning your ſteaks quick till they are done, for that keeps the gravy in them. When the ſteaks are enough, take them carefully off into your diſh, that none of the gravy be loſt; then have ready a hot diſh and cover, and carry them hot to table with the cover on. You may ſend a ſhalot in a plate, chopt fine.

To broil Mutton Chops.

CUT your ſteaks half an inch thick, when your gridiron is hot rub it with freſh ſuet, lay on your ſteaks, keep turning them as quick as poſſible; if you do not take great care the fat that drops from the ſteak will ſmoke them; when they are enough, put them into a hot diſh, rub them well with butter, ſlice a ſhalot very thin into a ſpoonful of water, pour it on them with a ſpoonful of muſhroom catchup and ſalt, ſerve them up hot, and in ſmall quantities, freſh and freſh.

To broil Pork Steaks.

OBSERVE the ſame as for mutton ſteaks, only pork requires more broiling; when they are enough put in a little good gravy; a little ſage rubbed very fine ſtrewed over them gives them a fine taſte.

To broil Chickens.

SLIT them down the back, and ſeaſon them with pepper and ſalt; lay them on a very clear fire, and at a great diſtance. Let the inſide lie next the fire till it is above half done; then turn them, and take great care the fleſhy ſide do not burn, and let them be of a fine brown. Let your ſauce be good gravy, with muſhrooms, and garniſh with lemon and the livers broiled, the gizzards cut, ſlaſhed, and broiled with pepper and ſalt.

Or this ſauce: take a handful of ſorrel dipped in boiling water, drain it, and have ready half a pint of good gravy, a ſhalot ſhred ſmall, and ſome parſley boiled very green; thicken it it with a piece of butter rolled in flour, and add a glaſs of red wine; then lay your ſorrel in heaps round the fowls, and pour the ſauce over them. Garniſh with lemon.

Note, You may make juſt what ſauce you fancy.

To broil Pigeons.

TAKE young pigeons, pick and draw them, ſplit them down the back, and ſeaſon them with pepper and ſalt, lay them on the gridiron with the breaſt upward. Take care your fire is very clear, and ſet your gridiron high, that they may not burn; turn them, rub them over with butter, and keep turning them till they are enough; diſh them up, and lay round them criſped parſley, and pour over them melted butter or gravy, which you pleaſe, and ſend them up.

FRYING.

To fry Beef Steaks.

TAKE rump ſteaks, pepper and ſalt them, fry them in a little butter very quick and brown; take them out and put them into a diſh, pour the fat out of the frying-pan, and then take half a pint of hot gravy; if no gravy, half a pint of hot water, and put into the pan, and a little butter rolled in flour, a little pepper and ſalt, and two or three ſhalots chopped fine; boil them up in your pan for two minutes, then put it over the ſteaks, and ſend them to table.

A ſecond Way to fry Beef-Steaks.

CUT the lean by itſelf, and beat them well with the back of a knife, fry them in juſt as much butter as will moiſten the pan, pour out the gravy as it runs out of the meat, turn them often, do them over a gentle fire, then fry the fat by itſelf and lay upon the meat, and put to the gravy a glaſs of red wine, half an anchovy, a little nutmeg, a little beaten pepper, and a ſhalot cut ſmall; give it two or three little boils, ſeaſon it with ſalt to your palate, pour it over the ſteaks, and ſend them to table.

To fry Tripe.

CUT your tripe in long pieces of about three inches wide, and all the breadth of the double; put it in ſome ſmall-beer batter, or yolks of eggs; have a large pan of good fat, and fry it brown, then take it out and put it to drain; diſh it up with plain butter in a cup.

To fry Sauſages.

CUT them in ſingle links, and fry them in freſh butter, then take a ſlice of bread and fry it a good brown in the butter you fried

fried the ſauſages in, and lay it in the bottom of your diſh, put the ſauſages on the toaſt, in four parts.

B O I L I N G.

General Directions concerning Boiling.

To all ſorts of boiled meats, allow a quarter of an hour to every pound; be ſure the pot is very clean, and ſkim it well, for every thing will have a ſcum riſe, and if that boils down, it makes the meat black. All ſorts of freſh meat you are to put in when the water boils, but ſalt meat when the water is warm.

To boil a Ham.

When you boil a ham, put it into your copper when the water is pretty warm, for cold water draws the colour out; when it boils, be careful it boils very ſlowly. A ham of twenty pounds takes four hours and a half, larger and ſmaller in proportion. Keep the copper well ſkimmed. A green ham wants no ſoaking, but an old ham muſt be ſoaked ſixteen hours in a large tub of ſoft water.

To boil a Tongue.

A tongue, if ſalt, ſoak it in ſoft water all night, boil it three hours; if freſh out of the pickle, two hours and an half, and put it in when the water boils; take it out and pull it, trim it, garniſh with greens and carrots.

To boil a Round of Beef.

Take a round of beef, ſalt it well with common ſalt, let it lay ten days, turning it over and rubbing it with the brine every other day, then waſh it in ſoft water, tie it up as round as you can, and put it into cold ſoft water, boil it very gently, if it weighs thirty pounds, it will take three hours and a half; if you ſtuff it, do it thus; take half a pound of beef ſuet, ſome green beet, parſley, pot-marjoram, thyme, and leeks; chop all theſe very fine, put to them a handful of ſtale bread crumbs, pepper and ſalt, mix theſe well together, make holes in your beef and put it in, tie it up in a cloth.

To boil a Briſket of Beef.

Take a thick piece of the briſket, ſalt it well with common ſalt, rub it with the brine every other day, and turn it over, let it lay a fortnight or three weeks, if you think it will be too ſalt, ſteep it all night in cold water; ſet it on to boil in cold water, keep it cloſe covered, and ſtew it gently four hours, but if it be very thick it will take more; mind to ſkim your pot well

well when it begins to boil, which muſt be carefully obſerved in all kinds of boiled meats; if you take out the bones and roll it like collared meat, it will look much handſomer, particularly to eat cold.

To dreſs a Calf's Head plain.

TAKE a calf's head when freſh killed, ſplit and clean it well, take care of the brains, waſh it in ſoft water juſt aired, then put it into cold ſoft water, let it ſtand three or four hours, or all night if you have time, wrap it in a cloth and boil it in milk and ſoft water, if a large head it will take near two hours; tie the brains in a cloth with a few ſage leaves and a little parſley, an hour will boil them; take them out and chop the ſage and parſley well, and the brains a little, put them into a ſauce-pan, with a little good melted butter and a little ſalt, make them hot, then take up half the head, ſcore it and do it over with the yolk of egg, ſeaſon it with a little pepper and ſalt, ſtrew over a few ſtale bread crumbs mixed with a little chopped parſley, ſet it before the fire till brown, baſte it, but do not let it burn, then diſh it up, lay the boiled and broiled both on a diſh, and garniſh with greens, ſkin the tongue and ſplit it, lay the brains on a diſh and the tongue upon them; it is common to ſend up greens and bacon with it.

To boil a Lamb's Head.

BOIL the head and pluck tender, but do not let the liver be too much done. Take the head up, hack it croſs and croſs with a knife, grate ſome nutmeg over it, and lay it in a diſh before a good fire; then grate ſome crumbs of bread, ſome ſweet herbs rubbed, a little lemon-peel chopped fine, a very little pepper and ſalt, and baſte it with a little butter; then throw a little flour over it, and juſt before it is done do the ſame, baſte it and dredge it. Take half the liver, the lights, the heart, and tongue, chop them very ſmall, with ſix or eight ſpoonfuls of gravy or water; firſt ſhake ſome flower over the meat, and ſtir it together, then put in the gravy or water, a good piece of butter rolled in a little flour, a little pepper and ſalt, and what runs from the head in the diſh; ſimmer all together a few minutes, and add half a ſpoonful of vinegar, pour it into your diſh, lay the head in the middle of the mince-meat, have ready the other half of the liver cut thin, with ſome ſlices of bacon broiled, and lay round the head. Garniſh the diſh with lemon, and ſend it to table.

Boiled Leg of Lamb and the Loin fried round it.

LET the leg be boiled very white. An hour will do it. Cut the loin into ſteaks, dip them into a few crumbs of bread and

egg,

egg, fry them nice and brown, boil a good deal of ſpinage, and lay in the diſh; put the leg in the middle, lay the loin round it, cut an orange in four and garniſh the diſh, and have butter in a cup. Some love the ſpinage boiled, then drained, put into a ſauce-pan with a good piece of butter, and ſtewed.

To boil a Leg of Pork.

TAKE a leg of pork that has been ſalted a fortnight or three weeks, about eight pounds weight, put it into cold ſoft water, and boil it three hours and a quarter, then take off the ſkin. All ſalt meats require gently boiling. It is common to ſend up peaſe pudding with boiled pork.

To boil Pickled Pork.

BE ſure you put it in when the water boils. If a middling piece, an hour will boil it; if a very large piece, an hour and a half, or two hours. If you boil pickled pork too long, it will go to a jelly. You will know when it is done by trying it with a fork.

POULTRY.

To boil a Turkey.

TAKE a turkey, cut off the legs and head, truſs it as you would a fowl for boiling; lay it in milk and water an hour or two, drain it well, put ſome force-meat into the craw, made of beef ſuet ſhred fine, ſtale bread crumbs an equal quantity, a bit of lean veal the ſize of an egg, beat it in a marble mortar, pick the ſkins out, put to it an anchovy chopped, a little beaten mace, a little nutmeg, chyan, ſalt, lemon-peel ſhred fine, and a little lemon juice, mix theſe all together with an egg; ſew up the craw, rub the breaſt well with lemon juice, dredge it a little, pin it up in a clean cloth, boil it in ſoft water and milk; put your turkey in when it boils, boil it gently, if it is a large one it will take an hour and a quarter, if a middling ſize, an hour; diſh it up, and garniſh with lemon; you may ſerve it up with oyſter ſauce, celery, or white ſauce; you may dreſs a full grown fowl the ſame way.

To boil young Chickens.

TAKE chickens, pull and pick them clean whilſt warm, let them hang one night, then drain them, cut off the heads and legs, then truſs them, if your chickens be fat do not break the breaſt-bone; lay them into milk and water two hours, rub their breaſts with lemon juice, dredge them and put them into boiling milk and water; if they are fine chickens half an hour, if ſmall twenty minutes; diſh them up, and pour the ſauce over them, garniſh with ſliced lemon and chopped parſley.

To boil Fowls and House Lamb.

Boil these in a pot by themselves, with a good deal of water, scum the pot carefully; they will be both sweeter and whiter than if boiled in a cloth. A fowl takes half an hour.

To dress GREENS, ROOTS, *&c.*

Always be very careful that your greens be nicely picked and washed. You should lay them in a clean pan, for fear of sand or dust which is apt to hang round wooden vessels. Boil all your greens in a copper or sauce-pan, by themselves, with a great quantity of water. Boil no meat with them, for that discolours them. Use no iron pans, &c. for they are not proper; but let them be copper, brass, or silver.

Most people spoil garden things by over-boiling them. All things that are green should have a little crispness, for if they are over-boiled, they neither have any sweetness or beauty.

To dress Spinage.

Pick it very clean, and wash it in five or six waters; put it in a sauce-pan that will just hold it, throw a little salt over it, and cover the pan close. Do not put any water in, but shake the pan often. You must put your sauce-pan on a clear quick fire. As soon as you find the greens are shrunk and fallen to the bottom, and that the liquor which comes out of them boils up, they are enough. Throw the spinage into a clean sieve to drain, and squeeze it well between two plates, and cut it in any form you like. Lay it in a plate, or small dish, and never put any butter on it, but put it in a cup or boat.

To dress Cabbage, &c.

Cabbage, and all sorts of young sprouts, must be boiled in a great deal of water. When the stalks are tender, or fall to the bottom, they are enough; then take them off, before they lose their colour. Always throw salt in your water before you put your greens in. Young sprouts you send to table just as they are, but cabbage is best chopped and put into a sauce-pan with a good piece of butter, stirring it for about five or six minutes, till the butter is all melted, and then send it to table.

To dress Carrots.

Let them be scraped very clean, and when they are enough, rub them in a clean cloth, then slice them into a plate, and pour some melted butter over them. If they are young spring carrots, half an hour will boil them; if large, an hour; but old Sandwich carrots will take two hours.

To dreſs Turnips.

THEY eat beſt boiled in the pot with the meat, and, when enough, which you will know by trying them with a fork, take them out and put them in a pan, and maſh them with butter, a little cream, and a little ſalt, and ſend them to table. But you may do them thus: pare your turnips and cut them into dice, as big as the top of one's finger; put them into a clean ſauce-pan, and juſt cover them with water. When enough, throw them into a ſieve to drain, and put them into a ſauce-pan with a good piece of butter and a little cream; ſtir them over the fire for five or ſix minutes, and ſend them to table.

To dreſs Parſnips.

THEY ſhould be boiled in a great deal of water, and when you find they are ſoft, (which you will know by running a fork into them,) take them up, and carefully ſcrape all the dirt off them, and then with a knife ſcrape them all fine, throwing away all the ſticky parts, and ſend them up plain in a diſh with melted butter.

To dreſs Broccoli.

STRIP all the little branches off till you come to the top one, then with a knife peel off all the hard outſide ſkin, which is on the ſtalks and little branches, and throw them into water. Have a ſtew-pan of water with ſome ſalt in it; when it boils put in the broccoli, and when the ſtalks are tender it is enough, then ſend it to table with a piece of toaſted bread ſoaked in the water the broccoli is boiled in under it, the ſame way as aſparagus, with butter in a cup. The French eat oil and vinegar with it.

To dreſs Potatoes.

YOU muſt boil them in as little water as you can, without burning the ſauce-pan. Cover the ſauce-pan cloſe, and when the ſkin begins to crack they are enough. Drain all the water out, and let them ſtand covered for a minute or two; then peel them, lay them in your plate, and pour ſome melted butter over them. The beſt way to do them is, when they are peeled to lay them on a gridiron till they are of a fine brown, and ſend them to table. Another way is to put them into a ſauce-pan with ſome good beef dripping, cover them cloſe, and ſhake the ſauce-pan often for fear of burning to the bottom. When they are of a fine brown, and criſp, take them up in a plate, then put them into another for fear of the fat, and put butter in a cup.

To dreſs Cauliflowers.

TAKE your flowers, cut off all the green part, and then cut the flowers into four, and lay them into water for an hour; then

then have ſome milk and water boiling, put in the cauliflowers, and be ſure to ſkim the ſauce-pan well. When the ſtalks are tender, take them carefully up, and put them into a cullender to drain; then put a ſpoonful of water into a clean ſtew-pan with a little duſt of flour, about a quarter of a pound of butter, and ſhake it round till it is all finely melted, with a little pepper and ſalt; then take half the cauliflower and cut it as you would for pickling, lay it into the ſtew-pan, turn it, and ſhake the pan round. Ten minutes will do it. Lay the ſtewed in the middle of your plate, and the boiled round it. Pour the butter you did it in over it, and ſend it to table.

To boil them in the common Way.

CUT the cauliflower ſtalks off, leave a little green on, and boil them in ſpring water and ſalt; about fifteen minutes will do them. Take them out and drain them; ſend them whole in a diſh, with ſome melted butter in a cup.

To dreſs French Beans.

FIRST ſtring them, then cut them in two, and afterwards acroſs; but if you would do them nice, cut the bean into four, and then acroſs, which is eight pieces. Lay them into water and ſalt, and when your pan boils put in ſome ſalt and the beans; when they are tender they are enough; they will be ſoon done. Take care they do not loſe their fine green. Lay them in a plate, and have butter in a cup.

To dreſs Artichokes.

WRING off the ſtalks, and put the artichokes into cold water, and waſh them well, then put them in, when the water boils, with the tops downwards, that all the duſt and ſand may boil out. An hour and a half will do them.

To dreſs Aſparagus.

SCRAPE all the ſtalks very carefully till they look white, then cut all the ſtalks even alike, throw them into water, and have ready a ſtew-pan boiling. Put in ſome ſalt, and tie the aſparagus in little bundles. Let the water keep boiling, and when they are a little tender take them up. If you boil them too much you loſe both colour and taſte. Cut the round of a ſmall loaf, about half an inch thick, toaſt it brown on both ſides, dip it in the aſparagus liquor, and lay it in your diſh; pour a little butter over the toaſt, then lay your aſparagus on the toaſt all round the diſh, with the white tops outward. Do not pour butter over the aſparagus, for that makes them greaſy to the fingers, but have your butter in a baſon, and ſend it to table.

To

To boil green Peaſe.

SHELL your peaſe juſt before you want them, put them into a very ſmall quantity of boiling water, with a little ſalt and a lump of loaf ſugar, when they begin to dent in the middle they are enough, ſtrain them in a ſieve, put a good lump of butter into a mug or ſmall diſh, give your peaſe a ſhake up with the butter, put them on a diſh, and ſend them to table. Boil a ſprig of mint in another water, chop it fine, and lay it in lumps round the edge of your diſh.

To dreſs Beans and Bacon.

WHEN you dreſs beans and bacon, boil the bacon by itſelf and the beans by themſelves, for the bacon will ſpoil the colour of the beans. Always throw ſome ſalt into the water, and ſome parſley, nicely picked. When the beans are enough, (which you will know by their being tender,) throw them into a cullender to drain. Take up the bacon and ſkin it; throw ſome raſpings of bread over the top, and if you have an iron, make it red hot and hold over it, to brown the top of the bacon; if you have not one, hold it to the fire to brown; put the bacon in the middle of the diſh, and the beans all round, cloſe up to the bacon, and ſend them to table, with parſley and butter in a baſon.

CHAP. IV.

SAUCES FOR ALL THE DISHES MENTIONED IN THE FOREGOING CHAPTER.

To melt Butter.

IN melting of butter you muſt be very careful; let your ſauce-pan be well tinned; take a ſpoonful of cold water, a little duſt of flour, and a piece of butter ſufficient for your purpoſe, cut to pieces; be ſure to keep ſhaking your pan one way, for fear it ſhould oil; when it is all melted, let it boil, and it will be ſmooth and fine. A ſilver pan is beſt, if you have one.

To make Veal, Mutton, or Beef Gravy.

TAKE a raſher or two of bacon or ham, lay it at the bottom of your ſtew-pan; put your meat, cut in thin ſlices, over it; and cut ſome onions, turnips, carrots, and celery, a little thyme, and put over the meat, with a little all-ſpice; put a little water at the bottom, then ſet it on the fire, which muſt be a gentle one, and draw it till it is brown at the bottom

(which

(which you may know by the pan's hiffing), then pour boiling water over it, and ftew it gently for one hour and a half: if a fmall quantity, lefs time will do it. Seafon it with falt.

To make Gravy.

If you live in the country, where you cannot always have gravy meat, when your meat comes from the butcher's, take a piece of beef, a piece of veal, and a piece of mutton; cut them into as fmall pieces as you can, and take a large deep fauce-pan with a cover, lay your beef at bottom, then your mutton, then a very little piece of bacon, a flice or two of carrot, fome mace, cloves, whole pepper black and white, a large onion cut in flices, a bundle of fweet herbs, and then lay in your veal. Cover it clofe over a flow fire for fix or feven minutes, fhaking the fauce-pan now and then: then fhake fome flour in, and have ready fome boiling water; pour it in till you cover the meat and fomething more. Cover it clofe, and let it ftew till it is quite rich and good; then feafon it to your tafte with falt, and ftrain it off. This will do for moft things.

Different Sorts of Sauce for a Pig.

There are feveral ways of making fauce for a pig. Some do not love any fage in the pig, only a cruft of bread; but then you fhould have a little dried fage rubbed and mixed with the gravy and butter. Some love bread-fauce in a bafon, made thus: take a pint of water, put in a good piece of crumb of bread, a blade of mace, and a little whole pepper; boil it for about five or fix minutes, and then pour the water off; take out the fpice, and beat up the bread with a good piece of butter, and a little milk or cream. Some love a few currants boiled in it, a glafs of wine, and a little fugar; but that you muft do juft as you like it. Others take half a pint of good beef gravy, and the gravy which comes out of the pig, with a piece of butter rolled in flour, two fpoonfuls of catchup, and boil them all together; then take the brains of the pig and bruife them fine; put all thefe together, with the fage in the pig, and pour into your difh. It is a very good fauce. When you have not gravy enough comes out of your pig with the butter for fauce, take about half a pint of veal gravy and add to it; or ftew the pettitoes, and take as much of that liquor as will do for fauce, mixed with the other.—*N. B.* Some like the fauce fent in a boat, or bafon.

Different Sorts of Sauce for Venifon.

You may take either of thefe fauces for venifon: Currant-jelly warmed; or a pint of red wine, with a quarter of a pound of fugar, fimmered over a clear fire for five or fix minutes; or a pint of vinegar, and a quarter of a pound of ſugar, ſimmered till it is a ſyrup.

Sauce for a Gooſe.

FOR a gooſe make a little good gravy, and put it into a baſon by itſelf, and ſome apple-ſauce into another, made thus:

Apple-Sauce.

PARE, core, and ſlice your apples, put them in a ſauce-pan with as much water as will keep them from burning, ſet them over a very ſlow fire, keep them cloſe covered till they are all of a pulp, then put in a lump of butter, and ſugar to your taſte, beat them well, and ſend them to the table in a china baſon. Add a piece of lemon-peel.

Sauce for a Turkey.

FOR a turkey, good gravy in the diſh, and either bread or onion ſauce in a baſon, or both.

Sauce for Ducks.

FOR ducks, a little gravy in the diſh, and onion-ſauce in a cup, if liked.

Sauce for Fowls.

TO fowls you ſhould put good gravy in the diſh, and either bread, parſley, or egg ſauce in a baſon.

Sauce for Pheaſants and Partridges.

PHEASANTS and partridges ſhould have gravy in the diſh, and bread-ſauce in a cup, and poivrade-ſauce, which is made, either hot or cold, as under.

To make hot Poivrade-Sauce.

TAKE two anchovies, take out the bones, waſh them, and chop them fine with two or three ſhalots, ſix ſpoonfuls of gravy, and ſix of vinegar; boil theſe two minutes; keep ſtirring it. You may either ſend it up ſtrained, or with the ingredients.

To make cold Poivrade-Sauce.

TAKE two anchovies, take out the bones, chop them well, put them into a baſon with two table-ſpoonfuls of the beſt ſallad-oil, a tea-ſpoonful of made muſtard; rub theſe well with the back of a ſpoon; add two large ſhalots ſhred fine, and ſhred parſley. Mix theſe well together with vinegar to your taſte.

Different

Different Sorts of Sauce for a Hare.

TAKE for ſauce, a pint of cream and half a pound of freſh butter; put them in a ſauce-pan, and keep ſtirring it with a ſpoon till the butter is melted and the ſauce is thick; then take up the hare, and pour the ſauce into the diſh. Another way to make ſauce for a hare is, to make good gravy, thickened with a little piece of butter rolled in flour, and pour it into your diſh. You may leave the butter out, if you do not like it, and have ſome currant-jelly warmed in a cup, or red wine and ſugar boiled to a ſyrup, done thus: take a pint of red wine, a quarter of a pound of ſugar, and ſet it over a ſlow fire to ſimmer for about a quarter of an hour. You may do half the quantity, and put it into your ſauce-boat or baſon.

To make Gravy for a Turkey, or any Sort of Fowls.

TAKE a pound of the lean part of the beef, hack it with a knife; flour it well; have ready a ſtew-pan with a piece of freſh butter. When the butter is melted, put in the beef, fry it till it is brown, and then pour in a little boiling water; ſhake it round, and then fill up with a tea-kettle of boiling water. Stir it all together, and put in two or three blades of mace, four or five cloves, ſome whole pepper, an onion, a bundle of ſweet herbs, a little cruſt of bread baked brown, and a little piece of carrot. Cover it cloſe, and let it ſtew till it is as good as you would have it. This will make a pint of rich gravy.

Turkies, Pheaſants, &c. may be larded.

YOU may lard a turkey or pheaſant, or any thing, juſt as you like it.

Directions concerning the Sauce for Steaks.

IF you love pickles or horſe-raddiſh with ſteaks, never garniſh your diſh; becauſe both the garniſhing will be dry and the ſteaks will be cold; but lay thoſe things on little plates, and carry to table. The great nicety is to have them hot and full of gravy.

Sauce for a boiled Turkey.

THE beſt ſauce for a boiled turkey is good oyſter and cellery ſauce. Make OYSTER-SAUCE thus: Take as many oyſters as you want, and ſet them off, ſtrain the liquor from them, put them in cold water, and waſh and beard them; put them into the liquor which came from them in a ſtew-pan, with a blade of mace, and ſome butter rolled in flour, and a little lemon; boil them up, then put in cream in proportion, and boil it all together gently; take the lemon and mace out, ſqueeze the juice of the lemon into the ſauce, then ſerve it in your

 boats

boats or basons. Make CELLERY-SAUCE thus: Take the white part of the cellery; cut it about one inch long; boil it in some water till it is tender, then take as much veal broth as you want, a blade of mace, and thicken it with a little flour and butter; put in as much cream as broth; boil them up gently together; put in your cellery, and boil it up; then pour it into your boats.

Sauce for a boiled Goose.

SAUCE for a boiled goose must be either onions or cabbage, first boiled, and then stewed in butter for five minutes.

Sauce for boiled Ducks or Rabbits.

OVER boiled ducks or rabbits you must pour boiled onions, which do thus: Take the onions, peel them, and boil them in a great deal of water; shift your water, then let them boil about two hours; take them up, and throw them into a cullender to drain, then with a knife chop them on a board, and rub them through a cullender; put them into a sauce-pan, just shake a little flour over them, put in a little milk or cream, with a good piece of butter, and a little salt; set them over the fire, and when the butter is melted they are enough. But if you would have onion-sauce in half an hour, take your onions, peel them, and cut them in thin slices, put them into milk and water, and when the water boils, they will be done in twenty minutes, then throw them into a cullender to drain, and chop them and put them into a sauce-pan; shake in a little flour, with a little cream if you have it, and a good piece of butter; stir all together over the fire till the butter is melted, and they will be very fine. This sauce is very good with roast mutton, and it is the best way of boiling onions.

To bake a Leg of Beef.

Do it just in the same manner as before directed in the making gravy for soups, &c.; and when it is baked, strain it through a coarse sieve. Pick out all the sinews and fat, put them into a sauce-pan with a few spoonfuls of the gravy, a little red wine, a piece of butter rolled in flour, and some mustard; shake your sauce-pan often, and when the sauce is hot and thick, dish it up, and send it to table. It is a pretty dish.

To bake an Ox's Head.

Do just in the same manner as the leg of beef is directed to be done in making the gravy for soups, &c. and it does full as well for the same uses. If it should be too strong for any thing you want it for, it is only putting some hot water to it. Cold water will spoil it.

CHAP.

CHAP. V.

MADE-DISHES.

Rules to be obſerved in all Made-Diſhes.

FIRST, that the ſtew-pans, or ſauce-pans, and covers, be very clean, free from ſand, and well tinned; and that all the white ſauces have a little tartneſs; put every ingredient into your white ſauce, and have it of a proper thickneſs and well boiled before any eggs and cream are put in, for they add but little to the thickneſs; do not ſtir it with a ſpoon after they are in, nor ſet your pan on the fire, or it will gather at the bottom, and be in lumps; but hold your pan a good height from the fire, and keep ſhaking the pan round one way, it will keep the ſauce from curdling; and be ſure you do not let it boil.

And as to brown ſauce, take great care no fat ſwims at the top, but that it be all ſmooth alike, and about as thick as good cream, and not to taſte of one thing more than another. As to pepper and ſalt, ſeaſon to your palate, but do not put too much of either, for that will take away the fine flavour of every thing.

When you uſe fried force-meat balls, put them on a ſieve to drain the fat from them, and never let them boil in your ſauce, it will give them a greaſy look, and ſoften the balls; the beſt way is to put them in after your meat is diſhed up.

As to moſt made-diſhes, you muſt put in what you think proper to enlarge it, or make it good; as muſhrooms pickled, dried, freſh, or powdered; truffles, morels, cock's-combs ſtewed, ox-palates cut in ſmall bits, artichoke-bottoms, either pickled, freſh boiled, or dried ones ſoftened in warm water, each cut in four pieces, aſparagus-tops, the yolks of hard eggs, force-meat balls, &c. The beſt things to give a ſauce tartneſs are muſhroom-pickle, white walnut-pickle, elder-vinegar, lemon-juice, or lemon-pickle.

To make Lemon-Pickle.

TAKE two dozen of lemons, grate off the out-rinds very thin, cut them in four quarters, but leave the bottoms whole, rub on them equally half a pound of bay ſalt, and ſpread them on a large pewter diſh, put them in a cool oven, or let them dry gradually by the fire till all the juice is dried into the peels, then put them into a pitcher well glazed; with one ounce of mace, half an ounce of cloves beat fine, one ounce of nutmeg cut in thin ſlices, four ounces of garlic peeled, half a pint of muftard-feed bruifed a little, and tied in a muflin bag; pour two quarts of boiling white wine vinegar upon them, clofe the pitcher well up, and let it ftand five or fix days by the fire; fhake it well up every day, then tie it up, and let it ftand for three months to take off the bitter; when you bottle it, put the pickle and lemon in a hair fieve, prefs them well to get out the liquor, and let it ftand till another day, then pour off the fine, and bottle it; let the other ftand three or four days, and it will refine itfelf, pour it off and bottle it, let it ftand again and bottle it, till the whole is refined. It may be put in any white fauce, and will not hurt the colour. It is very good for fifh-fauce and made-difhes; a tea-fpoonful is enough for white, and two for brown fauce for a fowl; it is a moft ufeful pickle, and gives a pleafant flavour. Be fure you put it in before you thicken the fauce or put any cream in, left the fharpnefs make it curdle.

Browning for Made-Difhes.

BEAT fmall a quarter of a pound of treble-refined fugar, put it in a clean iron frying-pan, with an ounce of butter, fet it over a clear fire, mix it very well together all the time; when it begins to be frothy, the fugar is melted; hold it higher over the fire; have ready a pint of red wine; when the fugar and butter is of a deep brown, pour in a little of the wine, and ftir it well together, then add more wine, keep it ftirring all the time, put in half an ounce of Jamaica pepper, fix cloves, four quarters of chalots peeled, two or three blades of mace, three fpoonfuls of mufhroom catchup, a little falt, the rind of a lemon pared thin; boil them flowly for ten minutes, pour it into a bafon, and when cold take off the fcum and bottle the liquor.

To drefs Scotch Collops.

TAKE a piece of fillet of veal, cut it in thin pieces, about as big as a crown-piece, but very thin; fhake a little flour over it, then put a little butter in a frying-pan, and melt it; put in your collops, and fry them quick till they are brown, then lay them in a difh: have ready a good ragoo made thus: Take a little butter in your ftew-pan, and melt it, then add a fpoonful of flour, ftir it about till it is fmooth, then put in a fufficient quantity of good brown gravy; feafon it with pepper and falt, put in fome veal fweet-breads, force-meat balls, truffles and morels, ox palates, and mufhrooms; ftew them gently for half an hour, add the juice of half a lemon to it; put it over the collops, and garnifh with fmall rafhers of bacon curled round a fkewer. Some like the Scotch collops made thus: Put the collops into the ragoo, and ftew them for five minutes.

To dreſs White Collops.

CUT the veal the ſame as for Scotch collops; throw them into a ſtew-pan; put ſome boiling water over them, and ſtir them about, then ſtrain them off; take a little good veal broth, and thicken it; add a bundle of ſweet herbs, with ſome mace; put ſweetbread, force-meat balls, and freſh muſhrooms; if no freſh to be had, uſe pickled ones waſhed in warm water; ſtew them about fifteen minutes; add the yolk of an egg, and ſome cream; beat them well together with ſome nutmeg grated, and keep ſtirring it till it boils up; add a ſqueeze of a lemon, then put it in your diſh. Garniſh with lemon.

To dreſs a Fillet of Veal with Collops.

FOR an alteration, take a ſmall fillet of veal, cut what collops you want, then take the udder, and fill it with force-meat, roll it round, tie it with a pack-thread acroſs, and roaſt it; lay your collops in the diſh, and lay your udder in the middle. Garniſh your diſhes with lemon.

Scotch Collops à la Françoiſe.

TAKE a leg of veal, cut it very thin, lard it with bacon, then take half a pint of ale boiling, and pour over it till the blood is out, and then pour the ale into a baſon; take a few ſweet herbs chopped ſmall, ſtrew them over the veal, and fry it in butter, flour it a little till enough, then pour it into a diſh, and pour the butter away, toaſt little thin pieces of bacon and lay round, pour the ale into the ſtew-pan with two anchovies, then beat up the yolks of two eggs and ſtir in, with a little nutmeg, ſome pepper, and a piece of butter; ſhake all together till thick, and then pour it into the diſh. Garniſh with lemon.

To make a Savoury Diſh of Veal.

CUT large collops out of a leg of veal, ſpread them abroad on a dreſſer, hack them with the back of a knife, and dip them in the yolks of eggs; ſeaſon them with cloves, mace, nutmeg, and pepper, beat fine; make force-meat with ſome of your veal, beef-ſuet, oyſters chopped, ſweet herbs ſhred fine, and the aforeſaid ſpice; ſtrew all theſe over your collops, roll and tie them up, put them on ſkewers, tie them to a ſpit, and roaſt them; to the reſt of your force-meat add a raw egg or two, roll them in balls, and fry them; put them in your diſh with your meat when roaſted, and make the ſauce with ſtrong broth, an anchovy, a ſhalot, a little white wine, and ſome ſpice. Let it ſtew, and thicken it with a piece of butter rolled in flour; pour the fauce into the difh, lay the meat in, and garnifh with lemon.

Italian Collops.

PREPARE a fillet of veal, cut into thin flices, cut off the fkin and fat, lard them with bacon, fry them brown, then take them out and lay them in a difh, pour out all the butter, take a quarter of a pound of butter and melt it in the pan, then ftrew in a large fpoonful of flour; ftir it till it is brown, and pour in three pints of good gravy, a bundle of fweet herbs, and an onion, which you muft take out foon; let it boil a little, then put in the collops, let them ftew half a quarter of an hour, put in fome force-meat balls fried, and a few pickled mufhrooms, truffles and morels; ftir all together for a minute or two till it is thick, and then difh it up. Garnifh with lemon.

To do them White.

AFTER you have cut your veal in thin flices, lard it with bacon; feafon it with cloves, mace, nutmeg, pepper and falt, fome grated bread, and fweet herbs. Stew the knuckle in as little liquor as you can, a bunch of fweet herbs, fome whole pepper, a blade of mace, and four cloves; then take a pint of the broth, ftew the cutlets in it, and add to it fome mufhrooms, a piece of butter rolled in flour, and the yolk of an egg, and a gill of cream; ftir all together till it is thick, and then difh it up. Garnifh with lemon.

Beef Collops.

TAKE fome rump fteaks, or any tender piece, cut like Scotch collops, only larger, hack them a little with a knife, and flour them; put a little butter in a ftew-pan, and melt it, then put in your collops, and fry them quick for about two minutes; put in a pint of gravy, a little butter rolled in flour; feafon with pepper and falt; cut four pickled cucumbers in thin flices, half a walnut, and a few capers, a little onion fhred very fine; ftew them five minutes, then put them into a hot difh, and fend them to table. You may put half a glafs of white wine into it.

To make Force-Meat Balls.

FORCE-MEAT balls are a great addition to all made-difhes, made thus: Take half a pound of veal, and half a pound of fuet, cut fine, and beat in a marble mortar or wooden bowl; have a few fweet herbs and parfley fhred fine, a little mace dried and beat fine, a fmall nutmeg grated, or half a large one, a little lemon-peel cut very fine, a little pepper and falt, and the yolks of two eggs; mix all thefe well together, then roll them in little round balls, and ſome in little long balls; roll them in flour, and fry them brown. If they are for any thing of white ſauce, put a little water in a ſauce-pan, and when the water boils put them in, and let them boil for a few minutes, but never fry them for white ſauce.

A leſs quantity may be made, by uſing the ingredients in proportion.

Truffles and Morels, good in Sauces and Soups.

TAKE half an ounce of truffles and morels, let them be well waſhed in warm water, to get the ſand and dirt out, then ſimmer them in two or three ſpoonfuls of water for a few minutes, then put them with the liquor into the ſauce. They thicken both ſauce and ſoup, and give it a fine flavour.

To ſtew Ox Palates.

STEW them very tender, which muſt be done by putting them into cold water, and letting them ſtew very ſoftly over a ſlow fire; then take off the two ſkins, cut them in pieces, and put them either into your made-diſh or ſoup; and cock's-combs and artichoke-bottoms, cut ſmall, and put into the made-diſh. Garniſh your diſhes with lemon, ſweet breads ſtewed for white diſhes, and fried for brown ones, and cut in little pieces.

To ragoo Ox Palates.

TAKE four ox palates, and boil them very tender, clean them well, cut ſome in ſquare pieces, and ſome long; then make a rich cooley thus: Put a piece of butter in your ſtew-pan, and melt it, put a large ſpoonful of flour to it, ſtir it well till it is ſmooth; then put a quart of good gravy to it, chop three ſhalots, and put in a gill of Liſbon, cut ſome lean ham very fine and put in, alſo half a lemon; boil them twenty minutes, then ſtrain it through a ſieve, put it into your pan, and the palates, with ſome force-meat balls, truffles and morels, pickled or freſh muſhrooms ſtewed in gravy; ſeaſon with pepper and ſalt to your liking, and toſs them up five or ſix minutes; then diſh them up. Garniſh with lemon or beet-root.

To fricaſſee Ox Palates.

AFTER boiling your palates very tender, (which you muſt do by ſetting them on in cold water, and letting them do ſoftly,) then blanch and ſcrape them clean; take mace, nutmeg, cloves, and pepper beat fine, rub them all over with thoſe, and with crumbs of bread; have ready ſome butter in a ſtew-pan, and when it is hot put in the palates; fry them brown on both ſides, then pour out the fat, and put to them ſome mutton or beef

gravy,

gravy, enough for ſauce, an anchovy, a little nutmeg, a little piece of butter rolled in flour, and the juice of a lemon; let it ſimmer all together for a quarter of an hour; diſh it up, and garniſh with lemon.

To roaſt Ox Palates.

HAVING boiled your palates tender, blanch them, cut them into ſlices about two inches long, lard half with bacon, then have ready two or three pigeons, and two or three chicken-peepers, draw them, truſs them, and fill them with force-meat; let half of them be nicely larded; ſpit them on a bird-ſpit in this order: a bird, a palate, a ſage-leaf, and a piece of bacon; and ſo on; take cock's-combs and lamb-ſtones, parboiled and blanched, lard them with little bits of bacon, large oyſters parboiled, and each one larded with one piece of bacon; put theſe on a ſkewer, with a little piece of bacon and a ſage-leaf between them, tie them on a ſpit, and roaſt them, then beat up the yolks of three eggs, ſome nutmeg, a little ſalt, and crumbs of bread; baſte them with theſe all the time they are roaſting, and have ready two ſweetbreads, each cut in two, ſome artichoke-bottoms cut into four and fried, and then rub the diſh with ſhalots: lay the birds in the middle, piled upon one another, and lay the other things all ſeparate by themſelves round about in the diſh. Have ready for ſauce a pint of good gravy, a quarter of a pint of red wine, an anchovy, the oyſter liquor, a piece of butter rolled in flour; boil all theſe together and pour into the diſh, with a little juice of lemon. Garniſh your diſh with lemon.

To fricando Ox Palates.

WHEN you have waſhed and cleaned your palates, cut them in ſquare pieces, lard them with little bits of bacon, fry them in hog's lard, a pretty brown, and put them in a ſieve to drain the fat from them, then take better than half a pint of beef gravy, one ſpoonful of red wine, half as much of browning, a little lemon-pickle, one anchovy, a ſhalot, and a bit of horſe-radiſh; give them a boil, and ſtrain your gravy, then put in your palates, and ſtew them half an hour, make your ſauce pretty thick, diſh them up, and lay round them ſtewed ſpinage preſſed and cut like little ſippets, and ſerve them up.

To make a Brown Fricaſſee.

YOU muſt take your rabbits and chickens, and ſkin the rabbits, but not the chickens, then cut them into ſmall pieces, and rub them over with yolks of eggs. Have ready ſome grated bread, a little beaten mace, and a little grated nutmeg mixed together, and then roll them in it; put a little butter into a ſtew-

ſtew-pan, and when it is melted put in your meat. Fry it of a fine brown, and take care they do not ſtick to the bottom of the pan; then pour the butter from them, and pour in half a pint of brown gravy, a glaſs of white wine, a few muſhrooms, or two ſpoonfuls of the pickle, a little ſalt (if wanted), and a piece of butter rolled in flour. When it is of a fine thickneſs, diſh it up, and ſend it to table. You may add truffles and morels, and cock's-combs.

To make a White Fricaſſee.

TAKE two chickens, and cut them in ſmall pieces; put them in warm water to draw out the blood, then put them into ſome good veal broth; if no veal broth, a little boiling water, and ſtew them gently with a bundle of ſweet herbs, and a blade of mace, till they are tender; then take out the ſweet herbs, add a little flour and butter, boiled together, to thicken it a little, then add a quarter of a pint of cream, and the yolk of an egg beat very fine; ſome pickled muſhrooms: the beſt way is to put ſome freſh muſhrooms in at firſt; if no freſh, then pickled; keep ſtirring it till it boils up, then add the juice of half a lemon, ſtir it well to keep it from curdling, then put it in your diſh. Garniſh with lemon.

To fricaſſee Rabbits, Lamb, or Veal.

OBSERVE the directions given in the preceding article.

A ſecond Way to make a White Fricaſſee.

YOU muſt take two or three rabbits, or chickens, ſkin them, and lay them in warm water, and dry them with a clean cloth. Put them into a ſtew-pan with a blade or two of mace, a little black and white pepper, an onion, a little bundle of ſweet herbs, and do but juſt cover them with water; ſtew them till they are tender, then with a fork take them out, ſtrain the liquor, and put them into the pan again with half a pint of the liquor, and half a pint of cream, the yolks of two eggs beat well, half a nutmeg grated, a glaſs of white wine, a little piece of butter rolled in flour, and a gill of muſhrooms; keep ſtirring all together, all the while one way, till it is ſmooth and of a fine thickneſs, and then diſh it up. Add what you pleaſe.

A third Way of making a White Fricaſſee.

TAKE three chickens, ſkin them, cut them into ſmall pieces, that is, every joint aſunder; lay them in warm water for a quarter of an hour, take them out and dry them with a cloth, then put them into a ſtew-pan with milk and water, and boil them tender; take a pint of good cream, a quarter of a pound of of butter, and ſtir it till it is thick, then let it ſtand till it is cool, and put to it a little beaten mace, half a nutmeg grated, a little ſalt, and a few muſhrooms; ſtir all together, then take the chickens out of the ſtew-pan, throw away what they are boiled in, clean the pan, and put in the chickens and ſauce together; keep the pan ſhaking round till they are quite hot, and diſh them up. Garniſh with lemon.

To fricaſſee Rabbits, Lamb, Sweetbreads, or Tripe.

Do them the ſame way.

Another Way to fricaſſee Tripe.

TAKE a piece of double tripe, and cut it in pieces of about two inches; put them into a ſauce-pan of water, with an onion and a bundle of ſweet herbs; boil it till it is quite tender, then have ready a biſhemel made thus: Take ſome lean ham, cut it in thin pieces, and put it in a ſtew-pan, and ſome veal, having firſt cut off all the fat, put it over the ham; cut an onion in ſlices, ſome carrot and turnip, a little thyme, cloves, and mace, and ſome freſh muſhrooms chopped; put a little milk at the bottom, and draw it gently over the fire; be careful it does not ſcorch; then put in a quart of milk, and half a pint of cream, ſtew it gently for an hour, thicken it with a little flour and milk, ſeaſon it with ſalt and a very little Cayenne pepper, then ſtrain it off through a tammy, put your tripe into it, toſs it up, and add ſome force-meat balls, muſhrooms, and oyſters blanched; then put it into your diſh, and garniſh with fried oyſters, or ſweetbreads, or lemons.

To make a Fricaſſee of Calves' Feet and Chaldron, after the Italian Way.

TAKE the crumb of half a quartern loaf, one pound of ſuet, a large onion, two or three handfuls of parſley, mince it very ſmall, ſeaſon it with ſalt and pepper, three or four cloves of garlic, mix with eight or ten eggs; then ſtuff the chaldron; take the feet, and put them into a deep ſtew-pan: it muſt ſtew upon a ſlow fire till the bones are looſe; then take two quarts of green peas, and put in the liquor; and when done, you muſt thicken it with the yolks of two eggs, and the juice of a lemon. It muſt be ſeaſoned with pepper, ſalt, mace, and onion, ſome parſley, and garlic. You muſt ſerve it up with the abovesaid pudding in the middle of the diſh, and garniſh the diſh with fried ſuckers and ſliced onion.

A Fricaſſee of Pigeons.

TAKE eight pigeons new killed, cut them in ſmall pieces, and put them into a ſtew-pan with a pint of white wine and a pint

pint of water. Seaſon your pigeons with ſalt and pepper, a blade or two of mace, an onion, a bundle of ſweet herbs, a good piece of butter juſt rolled in a very little flour; cover it cloſe, and let them ſtew till there is juſt enough for ſauce, and then take out the onion and ſweet herbs, beat up the yolks of three eggs, grate half a nutmeg in, and with your ſpoon puſh the birds all to one ſide of the pan, and the gravy to the other ſide, and ſtir in the eggs; keep them ſtirring for fear of turning to curds; and when the ſauce is fine and thick, ſhake all together, and then put the pigeons into the diſh, pour the ſauce over them, and have ready ſome ſlices of bacon toaſted, and fried oyſters; throw the oyſters all over, and lay the bacon round. Garniſh with lemon.

A Fricaſſee of Lamb ſtones and Sweetbreads.

HAVE ready ſome lamb-ſtones blanched, parboiled, and ſliced, and flour two or three ſweetbreads; if very thick, cut them in two; the yolks of ſix hard eggs whole, a few piſtachio-nut kernels, and a few large oyſters: fry theſe all of a fine brown, then pour out all the butter, and add a pint of drawn gravy, the lamb-ſtones, ſome aſparagus-tops about an inch long, ſome grated nutmeg, a little pepper and ſalt, two ſhalots ſhred ſmall, and a glaſs of white wine. Stew all theſe together for ten minutes, then add the yolks of three eggs beat very fine, with a little cream, and a little beaten mace; ſtir all together till it is of a fine thickneſs, and then diſh it up. Garniſh with lemon.

Lamb Cutlets fricaſſeed.

TAKE a leg of lamb, cut it in thin cutlets acroſs the grain, put them in a ſtew-pan; in the mean time make ſome good broth with the bones and ſhank, &c. enough to cover the meat, put it into the cover with a bundle of ſweet herbs, an onion, a little cloves and mace tied in a muſlin rag; ſtew them gently for ten minutes; take out the meat, ſkim the fat off, and take out the ſweet herbs and mace, thicken it with butter rolled in flour, ſeaſon it with ſalt and a little Cayenne pepper, put in a few muſhrooms, truffles and morels clean waſhed, ſome force-meat balls, three yolks of eggs beat up in half a pint of cream, ſome nutmeg grated; keep ſtirring it one way till it is thick and ſmooth; put in your cutlets, give them a toſs up, take them out with a fork and lay them in a diſh, pour the ſauce over them. Garniſh with lemon and beet-root.

To haſh a Calf's Head.

BOIL the head almoſt enough, then take the beſt half, and with a ſharp knife take it nicely from the bone, with the two eyes.

eyes. Lay it in a little deep diſh before a good fire, and take great care no aſhes fall into it, and then hack it with a knife croſs and croſs; grate ſome nutmeg all over, the yolks of two eggs, a very little pepper and ſalt, a few ſweet herbs, ſome crumbs of bread, and a little lemon-peel chopped very fine, baſte it with a little butter, then baſte it again; keep the diſh turning that it may be all brown alike; cut the other half and tongue into little thin bits, and ſet on a pint of drawn gravy in a ſauce-pan, a little bundle of ſweet herbs, an onion, a little pepper and ſalt, a glaſs of white wine, and two ſhalots; boil all theſe together a few minutes, then ſtrain it through a ſieve, and put it into a clean ſtew-pan with the haſh. Flour the meat before you put it in, and put in a few muſhrooms, a ſpoonful of pickle, two ſpoonfuls of catchup, and a few truffles and morels; ſtir all theſe together for a few minutes, then beat up half the brains, and ſtir into the ſtew-pan, and a little piece of butter rolled in flour. Take the other half of the brains, and beat them up with a little lemon-peel cut fine, a little nutmeg grated, a little beaten mace, a little thyme ſhred ſmall, a little parſley, the yolk of an egg, and have ſome good dripping boiling in a ſtew-pan; then fry the brains in little cakes, about as big as a crown-piece. Fry about twenty oyſters dipped in the yolk of an egg, toaſt ſome ſlices of bacon, fry a few force-meat balls, and have ready a hot diſh; if pewter, over a few coals; if china, over a pan of hot water. Pour in your haſh, then lay in your toaſted head, throw the force-meat balls over the haſh, and garniſh the diſh with fried oyſters, the fried brains, and lemon; throw the reſt over the haſh, lay the bacon round the diſh, and ſend it to table.

To haſh a Calf's Head white.

TAKE a pint of white gravy, a large wine-glaſs of white wine, a little beaten mace, a little nutmeg, and a little ſalt; throw into your haſh a few muſhrooms, a few truffles and morels firſt parboiled; a few artichoke-bottoms, and aſparagus-tops, (if you have them,) a good piece of butter rolled in flour, the yolks of two eggs, half a pint of cream, and one ſpoonful of muſhroom catchup; ſtir it all together very carefully till it is of a fine thickneſs; then pour it into your diſh, and lay the other half of the head, as before mentioned, in the middle, and garniſh as before directed, with fried oyſters, brains, lemon, and force-meat balls fried.

Calf's Head Haſh another Way, leſs expenſive and troubleſome.

PARBOIL a calf's head; cut out the cheek-bones to broil, cut all the reſt to pieces, ſeaſon with cloves, mace, pepper, and falt; tofs it up in fome good gravy till enough. You may add fome ox palates, fweetbreads, mufhrooms, force-meat balls, &c. Then make the gravy a proper thicknefs, and tofs it up a fecond time, and it is fit for the table. Fry the brains in butter to lay round the difh; garnifh with lemon.

To hafh Venifon.

TAKE it when cold, cut it into thin flices, lay it into a ftew-pan, with a little fhalot chopped fine, a little chyan, and falt; its own gravy or any other good gravy, as much red wine as you have gravy, let there be as much as will cover it, juft give it a boil, lay it on a hot difh, and fend up currant-jelly with it.

To hafh Beef.

CUT your beef in very thin flices, take a little of your gravy that runs from it, put it into a toffing-pan with a tea-fpoonful of lemon-pickle, a large one of walnut-catchup, the fame of browning, flice a fhalot in, and put it over the fire; when it boils, put in your beef; fhake it over the fire till it is quite hot, the gravy is not to be thickened, flice in a fmall pickled cucumber; garnifh with fcraped horfe-radifh or pickled onions.

To make a Mutton Hafh.

CUT your mutton in little bits as thin as you can, ftrew a little flour over it, have ready fome gravy (enough for fauce) wherein fweet herbs, onions, pepper, and falt, have been boiled; ftrain it, put in your meat, with a little piece of butter rolled in flour, and a little falt, a fhalot cut fine, a few capers and gerkins chopped fine; tofs all together for a minute or two; have ready fome bread toafted and cut into thin fippets, lay them round the difh, and pour in your hafh. Garnifh your difh with pickles and horfe-radifh.

N. B. Some love a glafs of red wine, or walnut-pickle. You may put juft what you will into a hafh. If the fippets are toafted, it is better.

To hafh Veal.

CUT your veal in thin round flices, the fize of a half-crown; put into a fauce-pan a little gravy and lemon-peel cut very fine, a tea-fpoonful of lemon-pickle, put it over the fire, thicken it with flour and butter; when it boils, put in your veal; juft before you difh it, put in a fpoonful of cream; lay fippets round your difh, and ferve it up.

To hafh a Turkey.

TAKE off the legs, cut the thighs in two pieces, cut off the pinions and breaft in pretty large pieces, take off the fkin, or it will give the gravy a greafy tafte, put it into a ftew-pan, with a pint of gravy, a tea-fpoonful of lemon-pickle, a flice of the end of a lemon, and a little beaten mace; boil your turkey fix or feven minutes, (if you boil it any longer it will make it hard,) then put it on your difh, thicken your gravy with flour and butter, mix the yolks of two eggs with a fpoonful of thick cream, put it in your gravy, fhake it over your fire till it is quite hot, but do not let it boil, ftrain it, and pour it over your turkey; lay fippets round, ferve it up, and garnifh with lemon or parfley.

To hafh a Fowl.

CUT it up as for eating, put it in a toffing-pan, with half a pint of gravy, a tea-fpoonful of lemon-pickle, a little mufhroom catchup, a flice of lemon, thicken it with flour and butter; juft before you difh it up, put in a fpoonful of good cream; lay fippets round your difh, and ferve it up.

To hafh a Woodcock.

CUT your woodcock up as for eating, work the entrails very fine with the back of a fpoon, mix it with a fpoonful of red wine, the fame of water, half a fpoonful of vinegar, cut an onion in flices and pull it into rings, roll a little butter in flour, put them all in your toffing-pan, and fhake it over the fire till it boils, then put in your woodcock, and when it is thoroughly hot, lay it in your difh with fippets round it, ftrain the fauce over the woodcock, and lay on the onion in rings; it is a pretty corner-difh for dinner or fupper.

To hafh a Wild Duck.

CUT it up as for eating, put it in a toffing-pan, with a fpoonful of good gravy, the fame of red wine, a little of your onion-fauce, or an onion fliced exceeding thin; when it has boiled two or three minutes, lay the duck in your difh, pour the gravy over it, it muft not be thickened, you may add a tea-fpoonful of caper liquor, or a little browning.

To hafh a Hare.

CUT your hare in fmall pieces, if you have any of the pudding left, rub it fmall, put to it a large glafs of red wine, the fame quantity of water, half an anchovy chopped fmall, an onion ftuck with four cloves, a quarter of a pound of butter rolled in flour, fhake them all together over a flow fire, till your hare is thoroughly hot; it is a bad cuftom to let any kind of hafh boil longer, it makes the meat eat hard; fend your hare to the table in a deep difh, lay fippets round it, but take out the onion, and ferve it up.

To bake a Calf's Head.

TAKE the head, pick it and wash it very clean; take an earthen dish large enough to lay the head on, rub a little piece of butter all over the dish, then lay some long iron skewers across the top of the dish, and lay the head on them; skewer up the meat in the middle that it do not lie on the dish, then grate some nutmeg all over it, a few sweet herbs shred small, some crumbs of bread, a little lemon-peel cut fine, and then flour it all over; stick pieces of butter in the eyes and all over the head, and flour it again. Let it be well baked, and of a fine brown; you may throw a little pepper and salt over it, and put into the dish a piece of beef cut small, a bundle of sweet herbs, an onion, some whole pepper, a blade of mace, two cloves, a pint of water, and boil the brains with some sage. When the head is enough, lay it on a dish, and set it to the fire to keep warm, then stir all together in the dish, and boil it in a sauce-pan; strain it off, put it into the sauce-pan again, add a piece of butter rolled in flour, and the sage in the brains chopped fine, a spoonful of catchup, and two spoonfuls of red wine; boil them together; take the brains, beat them well, and mix them with the sauce; pour it into the dish, and send it to table. You must bake the tongue with the head, and do not cut it out; it will lie the handsomer in the dish.

To bake a Sheep's Head.

Do it the same way, and it eats very well.

To dress a Lamb's Head.

BOIL the head and pluck tender, but do not let the liver be too much done. Take the head up, hack it cross and cross with a knife, grate some nutmeg over it, and lay it in a dish, before a good fire; then grate some crumbs of bread, some sweet herbs rubbed, a little lemon-peel chopped fine, a very little pepper and salt, and baste it with a little butter; then throw a little flour over it, and just as it is done do the same, baste it and dredge it. Take half the liver, the lights, the heart and tongue, chop them very small, with six or eight spoonfuls of gravy or water; first shake some flour over the meat, and stir it together, then put in the gravy or water, a good piece of butter rolled in a little flour, a little pepper and salt, and what runs from the head in the dish; simmer all together a few minutes, and add half a spoonful of vinegar, pour it into your dish, lay the head in the middle of the mince-meat, have ready the other half of the liver cut thin, with some slices of bacon broiled, and lay round the head. Garnish the dish with lemon, and send it to table.

Calf's Head Surprize.

TAKE a calf's head with the ſkin on, take a ſharp knife and raiſe off the ſkin with as much meat from the bone as you can poſſibly get, ſo that it may appear like a whole head when ſtuffed, then make a force-meat in the following manner: take half a pound of veal, a pound of beef-ſuet, the crumb of a ſmall loaf, half a pound of fat bacon, beat them well in a mortar, with ſome ſweet herbs and parſley ſhred fine, ſome cloves, mace and nutmeg beat fine, ſome ſalt and Cayenne pepper enough to ſeaſon it, the yolks of four eggs beat up and mixt all together in a force-meat; ſtuff the head with it, and ſkewer it tight at each end; then put into a deep pot or pan, and put two quarts of water, half a pint of white wine, a blade or two of mace, a bundle of ſweet herbs, and an anchovy, two ſpoonfuls of walnut and muſhroom catchup, the ſame quantity of lemon-pickle, a little ſalt and pepper; lay a coarſe paſte over it to keep in the ſteam, and put it for two hours and a half in a quick oven; when you take it out, lay the head in a ſoup-diſh, ſkim off the fat from the gravy and ſtrain it through a ſieve into a ſtew-pan, thicken it with butter rolled in flour; and when it has boiled a few minutes, put in the yolks of four eggs well beaten and minced with half a pint of cream; have ready boiled ſome force-meat balls, half an ounce of truffles and morels, but do not put them into the gravy; pour the gravy over the head, and garniſh with force-meat balls, truffles, morels, and muſhrooms.

A Calf's Head dreſſed after the Dutch Way.

TAKE half a pound of Spaniſh peas, lay them in water a night; then one pound of whole rice, mix the peas and rice together, and lay it round the head in a deep diſh; then take two quarts of water ſeaſoned with pepper and ſalt, and coloured with ſaffron; then ſend it to bake.

To ſtew a Lamb's or Calf's Head.

FIRST waſh it and pick it very clean, lay it in water for an hour, take out the brains, and with a ſharp penknife carefully take out the bones and the tongue, but be careful you do not break the meat; then take out the two eyes, and take two pounds of veal and two pounds of beef-ſuet, a very little thyme, a good piece of lemon-peel minced, a nutmeg grated, and two anchovies; chop all very well together, grate two ſtale rolls, and mix all together with the yolks of four eggs; ſave enough of this meat to make about twenty balls, take half a pint of freſh muſhrooms clean peeled and waſhed, the yolks of ſix eggs chopped, half a pint of oyſters clean waſhed, or pickled

pickled cockles; mix all theſe together; but firſt ſtew your oyſters, put the force-meat into the head and cloſe it, tie it tight with packthread and put it into a deep ſtew-pan, and put to it two quarts of gravy, with a blade or two of mace. Cover it cloſe, and let it ſtew two hours; in the mean time beat up the brains with ſome lemon-peel cut fine, a little parſley chopped, half a nutmeg grated, and the yolk of an egg; have ſome dripping boiling, fry half the brains in little cakes, and fry the balls, keep them both hot by the fire; take half an ounce of truffles and morels, then ſtrain the gravy the head was ſtewed in, put the truffles and morels to it with the liquor, and a few muſhrooms; boil all together, then put in the reſt of the brains that are not fried, ſtew them together for a minute or two, pour it over the head, and lay the fried brains and balls round it. Garniſh with lemon. You may fry about twelve oyſters and put over.

To grill a Calf's Head.

WASH your calf's head clean, and boil it almoſt enough, then take it up and haſh one half, the other half rub over with the yolk of an egg, a little pepper and ſalt, ſtrew over it bread crumbs, parſley chopped ſmall, and a little grated lemon-peel, ſet it before the fire, and keep baſting it all the time to make the froth riſe; when it is a fine light brown, diſh up your haſh, and lay the grilled ſide upon it.

Blanch your tongue, ſlit it down the middle, and lay it on a ſoup-plate; ſkin the brains, boil them with a little ſage and parſley; chop them fine, and mix them with ſome melted butter and a ſpoonful of cream, make them hot, and pour them over the tongue, ſerve them up, and they are ſauce for the head.

A Breaſt of Veal in Hodge-podge.

TAKE a breaſt of veal, cut the briſket into little pieces, and every bone aſunder, then flour it, and put half a pound of good butter into a ſtew-pan; when it is hot, throw in the veal, fry it all over of a fine light brown, and then have ready a tea-kettle of water boiling; pour it in the ſtew-pan, fill it up and ſtir it round, throw in a pint of green peas, a fine lettuce whole, clean waſhed, two or three blades of mace, a little whole pepper tied in a muſlin rag, a little bundle of ſweet herbs, a ſmall onion ſtuck with a few cloves, and a little ſalt. Cover it cloſe, and let it ſtew an hour, or till it is boiled to your palate, if you would have ſoup made of it; if you would only have ſauce to eat with the veal, you muſt ſtew it till there is juſt as much as you would have for ſauce, and ſeaſon it with ſalt to your palate; take out the onion, ſweet herbs, and ſpice, and pour it all together into your diſh. It is a fine diſh. If you have no peas, pare three or four cucumbers, ſcoop out the pulp, and cut it into little pieces, and take four or five heads of celery, clean waſhed, and cut the white part ſmall; when you have no lettuces, take the little hearts of ſavoys, or the little young ſprouts that grow on the old cabbage-ſtalks, about as big as the top of your thumb.

N. B. If you would make a very fine diſh of it, fill the inſide of your lettuce with force meat, and tie the top cloſe with a thread; ſtew it till there is but juſt enough for ſauce; ſet the lettuce in the middle and the veal round, and pour the ſauce all over it. Garniſh your diſh with raſped bread made into figures with your fingers. This is the cheapeſt way of dreſſing a breaſt of veal to be good, and ſerve a number of people.

To collar a Breaſt of Veal.

TAKE a very ſharp knife, and nicely take out all the bones, but take great care you do not cut the meat through: pick all the fat and meat off the bones, then grate ſome nutmeg all over the inſide of the veal, a very little beaten mace, a little pepper and ſalt, a few ſweet herbs ſhred ſmall, ſome parſley, a little lemon-peel ſhred ſmall, a few crumbs of bread, and the bits of fat picked off the bones; roll it up tight, ſtick one ſkewer in to hold it together, but do it cleverly, that it ſtands upright in the diſh; tie a packthread acroſs it to hold it together, ſpit it, then roll the caul all round it, and roaſt it. An hour and a quarter will do it. When it has been about an hour at the fire, take off the caul, dredge it with flour, baſte it well with freſh butter, and let it be of a fine brown. For ſauce take two-pennyworth of gravy-beef, cut it and hack it well, then flour it, fry it a little brown, then pour into your ſtew-pan ſome boiling water, ſtir it well together, then fill your pan two parts full of water; put in an onion, a bundle of ſweet herbs, a little cruſt of bread toaſted, two or three blades of mace, four cloves, ſome whole pepper, and the bones of the veal. Cover it cloſe, and let it ſtew till it is quite rich and thick; then ſtrain it, boil it up with ſome truffles and morels, a few muſhrooms, a ſpoonful of catchup, two or three bottoms of artichokes, if you have them; add a little ſalt, juſt enough to ſeaſon the gravy, take the packthread off the veal, and ſet it upright in the diſh; cut the ſweetbread into four, and broil it of a fine brown, with a few forcemeat balls fried; lay theſe round the diſh, and pour in the ſauce. Garniſh the diſh with lemon, and ſend it to table.

To collar a Breaſt of Mutton.

DO it the ſame way, and it eats very well; but you muſt take off the ſkin.

Another

Another good Way to drefs a Breaft of Mutton.

COLLAR as before; roaft it, and bafte it with half a pint of red wine, when that is all foaked in, bafte it well with butter, have a little good gravy, fet the mutton upright in the difh, pour in the gravy, have fweet-fauce as for venifon, and fend it to table. Do not garnifh the difh, but be fure to take the fkin off the mutton.

The infide of a furloin of beef is very good done this way. If you do not like the wine, a quart of milk and a quarter of a pound of butter put into the dripping-pan does full as well to bafte it.

To ragoo a Leg of Mutton.

TAKE all the fkin and fat off, cut it very thin the right way of the grain, then butter your ftew-pan, and fhake fome flour into it; flice half a lemon and half an onion, cut them very fmall, a little bundle of fweet herbs, and a blade of mace. Put all together with your meat into the pan, ftir it a minute or two, and then put in fix fpoonfuls of gravy, and have ready an anchovy minced fmall; mix it with fome butter and flour, ftir it all together for fix minutes, and then difh it up.

To ragoo Hogs' Feet and Ears.

TAKE your ears out of the pickle they are foufed in, or boil them till they are tender, then cut them into little thin bits, about two inches long, and about as thick as a quill; put them into your ftew-pan with half a pint of good gravy, or as much as will cover them, a glafs of white wine, a good deal of muftard, a good piece of butter rolled in flour, and a little pepper and falt; ftir all together till it is of a fine thicknefs, and then difh it up. The hogs' feet muft not be ftewed but boiled tender, then flit them in two, and put the yolk of an egg over and crumbs of bread, and broil or fry them; put the ragoo of ears in the middle, and the feet round it.

N.B. They make a very pretty difh fried with butter and muftard, and a little good gravy, if you like it. Then only cut the feet and ears in two. You may add half an onion, cut fmall.

To ragoo a Neck of Veal.

CUT a neck of veal into fteaks, flatten them with a rolling-pin, feafon them with falt, pepper, cloves, and mace, lard them with bacon, lemon-peel, and thyme, dip them in the yolks of eggs, make a fheet of ftrong foolfcap-paper up at the four corners in the form of a dripping-pan; pin up the corners, butter the paper and alfo the gridiron, and fet it over a fire of charcoal; put in your meat, let it do leifurely, keep it bafting and

and turning to keep in the gravy; and when it is enough have ready half a pint of ſtrong gravy, ſeaſon it high, put in muſhrooms and pickles, force-meat balls dipped in the yolks of eggs, oyſters ſtewed and fried, to lay round and at the top of your diſh, and then ſerve it up. If for a brown ragoo, put in red wine. If for a white one, put in white wine, with the yolks of eggs beat up with two or three ſpoonfuls of cream.

To ragoo a Breaſt of Veal.

TAKE your breaſt of veal, put it into a large ſtew-pan, put in a bundle of ſweet herbs, an onion, ſome black and white pepper, a blade or two of mace, two or three cloves, a very little piece of lemon-peel, and juſt cover it with water: when it is tender take it up, bone it, put in the bones, boil it up till the gravy is very good, then ſtrain it off, and if you have a little rich beef-gravy, add a quarter of a pint, put in half an ounce of truffles and morels, a ſpoonful or two of catchup, two or three ſpoonfuls of white wine, and let them all boil together: in the mean time flour the veal, and fry it in butter till it is of a fine brown, then drain out all the butter, and pour the gravy you are boiling to the veal, with a few muſhrooms; boil all together till the ſauce is rich and thick, and cut the ſweetbread into four. A few force-meat balls are proper in it. Lay the veal in the diſh, and pour the ſauce all over it. Garniſh with lemon.

Or thus: Half roaſt a breaſt of veal, then cut it in ſquare pieces; put it into a ſtew-pan, with half a pint of gravy, a pint of water, a bundle of ſweet herbs, an onion ſtuck with cloves, a little mace, and ſtew it till it is tender; then take it out, and pull out all the bones, ſtrain the gravy through a ſieve, then put it into the ſtew-pan again, with a ſpoonful of muſtard, ſome truffles and morels, a ſweetbread cut in pieces, one artichoke-bottom, about twenty force-meat balls, ſome butter rolled in flour, enough to thicken it; boil it up till it is of a proper thickneſs; ſeaſon it with pepper and ſalt, then put in your veal, ſtew it for five minutes, add the juice of half a lemon, then put your meat into the diſh, the ragoo all over it. Garniſh with lemon and beet-root.

Another Way to ragoo a Breaſt of Veal.

YOU may bone it nicely, flour it, and fry it of a fine brown, then pour the fat out of the pan, and the ingredients as above, with the bones; when enough, take it out, and ſtrain the liquor, then put in your meat again, with the ingredients, as before directed.

To

To ragoo a Fillet of Veal.

LARD your fillet and half roaſt it, then put it in a toſſing-pan, with two quarts of good gravy, cover it cloſe and let it ſtew till tender, then add one ſpoonful of white wine, one of browning, one of catchup, a tea-ſpoonful of lemon-pickle, a little caper liquor, half an ounce of morels, thicken with flour and butter, lay round it a few yolks of eggs.

To ragoo Sweetbreads.

RUB them over with the yolk of an egg, ſtrew over them bread-crumbs, parſley, thyme, and ſweet-marjoram ſhred ſmall, and pepper and ſalt, make a roll of force-meat like a ſweet-bread, and put it in a veal caul, and roaſt them in a Dutch oven; take ſome brown gravy, and put to it a little lemon-pickle, muſhroom-catchup, and the end of a lemon, boil the gravy, and when the ſweetbreads are enough, lay them in a diſh, with a force-meat in the middle, take the end of the lemon out, and pour the gravy into the diſh, and ſerve them up.

To make a Ragoo of Lamb.

TAKE a fore-quarter of lamb, cut the knuckle-bone off, lard it with little thin bits of bacon, flour it, fry it of a fine brown, and then put it into an earthen pot or ſtew-pan; put to it a quart of broth or good gravy, a bundle of herbs, a little mace, two or three cloves, and a little whole pepper; cover it cloſe, and let it ſtew pretty faſt for half an hour; pour the liquor all out, ſtrain it, keep the lamb hot in the pot till the ſauce is ready. Take half a pint of oyſters, flour them, fry them brown, drain out all the fat clean that you fried them in, ſkim all the fat off the gravy, then pour it in to the oyſters, put in an anchovy, and two ſpoonfuls of either red or white wine; boil all together till there is juſt enough for ſauce, add ſome freſh muſhrooms (if you can get them) and ſome pickled ones, with a ſpoonful of the pickle, or the juice of half a lemon. Lay your lamb in the diſh, and pour the ſauce over it. Garniſh with lemon.

To ragoo a Piece of Beef.

TAKE a large piece of the flank, which has fat at the top, cut ſquare, or any piece that has fat at the top, but no bones. The rump does well. Cut all nicely off the bone (which makes fine ſoup); then take a large ſtew-pan, and with a good piece of butter fry it a little brown all over, flouring your meat well before you put it into the pan, then pour in as much gravy as will cover it, made thus; take about a pound of coarſe beef, a little piece of veal cut ſmall, a bundle of ſweet herbs, an onion,

onion, ſome whole black pepper and white pepper, two or three large blades of mace, four or five cloves, a piece of carrot, a little piece of bacon ſteeped in vinegar a little while, a cruſt of bread toaſted brown; put to this a quart of white wine, and let it boil till half is waſted. While this is making, pour a quart of boiling water into the ſtew-pan, cover it cloſe, and let it be ſtewing ſoftly; when the gravy is done, ſtrain it, pour it into the pan where the beef is, take an ounce of truffles and morels cut ſmall, ſome freſh or dried muſhrooms cut ſmall, two ſpoonfuls of catchup, and cover it cloſe. Let all this ſtew till the ſauce is rich and thick; then have ready ſome artichoke-bottoms cut into four, and a few pickled muſhrooms, give them a boil or two, and when your meat is tender, and your ſauce quite rich, lay the meat into a diſh and pour the ſauce over it. You may add a ſweetbread cut in ſix pieces, a palate ſtewed tender cut into little pieces, ſome cock's-combs, and a few force-meat balls. Theſe are a great addition, but it will be good without.

N. B. For variety, when the beef is ready, and the gravy put to it, add a large bunch of celery cut ſmall and waſhed clean, two ſpoonfuls of catchup, and a glaſs of red wine. Omit all the other ingredients. When the meat and celery are tender, and the ſauce rich and good, ſerve it up. It is alſo very good this way: take ſix large cucumbers, ſcoop out the ſeeds, pare them, cut them into ſlices, and do them juſt as you do the celery.

To force the Inſide of a Sirloin of Beef.

TAKE a ſharp knife, and carefully lift up the fat of the inſide, take out all the meat cloſe to the bone, chop it ſmall, take a pound of ſuet and chop fine, about as many crumbs of bread, a little thyme and lemon-peel, a little pepper and ſalt, half a nutmeg grated, and two ſhalots chopped fine; mix and beat all very fine in a marble mortar, with a glaſs of red wine, then put it into the ſame place, cover it with the ſkin and fat, ſkewer it down with fine ſkewers, and cover it with paper. Do do not take the paper off till the meat is on the diſh. Take a quarter of a pint of red wine, two ſhalots ſhred ſmall, boil them, and pour into the diſh, with the gravy which comes out of the meat; it eats well. Spit your meat before you take out the inſide.

Another Way to force a Sirloin.

WHEN it is quite roaſted, take it up, and lay it in the diſh with the inſide uppermoſt; with a ſharp knife lift up the ſkin, hack and cut the inſide very fine, ſhake a little pepper and ſalt over it, with two ſhalots, cover it with the ſkin, and ſend it to table. You may add red wine or vinegar, juſt as you like.

Sirloin

Sirloin of Beef en Epigram.

ROAST a ſirloin of beef, take it off the ſpit, then raiſe the ſkin carefully off, and cut the lean part of the beef out, but obſerve not to cut near the ends or ſides; haſh the meat in the following manner: cut it into pieces about as big as a crown-piece, put half a pint of gravy into a toſs-pan, an onion chopt fine, two ſpoonfuls of catchup, ſome pepper and ſalt, ſix ſmall pickled cucumbers cut in thin ſlices, and the gravy that comes from the beef, a little butter rolled in flour, put the meat in, and toſs it up for five minutes, put it on the ſirloin, and then put the ſkin over, and ſend it to table. Garniſh with horſe-radiſh.

You may do the inſide inſtead of the outſide, if you pleaſe.

To force the Inſide of a Rump of Beef.

YOU may do it juſt in the ſame manner, only lift up the outſide ſkin, take the middle of the meat, and do as before directed; put it into the ſame place, and with fine ſkewers put it down cloſe.

To force a Round of Beef.

TAKE a good round of beef, and rub over it a quarter of an hour with two ounces of ſaltpetre, the ſame of bay-ſalt, half a pound of brown ſugar, and a pound of common ſalt, let it lie in it for ten or twelve days, turn it once every day in the brine, then waſh it well, and make holes in it with a penknife about an inch one from another, and fill one hole with ſhred parſley, a ſecond with fat pork cut in ſmall pieces, and a third with bread-crumbs, beef-marrow, a little mace, nutmeg, pepper, and ſalt mixed together; then parſley, and ſo on till you have filled all the holes; then wrap your beef in a cloth, and bind it with a fillet, and boil it four hours; when it is cold, bind it over again, and cut a thin ſlice off before you ſend it to the table; garniſh with parſley and red cabbage.

A forced Leg of Lamb.

TAKE a large leg of lamb, cut a long ſlit on the back ſide and take out the meat, but take great care you do not deface the other ſide; then chop the meat ſmall with marrow, half a pound of beef-ſuet, ſome oyſters, an anchovy waſhed, an onion, ſome ſweet herbs, a little lemon-peel, and ſome beaten mace and nutmeg; beat all theſe together in a mortar, ſtuff it up in the ſhape it was before, ſew it up, and rub it over with the yolks of eggs beaten, ſpit it, flour it all over, lay it to the fire, and baſte it with butter. An hour will roaſt it. You may bake it, if you pleaſe, but then you muſt butter the diſh, and lay the butter over it: cut the loin into ſteaks, ſeaſon them with pepper,

per, ſalt, and nutmeg, lemon-peel cut fine, and a few ſweet herbs; fry them in freſh butter of a fine brown, then pour out all the butter, put in a quarter of a pint of white wine, ſhake it about, and put in half a pint of ſtrong gravy, wherein good ſpice has been boiled, a quarter of a pint of oyſters and the liquor, ſome muſhrooms, and a ſpoonful of the pickle, a piece of butter rolled in flour, and the yolk of an egg beat; ſtir all theſe together till thick, then lay your leg of lamb in the diſh, and the loin round it; pour the ſauce over it, and garniſh with lemon.

To force a Leg of Lamb another Way.

WITH a ſharp knife carefully take out all the meat, and leave the ſkin whole and the fat on it, make the lean you cut out into force-meat thus: to two pounds of meat add two pounds of beef-ſuet cut fine, and beat in a marble mortar till it is very fine, and take away all the ſkin of the meat and ſuet, then mix it with four ſpoonfuls of grated bread, eight or ten cloves, five or ſix large blades of mace dried and beat fine, half a large nutmeg grated, a little pepper and ſalt, a little lemon-peel cut fine, a very little thyme, ſome parſley, and four eggs; mix all together, put it into the ſkin again juſt as it was, in the ſame ſhape, ſew it up, roaſt it, baſte it with butter, cut the loin into ſteaks and fry it nicely, lay the leg in the diſh and the loin round it, with ſtewed cauliflower all round upon the loin; pour a pint of good gravy into the diſh, and ſend it to table. If you do not like the cauliflower, it may be omitted.

To force a large Fowl.

CUT the ſkin down the back, and carefully ſlit it up ſo as to take out all the meat, mix it with one pound of beef-ſuet, cut it ſmall, and beat them together in a marble mortar; take a pint of large oyſters cut ſmall, two anchovies cut ſmall, one ſhalot cut fine, a few ſweet herbs, a little pepper, a little nutmeg grated, and the yolks of four eggs; mix all together and lay this on the bones, draw over the ſkin, and ſew up the back, put the fowl into a bladder, boil it an hour and a quarter, ſtew ſome oyſters in good gravy thickened with a piece of butter rolled in flour; take the fowl out of the bladder, lay it in your diſh, and pour the ſauce over it. Garniſh with lemon.

It eats much better roaſted with the ſame ſauce.

To roaſt a Turkey the genteel Way.

FIRST cut it down the back, and with a ſharp penknife, bone it, then make your force-meat thus: take a large fowl or a pound of veal, as much grated bread, half a pound of ſuet cut and beat very fine, a little beaten mace, two cloves, half a nutmeg

nutmeg grated, about a large tea-ſpoonful of lemon-peel, and the yolks of two eggs; mix all together with a little pepper and ſalt, fill up the places where the bones came out, and fill the body, that it may look juſt as it did before, ſew up the back, and roaſt it. You may have oyſter-ſauce, celery-ſauce, or juſt as you pleaſe; put good gravy in the diſh, and garniſh with lemon is as good as any thing. Be ſure to leave the pinions on.

To ſtew a Knuckle of Veal.

BE ſure let the pot or ſauce-pan be very clean, lay at the bottom four clean wooden ſkewers, waſh and clean the knuckle very well, then lay it in the pot with two or three blades of mace, a little whole pepper, a little piece of thyme, a ſmall onion, a cruſt of bread, and two quarts of water. Cover it down cloſe, make it boil, then only let it ſimmer for two hours, and when it is enough take it up, lay it in a diſh, and ſtrain the broth over it.

Another Way to ſtew a Knuckle of Veal.

CLEAN it as before directed, and boil it till there is juſt enough for ſauce, add one ſpoonful of catchup, one of red wine, and one of walnut-pickle, ſome truffles and morels, or ſome dried muſhrooms cut ſmall; boil all together. Take up the knuckle, lay it in a diſh, pour the ſauce over it, and ſend it up.

To ſtew a Fillet of Veal.

TAKE a fillet of a cow-calf, ſtuff it well under the udder, at the bone and quite through to the ſhank, put it in the oven, with a pint of water under it, till it is a fine brown, then put it in a ſtew-pan with three pints of gravy, ſtew it tender, put in a few morels, truffles, a tea-ſpoonful of lemon-pickle, a large one of browning, and one of catchup, and a little Cayenne pepper, thicken with a lump of butter rolled in flour, diſh up your veal, ſtrain your gravy over, lay round force-meat balls: garniſh with pickles and lemon.

Beef Tremblant.

TAKE the fat end of a briſket of beef, and tie it up cloſe with pack-thread; put it in a pot of water, and boil it ſix hours very gently; ſeaſon the water with a little ſalt, a handful of all-ſpice, two onions, two turnips, and a carrot: in the mean while put a piece of butter in a ſtew-pan and melt it, then put in two ſpoonfuls of flour, and ſtir it till it is ſmooth; put in a quart of gravy, a ſpoonful of catchup, the ſame of browning, a gill of white wine, carrots and turnips, and cut the ſame as for harrico of mutton; ſtew them gently till the roots are tender, ſeaſon with pepper and ſalt, ſkim all the fat clean off,

put

put the beef in the diſh, and pour the ſauce all over. Garniſh with pickle of any ſort; or make a ſauce thus: chop a handful of parſley, one onion, four pickled cucumbers, one walnut and a gill of capers; put them in a pint of good gravy, and thicken it with a little butter rolled in flour, and ſeaſon it with pepper and ſalt; boil it up for ten minutes, and then put over the beef; or you may put the beef in a diſh, and put greens and carrots round it.

Beef à la Daub.

TAKE a rump and bone it, or a part of the leg-of-mutton-piece, or a piece of the buttock; cut ſome fat bacon as long as the beef is thick, and about a quarter of an inch ſquare; take eight cloves, four blades of mace, a little all-ſpice, and half a nutmeg beat very fine; chop a good handful of parſley fine, ſome ſweet herbs of all ſorts chopped fine, and ſome pepper and ſalt; roll the bacon in theſe, and then take a large larding-pin, or a ſmall bladed knife, and put the bacon through and through the beef with the larding-pin or knife; when that is done, put it in a ſtew-pan, with brown gravy enough to cover it. Chop three blades of garlic very fine, and put in ſome freſh muſhrooms or champignons, two large onions, and a carrot: ſtew it gently for ſix hours; then take the meat out, ſtrain off the gravy, and ſkim all the fat off. Put your meat and gravy into the pan again; put a gill of white wine into the gravy, and if it wants ſeaſoning, ſeaſon with pepper and ſalt; ſtew them gently for half an hour; add ſome artichoke-bottoms, truffles and morels, oyſters, and a ſpoonful of vinegar. Put the meat in a ſoup-diſh, and the ſauce over it; or you may put turnips cut in round pieces, and carrots cut round, ſome ſmall onions, and thicken the ſauce; then put the meat in, and ſtew it gently for half an hour with a gill of white wine. Some like ſavoys or cabbage ſtewed and put into the ſauce.

To make Beef Alamode.

TAKE a ſmall buttock, or leg-of-mutton-piece of beef, or a clod, or a piece of buttock of beef, alſo two dozen of cloves, as much mace, and half an ounce of all ſpice beat fine; chop a large handful of parſley, and all ſorts of ſweet herbs fine (cut fat bacon as for beef à la Daub, and put it into the ſpice, &c. and into the beef the ſame); put it into a pot, and cover it with water; chop four large onions very fine, and ſix cloves of garlic, ſix bay-leaves, and a handful of champignons or freſh muſhrooms; put all into the pot with a pint of porter or ale, and half a pint of red wine; put in ſome pepper and ſalt, ſome Cayenne pepper, a ſpoonful of vinegar, ſtrew three handfuls of bread raſpings, ſifted fine, over all; cover the pot cloſe, and ſtew it for ſix hours, or according to the ſize of the piece; if a large piece, eight hours; then take the beef out and put it in a deep diſh, and keep it hot over ſome boiling water; ſtrain the gravy through a ſieve, and pick out the champignons or muſhrooms; ſkim all the fat off clean, put it into your pot again, and give it a boil up; if not ſeaſoned enough, ſeaſon it to your liking; then put the gravy over your beef, and ſend it to table hot; or you may cut it in ſlices if you like it beſt, or put it to get cold, and cut it in ſlices with the gravy over it; for when the gravy is cold, it will be in a ſtrong jelly.

N. B. This makes an excellent diſh, but many of the ingredients, ſuch as the garlic, muſhrooms, &c. may be left out.

Beef Alamode in Pieces.

YOU muſt take a buttock of beef, cut it into two-pound pieces, lard them with bacon, fry them brown, put them into a pot that will juſt hold them, put in two quarts of broth or gravy, a few ſweet herbs, an onion, ſome mace, cloves, nutmeg, pepper and ſalt; when that is done, cover it cloſe, and ſtew it till it is tender, ſkim off all the fat, lay the meat in the diſh, and ſtrain the ſauce over it. You may ſerve it up hot or cold.

To ſtew Beef-Steaks.

TAKE rump-ſteaks, pepper and ſalt them, lay them in a ſtew-pan, pour in half a pint of water, a blade or two of mace, two or three cloves, a little bundle of ſweet herbs, an anchovy, a piece of butter rolled in flour, a glaſs of white wine, and an onion; cover them cloſe, and let them ſtew ſoftly till they are tender; then take out the ſteaks, flour them, fry them in freſh butter, and pour away all the fat, ſtrain the ſauce they were ſtewed in, and pour into the pan; toſs it all up together till the ſauce is quite hot and thick. If you add a quarter of a pint of oyſters, it will make it the better. Lay the ſteaks into the diſh, and pour the ſauce over them. Garniſh with any pickle you like.

Beef-Steaks after the French Way.

TAKE ſome beaf-ſteaks, broil them till they are half done, while the ſteaks are doing, have ready in a ſtew-pan ſome red wine, a ſpoonful or two of gravy, ſeaſon it with ſalt, pepper, ſome ſhalots; then take the ſteaks, and cut in ſquares, and put in the ſauce; you muſt put ſome vinegar, cover it cloſe, and let it ſimmer on a ſlow fire half an hour.

A pretty Side-diſh of Beef.

ROAST a tender piece of beef, lay fat bacon all over it, and roll it in paper, baſte it, and when it is roaſted cut about two pounds

in

in thin ſlices, lay them in a ſtew-pan, and take ſix large cucumbers, peel them, and chop them ſmall, lay over them a little pepper and ſalt, and ſtew them in butter for about ten minutes, then drain out the butter, and ſhake ſome flour over them; toſs them up, pour in half a pint of gravy, let them ſtew till they are thick, and diſh them up.

To ſtew a Rump of Beef.

HAVING boiled it till it is little more than half enough, take it up, and peel off the ſkin: take ſalt, pepper, beaten mace, grated nutmeg, a handful of parſley, a little thyme, winter-ſavory, ſweet-marjoram, all chopped fine and mixed, and ſtuff them in great holes in the fat and lean, the reſt ſpread over it, with the yolks of two eggs; ſave the gravy that runs out, put to it a pint of claret, and put the meat in a deep pan, pour the liquor in, cover it cloſe, and let it bake two hours, then put it into the diſh, ſtrain the liquor through a ſieve, and ſkim off the fat very clean, then pour it over the meat, and ſend it to table.

Another Way to ſtew a Rump of Beef.

YOU muſt cut the meat off the bone, lay it in your ſtew-pan, cover it with half gravy and half water, put in a ſpoonful of whole pepper, two onions, a bundle of ſweet herbs, ſome ſalt, and a pint of red wine; cover it cloſe, ſet it over a ſtove or ſlow fire for four hours, ſhaking it ſometimes, and turning it four or five times; keep it ſtirring till dinner is ready: take ten or twelve turnips, cut them into ſlices the broad way, then cut them into four, flour them, and fry them brown in beef-dripping. Be ſure to let your dripping boil before you put them in; then drain them well from the fat, lay the beef in your ſoup diſh, toaſt a little bread very nice and brown, cut in three corner dice, lay them into the diſh, and the turnips likewiſe; ſkim the fat off clean, ſtrain in the gravy, and ſend it to table. If you have the convenience of a ſtove, put the diſh over it for five or ſix minutes; it gives the liquor a fine flavour of the turnips, makes the bread eat better, and is a great addition. Seaſon it with pepper and ſalt to your palate.

Portugal Beef.

TAKE a rump of beef, cut it off the bone, cut it acroſs, flour it, fry the thin part brown in butter, the thick end ſtuff with ſuet, boiled cheſnuts, an anchovy, an onion, and a little pepper. Stew it in a pan of ſtrong broth, and when it is tender, lay both the fried and ſtewed together in your diſh; cut the fried in two and lay on each ſide of the ſtewed, ſtrain the gravy it was ſtewed in, put to it ſome pickled gerkins chopped, and boiled chefnuts, thicken it with a piece of butter rolled in flour, a fpoonful of browning, give it two or three boils up, feafon it with falt to your palate, and pour it over the beef. Garnifh with lemon.

To ftew a Rump of Beef, or Brifket, the French Way.

TAKE a rump of beef, cut it from the bone; take half a pint of white port, and half a pint of red, a little vinegar, fome cloves and mace, half a nutmeg beat fine, fome parfley chopped, and all forts of fweet herbs, a little pepper and falt; mix the herbs, fpice, and wine all together; lay your beef in an earthen pan, put the mixture over it, and let it lay all night, then take the beef and put it into a deep ftew-pan, with two quarts of good gravy, the wine, &c. an onion chopped fine, fome carrot, and two or three bay-leaves; you may put in fome thick rafhers of bacon at the bottom of your pan; ftew it very gently for five hours, if twelve pounds; if eight or nine, four hours, and keep the ftew-pan clofe covered: then take the meat out and ftrain the liquor through a fieve, fkim all the fat off, put it into your ftew-pan with fome truffles and morels, artichoke-bottoms blanched and cut in pieces, or fome carrots and turnips cut as for harrico of mutton, or a few favoys tied up in quarters and ftewed till tender; boil it up, feafon it with a little Cayenne pepper and falt to your palate, then put the meat in juft to make it hot: difh it up. Garnifh with fried fippets, or lemon and beet-root.

To ftew Beef-Gobbets.

GET any piece of beef except the leg, cut it in pieces about the bignefs of a pullet's egg, put them in a ftew-pan, cover them with water, let them ftew, fkim them clean, and when they have ftewed an hour, take mace, cloves, and whole pepper tied in a muflin rag loofe, fome celery cut fmall, put them into the pan with fome falt, turnips and carrots pared and cut in flices, a little parfley, a bundle of fweet herbs, and a large cruft of bread. You may put in an ounce of barley or rice, if you like it. Cover it clofe, and let it ftew till it is tender; take out the herbs, fpices, and bread, and have ready fried a French roll cut in four. Difh up all together, and fend it to table.

Beef Royal.

TAKE a firloin of beef, or a large rump, bone it and beat it very well, then lard it with bacon, feafon it all over with falt, pepper, mace, cloves, and nutmeg, all beat fine, fome lemon-peel cut fmall, and fome fweet herbs; in the mean time make a ftrong broth of the bones; take a piece of butter with a little flour,

flour, brown it, put in the beef; keep it turning often till it is brown, then ſtrain the broth, put all together into a pot, put in a bay-leaf, a few truffles, and ſome ox-palates cut ſmall; cover it cloſe, and let it ſtew till it is tender; take out the beef, ſkim off all the fat, pour in a pint of claret, ſome fried oyſters, an anchovy, and ſome gerkins ſhred ſmall; boil all together, put in the beef to warm, thicken your ſauce with a piece of butter rolled in flour or muſhroom powder. Lay your meat in the diſh, pour the ſauce over it, and ſend it to table. This may be eat either hot or cold.

To make Stew of Ox-Cheek.

TAKE an ox-cheek when freſh killed, take out the teeth and looſe bones, rub it with a little ſalt, put it into ſoft water juſt warm, let it lay three or four hours, then put it into cold water, let it ſtand all night, waſh it clean and drain it well, ſeaſon it with ground-pepper and ſalt, put it into a kettle well tinned, put to it five quarts of ſoft water; before it boils you muſt take care to ſkim it well, then put in ſix large onions, a ſmall bunch of ſweet herbs, ſtew it gently five or ſix hours, take out the herbs and let it ſtand all night, then take off all the fat, put in celery, carrots, and turnips cut in pieces, alſo Cayenne pepper, and ſalt, to your taſte; ſtew it two hours more; ſend up all together in a tureen, and dry toaſt on a plate. Make ſtew of tongue roots the ſame way.

To make Stew of a Shank of Beef.

TAKE a ſhank of beef ſeven or eight pounds weight, break the bone well, put it into a kettle well tinned, put to it ſix quarts of ſoft water, ſeaſon it with pepper and ſalt, ſkim it when it boils; ſtew it five or ſix hours, let it ſtand all night, then take off the fat, and put in celery, carrots, turnips, Cayenne, and ſalt; ſtew it two hours more, then ſend it up as the other ſtew.

To ſtew a Turkey or Fowl.

FIRST let your pot be very clean, lay four clean ſkewers at the bottom, lay your turkey or fowl upon them, put in a quart of gravy, take a bunch of celery, cut it ſmall, and waſh it very clean, put it into your pot, with two or three blades of mace, let it ſtew ſoftly till there is juſt enough for ſauce, then add a good piece of butter rolled in flour, two ſpoonfuls of red-wine, two of catchup, and juſt as much pepper and ſalt as will ſeaſon it; lay your fowl or turkey in the diſh, pour the ſauce over it, and ſend it to table. If the fowl or turkey is enough before the ſauce, take it up, and keep it up till the ſauce is boiled enough, then put it in, and let it boil a minute or two, and diſh it up.

A rolled Rump of Beef.

CUT the meat all off the bone whole, ſlit the inſide down from top to bottom, but not through the ſkin, ſpread it open; take the fleſh of two fowls and beef-ſuet, an equal quantity, and as much cold boiled ham (if you have it), a little pepper, an anchovy, a nutmeg grated, a little thyme, a good deal of parſley, a few muſhrooms, and chop them all together, beat them in a mortar, with a half-pint baſon full of crumbs of bread; mix all theſe together, with four yolks of eggs, lay it into the meat, cover it up, and roll it round, ſtick one ſkewer in, and tie it with a packthread croſs and croſs to hold it together; take a pot or large ſauce-pan that will juſt hold it, lay a layer of bacon and a layer of beef cut in thin ſlices, a piece of carrot, ſome whole pepper, mace, ſweet herbs, and a large onion; lay the rolled beef on it; juſt water enough to cover the top of the beef; cover it cloſe, and let it ſtew very ſoftly on a ſlow fire for eight or ten hours, but not too faſt. When you find the beef tender, which you will know by running a ſkewer into the meat, then take it up, cover it up hot, boil the gravy till it is good, then ſtrain it off, and add ſome muſhrooms chopped, ſome truffles and morels cut ſmall, two ſpoonfuls of red or white wine, the yolks of two eggs, and a piece of butter rolled in flour; boil it together, ſet the meat before the fire, baſte it with butter, and throw crumbs of bread all over it; when the ſauce is enough, lay the meat into the diſh, and pour the ſauce over it. Take care the eggs do not curdle; or you may omit the eggs.

To boil a Rump of Beef the French Faſhion.

TAKE a rump of beef, boil it half an hour, take it up, lay it into a large deep pewter diſh or ſtew-pan, cut three or four gaſhes in it all along the ſide, rub the gaſhes with pepper and ſalt, and pour into the diſh a pint of red wine, as much hot water, two or three large onions cut ſmall, the hearts of eight or ten lettuces cut ſmall, and a good piece of butter rolled in a little flour; lay the fleſhy part of the meat downwards, cover it cloſe, let it ſtew two hours and a half over a charcoal fire, or a very ſlow coal fire. Obſerve that the butcher chops the bone ſo cloſe that the meat may lie as flat as it can in the diſh. When it is enough, take the beef, lay it in the diſh, and pour the ſauce over it.

N.B. When you do it in a pewter diſh, it is beſt done over a chafing-diſh of hot coals, with a bit or two of charcoal to keep it alive.

Beef-Efcarlot.

TAKE a brifket of beef, half a pound of coarfe fugar, two ounces of bay-falt, one ounce of faltpetre, a pound of common falt; mix all together, and rub the beef; lay it in an earthen pan, and turn it every day. It may lie a fortnight in the pickle; then boil it, and ferve it up either with favoys, cabbage, or greens, or peas-pudding.

N. B. It eats much finer cold, cut into flices, and fent to table.

A Fricando of Beef.

CUT a few flices of beef five or fix inches long, and half an inch thick, lard it with bacon, dredge it well with flour, and fet it before a brifk fire to brown, then put it in a toffing-pan, with a quart of gravy, a few morels and truffles, half a lemon, and ftew them half an hour, then add one fpoonful of catchup, the fame of browning, and a littte Cayenne, thicken your fauce and pour it over your fricando, lay round them force-meat balls, and the yolks of hard eggs.

Beef Olives.

TAKE a rump of beef, cut it into fteaks of half an inch thick, cut them as fquare as you can, and about ten inches long, cut a piece of fat bacon as wide as the beef, and about three parts as long, put fome yolk of an egg on the beef, put the bacon on it, and the yolk of an egg on the bacon, and fome good favoury force-meat on that, fome yolk of an egg on the force-meat, then roll them up and tie them round with a ftring in two places; put fome yolk of an egg on them and fome crumbs of bread, then fry them brown in a large pan of good beef-dripping; take them out and put them to drain; take fome butter and put into a ftew-pan, melt it, and put in a fpoonful of flour, ftir it well till it is fmooth; then put a pint of good gravy in, and a gill of white wine, put in the olives and ftew them for an hour; add fome mufhrooms, truffles and morels, force-meat balls and fweetbreads, cut in fmall fquare pieces, fome ox-palates; feafon with pepper and falt, and fqueeze the juice of half a lemon; tofs them up. Be careful to fkim all the fat off, then put them in your difh. Garnifh with beet-root and lemon.

To drefs a Fillet of Beef.

IT is the infide of a firloin. You muft carefully cut it all out from the bone, grate fome nutmeg over it, a few crumbs of bread, a little pepper and falt, a little lemon-peel, a little thyme, fome parfley fhred fmall, and roll it up tight; tie it with a packthread, roaft it, put a quart of milk and a quarter of of a pound of butter into the dripping-pan, and bafte it; when it is enough take it up, untie it, leave a little fkewer in it to hold it together, have a little good gravy in the difh, and fome fweet fauce in a cup. You may bafte it with red-wine and butter, if you like it better; or it will do very well with butter only.

Beef-Steaks rolled.

TAKE three or four beef-fteaks, flat them with a cleaver, and make a force-meat thus: take a pound of veal beat fine in a mortar, the flefh of a large fowl cut fmall, half a pound of cold ham chopped fmall, the kidney-fat of a loin of veal chopped fmall, a fweetbread cut in little pieces, an ounce of truffles and morels firft ftewed and then cut fmall, fome parfley, the yolks of four eggs, a nutmeg grated, a very little thyme, a little lemon-peel cut fine, a little pepper and falt, and half a pint of cream: mix all together, lay it on your fteaks, roll them up firm, of a good fize, and put a little fkewer into them, put them into the ftew-pan and fry them of a nice brown; and pour all the fat quite out, and put in a pint of good fried gravy, put one fpoonful of catchup, two fpoonfuls of red wine, a few mufhrooms, and let them ftew for half an hour. Take up the fteaks, cut them in two, lay the cut fide uppermoft, and pour the fauce over it. Garnifh with lemon.

N. B. Before you put the force-meat into the beef, you are to ftir it all together over a flow fire for eight or ten minutes.

To drefs the Infide of a cold Sirloin of Beef.

CUT out all the infide (free from fat) of the firloin in pieces as thick as your finger and about two inches long, dredge it with a little flour, and fry it in nice butter of a light brown, then drain it, and tofs it up in rich gravy that has been well feafoned with pepper, falt, fhalot, and an anchovy; juft before you fend it up, add two fpoonfuls of vinegar taken from pickled capers; garnifh with fried oyfters, or what you pleafe.

Boullie Beef.

TAKE the thick end of a brifket of beef, put it into a kettle of water quite covered over, let it boil faft for two hours, then keep ftewing it clofe by the fire for fix hours more, and as the water waftes fill up the kettle, put in with the beef fome turnips cut in little balls, carrots, and fome celery cut in pieces; an hour before it is done take out as much broth as will fill your foup-difh, and boil in it for that hour turnips and carrots cut out in balls or in little fquare pieces, with fome celery, falt and pepper to your tafte, ferve it up in two difhes, the beef by itfelf, and the foup by itfelf; you may put pieces of fried bread, if you like it, in your ſoup, boil in a few knots of greens, and if you think your ſoup will not be rich enough, you may add a pound or two of fried mutton chops to your broth when you take it from the beef, and let it ſtew for that hour in the broth, but be ſure to take out the mutton when you ſend it to the table: the ſoup muſt be very clear.

To make Mock-Hare of a Beaſt's Heart.

WASH a large beaſt's heart clean, and cut off the deaf-ears, and ſtuff it with ſome force-meat, as you do a hare, lay a caul of veal or paper over the top, to keep in the ſtuffing, roaſt it either in a cradle-ſpit or hanging one, it will take an hour and a half before a good fire, baſte it with red wine; when roaſted, take the wine out of the dripping-pan and ſkim off the fat, and add a glaſs more of wine; when it is hot, put in ſome lumps of red-currant jelly, and pour it in the diſh; ſerve it up, and ſend in red-currant jelly cut in ſlices on a ſaucer.

Tripe à la Kilkenny.

THIS is a favourite Iriſh diſh, and is done thus: take a piece of double tripe cut in ſquare pieces, have twelve large onions peeled and waſhed clean, cut them in two, and put them on to boil in clean water till they are tender; then put in your tripe and boil it ten minutes; pour off almoſt all the liquor, ſhake a little flour in, and put ſome butter in, and a little ſalt and muſtard; ſhake it all over the fire till the butter is melted; then put it in your diſh, and ſend it to table as hot as poſſible. Garniſh with barberries or lemon.

A Tongue and Udder forced.

FIRST parboil the tongue and udder, blanch the tongue and ſtick it with cloves; as for the udder, you muſt carefully raiſe it, and fill it with force-meat made with veal: firſt waſh the inſide with the yolk of an egg, then put in the force-meat, tie the ends cloſe and ſpit them, roaſt them, and baſte them with butter; when enough, have good gravy in the diſh, and ſweet ſauce in a cup.

N. B. For variety, you may lard the udder.

To fricaſſee Neats' Tongues brown.

TAKE neats' tongues, boil them tender, peel them, cut them into thin ſlices, and fry them in freſh butter; then pour out the butter, put in as much gravy as you ſhall want for ſauce, a bundle of ſweet herbs, an onion, ſome pepper and ſalt, and a blade or two of mace, a glaſs of white wine, ſimmer all together half an hour; then take out your tongue, ſtrain the gravy,

gravy, put it with the tongue in the ſtew-pan again, beat up the yolks of two eggs, a little grated nutmeg, a piece of butter as big as a walnut, rolled in flour; ſhake all together for four or five minutes. Diſh it up and ſend it to table.

To force a Tongue.

BOIL it till it is tender; let it ſtand till it is cold, then cut a hole at the root end of it, take out ſome of the meat, chop it with as much beef-ſuet, a few pippins, ſome pepper and ſalt, a little mace beat, ſome nutmeg, a few ſweet herbs, and the yolks of two eggs; beat all together well in a marble mortar; ſtuff it, cover the end with a veal caul or buttered paper, roaſt it, baſte it with butter, and diſh it up. Have for ſauce good gravy, a little melted butter, the juice of an orange or lemon, and ſome grated nutmeg; boil it up, and pour it into the diſh.

To ſtew Neats' Tongues whole.

TAKE two tongues, let them ſtew in water juſt to cover them for two hours, then peel them, put them in again with a pint of ſtrong gravy, half a pint of white wine, a bundle of ſweet herbs, a little pepper and ſalt, ſome mace, cloves, and whole pepper tied in a muſlin rag, a ſpoonful of capers chopped, turnips and carrots ſliced, and a piece of butter rolled in flour; let all ſtew together very ſoftly over a ſlow fire for two hours, then take out the ſpice and ſweet herbs, and ſend it to table. You may leave out the turnips and carrots, or boil them by themſelves, and lay them in a diſh, juſt as you like.

To dreſs a Leg of Mutton à la Royale.

HAVING taken off all the fat, ſkin, and ſhank-bone, lard it with bacon, ſeaſon it with pepper and ſalt, and a round piece of about three or four pounds of beef or leg of veal, lard it, have ready ſome hog's-lard boiling, flour your meat, and give it a colour in the lard, then take the meat out and put it into a pot, with a bundle of ſweet herbs, ſome parſley, an onion ſtuck with cloves, two or three blades of mace, ſome whole pepper, and three quarts of gravy; cover it cloſe, and let it boil very ſoftly for two hours, meanwhile get ready a ſweet-bread ſplit, cut into four, and broiled, a few truffles and morels ſtewed in a quarter of a pint of ſtrong gravy, a glaſs of red wine, a few muſhrooms, two ſpoonfuls of catchup, and ſome aſparagus-tops; boil all theſe together, then lay the mutton in the middle of the diſh, cut the beef or veal into ſlices, make a rim round your mutton with the ſlices, and pour the ragoo over it; when you have taken the meat out of the pot, ſkim all the fat off the gravy; ſtrain it, and add as much to the other as will fill the diſh. Garniſh with lemon.

A Leg of Mutton à la Haut Goût.

LET it hang a fortnight in an airy place, then have ready ſome cloves of garlic, and ſtuff it all over, rub it with pepper and ſalt; roaſt it, have ready ſome good gravy and red wine in the diſh, and ſend it to table.

To roaſt a Leg of Mutton with Oyſters.

TAKE a leg about two or three days killed, ſtuff it all over with oyſters, and roaſt it. Garniſh with horſe radiſh.

A ſecond Way to roaſt a Leg of Mutton with Oyſters.

STUFF a leg of mutton with mutton-ſuet, ſalt, pepper, nutmeg, and the yolks of eggs; then roaſt it, ſtick it all over with cloves, and when it is about half done, cut off ſome of the under-ſide of the fleſhy end in little bits, put theſe into a pipkin with a pint of oyſters, liquor and all, a little ſalt and mace, and half a pint of hot water: ſtew them till half the liquor is waſted, then put in a piece of butter rolled in flour, ſhake all together, and when the mutton is enough, take it up; pour this ſauce over it, and ſend it to table.

To roaſt a Leg of Mutton with Cockles.

STUFF it all over with cockles, and roaſt it. Garniſh with horſe-radiſh.

A Shoulder of Mutton en Epigram.

ROAST it almoſt enough, then very carefully take off the ſkin about the thickneſs of a crown-piece, and the ſhank-bone with it at the end; then ſeaſon that ſkin and ſhank-bone with pepper and ſalt, a little lemon-peel cut ſmall, and a few ſweet herbs and crumbs of bread, then lay this on the gridiron, and let it be of a fine brown; in the mean time take the reſt of the meat and cut it like a haſh about the bigneſs of a ſhilling; ſave the gravy and put to it, with a few ſpoonfuls of ſtrong gravy, half an onion cut fine, a little nutmeg, a little pepper and ſalt, a little bundle of ſweet herbs, ſome gerkins cut very ſmall, a few muſhrooms, two or three truffles cut ſmall, two ſpoonfuls of wine, either red or white, and throw a little flour over the meat: let all theſe ſtew together very ſoftly for five or ſix minutes, but be ſure it does not boil; take out the ſweet herbs, and put the haſh into the diſh, lay the broiled upon it, and ſend it to table.

A Harrico of Mutton.

TAKE a neck or loin of mutton, cut it into thick chops, flour them, and fry them brown in a little butter; take them out, and lay them to drain on a ſieve, then put them into a ſtew-

ſtew-pan, and cover them with gravy; put in a whole onion and a turnip or two, and ſtew them till tender; then take out the chops, ſtrain the liquor through a ſieve, and ſkim off all the fat; put a little butter in the ſtew-pan and melt it, with a ſpoonful of flour, ſtir it well till it is ſmooth, then put the liquor in, and ſtir it well all the time you are pouring it, or it will be in lumps; put in your chops and a glaſs of Liſbon; have ready ſome carrot about three quarters of an inch long, and cut round with an apple-corer, ſome turnips cut with a turnip-ſcoop, a dozen ſmall onions all blanched well; put them to your meat, and ſeaſon with pepper and ſalt; ſtew them very gently for fifteen minutes, then take out the chops with a fork, lay them in your diſh, and pour the ragoo over it. Garniſh with beet-root. The wine may be omitted.

To French a Hind-Saddle of Mutton.

IT is the two chumps of the loins. Cut off the rump, and carefully lift up the ſkin with a knife: begin at the broad end, but be ſure you do not crack it nor take it quite off; then take ſome ſlices of ham or bacon chopped fine, a few truffles, ſome young onions, ſome parſley, a little thyme, ſweet-marjoram, winter-ſavory, a little lemon-peel, all chopped fine, a little mace and two or three cloves beat fine, half a nutmeg, and a little pepper and ſalt; mix all together, and throw over the meat where you took off the ſkin, then lay on the ſkin again, and faſten it with two fine ſkewers at each ſide, and roll it in well-buttered paper. It will take two hours roaſting: then take off the paper, baſte the meat, ſtrew it all over with crumbs of bread, and when it is of a fine brown take it up. For ſauce take ſix large ſhalots, cut them very fine, put them into a ſauce-pan with two ſpoonfuls of vinegar and two of white wine; boil them for a minute or two, pour it into the diſh, and garniſh with horſe-radiſh.

Another French Way, called St. Menehout.

TAKE the hind-part of a chine of mutton, take off the ſkin, lard it with bacon, ſeaſon it with pepper, ſalt, mace, cloves beat, and nutmeg, ſweet herbs, young onions, and parſley, all chopped fine; take a large oval or a large gravy-pan, lay layers of bacon, and then layers of beef all over the bottom; lay in the mutton; then lay layers of bacon on the mutton, and then a layer of beef, put in a pint of wine, and as much good gravy as will ſtew it, put in a bay-leaf and two or three ſhalots, cover it cloſe, put fire over and under it (if you have a cloſe-pan), and let it ſtand ſtewing for two hours; when done, take it out, ſtrew crumbs of bread all over it, and put it into the oven to brown, ſtrain the gravy it was ſtewed in, and boil it till there is juſt enough for ſauce; lay the mutton into a diſh, pour the ſauce in, and ſerve it up. You muſt brown it before a fire, if you have not an oven.

Cutlets à la Maintenon. A very good Diſh.

TAKE a neck of mutton, cut it into chops, in every chop muſt be a long bone; take the fat off the bone, and ſcrape it clean; have ſome bread-crumbs, parſley, marjoram, thyme, winter-ſavory, and baſil, all chopped fine, grate ſome nutmeg on it, ſome pepper and ſalt; mix theſe all together, melt a little butter in a ſtew-pan, dip the chop in the butter, then roll them in the herbs, and put them in half ſheets of buttered paper; leave the end of the bone bare, then broil them on a clear fire for twenty minutes: ſend them up in the paper with poivrade-ſauce in a boat.

Mutton-Chops in Diſguiſe.

TAKE as many mutton-chops as you want, rub them with pepper, ſalt, nutmeg, and a little parſley; roll each chop in half a ſheet of white paper, well buttered on the inſide, and rolled on each end cloſe. Have ſome hog's-lard, or beef-dripping, boiling in a ſtew-pan; put in the ſteaks, fry them of a fine brown, lay them in your diſh, and garniſh with fried parſley; throw ſome all over, have a little good gravy in a cup; but take great care you do not break the paper, nor have any fat in the diſh; but let them be well drained.

To dreſs a Leg of Mutton to eat like Veniſon.

TAKE a hind-quarter of mutton, and cut the leg in the ſhape of a haunch of veniſon, ſave the blood of the ſheep and ſteep the haunch in it for five or ſix hours, then take it out and roll it in three or four ſheets of white paper well buttered on the inſide, tie it with a packthread, and roaſt it, baſting it with good beef-dripping or butter. It will take two hours at a good fire, for your mutton muſt be fat and thick. About five or ſix minutes before you take it up, take off the paper, baſte it with a piece of butter, and ſhake a little flour over it to make it have a fine froth, and then have a little good drawn gravy in a baſon, and ſweet ſauce in another. Do not garniſh with any thing.

To dreſs Mutton the Turkiſh Way.

FIRST cut your meat into thin ſlices, then waſh it in vinegar, and put it into a pot or ſauce-pan that has a cloſe cover to it, put in ſome rice, whole pepper, and three or four whole onions; let all theſe ſtew together, ſkimming it frequently;

when it is enough, take out the onions, and ſeaſon it with ſalt to your palate, lay the mutton in the diſh, and pour the rice and liquor over it.

N. B. The neck or leg are the beſt joints to dreſs this way; put to a leg four quarts of water, and a quarter of a pound of rice; to a neck, two quarts of water, and two ounces of rice. To every pound of meat allow a quarter of an hour, being cloſe covered. If you put in a blade or two of mace, and a bundle of ſweet herbs, it will be a great addition. When it is juſt enough, put in a piece of butter, and take care the rice do not burn to the pot. In all theſe things you ſhould lay ſkewers at the bottom of the pot to lay your meat on, that it may not ſtick.

A Hodge-podge of Mutton.

CUT a neck or loin of mutton into ſteaks, take off all the fat, then put the ſteaks into a pitcher, with lettuce, turnips, carrots, two cucumbers cut in quarters, four or five onions, and pepper and ſalt; you muſt not put any water to it, and ſtop the pitcher very cloſe, then ſet it in a pan of boiling water, let it boil four hours, keep the pan ſupplied with freſh boiling water as it waſtes.

A Shoulder of Mutton with a Ragoo of Turnips.

TAKE a ſhoulder of mutton, get the blade bone taken out as neat as poſſible, and in the place put a ragoo, done thus: take one or two ſweetbreads, ſome cock's-combs, half an ounce of truffles, ſome muſhrooms, a blade or two of mace, a little pepper and ſalt; ſtew all theſe in a quarter of a pint of good gravy, and thicken it with a piece of butter rolled in flour, or yolks of eggs, which you pleaſe: let it be cold before you put it in, and fill up the place where you took the bone out juſt in the form it was before, and ſew it up tight: take a large deep ſtew-pan, or one of the round deep copper pans with two handles, lay at the bottom thin ſlices of bacon, then ſlices of veal, a bundle of parſley, thyme, and ſweet herbs, ſome whole pepper, a blade or two of mace, three or four cloves, a large onion, and put in juſt thin gravy enough to cover the meat; cover it cloſe, and let it ſtew two hours, then take eight or ten turnips, pare them, and cut them into what ſhape you pleaſe, put them into boiling water, and let them be juſt enough; throw them into a ſieve to drain over the hot water that they may keep warm; then take up the mutton, drain it from the fat, lay it in a diſh, and keep it hot covered; ſtrain the gravy it was ſtewed in, and take off all the fat, put in a little ſalt, a glaſs of white wine, two ſpoonfuls of catchup, and a piece of butter rolled in flour, boil them together

gether till there is juſt enough for ſauce; then put in the turnips, give them a boil up, pour them over the meat, and ſend it to table. You may fry the turnips of a light brown, and toſs them up with the ſauce; but that is according to your palate.

Note: For a change you may leave out the turnips, and add a bunch of celery cut and waſhed clean, and ſtewed in a very little water, till it is quite tender, and the water almoſt boiled away. Pour the gravy, as before directed, into it, and boil it up till the ſauce is good: or you may leave both theſe out, and add truffles, morels, freſh and pickled muſhrooms, and artichoke-bottoms.

N. B. A ſhoulder of veal without the knuckle, half roaſted, very quick and brown, and then done like the mutton, eats well. Do not garniſh your mutton, but garniſh your veal with lemon.

To ſtuff a Leg or Shoulder of Mutton.

TAKE a little grated bread, ſome beef-ſuet, the yolks of three hard eggs, three anchovies, a bit of onion, ſome pepper and ſalt, a little thyme and winter-ſavory, twelve oyſters, and ſome nutmeg grated; mix all theſe together, ſhred them very fine, work them up with raw eggs like a paſte, ſtuff your mutton under the ſkin in the thickeſt place, or where you pleaſe, and roaſt it: for ſauce, take ſome of the oyſter-liquor, ſome claret, one anchovy, a little nutmeg, a bit of onion, and a few oyſters; ſtew all theſe together, then take out your onion, pour ſauce under your mutton, and ſend it to table. Garniſh with horſe-radiſh.

Oxford John.

KEEP a leg of mutton till it is ſtale, cut it into thin collops, and take out all the ſinews and fat, ſeaſon them with pepper and ſalt, a little beaten mace, and ſtrew among them a little ſhred parſley, thyme, and three or four ſhalots; put about a quarter of a pound of butter in a ſtew-pan, and make it hot, put all your collops in, keep them ſtirring with a wooden ſpoon till they are three parts done, and then add a pint of gravy, a little juice of lemon, and thicken it with butter rolled in flour; let it ſimmer four or five minutes, and they will be enough. Take care you do not let them boil, nor have them ready before you want them, for they will grow hard; fry ſome bread ſippets, and throw over and round them, and ſend them up hot.

Mutton-Rumps à la Braiſe.

TAKE ſix mutton-rumps, and boil them for fifteen minutes in water; take them out, cut them in two, and put them into a ſtew-pan with half a pint of good gravy, a gill of white wine, an onion ſtuck with cloves, a little ſalt and Cayenne pepper, cover them cloſe and ſtew them till tender; take them out and the onion, ſkim off all the fat, thicken the gravy with a little butter rolled in flour, a ſpoonful of browning, the juice of half a lemon; boil it up till it is ſmooth, but not too thick; put in your rumps, give them a toſs or two, diſh them up hot. Garniſh with horſe-radiſh and beet-root.

For variety, you may leave the rumps whole, and lard ſix kidneys on one ſide, and do them the ſame as the rumps, only not boil them, and put the rumps in the middle of the diſh, and kidneys round them, with ſauce over all. The kidneys make a pretty ſide-diſh of themſelves.

Sheeps' Rumps with Rice.

TAKE ſix rumps, put them into a ſtew-pan, with ſome mutton gravy enough to fill it; ſtew them about half an hour; take them up and let them ſtand to cool, then put into the liquor a quarter of a pound of rice, an onion ſtuck with cloves, and a blade or two of mace; let it boil till the rice is as thick as a pudding, but take care it does not ſtick to the bottom, which you muſt prevent by ſtirring it often; in the mean time take a clean ſtew-pan, put a piece of butter into it; dip your rumps in the yolks of eggs beat, and then in crumbs of bread with a little nutmeg, lemon-peel, and a very little thyme in it, fry them in the butter of a fine brown, then take them out, lay them in a diſh to drain, pour out all the fat, and toſs the rice into that pan; ſtir it all together for a minute or two, then lay the rice into the diſh, and the rumps all round upon the rice; have ready four eggs boiled hard, cut them into quarters, lay them round the diſh with fried parſley between them, and ſend it to table.

Mutton Kebobbed.

TAKE a loin of mutton and joint it between every bone; ſeaſon it with pepper and ſalt moderately, grate a ſmall nutmeg all over, dip the chops in the yolks of three eggs, and have ready crumbs of bread and ſweet herbs, dip them in, and clap them together in their former ſhape again, and put it on a ſmall ſpit; roaſt it before a quick fire, ſet a diſh under, and baſte it with a little piece of butter, and then keep baſting with what comes from it, and throw ſome crumbs of bread and ſweet herbs all over it while roaſting; when it is enough take it up, lay it in the diſh, and have ready half a pint of good made gravy and what comes from the mutton; take two ſpoonfuls of catchup, and mix a tea-ſpoonful of flour with it and put to the gravy, ſtir it together and give it a boil, and pour over the mutton.

N. B.

N. B. You muſt obſerve to take off all the fat of the inſide, and the ſkin of the top of the meat, and ſome of the fat, if there be too much. When you put what comes from your meat into the gravy, obſerve to pour out all the fat.

A Neck of Mutton, called The Haſty Diſh.

TAKE a large pewter or ſilver diſh, made like a deep ſoup-diſh, with an edge about an inch deep on the inſide, on which the lid fixes (with an handle at top) ſo faſt that you may lift it up full by that handle without falling. This diſh is called a necromancer. Take a neck of mutton about ſix pounds, take off the ſkin, cut it into chops, not too thick, ſlice a French roll thin, peel and ſlice a very large onion, pare and ſlice three or four turnips, lay a row of mutton in the diſh, on that a row of roll, then a row of turnips, and then onions, a little ſalt, then the meat, and ſo on; put in a little bundle of ſweet herbs, and two or three blades of mace; have a tea-kettle of water boiling, fill the diſh, and cover it cloſe, hang the diſh on the back of two chairs by the rim, have ready three ſheets of brown paper, tear each ſheet into five pieces, and draw them through your hand, light one piece and hold it under the bottom of the diſh, moving the paper about, as faſt as the paper burns; light another till all is burnt, and your meat will be enough. Fifteen minutes juſt does it. Send it to table hot in the diſh.

N. B. This diſh was firſt contrived by Mr. Rich, and is much admired by the nobility.

To bake Lamb and Rice.

TAKE a neck or loin of lamb, half roaſt it, take it up, cut it into ſteaks, then take half a pound of rice boiled in a quart of water ten minutes, put it into a quart of good gravy, with two or three blades of mace, and a little nutmeg. Do it over a ſtove or ſlow fire till the rice begins to be thick; then take it off, ſtir in a pound of butter, and when that is quite melted, ſtir in the yolks of ſix eggs, firſt beat; then take a diſh and butter it all over, take the ſteaks and put a little pepper and ſalt over them, dip them in a little melted butter, lay them into the diſh, pour the gravy which comes out of them over them, and then the rice; beat the yolks of three eggs and pour all over, ſend it to the oven, and bake it better than half an hour.

To fry a Loin of Lamb.

CUT your lamb into chops, rub it over on both ſides with the yolk of an egg, and ſprinkle ſome bread crumbs, a little parſley, thyme, marjoram, and winter-ſavory chopped very fine, and a little lemon-peel chopped fine; fry it in butter of a nice light

light brown, send it up in a dish by itself. Garnish with a good deal of fried parsley.

Another Way of frying a Neck or Loin of Lamb.

CUT it into thin steaks, beat them with a rolling-pin, fry them in half a pint of ale, season them with a little salt, and cover them close; when enough, take them out of the pan, lay them in a plate before the fire to keep hot, and pour all out of the pan into a bason; then put in half a pint of white wine, a few capers, the yolks of two eggs beat, with a little nutmeg and a little salt; add to this the liquor they were fried in, and keep stirring it one way all the time till it is thick, then put in the lamb, keep shaking the pan for a minute or two, lay the steaks into the dish, pour the sauce over them, and have some parsley in a plate before the fire to crisp. Garnish your dish with that and lemon.

Lamb-Chops larded.

CUT the best end of a neck of lamb in chops, and lard one side, season them with beaten cloves, mace and nutmeg, a little pepper and salt; put them into a stew-pan, the larded side uppermost; put in half a pint of gravy, a gill of white wine, an onion, a bundle of sweet herbs, stew them gently till tender; take the chops out, skim the fat clean off, and take out the onion and sweet herbs; thicken the gravy with a little butter rolled in flour, add a spoonful of browning, a spoonful of catchup, and one of lemon-pickle. Boil it up till it is smooth, put in the chops larded side down, stew them up gently for a minute or two; take the chops out and put the larded side uppermost in the dish, and the sauce over them. Garnish with lemon and pickles of any sort; you may add truffles and morels and pickled mushrooms in the sauce, if you please; or you may do the chops without larding.

Lamb-Chops en Casorole.

CUT a loin of lamb in chops, put yolk of egg on both sides, and strew bread crumbs over, with a little cloves and mace, pepper and salt mixed; fry them of a nice light brown, and put them round in a dish close as you can, and leave a hole in the middle to put the following sauce in: all sorts of sweet herbs and parsley chopt fine, stewed a little in some good thick gravy. Garnish with fried parsley.

To dress a Dish of Lambs' Bits.

SKIN the stones and split them, lay them on a dry cloth with the sweetbreads and liver, and dredge them well with flour, and

and fry them in boiling lard, or butter, a light brown, then lay them on a ſieve to drain, fry a good quantity of parſley, lay your bits on the diſh, and the parſley in lumps over it, pour melted butter round them.

To dreſs Veal à la Bourgeoiſe.

CUT pretty thick ſlices of veal, lard them with bacon, and ſeaſon them with pepper, ſalt, beaten mace, cloves, nutmeg, and chopped parſley; then take the ſtew-pan and cover the bottom with ſlices of fat bacon, lay the veal upon them, cover it, and ſet it over a very ſlow fire for eight or ten minutes, juſt to be hot and no more, then briſk up your fire, and brown your veal on both ſides, then ſhake ſome flour over it and brown it; pour in a quart of good broth or gravy, cover it cloſe, and let it ſtew gently till it is enough; when enough, take out the ſlices of bacon, and ſkim all the fat off clean, and beat up the yolks of three eggs with ſome of the gravy; mix all together, and keep it ſtirring one way till it is ſmooth and thick, then take it up, lay your meat in the diſh, and pour the ſauce over it. Garniſh with lemon.

A diſguiſed Leg of Veal and Bacon.

LARD your veal all over with ſlips of bacon and a little lemon-peel, and boil it with a piece of bacon; when enough, take it up, cut the bacon into ſlices, and have ready ſome dried ſage and pepper rubbed fine; rub over the bacon, lay the veal in the diſh and the bacon round it, ſtrew it all over with fried parſley, and have green-ſauce in cups, made thus: take two handfuls of ſorrel, pound it in a mortar, and ſqueeze out the juice, put it into a ſauce-pan with ſome melted butter, a little ſugar, and the juice of a lemon. Or you may make it thus: beat two handfuls of ſorrel in a mortar, with two pippins quartered, ſqueeze the juice out, with the juice of a lemon, or vinegar, and ſweeten it with ſugar.

Loin of Veal en Epigram.

ROAST a fine loin of veal as directed in the chapter for roaſting; take it up, and carefully take the ſkin off the back part without breaking; take and cut out all the lean meat, but mind and leave the ends whole, that it may hold the following mince-meats: mince all the meat very fine with the kidney part, put it in a little veal gravy, enough to moiſten it with the gravy that comes from the loin; put in a little pepper and ſalt, ſome lemon-peel ſhred fine, the yolks of three eggs, a ſpoonful of catchup, and thicken it with a little butter rolled in flour; give it a ſhake or two over the fire and put it into the loin, and then

then pull the ſkin over; if the ſkin ſhould not quite cover it, give it a brown with a hot iron, or put it in an oven for fifteen minutes. Send it up hot, and garniſh with barberries and lemon.

To make a Porcupine of a Breaſt of Veal.

BONE the fineſt and largeſt breaſt of veal you can get, rub it over with the yolks of two eggs, ſpread it on a table, lay over it a little bacon cut as thin as poſſible, a handful of parſley ſhred fine, the yolks of five hard-boiled eggs chopped ſmall, a little lemon-peel cut fine, nutmeg, pepper, and ſalt to your taſte, and the crumb of a penny loaf ſteeped in cream, roll the breaſt cloſe, and ſkewer it up, then cut fat bacon and the lean of ham that has been a little boiled, or it will turn the veal red, and pickled cucumbers about two inches long to anſwer the other lardings, and lard it in rows, firſt ham, then bacon, then cucumbers, till you have larded it all over the veal; put it in a deep earthen pot with a pint of water, and cover it and ſet it in a ſlow oven two hours; when it comes from the oven ſkim the fat off, and ſtrain the gravy through a ſieve into a ſtew-pan; put in a glaſs of white wine, a little lemon-pickle, and caper-liquor, a ſpoonful of muſhroom catchup, thicken it with a little butter rolled in flour, lay your porcupine on the diſh, and pour it hot upon it, cut a roll of force-meat in four ſlices, lay one at each end and the other at the ſides; have ready your ſweet-bread cut in ſlices and fried, lay them round it with a few muſhrooms. It is a grand bottom-diſh when game is not to be had.

N. B. Make the force-meat of a few chopped oyſters, the crumbs of a penny loaf, half a pound of beef-ſuet ſhred fine, and the yolks of four eggs; mix them well together with nutmegs, Cayenne pepper, and ſalt to your taſte, ſpread it on a veal caul, and roll it up cloſe like a collared eel, bind it in a cloth, and boil it one hour.

A Pillaw of Veal.

TAKE a neck or breaſt of veal, half roaſt it, then cut it into ſix pieces, ſeaſon it with pepper, ſalt, and nutmeg; take a pound of rice, put to it a quart of broth, ſome mace, and a little ſalt, do it over a ſtove or very ſlow fire till it is thick, but butter the bottom of the diſh or pan you do it in; beat up the yolks of ſix eggs and ſtir into it; then take a little round deep diſh, butter it, lay ſome of the rice at the bottom, then lay the veal on a round heap, and cover it all over with rice, waſh it over with the yolks of eggs, and bake it an hour and a half; then open the top and pour in a pint of rich good gravy. Garniſh with a Seville orange cut in quarters, and ſend it to table hot.

To

To make a Fricando of Veal.

CUT ſteaks half an inch thick and ſix inches long out of the thick part of a leg of veal, lard them with ſmall cardoons, and duſt them with flour, put them before the fire to broil a fine brown, then put them into a large toſſing-pan, with a quart of good gravy, and let it ſtew half an hour, then put in two tea-ſpoonfuls of lemon-pickle, a meat-ſpoonful of walnut-catchup, the ſame of browning, a ſlice of lemon, a little anchovy and Cayenne, a few morels and truffles; when your fricandos are tender, take them up, and thicken your gravy with flour and butter, ſtrain it, place your fricandos in the diſh, pour your gravy on them: garniſh with lemons and barberries. You may lay round them force-meat balls fried, or force meat rolled in a veal caul, and yolks of eggs boiled hard.

Bombarded Veal.

GET a fillet of veal, cut out of it five lean pieces as thick as your hand, round them up a little, then lard them very thick on the round ſide with little narrow thin pieces of bacon, take five ſheeps' tongues (being firſt boiled and blanched), lard them here and there with very little bits of lemon peel, and make a well-ſeaſoned force-meat of veal, bacon, ham, beef-ſuet, and anchovy beat well; make another tender force-meat of veal, beef-ſuet, muſhrooms, ſpinage, parſley, thyme, ſweet-marjoram, winter-ſavory, and green onions. Seaſon with pepper, ſalt, and mace; beat it well, make a round ball of the other force-meat and ſtuff in the middle of this, roll it up in a veal caul, and bake it; what is left, tie up like a Bologna ſauſage and boil it, but firſt rub the caul with the yolk of an egg; put the larded veal into a ſtew-pan with ſome good gravy, and ſtew it gently till it is enough; ſkim off the fat, put in ſome truffles and morels, and ſome muſhrooms. Your force-meat being baked enough, lay it in the middle, the veal round it, and the tongues fried, and laid between; the boiled cut into ſlices and fried, and throw all over. Pour on them the ſauce. You may add artichoke-bottoms, ſweetbreads, and cock's-combs, if you pleaſe. Garniſh with lemon.

Veal Rolls.

TAKE ten or twelve little thin ſlices of veal, lay on them ſome force-meat, according to your fancy, roll them up, and tie them juſt acroſs the middle with coarſe thread, put them on a bird-ſpit, rub them over with the yolks of eggs, flour them, and baſte them with butter. Half an hour will do them. Lay them into a diſh, and have ready ſome good gravy with a few

truffles

truffles and morels, and ſome muſhrooms. Garniſh with lemon.

Veal Olives.

CUT them out of a leg of veal, and do them the ſame as beef olives, with the ſame ſauce and garniſh.

Or thus: cut ſome ſlices of a leg of veal, about three inches long, and two broad, cut them thin, ſpread them on the table, and hack them with the back of a knife; put ſome yolk of egg over them, and ſome ſavoury force-meat on the egg as thick as the veal, then ſome yolk of egg over it; roll them up tight, and tie them with a ſtring; rub them all over with yolk of egg, and ſtrew bread-crumbs over them; have ready a pan of boiling fat; fry them of a gold colour, put them before the fire to drain. Have ready the following ragoo: put about two ounces of butter in your ſtew-pan, and melt it, put a ſpoonful of flour, and ſtir it about till it is ſmall; put a pint of gravy, a glaſs of white wine, ſome pepper and ſalt, a little cloves and mace, a little ham or lean bacon cut fine, two ſhalots cut fine, and half a lemon, ſtew them gently for ten minutes, ſtrain it through a ſieve, ſkim off the fat, then put it into your pan again, add a ſweetbread cut in pieces, artichoke-bottoms cut in pieces, ſome force-meat balls, a few truffles and morels, and muſhrooms, a ſpoonful of catchup, give them a boil up; put your olives in the diſh, and pour the ragoo over them. Garniſh with lemon.

Olives of Veal the French Way.

TAKE two pounds of veal, ſome marrow, two anchovies, the yolks of two hard eggs, a few muſhrooms, and ſome oyſters, a little thyme, marjoram, parſley, ſpinage, lemon-peel, ſalt, pepper, nutmeg, and mace, finely beaten, take your veal caul, lay a layer of bacon and a layer of the ingredients, roll it in the veal caul, and either roaſt it or bake it. An hour will do either. When enough, cut it into ſlices, lay it into your diſh, and pour good gravy over it. Garniſh with lemon.

Veal Blanquets.

ROAST a piece of fillet of veal, cut off the ſkin and nervous parts, cut it into little thin bits, put ſome butter into a ſtew-pan over the fire with ſome chopped onions, fry them a little, then add a duſt of flour, ſtir it together, and put in ſome good broth or gravy, and a bundle of ſweet herbs; ſeaſon it with ſpice, make it of a good taſte, and then put in your veal, the yolks of two eggs beat up with cream and grated nutmeg, ſome chopped parſley, a ſhalot, ſome lemon-peel grated, and a little juice of lemon. Keep it ſtirring one way; when enough, diſh it up.

A Shoulder of Veal à la Piedmontoife.

TAKE a fhoulder of veal, cut off the fkin that it may hang at one end, then lard the meat with bacon and ham, and feafon it with pepper, falt, mace, fweet herbs, parfley, and lemon-peel; cover it again with the fkin, ftew it with gravy, and when it is juft tender, take it up; then take forrel, fome lettuce chopped fmall, and ftew them in fome butter with parfley, onions, and mufhrooms; the herbs being tender put to them fome of the liquor, fome fweetbreads and fome bits of ham. Let all ftew together a little while; then lift up the fkin, lay the ftewed herbs over and under, cover it with the fkin again, wet it with melted butter, ftrew it over with crumbs of bread, and fend it to the oven to brown; ferve it hot, with fome good gravy in the difh: The French ftrew it over with Parmefan before it goes to the oven.

Sweetbreads of Veal à la Dauphiné.

TAKE the largeft fweetbreads you can get, and lard them; open them in fuch a manner as you can ftuff in force-meat, three will make a fine difh: make your force-meat with a large fowl or young cock; fkin it, and pluck off all the flefh; take half a pound of fat and lean bacon, cut thefe very fine and beat them in a mortar; feafon it with an anchovy, fome nutmeg, a little lemon-peel, a very little thyme, and fome parfley; mix thefe up with the yolks of two eggs, fill your fweetbreads and faften them with fine wooden fkewers; take the ftew-pan, lay layers of bacon at the bottom of the pan, feafon them with pepper, falt, mace, cloves, fweet herbs, and a large onion fliced; upon that lay thin flices of veal, and then lay on your fweetbreads; cover it clofe, let it ftand eight or ten minutes over a flow fire, and then pour in a quart of boiling water or broth; cover it clofe, and let it ftew two hours very foftly; then take out the fweetbreads, keep them hot, ftrain the gravy, fkim all the fat off, boil it up till there is about half a pint, put in the fweetbreads, and give them two or three minutes ftew in the gravy, then lay them in the difh, and pour the gravy over them. Garnifh with lemon.

Another Way to drefs Sweetbreads.

Do not put any water or gravy into the ftew-pan, but put the fame veal and bacon over the fweetbreads, and feafon as under directed; cover them clofe, put fire over as well as under, and when they are enough, take out the fweetbreads, put in a ladleful of gravy, boil it, and ftrain it, fkim off all the fat, let it boil till it jellies, then put in the fweetbreads to glaze;

glaze; lay effence of ham in the difh, and lay the fweetbreads upon it; or make a very rich gravy with mufhrooms, truffles, and morels, a glafs of white wine, and two fpoonfuls of catchup. Garnifh with cock's-combs forced, and ftewed in the gravy.

N. B. You may add to the firft, truffles, morels, mufhrooms, cock's-combs, palates, artichoke-bottoms, two fpoonfuls of white wine, two of catchup, or juft as you pleafe.

*** There are many ways of dreffing fweetbreads: you may lard them with thin flips of bacon, and roaft them with what fauce you pleafe; or you may marinate them, cut them into thin flices, flour them and fry them. Serve them up with fried parfley, and either butter or gravy. Garnifh with lemon.

Sweetbreads en Cordonnier.

TAKE three fweetbreads and parboil them, take a ftew-pan and lay layers of bacon or ham and veal, over that lay the fweetbreads on with the upper fide downwards, put a layer of veal and bacon over them, a pint of veal broth, three or four blades of mace, ftew them gently three quarters of an hour; take the fweetbreads out, ftrain off the gravy through a fieve, and fkim off the fat; make an amlet of yolks of eggs in the following manner: beat up four yolks of eggs, put two in a plate, and put them over a ftew-pan of water boiling on the fire, put another plate over them, and they will foon be done; put a little fpinage-juice into the other half and ferve it the fame; cut it out in fprigs or what form you pleafe, and put it over the fweetbreads in the difh, and keep them as hot as you can; put fome butter rolled in flour to thicken the gravy, two yolks of eggs beat up in a gill of cream; put it over the fire and keep ftirring it one way till it is thick and fmooth; put it under the fweetbreads and fend them up. Garnifh with lemon and beet-root.

Calf's Chitterlings, or Andouilles.

TAKE fome of the largeft calf's nuts, cleanfe them, cut them in pieces proportionable to the length of the puddings you defign to make, and tie one end to thofe pieces; then take fome bacon, with a calf's udder and chaldron blanched and cut into dice or flices, put them into a ftew-pan and feafon with fine fpice pounded, a bay leaf, fome falt, pepper, and fhalot cut fmall, and about half a pint of cream; tofs it up take off the pan and thicken your mixture with four or five yolks of eggs, add fome crumbs of bread, then fill up your chitterlings with the ftuffing; keep it warm, tie the other ends with packthread, blanch and boil them like hog's chitterlings, let them grow cold in their own liquor before you ferve them up; broil them over a moderate fire, and ferve them up pretty hot. This fort of andouilles or puddings muft be made in fummer, when hogs are feldom killed.

To drefs Calf's Chitterlings curioufly.

CUT a calf's nut in flices of its length, and the thicknefs of a finger, together with fome ham, bacon, and the white of chickens cut after the fame manner; put the whole into a ftew-pan feafoned with falt, pepper, fweet herbs, and fpice; then take the guts cleanfed, cut and divide them in parcels, and fill them with your flices; then lay in the bottom of a kettle or pan fome flices of bacon and veal, feafon them with fome pepper, falt, a bay-leaf, and an onion, and lay fome bacon and veal over them; then put in a pint of white wine, and let it ftew foftly, clofe covered, with fire over and under it, if the pot or pan will allow it; then broil the puddings on a fheet of white paper, well buttered on the infide.

To drefs a Calf's Liver in a Caul.

TAKE off the under-fkins, and fhred the liver very fmall, then take an ounce of truffles and morels chopped fmall, with parfley; roaft two or three onions, take off their outermoft coats, pound fix cloves and a dozen coriander-feeds, add them to the onions, and pound them together in a marble mortar; then take them out, and mix them with the liver; take a pint of cream, half a pint of milk, and feven or eight new-laid eggs; beat them together, boil them, but do not let them curdle, fhred a pound of fuet as fmall as you can, half melt it in a pan, and pour it into your egg and cream, then pour it into your liver, then mix all well together, feafon it with pepper, falt, nutmeg, and a little thyme, and let it ftand till it is cold; fpread a caul over the bottom and fides of the ftew-pan, and put in your hafhed liver and cream all together, fold it up in the caul in the fhape of a calf's liver, then turn it upfide down carefully, lay it in a difh that will bear the oven, and do it over with beaten egg, dredge it with grated bread, and bake it in an oven. Serve it up hot for a firft courfe.

To roaft a Calf's Liver.

LARD it with bacon, fpit it firft, and roaft it: ferve it up with good gravy.

Calves' Feet ftewed.

CUT a calf's foot into four pieces, put it into a fauce-pan with half a pint of foft water and a middling potatoe; fcrape the outfide fkin clean off, flice it thin, and a middling onion peeled and fliced thin, fome beaten pepper and falt, cover it clofe, close, and let it ftew very foftly for about two hours after it boils; be fure to let it fimmer as foftly as you can; eat it without any other fauce: it is an excellent difh.

To make Fricandillas.

TAKE two pounds of lean veal and half a pound of kidney-fuet chopped fmall, the crumb of a two-penny French roll foaked in hot milk; fqueeze the milk out and put it to the veal; feafon it pretty high with pepper and falt, and grated nutmeg; make it into balls as big as a tea-cup, with the yolks of eggs over it, and fry them in butter till they are of a fine light brown; have a quart of veal broth in a ftew-pan, ftew them gently three quarters of an hour, thicken it with butter rolled in flour, and add the juice of half a lemon; put it in a difh with the fauce over, and garnifh with notched lemon and beet root.

To make a Scotch Haggafs.

TAKE the lights, heart, and chitterlings of a calf, chop them very fine, and a pound of fuet chopped fine; feafon with pepper and falt to your palate; mix in a pound of flour or oatmeal, roll it up, and put it into a calf's bag, and boil it; an hour and a half will do it. Some add a pint of good thick cream, and put in a little beaten mace, cloves, or nutmeg; or all-fpice is very good in it.

To make it fweet with Fruit.

TAKE the meat and fuet as above, and flour, with beaten mace, cloves, and nutmeg to your palate, a pound of currants wafhed very clean, a pound of raifins ftoned and chopped fine, half a pint of fack; mix all well together, and boil it in the calf's bag two hours. You muft carry it to table in the bag it was boiled in.

To drefs a Ham à la Braife.

CLEAR the knuckle, take off the fwerd, and lay it in water to frefhen; then tie it about with a ftring; take flices of bacon and beef, beat and feafon them well with fpice and fweet herbs; then lay them in the bottom of a kettle, with onions, parfnips, and carrots fliced, with fome cives and parfley; lay in your ham the fat fide uppermoft, and cover it with flices of beef, and over that with flices of bacon; then lay on fome fliced roots and herbs the fame as under it: cover it clofe, and ftop it clofe with pafte; put fire both over and under it, and let it ftew with a very flow fire twelve hours; put it in a pan, dredge it well with grated bread, and brown it with a hot iron; or put it in the oven, and bake it one hour: then ferve it upon a clean napkin. Garnifh with raw parfley.

N. B. If you eat it hot, make a ragoo thus: take a veal ſweetbread, ſome livers of fowls, cocks-combs, muſhrooms, and truffles; toſs them up in a pint of good gravy, ſeaſoned with ſpice as you like it; thicken it with a piece of butter rolled in flour, and a glaſs of red wine; then brown your ham as above, and let it ſtand a quarter of an hour to drain the fat out; take the liquor it was ſtewed in, ſtrain it, ſkim all the fat off, put it to the gravy, and boil it up with a ſpoonful of browning. It will do as well as the eſſence of ham. Sometimes you may ſerve it up with a ragoo of crawfiſh, and ſometimes with carp-ſauce.

To roaſt a Ham or Gammon.

TAKE off the ſwerd, or what we call the ſkin, or rind, and lay it in lukewarm water for two or three hours; then lay it in a pan, pour upon it a quart of canary, and let it ſteep in it for ten or twelve hours. When you have ſpitted it, put ſome ſheets of white paper over the fat ſide, pour the canary in which it was ſoaked in the dripping-pan, and baſte it all the time it is roaſting; when it is roaſted enough pull off the paper, and dredge it well with crumbled bread and parſley ſhred fine; make the fire briſk, and brown it well. If you heat it hot, garniſh it with raſpings of bread: if cold, ſerve it on a clean napkin, and garniſh it with parſley for a ſecond courſe.

Or thus: take off the ſkin of the ham or gammon, when you have half-boiled it, and dredge it with oatmeal ſifted very fine, baſte it with butter, then roaſt it gently two hours; ſtir up your fire, and brown it quick; when ſo done, diſh it up, and pour brown gravy in the diſh. Garniſh with bread raſpings, if hot; if cold, garniſh with parſley.

To make Eſſence of Ham.

TAKE a ham, and cut off all the fat, cut the lean in thin pieces, and lay them in the bottom of your ſtew pan; put over them ſix onions ſliced, two carrots, and one parſnip, two or three leeks, a few freſh muſhrooms, a little parſley and ſweet-herbs, four or five ſhalots, and ſome cloves and mace; put a little water at the bottom; ſet it on a gentle ſtove till it begins to ſtick; then put in a gallon of veal broth to a ham of fourteen pounds, (more or leſs broth, according to the ſize of the ham,) let it ſtew very gently for one hour; then ſtrain it off, and put it away for uſe.

To ſtuff a Chine of Pork.

MAKE a ſtuffing of the fat leaf of pork, parſley, thyme, ſage, eggs, crumbs of bread; ſeaſon it with pepper, ſalt, ſhalot,

lot, and nutmeg, and ſtuff it thick; then roaſt it gently, and when it is about a quarter roaſted, cut the ſkin in ſlips: and make your ſauce with apples, lemon-peel, two or three cloves, and a blade of mace; ſweeten it with ſugar, put ſome butter in, and have muſtard in a cup.

To barbecue a Leg of Pork.

LAY down your leg to a good fire, put into the dripping-pan two bottles of red wine, baſte your pork with it all the time it is roaſting; when it is enough, take up what is left in the pan, put to it two anchovies, the yolks of three eggs boiled hard and pounded fine, with a quarter of a pound of butter and half a lemon, a bunch of ſweet herbs, a tea-ſpoonful of lemon-pickle, a ſpoonful of catchup, and one of tarragon vinegar, or a little tarragon ſhred ſmall, boil them a few minutes, then draw your pork, and cut the ſkin down from the bottom of the ſhank in rows an inch broad, raiſe every other row, and roll it to the ſhank, ſtrain your ſauce, and pour it on boiling hot; lay oyſter-patties all round the pork, and ſprigs of green parſley.

Various Ways of dreſſing a Pig.

FIRST ſkin your pig up to the ears whole, then make a good plumb-pudding batter, with good beef fat, fruit, eggs, milk, and flour; fill the ſkin, and ſew it up; it will look like a pig; but you muſt bake it, flour it very well, and rub it all over with butter, and when it is near enough, draw it to the oven's mouth, rub it dry, and put it in again for a few minutes; lay it in the diſh, and let the ſauce be ſmall gravy and butter in the diſh: cut the other part of the pig into four quarters, roaſt them as you do lamb, throw mint and parſley on it as it roaſts; then lay them on water-creſſes, and have mint-ſauce in a baſon. Any one of theſe quarters will make a pretty ſide-diſh: or take one quarter and roaſt, cut the other in ſteaks, and fry them fine and brown. Have ſtewed ſpinage in the diſh, and lay the roaſt upon it, and the fried in the middle. Garniſh with hard eggs and Seville oranges cut into quarters, and have ſome butter in a cup: or for change, you may have good gravy in the diſh, and garniſh with fried parſley and lemon; or you may make a ragoo of ſweetbreads, artichoke-bottoms, truffles, morels, and good gravy, and pour over them. Garniſh with lemon. Either of theſe will do for a top-diſh of a firſt courſe. You may fricaſſee it white for a ſecond courſe at top, or a ſide-diſh.

You may take a pig, ſkin him, and fill him with force-meat made thus: take two pounds of young pork, fat and all, two pounds of veal the ſame, ſome ſage, thyme, parſley, a little lemon-

lemon-peel, pepper, ſalt, mace, cloves, and a nutmeg: mix them and beat them fine in a mortar, then fill the pig, and ſew it up. You may either roaſt or bake it. Have nothing but good gravy in the diſh. Or you may cut it into ſlices, and lay the head in the middle. Save the head whole with the ſkin on, and roaſt it by itſelf: when it is enough, cut it in two and lay it in your diſh: have ready ſome good gravy and dried ſage rubbed in it, thicken it with a piece of butter rolled in flour, take out the brains, beat them up with the gravy, and pour them into the diſh.

N. B. You may make a very good pie of it, as you may ſee in the directions for pies, which you may either make a bottom or ſide-diſh.

You muſt obſerve in your white fricaſſee that you take off the fat. Or you may make a very good diſh thus: take a quarter of a pig ſkinned, cut it into chops, ſeaſon them with ſpice, and waſh them with the yolks of eggs, butter the bottom of a diſh, lay theſe ſteaks on the diſh, and upon every ſteak lay ſome force-meat the thickneſs of half a crown, made thus: Take half a pound of veal, and of fat pork the ſame quantity, chop them very well together, and beat them in a mortar fine; add ſome ſweet herbs and ſage, a little lemon-peel, nutmeg, pepper, and ſalt, and a little beaten mace; upon this lay a layer of bacon or ham, and then a bay leaf; take a little fine ſkewer and ſtick it juſt in about two inches long to hold them together, then pour a little melted butter over them, and ſend them to the oven to bake: when they are enough, lay them in your diſh, and pour good gravy over them, with muſhrooms, and garniſh with lemon.

A Pig in Jelly.

CUT it into quarters, and lay it into your ſtew-pan; put in one calf's foot and the pig's feet, a pint of Rheniſh wine, the juice of four lemons, and one quart of water, three or four blades of mace, two or three cloves, ſome ſalt, and a very little piece of lemon-peel; ſtove it, or do it over a ſlow fire two hours; then take it up, lay the pig into the diſh you intended for it, then ſtrain the liquor, and when the jelly is cold, ſkim off the fat, and leave the ſettling at the bottom. Beat up the whites of ſix eggs, and boil up with the jelly about ten minutes, and put it through a bag till it is clear, then pour the jelly over the pig; then ſerve it up cold in the jelly.

Collared Pig.

KILL a fine young roaſting pig, dreſs off the hair and draw it, and waſh it clean, rip it open from one end to the other, and take out all the bones; rub it all over with pepper and ſalt, a little cloves and mace beat fine, fix fage leaves and fweet herbs chopped fmall; roll up your pig tight, and bind it with a fillet; fill the pot you intend to boil it in with foft water, a bunch of fweet herbs, fome pepper-corns, fome cloves and mace, a handful of falt, and a pint of vinegar; when the liquor boils, put in your pig; boil it till it is tender; take it up, and when it is almoft cold bind it over again, put it into an earthen pan and pour the liquor your pig was boiled in over it, and always keep it covered; when you want it, take it out of the pan, untie the fillet as far as you want to cut it; then cut it in flices and lay it in your difh. Garnifh with parfley.

To drefs a Pig the French Way.

SPIT your pig, lay it down to the fire, let it roaft till it is thoroughly warm, then cut it off the fpit, and divide it in twenty pieces. Set them to ftew in half a pint of white wine and a pint of ftrong broth, feafoned with grated nutmeg, pepper, two onions cut fmall, and fome ftripped thyme. Let it ftew an hour, then put to it half a pint of ftrong gravy, a piece of butter rolled in flour, fome anchovies, and a fpoonful of vinegar or mufhroom-pickle; when it is enough, lay it in your difh, and pour the gravy over it, then garnifh with orange and lemon.

To drefs a Pig au Pere Douillet.

CUT off the head, and divide it into quarters, lard them with bacon, feafon them well with mace, cloves, pepper, nutmeg, and falt. Lay a layer of fat bacon at the bottom of a kettle, lay the head in the middle, and the quarters round; then put in a bay-leaf, an onion fliced, lemon, carrots, parfnips, parfley, and cives; cover it again with bacon, put in a quart of broth, ftew it over the fire for an hour, and then take it up; put your pig into a ftew-pan or kettle, pour in a bottle of white wine, cover it clofe, and let it ftew for an hour very foftly. If you would ferve it cold, let it ftand till it is fo; then drain it well, and wipe it, that it may look white, and lay it in a difh with the head in the middle and the quarters round, then throw fome green parfley all over: or any one of the quarters is a very pretty difh, laid on water-creffes. If you would have it hot, whilft your pig is ftewing in the wine, take the firft gravy it was ftewed in, and ftrain it, fkim of all the fat, then take a fweetbread cut into five or fix flices, fome truffles, morels, and mufhrooms; ftew all together till they are enough, thicken it with the yolks of two eggs, or a piece of butter rolled in flour, and when your pig is enough take it out, and lay it in your difh; put the wine it was ftewed in to the ragoo, then pour all over the pig, and garnifh with lemon.

A Pig

A Pig Matelote.

GUT and fcald your pig, cut off the head and pettitoes, then cut your pig in four quarters, put them with the head and toes into cold water; cover the bottom of a ftew-pan with flices of bacon, and place over them the faid quarters, with the pettitoes, and the head cut in two. Seafon the whole with pepper, falt, thyme, bay leaf, an onion, and a bottle of white wine; lay over more flices of bacon, put over it a quart of water, and let it boil. Take two large eels, fkin and gut them, and cut them about five or fix inches long; when your pig is half done, put in your eels, then boil a dozen of large crawfifh, cut off the claws, and take off the fhells of the tails; and when your pig and eels are enough, lay firft your pig and the pettitoes round it, but do not put in the head, (it will be a pretty difh cold,) then lay your eels and crawfifh over them, and take the liquor they were ftewed in, fkim off all the fat, then add to it half a pint of ftrong gravy, thickened with a little piece of butter rolled in flour, and a fpoonful of browning, and pour over it, then garnifh with crawfifh and lemon. This will do for a firft courfe or remove. Fry the brains and lay round, and all over the difh.

To drefs a Pig like a fat Lamb.

TAKE a fat pig, cut off his head, flit and trufs him up like a lamb; when he is flit through the middle and fkinned, parboil him a little, then throw fome parfley over him, roaft it and dredge it. Let your fauce be half a pound of butter and a pint of cream, ftirring all together till it is fmooth; then pour it over and fend it to table.

Barbecued Pig.

HAVING dreffed a pig ten or twelve weeks old, as if you intended to roaft it, make a force-meat in the following manner: take the liver of the pig, two anchovies, and fix fage leaves chopped fmall; put them into a marble mortar with the crumbs of a penny-loaf, half a pint of Madeira wine, four ouces of butter, and half a tea-fpoonful of Cayenne pepper, beat them all together to a pafte, put it into your pig's belly, and few it up; lay your pig down, at a good diftance, before a large brifk fire; put into your dripping-pan two bottles of red wine and one of Madeira, bafte it with the wine all the time it is roafting, and when it is half roafted, put two penny loaves under the pig; if there is not wine enough put in more, and when the pig is near done, take the loaves and fauce out of the pan, and put to the fauce half a lemon, a bundle of fweet herbs, an anchovy chopped

chopped ſmall, boil it five minutes, and then draw your pig when it has roaſted four hours; put into the pig's mouth an orange or lemon, and a loaf on each ſide; ſkim off the fat, and ſtrain your ſauce through a ſieve, and pour over the pig boiling hot; ſerve it up garniſhed with lemon and barberries; or you may bake it, only keep it baſting with wine.

To dreſs Pigs' Pettitoes.

PUT your pettitoes into a ſauce-pan with half a pint of water, a blade of mace, a little whole pepper, a bundle of ſweet herbs, and an onion. Let them boil five minutes, then take out the liver, lights, and heart, mince them very fine, grate a little nutmeg over them, and ſhake a little flour on them; let the feet do till they are tender, then take them out and ſtrain the liquor, put all together with a little ſalt and a piece of butter as big as a walnut, ſhake the ſauce-pan often, let it ſimmer five or ſix minutes, then cut ſome toaſted ſippets and lay round the diſh, lay the mince-meat and ſauce in the middle, and the pettitoes ſplit round it. You may add the juice of half a lemon, or a very little vinegar.

To make a pretty Diſh of a Breaſt of Veniſon.

TAKE half a pound of butter, flour your veniſon, and fry it of a fine brown on both ſides; then take it up and keep it hot covered in the diſh; take ſome flour and ſtir it into the butter till it is quite thick and brown (but take great care it do not burn), ſtir in it half a pound of lump-ſugar beat fine, and pour in as much red wine as will make it of the thickneſs of a ragoo; ſqueeze in the juice of a lemon, give it a boil up, and pour it over the veniſon. Do not garniſh the diſh, but ſend it to table.

To boil a Haunch or Neck of Veniſon.

LAY it in ſalt for a week, then boil it in a cloth well floured; for every pound of veniſon allow a quarter of an hour for the boiling. For ſauce you muſt boil ſome cauliflowers, pulled into little ſprigs, in milk and water, ſome fine white cabbage, ſome turnips cut into dice, with ſome beet-root cut into long narrow pieces about an inch and a half long and half an inch thick; lay a ſprig of cauliflower, and ſome of the turnips maſhed with ſome cream and a little butter; let your cabbage be boiled and then beat in a ſauce-pan with a piece of butter and ſalt, lay that next the cauliflower, then the turnips, then cabbage, and ſo on till the diſh is full; place the beet-root here and there, juſt as you fancy: it looks very pretty, and is a fine diſh. Have a little melted butter in a cup, if wanted.

N. B. A

N. B. A leg of mutton cut veniſon-faſhion, and dreſſed the ſame way, is a pretty diſh: or a fine neck, with the ſcrag cut off. This eats well boiled or haſhed, with gravy and ſweet ſauce, next day.

CHAP. VI.

To dress POULTRY, GAME, &c.

To roaſt a Turkey.

THE beſt way to roaſt a turkey is to looſen the ſkin on the breaſt, and fill it with force-meat, made thus: take a quarter of a pound of beef-ſuet, as much of crumbs of bread, a little lemon-peel, an anchovy, ſome nutmeg, pepper, parſley, and a little thyme. Chop and beat them all well together, mix them with the yolk of an egg, and ſtuff up the breaſt; when you have no ſuet, butter will do: or you may make your force-meat thus: ſpread bread and butter thin, and grate ſome nutmeg over it; when you have enough roll it up, and ſtuff the breaſt of the turkey; then roaſt it of a fine brown, but be ſure to pin ſome white paper on the breaſt till it is near enough. You muſt have good gravy in the diſh, and bread-ſauce, made thus: take a good piece of crumb, put it into a pint of water, with a blade or two of mace, two or three cloves, and ſome whole pepper. Boil it up five or ſix times, then with a ſpoon take out the ſpice you had before put in, and then you muſt pour off the water (you may boil an onion in it, if you pleaſe); then beat up the bread with a good piece of butter and a little ſalt. Or onion-ſauce, made thus: take ſome onions, peel them, and cut them into thin ſlices, and boil them half an hour in milk and water; then drain the water from them, and beat them up with a good piece of butter; ſhake a little flour in, and ſtir it all together with a little cream (if you have it), or milk will do; put the ſauce into boats, and garniſh with lemon.

Another way to make ſauce: take half a pint of oyſters, ſtrain the liquor, and put the oyſters with the liquor into a ſauce-pan, with a blade or two of mace; let them juſt lump, then pour in a glaſs of white wine, let it boil once, and thicken it with a piece of butter rolled in flour. Serve this up in a baſon by itſelf, with good gravy in the diſh, for every body does not love oyſter-ſauce. This makes a pretty ſide-diſh for ſupper, or a corner-diſh of a table for dinner. If you chafe it in the diſh, add half a pint of gravy, and boil it up together. This ſauce

ſauce is good either with boiled or roaſted turkies or fowls; but you may leave the gravy out, adding as much butter as will do for ſauce, and garniſhing with lemon.

Another bread-ſauce: take ſome crumbs of bread, rubbed through a fine cullender, put to it a pint of milk, a little butter, and ſome ſalt, a few corns of white pepper, and an onion; boil them for fifteen minutes, take out the onion and beat it up well, then toſs it up and put it in your ſauce-boats.

A white Sauce for Fowls or Chickens.

TAKE a little ſtrong veal gravy, with a little white pepper, mace, and ſalt boiled in it; have it clear from any ſkin or fat; as much cream, with a little flour mixed in the cream, a little mountain wine to your liking; boil it up gently for five minutes, then ſtrain it over your chickens or fowls, or in boats.

To make Mock Oyſter-Sauce, either for Turkies or Fowls boiled.

FORCE the turkies or fowls as above, and make your ſauce thus: take a quarter of a pint of water, an anchovy, a blade or two of mace, a piece of lemon-peel, and five or ſix whole pepper-corns; boil theſe together, then ſtrain them, add as much butter with a little flour as will do for ſauce; let it boil, and lay ſauſages round the fowl or turkey. Garniſh with lemon.

To make Muſhroom-Sauce for white Fowls of all Sorts.

TAKE a quart of freſh muſhrooms, well cleaned and waſhed, cut them in two, put them in a ſtew-pan, with a little butter, a blade of mace, and a little ſalt; ſtew it gently for half an hour, then add a pint of cream and the yolks of two eggs beat very well, and keep ſtirring it till it boils up; then ſqueeze half a lemon, put it over your fowls or turkies, or in baſons, or in a diſh, with a piece of French bread, firſt buttered then toaſted brown, and juſt dip it in boiling water; put it in the diſh, and the muſhrooms over.

Muſhroom-Sauce for white Fowls boiled.

TAKE half a pint of cream and a quarter of a pound of butter, ſtir them together one way till it is thick; then add a ſpoonful of muſhroom-pickle, pickled muſhrooms, or freſh, if you have them. Garniſh only with lemon.

To make Celery-Sauce, either for roaſted or boiled Fowls, Turkies, Partridges, or any other Game.

TAKE a large bunch of celery, waſh and pare it very clean, cut it into little thin bits, and boil it ſoftly in a little water till it is tender; then add a little beaten mace, ſome nutmeg, pepper,

per, and ſalt, thickened with a good piece of butter rolled in flour; then boil it up and pour in your diſh.

You may make it with cream thus: boil your celery as above, and add ſome mace, nutmeg, a piece of butter as big as a walnut rolled in flour, and half a pint of cream; boil them all together.

To make brown Celery-Sauce.

STEW the celery as above, then add mace, nutmeg, pepper, ſalt, a piece of butter rolled in flour, with a glaſs of red wine, a ſpoonful of catchup, and half a pint of good gravy; boil all theſe together, and pour into the diſh. Garniſh with lemon.

To ſtew a Turkey or Fowl in Celery Sauce.

YOU muſt judge according to the largeneſs of your turkey or fowl what celery or ſauce you want. Take a large fowl, put it into a ſauce pan or pot, and put to it one quart of good broth or gravy, a bunch of celery waſhed clean and cut ſmall, with ſome mace, cloves, pepper, and all-ſpice, tied looſe in a muſlin rag; put in an onion and a ſprig of thyme, a little ſalt and Cayenne pepper; let theſe ſtew ſoftly till they are enough, then add a piece of butter rolled in flour; take up your fowl and pour the ſauce over it. An hour will do a large fowl, or a ſmall turkey; but a very large turkey will take two hours to do it ſoftly. If it is over-done or dry, it is ſpoiled; but you may be a judge of that if you look at it now and then. Mind to take out the onion, thyme, and ſpice before you ſend it to table.

N. B. A neck of veal done this way is very good, and will take two hours doing.

To make Egg-Sauce proper for roaſted Chickens.

MELT your butter thick and fine, chop two or three hard-boiled eggs fine, put them into a baſon, pour the butter over them, and have good gravy in the diſh.

Shalot-Sauce for roaſted Fowls.

TAKE ſix ſhalots chopped fine, put them into a ſauce-pan with a gill of gravy, a ſpoonful of vinegar, ſome pepper and ſalt, ſtew them for a minute; then pour them into your diſh, or put it in ſauce-boats.

Carrier-Sauce.

TAKE a Spaniſh onion, and cut it in thin ſlices, put it into a deep plate, take half a pint of boiling water, with a ſpoonful of vinegar, a little pepper and ſalt, and pour it over the onion.

Shalot-Sauce for a Scrag of Mutton boiled.

TAKE two ſpoonfuls of the liquor the mutton is boiled in, two ſpoonfuls of vinegar, two or three ſhalots cut fine, with a little ſalt; put it into a ſauce-pan, with a piece of butter as big as a walnut rolled in a little flour; ſtir it together, and give it a boil. For thoſe who love ſhalot, it is the pretrieſt ſauce that can be made to a ſcrag of mutton.

To dreſs Livers with Muſhroom-Sauce.

TAKE ſome pickled or freſh muſhrooms cut ſmall (both if you have them), and let the livers be bruiſed fine, with a good deal of parſley chopped ſmall, a ſpoonful or two of catchup, a glaſs of white wine, and as much good gravy as will make ſauce enough; thicken it with a piece of butter rolled in flour. This does either for roaſted or boiled.

A pretty little Sauce.

TAKE the liver of the fowl, bruiſe it with a little of the liquor, cut a little lemon-peel fine, melt ſome good butter, and mix the liver by degrees; give it a boil, and pour it into the diſh.

To make Lemon-Sauce for boiled Fowls.

TAKE a lemon and pare off the rind, cut it into ſlices, and take the kernels out, cut it into ſquare bits, blanch the liver of the fowl, and chop it fine; mix the lemon and liver together in a boat, and pour ſome hot melted butter on it, and ſtir it up. Boiling of it will make it go to oil.

A German Way of dreſſing Fowls.

TAKE a turkey or fowl, ſtuff the breaſt with what force-meat you like, and fill the body with roaſted cheſnuts peeled. Roaſt it, and have ſome more roaſted cheſnuts peeled, put them in half a pint of good gravy, with a little piece of butter rolled in flour; boil theſe together with ſome ſmall turnips and ſauſages cut in ſlices, and fried or boiled. Garniſh with cheſnuts. You may leave the turnips out.

N. B. You may dreſs ducks the ſame way.

To dreſs a Turkey or Fowl to Perfection.

BONE them, and make a force-meat thus: take the fleſh of a fowl, cut it ſmall, then take a pound of veal, beat it in a mortar with half a pound of beef-ſuet, as much crumbs of bread, ſome muſhrooms, truffles, and morels cut ſmall, a few ſweet herbs and parſley, with ſome nutmeg, pepper, and ſalt, a little mace beaten, ſome lemon-peel cut fine; mix all theſe together

together with the yolks of two eggs, then fill your turkey and roast it. This will do for a large turkey, and so in proportion for a fowl. Let your sauce be good gravy, with mushrooms, truffles, and morels in it: then garnish with lemon, and for variety sake, you may lard your fowl or turkey.

To stew a Turkey brown.

TAKE your turkey after it is nicely picked and drawn, fill the skin of the breast with force-meat, and put an anchovy, a shalot, and a little thyme in the belly; lard the breast with bacon, then put a good piece of butter in the stew-pan, flour the turkey, and fry it just of a fine brown; then take it out, and put it into a deep stew-pan, or little pot, that will just hold it, and put in as much gravy as will barely cover it, a glass of white wine, some whole pepper, mace, two or three cloves, and a little bundle of sweet herbs; cover it close, and stew it for an hour, then take up the turkey, and keep it hot covered by the fire, and boil the sauce to about a pint, strain it off, add the yolks of two eggs and a piece of butter rolled in flour; stir it till it is thick, and then lay your turkey in the dish and pour your sauce over it. You may have ready some little French loaves about the bigness of an egg, cut off the tops, and take out the crumb; then fry them of a fine brown, fill them with stewed oysters, lay them round the dish, and garnish with lemon.

To stew a Turkey brown the nice Way.

BONE it, and fill it with a force-meat made thus: take the flesh of a fowl, half a pound of veal, and the flesh of two pigeons, with a well-picked or dry tongue, peel it, and chop it all together, then beat it in a mortar, with the marrow of a beef bone, or a pound of the fat of a loin of veal; season it with two or three blades of mace, two or three cloves, and half a nutmeg dried at a good distance from the fire, and pounded, with a little pepper and salt; mix all these well together, fill your turkey, fry it of a fine brown, and put it into a little pot that will just hold it; lay four or five skewers at the bottom of the pot to keep the turkey from sticking; put in a quart of good beef and veal gravy wherein was boiled spice and sweet herbs, cover it close, and let it stew half an hour; then put in a glass of white wine, one spoonful of catchup, a large spoonful of pickled mushrooms, and a few fresh ones (if you have them), a few truffles and morels, a piece of butter as big as a walnut rolled in flour; cover it close, and let it stew half an hour longer; get the little French rolls ready fried, take some oysters and strain the liquor from them, then put the oysters and liquor into a sauce-pan, with a blade of mace, a little

little white wine, and a piece of butter rolled in flour; let them stew till thick, then fill the loaves, lay the turkey in the dish, and pour the sauce over it. If there is any fat on the gravy take it off, and lay the loaves on each side of the turkey. Garnish with lemon when you have no loaves, and take oysters dipped in butter and fried.

N. B. The same will do for any white fowl.

Turkies and Chickens dressed after the Dutch Way.

BOIL them, season them with salt, pepper, and cloves; then to every quart of broth put a quarter of a pound of rice or vermicelli: it is eat with sugar and cinnamon. The two last may be left out.

A Turkey stuffed after the Hamburgh Way.

TAKE one pound of beef, three quarters of a pound of suet, mince it very small, season it with salt, pepper, cloves, mace, and sweet-marjoram; then mix two or three eggs with it, loosen the skin all round the turkey, and stuff, and roast it.

A Turkey à la daub, to be sent up hot.

CUT the turkey down the back just enough to bone it, without spoiling the look of it, then stuff it with a nice force-meat made of oysters chopped fine, crumbs of bread, pepper, salt, shalots, a very little thyme, parsley and butter, fill it as full as you like, and sew it up with a thread, tie it up in a clean cloth and boil it very white, but not too much. You may serve it up with oyster-sauce made good, or take the bones with a piece of veal, mutton, and bacon, and make a rich gravy seasoned with pepper, salt, shalots, and a little bit of mace, strain it off through a sieve, and stew your turkey in it, (after it is half boiled,) just half an hour, dish it up in the gravy after it is well skimmed, strained, and thickened with a few mushrooms stewed white, or stewed pallets, force-meat balls, fried oysters, or sweetbreads, and pieces of lemon. Dish it up with the breast upwards; if you send it up garnished with pallets, take care to have them stewed tender first; before you add them to the turkey, you may put a few morels and truffles in your sauce, if you like it, but take care to wash them clean.

Turkey à la daub, to be sent up cold.

BONE the turkey, and season it with pepper and salt, then spread over it some slices of ham, upon that some force-meat, upon that a fowl, boned and seasoned as above, then more ham and force-meat, then sew it up with thread; cover the bottom of the stew-pan with veal and ham, then lay in the turkey the breast

breaſt down, chop all the bones to pieces, and put them on the turkey, cover the pan and ſet it on the fire five minutes, then put in as much clear broth as will cover it, let it boil two hours, when it is more than half done, put in one ounce of iſing-glaſs and a bundle of herbs. When it is done enough, take out the turkey, and ſtrain the jelly through a hair ſieve, ſkim off all the fat, and when it is cold, lay the turkey upon it, the breaſt down, and cover it with the reſt of the jelly. Let it ſtand in ſome cold place; when you ſerve it up, turn it on the diſh it is to be ſerved in: if you pleaſe, you may ſpread butter over the turkey's breaſt, and put ſome green parſley or flowers, or what you pleaſe, and in what form you like.

A Turkey, &c. in Jelly.

Boil a turkey, or a fowl, as white as you can, let it ſtand till cold, and have ready a jelly made thus: take a fowl, ſkin it, take off all the fat, do not cut it to pieces, nor break the bones; take four pounds of a leg of veal, without any fat or ſkin, put it into a well-tinned ſauce-pan, put to it full three quarts of water, ſet it on a very clear fire till it begins to ſimmer; be ſure to ſkim it well, but take great care it does not boil. When it is well ſkimmed, ſet it ſo as it will but juſt ſeem to ſimmer; put to it two large blades of mace, half a nutmeg, and twenty corns of white pepper, a little bit of lemon-peel as big as a ſixpence. This will take ſix or ſeven hours doing. When you think it is a ſtiff jelly, which you will know by taking a little out to cool; be ſure to ſkim off all the fat, if any, and be ſure not to ſtir the meat in the ſauce-pan. A quarter of an hour before it is done, throw in a large tea-ſpoonful of ſalt, ſqueeze in the juice of half a fine Seville orange or lemon; when you think it is enough, ſtrain it off through a clean ſieve, but do not pour it off quite to the bottom, for fear of ſettlings. Lay the turkey or fowl in the diſh you intend to ſend it to the table in, beat up the whites of ſix eggs to a froth, and put the liquor to it, then boil it five or ſix minutes, and run it through a jelly-bag till it is very clear, then pour the liquor over it, let it ſtand till quite cold; colour ſome of the jelly in different colours, and when it is near cold, with a ſpoon ſprinkle it over, in what form or fancy you pleaſe, and ſend it to table; a few naſtertium flowers ſtuck here and there, look pretty, if you can get them, but theſe as well as lemon, &c. are entirely fancy. This is a very pretty diſh for a cold collation or a ſupper. All ſorts of birds or fowls may be done this way.

A Fowl à la Braiſe.

Truss your fowl, with the legs turned into the belly, ſeaſon it both inſide and out, with beaten mace, nutmeg, pepper, and ſalt, lay a layer of bacon at the bottom of a deep ſtew-pan, then a layer of veal, and afterwards the fowl, then put in an onion, two or three cloves ſtuck in a little bundle of ſweet herbs, with a piece of carrot, then put at the top a layer of bacon, another of veal, and a third of beef, cover it cloſe, and let it ſtand over the fire for two or three minutes, then pour in a pint of broth, or hot water; cover it cloſe, and let it ſtew an hour; afterwards take up your fowl, ſtrain the ſauce, and after you have ſkimmed off the fat, boil it down till it is of a glaze, then put it over the fowl. You may add juſt what you pleaſe to the ſauce. A ragoo of ſweetbreads, cocks'-combs, truffles, and morels, or muſhrooms, with force-meat balls, look very pretty, or any of the ſauces above.

A Capon done after the French Way.

TAKE a quart of white wine, ſeaſon the capon with ſalt, cloves, and whole pepper, and a few ſhalots; then put the capon in an earthen pan; you muſt take care it has not room to ſhake; it muſt be covered cloſe, and done on a ſlow charcoal fire.

To roaſt a Fowl with Cheſnuts.

FIRST take ſome cheſnuts, roaſt them very carefully, ſo as not to burn them; take off the ſkin and peel them; take about a dozen of them cut ſmall, and bruiſe them in a mortar; parboil the liver of the fowl, bruiſe it, cut about a quarter of a pound of ham or bacon, and pound it; then mix them all together, with a good deal of parſley chopped ſmall, a little ſweet herbs, ſome mace, pepper, ſalt, and nutmeg; mix theſe together and put into your fowl, and roaſt it. The beſt way of doing it is to tie the neck, and hang it up by the legs to roaſt with a ſtring, and baſte it with butter. For ſauce, take the reſt of the cheſnuts peeled and ſkinned; put them into ſome good gravy, with a little white wine, and thicken it with a piece of butter rolled in flour; then take up your fowl, lay it in the diſh, and pour in the ſauce. Garniſh with lemon.

To marinate Fowls.

TAKE a fine large fowl or turkey, raiſe the ſkin from the breaſt-bone with your finger; then take a veal ſweetbread and cut it ſmall, a few oyſters, a few muſhrooms, an anchovy, ſome pepper, a little nutmeg, ſome lemon-peel, and a little thyme; chop all together ſmall, and mix it with the yolk of an egg, ſtuff it in between the ſkin and the fleſh, but take great care you do not break the ſkin; and then ſtuff what oyſters you pleaſe into the body of the fowl. You may lard the breaſt of the fowl with bacon, if you chuſe it. Paper the breaſt, and roaſt it. Make good gravy, and garniſh with lemon. You may add a few muſhrooms to the ſauce.

To make a Frangas Incopades.

Take three quarters of a pound of lean bacon or ham, two large onions ſliced, four ſhalots, and two quarts of water, with a little beaten pepper, cloves, and mace, and a pennyworth of ſaffron, ſtew it gently till it is reduced to three pints, and ſtrain it through a ſieve; cut two fowls, as for a fricaſſee, and ſtew them in the broth till they are tender; mix two ſpoonfuls of flour in two ſpoonfuls of vinegar, and beat it up with ſome of the liquor till it is quite ſmooth; and mix the whole together, and boil it for ten minutes gently; put ſippets in a ſoup-diſh, and pour it all over them. You may add ſmall force-meat balls, if you pleaſe, in it; or you may make it of veal in the form of veal olives; and you may ſend it in a tureen, if you like.

Pullets à la Sainte Menehout.

After having truſſed the legs in the body, ſlit them along the back, ſpread them open on a table, take out the thigh-bones, and beat them with a rolling-pin; then ſeaſon them with pepper, ſalt, mace, nutmeg, and ſweet herbs; after that take a pound and a half of veal, cut it into thin ſlices, and lay it in a ſtew-pan, of a convenient ſize, to ſtew the pullets in; cover it, and ſet it over a ſtove or ſlow fire; and when it begins to cleave to the pan, ſtir in a little flour, ſhake the pan about till it be a little brown; then pour in as much broth as will ſtew the fowls, ſtir it together, put in a little whole pepper, an onion, and a little piece of bacon or ham; then lay in your fowls, cover them cloſe, and let them ſtew half an hour; then take them out, lay them on the gridiron to brown on the in-ſide; then lay them before the fire to do on the outſide; ſtrew them over with the yolk of an egg, ſome crumbs of bread, and baſte them with a little butter; let them be of a fine brown, and boil the gravy till there is about enough for ſauce; ſtrain it, put a few muſhrooms in, and a little piece of butter rolled in flour; lay the pullets in the diſh, and pour in the ſauce. Garniſh with lemon.

N. B. You may brown them in an oven, or fry them, which you pleaſe.

Chicken-Surprize.

If a ſmall diſh, one large fowl will do; roaſt it, and take the lean from the bone; cut it in thin ſlices, about an inch long, toſs it up with ſix or ſeven ſpoonfuls of cream, and a piece of butter rolled in flour, as big as a walnut. Boil it up and ſet it to cool; then cut ſix or ſeven thin ſlices of bacon round,

round, place them in a patty-pan, and put ſome force-meat on each ſide; work them up in the form of a French roll, with a raw egg in your hand, leaving a hollow place in the middle; put in your fowl, and cover them with ſome of the ſame force-meat, rubbing them ſmooth with your hand and a raw egg; make them of the height and bigneſs of a French roll, and throw a little fine grated bread over them. Bake them three quarters or an hour, in a gentle oven, or under a baking cover, till they come to a fine brown, and place them on your mazarine, that they may not touch one another; but place them ſo that they may not fall flat in the baking; or you may form them on your table with a broad kitchen knife, and place them on the thing you intend to bake them on. You may put the leg of a chicken into one of the loaves you intend for the middle. Let your ſauce be gravy, thickened with butter and a little juice of lemon. This is a pretty ſide-diſh for a firſt courſe, ſummer or winter, if you can get them.

Chickens in Savoury Jelly.

ROAST two chickens, then boil a gang of calf's-feet to a ſtrong jelly, take out the feet, ſkim off the fat, beat the whites of three eggs very well, then mix them with half a pint of white wine vinegar, the juice of three lemons, a blade or two of mace, a few pepper-corns, and a little ſalt, put them to your jelly; when it has boiled five or ſix minutes, run it through a jelly-bag ſeveral times till it is very clear, then put a little in the bottom of a bowl that will hold your chickens; when they are cold, and the jelly quite ſet, lay them in with their breaſts down, then fill up your bowl quite full with the reſt of your jelly, which you muſt take care to keep from ſetting, (ſo that when you pour it into your bowl it will not break,) let it ſtand all night, the next day put your baſon into warm water, pretty near the top; as ſoon as you find it looſe in the baſon, lay your diſh over it, and turn it out upon it.

Chickens roaſted with Force-meat and Cucumbers.

TAKE two chickens, dreſs them very neatly, break the breaſt-bone; and make force-meat thus: take the fleſh of a fowl, and of two pigeons, with ſome ſlices of ham or bacon; chop them all well together, take the crumb of a penny-loaf ſoaked in milk and boiled, then ſet to cool; when it is cool, mix it all together; ſeaſon it with beaten mace, nutmeg, pepper, and a little ſalt, a very little thyme, ſome parſley, and a little lemon-peel, with the yolks of two eggs; then fill your fowls, ſpit them, and tie them at both ends; after you have papered the breaſt, take four cucumbers, cut them in two, and lay them in falt and water two or three hours before; then dry them, and fill them with fome of the force-meat, (which you muft take care to fave,) and tie them with a packthread; flour them, and fry them of a fine brown; when your chickens are enough, lay them in the difh, and untie your cucumbers; but take care the meat do not come out; then lay them round the chickens, with the flat fide downwards, and the narrow end upwards. You muft have fome rich fried gravy, and pour into the difh; then garnifh with lemon.

N.B. One large fowl done this way, with the cucumbers laid round it, looks pretty, and is a very good difh.

Chickens à la Braife.

TAKE a couple of fine chickens, lard them, and feafon them with pepper, falt, and mace; then lay a layer of veal in the bottom of a deep ftew-pan, with a flice or two of bacon, an onion cut to pieces, a piece of carrot, and a layer of beef; then lay in the chickens with the breaft downward, and a bundle of fweet herbs; after that, a layer of beef, and put in a quart of broth or water; cover it clofe, let it ftew very foftly for an hour, after it begins to fimmer. In the mean time, get ready a ragoo made thus: take a good veal fweetbread or two, cut them fmall, fet them on the fire, with a very little broth or water, a few cocks'-combs, truffles, and morels, cut fmall, with an ox-palate, if you have it; ftew them all together till they are enough; and when your chickens are done, take them up, and keep them hot; then ftrain the liquor they were ftewed in, fkim the fat off, and pour into your ragoo; add a glafs of red wine, a fpoonful of catchup, and a few mufhrooms; then boil all together with a few artichoke-bottoms cut in four, and afparagus-tops. If your fauce is not thick enough, take a little piece of butter rolled in flour; and when enough, lay your chickens in the difh, and pour the ragoo over them. Garnifh with lemon.

Or, you may make your fauce thus: take the gravy the fowls were ftewed in, ftrain it, fkim off the fat; have ready half a pint of oyfters with the liquor ftrained; put them to your gravy with a glafs of white wine, a good piece of butter rolled in flour; then boil them all together, and pour over your fowls. Garnifh with lemon.

To broil Chickens.

SLIT them down the back, and feafon them with pepper and falt; lay them on a very clear fire, and at a great diftance. Let the infide lie next the fire till it is above half done; then turn them, and take great care the flefhy fide do not burn, and let them be of a fine brown. Let your fauce be good gravy,

gravy, with muſhrooms, and garniſh with lemon and the livers broiled, the gizzards cut, ſlaſhed, and broiled with pepper and ſalt.

Or this ſauce: take a handful of ſorrel dipped in boiling water, drain it, and have ready half a pint of good gravy, a ſhalot ſhred ſmall, and ſome parſley boiled very green, thicken it with a piece of butter rolled in flour, and add a glaſs of red wine; then lay your ſorrel in heaps round the fowls, and pour the ſauce over them. Garniſh with lemon.

N. B. You may make juſt what ſauce you fancy.

Pulled Chickens.

TAKE three chickens, boil them juſt fit for eating, but not too much; when they are boiled enough, flay all the ſkin off, and take the white fleſh off the bones, pull it into pieces about the ſize of a large quill, and half as long as your finger. Have ready a quarter of a pint of good cream, and a piece of freſh butter about as big as an egg; ſtir them together till the butter is all melted, and then put in your chicken with the gravy that came from them; give them two or three toſſes round on the fire, put them into a diſh, and ſend them up hot.

N. B. The legs, pinions, and rump muſt be peppered and ſalted, done over with the yolk of an egg and bread crumbs, and broiled on a clear fire; put the white meat, with the rump, in the middle, and the legs and pinions round.

Chickens Chiringrate.

CUT off their feet, break the breaſt-bone flat with a rolling-pin; but take care you do not break the ſkin; flour them, fry them of a fine brown in butter, then drain all the fat out of the pan, but leave the chickens in. Lay a pound of gravy-beef, cut very thin, over your chickens, and a piece of veal cut very thin, a little mace, two or three cloves, ſome whole-pepper, an onion, a little bundle of ſweet herbs, and a piece of carrot, and then pour in a quart of boiling water; cover it cloſe, let it ſtew for a quarter of an hour; then take out the chickens and keep them hot: let the gravy boil till it is quite rich and good; then ſtrain it off, and put it into your pan again, with two ſpoonfuls of red wine and a few muſhrooms; put in your chickens to heat, then take them up, lay them into your diſh, and pour your ſauce over them. Garniſh with lemon, and a few ſlices of cold ham broiled.

N. B. You may fill your chickens with force-meat, and lard them with bacon, and add truffles, morels, and ſweetbreads, cut ſmall; but then it will be a very high diſh.

Chickens dressed the French Way.

QUARTER, then broil them, crumble over them a little bread and parsley; when they are half done, put them in a stew-pan, with three or four spoonfuls of gravy, and double the quantity of white wine, salt, and pepper, some fried veal-balls, and some suckers, onions, shalots, and some green gooseberries or grapes when in season; cover the pan close, and let it stew on a charcoal fire for an hour; thicken the liquor with the yolks of eggs, and the juice of lemon; garnish the dish with fried suckers, sliced lemon, and the livers.

Chickens boiled with Bacon and Celery.

BOIL two chickens very white in a pot by themselves, and a piece of ham, or good thick bacon; boil two bunches of celery tender; then cut them about two inches long, all the white part; put it into a sauce-pan, with half a pint of cream, a piece of butter rolled in flour, and some pepper and salt; set it on the fire, and shake it often: when it is thick and fine, lay your chickens in the dish, and pour your sauce in the middle, that the celery may lie between the fowls; and garnish the dish all round with slices of ham or bacon.

N. B. If you have cold ham in the house, that, cut into slices and broiled, does full as well, or better, to lay round the dish.

Chickens with Tongues. A good Dish for a great deal of Company.

TAKE six small chickens, boiled very white, six hogs tongues boiled and peeled, a cauliflower boiled very white in milk and water whole, and a good deal of spinage boiled green; then lay your cauliflower in the middle, the chickens close all round, and the tongues round them with the roots outward, and the spinage in little heaps between the tongues. Garnish with little pieces of bacon toasted, and lay a little piece on each of the tongues.

Scotch Chickens.

FIRST wash your chickens, dry them in a clean cloth, and singe them; then cut them into quarters; put them into a stew-pan or sauce-pan, and just cover them with water; put in in a blade or two of mace, and a little bundle of parsley; cover them close, and let them stew half an hour; then chop half a handful of clean washed parsley, and throw in, and have ready six eggs, whites and all, beat fine. Let your liquor boil up, and pour the eggs all over them as it boils; then send all together hot in a deep dish, but take out the bundle of parsley first.

first. You must be sure to skim them well before you put in your mace, and the broth will be fine and clear.

N. B. This is also a very pretty dish for sick people; but the Scotch gentlemen are very fond of it.

To stew Chickens the Dutch Way.

TAKE two chickens, truss them as for boiling; beat fine six cloves, and four blades of mace, a handful of parsley shred fine, some pepper and salt; mix all together, and put into the inside of your chickens; singe them and flour them; put them into a stew-pan; clarify as much butter as will cover them; stew them gently one hour; put them into a china bowl with the butter, and send them up hot.

To stew Chickens.

TAKE two chickens, cut them into quarters, wash them clean, and then put them into a sauce-pan; put to them a quarter of a pint of water, half a pint of red wine, some mace, pepper, a bundle of sweets herbs, an onion, and a few raspings; cover them close, let them stew half an hour; then take a piece of butter about as big as an egg, rolled in flour, put in, and cover it close for five or six minutes; shake the sauce-pan about, then take out the sweet herbs and onion. You may take the yolks of two eggs, beat and mixed with them, or leave them out. Garnish with lemon.

A pretty Way of stewing Chickens.

TAKE two fine chickens, half boil them, then take them up in a pewter, or silver dish; cut up your fowls, and separate all the joint-bones one from another, and then take out the breast-bones. If there is not liquor enough from the fowls, add a few spoonfuls of the water they were boiled in, put in a blade of mace, and a little salt; cover it close with another dish; set it over a stove, or chafing-dish of coals; let it stew till the chickens are enough, and then send them hot to the table in the same dish they were stewed in.

Note: This is a very pretty dish for any sick person, or for a lying-in lady. For change it is better than butter, and the sauce is very agreeable and pretty.

N. B. You may do rabbits, partridges, or moor-game this way.

Ducks Alamode.

TAKE two fine ducks, cut them into quarters, fry them in butter a little brown; then pour out all the fat, and throw a little flour over them, and half a pint of good gravy, a quarter of a pint of red wine, two shalots, an anchovy, and a bundle of ſweet herbs; cover them cloſe, and let them ſtew a quarter of an hour; take out the herbs, ſkim off the fat, and let your ſauce be as thick as cream; ſend it to table, and garniſh with lemon.

To ſtew Ducks with green Peas.

HALF roaſt your ducks, then put them into a ſtew-pan with a pint of good gravy, a little mint, and three or four ſage leaves chopped ſmall, cover them cloſe and ſtew them half an hour, boil a pint of green peas, as for eating, and put them in after you have thickened the gravy; diſh up your ducks, and pour the gravy and peas over them.

To dreſs a Wild Duck the beſt Way.

FIRST half roaſt it, then lay it in a diſh, carve it, but leave the joints hanging together; throw a little pepper and ſalt, and ſqueeze the juice of a lemon over it; turn it on the breaſt, and preſs it hard with a plate, and add to its own gravy two or three ſpoonfuls of good gravy; cover it cloſe with another diſh, and ſet it over a ſtove ten minutes; then ſend it to table hot in the diſh it was done in, and garniſh with lemon. You may add a little red wine, and a ſhalot cut ſmall, if you like it; but it is apt to make the duck eat hard, unleſs you firſt heat the wine, and pour it in juſt as it is done.

Another Way to dreſs a Wild Duck.

TAKE a wild duck, put ſome pepper and ſalt in the inſide, and half roaſt it; have ready the following ſauce: a gill of good gravy, and a gill of red wine; put it in a ſtew-pan, with three or four ſhalots cut fine; boil it up; then cut the duck in ſmall pieces, and put it in with a little Cayenne pepper and ſalt; be careful to put in all the gravy that comes from the duck; ſimmer it for three minutes, and ſqueeze in a Seville orange or lemon; put it in the diſh, and garniſh with lemon.

To boil a Duck or a Rabbit with Onions.

BOIL your duck, or rabbit, in a good deal of water; be ſure to ſkim your water; for there will always riſe a ſcum, which, if it boils down, will diſcolour your fowls, &c. They will take about half an hour boiling. For ſauce, your onions muſt be peeled, and throw them into water as you peel them; then cut them into thin ſlices, boil them in milk and water, and ſkim the liquor. Half an hour will boil them. Throw them into a clean ſieve to drain; chop them and rub them through a cullender; put them into a ſauce-pan, ſhake in a little flour; put to them two or three ſpoonfuls of cream, a good piece of butter; ſtew all together over the fire till they are thick and fine; lay the duck or rabbit in the diſh, and pour the ſauce all over: if a rabbit, you muſt pluck out the jaw-bones, and ſtick one in each eye, the ſmall end inwards.

Or you may make this ſauce for change: take one large onion, cut it ſmall, half a handful of parſley clean waſhed and picked, chop it ſmall, a lettuce cut ſmall, a quarter of a pint of good gravy, a good piece of butter rolled in a little flour; add a little juice of lemon, a little pepper and ſalt; let all ſtew together for half an hour; then add two ſpoonfuls of red wine. This ſauce is moſt proper for a duck; lay your duck in the diſh, and pour your ſauce over it.

To dreſs a Duck with Green Peas.

PUT a deep ſtew-pan over the fire, with a piece of freſh butter; ſinge your duck and flour it, turn it in the pan two or three minutes; then pour out all the fat, but let the duck remain in the pan; put to it a pint of good gravy, a pint of peas, two lettuces cut ſmall, a ſmall bundle of ſweet herbs, a little pepper and ſalt; cover them cloſe, and let them ſtew for half an hour; now and then give the pan a ſhake; when they are juſt done, grate in a little nutmeg, and put in a very little beaten mace, and thicken it either with a piece of butter rolled in flour, or the yolk of an egg beat up with two or three ſpoonfuls of cream; ſhake it all together for three or four minutes, take out the ſweet herbs, lay the duck in the diſh, and pour the ſauce over it. You may garniſh with boiled mint chopped, or let it alone.

To dreſs a Duck with Cucumbers.

TAKE three or four cucumbers, pare them, take out the ſeeds, cut them into little pieces, lay them in vinegar for two or three hours before, with two large onions peeled and ſliced; then do your duck as above; then take the duck out, and put in the cucumbers and onions, firſt drain them in a cloth, let them be a little brown; ſhake a little flour over them. In the mean time let your duck be ſtewing in the ſauce-pan with a pint of gravy, for a quarter of an hour; then add to it the cucumbers and onions, with pepper and ſalt to your palate, a good piece of butter rolled in flour, and two or three ſpoonfuls of red wine; ſhake all together, and let it ſtew for eight or ten minutes; then take up your duck, and pour the ſauce over it.

Or, you may roaſt your duck, and make this ſauce, and pour over it; but then half a pint of gravy will be enough.

To dreſs a Duck à la Braiſe.

TAKE a duck, lard it with little pieces of bacon, ſeaſon it inſide and out with pepper and ſalt; lay a layer of bacon, cut thin,

thin, in the bottom of a ſtew-pan, and then a layer of lean beef, cut thin; then lay your duck with ſome carrot, an onion, a little bundle of ſweet herbs, a blade or two of mace, and a thin layer of beef over the duck; cover it cloſe, and ſet it over a ſlow fire for eight or ten minutes; then take off the cover and ſhake in a little flour, give the pan a ſhake; pour in a pint of ſmall broth, or boiling water; give the pan a ſhake or two, cover it cloſe again, and let it ſtew half an hour; then take off the cover, take out the duck, and keep it hot; let the ſauce boil till there is about a quarter of a pint, or a little better; then ſtrain it, and put it into the ſtew-pan again, with a glaſs of red wine; put in your duck, ſhake the pan, and let it ſtew four or five minutes; then lay your duck in the diſh, and pour the ſauce over it, and garniſh with lemon. If you love your duck very high, you may fill it with the following ingredients; take a veal ſweetbread cut in eight or ten pieces, a few truffles, ſome oyſters, a few ſweet herbs and parſley chopped fine, a little pepper, ſalt, and beaten mace; fill your duck with the above ingredients, tie both ends tight, and dreſs as above. Or, you may fill it with force-meat made thus: take a little piece of veal, take all the ſkin and fat off, beat it in a mortar, with as much ſuet, and an equal quantity of crumbs of bread, a few ſweet herbs, ſome parſley chopped, a little lemon-peel, pepper, ſalt, beaten mace, and nutmeg, and mix it up with the yolk of an egg.

You may ſtew an ox's palate tender, and cut it into pieces, with ſome artichoke-bottoms cut into four, and toſſed up in the ſauce. You may lard your duck, or let it alone, juſt as you pleaſe: for my part I think it beſt without.

To boil Ducks the French Way.

LET your ducks be larded, and half roaſted; then take them off the ſpit, put them into a large earthen pipkin, with half a pint of red wine, and a pint of good gravy, ſome cheſnuts, firſt roaſted and peeled, half a pint of large oyſters, the liquor ſtrained, and the beards taken off, two or three little onions minced ſmall, a very little ſtripped thyme, mace, pepper, and a little ginger beat fine; cover it cloſe, and let them ſtew half an hour over a ſlow fire; add the cruſt of a French roll grated when you put in your gravy and wine. When they are enough, take them up, and pour the ſauce over them.

To dreſs a Gooſe with Onions and Cabbage.

SALT the gooſe for a week, then boil it. It will take an hour. You may either make onion-ſauce, as we do for ducks or cabbage boiled, chopped and ſtewed in butter, with a little pepper and ſalt; lay the gooſe in the diſh, and pour the ſauce over it. It eats very good with either.

Directions for roaſting a Gooſe.

TAKE ſome ſage, waſh and pick it clean, and an onion; chop them very fine, with ſome pepper and ſalt, and put them into the belly; let your gooſe be clean picked, and wiped dry with a dry cloth, inſide and out; put it down to the fire, and roaſt it brown: one hour will roaſt a large gooſe, three quarters of an hour, a ſmall one. Serve it in your diſh with ſome brown gravy, apple-ſauce in a boat, and ſome gravy in another.

A Green Gooſe.

NEVER put any thing but a little pepper and ſalt, unleſs deſired; put gravy in the diſh, and green ſauce in a boat; made thus: take half a pint of the juice of ſorrel; if no ſorrel, ſpinage-juice: have ready a cullis of veal broth, about half a pint, ſome ſugar, the juice of an orange or lemon; boil it up for five or ſix minutes, then put your ſorrel-juice in, and juſt boil it up. Be careful to keep it ſtirring all the time, or it will curdle; then put it in your boat.

To dreſs a Stubble Gooſe.

TAKE a gooſe, kill, and hang it up in the feathers, two or three nights, as it ſuits you; when you dreſs it, ſeaſon it well with pepper and ſalt, take two middle ſized onions, half a ſour apple, a few ſage leaves, chop theſe well, and put them into the inſide with a lump of butter, the ſize of an egg, and a tea-cup full of water, tie it up cloſe at both ends; if a large gooſe, it will take an hour and a half, if a ſmall one, an hour, and ſo on in proportion; diſh it up, pour into your diſh ſome brown-gravy, with two ſpoonfuls of red wine, the ſame of ale, ſerve it up with apple-ſauce.

To dry a Gooſe.

GET a fat gooſe, take a handful of common ſalt, a quarter of an ounce of ſalt-petre, a quarter of a pound of coarſe ſugar; mix all together, and rub your gooſe very well; let it lie in this pickle a fortnight, turning and rubbing it every day; then roll it in bran, and hang it up in a chimney where wood-ſmoke is, for a week. If you have not that conveniency, ſend it to the baker's: the ſmoke of the oven will dry it: or you may hang it in your own chimney, not too near the fire, but make a fire under it, and lay horſe-dung and ſaw-duſt on it, and that will ſmother and ſmoke-dry it; when it is well dried, keep it in a dry place; you my keep it two or three months, or more; when you boil it, put in a good deal of water, and be ſure to ſkim it well.

N. B.

N. B. You may ſend it up with boiled turnips, or cabbage, boiled and ſtewed in butter, or onion-ſace.

To dreſs a Gooſe in Ragoo.

FLAT the breaſt down with a cleaver, then preſs it down with your hand, ſkin it, dip it into ſcalding water; let it be cold, lard it with bacon, ſeaſon it well with pepper, ſalt, and a little beaten mace; then flour it all over, take a pound of good beef-ſuet cut ſmall, put it into a deep ſtew-pan, let it be melted, then put in your gooſe; let it be brown on both ſides; when it is brown, put in a quart of boiling gravy, an onion or two, a bundle of ſweet herbs, a bay leaf, ſome whole pepper, and a few cloves; cover it cloſe, and let it ſtew ſoftly till it is tender. About an hour will do it, if ſmall; if a large one, an hour and a half. In the mean time make a ragoo: boil ſome turnips almoſt enough, ſome carrots and onions quite enough; cut your turnips and carrots the ſame as for a harrico of mutton, put them into a ſauce-pan with half a pint of good beef gravy, a little pepper and ſalt, a piece of butter rolled in flour, and let this ſtew all together a quarter of an hour. Take the gooſe and drain it well; then lay it in the diſh, and pour the ragoo over it.

Where the onion is diſliked, leave it out. You may add cabbage boiled and chopped ſmall.

A Gooſe Alamode.

TAKE a large fine gooſe, pick it clean, ſkin it, bone it nicely, take the fat off; then take a dried tongue, boil it, and peel it: take a fowl, and do it in the ſame manner as the gooſe; ſeaſon it with pepper, ſalt, and beaten mace, roll it round the tongue; ſeaſon the gooſe with the ſame; put the tongue and fowl in the gooſe, with ſome ſlices of ham or good bacon between them; put it into a little pot that will juſt hold it; put to it two quarts of beef gravy, a bundle of ſweet herbs, and an onion; cover it cloſe, and let it ſtew an hour over a good fire: when it begins to boil, let it do very ſoftly; then take up your gooſe, and ſkim off all the fat; ſtrain it, put in a glaſs of red wine, two ſpoonfuls of catchup, a veal ſweetbread cut ſmall, ſome truffles, morels and muſhrooms, a a piece of butter rolled in flour, and ſome pepper and ſalt, if wanted; put in the gooſe again, cover it cloſe, and let it ſtew half an hour longer; then take it up, and pour the ragoo over. Garniſh with lemon.

Note: This is a very fine diſh. You muſt mind to ſave the bones of the gooſe and fowl, and put them into the gravy when it is firſt ſet on; and it will be better if you roll ſome beef-

marrow

marrow between the tongue and the fowl. and between the fowl and goose, it will make them mellow and eat fine. You may add six or seven yolks of hard eggs whole in the dish; they are a pretty addition. Take care to skim off the fat.

N. B. The best method to bone a goose or fowl of any sort, is to begin at the breast, and take all off the bones without cutting the back; for when it is sewed up, and you come to stew it, it generally bursts in the back, and spoils the shape of it.

To stew Giblets.

LET them be nicely scalded and picked, cut the pinions in two; cut the head, and the neck, and legs in two, and the gizzards in four; wash them very clean, put them into a stew-an or soup-pot, with three pounds of scrag of veal, just cover them with water; let them boil up, take all the scum clean off; then put three onions, two turnips, one carrot, a little thyme and parsley, stew them till they are tender, strain them through a sieve, wash the giblets clean with some warm water out of the herbs, &c.; then take a piece of butter as big as a large walnut, put it in a stew-pan, melt it, and put in a large spoonful of flour, keep it stirring till it is smooth; then put in your broth and giblets, stew them for a quarter of an hour; season with salt: or, you may add a gill of Lisbon, and just before you serve them up, chop a handful of green parsley and put in; give them a boil up, and serve them in a tureen or soup dish.

N. B. Three pair will make a handsome tureen-ful:

To make Giblets à la Turtle.

LET three pair of giblets be done as before (well cleaned), put them into your stew-pan with four pounds of scrag of veal, and two pounds of lean beef, covered with water; let them boil up, and skim them very clean; then put in six cloves, four blades of mace, eight corns of all-spice, beat very fine, some basil, sweet-marjoram, winter-savoury, and a little thyme chopped very fine, three onions, two turnips, and one carrot; stew them till tender, then strain them through a sieve, and wash them clean out of the herbs in some warm water; then take a piece of butter, put it in your stew-pan, melt it, and put in as much flour as will thicken it, stir it till it is smooth, then put your liquor in, and keep stirring it all the time you pour it in, or else it will go into lumps, which, if it happens, you must strain it through a sieve; then put in a pint of Madeira wine, some pepper and salt, and some Cayenne pepper; stew it for ten minutes, then put in your giblets, add the juice of a lemon, and stew them fifteen minutes;

nutes; then ſerve them in a tureen. You may put in ſome egg-balls, made thus: boil ſix eggs hard, take out the yolks, put them in a mortar and beat them, throw in a ſpoonful of flour, and the yolk of a raw egg, beat them together till ſmooth; then roll them in little balls, and ſcald them in boiling water, and juſt before you ſerve the giblets up, put them in.

N. B. Never put your livers in at firſt, but boil them in a ſauce-pan of water by themſelves.

To roaſt Pigeons.

Fill them with parſley, clean waſhed and chopped, and ſome pepper and ſalt rolled in butter; fill the bellies, tie the neck-end cloſe, ſo that nothing can run out; put a ſkewer through the legs, and have a little iron on purpoſe, with ſix hooks to it, and on each hook hang a pigeon; faſten one end of the ſtring to the chimney, and the other end to the iron (this is what we call the poor man's ſpit); flour them, baſte them with butter, and turn them gently for fear of hitting the bars. They will roaſt nicely, and be full of gravy. Take care how you take them off, not to loſe any of the liquor. You may melt a very little butter, and put into the diſh. Your pigeons ought to be quite freſh, and not too much done, This is by much the beſt way of doing them, for then they will ſwim in their own gravy, and a very little melted butter will do.

N. B. You may ſpit them on a long ſmall ſpit, only tie both ends cloſe; and ſend parſley and butter in one boat and gravy in another.

When you roaſt them on a ſpit, all the gravy runs out; or if you ſtuff them and broil them whole, you cannot ſave the gravy ſo well; though they will be very good with parſley and butter in the diſh; or ſplit and broiled, with pepper and ſalt.

To boil Pigeons.

Boil them by themſelves for fifteen minutes; then boil a handſome ſquare piece of bacon and lay in the middle; ſtew ſome ſpinage to lay round; and lay the pigeons on the ſpinage. Garniſh your diſh with parſley, laid on a plate before the fire to criſp. Or, you may lay one pigeon in the middle, and the reſt round, and the ſpinage between each pigeon, and a ſlice of bacon on each pigeon. Garniſh with ſlices of bacon, and melted butter in a cup.

To à la daub Pigeons.

Take a large ſauce-pan, lay a layer of bacon, then a layer of veal, a layer of coarſe beef, and another little layer of veal,

veal, about a pound of veal and a pound of beef cut very thin, a piece of carrot, a bundle of ſweet herbs, an onion, ſome black and white pepper, a blade or two of mace, four or five cloves; cover the ſauce-pan cloſe, ſet it over a ſlow fire, draw it till it is brown to make the gravy of a fine light brown; then put in a quart of boiling water, and let it ſtew till the gravy is quite rich and good; then ſtrain it off, and ſkim off all the fat. In the mean time ſtuff the bellies of the pigeons with force-meat, made thus: take a pound of veal, a pound of beef-ſuet, beat both in a mortar fine, an equal quantity of crumbs of bread, ſome pepper, ſalt, nutmeg, beaten mace, a little lemon-peel cut ſmall, ſome parſley cut ſmall, and a very little thyme ſtripped; mix all together with the yolks of two eggs; fill the pigeons and flat the breaſt down, flour them and fry them in freſh butter a little brown; then pour the fat clean out of the pan, and put the gravy to the pigeons; cover them cloſe and let them ſtew a quarter of an hour, or till you think they are quite enough; then take them up, lay them in a diſh, and pour in your ſauce; on each pigeon lay a bay-leaf, and on the leaf a ſlice of bacon. You may garniſh with a lemon notched, or let it alone.

N. B. You may leave out the ſtuffing; they will be very rich and good without it, and it is the beſt way of dreſſing them for a fine made-diſh.

Pigeons au Poire.

MAKE a good force-meat as above, cut the feet quite off, ſtuff them in the ſhape of a pear, roll them in the yolk of an egg and then in crumbs of bread, ſtick the leg at the top, and butter a diſh to lay them in; then ſend them to an oven to bake, but do not let them touch each other; when they are enough, lay them in a diſh, and pour in good gravy thickened with the yolk of an egg, or butter rolled in flour; do not pour your gravy over the pigeons. You may garniſh with lemon. It is a pretty genteel diſh: or, for change, lay one pigeon in the middle, the reſt round, and ſtewed ſpinage between; poached eggs on the ſpinage. Garniſh with notched lemon and orange cut into quarters, and have melted butter in boats.

Or thus: bone your pigeons, and ſtuff them with force-meat; make them in the ſhape of a pear, with one foot ſtuck at the ſmall end to appear like the ſtalk of a pear; rub them over with the yolk of an egg, and ſtrew ſome crumbs of bread on; fry them in a pan of good dripping a nice light brown; put them in a drainer to drain all the fat off; then put them in a ſtew-pan with a pint of gravy, a gill of white wine, an onion ſtuck with cloves; cover them cloſe and ſtew them for half an hour; take them out, ſkim off all the fat, and take out the onion; put in ſome butter rolled in flour, a ſpoonful of catchup, the ſame of browning, ſome truffles and morels, pickled muſhrooms, two artichoke-bottoms cut in ſix pieces each, a little ſalt and Cayenne pepper, the juice of half a lemon; ſtew it five minutes, put in your pigeons and make them hot; put them in your diſh and pour the ſauce over them. Garniſh with fried force-meat balls, or with a lemon cut in quarters.

Pigeons ſtoved.

TAKE a ſmall cabbage-lettuce, juſt cut out the heart, and make a force-meat as before, only chop the heart of the lettuce and mix with it; then fill up the place, and tie it acroſs with a packthread; fry it of a light brown in freſh butter, pour out all the fat, lay the pigeons round, flat them with your hand, ſeaſon them a little with pepper, ſalt, and beaten mace, (take great care not to put too much ſalt,) pour in half a pint of Rheniſh wine, cover it cloſe, and let it ſtew about five or ſix minutes; then put in half a pint of good gravy, cover them cloſe, and let them ſtew half an hour. Take a good piece of butter rolled in flour, ſhake it in; when it is fine and thick take it up, untie it, lay the lettuce in the middle, and the pigeons round; ſqueeze in a little lemon-juice, and pour the ſauce all over them. Stew a little lettuce, and cut it into pieces for garniſh, with pickled cabbage.

N. B. Or for change, you may ſtuff your pigeons with the ſame force-meat, and cut two cabbage-lettuces into quarters, and ſtew it as above; ſo lay the lettuce between each pigeon, and one in the middle with the lettuce round it, and pour the ſauce all over them.

Pigeons Surtout.

FORCE your pigeons as above, then lay a ſlice of bacon on the breaſt, and a ſlice of veal beat with the back of a knife, and ſeaſoned with mace, pepper, and ſalt; tie them on with a ſmall packthread, or two little fine ſkewers are better; ſpit them on a fine bird-ſpit, roaſt them, and baſte with a piece of butter, then with the yolk of an egg, and then baſte them again with crumbs of bread, a little nutmeg and ſweet herbs; when enough, lay them in your diſh, have good gravy ready, with truffles, morels, and muſhrooms, to pour into your diſh. Garniſh with lemon.

Pigeons Compote.

TAKE ſix young pigeons and ſkewer them as for boiling; make a force-meat thus: grate the crumb of a penny loaf, half a pound of fat bacon, ſhred ſome ſweet herbs and parſley fine,

 two

two ſhalots, or a little onion, a little lemon-peel, a little grated nutmeg, ſeaſon it with pepper and ſalt, and mix it up with the yolk of two eggs; put it into the craws and bellies, lard them down the breaſt, and fry them brown with a little butter; then put them in a ſtew-pan, with a pint of ſtrong brown gravy, a gill of white wine; ſtew them three quarters of an hour, thicken it with a little butter rolled in flour, ſeaſon with ſalt and Cayenne pepper, put the pigeons in the diſh, and ſtrain the gravy over them. Lay ſome hot force-meat balls round them, and ſend them up hot.

A French Pupton of Pigeons.

TAKE ſavoury force-meat rolled out like paſte, put it in a butter-diſh, lay a layer of very thin bacon, ſquab pigeons, ſliced ſweetbread, aſparagus-tops, muſhrooms, cock's-combs, a palate boiled tender and cut into pieces, and the yolks of hard eggs; make another force-meat and lay over like a pie, bake it, and when enough turn it into a diſh, and pour gravy round it.

Pigeons boiled with Rice.

TAKE ſix pigeons, ſtuff their bellies with parſley, pepper, and ſalt rolled in a very little piece of butter; put them into a quart of mutton broth, with a little beaten mace, a bundle of ſweet herbs, and an onion; cover them cloſe, and let them boil a full quarter of an hour; then take out the onion and ſweet herbs, and take a good piece of butter rolled in flour, put it in and give it a ſhake, ſeaſon it with ſalt (if it wants it), then have ready half a pound of rice boiled tender in milk; when it begins to be thick (but take great care it does not burn), take the yolks of two or three eggs beat up with two or three ſpoonfuls of cream and a little nutmeg, ſtir it together till it is quite thick; then take up the pigeons and lay them in a diſh; pour the gravy to the rice, ſtir all together and pour over the pigeons. Garniſh with hard eggs cut into quarters.

Pigeons tranſmogrified.

TAKE your pigeons, ſeaſon them with pepper and ſalt, take a large piece of butter, make a puff-paſte, and roll each pigeon in a piece of paſte; tie them in a cloth ſo that the paſte do not break, boil them in a good deal of water; they will take an hour and a half boiling; untie them carefully that they do not break; lay them in the diſh, and you may pour a little good gravy in the diſh. They will eat exceeding good and nice, and will yield ſauce enough of a very agreeable reliſh.

Pigeons transmogrified, a second Way.

PICK and clean six small young pigeons, but do not cut off their heads, cut off their pinions, and boil them ten minutes in water, then cut off the ends of six large cucumbers and scrape out the seeds, put your pigeons into the cucumbers, but let the heads be out at the ends, and stick a bunch of barberries in their bills, and then put them in a tossing-pan with a pint of veal gravy, a little anchovy, a glass of red wine, a spoonful of browning, a little slice of lemon, Cayenne and salt to your taste, stew them seven minutes, take them out, thicken your gravy with a little butter rolled in flour, boil it up and strain it over your pigeons, and serve them up.

Pigeons in Fricando.

AFTER having trussed your pigeons with their legs in their bodies, divide them in two, and lard them with bacon; then lay them in a stew-pan with the larded side downwards, and two whole leeks cut small, two ladlefuls of mutton broth or veal gravy; cover them close over a very slow fire, and when they are enough make your fire very brisk to waste away what liquor remains: when they are of a fine brown take them up and pour out all the fat that is left in the pan; then pour in some veal gravy to loosen what sticks to the pan, and a little pepper; stir it about for two or three minutes, and pour it over the pigeons. This is a pretty little side-dish.

To roast Pigeons with a Farce.

MAKE a farce with the livers minced small, as much sweet suet or marrow, grated bread, and hard eggs, an equal quantity of each; season with beaten mace, nutmeg, or a little pepper, salt, and sweet herbs; mix all these together with the yolk of an egg, then cut the skin of your pigeon between the legs and body, and very carefully with your fingers raise the skin from the flesh, but take care you do not break it; then force them with this farce between the skin and flesh, then truss the legs close to keep it in; spit them and roast them, dredge them with a little flour, and baste them with a piece of butter, save the gravy which runs from them and mix it up with a little red wine, a little of the force-meat, and some nutmeg; let it boil, then thicken it with a piece of butter rolled in flour, and the yolk of an egg beat up, and some minced lemon: when enough, lay the pigeons in the dish, and pour in the sauce. Garnish with lemon.

Pigeons in Savoury Jelly.

ROAST your pigeons with the head and feet on, put a sprig of myrtle in their bills, make a jelly for them the same way as

for

for the chickens, pour a little into a bason, when it is set lay in the pigeons with their breasts down, fill up your bowl with jelly, and turn it out.

Pigeons à la Soussel.

TAKE four pigeons and bone them; make a force-meat as for pigeons Compote, and stuff them, put them in a stew-pan with a pint of veal gravy, stew them half an hour very gently, then take them out; in the mean time make a veal force-meat and wrap all round them, rub it over with the yolk of an egg, and fry them in good dripping of a nice brown; take the gravy they were stewed in, skim off the fat, thicken it with a little butter rolled in flour, the yolk of an egg, and a gill of cream beat up, season it with pepper and salt, mix it all together, and keep it stirring one way till it is smooth; strain it into your dish, and put the pigeons on. Garnish with plenty of fried parsley; you may leave out the egg and cream, and put in a spoonful of browning, a little lemon pickle and catchup, if you like best.

Pigeons in Pimlico.

TAKE the livers, with some fat and lean of ham or bacon, mushrooms, truffles, parsley, and sweet herbs; season with beaten mace, pepper, and salt; beat all these together with two raw eggs, put it into the bellies, roll them all in a thin slice of veal, over that a thin slice of bacon; wrap them up in white paper, spit them on a small spit, and roast them. In the mean time make for them a ragoo of truffles and mushrooms chopped small, with parsley cut small; put to it half a pint of good veal gravy, thicken with a piece of butter rolled in flour; an hour will do your pigeons; baste them, when enough lay them in your dish, take off the paper, and pour your sauce over them. Garnish with patties, made thus: take veal and cold ham, beef-suet, an equal quantity, some mushrooms, sweet herbs, and spice; chop them small, set them on the fire, and moisten with milk or cream; then make a little puff-paste, roll it, and make little patties about an inch deep and two inches long; fill them with the above ingredients, cover them close and bake them; lay six of them round a dish. This makes a fine dish for a first course.

Pigeons in a Hole.

PICK, draw, and wash four young pigeons; stick their legs in their belly as you do boiled pigeons, season them with pepper, salt, and beaten mace; put into the belly of every pigeon a lump of butter the size of a walnut, lay your pigeons in a pie, dish, pour over them a batter made of three eggs, two spoonfuls of flour, and half a pint of good milk; bake it in a moderate oven, and ſerve them to table in the ſame diſh.

To jug Pigeons.

PULL, crop, and draw pigeons, but do not waſh them; ſave the livers and put them in ſcalding water, and ſet them on the fire for a minute or two: then take them out and mince them ſmall, and bruiſe them with the back of a ſpoon; mix them with a little pepper, ſalt, grated nutmeg, and lemon-peel ſhred very fine, chopped parſley, and two yolks of eggs very hard; bruiſe them as you do the liver, and put as much ſuet as liver, ſhaved exceeding fine, and as much grated bread; work theſe together with raw eggs, and roll it in freſh butter; put a piece into the crops and bellies, and ſew up the neck and vents; then dip your pigeons in water, and ſeaſon them with pepper and ſalt as for a pie; put them in your jug, with a piece of celery, a bundle of ſweet herbs, four cloves, and three blades of mace beat fine, ſtop them cloſe and ſet them in a kettle of cold water; firſt cover them cloſe, and lay a tile on the top of the jug, and let it boil three hours; then take them out of the jug and lay them in a diſh, take out the celery and ſweet herbs, put in a piece of butter rolled in flour, ſhake it about till it is thick, and pour it on your pigeons. Garniſh with lemon.

To ſtew Pigeons.

SEASON your pigeons with pepper and ſalt, a few cloves and mace, and ſome ſweet herbs; wrap this ſeaſoning up in a piece of butter, and put it in their bellies; then tie up the neck and vent, and half roaſt them: put them in a ſtew-pan, with a quart of good gravy, a little white wine, a few pepper-corns, three or four blades of mace, a bit of lemon, a bunch of ſweet herbs, and a ſmall onion; ſtew them gently till they are enough; then take the pigeons out, and ſtrain the liquor through a ſieve; ſkim it, and thicken it in your ſtew-pan; put in the pigeons, with ſome pickled muſhrooms and oyſters, ſtew it five minutes, and put the pigeons in a diſh, and the ſauce over.

To ſtew Pigeons another Way.—An excellent Receipt.

MAKE a pudding of bread, ſuet, the livers of the pigeons, lemon, thyme, parſley, and ſweet marjoram, moiſtened with an egg and a bit of butter; put in nutmeg, pepper, and ſalt; ſtuff the pigeons and ſew them up, then fry them in butter till they look brown; then put them into ſome good gravy with an onion ſtuck with cloves, ſtew them till they are tender; when they are ſo take them out, and add a little red wine and catchup

catchup to your taſte; thicken with butter and toſs them together; add ſome morels and truffles, which muſt be boiled a quarter of an hour before they go in. Pickled muſhrooms and artichoke-bottoms are an improvement; but they and the truffles and morels may be done without.

To fricaſſee Pigeons the Italian Way.

QUARTER them, and fry them in oil; take ſome green peas and let them fry in the oil till they are almoſt ready to burſt, then put ſome boiling water to them; ſeaſon it with ſalt, pepper, onions, garlic, parſley, and vinegar. Veal and lamb do the ſame way, and thicken with yolks of eggs.

To make Force-meat for Pigeons.

TAKE a little fat bacon, beat it in a marble mortar, take two anchovies, two or three of the pigeons' livers, chop them together; add a little lemon-peel ſhred, a little beaten mace, nutmeg, Cayenne, ſtale bread crumbs, and beef-ſuet an equal quantity, mix all together with an egg.

To boil Partridges.

PUT them in a good deal of water, let them boil quick; fifteen minutes will be ſufficient. For ſauce, take a quarter of a pint of cream and a piece of freſh butter as big as a walnut, ſtir it one way till it is melted, and pour it into the diſh.

Or this ſauce: take a bunch of celery clean waſhed, cut all the white very ſmall, waſh it again very clean, put it into a ſauce-pan with a blade of mace, a little beaten pepper, and a very little ſalt; put to it a pint of water, let it boil till the water is juſt waſted away, then add a quarter of a pint of cream and a piece of butter rolled in flour; ſtir all together, and when it is thick and fine pour it over the birds.

Or this ſauce: take the livers and bruiſe them fine, ſome parſley chopped fine, melt a little nice freſh butter, and then add the livers and parſley to it, ſqueeze in a little lemon, juſt give it a boil, and pour over the birds.

Or this ſauce: take a quarter of a pint of cream, the yolk of an egg beat fine, a little grated nutmeg, a little beaten mace, a piece of butter as big as a nutmeg rolled in flour, and one ſpoonful of white wine; ſtir all together one way, when fine and thick pour it over the birds. You may add a few muſhrooms.

Or this ſauce: take a few muſhrooms freſh peeled and waſh them clean, put them in a ſauce-pan with a little ſalt, put them over a quick fire, let them boil up, then put in a quarter of a pint of cream and a little nutmeg; ſhake them together with a very little piece of butter rolled in flour, give it two or three ſhakes over the fire, three or four minutes will do; then pour it over the birds.

Or this ſauce: boil half a pound of rice very tender in beef-gravy; ſeaſon it with pepper and ſalt, and pour over your birds. Theſe ſauces do for boiled fowls; a quart of gravy will be enough, and let it boil till it is quite thick.

To dreſs Partridges à la Braiſe.

TAKE two brace, truſs the legs into the bodies, lard them, ſeaſon with beaten mace, pepper, and ſalt; take a ſtew-pan, lay ſlices of bacon at the bottom, then ſlices of beef, and then ſlices of veal, all cut thin, a piece of carrot, an onion cut ſmall, a bundle of ſweet herbs, and ſome whole pepper; lay the partridges with the breaſt downwards, lay ſome thin ſlices of beef and veal over them, and ſome parſley ſhred fine; cover them and let them ſtew eight or ten minutes over a ſlow fire, then give your pan a ſhake, and pour in a pint of boiling water; cover it cloſe and let it ſtew half an hour over a little quicker fire; then take out your birds, keep them hot, pour into the pan a pint of thin gravy, let them boil till there is about half a pint, then ſtrain it off, and ſkim off all the fat: in the mean time have a veal ſweetbread cut ſmall, truffles and morels, cock's-combs and fowls livers, ſtewed in a pint of good gravy half an hour, ſome artichoke-bottoms and aſparagus-tops, both blanched in warm water, and a few muſhrooms; then add the other gravy to this, and put in your partridges to heat; if it is not thick enough, take a piece of butter rolled in flour and toſs up in it; if you will be at the expence, thicken it with veal and ham cullis, but it will be full as good without.

To make Partridge Panes.

TAKE two roaſted partridges and the fleſh of a large fowl, a little parboiled bacon, a little marrow or ſweet ſuet chopped very fine, a few muſhrooms and morels chopped fine, truffles and artichoke-bottoms; ſeaſon with beaten mace, pepper, a little nutmeg, ſalt, ſweet herbs chopped fine, and the crumb of a two-penny loaf ſoaked in hot gravy; mix all well together with the yolks of two eggs, make your panes on paper of a round figure and the thickneſs of an egg, at a proper diſtance one from another, dip the point of a knife in the yolk of an egg in order to ſhape them, bread them neatly, and bake them a quarter of an hour in a quick oven: obſerve that the truffles and morels be boiled tender in the gravy you ſoak the bread in. Serve them up for a ſide-diſh, or they will ſerve to garniſh the above diſh, which will be a very fine one for a firſt courſe.

N. B. When

N. B. When you have cold fowls in the house, this makes a pretty addition in an entertainment.

To ſtew Partridges.

TRUSS your partridges as for roaſting, ſtuff the craws, and lard them down each ſide of the breaſt; then roll a lump of butter in pepper, ſalt, and beaten mace, and put it into the bellies, ſew up the vents, dredge them well and fry them a light brown; then put them into a ſtew-pan with a quart of good gravy, a ſpoonful of Madeira wine, the ſame of muſhroom catchup, a tea-ſpoonful of lemon-pickle, and half the quantity of muſhroom powder, one anchovy, half a lemon, a ſprig of ſweet marjoram; cover the pan cloſe and ſtew them half an hour, then take them out and thicken the gravy, boil it a little and pour it over the partridges, and lay round them artichoke-bottoms boiled and cut in quarters, and the yolks of four hard eggs, if agreeable.

To ſtew Partridges, a ſecond Way—much more expenſive.

TAKE three partridges when dreſſed, ſinge them, blanch and beat three ounces of almonds, and grate the ſame quantity of fine white bread, chop three anchovies, mix them with ſix ounces of butter, ſtuff the partridges, and ſew them up at both ends; truſs them and wrap ſlices of fat bacon round them, half roaſt them, then take one and pull the meat off the breaſt, and beat it in a marble mortar with the force-meat it was ſtuffed with; have ready a ſtrong gravy made of ham and veal, ſtrain it into a ſtew-pan, then take the bacon off the other two, wipe them clean and put them into the gravy with a good deal of ſhalots, let them ſtew till tender, then take them out, and boil the gravy till it is almoſt as thick as bread ſauce, then add to it a glaſs of ſweet oil, the ſame of Champagne, and the juice of a China orange; put your partridges in and make them hot. Garniſh with ſlices of bacon and lemon.

To ſtew Partridges or Pigeons with red or white Cabbage.

SKEWER them neatly, ſeaſon them with Cayenne, ſalt, and beaten mace, fry them in butter not too brown, put them into a ſtew-pan with a little brown gravy, cover them cloſe, and ſtew them gently till tender, keep turning them over. Prepare the cabbage thus: take red cabbage when touched with froſt, cut it round as you would to pickle, waſh it, put it into a ſtew-pan, with three ounces of butter, a pint of ſpring water, a little Cayenne and ſalt, a halfpenny worth of cochineal beat, cover it cloſe, ſtew it gently quite tender, pour out ſome of the liquor, and put in ſome of the gravy that the pigeons are ſtewed in, ſqueeze

ſqueeze in juice of lemon ſo as to make it taſte, and a ſpoonful of melted butter, and give it a boil, lay your pigeons or partridges on the diſh, with the remainder of the gravy they were ſtewed in; lay the cabbage over and about them, ſo ſend them up; do white or green cabbage the ſame way cut into quarters, leaving out the cochineal; this may be ſent up without meat, but remember to uſe a little gravy.

To roaſt Pheaſants.

PICK and draw a brace of pheaſants, and ſinge them, lard one with bacon but not the other, ſpit them, roaſt them fine, and paper them all over the breaſt; when they are juſt done, flour and baſte them with a little nice butter, and let them have a fine white froth; then take them up, and pour good gravy in the diſh, and bread-ſauce in boats or baſons.

Or you may put water-creſſes, with gravy in the diſh, and lay the creſſes under the pheaſants.

Or you may make celery-ſauce, ſtewed tender, ſtrained and mixed with cream, and poured into the diſh.

If you have but one pheaſant, take a large fowl about the bigneſs of a pheaſant, pick it nicely with the head on, draw it, and truſs it with the head turned as you do a pheaſant's, lard the fowl all over the breaſt and legs with bacon cut in little pieces; when roaſted put them both in a diſh, and nobody will know it. They will take three quarters of an hour doing, and the fire muſt not be too briſk. Put gravy in the diſh, and garniſh with water-creſſes.

A ſtewed Pheaſant.

TAKE your pheaſant and ſtew it in veal gravy, take artichoke-bottoms parboiled, ſome cheſnuts, roaſted and blanched; when your pheaſant is enough (but it muſt ſtew till there is juſt enough for ſauce, then ſkim it), put in the cheſnuts and artichoke-bottoms, a little beaten mace, pepper and ſalt enough to ſeaſon it, and a glaſs of white wine; if you do not think it thick enough, thicken it with a little piece of butter rolled in flour: ſqueeze in a little lemon, pour the ſauce over the pheaſant, and have ſome force-meat balls fried and put into the diſh.

N. B. A good fowl will do full as well, truſſed with the head on like a pheaſant. You may fry ſauſages inſtead of force-meat balls.

To dreſs a Pheaſant à la Braiſe.

LAY a layer of beef all over your pan, then a layer of veal, a little piece of bacon, a piece of carrot, an onion ſtuck with cloves,

cloves, a blade or two of mace, a ſpoonful of pepper black and white, and a bundle of ſweet herbs; then lay in the pheaſant, lay a layer of veal and then a layer of beef to cover it, ſet it on the fire five or ſix minutes, then pour in two quarts of boiling gravy; cover it cloſe and let it ſtew very ſoftly an hour and a half, then take up your pheaſant, keep it hot, and let the gravy boil till there is about a pint; then ſtrain it off and put it in again, and put in a veal ſweetbread, firſt being ſtewed with the pheaſant; then put in ſome truffles and morels, ſome livers of fowls, artichoke-bottoms, and aſparagus-tops (if you have them); let theſe ſimmer in the gravy about five or ſix minutes, then add two ſpoonfuls of catchup, two of red wine, and a little piece of butter rolled in flour, a ſpoonful of browning, ſhake all together, put in your pheaſant, let them ſtew all together with a few muſhrooms about five or ſix minutes more, then take up your pheaſant and pour your ragoo all over, with a few force-meat balls. Garniſh with lemon. You may lard it, if you chooſe.

To boil a Pheaſant.

TAKE a fine pheaſant, boil it in a good deal of water, keep your water boiling; half an hour will do a ſmall one, and three quarters of an hour a large one. Let your ſauce be celery ſtewed and thickened with cream, and a little piece of butter rolled in flour; take up the pheaſant, and pour the ſauce all over. Garniſh with lemon. Obſerve to ſtew your celery ſo that the liquor will not be all waſted away before you put your cream in; if it wants ſalt, put in ſome to your palate.

To ſalmec a Snipe or Woodcock.

HALF roaſt them and cut them in quarters, put them in a ſtew-pan with a little gravy, two ſhalots chopt fine, a glaſs of red wine, a little ſalt and Cayenne pepper, the juice of half a lemon; ſtew them gently for ten minutes, and put them on a toaſt ſerved the ſame as for roaſting, and ſend them up hot. Garniſh with lemon.

Snipes in a Surtout, or Woodcocks.

TAKE force-meat made with veal, as much beef-ſuet chopped and beat in a mortar, with an equal quantity of crumbs of bread; mix in a little beaten mace, pepper and ſalt, ſome parſley, and a little ſweet herbs, mix it with the yolk of an egg: lay ſome of this meat round the diſh, then lay in the ſnipes, being firſt drawn and half roaſted. Take care of the trail; chop it and throw it all over the diſh.

Take ſome good gravy, according to the bigneſs of your ſurtout, ſome truffles and morels, a few muſhrooms, a ſweetbread cut

cut into pieces, and artichoke-bottoms cut ſmall; let all ſtew together, ſhake them, and take the yolks of two or three eggs (according as you want them), beat them up with a ſpoonful or two of white wine; ſtir all together one way, when it is thick take it off, let it cool, and pour it into the ſurtout; have the yolks of a few hard eggs put in here and there; ſeaſon with beaten mace, pepper, and ſalt, to your taſte; cover it with the force-meat all over; rub the yolks of eggs all over to colour it, then ſend it to the oven. Half an hour does it, and ſend it hot to table.

To boil Snipes or Woodcocks.

Boil them in good ſtrong broth, or beef gravy made thus: take a pound of beef, cut it into little pieces, put it into two quarts of water, an onion, a bundle of ſweet herbs, a blade or two of mace, ſix cloves, and ſome whole pepper; cover it cloſe, let it boil till about half waſted, then ſtrain it off, put the gravy into a ſauce-pan with ſalt enough to ſeaſon it; take the ſnipes and gut them clean (but take care of the guts), put them into the gravy and let them boil, cover them cloſe, and ten minutes will boil them: in the mean time, chop the guts and liver ſmall, take a little of the gravy the ſnipes are boiling in, and ſtew the guts in, with a blade of mace; take ſome crumbs of bread, and have them ready fried in a little freſh butter criſp, of a fine light brown; you muſt take about as much bread as the inſide of a ſtale roll, and rub them ſmall into a clean cloth; when they are done, let them ſtand ready in a plate before the fire.

When your ſnipes are ready, take about half a pint of the liquor they are boiled in, and add to the guts two ſpoonfuls of red wine, and a piece of butter as big as a walnut, rolled in a little flour; ſet them on the fire, ſhake your ſauce-pan often (but do not ſtir it with a ſpoon) till the butter is all melted, then put in the crumbs, give your ſauce-pan a ſhake, take up your birds, lay them in the diſh, and pour this ſauce over them. Garniſh with lemon.

To dreſs Ortolans.

Spit them ſideways, with a vine-leaf between; baſte them with butter, and have fried crumbs of bread round the diſh. Dreſs quails the ſame way.

To dreſs Ruffs and Rees.

These birds are found in Lincolnſhire and the Iſle of Ely: the food proper for them is new milk boiled and put over white bread, or white bread boiled in milk, with a little fine ſugar;

fugar; and be careful to keep them in feparate cages: they feed very faft, and will die of their fat if not killed in time; when you kill them, flip the fkin off the head and neck with the feathers on, then pluck and draw them; when you roaft them, put them a good diftance from the fire, if the fire be good they will take about twelve minutes; when they are roafted, flip the fkin on again with the feathers on, fend them up with the gravy under them made the fame as for the pheafant, and bread-fauce in a boat, and crifp crumbs of bread round the edge of the difh.

To drefs Larks.

PUT them on a bird-fpit, tie them on another fpit, and roaft them twenty-five minutes with a gentle fire; put them in a difh with crumbs of bread fried brown, or you may put a toaft under with gravy and butter, or gravy only.

To drefs Larks Pear Fafhion.

YOU muft trufs the larks clofe and cut off the legs, feafon them with falt, pepper, cloves, and mace; make a force-meat thus: take a veal fweetbread, as much beef-fuet, a few morels and mufhrooms, chop all fine together, fome crumbs of bread, a few fweet herbs, and a little lemon-peel cut fmall, mix all together with the yolk of an egg, wrap up the larks in force-meat, and fhape them like a pear, ftick one leg on the top like the ftalk of a pear, rub them over with the yolk of an egg and crumbs of bread, bake them in a gentle oven, ferve them without fauce: or they will make a good garnifh to a very fine difh.

You may ufe veal, if you have not a fweetbread.

To drefs Plovers.

TO two plovers take two artichoke-bottoms boiled, fome chefnuts roafted and blanched, fome fkirrets boiled, cut all very fmall, mix it with fome marrow or beef-fuet, the yolks of two hard eggs, chop all together, feafon with pepper, falt, nutmeg, and a little fweet herbs; fill all the bodies of the plovers, lay them in a fauce-pan, put to them a pint of gravy, a glafs of white wine, a blade or two of mace, fome roafted chefnuts blanched, and artichoke-bottoms cut into quarters, two or three yolks of eggs, and a little juice of lemon; cover them clofe and let them ftew very foftly an hour. If you find the fauce is not thick enough, take a piece of butter rolled in flour and put into the fauce; fhake it round, and when it is thick take up your plovers, and pour the fauce over them. Garnifh with roafted chefnuts.

Ducks

Ducks are very good done this way.

If they are well fed they need no butter, being fat enough of themselves.

Or boil them in good celery-ſauce, either white or brown, juſt as you like.

The ſame way you may dreſs wigeons.

N. B. The beſt way to dreſs plovers, is to roaſt them the ſame as woodcocks, with a toaſt under them, and gravy and butter.

Jugged Hare.

CUT it into little pieces, lard them here and there with little ſlips of bacon, ſeaſon them with Cayenne pepper and ſalt, put them into an earthen jug, with a blade or two of mace, an onion ſtuck with cloves, and a bundle of ſweet herbs; cover the jug or jar you do it in ſo cloſe that nothing can get in, then ſet it in a pot of boiling water, and three hours will do it; then turn it out into the diſh, and take out the onion and ſweet herbs, and ſend it to table hot. If you do not like it larded, leave it out.

To jug a Hare, a ſecond Way.—An excellent Receipt.

CUT a hare to pieces, but do not waſh it; ſeaſon it with an onion ſhred fine, thyme, parſley, ſavoury, marjoram, lemon-peel, pepper, ſalt, and half a nutmeg; ſtrew all theſe over your hare, ſlice ſome fat bacon thin, then put the hare into an earthen jug, without any water, and put a layer of hare and a layer of bacon; ſtop it cloſe with a cloth tied on, and cover it with a tile, put it in a pot of cold water, and let it boil three hours. When you take it up, ſhake in ſome freſh butter till it is melted; garniſh with lemon.

Florendine Hare.

TAKE a full grown hare and let it hang four or five days before you caſe it; leave the ears on, and take out all the bones except the head, which muſt be left whole; lay the hare on the dreſſer, and put in the following force-meat; take the crumbs of a penny loaf, the liver ſhred fine, half a pound of fat bacon ſcraped, a glaſs of red wine, ſome ſweet herbs chopped fine, ſeaſon with pepper, ſalt, and nutmeg, an anchovy chopped fine, the yolks of two eggs, mix all together and put into your hare's belly, roll it up to the head, ſkewer it with the head and ears leaning back, and tie it with pack-thread as you would a collar of veal, wrap it in a cloth, and boil it one hour and a half in a ſtew-pan (covered cloſe), with two quarts of water; as ſoon as the liquor is reduced to a quart, add a pint of red wine, a ſpoonful of lemon-pickle, one

of

of catchup, and one of browning; then take out your hare, and stew the gravy till it is reduced to a pint, thicken it with butter rolled in flour; put the hare in the dish, and pour the sauce over it; pull the jaw-bones out, and put them in the eyes; put some force-meat balls and truffles round it; and garnish with water-cresses.

To scare a Hare.

LARD a hare, and put a pudding in the belly; put it into a pot or fish-kettle, then put to it two quarts of strong-drawn gravy, one of red wine, a whole lemon cut, a faggot of sweet herbs, nutmeg, pepper, a little salt, and six cloves; cover it close, and stew it over a slow fire till it is three parts done; then take it up, put it into a dish, and strew it over with crumbs of bread, sweet herbs chopped fine, some lemon-peel grated, and half a nutmeg; set it before the fire, and baste it till it is of a fine light brown; in the mean time, take the fat off your gravy, and thicken it with the yolk of an egg; take six eggs boiled hard and chopped small, some pickled cucumbers cut very thin: mix these with the sauce, and pour it into the dish.

A fillet of mutton or neck of venison may be done the same way.

N. B. You may do rabbits the same way, but it must be veal gravy and white wine, adding mushrooms for cucumbers.

To stew a Hare.

CUT it into pieces, and put it into a stew-pan, with a blade or two of mace, some whole pepper black and white, an onion stuck with cloves, a bundle of sweet herbs, and a nutmeg cut to pieces, and cover it with water; cover the stew-pan close, let it stew till the hare is tender, but not too much done: then take it up, and with a fork take out the hare into a clean pan, strain the sauce through a coarse sieve, empty all out of the pan, put in the hare again with the sauce, take a piece of butter as big as a walnut, rolled in flour, and put in likewise one spoonful of catchup and a gill of red wine; stew all together (with a few fresh mushrooms or pickled ones, if you have any) till it is thick and smooth; then dish it up and send it to table. You may cut a hare in two, and stew the fore-quarters thus, and roast the hind-quarters with a pudding in the belly.

To hodge-podge a Hare.

CUT the hare in pieces as you do for stewing, and put it into the pitcher, with two or three onions, some salt, and a little pepper, a bunch of sweet herbs, and a piece of butter: stop

ſtop the pitcher very cloſe, that no ſteam may get out, ſet it in a kettle full of boiling water, keep the kettle filled up as the water waſtes; let it ſtew four or five hours at leaſt. You may, when you firſt put in the hare into the kettle, put in lettuce, cucumbers, celery, and turnips, if you like it better.

A Hare Civet.

BONE the hare, and take out all the ſinews; cut one half in thin ſlices, and the other half in pieces an inch thick, flour them, and fry them in a little freſh butter as collops, quick, and have ready ſome gravy made good with the bones of the hare and beef, put a pint of it into the pan to the hare, ſome muſtard, and a little alder vinegar; cover it cloſe, and let it do ſoftly till it is as thick as cream, then diſh it up, with the head in the middle.

Portugueſe Rabbits.

GET ſome rabbits, truſs them chicken-faſhion, the head muſt be cut off, and the rabbit turned with the back upwards, and two of the legs ſtripped to the claw-end, and ſo truſſed with two ſkewers. Lard them, and roaſt them with what ſauce you pleaſe. If you want chickens, and they are to appear as ſuch, they muſt be dreſſed in this manner: ſend them up hot with gravy in the diſh, and garniſh with lemon and beet-root.

Rabbits Surpriſe.

ROAST two half-grown rabbits, cut off the heads cloſe to the ſhoulders and the firſt joints; then take off all the lean meat from the back-bones, cut it ſmall, and toſs it up with ſix or ſeven ſpoonfuls of cream and milk, and a piece of butter as big as a walnut, rolled in flour, a little nutmeg and a little ſalt, ſhake all together till it is as thick as good cream, and ſet it to cool: then make a force-meat, with a pound of veal, a pound of ſuet, as much crumbs of bread, two anchovies, a little piece of lemon-peel cut fine, a little ſprig of thyme, and a little nutmeg grated; let the veal and ſuet be chopped very fine and beat in a mortar, then mix it all together with the yolks of two raw eggs; place it all round the rabbits, leaving a long trough in the back-bone open that you think will hold the meat you cut out with the ſauce; pour it in and cover it with the force-meat, ſmooth it all over with your hand as well as you can with a raw egg, make it ſquare at both ends, throw on a little grated bread, and butter a mazarine, or pan, and take them from the dreſſer where you formed them, and place them on it very carefully. Bake them three quarters of an hour till they are of a fine brown colour. Let your ſauce be gravy thickened with butter and the juice of a lemon; lay them into the diſh,

 and

and pour in the ſauce. Garniſh with orange cut into quarters, and ſerve it up for a firſt courſe.

To dreſs Rabbits in Caſſerole.

DIVIDE the rabbits into quarters; you may lard them or not (juſt as you pleaſe), ſhake ſome flour over them and fry them with lard or butter, then put them into an earthen pipkin with a quart of good broth, a glaſs of white wine, a little pepper and ſalt (if wanted), a bunch of ſweet herbs, and a piece of butter as big as a walnut, rolled in flour; cover them cloſe and let them ſtew half an hour, then diſh them up and pour the ſauce over them. Garniſh with Seville orange, cut into thin ſlices and notched; the peel that is cut out lay prettily between the ſlices.

To make a Curry the Indian Way.

TAKE two ſmall chickens, ſkin them and cut them as for a fricaſſee, waſh them clean, and ſtew them in about a quart of water for about five minutes, then ſtrain off the liquor and put the chickens in a clean diſh; take three large onions, chop them ſmall and fry them in about two ounces of butter, then put in the chickens and fry them together till they are brown; take a quarter of an ounce of turmeric, a large ſpoonful of ginger and beaten pepper together, and a little ſalt to your palate, ſtrew all theſe ingredients over the chickens whilſt frying, then pour in the liquor and let it ſtew about half an hour, then put in a quarter of a pint of cream and the juice of two lemons, and ſerve it up. The ginger, pepper, and turmeric muſt be beat very fine.

To boil the Rice.

PUT two quarts of water to a pint of rice, let it boil till you think it is done enough, then throw in a ſpoonful of ſalt and turn it out into a cullender; then let it ſtand about five minutes before the fire to dry, and ſerve it up in a diſh by itſelf. Diſh it up and ſend it to table; the rice in a diſh by itſelf.

Another Way to make a Curry; eaſier, and much approved.

FRY your chickens or rabbits a light brown, fry three onions and put to them, add ſome water, Cayenne pepper, ſalt, and two large ſpoonfuls of curry powder; cover your pan cloſe and ſet it over the fire to ſtew all together till your gravy is thick, then put in a few pickles chopped ſmall, and half the juice of a lemon.

You may make it of veal or mutton the ſame way. The chickens or rabbits are to be cut up as for a fricaſſee.

To boil the Rice.

LET the rice be well picked and waſhed, put it into a tin pan that ſhuts cloſe, with water enough to cover it about an inch; let it boil with a little ſalt, very quick, till the water is reduced even with the rice, then ſet it high on the fire and keep it cloſe covered till ready for table. Send it up in a diſh by itſelf.

To make a Pellaw the Indian Way.

TAKE three pounds of rice, pick and waſh it very clean, put it into a cullender and let it drain very dry; take three quarters of a pound of butter and put it into a pan over a very ſlow fire till it melts, then put in the rice and cover it over very cloſe that it may keep all the ſteam in; add to it a little ſalt, ſome whole pepper, half a dozen blades of mace, and a few cloves; you muſt put in a little water to keep it from burning, then ſtir it up very often, and let it ſtew till the rice is ſoft. Boil two fowls, and a fine piece of bacon of about two pounds weight, as common, cut the bacon into two pieces, lay it in the diſh with the fowls, cover it over with the rice, and garniſh it with about half a dozen of hard eggs and a dozen of onions fried whole and very brown.

N. B. This is the true Indian way of dreſſing them.

Another Way to make a Pellaw.

TAKE a leg of veal about twelve or fourteen pounds weight, an old cock ſkinned, chop both to pieces, put it into a pot with five or ſix blades of mace, ſome whole white pepper, and three gallons of water, half a pound of bacon, two onions, and ſix cloves; cover it cloſe, and when it boils let it do very ſoftly till the meat is good for nothing and above two thirds waſted, then ſtrain it; the next day put this ſoup into a ſauce-pan with a pound of rice, ſet it over a very ſlow fire, take great care it do not burn; when the rice is very thick and dry turn it into a diſh. Garniſh with hard eggs cut in two, and have roaſted fowls in another diſh.

N. B. You are to obſerve, if your rice ſimmers too faſt it will burn when it comes to be thick. It muſt be very thick and dry, and the rice not boiled to a mummy.

CHAP.

CHAP. VII.

Read this CHAPTER, and you will find how expenſive a FRENCH COOK's Sauce is.

The French Way of dreſſing Partridges.

WHEN they are newly picked and drawn, ſinge them: you muſt mince their livers with a bit of butter, ſome ſcraped bacon, green truffles (if you have any), parſley, chimbol, ſalt, pepper, ſweet herbs, and all-ſpice; the whole being minced together, put it into the inſide of your partridges, then ſtop both ends of them, after which give them a fry in the ſtew pan; that being done, ſpit them, and wrap them up in ſlices of bacon and paper; then take a ſtew-pan, and having put in an onion cut into ſlices, a carrot cut into little bits, with a little oil, give them a few toſſes over the fire; then moiſten them with gravy, cullis, and a little eſſence of ham; put therein half a lemon cut in ſlices, four cloves of garlic, a little ſweet baſil, thyme, a bay-leaf, a little parſley, chimbol, two glaſſes of white wine, and four of the carcaſes of the partridges; let them be pounded, and put them in this ſauce; when the fat of your cullis is taken away be careful to make it reliſhing, and after your pounded livers are put into your cullis you muſt ſtrain them through a ſieve; your partridges being done, take them off, as alſo take off the bacon and paper, and lay them in your diſh with your ſauce over them.

This diſh I do not recommend; for I think it an odd jumble of traſh: by that time the cullis, the eſſence of ham, and all other ingredients are reckoned, the partridges will come to a fine penny. But ſuch receipts as this are what you have in moſt books of Cookery yet printed.

To make Eſſence of Ham.

TAKE the fat off a Weſtphalia ham, cut the lean in ſlices, beat them well and lay them in the bottom of a ſtew-pan, with ſlices of carrots, parſnips, and onions; cover your pan and ſet it over a gentle fire; let them ſtew till they begin to ſtick, then ſprinkle on a little flour and turn them; then moiſten with broth and veal gravy; ſeaſon with three or four muſhrooms, as many truffles, a whole leek, ſome baſil, parſley, and half a dozen cloves; or, inſtead of the leek, you may put a clove of garlic; put in ſome cruſts of bread, and let them ſimmer over the fire for three quarters of an hour. Strain it, and ſet it by for uſe.

A Cullis for all Sorts of Ragoo.

HAVING cut three pounds of lean veal and half a pound of ham into ſlices, lay it in the bottom of a ſtew-pan; put in carrots and parſnips, and an onion ſliced; cover it and ſet it a-ſtewing over a ſtove; when it has a good colour, and begins to ſtick, put to it a little melted butter, and ſhake in a little flour, keep it moving a little while till the flour is fried; then moiſten it with gravy and broth, of each a like quantity; then put in ſome parſley and baſil, a whole leek, a bay-leaf, ſome muſhrooms and truffles minced ſmall, three or four cloves, and the cruſt of two French rolls; let all theſe ſimmer together for three quarters of an hour; then take out the ſlices of veal, ſtrain it, and keep it for all ſorts of ragoos. Now compute the expence, and ſee if this diſh cannot be dreſſed full as well without this expence.

A Cullis for all Sorts of Butchers' Meat.

YOU muſt take meat according to your company; if ten or twelve, you cannot take leſs than a leg of veal and a ham, with all the fat, ſkin, and outſide cut off. Cut the leg of veal in pieces about the bigneſs of your fiſt, place them in your ſtew-pan, and then the ſlices of ham, two carrots, an onion cut in two; cover it cloſe, let it ſtew ſoftly at firſt, and as it begins to be brown take off the cover and turn it, to colour it on all ſides the ſame; but take care not to burn the meat; when it has a pretty brown colour, moiſten your cullis with broth made of beef, or other meat; ſeaſon your cullis with a little ſweet baſil, ſome cloves, and ſome garlic; pare a lemon, cut it in ſlices and put it into your cullis, with ſome muſhrooms; put into a ſtew-pan a good lump of butter and ſet it over a ſlow fire, put into it two or three handfuls of flour, ſtir it with a wooden ladle, and let it take a colour; if your cullis be pretty brown, you muſt put in ſome flour; your flour being brown with your cullis, pour it very ſoftly into your cullis, keeping it ſtirring with a wooden ladle; then let your cullis ſtew ſoftly, and ſkim off all the fat, put in two glaſſes of Champaign, or other white wine; but take care to keep your cullis very thin, ſo that you may take the fat well off and clarify it. To clarify it, you muſt put it in a ſtove that draws well, cover it cloſe, and let it boil without uncovering till it boils over; then uncover it and take off the fat that is round the ſtew-pan, then wipe it off the cover alſo, and cover it again. When your cullis is done, take out the meat and ſtrain your cullis through a ſilk ſtrainer. This cullis is for all ſorts of ragoos, fowls, pies, and terrines.

Cullis the Italian Way.

PUT into a ſtew-pan half a ladleful of cullis, as much eſſence of ham, half a ladleful of gravy, as much of broth, three or four onions cut into ſlices, four or five cloves of garlic, a little beaten coriander-ſeed, with a lemon pared and cut into ſlices, a little ſweet baſil, muſhrooms and good oil; put all over the fire, let it ſtew a quarter of an hour, take the fat well off; let it be of a good taſte, and you may uſe it with all ſorts of meat and fiſh, particularly with glazed fiſh. This ſauce will do for two chickens, ſix pigeons, quails, or ducklings, and all ſorts of tame and wild fowl. Now this Italian or French ſauce, is ſaucy.

Cullis of Craw-Fiſh.

YOU muſt get the middling ſort of craw-fiſh, put them over the fire ſeaſoned with ſalt, pepper, and onion cut in ſlices; being done, take them out, pick them, and keep the tails after they are ſcalded, pound the reſt together in a mortar; the more they are pounded the finer your cullis will be. Take a bit of veal the bigneſs of your fiſt, with a ſmall bit of ham, an onion cut into four, put it in to ſweat gently: if it ſticks but a very little to the pan, powder it a little. Moiſten it with broth, put in it ſome cloves, ſweet baſil in branches, ſome muſhrooms, with lemon pared and cut in ſlices: being done, ſkim the fat well off, let it be of a good taſte; then take out your meat with a ſkimmer, and go on to thicken it a little with eſſence of ham; then put in your craw-fiſh, and ſtrain it off. Being ſtrained, keep it for a firſt-courſe of craw-fiſh.

A White Cullis.

TAKE a piece of veal, cut it into ſmall bits, with ſome thin ſlices of ham, and two onions cut into four pieces; moiſten it with broth ſeaſoned with muſhrooms, a bunch of parſley, green onions, three cloves, and ſo let it ſtew. Being ſtewed, take out all your meat and roots with a ſkimmer, put in a few crumbs of bread, and let it ſtew ſoftly; take the white of a fowl, or two chickens, and pound it in a mortar; being well pounded, mix it in your cullis, but it muſt not boil, and your cullis muſt be very white; but if it is not white enough, you muſt pound two dozen of ſweet almonds blanched, and put into your cullis; then boil a glaſs of milk, and put it into your cullis; let it be of a good taſte, and ſtrain it off; then put it in a ſmall kettle and keep it warm. You may uſe it for white loaves, white cruſt of bread, and biſcuits.

Sauce for a Brace of Partridges, Pheasants, or any thing you please.

ROAST a partridge, pound it well in a mortar with the pinions of four turkies, with a quart of strong gravy, and the livers of the partridges, and some truffles, and let it simmer till it be pretty thick; let it stand in a dish for a while, then put two glasses of Burgundy into a stew-pan, with two or three slices of onions, a clove or two of garlic, and the above sauce. Let it simmer a few minutes, then press it through a hair-bag into a stew-pan, add the essence of ham, let it boil for some time, season it with good spice and pepper, lay your partridges, &c. in the dish, and pour your sauce in.

They will use as many fine ingredients to stew a pigeon, or fowl, as will make a very fine dish, which is equal to boiling a leg of mutton in Champaign.

It would be needless to name any more, though you have much more expensive sauce than this: however, I think here is enough to shew the folly of these fine French cooks. In their own country, they will make a grand entertainment with the expence of one of these dishes; but here they want the little petty profit; and by this sort of legerdemain, some fine estates are juggled into France.

CHAP. VIII.

To make a Number of pretty little Dishes fit for a Supper or Side-dish, and little Corner-dishes for a great Table; and the rest you have in the CHAPTER for LENT.

Hogs' Ears forced.

TAKE four hogs' ears and half boil them, or take them soused; make a force-meat thus: take half a pound of beef-suet, as much crumbs of bread, an anchovy, some sage; boil and chop very fine a little parsley: mix all together with the yolk of an egg and a little pepper; slit your ears very carefully to make a place for your stuffing; fill them, flour them, and fry them in fresh butter till they are of a fine brown; then pour out all the fat clean, and put to them half a pint of gravy, a glass of white wine, three tea-spoonfuls of mustard, a piece of butter as big as a nutmeg rolled in flour, a little pepper, a small onion whole; cover them close, and let them stew softly for half an hour, shaking your pan now and then. When they are enough, lay them in your dish, and pour your sauce over them,

them, but firſt take out the onion. This makes a very pretty diſh; but if you would make a fine large diſh, take the feet, and cut all the meat in ſmall thin pieces, and ſtew with the ears. Seaſon with ſalt to your palate.

To force Cock's-Combs.

PARBOIL your cock's-combs, then open them with a point of a knife at the great end: take the white of a fowl, as much bacon and beef-marrow, cut theſe ſmall, and beat them fine in a marble mortar; ſeaſon them with ſalt, pepper, and grated nutmeg, and mix it with an egg; fill the cock's-combs, and ſtew them in a little ſtrong gravy ſoftly for half an hour; then ſlice in ſome freſh muſhrooms and a few pickled ones; then beat up the yolk of an egg in a little gravy, ſtirring it. Seaſon with ſalt. When they are enough, diſh them up in little diſhes or plates.

A forced Cabbage.

TAKE a fine white-heart cabbage about as big as a quarter of a peck, lay it in water two or three hours, then half boil it, ſet it in a cullender to drain, then very carefully cut out the heart, but take great care not to break off any of the outſide leaves, fill it with force-meat made thus: take a pound of veal, half a pound of bacon, fat and lean together, cut them ſmall, and beat them fine in a mortar, with four eggs boiled hard. Seaſon it with pepper and ſalt, a little beaten mace, a very little lemon-peel cut fine, ſome parſley chopped fine, a very little thyme, and two anchovies: when they are beat fine, take the crumb of a ſtale roll, ſome muſhrooms (if you have them) either pickled or freſh, and the heart of the cabbage you cut out chopped fine; mix all together with the yolk of an egg, then fill the hollow part of the cabbage, and tie it with a packthread; then lay ſome ſlices of bacon to the bottom of a ſtew-pan or ſauce-pan, and on that a pound of coarſe lean beef cut thin; put in the cabbage, cover it cloſe and let it ſtew over a ſlow fire till the bacon begins to ſtick to the pan, ſhake in a little flour, then pour in a quart of broth, an onion ſtuck with cloves, two blades of mace, ſome whole pepper, a little bundle of ſweet herbs; cover it cloſe and let it ſtew very ſoftly an hour and a half, put in a glaſs of red wine, give it a boil, then take it up, lay it in the diſh, and ſtrain the gravy and pour over: untie it firſt. This is a fine ſide-diſh, and the next day makes a fine haſh, with a veal-ſteak nicely broiled and laid on it.

Savoys forced and ſtewed.

TAKE two ſavoys, fill one with force-meat and the other without; ſtew them with gravy; ſeaſon them with pepper and

 ſalt,

ſalt, and when they are near enough, take a piece of butter as big as a large walnut, rolled in flour, and put in; let them ſtew till they are enough, and the ſauce thick; then lay them in your diſh, and pour the ſauce over them. Theſe things are beſt done on a ſtove.

Forced Eggs.

Boil the eggs hard and peel the ſhells off, wrap them up in force-meat and fry them a fine brown, then cut them length-ways with the yolks, put fine brown gravy into the diſh thick-ened a little; do not pour it over the eggs.

To force Cucumbers.

Take three large cucumbers, ſcoop out the pith, fill them with fried oyſters ſeaſoned with pepper and ſalt; put on the piece again you cut off, ſew it with a coarſe thread, and fry them in the butter the oyſters are fried in: then pour out the butter and ſhake in a little flour, pour in half a pint of gravy, ſhake it round and put in the cucumbers; ſeaſon it with a little pepper and ſalt; let them ſtew ſoftly till they are tender, then lay them in a plate and pour the gravy over them: or you may force them with any ſort of force-meat you fancy, and fry them in hog's lard, and then ſtew them in gravy and red wine.

To preſerve Cock's-Combs.

Let them be well cleaned, then put them into a pot, with ſome melted bacon, and boil them a little; about half an hour after add a little bay-ſalt, ſome pepper, a little vinegar, a lemon ſliced, and an onion ſtuck with cloves; when the bacon begins to ſtick to the pot, take them up, put them into the pan you would keep them in, lay a clean linen cloth over them, and pour melted butter clarified over them to keep them cloſe from the air. Theſe make a pretty plate at a ſupper.

To preſerve or pickle Pig's Feet and Ears.

Take your feet and ears ſingle and waſh them well, ſplit the feet in two, put a bay-leaf between every foot, put in almoſt as much water as will cover them; when they are well ſteamed, add to them cloves, mace, whole pepper, and ginger, coriander-ſeed and ſalt, according to your diſcretion; put to them a bot-tle or two of Rheniſh wine (according to the quantity you do), half a ſcore of bay-leaves, and a bunch of ſweet herbs; let them boil ſoftly till they are very tender, then take them out of the liquor, lay them in an earthen pot, then ſtrain the liquor over them; when they are cold, cover them down cloſe and keep them for uſe.

You ſhould let them ſtand to be cold; ſkim off all the fat, and then put in the wine and ſpice.

Pig's Feet and Ears another Way.

TAKE two pig's ears ſouſed, cut them into long ſlips about three inches, and about as thick as a gooſe quill; put them in a ſtew-pan with a pint of good gravy and half an onion cut very fine, ſtew them till they are tender; then add a little butter rolled in flour, a ſpoonful of muſtard, ſome pepper and ſalt, a little alder vinegar; toſs them up and put them in a diſh: have the feet cut in two, and put a bay-leaf between; tie them up, and boil them very tender in water and a little vinegar, with an onion or two, rub them over with the yolk of an egg, and ſprinkle bread crumbs on them; broil or fry them, and put them round the ears.

To pickle Ox Palates.

TAKE your palates, waſh them well with ſalt and water, and put them in a pipkin with water and ſome ſalt; and when they are ready to boil, ſkim them well, and put to them pepper, cloves, and mace, as much as will give them a quick taſte; when they are boiled tender (which will require four or five hours), peel them and cut them into ſmall pieces, and let them cool; then make the pickle of white wine and vinegar, an equal quantity; boil the pickle and put in the ſpices that were boiled in the palates; when both the pickle and palates are cold, lay your palates in a jar and put to them a few bay-leaves and a little freſh ſpice; pour the pickle over them, cover them cloſe and keep them for uſe.

Of theſe you may at any time make a pretty little diſh, either with brown ſauce or white, or butter and muſtard and a ſpoonful of white wine; or they are ready to put in made-diſhes.

To ſtew Cucumbers.

TAKE ſix cucumbers, pare them and cut them in two length-ways, take out the ſeeds; take a dozen of ſmall round-headed onions peeled; put ſome butter in a ſtew-pan, melt it, put in your onions and fry them brown; then put a ſpoonful of flour in, ſtir it till it is ſmooth, put in three quarters of a pint of brown gravy, and ſtir it all the time; then put in your cucumbers with a glaſs of Liſbon, ſtew them till they are tender; ſeaſon with pepper and ſalt and a little Cayenne pepper to your liking: obſerve to ſkim it well, becauſe the butter will riſe to the top. Send them to table in a diſh or under your meat.

Stewed Red Cabbage.

TAKE a red cabbage, lay it in cold water an hour, then cut it into thin ſlices acroſs and cut it into little pieces; put it into a ſtew-a ſtew-pan with a pound of ſauſages, a pint of gravy, a little bit of ham or lean bacon; cover it cloſe and let it ſtew half an hour; then take the pan off the fire and ſkim off the fat, ſhake in a little flour and ſet it on again; let it ſtew two or three minutes, then lay the ſauſages in your diſh and pour the reſt all over. You may, before you take it up, put in half a ſpoonful of vinegar.

Stewed Peas and Lettuce.

TAKE a quart of green peas, two large cabbage-lettuces cut ſmall acroſs and waſhed very clean, put them in a ſtew-pan with a quart of gravy, and ſtew them till tender; put in ſome butter rolled in flour, ſeaſon with pepper and ſalt: when of a proper thickneſs diſh them up.

N. B. Some like them thickened with the yolks of four eggs; others like an onion chopped very fine and ſtewed with them, with two or three raſhers of lean ham.

Another Way to ſtew Peas.

TAKE a pint of peas, put them in a ſtew-pan with a handful of chopped parſley; juſt cover them with water, ſtew them till tender; then beat up the yolks of two eggs, put in ſome double-refined ſugar to ſweeten them, put in the eggs and toſs them up; then put them in your diſh.

Stewed Spinage and Eggs.

PICK and waſh your ſpinage very clean, put it into a ſaucepan with a little ſalt, cover it cloſe, ſhake the pan often; when it is juſt tender and whilſt it is green throw it into a ſieve to drain, lay it into your diſh: in the mean time have a ſtew-pan of water boiling, break as many eggs into cups as you would poach; when the water boils put in the eggs, have an egg-ſlice ready to take them out with, lay them on the ſpinage, and garniſh the diſh with orange cut into quarters, with melted butter in a cup.

To ſtew Muſhrooms.

TAKE large buttons, wipe them with a wet flannel, put them in a ſtew-pan with a little water, let them ſtew a quarter of an hour, then put in a little ſalt, work a little flour and butter to make it as thick as cream, let it boil five minutes; when you diſh it up put two large ſpoonfuls of cream mixed with the yolk of an egg, ſhake it over the fire about a minute or two, but do not let it boil for fear of curdling; put ſippets round the inſide of the rim of the diſh, but not toaſted, and ſerve it up. It is proper for a ſide-diſh for ſupper, or a corner for dinner.

Another Way to stew Mushrooms.

PUT your mushrooms in salt and water, wipe them with a flannel and put them again in salt and water, then throw them into a sauce-pan by themselves and let them boil up as quick as possible, then put in a little Cayenne pepper, a little mace (if you like the flavour), let them stew in this a quarter of an hour, then add a tea-cupful of cream, with a little flour and butter the size of a walnut; let them be served up as soon as done.

To stew Chardoons.

TAKE the inside of your chardoons, wash them well, boil them in salt and water, put them into a tossing-pan with a little veal gravy, a tea-spoonful of lemon-pickle, a large one of mushroom catchup, pepper and salt (to your taste), thicken it with flour and butter, boil it a little, and serve it up in a soup-plate.

To dress Windsor-Beans.

TAKE the seed, boil them till they are tender; then blanch them, and fry them in clarified butter; melt butter, with a little vinegar, and pour over them; stew them with salt, pepper, and nutmeg.

Or you may eat them with butter, sack, sugar, and a little powder of cinnamon.

To make Jumballs.

TAKE a pound of fine flour and a pound of fine powder-sugar, make them into a light paste, with whites of eggs beat fine; then add half a pint of cream, half a pound of fresh butter melted, and a pound of blanched almonds well beat; knead them all together thoroughly with a little rose-water, and cut out your jumballs in what figures you fancy; and either bake them in a gentle oven or fry them in fresh butter, and they make a pretty side or corner-dish. You may melt a little butter with a spoonful of sack, throw fine sugar all over the dish. If you make them in pretty figures, they make a fine little dish.

To ragoo Cucumbers.

TAKE two cucumbers and two onions, slice them and fry them in a little butter, then drain them in a sieve; put them into a sauce-pan, add six spoonfuls of gravy, two of white wine, a blade of mace; let them stew five or six minutes; then take a piece of butter as big as a walnut, rolled in flour, a little salt and Cayenne pepper; shake them together, and when it is thick, dish them up.

To

To make a Ragoo of Onions.

TAKE a pint of little young onions, peel them, and take four large ones, peel them, and cut them very ſmall; put a quarter of a pound of good butter into a ſtew-pan, when it is melted and done making a noiſe, throw in your onions, and fry them till they begin to look a little brown; then ſhake in a little flour, and ſhake them round till they are thick; throw in a little ſalt, a little beaten pepper, a quarter of a pint of good gravy, and a tea-ſpoonful of muſtard; ſtir all together, and when it is well-taſted and of a good thickneſs pour it into your diſh, and garniſh it with fried crumbs of bread. They make a pretty little diſh, and are very good. You may ſtew raſpings in the room of flour, if you pleaſe.

A Ragoo of Oyſters.

OPEN twenty large oyſters, take them out of the liquor, ſave the liquor, and dip the oyſters in a batter made thus: take two eggs, beat them well, a little lemon-peel grated, a little nutmeg grated, a blade of mace pounded fine, a little parſley chopped fine, beat all together with a little flour, have ready ſome butter or dripping in a ſtew-pan; when it boils, dip in your oyſters one by one into the batter, and fry them of a fine brown; then with an egg-ſlice take them out, and lay them in a diſh before the fire; pour the fat out of the pan, and ſhake a little flour over the bottom of the pan, then rub a little piece of butter (as big as a ſmall walnut) all over with your knife whilſt it is over the fire; then pour in three ſpoonfuls of the oyſter-liquor ſtrained, one ſpoonful of white wine, and a quarter of a pint of gravy; grate a little nutmeg, ſtir all together, throw in the oyſters, give the pan a toſs round, and when the ſauce is of a good thickneſs, pour all into the diſh, and garniſh with raſpings.

A Ragoo of Aſparagus.

SCRAPE a hundred of graſs very clean, and throw them into cold water; when you have ſcraped all, cut as far as is good and green about an inch long, and take two heads of endive clean waſhed and picked, cut it very ſmall, a young lettuce clean waſhed and cut ſmall, a large onion peeled and cut ſmall, put a quarter of a pound of butter into a ſtew-pan, when it is melted throw in the above things: toſs them about, and fry them ten minutes; then ſeaſon them with a little pepper and ſalt, ſhake in a little flour, toſs them about, then pour in half a pint of gravy; let them ſtew till the ſauce is very thick and good; then pour all into your diſh. Save a few of the little tops of the graſs to garniſh the diſh.

N. B. You

N. B. You muſt not fry the aſparagus: boil it in a little water and put them in your ragoo, and then they will look green.

A Ragoo of Livers.

TAKE as many livers as you would have for your diſh. A turkey's liver and ſix fowls' livers will make a pretty diſh. Pick the galls from them, and throw them into cold water; take the ſix livers, put them into a ſauce-pan with a quarter of a pint of gravy, a ſpoonful of muſhrooms (either pickled or freſh), a ſpoonful of catchup, a little piece of butter as big as a nutmeg, rolled in flour; ſeaſon them with pepper and ſalt to your palate; let them ſtew ſoftly ten minutes; in the mean while, butter one ſide of a piece of writing paper and wrap the turkey's liver in it, and broil it nicely, lay it in the middle, and the ſtewed livers round; pour the ſauce all over, and garniſh with lemon.

To ragoo Cauliflowers.

TAKE a large cauliflower, waſh it very clean and pick it in pieces, as for pickling; make a nice brown cullis, and ſtew them till tender, ſeaſon with pepper and ſalt, put them into your diſh with the ſauce over; boil a few ſprigs of the cauliflower in water, to garniſh with.

Fried Sauſages.

TAKE half a pound of ſauſages, and ſix apples, ſlice four about as thick as a crown, cut the other two in quarters, fry them with the ſauſages of a fine light brown, lay the ſauſages in the middle of the diſh, and the apples round. Garniſh with the quartered apples.

Stewed cabbage and ſauſages fried is a good diſh.

Collops and Eggs.

CUT either bacon, hung-beef, or hung-mutton into thin ſlices, broil them nicely, lay them in a diſh before the fire, have ready a ſtew-pan of water boiling, break as many eggs as you have collops, break them one by one in a cup, and pour them into the ſtew-pan; when the whites of the eggs begin to harden, and all look of a clear white, take them up one by one in an egg-ſlice, lay them on the collops.

To dreſs cold Fowl or Pigeon.

CUT them in four quarters, beat up an egg or two (according to what you dreſs), grate a little nutmeg in, a little ſalt, ſome parſley chopped, a few crumbs of bread, beat them well together, dip them in this batter, and have ready ſome dripping hot in a ſtew-pan, in which fry them of a fine light brown; have

have ready a little good gravy, thickened with a little flour, mixed with a ſpoonful of catchup; lay the fry in the diſh and pour the ſauce over. Garniſh with lemon, and a few muſh-rooms, if you have any. A cold rabbit eats well done thus.

To fry cold Veal.

CUT it in pieces about as thick as half-a-crown, and as long as you pleaſe, dip them in the yolk of an egg, and then in crumbs of bread, with a few ſweet herbs, and ſhred lemon-peel in it; grate a little nutmeg over them, and fry them in freſh butter. The butter muſt be hot, juſt enough to fry them in: in the mean time, make a little gravy of the bone of the veal; when the meat is fried take it out with a fork, and lay it in a diſh before the fire, then ſhake a little flour into the pan and ſtir it round; then put in a little gravy, ſqueeze in a little lemon, and pour it over the veal. Garniſh with lemon.

To toſs up cold Veal white.

CUT the veal into little thin bits, put milk enough to it for ſauce, grate in a little nutmeg, a very little ſalt, a little piece of butter rolled in flour: to half a pint of milk, the yolks of two eggs well beat, a ſpoonful of muſhroom-pickle, ſtir all together till it is thick; then pour it into your diſh, and garniſh with lemon.

Cold fowl ſkinned, and done this way, eats well: or the beſt end of a cold breaſt of veal; firſt fry it, drain it from the fat, then pour this ſauce to it.

To haſh cold Mutton.

CUT your mutton with a very ſharp knife in very little bits, as thin as poſſible; then boil the bones with an onion, a little ſweet herbs, a blade of mace, a very little whole pepper, a little ſalt, a piece of cruſt toaſted very criſp; let it boil till there is juſt enough for ſauce, ſtrain it and put it into a ſauce-pan with a piece of butter rolled in flour; put in the meat; when it is very hot it is enough; ſeaſon with pepper and ſalt; have ready ſome thin bread toaſted brown, cut three-corner ways, lay them round the diſh, and pour in the haſh. As to walnut-pickle, and all ſorts of pickles, you muſt put in according to your fancy. Garniſh with pickles. Some love a ſmall onion peeled and cut very ſmall, and done in the haſh. Or you may uſe made-gravy, if you have not time to boil the bones.

To haſh Mutton like Veniſon.

CUT it very thin as above; boil the bones as above; ſtrain the liquor, where there is juſt enough for the haſh; to a quarter of of a pint of gravy put a large ſpoonful of red wine, an onion peeled and chopped fine, a very little lemon-peel ſhred fine, a piece of butter as big as a ſmall walnut, rolled in flour; put it into a ſauce-pan with the meat, ſhake it all together, and when it is thoroughly hot pour it into your diſh. Haſh beef the ſame way.

To make Collops of cold Beef.

IF you have any cold inſide of a ſirloin of beef, take off all the fat, cut it very thin in little bits, cut an onion very ſmall; boil as much water or gravy as you think will do for ſauce; ſeaſon it with a little pepper and ſalt and a bundle of ſweet herbs; let the water boil, then put in the meat, with a good piece of butter rolled in flour, ſhake it round and ſtir it. When the ſauce is thick and the meat done, take out the ſweet herbs, and pour it into your diſh. They do better than freſh meat.

To mince Veal.

CUT your veal as fine as poſſible, but do not chop it; grate a little nutmeg over it, ſhred a little lemon-peel very fine, throw a very little ſalt on it, dredge a little flour over it. To a large plate of veal, take four or five ſpoonfuls of water, let it boil, then put in the veal with a piece of butter as big as an egg, ſtir it well together; when it is all thorough hot, it is enough. Have ready a very thin piece of bread toaſted brown, cut it into three-corner ſippets, lay it round the plate, and pour in the veal. Juſt before you pour it in, ſqueeze in half a lemon, or half a ſpoonful of vinegar. Garniſh with lemon. You may put gravy in the room of water, if you love it ſtrong; but it is better without.

To make a Florentine of Veal.

TAKE two kidneys of veal, fat and all, and mince them very fine, then chop a few herbs and put to them, and add a few currants; ſeaſon with cloves, mace, nutmeg, and a little ſalt, four or five yolks of eggs chopped fine, and ſome crumbs of bread, a pippin or two chopped, ſome candied lemon-peel cut ſmall, a little ſack, and orange-flower water. Lay a ſheet of puff-paſte at the bottom of your diſh and put in the ingredients, and cover it with another ſheet of puff-paſte. Bake it in a ſlack oven, ſcrape ſugar on the top, and ſerve it up hot.

A Salmagundy.

TAKE two pickled herrings and bone them, a handful of parſley, four eggs boiled hard, the white of one roaſted chicken or fowl; chop all very fine ſeparately, that is, the yolks of eggs by themſelves, and the whites the ſame; ſcrape ſome lean boiled ham very fine, hung-beef or Dutch beef ſcraped; turn a ſmall china

china baſon, or deep ſaucer, into your diſh; make ſome butter into the ſhape of a pine-apple, or any other ſhape you pleaſe, and ſet on the top of the baſon or ſaucer; lay round your baſon a ring of ſhred parſley, then whites of eggs, then ham, then chickens, then beef, then yolks of eggs, then herrings, till you have covered the baſon and uſed all your ingredients. Garniſh the diſh with whole capers and pickles of any ſort you chooſe, chopped fine; or you may leave out the butter and put the ingredients on, and put a flower of any ſort at the top, or a ſprig of myrtle.

Another Way.

MINCE veal or fowl very ſmall, a pickled herring boned and picked ſmall, cucumbers minced ſmall, apples minced ſmall, an onion peeled and minced ſmall, ſome pickled red-cabbage chopped ſmall, cold pork minced ſmall, or cold duck or pigeons minced ſmall, boiled parſley chopped fine, celery cut ſmall, the yolks of hard eggs chopped ſmall, and the whites chopped ſmall, and either lay all the ingredients by themſelves ſeparate on ſaucers, or in heaps in a diſh. Diſh them out with what pickles you have, and ſliced lemon nicely cut; and if you can get naſtertium-flowers, lay them round it. This is a fine middle-diſh for ſupper; but you may always make ſalmagundy of ſuch things as you have, according to your fancy. The other ſorts are in the Chapter of Lent.

To make little Paſties.

TAKE the kidney of a loin of veal cut very fine, with as much of the fat, the yolks of two hard eggs, ſeaſoned with a little ſalt, and half a ſmall nutmeg; mix them well together, then roll it well in a puff-paſte cruſt; make three of it, and fry them nicely in hog's-lard or butter.

They make a pretty little diſh for a change. You may put in ſome carrots, and a little ſugar and ſpice, with the juice of an orange, and ſometimes apples, firſt boiled and ſweetened, with a little juice of lemon, or any fruit you pleaſe.

Petit Paſties for garniſhing Diſhes.

MAKE a ſhort cruſt, roll it thick, make them about as big as the bowl of a ſpoon and about an inch deep; take a piece of veal, enough to fill the patty, as much bacon and beef-ſuet, ſhred them all very fine, ſeaſon them with pepper and ſalt, and a little ſweet herbs; put them into a little ſtew-pan, keep turning them about, with a few muſhrooms chopped ſmall, for eight or ten minutes; then fill your petty-patties and cover them with ſome cruſt; colour them with the yolk of an egg, and bake them. Sometimes fill them with oyſters for fiſh, or the

the melts of the fiſh pounded, and ſeaſoned with pepper and ſalt; fill them with lobſters, or what you fancy. They make a fine garniſhing, and give a diſh a fine look: if for a calf's head, the brains ſeaſoned is moſt proper, and ſome with oyſters.

CHAP. IX.

Turtle, Mock-Turtle, &c.

As all the articles contained in the Chapter formerly diſtinguiſhed by the name of Additions are (in this edition) put in their proper places, a ſeparate Chapter is allotted to the King of Fiſh; and if little alteration is made from the manner of dreſſing it and making mock-turtle, given in former editions, it is becauſe ſuch alterations have more affectation than uſe in them; the receipts here given being, in reality, the beſt extant.

To dreſs a Turtle the Weſt India Way.

Take the turtle out of water the night before you dreſs it, and lay it on its back, in the morning cut its head off, and hang it up by its hind-fins for it to bleed till the blood is all out; then cut out the callapee (which is the belly) round, and raiſe it up; cut as much meat to it as you can; throw it into ſpring-water with a little ſalt, cut the fins off and ſcald them with the head; take off all the ſcales, cut all the white meat out and throw it into ſpring-water and ſalt; the guts and lungs muſt be cut out; waſh the lungs very clean from the blood; then take the guts and maw and ſlit them open, waſh them very clean, and put them on to boil in a large pot of water, and boil them till they are tender; then take off the inſide ſkin, and cut them in pieces of two or three inches long. Have ready a good veal broth made as follows: take one large or two ſmall knuckles of veal and put them on in three gallons of water; let it boil, ſkim it well, ſeaſon with turnips, onions, carrots, and celery, and a good large bundle of ſweet herbs; boil it till it is half waſted, then ſtrain it off. Take the fins and put them in a ſtew-pan, cover them with veal broth, ſeaſon with an onion chopped fine, all ſorts of ſweet herbs chopped very fine, half an ounce of cloves and mace, half a nutmeg beat very fine, ſtew it very gently till tender; then take the fins out, and put in a pint of Madeira wine, and ſtew it for fifteen minutes; beat up the whites of ſix eggs, with the juice of two lemons; put the liquor in and boil it up, run it through a flannel bag, make it hot, waſh the fins very clean and put them in. Take a piece of butter and put at the bottom of a ſtew-pan, put your white meat in, and ſweat it gently till it is almoſt tender. Take the lungs and heart and cover them with veal broth, with an onion, herbs, and ſpice; as for the fins, ſtew them till tender; take out the lungs, ſtrain the liquor off, thicken it, and put in a bottle of Madeira wine, ſeaſon with Cayenne pepper and ſalt pretty high; put in the lungs and white meat, ſtew them up gently for fifteen minutes; have ſome force-meat balls made out of the white part inſtead of veal, as for Scotch collops: if the turtle has any eggs, ſcald them; if not, take twelve hard yolks of eggs, made into egg-balls; have your callapaſh, or deep ſhell, done round the edges with paſte, ſeaſon it in the inſide with Cayenne pepper and ſalt, and a little Madeira wine, bake it half an hour, then put in the lungs and white meat, force-meat, and eggs over, and bake it half an hour; take the bones, and three quarts of veal broth, ſeaſoned with an onion, a bundle of ſweet herbs, two blades of mace, ſtew it an hour, ſtrain it through a ſieve, thicken it with flour and butter, put in half a pint of Madeira wine, ſtew it half an hour; ſeaſon with Cayenne pepper and ſalt to your liking: this is the ſoup. Take the callapee, run your knife between the meat and ſhell, and fill it full of force-meat; ſeaſon it all over with ſweet herbs chopped fine, a ſhalot chopped, Cayenne pepper and ſalt, and a little Madeira wine; put a paſte round the edge, and bake it an hour and a half; take the guts and maw, put them in a ſtew-pan, with a little broth, a bundle of ſweet herbs, two blades of mace beat fine; thicken with a little butter rolled in flour; ſtew them gently for half an hour, ſeaſon with Cayenne pepper and ſalt, beat up the yolks of two eggs in half a pint of cream, put it in, and keep ſtirring it one way till it boils up; then diſh them up as follows:

Callapee.
Fricaſſee. Soup. Fins.
Callapaſh.

The fins eat fine when cold, put by in the liquor.

Another Way to dreſs a Turtle.

KILL your turtle as before, then cut the belly-ſhell clean off, cut off the fins, take all the white meat out, and put it into ſpring-water; take the guts and lungs out; do the guts as before; waſh the lungs well, ſcald the fins, head, and belly-ſhell; take a ſaw and ſaw the ſhell all round about two inches deep, ſcald it, and take the ſhell off, cut it in pieces; take the ſhells, fins, and head and put them in a pot, cover them with veal broth; ſeaſon with two large onions chopped fine, all ſorts of ſweet herbs chopped fine, half an ounce of cloves and mace, a whole a whole nutmeg, ftew them till tender; take out all the meat, and ftrain the liquor through a fieve, cut the fins in two or three pieces; take all the brawn from the bones, cut it in pieces of about two inches fquare; take the white meat, put fome butter at the bottom of a ftew-pan, put your meat in, and fweat it gently over a flow fire till almoft done; take it out of the liquor, and cut it in pieces about the bignefs of a goofe's egg; take the lungs and heart and cover them with veal broth; feafon with an onion, fweet herbs, and a little beat fpice (always obferve to boil the liver by itfelf); ftew it till tender, take the lungs out, and cut them in pieces; ftrain off the liquor through a fieve; take a pound of butter and put in a large ftew-pan (big enough to hold all the turtle) and melt it; put half a pound of flour in, and ftir it till it is fmooth; put in the liquor, and keep ftirring it till it is well mixed, if lumpy, ftrain it through a fieve; put in your meat of all forts, a great many force-meat balls and egg-balls, and put in three pints of Madeira wine; feafon with pepper and falt, and Cayenne pepper, pretty high; ftew it three quarters of an hour, add the juice of two lemons; have your deep fhell baked, put fome into the fhells, and bake it or brown it with a hot iron, and ferve the reft in tureens.

N. B. This is for a turtle of fixty pounds weight.

To make a Mock-Turtle.

TAKE a large calf's head with the fkin on, well fcalded and cleaned, boil it three quarters of an hour; take it out, and flit down the face, take all the fkin and meat from the bones as clean as poffible, be careful you do not break off the ears; lay it on the dreffer, and fill the ears full of force-meat, tie them round with a cloth; take out the eyes, and pick all the meat from the bones, put it in a large ftew-pan with the beft and fatteft parts of another head without the fkin, boiled as long as the above, and three quarts of veal gravy; lay the fkin on the meat, with the flefh fide up, cover the pan clofe, and let it ftew one hour over a moderate fire; put in three fweetbreads cut in pieces, two ounces of truffles and morels, four artichoke-bottoms boiled and cut in four pieces each, an anchovy boned and chopped fmall, feafon it pretty high with falt and Cayenne pepper, put in half a lemon, three pints of Madeira wine, two fpoonfuls of catchup, one of lemon-pickle, half a pint of pickled or frefh mufhrooms, a quarter of a pound of butter rolled in flour, and let it all ftew half an hour longer; take the yolks of four eggs boiled hard, and the brains of both heads boiled, cut the brains in pieces of the fize of a nutmeg, make a rich force-meat, and roll it up in a veal caul, and

 then

then in a cloth, and boil it one hour; cut it in three parts, the middle piece the largest; put the meat into the dish and lay the head over it, the skin side uppermost; put the largest piece of force-meat between the ears, the other two slices at the narrow end opposite each other; put the brains, eggs, mushrooms, &c. over and round it, and pour the liquor hot upon it, and send it up as quick as possible, as it soon gets cold.

To make Mock-Turtle Soup.

TAKE a calf's head and scald the hair off as you would a pig, and wash it very clean; boil it in a large pot of water half an hour; then cut all the skin off by itself, take the tongue out; take the broth made of a knuckle of veal, put in the tongue and skin with three large onions, half an ounce of cloves and mace and half a nutmeg beat fine, all sorts of sweet herbs chopped fine, and three anchovies, stew it till tender, then take out the meat and cut it in pieces about two inches square, and the tongue in slices; mind to skin the tongue; strain the liquor through a sieve; take half a pound of butter and put in the stew-pan, melt it and put in a quarter of a pound of flour, keep it stirring till it is smooth; then put in the liquor, keeping it stirring till all is in, if lumpy strain it through a sieve; then put to your meat a bottle of Madeira wine, season with pepper and salt and Cayenne pepper pretty high; put in force-meat balls and egg-balls boiled, the juice of two lemons, stew it one hour gently, and then serve it up in tureens.

N. B. If it is too thick put some more broth in before you stew it the last time.

CHAP. X.

FISH.

To boil a Turbot.

LAY it in a good deal of salt and water an hour or two, and if it is not quite sweet shift your water five or six times; first put a good deal of salt in the mouth and belly.

In the mean time set on your fish-kettle with clean spring-water and salt, a little vinegar, and a piece of horse-radish; when the water boils lay the turbot on a fish-plate, put it into the kettle, let it be well boiled, but take great care it is not too much done; when enough take off the fish-kettle, set it before the fire, then carefully lift up the fish-plate and set it across the kettle to drain: in the mean time melt a good deal of fresh butter, and bruise in either the spawn of one or two lobsters, and the

the meat cut ſmall, with a ſpoonful of anchovy-liquor; then give it a boil, and pour it into baſons. This is the beſt ſauce; but you may make what you pleaſe. Lay the fiſh in the diſh. Garniſh with ſcraped horſe-radiſh and lemon.

To bake a Turbot.

TAKE a diſh the ſize of your turbot, rub butter all over it thick, throw a little ſalt, a little beaten pepper, and half a large nutmeg, ſome parſley minced fine and thrown all over, pour in a pint of white wine, cut off the head and tail, lay the turbot in the diſh, pour another pint of white wine all over, grate the other half of the nutmeg over it, and a little pepper, ſome ſalt, and chopped parſley; lay a piece of butter here and there all over, and throw a little flour all over, and then a good many crumbs of bread: bake it, and be ſure that it is of a fine brown; then lay it in your diſh, ſtir the ſauce in your diſh all together, pour it into a ſauce-pan, ſhake in a little flour, let it boil, then ſtir in a piece of butter and two ſpoonfuls of catchup, let it boil, and pour it into baſons. Garniſh your diſh with lemon; and you may add what you fancy to the ſauce, as ſhrimps, anchovies, muſhrooms, &c. If a ſmall turbot half the wine will do. It eats finely thus: lay it in a diſh, ſkim off all the fat, and pour the reſt over it. Let it ſtand till cold and it is good with vinegar, and a fine diſh to ſet out a cold table.

To dreſs a Brace of Carp.

TAKE a piece of butter and put into a ſtew-pan, melt it and put in a large ſpoonful of flour, keep it ſtirring till it is ſmooth; then put in a pint of gravy and a pint of red port or claret, a little horſe-radiſh ſcraped, eight cloves, four blades of mace, and a dozen corns of all-ſpice, tie them in a little linen rag, a bundle of ſweet herbs, half a lemon, three anchovies, a little onion chopped very fine; ſeaſon with pepper, ſalt, and Cayenne pepper, to your liking; ſtew it for half an hour, then ſtrain it through a ſieve into the pan you intend to put the fiſh in; let your carp be well cleaned and ſcaled, then put the fiſh in with the ſauce and ſtew them very gently for half an hour, then turn them and ſtew them fifteen minutes longer; put in along with your fiſh ſome truffles and morels ſcalded, ſome pickled muſhrooms, an artichoke-bottom, and about a dozen large oyſters, ſqueeze the juice of half a lemon in, ſtew it five minutes; then put your carp in your diſh and pour all the ſauce over. Garniſh with fried ſippits and the roe of the fiſh done thus: beat the roe up well with the yolks of two eggs, a little flour, a little lemon-peel chopped fine, ſome pepper, ſalt, and a little anchovy liquor; have ready a pan of beef-dripping boiling, drop the roe in to be

 about

about as big as a crown-piece, fry it of a light brown and put it round the diſh, with ſome oyſters fried in batter and ſome ſcraped horſe-radiſh.

N. B. Stick your fried ſippits in the fiſh.

You may fry the carp firſt if you pleaſe, but the above is the moſt modern way.

Or if you are in a great hurry, while the ſauce is making you may boil the fiſh with ſpring-water, half a pint of vinegar, a little horſe-radiſh, and bay-leaf; put your fiſh in the diſh, and pour the ſauce over.

To dreſs Carp au Beu.

TAKE a brace of carp alive and gut them, but do not waſh or ſcale them; tie them to a fiſh-drainer, and put them into a fiſh-kettle, and pour boiling vinegar over till they are blue, or you may hold them down in a fiſh-kettle with two forks, and another perſon pour the vinegar over them; put in a quart of boiling water, a handful of ſalt, ſome horſe-radiſh cut in ſlices; boil them gently twenty minutes: put a fiſh-plate in the diſh, a napkin over that, and ſend them up hot. Garniſh with horſe-radiſh. Boil half a pint of cream and ſweeten it with ſome ſugar, for ſauce, in a boat or baſon.

To ſtew a Brace of Carp.

SCRAPE them very clean, then gut them, waſh them and the roes in a pint of good ſtale beer to preſerve all the blood, and boil the carp with a little ſalt in the water.

In the mean time ſtrain the beer and put it into a ſauce-pan with a pint of red wine, two or three blades of mace, ſome whole pepper black and white, an onion ſtuck with cloves, half a nutmeg bruiſed, a bundle of ſweet herbs, a piece of lemon-peel as big as a ſixpence, an anchovy, a little piece of horſe-radiſh; let theſe boil together ſoftly for a quarter of an hour, covered cloſe; then ſtrain it and add to it half the hard roe beat to pieces, two or three ſpoonfuls of catchup, a quarter of a pound of freſh butter, and a ſpoonful of muſhroom-pickle, let it boil and keep ſtirring it till the ſauce is thick and enough; if it wants any ſalt you muſt put ſome in; then take the reſt of the roe and beat it up with the yolk of an egg, ſome nutmeg, and a little lemon-peel cut ſmall; fry them in freſh butter in little cakes, and ſome pieces of bread cut three-cornerways and fried brown. When the carp are enough take them up, pour your ſauce over them, lay the cakes round the diſh, with horſe-radiſh ſcraped fine, and fried parſley; the reſt lay on the carp, and ſtick the bread about them and lay round them, then ſliced lemon notched and lay round the diſh, and two or three pieces on the carp. Send them to table hot.

If you would have your ſauce white, put in good fiſh-broth inſtead of beer, and white wine in the room of red wine. Make your broth with any ſort of freſh fiſh you have, and ſeaſon it as you do gravy.

To fry Carp.

FIRST ſcale and gut them, waſh them clean, lay them in a cloth to dry, then flour them and fry them of a fine light brown; fry ſome toaſt cut three-cornerways and the roes; when your fiſh is done lay them on a coarſe cloth to drain: let your ſauce be butter and anchovy, with the juice of lemon. Lay your carp in the diſh, the roes on each ſide, and garniſh with the fried toaſt and lemon.

To bake Carp.

SCALE, waſh, and clean a brace of carp very well; take an earthen pan deep enough to lie cloſely in, butter the pan a little, lay in your carp; ſeaſon with mace, clove, nutmeg, and black and white pepper, a bundle of ſweet herbs, an onion, and anchovy; pour in a bottle of white wine, cover it cloſe and let them bake an hour in a hot oven, if large; if ſmall, a leſs time will do them; when they are enough, carefully take them up and lay them in a diſh; ſet it over hot water to keep it hot, and cover it cloſe, then pour all the liquor they were baked in into a ſauce-pan; let it boil a minute or two, then ſtrain it and add half a pound of butter rolled in flour; let it boil, keep ſtirring it, ſqueeze in the juice of half a lemon and put in what ſalt you want; pour the ſauce over the fiſh, lay the roes round, and garniſh with lemon. Obſerve to ſkim all the fat off the liquor.

To ſtew Carp or Tench.

GUT and ſcale your fiſh, waſh and dry them well with a clean cloth, dredge them well with flour, fry them in dripping or ſweet rendered ſuet until they are a light brown, and then put them in a ſtew-pan with a quart of water and one quart of red wine, a meat-ſpoonful of walnut or mum catchup, a little muſhroom-powder, and Cayenne to your taſte, a large onion ſtuck with cloves, and a ſtick of horſe-radiſh, cover your pan cloſe to keep in the ſteam, let them ſtew gently over a ſtove fire till your gravy is reduced to juſt enough to cover your fiſh in the diſh; then take the fiſh out and put them on the diſh you intend for table, ſet the gravy on the fire and thicken it with flour and a large lump of butter, boil it a little and ſtrain it over your fiſh. Garniſh them with pickled muſhrooms and ſcraped horſe-radiſh, put a bunch of pickled barberries or a ſprig of myrtle in their mouths, and ſend them to the table.

It is a top diſh for a grand entertainment.

To fry Tench.

SLIME your tenches, ſlit the ſkin along the backs, and with the point of your knife raiſe it up from the bone, then cut the ſkin acroſs at the head and tail, then ſtrip it off and take out the bone; then take another tench or carp and mince the fleſh ſmall with muſhrooms, cives, and parſley; ſeaſon them with ſalt, pepper, beaten mace, nutmeg, and a few ſavoury herbs minced ſmall; mingle all theſe well together, then pound them in a mortar, with crumbs of bread as much as two eggs ſoaked in cream, the yolks of three or four eggs, and a piece of butter; when theſe have been well pounded, ſtuff the tenches with this ſauce: take clarified butter and put it in a pan ſet over the fire, when it is hot flour your tenches, and put them into the pan one by one and fry them brown; then take them up, lay them in a coarſe cloth before the fire to keep hot; in the mean time pour all the greaſe and fat out of the pan, put in a quarter of a pound of butter, ſhake ſome flour all over the pan, keep ſtirring with a ſpoon till the butter is a little brown; then pour in half a pint of white wine, ſtir it together, pour in half a pint of boiling water, an onion ſtuck with cloves, a bundle of ſweet herbs, and two blades of mace; cover them cloſe and let them ſtew as ſoftly as you can for a quarter of an hour; then ſtrain off the liquor, put it into the pan again, add two ſpoonfuls of catchup, have ready an ounce of truffles or morels boiled in half a pint of water tender, pour in truffles, water, and all into the pan, a few muſhrooms, and either half a pint of oyſters clean waſhed in their own liquor and the liquor and all put into the pan, or ſome craw-fiſh; but then you muſt put in the tails, and after clean picking them boil them in half a pint of water, then ſtrain the liquor and put into the ſauce; or take ſome fiſh-melts and toſs up in your ſauce. All this is as you fancy.

When you find your ſauce is very good put your tench into the pan, make them quite hot, then lay them into your diſh and pour the ſauce over them. Garniſh with lemon.

Or you may, for change, put in half a pint of ſtale beer inſtead of water. You may dreſs tench juſt as you do carp.

To roaſt a Cod's Head.

WASH it very clean and ſcore it with a knife, ſtrew a little ſalt on it, and lay it in a ſtew-pan before the fire, with ſomething behind it that the fire may roaſt it; all the water that comes from it the firſt half hour throw away, then throw on it a little nutmeg, cloves, mace beat fine, and ſalt; flour it and baſte it with butter; when this has lain ſome time, turn and ſeaſon it, and baſte the other ſide the ſame; turn it often, then baſte it with

with butter and crumbs of bread: if it is a large head it will take four or five hours roasting; have ready some melted butter with an anchovy, some of the liver of the fish boiled and bruised fine; mix it well with the butter and two yolks of eggs beat fine and mixed with the butter, then strain them through a sieve and put them into the sauce-pan again with a few shrimps or pickled cockles, two spoonfuls of red wine and the juice of a lemon; pour it into the pan the head was roasted in and stir it all together, pour it into the sauce-pan, keep it stirring, and let it boil; pour it into a bason. Garnish the head with fried fish, lemon, and scraped horse-radish. If you have a large tin oven it will do better.

To boil a Cod's Head.

SET a fish-kettle on the fire with water enough to boil it, a good handful of salt, a pint of vinegar, a bundle of sweet herbs, and a piece of horse-radish; let it boil a quarter of an hour, then put in the head, and when you are sure it is enough lift up the fish-plate with the fish on it, set it across the kettle to drain, then lay it in your dish and lay the liver on one side. Garnish with lemon and horse-radish scraped; melt some butter with a little of the fish-liquor, an anchovy, oysters or shrimps, or just what you fancy.

To stew Cod.

CUT your cod into slices an inch thick, lay them in the bottom of a large stew-pan; season them with nutmeg, beaten pepper and salt, a bundle of sweet herbs and an onion, half a pint of white wine, and a quarter of a pint of water, cover it close and let it simmer softly for five or six minutes, then squeeze in the juice of a lemon, put in a few oysters and the liquor strained, a piece of butter as big as an egg, rolled in flour, and a blade or two of mace; cover it close and let it stew softly, shaking the pan often; when it is enough take out the sweet herbs and onion and dish it up, pour the sauce over it and garnish with lemon.

To fricassee Cod.

GET the sounds, blanch them, then make them very clean and cut them into little pieces; if they be dry sounds you must first boil them tender; get some of the roes, blanch them and wash them clean, cut them into round pieces about an inch thick, with some of the livers, an equal quantity of each to make a handsome dish, and a piece of cod (about one pound) in the middle; put them into a stew-pan, season them with a little beaten mace, grated nutmeg, and salt, a little bundle of sweet herbs, an onion, and a quarter of a pint of fish-broth or boiling water;

water; cover them close and let them stew a few minutes, then put in half a pint of red wine, a few oysters with the liquor strained, a piece of butter rolled in flour; shake the pan round and let them stew softly till they are enough, take out the sweet herbs and onion and dish it up. Garnish with lemon. Or you may do them white thus: instead of red wine add white, and a quarter of a pint of cream.

To bake a Cod's Head.

BUTTER the pan you intend to bake it in, make your head very clean, lay it in the pan, put in a bundle of sweet herbs, an onion stuck with cloves, three or four blades of mace, half a large spoonful of black and white pepper, a nutmeg bruised, a quart of water, a little piece of lemon-peel, and a little piece of horse-radish; flour your head, grate a little nutmeg over it, stick pieces of butter all over it, and throw raspings all over that; send it to the oven to bake; when it is enough take it out of that dish and lay it carefully into the dish you intend to serve it up in; set the dish over boiling water and cover it up to keep it hot; in the mean time be quick, pour all the liquor out of the dish it was baked in into a sauce-pan, set it on the fire to boil three or four minutes, then strain it and put to it a gill of red wine, two spoonfuls of catchup, a pint of shrimps, half a pint of oysters or muscles, liquor and all, but first strain it; a spoonful of mushroom-pickle, a quarter of a pound of butter rolled in flour, stir it all together till it is thick and boils; then pour it into the dish, have ready some toast cut three-corner-ways and fried crisp; stick pieces about the head and mouth and lay the rest round the head. Garnish with lemon notched, scraped horse-radish, and parsley crisped in a plate before the fire. Lay one slice of lemon on the head and serve it up hot.

To crimp Cod the Dutch Way.

TAKE a gallon of pump-water and a pound of salt, mix them well together; take your cod whilst alive and cut it in slices of one inch and a half thick, throw it into the salt and water for half an hour; then take it out and dry it well with a clean cloth, flour it and broil it; or have a stew-pan with some pump-water and salt boiling, put in your fish and boil it quick for five minutes; send oyster-sauce, anchovy-sauce, shrimp-sauce, or what sauce you please. Garnish with horse-radish and green parsley.

To broil Cod-Sounds.

YOU must first lay them in hot water a few minutes; take them out and rub them well with salt to take off the skin and black dirt, then they will look white, then put them in water and

and give them a boil. Take them out and flour them well, pepper and ſalt them and broil them; when they are enough lay them in your diſh and pour melted butter and muſtard into the diſh. Broil them whole.

Cod-Sounds broiled with Gravy.

SCALD them in hot water and rub them with ſalt well, blanch them, that is, take off the black dirty ſkin, then ſet them on in cold water, and let them ſimmer till they begin to be tender; take them out and flour them and broil them on a gridiron; in the mean time take a little good gravy, a little muſtard, a little bit of butter rolled in flour, give it a boil, ſeaſon it with pepper and ſalt; lay the ſounds in your diſh and pour your ſauce over them.

To fricaſſee Cod-Sounds.

CLEAN them very well as above, then cut them into little pretty pieces, boil them tender in milk and water, then throw them into a cullender to drain, pour them into a clean ſauce-pan, ſeaſon them with a little beaten mace and grated nutmeg, and a very little ſalt; pour to them juſt cream enough for ſauce and a good piece of butter rolled in flour, keep ſhaking your ſauce-pan round all the time till it is thick enough; then diſh it up and garniſh with lemon.

To broil Crimp-Cod, Salmon, Whiting, or Haddock.

FLOUR it, have a quick clear fire and ſet your gridiron high, broil it of a fine brown, lay it in your diſh, and for ſauce have good melted butter; take a lobſter, bruiſe the ſpawn in the butter, cut the meat ſmall, put all together into the melted butter, make it hot and pour it into your diſh or into baſons. Garniſh with horſe-radiſh and lemon.

To dreſs little Fiſh.

AS to all ſorts of little fiſh, ſuch as ſmelts, roach, &c. they ſhould be fried dry and of a fine brown, and nothing but plain butter. Garniſh with lemon.

And with all boiled fiſh you ſhould put a good deal of ſalt and horſe-radiſh in the water, except mackarel, with which put ſalt, parſley, and fennel, which you muſt chop to put into the butter; and ſome love ſcalded gooſeberries with them; and be ſure to boil your fiſh well, but take great care they do not break.

To broil Mackarel.

CLEAN them, ſplit them down the back, ſeaſon them with pepper and ſalt, ſome parſley and fennel chopped very fine, and flour

flour them; broil them of a fine light brown, put them on a diſh and ſtrainer. Garniſh with parſley; let your ſauce be fennel and butter in a boat.

To broil Mackarel whole.

CUT off their heads, gut them, waſh them clean, pull out the roe at the neck-end, boil it in a little water, then bruiſe it with a ſpoon, beat up the yolk of an egg, with a little nutmeg, a little lemon-peel cut fine, a little thyme, ſome parſley boiled and chopped fine, a little pepper and ſalt, a few crumbs of bread: mix all well together and fill the mackarel; flour it well, and broil it nicely: let your ſauce be plain butter, with a little catchup or walnut-pickle.

Mackarel à la Maitre d'Hotel.

TAKE three mackarel, and wipe them very dry with a clean cloth, cut them down the back from head to tail, but not open them; flour them and broil them nicely; chop a handful of parſley and a handful of green onions very fine, mix them up with butter, and pepper and ſalt; put your mackarel in the diſh, and put the parſley, &c. into the cut in the back, and put them before the fire till the butter is melted. Squeeze the juice of two lemons over them, and ſend them up hot.

To boil Mackarel.

GUT your mackarel and dry them carefully with a clean cloth, then rub them ſlightly over with a little vinegar, and lay them ſtraight on your fiſh-plate (for turning them round often breaks them); put a little ſalt in the water when it boils; put them into your fiſh-pan and boil them gently fifteen minutes, then take them up and drain them well, and put the water that runs from them into a ſauce-pan, with two tea-ſpoonfuls of lemon-pickle, one meat-ſpoonful of walnut-catchup, the ſame of browning, a blade or two of mace, one anchovy, a ſlice of lemon; boil them all together a quarter of an hour, then ſtrain it through a hair-ſieve, and thicken it with flour and butter; ſend it in a ſauce-boat, and parſley-ſauce in another; diſh up your fiſh with the tails in the middle; garniſh it with ſcraped horſe-radiſh and barberries. Or, inſtead of all this ſauce, a little melted butter and fennel and parſley.

To broil Weavers.

GUT them and waſh them clean, dry them in a clean cloth, flour, then broil them, and have melted butter in a cup: they are fine fiſh, and cut as firm as a ſole; but you muſt take care not to hurt yourſelf with the two ſharp bones in the head.

To dress a Jowl of Pickled Salmon.

LAY it in fresh water all night, then lay it in a fish-plate, put it into a large stew-pan, season it with a little whole pepper, a blade or two of mace tied in a coarse muslin-rag, a whole onion, a nutmeg bruised, a bundle of sweet herbs and parsley, a little lemon-peel, put to it three large spoonfuls of vinegar, a pint of white wine, and a quarter of a pound of fresh butter rolled in flour; cover it close and let it simmer over a slow fire for a quarter of an hour, then carefully take up your salmon and lay it in your dish; set it over hot water and cover it; in the mean time let your sauce boil till it is thick and good; take out the spice, onion, and sweet herbs, and pour it over the fish. Garnish with lemon.

To broil Salmon.

CUT fresh salmon into thick pieces, flour them and broil them, lay them in your dish, and have plain melted butter in a cup; or anchovy and butter.

Baked Salmon.

TAKE a little piece cut into slices about an inch thick, butter the dish that you would serve it to table on, lay the slices in the dish, take off the skin, and make a force-meat thus: take the flesh of an eel, the flesh of a salmon, an equal quantity, beat in a mortar, season it with beaten pepper, salt, nutmeg, two or three cloves, some parsley, a few mushrooms, a piece of butter, and ten or a dozen coriander-seeds beat fine; beat all together, boil the crumb of a halfpenny-roll in milk, beat up four eggs, stir it together till it is thick, let it cool and mix it well together with the rest; then mix all together with four raw eggs; on every slice lay this force-meat all over, pour a very little melted butter over them, and a few crumbs of bread, lay a crust round the edge of the dish, and stick oysters round upon it; bake it in an oven, and when it is of a very fine brown serve it up; pour a little plain butter (with a little red wine in it) into the dish, and the juice of a lemon: or you may bake it in any dish, and when it is enough lay the slices into another dish; pour the butter and wine into the dish it was baked in; give it a boil, and pour it into the dish. Garnish with lemon. This is a fine dish: squeeze the juice of a lemon in.

To dress Salmon au Court Bouillon.

AFTER having washed and made your salmon very clean, score the side pretty deep that it may take the seasoning; take a quarter of an ounce of mace, a quarter of an ounce of cloves, a nutmeg, a nutmeg, dry them and beat them fine, a quarter of an ounce of black pepper beat fine, and an ounce of ſalt; lay the ſalmon in a napkin, ſeaſon it well with this ſpice, cut ſome lemon-peel fine, and parſley, throw all over, and in the notches put about a pound of freſh butter rolled in flour, roll it up tight in the napkin, and bind it about with packthread; put it in a fiſh-kettle juſt big enough to hold it; pour in a quart of white wine, a quart of vinegar, and as much water as will juſt boil it; ſet it over a quick fire, cover it cloſe; when it is enough (which you muſt judge by the bigneſs of your ſalmon), ſet it over a ſtove to ſtew till you are ready; then have a clean napkin folded in the diſh it is to lay in, turn it out of the napkin it was boiled in, on the other napkin. Garniſh the diſh with a good deal of parſley criſped before the fire.

For ſauce have nothing but plain butter in a cup, or horſe-radiſh and vinegar. Serve it up for a firſt courſe.

To dreſs Salmon à la Braiſe.

TAKE a fine large piece of ſalmon, or a large ſalmon-trout; make a pudding thus; take a large eel, make it clean, ſlit it open, take out the bone, and take all the meat clean from the bone, chop it fine, with two anchovies, a little lemon-peel cut fine, a little pepper, and a grated nutmeg with parſley chopped, and a very little bit of thyme, a few crumbs of bread, the yolk of an hard egg chopped fine; roll it up in a piece of butter, and put it into the belly of the fiſh, ſew it up, lay it in an oval ſtew-pan, or little kettle that will juſt hold it, take half a pound of freſh butter, put it into a ſauce-pan, when it is melted ſhake in a handful of flour, ſtir it till it is a little brown, then pour to it a pint of fiſh-broth, ſtir it together, pour it to the fiſh, with a bottle of white wine; ſeaſon it with ſalt to your palate; put ſome mace, cloves, and whole pepper into a coarſe muſlin rag, tie it, put to the fiſh an onion and a little bundle of ſweet herbs; cover it cloſe, and let it ſtew very ſoftly over a ſlow fire, put in ſome freſh muſhrooms, or pickled ones cut ſmall, an ounce of truffles and morels cut ſmal. let them all ſtew together; when it is enough, take up your ſalmon carefully, lay it in your diſh, and pour the ſauce all over. Garniſh with ſcraped horſe-radiſh and lemon notched, ſerve it up hot: this is a fine diſh for a firſt courſe.

Salmon in Caſes.

CUT your ſalmon into little pieces, ſuch as will lay rolled in half ſheets of paper; ſeaſon it with pepper, ſalt, and nutmeg; butter the inſide of the paper well, fold the paper ſo as nothing can come out, then lay them in a tin-plate to be baked, pour a little

little melted butter over the papers, and then crumbs of bread all over them. Do not let your oven be too hot, for fear of burning the paper: a tin oven before the fire does beſt; when you think they are enough, ſerve them up juſt as they are: there will be ſauce enough in the papers; or put the ſalmon in buttered papers only, and broil them.

To boil Salmon-Crimp.

SCALE your ſalmon, take out the blood, waſh it well and lay it on a fiſh-plate, put your water in a fiſh-pan with a little ſalt; when it boils put in your fiſh for half a minute, then take it out for a minute or two; when you have done it four times, boil it until it be enough; when you take it out of the fiſh-pan, ſet it over the water to drain; cover it well with a clean cloth dipped in hot water; fry ſome ſmall fiſhes, or a few ſlices of ſalmon, and lay round it; garniſh with ſcraped horſe-radiſh and fennel.

To broil Herrings.

SCALE them, gut them, cut off their heads, waſh them clean, dry them in a cloth, flour them and broil them; lay the fiſh in the diſh, in a boat plain melted butter and muſtard: ſend them up hot and hot.

To fry Herrings.

CLEAN them as above, fry them in butter; have ready a good many onions peeled and cut thin; fry them of a light brown with the herrings; lay the herrings in your diſh, and the onions round, butter and muſtard in a cup. You muſt do them with a quick fire.

To bake Herrings.

WHEN you have cleaned your herrings as above, lay them on a board, take a little black and Jamaica pepper, a few cloves, mace, and a good deal of ſalt, mix them together, then rub it all over the fiſh, lay them ſtraight in a pot, cover them with vinegar, tie ſtrong paper over the pot, and bake them in a ſoaking oven; add a few bay-leaves, when cold, ſkim off the fat and fill them up with vinegar: you may eat them either hot or cold. If the vinegar be good they will keep three or four months.

To make Water-Sokey.

TAKE ſome of the ſmalleſt plaice or flounders you can get, waſh them clean, cut the fins cloſe, put them into a ſtew-pan with juſt water enough to boil them, a little ſalt, and a bunch of parſley; when they are enough ſend them to table in a ſoup-diſh, with the liquor to keep them hot; have parſley and butter in a cup.

To dreſs Flat Fiſh.

IN dreſſing all ſorts of flat fiſh, take great care in the boiling of them; be ſure to have them enough, but do not let them be broke; mind to put a good deal of ſalt and horſe-radiſh in the water, let your fiſh be well drained, and mind to cut the fins off: when you fry them let them be well drained in a cloth, and floured, and fry them of a fine light brown either in oil or butter; if there be any water in your diſh with the boiled fiſh, take it out with a ſpunge: as to your fried fiſh, a coarſe cloth is the beſt thing to drain it on.

To dreſs Salt Fiſh.

OLD ling (which is the beſt ſort of ſalt fiſh) lay in water twelve hours, then lay it twelve hours on a board, and then twelve more in water; when you boil it, put it into the water cold; if it is good, it will take about fifteen minutes boiling ſoftly: boil parſnips very tender, ſcrape them, and put them into a ſauce-pan, put to them ſome milk, ſtir them till thick, then ſtir in a good piece of butter and a little ſalt; when they are enough lay them in a plate, the fiſh by itſelf dry, and butter and hard eggs chopped in a baſon.

Water-cod need only be boiled and well ſkimmed.

Scotch haddocks you muſt lay in water all night. You may boil or broil them: if you broil, you muſt ſplit them in two.

You may garniſh your diſhes with hard eggs, parſnips, and potatoes.

The Manner of dreſſing various Sorts of Dried Fiſh, as Stock-Fiſh, Cod, Salmon, Whitings, &c.

The General RULE for ſteeping of Dried Fiſh, the Stock-Fiſh excepted.

ALL the kinds, except ſtock-fiſh, are ſalted, or either dried in the ſun, as the moſt common way, or in prepared kilns, or by the ſmoke of wood-fires in chimney-corners; and, in either caſe, require the being ſoftened and freſhened in proportion to their bulk, their nature, or dryneſs; the very dry ſort, as bacalao, cod-fiſh, or whiting, and ſuch like, ſhould be ſteeped in lukewarm milk and water: the ſteeping kept as near as poſſible to an equal degree of heat. The larger fiſh ſhould be ſteeped twelve hours; the ſmall, as whiting, &c. about two; the cod are therefore laid to ſteep in the evening, the whitings, &c. in the morning before they are to be dreſſed; after the time of ſteeping, they are to be taken out, and hung up by the tails until they are dreſſed; the reaſon of hanging them up is, that they ſoften equally as in the ſteeping, without extracting too

too much of the relish, which would make them insipid; when thus prepared, the small fish, as whiting, tusk, and such like, are floured and laid on the gridiron, and when a little hardened on the one side, must be turned and basted with oil upon a feather; and when basted on both sides, and well hot through, taken up, always observing that as sweet oil supples and supplies the fish with a kind of artificial juices, so the fire draws out those juices, and hardens them; therefore be careful not to let them broil too long; no time can be prescribed, because of the difference of fires, and various bigness of the fish. A clear charcoal-fire is much the best, and the fish kept at a good distance to broil gradually: the best way to know when they are enough is, they will swell a little in the basting, and you must not let them fall again.

The sauces are the same as usual to salt fish; and garnish with oysters fried in batter.

But for a supper, for those that like sweet oil, the best sauce is oil, vinegar, and mustard, beat up to a consistence, and served up in saucers.

If boiled, as the great fish usually are, it should be in milk and water, but not so properly boiled as kept just simmering over an equal fire; in which way, half an hour will do the largest fish, and five minutes the smallest. Some people broil both sorts after simmering, and some pick them to pieces, and then toss them up in a pan with fried onions and apples.

They are either way very good, and the choice depends on the weak or strong stomachs of the eaters.

Dried Salmon must be differently managed:

For though a large fish they do not require more steeping than a whiting; and when laid on the gridiron, should be moderately peppered.

The Dried Herring;

Instead of milk and water, should be steeped the like time as the whiting in small-beer; and to which, as to all kinds of broiled salt fish, sweet oil will always be found the best basting, and no ways affect even the delicacy of those who do not love oil.

Stock-Fish,

Are very different from those before mentioned; they being dried in the frost without salt, are in their kind very insipid, and are only eatable by the ingredients that make them so, and the art of Cookery: they should be first beat with a sledge-hammer on an iron anvil, or on a very solid smooth oaken block; and when reduced almost to atoms, the skin and bones taken away, and the remainder of the fish steeped in milk and warm water until very soft; then strained out, and put into a soup-dish with new milk, powdered cinnamon, mace, and nutmeg, the chief part cinnamon; a paste round the edge of the dish, and put in a temperate oven to simmer for about an hour, and then served up in the place of pudding.

N. B. The Italians eat the skin boiled, either hot or cold, and most usually with oil and vinegar, preferring the skin to the body of the fish.

To stew Eels.

SKIN, gut, and wash them very clean in six or eight waters, to wash away all the sand; then cut them in pieces, about as long as your finger, put just water enough for sauce, put in a small onion stuck with cloves, a little bundle of sweet herbs, a blade or two of mace, and some whole pepper in a thin muslin-rag: cover it close, and let them stew very softly.

Look at them now and then, put in a little piece of butter rolled in flour, and a little chopped parsley: when you find they are quite tender and well done, take out the onion, spice, and sweet herbs: put in salt enough to season it; then dish them up with the sauce.

To stew Eels with Broth.

CLEANSE your eels as above; put them into a sauce-pan with a blade or two of mace and a crust of bread; put just water enough to cover them close, and let them stew very softly: when they are enough, dish them up with the broth, and have a little plain melted butter and parsley in a cup to eat the eels with. The broth will be very good, and it is fit for weakly and consumptive constitutions.

To stew Eels excellently.

SKIN and clean the eel, cut it to pieces, stew it in just as much water as will cover it, an onion stuck with cloves, a bundle of sweet herbs, whole pepper, a blade of mace, and a little salt; cover it close, and when it begins to simmer put in red wine to your taste and let it stew till tender, then strain it; add a piece of butter the size of a walnut, rolled in flour, giving it a quick boil; pour out the sauce to the quantity you want, with wine. Garnish with lemon.

To dress Lampreys.

THE best of this sort of fish is taken in the river Severn; and, when they are in season, the fishmongers and others in London have them from Gloucester: but if you are where they are to be had fresh, you may dress them as you please.

To

To fry Lampreys.

BLEED them and ſave the blood, then waſh them in hot water to take off the ſlime, and cut them to pieces; fry them in a little freſh butter not quite enough, pour out the fat, put in a little white wine, give the pan a ſhake round, ſeaſon it with whole pepper, nutmeg, ſalt, ſweet herbs, and a bay-leaf, put in a few capers, a good piece of butter rolled up in flour, and the blood; give the pan a ſhake round often, and cover them cloſe; when you think they are enough take them out, ſtrain the ſauce, then give them a boil quick, ſqueeze in a little lemon and pour over the fiſh. Garniſh with lemon; and dreſs them juſt what way you fancy.

To pitchcock Eels.

TAKE a large eel and ſcour it well with ſalt to clean off all the ſlime; then ſlit it down the back, take out the bone, and cut it in three or four pieces; take the yolk of an egg and put over the inſide, ſprinkle crumbs of bread, with ſome ſweet herbs and parſley chopped very fine, a little nutmeg grated, and ſome pepper and ſalt, mixed all together; then put it on a grid-iron over a clear fire, broil it of a fine light brown, diſh it up, and garniſh with raw parſley and horſe radiſh; or put a boiled eel in the middle and the pitchcocked round. Garniſh as above with anchovy-ſauce, and parſley and butter in a boat.

To fry Eels.

MAKE them very clean, cut them into pieces, ſeaſon them with pepper and ſalt, flour them and fry them in butter; let your ſauce be plain melted butter, with the juice of lemon. Be ſure they be well drained from the fat before you lay them in the diſh.

To broil Eels.

TAKE a large eel, ſkin it and make it clean; open the belly, cut it into four pieces; take the tail end and ſtrip off the fleſh, beat it in a mortar, ſeaſon it with a little beaten mace, a little grated nutmeg, pepper and ſalt, a little parſley and thyme, a little lemon-peel, an equal quantity of crumbs of bread, roll it in a little piece of butter; then mix it again with the yolk of an egg, roll it up again, and fill the three pieces of belly with it; cut the ſkin of the eel, wrap the pieces in, and ſew up the ſkin; broil them well, have butter and an anchovy for ſauce, with the juice of a lemon. Or you may turn them round, and run a ſkewer through them, and broil them whole.

To farce Eels with White Sauce.

SKIN and clean your eels well, pick off all the fleſh clean from the bone, which you muſt leave whole to the head; take the fleſh, cut it ſmall and beat it in a mortar; then take half the quantity of crumbs of bread, beat it with the fiſh, ſeaſon it with nutmeg and beaten pepper, an anchovy, a good deal of parſley chopped fine, a few truffles boiled tender in a very little water, chop them fine, put them into the mortar with the liquor and a few muſhrooms: beat it well together, mix in a little cream, then take it out and mix it well together in your hand, lay it round the bone in the ſhape of the eel, lay it on a buttered pan, dredge it well with fine crumbs of bread, and bake it: when it is done, lay it carefully in your diſh; have ready half a pint of cream, a quarter of a pound of freſh butter, ſtir it one way till it is thick, pour it over your eels, and garniſh with lemon.

To dreſs Eels with Brown Sauce.

SKIN and clean a large eel very well, cut it in pieces, put it into a ſauce-pan or ſtew-pan, put to it a quarter of a pint of water, a bundle of ſweet herbs, an onion, ſome whole pepper, a blade of mace, and a little ſalt: cover it cloſe, and when it begins to ſimmer, put in a gill of red wine, a ſpoonful of muſh-room-pickle, a piece of butter as big as a walnut, rolled in flour; cover it cloſe, and let it ſtew till it is enough, which you will know by the eel being very tender: take up your eel, lay it in a diſh: you muſt make ſauce according to the largeneſs of your eel, more or leſs. Garniſh with lemon.

To dreſs a Pike.

SCALE and gut your pike, and waſh it very clean, then make a ſtuffing in the following manner: take the crumb of a penny loaf ſoaked in cream, a quarter of a pound of butter, an anchovy chopped fine, a handful of parſley, and a little ſweet herbs chopped fine; the liver or roe of the fiſh bruiſed, a little lemon-peel chopped fine, a little grated nutmeg, ſome pepper and ſalt, the yolks of two eggs; mix all together, and put it in the belly of your fiſh; ſew it up, and then make it in the form of an S; rub the yolk of an egg over, grate ſome nutmeg on it, and ſtrew ſome crumbs of bread on it; put ſome butter here and there on it; put it on an iron plate, and bake it, or roaſt it before the fire in a tin-oven; for ſauce, good an-chovies and butter, and plain melted butter. Garniſh with horſe-radiſh and barberries, or you may boil it without the ſtuffing.

To broil Haddocks, when they are in high Seaſon.

SCALE them, gut and waſh them clean; do not rip open their bellies, but take the guts out with the gills; dry them in a clean cloth very well: if there be any roe or liver take it out, but put it in again; flour them well, and have a clear good fire: let your gridiron be hot and clean, lay them on, turn them quick two or three times for fear of ſticking; then let one ſide be enough, and turn the other ſide: when that is done, lay them in a diſh, and have plain butter in a cup, or anchovy and butter.

They eat finely ſalted a day or two before you dreſs them, and hung up to dry, or boiled with egg-ſauce. Newcaſtle is a famous place for ſalted haddocks: they come in barrels, and keep a great while. Or you may make a ſtuffing the ſame as for the pike, and broil them.

To dreſs Haddocks after the Spaniſh Way.

TAKE a haddock, waſhed very clean and dried, and boil it nicely; then take a quarter of a pint of oil in a ſtew-pan, ſeaſon it with mace, cloves, and nutmeg, pepper and ſalt, two cloves of garlic (ſome love apples when in ſeaſon), a little vinegar; put in the fiſh, cover it cloſe, and let it ſtew half an hour over a ſlow fire.

Flounders done the ſame way are very good.

To dreſs Haddocks the Jews Way.

TAKE two large fine haddocks, waſh them very clean, cut them in ſlices about three inches thick, and dry them in a cloth; take a gill either of oil or butter in a ſtew-pan, a middling onion cut ſmall, a handful of parſley waſhed and cut ſmall; let it juſt boil up in either butter or oil, then put in the fiſh; ſeaſon it with beaten mace, pepper, and ſalt, half a pint of ſoft water; let it ſtew ſoftly till it is thoroughly done; then take the yolks of two eggs, beat up with the juice of a lemon, and juſt as it is done enough, throw it over, and ſend it to table.

To roaſt a Piece of freſh Sturgeon.

GET a piece of freſh ſturgeon of about eight or ten pounds, let it lay in water and ſalt ſix or eight hours, with its ſcales on; then faſten it on the ſpit, and baſte it well with butter for a quarter of an hour, then with a little flour, grate a nutmeg all over it, a little mace and pepper beaten fine, and ſalt thrown over it, and a few ſweet herbs dried and powdered fine, and then crumbs of bread; then keep baſting a little, and dredging with crumbs of bread and with what falls from it, till it is

 enough:

enough: in the mean time prepare this ſauce; take a pint of water, an anchovy, a little piece of lemon-peel, an onion, a bundle of ſweet herbs, mace, cloves, whole pepper black and white, a little piece of horſe-radiſh; cover it cloſe, let it boil a quarter of an hour, then ſtrain it, put it into the ſauce-pan again, pour in a pint of white wine, about a dozen of oyſters and the liquor, two ſpoonfuls of catchup, two of walnut-pickle, the inſide of a crab bruiſed fine, or lobſter, ſhrimps, or prawns, a good piece of butter rolled in flour, a ſpoonful of muſhroom-pickle, or juice of lemon; boil all together; when your fiſh is enough, lay it in your diſh, and pour the ſauce over it. Garniſh with fried toaſts and lemon.

To roaſt a Fillet or Collar of Sturgeon.

TAKE a piece of freſh ſturgeon, ſcale it, gut it, take out the bones, and cut it in lengths about ſeven or eight inches; then provide ſome ſhrimps and oyſters chopped ſmall, an equal quantity of crumbs of bread, and a little lemon-peel grated, ſome nutmeg, a little beaten mace, a little pepper and chopped parſley, a few ſweet herbs, an anchovy, mix them together; when this is done, butter one ſide of your fiſh, and ſtrew ſome of your mixture upon it; then begin to roll it up as cloſe as poſſible, and when the firſt piece is rolled up, roll upon that another, prepared in the ſame manner, and bind it round with a narrow fillet, leaving as much of the fiſh apparent as may be; but you muſt mind that the roll is not above four inches and a half thick, or elſe one part will be done before the inſide is warm; therefore we often parboil the inſide roll before we roll it: when it is enough, lay it in your diſh, and prepare ſauce as above. Garniſh with lemon.

To boil Sturgeon.

CLEAN your ſturgeon, and prepare as much liquor as will juſt boil it: to two quarts of water, a pint of vinegar, a ſtick of horſe-radiſh, two or three bits of lemon-peel, ſome whole pepper, a bay-leaf, add a ſmall handful of ſalt; boil your fiſh in this, and ſerve it with the following ſauce: melt a pound of butter, diſſolve an anchovy in it, put in a blade or two of mace, bruiſe the body of a crab in the butter, a few ſhrimps or crawfiſh, a little catchup, a little lemon-juice; give it a boil, drain your fiſh well, and lay it in your diſh. Garniſh with fried oyſters, ſliced lemon, and ſcraped horſe-radiſh; pour your ſauce into boats or baſons. So you may fry it, ragoo it, or bake it.

To Crimp Skate.

CUT it into long ſlips croſs-ways, about an inch broad, and put it into ſpring-water and ſalt, as above; then have ſpring-water and falt boiling, put it in, and boil it fifteen minutes. Shrimp-fauce, or what fauce you like.

To fricaffee Skate or Thornback white.

CUT the meat clean from the bone, fins, &c. and make it very clean; cut it into little pieces, about an inch broad and two inches long, lay it in your ftew-pan: to a pound of the fifh put a quarter of a pint of water, a little beaten mace, and grated nutmeg, a little bundle of fweet herbs, and a little falt; cover it, and let it boil fifteen minutes: take out the fweet herbs, put in a quarter of a pint of good cream, a piece of butter as big as a walnut, rolled in flour, a glafs of white wine, keep fhaking the pan all the while one way, till it is thick and fmooth; then difh it up, and garnifh with lemon.

To fricaffee it brown.

TAKE your fifh as above, flour it, and fry it of a fine brown in frefh butter; then take it up, lay it before the fire to keep warm, pour the fat out of the pan, fhake in a little flour, and with a fpoon ftir in a piece of butter as big as an egg; ftir it round till it is well mixed in the pan, then pour in a quarter of a pint of water, ftir it round, fhake in a very little beaten pepper, a little beaten mace; put in an onion, and a little bundle of fweet herbs, an anchovy, fhake it round and let it boil; then pour in a quarter of a pint of red wine, a fpoonful of catchup, a little juice of lemon, ftir it all together, and let it boil: when it is enough, take out the fweet herbs and onion, and put in the fifh to heat. Then difh it up, and garnifh with lemon.

To fricaffee Soals white.

SKIN, wafh, and gut your foals very clean, cut off their heads, dry them in a cloth, then with your knife very carefully cut the flefh from the bones and fins on both fides; cut the flefh longways and then acrofs, fo that each foal will be in eight pieces: take the heads and bones and put them into a fauce-pan with a pint of water, a bundle of fweet herbs, an onion, a little whole pepper, two or three blades of mace, a little falt, a very little piece of lemon-peel and a little cruft of bread: cover it clofe, let it boil till half is wafted, then ftrain it through a fine fieve, put it into a ftew-pan, put in the foals and half a pint of white wine, a little parfley chopped fine, a few mufhrooms cut fmall, a piece of butter as big as a hen's egg, rolled in flour, grate in a little nutmeg, fet all together on the fire, but keep fhaking the pan all the while till the fifh is enough. Then difh it up and garnifh with lemon.

To fricassee Soals brown.

CLEANSE and cut your soals, boil the water as in the foregoing receipt, flour your fish and fry them in fresh butter of a fine light brown. Take the flesh of a small soal, beat it in a mortar, with a piece of bread as big a hen's egg, soaked in cream, the yolks of two hard eggs and a little melted butter, a little bit of thyme, a little parsley, an anchovy, season it with nutmeg, mix all together with the yolk of a raw egg, and with a little flour, roll it up into little balls and fry them, but not too much; then lay your fish and balls before the fire, pour all the fat out of the pan, pour in the liquor which is boiled with the spice and herbs, stir it round the pan, then put in half a pint of red wine, a few truffles and morels, a few mushrooms, a spoonful of catchup, and the juice of half a small lemon: stir in all together and let it boil, then stir in a piece of butter rolled in flour; stir it round, when your sauce is of a fine thickness put in your fish and balls, and when it is hot dish it up, put in the balls, and pour your sauce over it. Garnish with lemon. In the same manner dress a small turbot, or any flat fish.

To boil Soals.

TAKE a pair of soals, make them clean, lay them in vinegar, salt, and water two hours; then dry them in a cloth, put them into a stew-pan, put to them a pint of white wine, a bundle of sweet herbs, an onion stuck with six cloves, some whole pepper and a little salt; cover them and let them boil: when they are enough, take them up, lay them in your dish, strain the liquor, and thicken it with butter and flour; pour the sauce over, and garnish with scraped horse-radish and lemon. In this manner dress a little turbot: it is a genteel dish for supper. You may add prawns, or shrimps, or muscles to the sauce.

Another Way to boil Soals.

TAKE three quarts of spring-water and a handful of salt, let it boil; then put in your soals, boil them gently for ten minutes; then dish them up in a clean napkin, with anchovy-sauce or shrimp-sauce in boats.

To make a Collar of Fish in Ragoo, to look like a Breast of Veal collared.

TAKE a large eel, skin it, wash it clean, and parboil it, pick off the flesh, and beat it in a mortar; season it with beaten mace, nutmeg, pepper, salt, a few sweet herbs, parsley, and a little lemon-peel chopped small; beat all well together with an equal quantity of crumbs of bread; mix it well together, then take

take a turbot, ſoals, ſkate, or thornback, or any flat fiſh that will roll cleverly: lay the flat fiſh on the dreſſer, take away all the bones and fins, and cover your fiſh with the farce; then roll it up as tight as you can, and open the ſkin of your eel, and bind the collar with it nicely, ſo that it may be flat top and bottom, to ſtand well in the diſh; then butter an earthen diſh and ſet it in upright; flour it all over, and ſtick a piece of butter on the top and round the edges, ſo that it may run down on the fiſh; and let it be well baked, but take great care it is not broke: let there be a quarter of a pint of water in the diſh.

In the mean time take the water the eel was boiled in, and all the bones of the fiſh, ſet them on to boil, ſeaſon them with mace, cloves, black and white pepper, ſweet herbs, an onion; cover it cloſe, and let it boil till there is about a quarter of a pint; then ſtrain it, add to it a few truffles and morels, a few muſhrooms, two ſpoonfuls of catchup, a gill of red wine, a piece of butter as big a large walnut, rolled in flour: ſtir all together, ſeaſon with ſalt to your palate: ſave ſome of the farce you make of the eel, and mix with the yolk of an egg, and roll them up in little balls with flour, and fry them of a light brown: when your fiſh is enough, lay it in your diſh, ſkim all the fat off the pan, and pour the gravy to your ſauce; let it all boil together till it is thick, then pour it it over the roll, and put in your balls. Garniſh with lemon.

This does beſt in a tin oven before the fire, becauſe then you can baſte it as you pleaſe. It is a fine bottom-diſh.

To butter Crabs or Lobſters.

TAKE two crabs or lobſters, being boiled, and cold, take all the meat out of the ſhells and bodies, mince it ſmall, and put it all together into a ſauce-pan; add to it a glaſs of white wine, two ſpoonfuls of vinegar, a nutmeg grated, then let it boil up till it is thoroughly hot: then have ready half a pound of freſh butter, melted with an anchovy, and the yolks of two eggs beat up and mixed with the butter; then mix crabs and butter all together, ſhaking the ſauce-pan conſtantly round till it is quite hot; then have ready the great ſhell either of a crab or lobſter; lay it in the middle of your diſh, pour ſome into the ſhell, and the reſt in little ſaucers round the ſhell, ſticking three-corner toaſts between the ſaucers and round the ſhell. This is a fine ſide-diſh at a ſecond courſe.

To butter Lobſters another Way.

PARBOIL your lobſters, then break the ſhells, pick out all the meat, cut it ſmall, take the meat out of the body, mix it fine with a ſpoon in a little white wine; for example, a ſmall lobſter, one ſpoonful of wine, put it into a ſauce-pan with the meat of the lobſter, four ſpoonfuls of white wine, a blade of mace, a little beaten pepper and ſalt; let it ſtew all together a few minutes, then ſtir in a piece of butter, ſhake your ſauce-pan round till your butter is melted, put in a ſpoonful of vinegar, and ſtrew in as many crumbs of bread as will make it thick enough: when it is hot, pour it into your plate, and garniſh with the chine of a lobſter cut in four, peppered, ſalted, and broiled. This makes a pretty plate, or a fine diſh, with two or three lobſters. You may add one tea-ſpoonful of fine ſugar to your ſauce.

To roaſt Lobſters.

BOIL your lobſters, then lay them before the fire, and baſte them with butter till they have a fine froth: diſh them up with plain melted butter in a cup. This is as good a way to the full as roaſting them alive, and not half the trouble, not to mention the cruelty.

To make a fine Diſh of Lobſters.

TAKE three lobſters, boil the largeſt as above, and froth it before the fire; take the other two boiled, and butter them as in the foregoing receipt; take the two body-ſhells, heat them hot, and fill them with the buttered meat; lay the large lobſter in the middle, and the two ſhells on each ſide, and the two great claws of the middle lobſter at each end; and the four pieces of chines of the two lobſters broiled and laid on each end. This, if nicely done, makes a pretty diſh.

To dreſs a Crab.

HAVING taken out the meat of a fine large crab, and cleanſed it from the ſkin, put it into a ſtew-pan, with half a pint of white wine, a little nutmeg, pepper, and ſalt over a ſlow fire; throw in a few crumbs of bread, beat up one yolk of an egg with one ſpoonful of vinegar, throw it in, then ſhake the ſauce-pan round a minute, and ſerve it up on a plate.

To ſtew Prawns, Shrimps, or Craw-fiſh.

PICK out the tails about the quantity of two quarts; take the bodies, give them a bruiſe and put them into a pint of white wine, with a blade of mace; let them ſtew a quarter of an hour, ſtir them together, and ſtrain them; then waſh out the ſauce-pan, put to it the ſtrained liquor and tails: grate a ſmall nutmeg in, add a little ſalt, and a quarter of a pound of butter rolled in flour; ſhake it all together, cut a pretty thin toaſt round a quartern loaf, toaſt it brown on both ſides, cut it into ſix pieces, lay it cloſe together in the bottom of your diſh, and pour

pour your fiſh and ſauce over it; ſend it to table hot. If it be craw-fiſh or prawns, garniſh your diſh with ſome of the biggeſt claws laid thick round. Water will do in the room of wine, only add a ſpoonful of vinegar.

Scolloped Oyſters.

PUT them on a gridiron over a good clear fire, let them remain till you think they are enough, then have ready ſome crumbs of bread rubbed in a clean napkin, fill your ſhells and ſet them before a good fire and baſte them with butter; let them be of a fine brown, keeping them turning to be brown all over alike; but a tin does them beſt before the fire. They eat much the beſt done this way, though moſt people ſtew the oyſters firſt in a ſauce-pan, with a blade of mace thickened with a bit of butter, and fill the ſhells, then cover them with crumbs, and brown them with a hot iron; but the bread has not the fine taſte of the former.

To ragoo Oyſters.

TAKE a quart of the largeſt oyſters you can get, open them, ſave the liquor and ſtrain it through a fine ſieve; waſh your oyſters in warm water; make a batter thus: take two yolks of eggs, beat them well, grate in half a nutmeg, cut a little lemon-peel ſmall, a good deal of parſley, a ſpoonful of the juice of ſpinage, two ſpoonfuls of cream or milk, beat it up with flour to a thick batter; have ready ſome butter in a ſtew-pan, dip your oyſters one by one into the batter, and have ready crumbs of bread, then roll them in it and fry them quick and brown; ſome with the crumbs of bread and ſome without; take them out of the pan and ſet them before the fire, then have ready a quart of cheſnuts ſhelled and ſkinned, fry them in the butter; when they are enough take them up, pour the fat out of the pan, ſhake a little flour all over the pan, and rub a piece of butter as big as a hen's egg all over the pan with your ſpoon till it is melted and thick; then put in the oyſter liquor, three or four blades of mace, ſtir it round, put in a few piſtachio nuts ſhelled, let them boil, then put in the cheſnuts and half a pint of white wine; have ready the yolks of two eggs beat up with four ſpoonfuls of cream; ſtir all well together; when it is thick and fine lay the oyſters in the diſh and pour the ragoo over them. Garniſh with cheſnuts and lemon.

You may ragoo muſcles the ſame way. You may leave out the piſtachio nuts if you do not like them, but they give the ſauce a fine flavour.

To fry Oyſters.

TAKE a quarter of an hundred of large oyſters, beat the yolk of two eggs, add a little nutmeg and a blade of mace pounded,

pounded, a ſpoonful of flour and a little ſalt, dip in your oyſters and fry them in hog's-lard a light brown; if you chooſe you may add a little parſley ſhred fine.

N. B. They are a proper garniſh for cod's head, calf's head, or moſt made-diſhes.

To ſtew Oyſters and all ſorts of Shell Fiſh.

WHEN you have opened your oyſters put their liquor into a toſſing-pan with a little beaten mace, thicken it with flour and butter, boil it three or four minutes, toaſt a ſlice of white bread and cut it into three-cornered pieces, lay them round your diſh, put in a ſpoonful of good cream, put in your oyſters and ſhake them round in your pan; you muſt not let them boil, for if they do it will make them hard and look ſmall; ſerve them up in a little ſoup diſh or plate.

N. B. You may ſtew cockles, muſcles, or any ſhell fiſh the ſame way.

To make Oyſter Loaves.

TAKE all the crumbs out of three French rolls, by cutting a piece of the top cruſt off, in ſuch a manner as it may fit again in the ſame place; fry the rolls out of which the crumb has been taken brown in freſh butter; take half a pint of oyſters, ſtew them in their own liquor, then take out the oyſters with a fork, ſtrain the liquor to them, put them into a ſauce-pan again with a glaſs of white wine, a little beaten mace, a little grated nutmeg, a quarter of a pound of butter rolled in flour; ſhake them well together, then put them into the rolls; and theſe make a pretty ſide-diſh for a firſt courſe. You may rub in the crumbs of two of the rolls and toſs up with the oyſters.

To ſtew Muſcles.

WASH them very clean from the ſand in two or three waters, put them into a ſtew-pan, cover them cloſe and let them ſtew till all the ſhells are opened; then take them out one by one, pick them out of the ſhells, and look under the tongue to ſee if there be a crab; if there is, you muſt throw away the muſcle; ſome will only pick out the crab and eat the muſcle, but this is dangerous; when you have picked them all clean put them into a ſauce-pan; to a quart of muſcles put half a pint of the liquor ſtrained through a ſieve, put in a blade or two of mace, a piece of butter as big as a large walnut, rolled in flour; let them ſtew; toaſt ſome bread brown and lay them round the diſh cut three-corner-ways; pour in the muſcles and ſend them to table hot.

Another Way to ſtew Muſcles.

CLEAN and ſtew your muſcles as in the foregoing receipt, only to a quart of muſcles put in a pint of liquor, and a quarter

ter of a pound of butter rolled in a very little flour; when they are enough have ſome crumbs of bread ready, and cover the bottom of your diſh thick, grate half a nutmeg over them, and pour the muſcles and ſauce all over the crumbs and ſend them to table.

A third Way to dreſs Muſcles.

STEW them as above and lay them in your diſh; ſtrew your crumbs of bread thick all over them, then ſet them before a good fire, turning the diſh round and round that they may be brown all alike; keep baſting them with butter that the crumbs may be criſp, and it will make a pretty ſide-diſh. You may do cockles the ſame way.

To ſtew Scollops.

BOIL them very well in ſalt and -ater, take them out and ſtew them in a little of the liquor, a little white wine, a little vinegar, two or three blades of mace, two or three cloves, a piece of butter rolled in flour, and the juice of a Seville orange; ſtew them well and diſh them up.

To grill Shrimps.

SEASON them well with ſalt and pepper, ſhred parſley, butter in ſcollop-ſhells; add ſome grated bread, and let them ſtew for half an hour; brown them with a hot iron and ſerve them up.

Buttered Shrimps.

STEW two quarts of ſhrimps in a pint of white wine with nutmeg; beat up eight eggs with a little white wine and half a pound of butter, ſhaking the ſauce-pan one way all the time over the fire till they are thick enough; lay toaſted ſippets round a diſh and pour them over it; ſo ſerve them up.

To fry Smelts.

LET your ſmelts be freſh caught, wipe them very dry with a cloth, beat up yolks of eggs and rub over them, ſtrew crumbs of bread on; have ſome clear dripping boiling in a frying-pan, and fry them quick of a fine gold colour; put them on a plate to drain, and then lay them in your diſh. Garniſh with fried parſley, with plain butter in a cup.

To dreſs White-bait.

TAKE your white-bait freſh caught and put them in a cloth with a handful of flour, and ſhake them about till they are

ſeparated

ſeparated and quite dry; have ſome hog's lard boiling quick, fry them two minutes, drain them and diſh up with plain butter and ſoy.

CHAP. XI.

SAUCES for FISH.

To make Quins Fiſh-Sauce.

TAKE a quart of walnut-pickle, put to it ſix anchovies with mace, cloves, and whole pepper, ſix bay-leaves, ſix ſhalots, boil them all together till the anchovies are diſſolved, when cold put in half a pint of red wine and bottle it up; when you uſe it give it a ſhake, two ſpoonfuls of this to a little rich melted butter makes good ſauce.

Quins Sauce another Way.

TAKE half a pint of muſhroom-catchup, a quarter of a pint of pickled walnut-liquor, three anchovies, two cloves of garlic pounded, a quarter of a tea-ſpoonful of Cayenne pepper, put all into a bottle and ſhake it well.

Lobſter-Sauce.

TAKE a fine hen lobſter, take out all the ſpawn and bruiſe it on a mortar very fine with a little butter; take all the meat out of the claws and tail and cut it in ſmall ſquare pieces; put the ſpawn and meat in a ſtew-pan with a ſpoonful of anchovy-liquor, and one ſpoonful of catchup, a blade of mace, a piece of a ſtick of horſe-radiſh, half a lemon, a gill of gravy, a little butter rolled in flour, juſt enough to thicken it; put in a ſufficient quantity of butter nicely melted, boil it gently up for ſix or ſeven minutes; take out the horſe-radiſh, mace, and lemon, and ſqueeze the juice of the lemon into the ſauce; juſt ſimmer it up and then put it in your boats.

Shrimp-Sauce.

TAKE half a pint of ſhrimps, waſh them very clean, put them in a ſtew-pan with a ſpoonful of fiſh-lear or anchovy-liquor, butter melted thick, boil it up for five minutes, and ſqueeze in half a lemon; toſs it up and then put it in your cups or boats.

To make Oyster-Sauce for Fish.

TAKE a pint of large oysters, scald them and then strain them through a sieve, wash the oysters very clean in cold water and take the beards off; put them in a stew-pan, pour the liquor over them, but be careful to pour the liquor gently out of the vessel you have strained it into and you will leave all the sediment at the bottom, which you must be careful not to put into your stew-pan; then add a large spoonful of anchovy-liquor, two blades of mace, half a lemon, some butter rolled in flour enough to thicken it; then put in half a pound of butter, boil it up till the butter is melted; then take out the mace and lemon, squeeze the lemon-juice into the sauce, give it a boil up, stir it all the time, and then put it into your boats or basons.

N. B. You may put in a spoonful of catchup or a spoonful of mountain wine.

To make Anchovy-Sauce.

TAKE a pint of gravy, put in an anchovy, take a piece of butter rolled in a little flour, and stir all together till it boils; you may add a little juice of a lemon, catchup, red wine, and walnut-liquor, just as you please.

Plain butter melted thick with a spoonful of walnut-pickle or catchup is good sauce, or anchovy; in short you may put as many things as you fancy into sauce.

To make Dutch Sauce.

TAKE a quarter of a pound of butter, four spoonfuls of water, dredge in a little flour, chop three anchovies and put in with three spoonfuls of good vinegar, a little scraped horse-radish, boil all together and send sent it up immediately, or else it will oil. This sauce is proper to all fresh-water fish.

To make Sauce for a Cod's Head.

TAKE a lobster, if it be alive stick a skewer in the vent of the tail to keep the water out, and throw a handful of salt in the water, when it boils put in the lobster and boil it half an hour; if it has spawn on, pick them off and pound them exceeding fine in a marble mortar, and put them into half a pound of good melted butter, then take the meat out of your lobster, pull it in bits and put it in your butter with a meat spoonful of lemon-pickle and the same of walnut-catchup, a slice of an end of a lemon, one or two slices of horse-radish, as much beaten mace as will lie on a sixpence, salt and Cayenne to your taste, boil them one minute, then take out the horse-radish and lemon, and serve it up in your sauce-boat.

N. B. If you can get no lobster you may make shrimp, cockle, or muscle sauce the same way; if there can be no kind of shell fish got, you then may add two anchovies cut small, a spoonful of walnut-liquor, a large onion stuck with cloves, strain it and put it in the sauce-boat.

To make a very nice Sauce for most Sorts of Fish.

TAKE a little gravy made of either veal or mutton, put to it a little of the water that drains from your fish, when it is boiled enough, put it in a sauce-pan, and put in a whole onion, one anchovy, a spoonful of catchup, and a glass of white wine, thicken it with a good lump of butter rolled in flour and a spoonful of cream; if you have oysters, cockles, or shrimps put them in after you take it off the fire (but it is very good without), you may use red wine instead of white by leaving out the cream.

To make White Fish-Sauce.

WASH two anchovies, put them into a sauce-pan with one glass of white wine and two of water, half a nutmeg grated, and a little lemon-peel; when it has boiled five or six minutes strain it through a sieve, add to it a spoonful of white wine vinegar, thicken it a little, then put in a pound of butter rolled in flour, boil it well and pour it hot upon your fish.

CHAP. XII.

SOUPS and BROTHS.

(Not included in the Lent Chapter on account of their being made with meat; but what Soups are not in this Chapter may be found there.)

Rules to be observed in making Soups and Broths.

FIRST take great care the pots or sauce-pans and covers be very clean and free from all grease and sand, and that they be well tinned, for fear of giving the broths or soups any brassy taste. If you have time to stew as softly as possible, it will both have a finer flavour and the meat will be tenderer; but then observe, when you make soups or broths for present use, if it is to be done softly, do not put much more water than you intend to have soup or broth; and if you have the convenience of an earthen pan or pipkin, set it on wood embers till it boils, then skim it, and put in your seasoning; cover it close and set it on embers, so ſo that it may do very ſoftly for ſome time, and both the meat and broths will be delicious. You muſt obſerve in all broths and ſoups that one thing does not taſte more than another, but that the taſte be equal, and that it has a fine agreeable reliſh, according to what you deſign it for; and you muſt be ſure that all the greens and herbs you put in be cleaned, waſhed, and picked.

To make ſtrong Broth for Soup or Gravy.

TAKE a ſhin of beef, a knuckle of veal, and a ſcrag of mutton, put them in five gallons of water, then let it boil up, ſkim it clean, and ſeaſon it with ſix large onions, four good leeks, four heads of celery, two carrots, two turnips, a bundle of ſweet herbs, ſix cloves, a dozen corns of all-ſpice and ſome ſalt; ſkim it very clean and let it ſtew gently for ſix hours; then ſtrain it off, and put it by for uſe.

When you want very ſtrong gravy, take a ſlice of bacon and lay it in a ſtew-pan; take a pound of beef, cut it thin, lay it on the bacon, ſlice a good piece of carrot in, an onion ſliced, a good cruſt of bread, a few ſweet herbs, a little mace, cloves, nutmeg, whole pepper, and an anchovy; cover it and ſet it on a ſlow fire for five or ſix minutes, and pour in a quart of the above gravy; cover it cloſe, and let it boil ſoftly till half is waſted: this will be a rich, high brown ſauce for fiſh, fowl, or ragoo.

Gravy for White Sauce.

TAKE a pound of any part of the veal, cut it into ſmall pieces, boil it in a quart of water, with an onion, a blade of mace, two cloves, and a few whole pepper-corns; boil it till it is as rich as you would have it.

Gravy for Turkey, Fowl, or Ragoo.

TAKE a pound of lean beef, cut and hack it well, then flour it well, put a piece of butter as big as an hen's egg in a ſtew-pan; when it is melted, put in your beef, fry it on all ſides a little brown, then pour in three pints of boiling water and a bundle of ſweet herbs, two or three blades of mace, three or four cloves, twelve whole pepper-corns, a little bit of carrot, a little piece of cruſt of bread toaſted brown; cover it cloſe, and let it boil till there is about a pint or leſs; then ſeaſon it with ſalt, and ſtrain it off.

Gravy for a Fowl, when you have no Meat nor Gravy ready.

TAKE the neck, liver and gizzard, boil them in half a pint of water, with a little piece of bread toaſted brown, a little pepper and ſalt, and a little bit of thyme; let them boil till there

there is about a quarter of a pint; then pour in half a glaſs of red wine, boil it and ſtrain it, then bruiſe the liver well in and ſtrain it again, thicken it with a little piece of butter rolled in flour, and it will be very good.

An ox's kidney makes good gravy, cut all to pieces and boiled with ſpice, &c. as in the foregoing receipts.

You have a receipt in the beginning of the book, in the preface for Gravies.

Vermicelli Soup.

TAKE three quarts of the broth and one of the gravy mixed together, a quarter of a pound of vermicelli blanched in two quarts of water; put it into the ſoup, boil it up for ten minutes and ſeaſon with ſalt, if it wants any; put it in your tureen, with a cruſt of a French roll baked.

Macaroni Soup.

TAKE three quarts of the ſtrong broth and one of the gravy mixed together; take half a pound of ſmall pipe macaroni and boil it in three quarts of water, with a little butter in it, till it is tender; then ſtrain it through a ſieve, cut it in pieces of about two inches long, put it in your ſoup, and boil it up for ten minutes, and then ſend it to table in a tureen, with the cruſt of a French roll toaſted.

Soup Creſſu.

TAKE a pound of lean ham and cut it into ſmall bits, and put at the bottom of a ſtew-pan, then cut a French roll and put over the ham; take two dozen heads of celery cut ſmall, ſix onions, two turnips, one carrot, cut and waſhed very clean, ſix cloves, four blades of mace, two handfuls of water-creſſes; put them all into the ſtew-pan with a pint of good broth; cover them cloſe, and ſweat it gently for twenty minutes, then fill it up with veal broth, and ſtew it four hours; rub it through a fine ſieve or cloth, put it in your pan again, ſeaſon it with ſalt and a little Cayenne pepper; give it a ſimmer up and ſend it to table hot with ſome French roll toaſted hard in it: boil a handful of creſſes till tender in water, and put in over the bread.

To make Mutton or Veal Gravy.

CUT and hack your meat well; ſet it on the fire with water, ſweet herbs, mace, and pepper: let it boil till it is as good as you would have it, then ſtrain it off. Your fine cooks always (if they can) chop a partridge or two and put into gravies.

To make a ſtrong Fiſh Gravy.

TAKE two or three eels, or any fiſh you have, ſkin or ſcale them, gut them and waſh them from grit, cut them into little pieces,

pieces, put them into a ſauce-pan, cover them with water, a little cruſt of bread toaſted brown, a blade or two of mace and ſome whole pepper, a few ſweet herbs, and a very little bit of lemon-peel: let it boil till it is rich and good, then have ready a piece of butter, according to your gravy, if a pint, as big as a walnut; melt it in the ſauce-pan, then ſhake in a little flour, and toſs it about till it is brown, and then ſtrain in the gravy to it; let it boil a few minutes, and it will be good.

To make Plumb-Porridge for Chriſtmas.

TAKE a leg and ſhin of beef, put them into eight gallons of water, and boil them till they are very tender, and when the broth is ſtrong ſtrain it out; wipe the pot and put in the broth again; then ſlice ſix penny-loaves thin, cut off the top and bottom, put ſome of the liquor to it, cover it up and let it ſtand a quarter of an hour, boil it and ſtrain it, and then put it into your pot; let it boil a quarter of an hour, then put in five pounds of currants, clean waſhed and picked; let them boil a little, and put in five pounds of raiſins of the ſun ſtoned, and two pounds of prunes, and let them boil till they ſwell; then put in three quarters of an ounce of mace, half an ounce of cloves, two nutmegs, all of them beat fine, and mix it with a little liquor cold, and put them in a very little while, and take off the pot, then put in three pounds of ſugar, a little ſalt, a quart of ſack, a quart of claret, and the juice of two or three lemons. You may thicken with ſago inſtead of bread (if you pleaſe); pour them into earthen pans, and keep them for uſe.

To make a ſtrong Broth to keep for Uſe.

TAKE part of a leg of beef and the ſcrag-end of a neck of mutton, break the bones in pieces, and put to it as much water as will cover it, and a little ſalt; and when it boils, ſkim it clean, and put into it a whole onion ſtuck with cloves, a bunch of ſweet herbs, ſome whole pepper, and a nutmeg quartered: let theſe boil till the meat is boiled in pieces, and the ſtrength boiled out of it; ſtrain it out, and keep it for uſe.

A Craw-fiſh Soup.

TAKE a gallon of water and ſet it a-boiling; put in it a bunch of ſweet herbs, three or four blades of mace, an onion ſtuck with cloves, pepper and ſalt; then have about two hundred craw-fiſh, ſave about twenty, then pick the reſt from the ſhells, ſave the tails whole; beat the body and ſhells in a mortar with a pint of peas (green or dry), firſt boiled tender in fair water; put your boiling water to it and ſtrain it boiling hot through a cloth till you have all the goodneſs out of it; ſet it over a ſlow fire or ſtew-hole, have ready a French roll cut very thin, and let it be very dry, put it to your ſoup, let it ſtew till half is waſted, then put a piece of butter as big as an egg into a ſauce-pan, let it ſimmer till it is done making a noiſe, ſhake in two tea-ſpoonfuls of flour, ſtirring it about, and an onion; put in the tails of the fiſh, give them a ſhake round, put to them a pint of good gravy, let it boil four or five minutes ſoftly, take out the onion, and put to it a pint of the ſoup, ſtir it well together, bruiſe the live ſpawn of a hen lobſter and put it all together, and let it ſimmer very ſoftly a quarter of an hour; fry a French roll very nice and brown, and the twenty craw-fiſh; pour your ſoup into the diſh, and lay the roll in the middle and the craw-fiſh round the diſh.

Fine cooks boil a brace of carp and tench, and perhaps a lobſter or two, and many more rich things, to make a craw-fiſh ſoup; but the above is full as good, and wants no addition.

To make Soup-Santea, or Gravy-Soup.

TAKE ſix good raſhers of lean ham, put it in the bottom of a ſtew-pan; then put over it three pounds of lean beef, and over the beef three pounds of lean veal, ſix onions cut in ſlices, two carrots, and two turnips ſliced, two heads of celery, and a bundle of ſweet herbs, ſix cloves, and two blades of mace; put a little water at the bottom, draw it very gently till it ſticks, then put in a gallon of boiling water; let it ſtew for two hours, ſeaſon with ſalt, and ſtrain it off; then have ready a carrot cut in ſmall ſlices of two inches long and about as thick as a gooſe-quill, a turnip, two heads of leeks, two heads of celery, two heads of endive cut acroſs, two cabbage-lettuces cut acroſs, a very little ſorrel and chervil; put them in a ſtew-pan and ſweat them for fifteen minutes gently, then put them in your ſoup, boil it up gently for ten minutes; put it in your tureen with the cruſt of a French roll.

N. B. You may boil the herbs in two quarts of water for ten minutes (if you like them beſt ſo); your ſoup will be the clearer; or you may take one quart of the broth, page 177, and one of the fowling gravy, and boil the herbs that are cut fine in it for a quarter of an hour.

A Green Peas Soup.

TAKE a knuckle of veal and one pound of lean ham, cut them in thin ſlices, lay the ham at the bottom of a ſoup-pot, the veal upon the ham; then cut ſix onions in ſlices and put on, two or three turnips, two carrots, three heads of celery cut ſmall, a little thyme, four cloves, and four blades of mace;

put

put a little water at the bottom, cover the pot close, and draw it gently but do not let it stick; then put in six quarts of boiling water, let it stew gently for four hours, and skim it well; take two quarts of green peas and stew them in some of the broth till tender; then strain them off, and put them in a marble mortar, and beat them fine, put the liquor in, and mix them up (if you have no mortar, you must bruise them in the best manner you can): take a tammy or a fine cloth and rub them through till you have rubbed all the pulp out, and then put your soup in a clean pot, with half a pint of spinage-juice, and boil it up for fifteen minutes; season with salt and a little pepper: if your soup is not thick enough, take the crumb of a French roll and boil it in a little of the soup, beat it in the mortar and rub it through your tammy cloth, then put it in your soup and boil it up; then put it in your tureen, with dice of bread toasted very hard.

Another Way to make Green Peas Soup.

TAKE a gallon of water, make it boil, then put in six onions, four turnips, two carrots, and two heads of celery cut in slices, four cloves, four blades of mace, four cabbage-lettuces cut small; stew them for an hour; then strain it off, and put in two quarts of old green peas and boil them in the liquor till tender; then beat or bruise them and mix them up with the broth, and rub them through a tammy or cloth, and put it in a clean pot, with half a pint of spinage-juice, and boil it up fifteen minutes, season with pepper and salt to your liking; then put your soup in your tureen, with small dice of bread toasted very hard.

A Peas-Soup for Winter.

TAKE about four pounds of lean beef, cut it in small pieces, about a pound of lean bacon, or pickled pork, set it on the fire with two gallons of water, let it boil, and skim it well; then put in six onions, two turnips, one carrot, and four heads of celery cut small, and put in a quart of split peas, boil it gently for three hours, then strain them through a sieve, and rub the peas well through; then put your soup in a clean pot, and put in some dried mint rubbed very fine to powder, cut the white of four heads of celery, and two turnips in dice, and boil them in a quart of water for fifteen minutes; then strain them off, and put them in your soup; take about a dozen of small rashers of bacon fried, and put them into your soup, season with pepper and salt to your liking, boil it up for fifteen minutes; then put it in your tureen, with dice of bread fried very crisp.

Another Way to make it.

WHEN you boil a leg of pork, or a good piece of beef, ſave the liquor; when it is cold take off the fat; the next day boil a leg of mutton, ſave the liquor, and when it is cold take off the fat, ſet it on the fire, with two quarts of peas; let them boil till they are tender, then put in the pork or beef liquor, with the ingredients as above, and let it boil till it is as thick as you would have it, allowing for the boiling again; then ſtrain it off, and add the ingredients as above. You may make your ſoup of veal or mutton gravy (if you pleaſe), that is according to your fancy.

A Cheſnut Soup.

TAKE half a hundred of cheſnuts, pick them, put them in an earthen pan, and ſet them in the oven half an hour, or roaſt them gently over a ſlow fire, but take care they do not burn; then peel them, and ſet them to ſtew in a quart of good beef, veal, or mutton broth, till they are quite tender; in the mean time, take a piece or ſlice of ham, or bacon, a pound of veal, a pigeon beat to pieces, a bundle of ſweet herbs, an onion, a little pepper and mace, and a piece of carrot; lay the bacon at the bottom of a ſtew-pan, and lay the meat and ingredients at top; ſet it over a ſlow fire till it begins to ſtick to the pan, then put in a cruſt of bread, and pour in two quarts of broth; let it boil ſoftly till one third is waſted, then ſtrain it off, and add to it the cheſnuts; ſeaſon it with ſalt, and let it boil till it is well taſted, ſtew two pigeons in it, and fry a French roll criſp; lay the roll in the middle of the diſh, and the pigeons on each ſide; pour in the ſoup, and ſend it away hot.

Hare Soup.

TAKE and cut a large hare into pieces, and put it into an earthen mug, with three blades of mace, two large onions, a little ſalt, a red herring, half a dozen large morels, a pint of red wine, and three quarts of water; bake it three hours in a quick oven, and then ſtrain it into a ſtew-pan; have ready boiled four ounces of French barley, and put in; juſt ſcald the liver and rub it through a ſieve with a wooden ſpoon; put it into the ſoup, ſet it over the fire, and keep it ſtirring, but it muſt not boil: ſend it up with criſp bread in it.

Soup à la Reine.

TAKE a pound of lean ham and cut it ſmall, and put it at the bottom of a ſoup-pot; cut a knuckle of veal into pieces and put in, and an old fowl cut in pieces; put three blades of mace, four onions, ſix heads of celery, two turnips, one carrot, a bundle

bundle of ſweet herbs waſhed clean; put in half a pint of water, and cover it cloſe, and ſweat it gently for half an hour, but be careful it does not burn, for that will ſpoil it; then pour in boiling water enough to cover it, and let it ſtew till all the goodneſs is out, then ſtrain it into a clean pan, and let it ſtand half an hour to ſettle, then ſkim it well, and pour it off the ſettlings into a clean pan; boil half a pint of cream and pour upon the crumb of a halfpenny roll, and let it ſoak well; take half a pound of almonds, blanch them and beat them in a mortar as fine as you can, putting now and then a little cream to keep them from oiling; take the yolks of ſix hard eggs and the roll and cream, and put to the almonds, and beat them up together in your broth; rub it through a fine hair ſieve or cloth till all the goodneſs is rubbed through, and put it into a ſtew-pan; keep ſtirring it till it boils, and ſkim off the froth as it riſes; ſeaſon with ſalt, and then pour it into your tureen, with three ſlices of French roll criſped before the fire.

To make Mutton-Broth.

TAKE a neck of mutton about ſix pounds, cut it in two, boil the ſcrag in a gallon of water, ſkim it well, then put in a little bundle of ſweet herbs, an onion, and a good cruſt of bread: let it boil an hour, then put in the other part of the mutton, take a turnip or two, ſome dried marigolds, a few cives chopped fine, a little parſley chopped ſmall, put theſe in about a quarter of an hour before your broth is enough; ſeaſon it with ſalt; or you may put in a quarter of a pound of barley or rice at firſt. Some love it thickened with oatmeal and ſome with bread, and ſome love it ſeaſoned with mace, inſtead of ſweet herbs and onion; all this is fancy and different palates. If you boil turnips for ſauce, do not boil all in the pot, it makes the broth too ſtrong of them, but boil them in a ſauce-pan.

Beef-Broth.

TAKE a leg of beef, crack the bone in two or three parts, waſh it clean, put it into a pot with a gallon of water, ſkim it well, then put in two or three blades of mace, a little bundle of parſley, and a good cruſt of bread; let it boil till the beef is quite tender, and the ſinews; toaſt ſome bread and cut it in dice, and put it in your tureen; lay in the meat, and pour the ſoup in.

To make Scotch Barley-Broth.

TAKE a leg of beef, chop it all to pieces, boil it in three gallons of water with a piece of carrot and a cruſt of bread, till it is half boiled away; then ſtrain it off, and put it into the pot again with half a pound of barley, four or five heads of celery washed clean and cut small, a large onion, a bundle of sweet herbs, a little parsley chopped small, and a few marigolds; let this boil an hour: take a cock or a large fowl clean picked and washed, and put into the pot, boil it till the broth is quite good, then season with salt, and send it to table with the fowl in the middle. This broth is very good without the fowl. Take out the onion and sweet herbs before you send it to table.

Some make this broth with a sheep's head instead of a leg of beef, and it is very good; but you must chop the head all to pieces. The thick flank (about six pounds to six quarts of water) makes good broth; then put the barley in with the meat, first skim it well, boil it an hour very softly, then put in the above ingredients with turnips and carrots clean scraped and pared and cut into little pieces; boil all together softly till the broth is very good; then season it with salt, and send it to table with the beef in the middle, turnips and carrots round, and pour the broth over all.

To make Hodge-Podge.

TAKE a piece of beef, fat and lean together, about a pound of veal, a pound of scrag of mutton, cut all into little pieces, set it on the fire, with two quarts of water, an ounce of barley, an onion, a little bundle of sweet herbs, three or four heads of celery washed clean and cut small, a little mace, two or three cloves, some whole pepper, tied all in a muslin rag, and put to the meat three turnips pared and cut in two, a large carrot scraped clean and cut in six pieces, a little lettuce cut small, put it all in the pot and cover it close: let it stew very softly over a slow fire five or six hours; take out the spice, sweet herbs, and onion, and pour all into a soup dish, and send it to table; first season it with salt. Half a pint of green peas, when it is the season for them, is very good. If you let this boil fast, it will waste too much; therefore you cannot do it too slow, if it does but simmer.

Hodge-Podge of Mutton.

TAKE a neck of mutton of about six pounds, cut about two pounds of the best end whole, cut the rest into chops, put them into a stew-pan or little pot; put in two large onions whole, two heads of celery, four turnips whole, a carrot cut in pieces, a small savoy or cabbage, all washed clean; stew it gently till you have drawn all the gravy out, but be sure it don't burn; put in about three quarts of boiling water, and let it stew gently for three hours; put in a spoonful of browning, and season it with salt; skim off all the fat clean. Put your meat in a soup-dish, and

and put the herbs over, and pour the ſoup over all. Garniſh with toaſted ſippets. You put only the beſt end in the diſh, and leave out the chops.

Partridge Soup.

TAKE two large old partridges, ſkin them and cut them into pieces, with three or four ſlices of ham, a little celery, and three large onions cut in ſlices; fry them in butter till they are brown; be ſure not to burn them; then put them to three quarts of boiling water, with a few pepper-corns, and a little ſalt; ſtew it very gently for two hours, then ſtrain it, and put ſome ſtewed celery and fried bread. Serve it up hot in a tureen.

To make Portable Soup.

TAKE two legs of beef, of about fifty pounds weight, take off all the ſkin and fat as well as you can, then take all the meat and ſinews clean from the bones, which meat put into a large pot, and put to it eight or nine gallons of ſoft water; firſt make it boil, then put in twelve anchovies, an ounce of mace, a quarter of an ounce of cloves, an ounce of whole pepper black and white together, ſix large onions peeled and cut in two, a little bundle of thyme, ſweet marjoram, and winter-ſavory, the dry hard cruſt of a two-penny loaf, ſtir it all together and cover it cloſe, lay a weight on the cover to keep it cloſe down, and let it boil ſoftly for eight or nine hours, then uncover it and ſtir it together; cover it cloſe again and let it boil till it is a very rich good jelly, which you will know by taking a little out now and then, and letting it cool: when you think it is a thick jelly, take it off, ſtrain it through a coarſe hair bag, and preſs it hard; then ſtrain it through a hair ſieve into a large earthen pan; when it is quite cold, take off the ſcum and fat, and take the fine jelly clear from the ſettlings at bottom, and then put the jelly into a large deep well-tinned ſtew-pan; ſet it over a ſtove with a ſlow fire, keep ſtirring it often, and take great care it neither ſticks to the pan or burns: when you find the jelly very ſtiff and thick, as it will be in lumps about the pan, take it out, and put it into large deep china cups, or well glazed earthen-ware. Fill the pan two-thirds full of water, and when the water boils ſet it in your cups. Be ſure no water gets into the cups, and keep the water boiling ſoftly all the time till you find the jelly is like a ſtiff glue; take out the cups, and when they are cool, turn out the glue into a coarſe new flannel; let it lay eight or nine hours, and then put it into the ſun till it is quite hard and dry. Put it into tin boxes, with a piece of writing paper between each piece, and keep them in a dry place.

When you uſe it, pour boiling water on it, and ſtir it all the time till it is melted: ſeaſon with ſalt to your palate. A piece as big as a large walnut will make a pint of water very rich; but as to that you are to make it as good as you pleaſe; if for ſoup, fry a French roll and lay it in the middle of the diſh, and when the glue is diſſolved in the water, give it a boil and pour it into a diſh. If you chooſe it for change, you may boil either rice or barley, vermicelli, celery cut ſmall, or truffles or morels; but let them be very tenderly boiled in the water before you ſtir in the glue, and then give it a boil all together. You may, when you would have it very fine, add force-meat balls, cock's-combs, or a palate boiled very tender, and cut into little bits; but it will be very rich and good without any of theſe ingredients.

If for gravy, pour the boiling water on to what quantity you think proper; and when it is diſſolved, add what ingredients you pleaſe, as in other ſauces. This is only in the room of a rich good gravy. You may make your ſauce either weak or ſtrong, by adding more or leſs; or you may make it of veal, or of mutton the ſame way.

To make an Ox Cheek Soup.

FIRST break the bones of an ox cheek, and waſh it in many waters, then lay it in warm water, throw in a little ſalt to fetch out the ſlime, waſh it out very well, then take a large ſtew-pan, put two ounces of butter at the bottom of the pan, and lay the fleſh ſide of the cheek down, add to it half a pound of a ſhank of ham cut in ſlices, and four heads of celery, pull off the leaves, waſh the heads clean, and cut them in with three large onions, two carrots and one parſnip ſliced, a few beets cut ſmall, and three blades of mace, ſet it over a moderate fire a quarter of an hour; this draws the virtue from the roots, which gives a pleaſant ſtrength to the gravy.

A good gravy may be made by this method, with roots and butter, only adding a little browning to give it a pretty colour; when the head has ſimmered a quarter of an hour, put to it ſix quarts of water, and let it ſtew till it is reduced to two quarts: if you would have it eat like ſoup, ſtrain and take out the meat and other ingredients, and put in the white part of a head of celery cut in ſmall pieces, with a little browning to make it a fine colour, take two ounces of vermicelli, give it a ſcald in the ſoup, and put the top of a French roll in the middle of a tureen, and ſerve it up.

To make Almond Soup.

TAKE a neck of veal, and the ſcrag-end of a neck of mutton, chop them in ſmall pieces, put them in a large toſſing-pan, cut in a turnip, with a blade or two of mace, and five quarts of water, ſet it over the fire, and let it boil gently till it is reduced to two quarts, ſtrain it through a hair ſieve into a clear pot, then put in ſix ounces of almonds blanched and beat fine, half a pint of thick cream, and Cayenne pepper to your taſte, have ready three ſmall French rolls, made for that purpoſe, the ſize of a ſmall tea-cup; if they are larger they will not look well, and drink up too much of the ſoup; blanch a few Jordan almonds, and cut them lengthways, ſtick them round the edge of the rolls ſlantways, then ſtick them all over the top of the rolls, and put them in the tureen; when diſhed up pour the ſoup upon the rolls: theſe rolls look like a hedge-hog: ſome French cooks give this ſoup the name of hedge-hog ſoup.

To make a Tranſparent Soup.

TAKE a leg of veal and cut off the meat as thin as you can; when you have cut off all the meat clean from the bone, break the bone in ſmall pieces, put the meat in a large jug, and the bones at top, with a bunch of ſweet herbs, a quarter of an ounce of mace, half a pound of Jordan almonds blanched and beat fine, pour on it four quarts of boiling water, let it ſtand all night by the fire covered cloſe, the next day put it into a well-tinned ſauce-pan, and let it boil ſlowly till it is reduced to two quarts; be ſure you take the ſcum and fat off as it riſes, all the time it is boiling; ſtrain it into a punch bowl, let it ſettle for two hours, pour it into a clean ſauce-pan clear from the ſediments, if any at the bottom; have ready three ounces of rice boiled in water; if you like vermicelli better, boil two ounces; when enough, put it in and ſerve it up.

To make Brown Pottage.

TAKE a piece of lean gravy-beef, and cut it into thin collops, and hack them with the back of a cleaver; have a ſtew-pan over the fire with a piece of butter, a little bacon cut thin; let them be brown over the fire, and put in your beef, let it ſtew till it be very brown; put in a little flour, and then have your broth ready, and fill up the ſtew-pan; put in two onions, a bunch of ſweet herbs, cloves, mace, and pepper; let all ſtew together an hour covered, then have your bread ready toaſted hard to put in your diſh, and ſtrain ſome of the broth to it through a fine ſieve; put a fowl of ſome ſort in the middle, with a little boiled ſpinage minced in it: garniſh your diſh with boiled lettuces, ſpinage, and lemon.

To make White Barley Pottage, with a large Chicken in the Middle.

FIRST make your ſtock with an old hen, a knuckle of veal, a ſcrag-end of mutton, ſome ſpice, ſweet herbs, and onions; boil all together till it be ſtrong enough, then have your barley ready boiled very tender and white, and ſtrain ſome of it

through

through a cullender; have your bread ready toasted in your dish, with some fine green herbs, minced chervil, spinage, sorrel; and put into your dish some of the broth to your bread, herbs, and chicken, then barley strained and re-strained; stew all together in the dish a little while: garnish your dish with boiled lettuces, spinage, and lemon.

CHAP. XIII.

PUDDINGS, PIES, &c.

(The Lent Chapter contains all the Puddings, &c. which are not in this; those which are here are either entirely of meat, or have suet or some other ingredient in them, which prevents their being included in the Lent Chapter.)

Rules to be observed in making Puddings, &c.

IN boiled puddings, take great care the bag or cloth be very clean, not soapy, but dipped in hot water, and well floured. If a bread-pudding, tie it loose; if a batter pudding, tie it close; and be sure the water boils when you put the pudding in, and you should move the puddings in the pot now and then, for fear they stick. When you make a batter-pudding, first mix the flour well with a little milk, then put in the ingredients by degrees, and it will be smooth and not have lumps; but for a plain batter-pudding, the best way is to strain it through a coarse hair sieve, that it may neither have lumps nor the treadles of the eggs: and for all other puddings strain the eggs when they are beat. If you boil them in wooden bowls, or China dishes, butter the inside before you put in your batter; and for all baked puddings, butter the pan or dish before the pudding is put in.

An Oat-Pudding to bake.

OF oats decorticated take two pounds, and new milk enough to drown it, eight ounces of raisins of the sun stoned, an equal quantity of currants neatly picked, a pound of sweet suet finely shred, six new laid eggs well beat; season with nutmeg, beaten ginger, and salt; mix it all well together: it will make a better pudding than rice.

To make a Calf's-Foot Pudding.

TAKE of calves feet one pound minced very fine, the fat and the brown to be taken out, a pound and an half of suet, pick

pick off all the ſkin and ſhred it ſmall, ſix eggs, but half the whites, beat them well, the crumb of a halfpenny-roll grated, a pound of currants clean picked and waſhed, and rubbed in a cloth; milk, as much as will moiſten it with the eggs, a handful of flour, a little ſalt, nutmeg, and ſugar, to ſeaſon it to your taſte; boil it nine hours with your meat; when it is done, lay it in your diſh, and pour melted butter over it. It is very good with white wine and ſugar in the butter.

To make a Pith-Pudding.

TAKE a quantity of the pith of an ox, and let it lie all night in water to ſoak out the blood; the next morning ſtrip it out of the ſkin and beat it with the back of a ſpoon in orange-water till it is as fine as pap; then take three pints of thick cream and boil in it two or three blades of mace, a nutmeg quartered, a ſtick of cinnamon; then take half a pound of the beſt Jordan almonds blanched in cold water, then beat them with a little of the cream, and as it dries put in more cream; and when they are all beaten, ſtrain the cream from them to the pith; then take the yolks of ten eggs, the white of but two, beat them very well and put them to the ingredients; take a ſpoonful of grated bread or Naples biſcuit, mingle all theſe together, with half a pound of fine ſugar, and the marrow of four large bones, and a little ſalt; fill them in a ſmall ox or hog's guts, or bake in a diſh, with a puff-paſte under it, and round the edges.

To make a Marrow Pudding.

TAKE a quart of cream or milk, and a quarter of a pound of Naples biſcuit, put them on the fire in a ſtew-pan, and boil them up; then take the yolks of eight eggs, the whites of four beat up very fine, a little moiſt ſugar, ſome marrow chopped; mix all well together, and put them on the fire, keep it ſtirring till it is thick, then take it off the fire and keep ſtirring it till it is cold; when it is almoſt cold, put in a ſmall glaſs of brandy, one of ſack, and a ſpoonful of orange-flower water; then have ready your diſh rimmed with puff-paſte, put your ſtuff in, ſprinkle ſome currants that have been well waſhed in cold water and rubbed clean in a cloth, ſome marrow cut in ſlices, and ſome candied lemon, orange, and citron, cut in ſhreds, and ſend it to the oven; three quarters of an hour will bake it: ſend it up hot.

A boiled Suet-Pudding.

TAKE a quart of milk, four ſpoonfuls of flour, a pound of ſuet ſhred ſmall, four eggs, one ſpoonful of beaten ginger, a tea-ſpoonful of ſalt; mix the eggs and flour with a pint of the milk very thick, and with the ſeaſoning mix in the reſt of the milk

milk and fuet. Let your batter be pretty thick, and boil it two hours.

A boiled Plumb-Pudding.

TAKE a pound of fuet cut in little pieces, not too fine, a pound of currants, and a pound of raifins ftoned, eight eggs, half the whites, half a nutmeg grated, and a tea-fpoonful of beaten ginger, a pound of flour, a pint of milk; beat the eggs firft, then half the milk, beat them together, and by degrees ftir in the flour, then the fuet, fpice, and fruit, and as much milk as will mix it well together very thick. Boil it five hours.

A Hunting-Pudding.

TAKE ten eggs, the whites of fix, and all the yolks, beat them up well with half a pint of cream, fix fpoonfuls of flour, one pound of beef fuet chopped fmall, a pound of currants well wafhed and picked, a pound of jar raifins ftoned and chopped fmall, two ounces of candied citron, orange, and lemon fhred fine, put two ounces of fine fugar, a fpoonful of rofe-water, a glafs of brandy, and half a nutmeg grated; mix all well together, tie it up in a cloth, and boil it four hours; be fure to put it in when the water boils, and keep it boiling all the time; turn it out into a difh, and garnifh with powder fugar.

A Yorkfhire Pudding.

TAKE a quart of milk and five eggs, beat them up well together, and mix them with flour till it is of a good pancake batter, and very fmooth; put in a little falt, fome grated nutmeg and ginger; butter a dripping or frying pan and put it under a piece of beef, mutton, or a loin of veal that is roafting, and then put in your batter, and when the top fide is brown, cut it in fquare pieces, and turn it, and then let the under fide be brown; then put it in a hot difh as clean of fat as you can, and fend it to table hot.

Vermicelli Pudding.

TAKE a quarter of a pound of vermicelli, and boil it in a pint of milk till it is tender, with a ftick of cinnamon, then take out the cinnamon, and put in half a pint of cream, a quarter of a pound of butter melted, a quarter of a pound of fugar, with the yolks of four eggs well beat; put it in a difh with or without pafte round the rim, and bake it three quarters of an hour; or if you like it, for variety, you may add half a pound of currants clean wafhed and picked, or a handful of marrow chopped fine, or both.

A Steak Pudding.

MAKE a good cruſt with ſuet ſhred fine with flour, and mix it up with cold water; ſeaſon it with a little ſalt, and make it pretty ſtiff; about two pounds of ſuet to a quarter of a peck of flour: let your ſteaks be either beef or mutton, well ſeaſoned with pepper and ſalt, make it up as you do an apple-pudding, tie it in a cloth, and put it into the water boiling. If it be a large pudding, it will take five hours; if a ſmall one, three hours. This is the beſt cruſt for an apple-pudding. Pigeons eat well this way.

Suet Dumplings.

TAKE a pint of milk, four eggs, a pound of ſuet, and a pound of currants, two tea-ſpoonfuls of ſalt, three of ginger; firſt take half the milk, and mix it like a thick batter, then put the eggs and the ſalt and ginger, then the reſt of the milk by degrees, with the ſuet and currants and flour, to make it like a light paſte: when the water boils, make them in rolls as big as a large turkey's egg, with a little flour; then flat them, and throw them into boiling water; move them ſoftly, that they do not ſtick together; keep the water boiling all the time, and half an hour will boil them.

An Oxford Pudding.

A QUARTER of a pound of biſcuit grated, a quarter of a pound of currants clean waſhed and picked, a quarter of a pound of ſuet ſhred ſmall, half a large ſpoonful of powder ſugar, a very little ſalt, and ſome grated nutmeg; mix all well together, then take two yolks of eggs, and make it up in balls as big as a turkey's egg: fry them in freſh butter of a fine light brown; for ſauce, have melted butter and ſugar, with a little ſack or white wine. You muſt mind to keep the pan ſhaking about, that they may be all of a fine light brown.

Obſervations on PIES.

RAISED pies ſhould have a quick oven, and well cloſed up, or your pie will fall in the ſides; it ſhould have no water put in till the minute it goes to the oven, it makes the cruſt ſad, and is a great hazard of the pie running.

To make a very fine ſweet Lamb or Veal Pie.

SEASON your lamb with ſalt, pepper, cloves, mace, and nutmeg, all beat fine, to your palate: cut your lamb or veal into little pieces; make a good puff-paſte cruſt, lay it into your diſh, then

then lay in your meat, ſtrew on it ſome ſtoned raiſins and currants clean waſhed, and ſome ſugar; then lay on it ſome force-meat balls made ſweet, and in the ſummer ſome artichoke-bottoms boiled, and ſcalded grapes in the winter; boil Spaniſh potatoes cut in pieces, candied citron, candied orange and lemon-peel, and three or four blades of mace; put butter on the top, cloſe up your pie, and bake it; have ready againſt it comes out of the oven a caudle made thus: take a pint of white wine and mix in the yolks of three eggs, ſtir it well together over the fire, one way all the time, till it is thick; then take it off, ſtir in ſugar enough to ſweeten it, and ſqueeze in the juice of a lemon; pour it hot into your pie, and cloſe it up again: ſend it hot to table.

A ſavoury Veal Pie.

TAKE a breaſt of veal, cut it into pieces, ſeaſon it with pepper and ſalt, lay it all into your cruſt, boil ſix or eight eggs hard, take only the yolks, put them into the pie here and there, fill your diſh almoſt full of water, put on the lid, and bake it well, or you may put ſome force meat balls in.

To make a ſavoury Lamb or Veal Pie.

MAKE a good puff-paſte cruſt, cut your meat into pieces, ſeaſon it to your palate with pepper, ſalt, mace, cloves, and nutmeg finely beat; lay it into your cruſt with a few lamb-ſtones and ſweetbreads ſeaſoned as your meat, alſo ſome oyſters and force-meat balls, hard yolks of eggs, and tops of aſparagus two inches long, firſt boiled green; put butter all over the pie, put on the lid, and ſet it in a quick oven an hour and a half, and then have ready the liquor, made thus: take a pint of gravy, the oyſter-liquor, a gill of red wine, and a little grated nutmeg; mix all together with the yolks of two or three eggs beat, and keep it ſtirring one way all the time; when it boils, pour it into your pie, put on the lid again; ſend it hot to table: you muſt make liquor according to your pie.

To make a Calf's-Foot Pie.

FIRST ſet your calf's-feet on in a ſauce-pan, in three quarts of water, with three or four blades of mace; let them boil ſoftly till there is about a pint and a half, then take out your feet, ſtrain the liquor, and make a good cruſt; cover your diſh, then pick off the fleſh from the bones, lay half in the diſh, ſtrew half a pound of currants clean waſhed and picked over, and half a pound of raiſins ſtoned; lay on the reſt of the meat, then ſkim the liquor, ſweeten it to the palate, and put in half a pint of white wine; pour it into the diſh, put on your lid, and bake it an hour and a half.

To make an Olive Pie.

MAKE your cruſt ready, then take the thin collops of the beſt end of a leg of veal, as many as you think will fill your pie, hack them with the back of a knife, and ſeaſon them with ſalt, pepper, cloves, and mace: waſh over your collops with a bunch of feathers dipped in eggs, and have in readineſs a good handful of ſweet herbs ſhred ſmall; the herbs muſt be thyme, parſley, and ſpinage, the yolks of eight hard eggs minced, and a few oyſters parboiled and chopped, ſome beef ſuet ſhred very fine; mix theſe together, and ſtrew them over your collops, then ſprinkle a little orange-flower water over them, roll the collops up very cloſe, and lay them in your pie, ſtrewing the ſeaſoning over what is left, put butter on the top, and cloſe your pie; when it comes out of the oven, have ready ſome gravy hot, with one anchovy diſſolved in the gravy; pour it in boiling hot. You may put in artichoke-bottoms and cheſnuts (if you pleaſe). You may leave out the orange-flower water (if you do not like it).

To ſeaſon an Egg-Pie.

BOIL twelve eggs hard, and ſhred them with one pound of beef ſuet or marrow ſhred fine; ſeaſon them with a little cinnamon and nutmeg beat fine, one pound of currants clean waſhed and picked, two or three ſpoonfuls of cream, and a little ſack and roſe-water mixed all together, and fill the pie; when it is baked, ſtir in half a pound of freſh butter, and the juice of a lemon.

To make a Mutton-Pie.

TAKE a loin of mutton, take off the ſkin and fat of the inſide, cut it into ſteaks, ſeaſon it well with pepper and ſalt to your palate; lay it into your cruſt, fill it, pour in as much water as will almoſt fill the diſh; then put on the cruſt, and bake it well.

A Beef-Steak Pie.

TAKE fine rump-ſteaks, beat them with a rolling-pin, then ſeaſon them with pepper and ſalt, according to your palate; make a good cruſt, lay in your ſteaks, fill your diſh, then pour in as much water as will half fill the diſh; put on the cruſt, and bake it well.

A Ham-Pie.

TAKE ſome cold boiled ham and ſlice it about half an inch thick, make a good cruſt, and thick, over the diſh, and lay a layer of ham, ſhake a little pepper over it, then take a large young fowl clean picked, gutted, waſhed, and ſinged; put a little pepper and ſalt in the belly, and rub a very little ſalt on the outſide; lay the fowl on the ham, boil ſome eggs hard, put in the yolks, and cover all with ham, then ſhake ſome pepper on the ham, and put on the top-cruſt; bake it well, have ready when it comes out of the oven ſome very rich beef gravy, enough to fill the pie; lay on the cruſt again, and ſend it to table hot: if you put two large fowls in, they will make a fine pie; but that is according to your company, more or leſs; the larger the pie the finer the meat eats; the cruſt muſt be the ſame you make for a veniſon-paſty; you ſhould pour a little ſtrong gravy into the pie when you make it, juſt to bake the meat, and then fill it up when it comes out of the oven; boil ſome truffles and morels and put into your pie, which is a great addition, and ſome freſh muſhrooms or dried ones.

To make a Pigeon-Pie.

MAKE a puff-paſte cruſt, cover your diſh, let your pigeons be very nicely picked and cleaned, ſeaſon them with pepper and ſalt, and put a good piece of fine freſh butter, with pepper and ſalt in their bellies; lay them in your pans, the necks, gizzards, livers, pinions, and hearts, lay between, with the yolk of a hard egg and beef-ſteak in the middle; put as much water as will almoſt fill the diſh, lay on the top-cruſt and bake it well; this is the beſt way to make a pigeon-pie; but the French fill the pigeons with a very high force meat, and lay force-meat balls round the inſide, with aſparagus-tops, artichoke-bottoms, muſhrooms, truffles and morels, and ſeaſon high; but that is according to different palates.

To make a Giblet-Pie.

TAKE two pair of giblets nicely cleaned, put all but the livers into a ſauce-pan; with two quarts of water, twenty corns of whole pepper, three blades of mace, a bundle of ſweet herbs, and a large onion; cover them cloſe, and let them ſtew very ſoftly till they are quite tender, then have a good cruſt ready, cover your diſh, lay a fine rump ſteak at the bottom, ſeaſoned with pepper and ſalt; then lay in your giblets with the livers, and ſtrain the liquor they were ſtewed in; ſeaſon it with ſalt, and pour into your pie; put on the lid, and bake it an hour and a half.

To make a Duck-Pie.

MAKE a puff-paſte cruſt, take two ducks, ſcald them and make them very clean, cut off the feet, the pinions, the neck and head, all clean picked and ſcalded, with the gizzards, livers and hearts; pick out all the fat of the inſide, lay a cruſt all over the diſh, ſeaſon the ducks with pepper and ſalt, inſide and out, lay them in your diſh, and the giblets at each end ſeaſoned; put in as much water as will almoſt fill the pie, lay on the cruſt, and bake it, but not too much.

To

To make a Chicken-Pie.

MAKE a puff-paste crust, take two chickens, cut them to pieces, season them with pepper and salt, a little beaten mace, lay a force-meat made thus round the side of the dish: take half a pound of veal, half a pound of suet, beat them quite fine in a marble mortar, with as many crumbs of bread; season it with a very little pepper and salt, an anchovy with the liquor, cut the anchovy to pieces, a little lemon-peel cut very fine and shred small, a very little thyme, mix all together with the yolk of an egg; make some into round balls, about twelve, the rest lay round the dish; lay in one chicken over the bottom of the dish, take two sweetbreads, cut them into five or six pieces, lay them all over, season them with pepper and salt, strew over them half an ounce of truffles and morels, two or three artichoke-bottoms cut to pieces, a few cock's-combs, (if you have them,) a palate boiled tender and cut to pieces; then lay on the other part of the chicken, put half a pint of water in, and cover the pie; bake it well, and when it comes out of the oven, fill it with good gravy, lay it on the crust, and send it to table.

To make a Cheshire Pork-Pie.

TAKE a loin of pork, skin it, cut it into steaks, season it with salt, nutmeg, and pepper; make a good crust, lay a layer of pork, then a large layer of pippins pared and cored, a little sugar, enough to sweeten the pie, then another layer of pork; put in half a pint of white wine, lay some butter on the top, and close your pie: if your pie be large, it will take a pint of white wine.

To make a Devonshire Squab-Pie.

MAKE a good crust, cover the dish all over, put at the bottom a layer of sliced pippins, then a layer of mutton-steaks cut from the loin, well seasoned with pepper and salt, then another layer of pippins; peel some onions and slice them thin, lay a layer all over the apples, then a layer of mutton, then pippins and onions, pour in a pint of water; so close your pie and bake it.

To make an Ox-Cheek-Pie.

FIRST bake your ox-cheek as at other times, but not too much, put it in the oven over night, and then it will be ready the next day; make a fine puff-paste crust, and let your side and top crust be thick; let your dish be deep to hold a good deal of gravy, cover your dish with crust, then cut off all the flesh, kernels, and fat of the head, with the palate cut in pieces, cut the meat into little pieces as you do for a hash, lay in the meat, take an ounce of truffles and morels and throw them over the meat, the yolks of six eggs boiled hard, a gill of pickled mushrooms, or fresh ones are better (if you have them); put in a good many force-meat balls, a few artichoke-bottoms and asparagus-tops (if you have any); season your pie with pepper and salt to your palate, and fill the pie with the gravy it was baked in: if the head be rightly seasoned when it comes out of the oven, it will want very little more; put on the lid, and bake it. When the crust is done your pie will be enough.

To make a Shropshire Pie.

FIRST make a good puff-paste crust, then cut two rabbits to pieces, with two pounds of fat pork cut into little pieces; season both with pepper and salt to your liking, then cover your dish with crust and lay in your rabbits; mix the pork with them, take the livers of the rabbits, parboil them and beat them in a mortar, with as much fat bacon, a little sweet herbs, and some oysters (if you have them); season with pepper, salt, and nutmeg; mix it up with the yolk of an egg, and make it into balls; lay them here and there in your pie, some artichoke-bottoms cut in dice, and cock's-combs (if you have them); grate a small nutmeg over the meat, then pour in half a pint of red wine, and half a pint of water; close your pie, and bake it an hour and a half in a quick, but not too fierce, oven.

To make a Yorkshire Christmas-Pie.

FIRST make a good standing crust, let the wall and bottom be very thick; bone a turkey, a goose, a fowl, a partridge, and a pigeon; season them all very well, take half an ounce of mace, half an ounce of nutmegs, a quarter of an ounce of cloves, and half an ounce of black pepper, all beat fine together, two large spoonfuls of salt, and then mix them together; open the fowls all down the back, and bone them; first the pigeon, then the partridge; cover them; then the fowl, then the goose, and then the turkey, which must be large; season them all well first, and lay them in the crust, so as it will look only like a whole turkey; then have a hare ready cased and wiped with a clean cloth; cut it to pieces, that is, joint it; season it, and lay it as close as you can on one side; on the other side woodcocks, moor game, and what sort of wild fowl you can get; season them well, and lay them close; put at least four pounds of butter into the pie, then lay on your lid, which must be a very thick one, and let it be well baked; it must have a very hot oven, and will take at least four hours.

This crust will take a bushel of flour. In this chapter you will see how to make it. These pies are often sent to London in a box, as presents; therefore the walls must be well built.

To make a Goose-Pie.

HALF a peck of flour will make the walls of a goose-pie, made as in the receipts for crust: raise your crust just big enough to hold a large goose; first have a pickled dried tongue boiled tender enough to peel, cut off the root, bone a goose and a large fowl; take a quarter of an ounce of mace beat fine, a large tea-spoonful of beaten pepper, three tea-spoonfuls of salt; mix all together, season your fowl and goose with it, then lay the fowl in the goose, and tongue in the fowl, and the goose in the same form as if whole; put half a pound of butter on the top, and lay on the lid. This pie is delicious, either hot or cold, and will keep a great while: a slice of this pie cut down across makes a pretty little side-dish for supper.

To make a Venison-Pasty.

TAKE a neck and breast of venison, bone it, season it with pepper and salt according to your palate; cut the breast in two or three pieces, but do not cut the fat off the neck if you can help it; lay in the breast and neck-end first, and the best end of the neck on the top, that the fat may be whole; make a good rich puff-paste crust, and rim your dish, then lay in your venison, put in half a pound of butter, about a quarter of a pint of water, then put a very thick paste over, and ornament it in any form you please with leaves, &c. cut in paste, and let it be baked three hours in a very quick oven; put a sheet of buttered paper over it to keep it from scorching. In the mean time set on the bones of the venison in two quarts of water, with two or three blades of mace, an onion, a little piece of crust baked crisp and brown, a little whole pepper; cover it close, and let it boil softly over a slow fire till above half is wasted, then strain it off; when the pasty comes out of the oven, lift up the lid and pour in the gravy.

When your venison is not fat enough, take the fat of a loin of mutton, steeped in a little rape-vinegar and red wine twenty-four hours, then lay it on the top of the venison, and close your pasty. It is a wrong notion of some people to think venison cannot be baked enough, and will first bake it in a false crust, and then bake it in the pasty; by this time the fine flavour of the venison is gone: no; if you want it to be very tender, wash it in warm milk and water, dry it in clean cloths till it is very dry, then rub it all over with vinegar, and hang it in the air; keep it as long as you think proper, it will keep thus a fortnight good; but be sure there be no moistness about it, if there is, you must dry it well and throw ginger over it, and it will keep a long time; when you use it, just dip it in lukewarm water, and dry it; bake it in a quick oven: if it is a large paſty, it will take three hours; then your veniſon will be tender, and have all the fine flavour: the ſhoulder makes a pretty paſty, boned and made as above with the mutton fat.

A loin of mutton makes a fine paſty: take a large fat loin of mutton, let it hang four or five days, then bone it, leaving the meat as whole as you can; lay the meat twenty-four hours in half a pint of red wine and half a pint of rape-vinegar; then take it out of the pickle, and order it as you do a paſty, and boil the bones in the ſame manner, to fill the paſty, when it comes out of the oven.

To make a Calf's-Head Pie.

CLEANSE your head very well, and boil it till it is tender; then carefully take off the fleſh as whole as you can, take out the eyes, and ſlice the tongue; make a good puff-paſte cruſt, cover the diſh, lay on your meat, throw over it the tongue, lay the eyes cut in two at each corner; ſeaſon it with a very little pepper and ſalt, pour in half a pint of the liquor it was boiled in, lay a thin top-cruſt on and bake it an hour in a quick oven; in the mean time boil the bones of the head in two quarts of liquor, with two or three blades of mace, half a quarter of an ounce of whole pepper, a large onion, and a bundle of ſweet herbs; let it boil till there is about a pint, then ſtrain it off, and add two ſpoonfuls of catchup, three of red wine, a piece of butter as big as a walnut, rolled in flour, half an ounce of truffles and morels; ſeaſon with ſalt to your palate; boil it, and have half the brains boiled with ſome ſage; beat them, and twelve leaves of ſage chopped fine, ſtir all together, and give it a boil; take the other part of the brains, and beat them with ſome of the ſage chopped fine, a little lemon-peel minced fine, and half a ſmall nutmeg grated; beat it up with an egg, and fry it in little cakes of a fine light brown; boil ſix eggs hard, take only the yolks; when your pie comes out of the oven take off the lid, lay the eggs and cakes over it, and pour the ſauce all over; ſend it to table hot without the lid. This is a fine diſh; you may put in it as many fine things as you pleaſe, but it wants no addition.

To make a Tort.

FIRST make a fine puff-paſte, cover your diſh with the cruſt, make a good force-meat thus: take a pound of veal and a pound of beef-ſuet, cut them ſmall, and beat them fine in a mortar; ſeaſon it with a ſmall nutmeg grated, a little lemon-peel ſhred fine, a few ſweet herbs, not too much, a little pepper and ſalt, juſt enough to ſeaſon it, the crumb of a penny-loaf rubbed fine; mix it up with the yolk of an egg, make one third into balls, and the reſt lay round the ſides of the diſh;

get

get two fine large veal ſweetbreads, cut each into ſour pieces; two pair of lamb's-ſtones, each cut in two; twelve cock's-combs, half an ounce of truffles and morels, four artichoke-bottoms, cut each into four pieces, a few aſparagus tops, ſome freſh muſhrooms and ſome pickled, put all together in your diſh: lay firſt your ſweetbreads, then the artichoke-bottoms, then the cock's-combs, then the truffles and morels, then the aſparagus, then the muſhrooms, and then the forçe-meat balls; ſeaſon the ſweetbreads with pepper and ſalt; fill your pie with water and put on the cruſt; bake it two hours.

To make Mince Pies the beſt Way.

TAKE three pounds of ſuet ſhred very fine, and chopped as ſmall as poſſible; two pounds of raiſins ſtoned and chopped as fine as poſſible; two pounds of currants nicely picked, waſhed, rubbed, and dried at the fire; half a hundred of fine pippins, pared, cored, and chopped ſmall; half a pound of fine ſugar pounded fine; a quarter of an ounce of mace, a quarter of an ounce of cloves, two large nutmegs, all beat fine; put all together into a great pan, and mix it well together with half a pint of brandy, and half a pint of ſack; put it down cloſe in a ſtone pot, and it will keep good four months. When you make your pies take a little diſh, ſomething bigger than a ſoup-plate, lay a very thin cruſt all over it, lay a thin layer of meat, and then a thin layer of citron cut very thin, then a layer of mince-meat, and a layer of orange-peel cut thin, over that a little meat, ſqueeze half the juice of a fine Seville orange or lemon, lay on your cruſt and bake it nicely. Theſe pies eat finely cold. If you make them in little patties, mix your meat and ſweetmeats accordingly: if you chooſe meat in your pies, parboil a neat's-tongue, peel it, and chop the meat as fine as poſſible, and mix with the reſt; or two pounds of the inſide of a ſirloin of beef boiled: but you muſt double the quantity of fruit when you uſe meat.

Mince Pies excellent.

TAKE about a pound of very tender beef, two pounds of ſuet, and about two pounds of currants; cloves and mace to your taſte; lemon-peel and the juice of two good lemons, white wine and red ſufficient to moiſten the meat; add ſome chopped nonpareils, and ſweetmeats (if you pleaſe); beat the ſpice with a little ſalt, and ſweeten with moiſt ſugar to your taſte.

Tort de Moy.

MAKE puff-paſte and lay round your diſh, then a layer of biſcuit and a layer of butter and marrow, and then a layer of all ſorts of ſweetmeats (or as many as you have), and ſo do till your diſh is full; then boil a quart of cream and thicken it with four eggs, and a ſpoonful of orange-flower water; ſweeten it with ſugar to your palate, and pour over the reſt: half an hour will bake it.

To make Orange or Lemon Tarts.

TAKE ſix large lemons and rub them very well with ſalt, and put them for two days in water, with a handful of ſalt in it; then change them into freſh water every day (without ſalt), for a fortnight, then boil them for two or three hours till they are tender, then cut them into half-quarters, and then cut them three-corner ways, as thin as you can; take ſix pippins pared, cored and quartered, and a pint of fair water: let them boil till the pippins break; put the liquor to your orange or lemon, and half the pulp of the pippins well broken and a pound of ſugar; boil theſe together a quarter of an hour, then put it in a gallipot, and ſqueeze an orange in it; if it be a lemon tart, ſqueeze a lemon; two ſpoonfuls is enough for a tart. Your patty-pans muſt be ſmall and ſhallow: put fine puff-paſte, and very thin; a little while will bake it. Juſt as your tarts are going into the oven, with a feather or bruſh do them over with melted butter, and then ſift double refined ſugar over them; and this is a pretty iceing on them.

To make different Sorts of Tarts.

IF you bake in tin patties butter them, and you muſt put a little cruſt all over, becauſe of the taking them out; if in China or glaſs, no cruſt but the top one; lay fine ſugar at the bottom, then your plums, cherries, or any other ſort of fruit, and ſugar at top; then put on your lid, and bake them in a ſlack oven. Mince-pies muſt be baked in tin patties, becauſe of taking them out, and puff-paſte is beſt for them; for ſweet tarts the beaten cruſt is beſt; but as you fancy. Apple, pear, apricot, &c. make thus: apples and pears, pare them, cut them into quarters, and core them; cut the quarters acroſs again, ſet them on in a ſauce-pan with juſt as much water as will barely cover them, let them ſimmer on a ſlow fire juſt till the fruit is tender; put a good piece of lemon-peel in the water with the fruit, then have your patties ready; lay fine ſugar at bottom, then your fruit, and a little ſugar at top; that you muſt put in at your diſcretion; pour over each tart a tea-ſpoonful of lemon-juice, and three tea-ſpoonfuls of the liquor they were boiled in; put on your lid, and bake them in a ſlack oven. Apricots do the ſame way, only do not uſe lemon.

As to preferved tarts, only lay in your preferved fruit, and put a very thin cruft at top, and let them be baked as little as poffible; but if you would make them very nice, have a large patty the fize you would have your tart; make your fugar cruft, roll it as thick as a halfpenny, then butter your patties and cover it; fhape your upper cruft on a hollow thing on purpofe, the fize of your patty, and mark it with a marking-iron for that purpofe, in what fhape you pleafe, to be hollow and open to fee the fruit through; then bake your cruft in a very flack oven, not to difcolour it, but to have it crifp; when the cruft is cold, very carefully take it out, and fill it with what fruit you pleafe, lay on the lid, and it is done; therefore if the tart is not eat, your fweetmeat is not the worfe, and it looks genteel.

Pafte for Tarts.

ONE pound of flour, three quarters of a pound of butter; mix up together, and beat well with a rolling-pin.

Another Pafte for Tarts.

HALF a pound of butter, half a pound of flour, and half a pound of fugar; mix it well together, and beat it with a rolling-pin well, then roll it out thin.

Puff-Pafte.

TAKE a quarter of a peck of flour, rub in a pound of butter very fine, make it up in a light pafte with cold water, juft ftiff enough to work it up; then roll it up about as thick as a crown-piece, put a layer of butter all over; fprinkle on a little flour, double it up, and roll it out again; double it, and roll it three times; then it is fit for all forts of pies and tarts that require a puff-pafte.

A good Cruft for great Pies.

To a peck of flour add the yolks of three eggs, then boil fome water, and put in half a pound of fried fuet, and a pound and a half of butter; fkim off the butter and fuet, and as much of the liquor as will make a light good cruft; work it up well, and roll it out.

A ftanding Cruft for great Pies.

TAKE a peck of flour, and fix pounds of butter boiled in a gallon of water; fkim it off into the flour, and as little of the liquor as you can; work it up well into a pafte, then pull it into pieces till it is cold; then make it up into what form you will have it: this is fit for the walls of a goofe-pie.

A cold

A cold Cruſt.

To three pounds of flour, rub in a pound and half of butter, break in two eggs, and make it up with cold water.

A dripping Cruſt.

TAKE a pound and a half of beef-dripping, boil it in water, ſtrain it, then let it ſtand to be cold, and take off the hard fat; ſcrape it, boil it ſo four or five times; then work it well up into three pounds of flour as fine as you can, and make it up up into paſte with cold water. It makes a very fine cruſt.

A Cruſt for Cuſtards.

TAKE half a pound of flour, ſix ounces of butter, the yolks of two eggs, three ſpoonfuls of cream; mix them together, and let them ſtand a quarter of an hour, then work it up and down and roll it very thin.

Paſte for Crackling Cruſt.

BLANCH four handfuls of almonds, and throw them into water, then dry them in a cloth, and pound them in a mortar very fine, with a little orange-flour water and the white of an egg; when they are well pounded, paſs them through a coarſe hair-ſieve, to clear them from all the lumps or clods; then ſpread it on a diſh till it is very pliable; let it ſtand for a while, then roll out a piece of the under cruſt, and dry it in the oven on the pie-pan, while other paſtry-works are making; as knots, cyphers, &c. for garniſhing your pies.

An Hottentot Pie.

BOIL and bone two calf's feet, clean very well a calf's chitterling, boil it and chop it ſmall, take two chickens and cut them up as for eating, put them in a ſtew-pan with two ſweetbreads, a quart of veal or mutton gravy, half an ounce of morels, Cayenne pepper and ſalt to your palate, ſtew them all together an hour over a gentle fire, then put in ſix force-meat balls that have been boiled, and the yolks of four hard eggs, and put them in a good raiſed cruſt that has been baked for it, ſtrew over the top of your pie a few green peas boiled as for eating; or peel and cut ſome young green brocoli ſtalks about the ſize of peas, give them a gentle boil, and ſtrew them over the top of your pie, and ſend it up hot without a lid, the ſame way as the French pie.

A Bride's Pie.

BOIL two calf's feet, pick the meat from the bones, and chop it very fine, ſhred ſmall one pound of beef ſuet, and a pound a pound of apples, wash and pick one pound of currants very small, dry them before the fire, stone and chop a quarter of a pound of jar raisins, a quarter of an ounce of cinnamon, the same of mace and nutmeg, two ounces of candied citron, two ounces of candied lemon cut thin, a glass of brandy and one of champagne, put them in a China dish with a rich puff paste over it, roll another lid and cut it in leaves, flowers, figures, and put a glass ring in it.

A Thatched House Pie.

TAKE an earthen dish that is pretty deep, rub the inside with two ounces of butter, then spread over it two ounces of vermicelli, make a good puff-paste, and roll it pretty thick, and lay it on the dish; take three or four pigeons, season them very well with pepper and salt, and put a good lump of butter in them, and lay them in the dish with the breast down, and put a thick lid over them, and bake it in a moderate oven; when enough, take the dish you intend for it and turn the pie on to it, and the vermicelli will appear like thatch, which gives it the name of thatched house pie. It is a pretty side or corner dish for a large dinner, or a bottom for a supper.

To make a French Pie.

TO two pounds of flour put three quarters of a pound of butter, make it into a paste, and raise the walls of the pie, then roll out some paste thin as for a lid, cut it into vine leaves, or the figures of any moulds you have, if you have no moulds, you may make use of a crocran, and pick out pretty shapes, beat the yolks of two eggs and rub the outside of the walls of the pie with it, and lay the vine leaves or shapes round the walls, and rub them over with the eggs, fill the pie with the bones of the meat to keep the steam in, that the crust may be well soaked; it is to go to table without a lid.

Take a calf's head, wash and clean it well, boil it half an hour, when it is cold cut it in thin slices and put it in a tossing-pan, with three pints of veal gravy and three sweet-breads cut thin, and let it stew one hour, with half an ounce of morels, and half an ounce of truffles, then have ready two calves feet boiled and boned, cut them in small pieces and put them into your tossing-pan, with a spoonful of lemon pickle and one of browning, Cayenne pepper, and a little salt; when the meat is tender thicken the gravy a little with flour and butter, strain it and put in a few pickled mushrooms, but fresh ones if you can get them; put the meat into the pie you took the bones out, and lay the nicest part at the top, have ready a quarter of an hundred of asparagus-heads, strew them over the top of the pie and serve it up.

A savoury Chicken Pie.

LET your chickens be small, season them with mace, pepper, and salt, put a lump of butter into every one of them, lay them in the dish with the breasts up, and lay a thin slice of bacon over them, it will give them a pleasant flavour, then put in a pint of strong gravy, and make a good puff-paste, lid it and bake it in a moderate oven: French cooks generally put morels and yolks of eggs chopped small.

Egg and Bacon Pie to eat cold.

STEEP a few thin slices of bacon all night in water to take out the salt, lay your bacon in the dish, beat eight eggs, with a pint of thick cream, put in a little pepper and salt, and pour it on the bacon, lay over it a good cold paste, bake it a day before you want it in a moderate oven.

To make a Pork Pie.

TAKE from a loin, neck, or any nice part, an equal quantity of fat and lean pork, cut it into pieces the size of a crown piece; shred some onion and apple not very small, season the meat with Cayenne, white pepper, salt, and dried sage, lay in your dish a layer of seasoning, and one of meat, alternately till filled, then add some lumps of butter, and put on the lid: you may make a raised pie.

To make savoury Patties.

TAKE one pound of the inside of a cold loin of veal, or the same quantity of cold fowl, that have been either boiled or roasted, a quarter of a pound of beef-suet, chop them as small as possible, with six or eight sprigs of parsley, season them well with half a nutmeg grated fine, pepper and salt, put them in a tossing-pan with half a pint of veal gravy, thicken the gravy with a little flour and butter, and two spoonfuls of cream, and shake them over the fire two minutes, and fill your patties. You must make your patties thus: raise them of an oval form, and bake them as for custards, cut some long narrow bits of paste and bake them on a dusting box, but not to go round, they are for handles; fill your patties when quite hot with the meat, then set your handles a-cross the patties; they will look like baskets if you have nicely pinched the walls of the patties, when you raised them; five will be a dish: you may make them with sugar and currants instead of parsley.

Common Patties.

TAKE the kidney part of a very fat loin of veal, chop the kidney, veal, and fat very small all together, season it with mace,

mace, pepper, and falt to your tafte, raife little patties the fize of a tea-cup, fill them with your meat, put thin lids on them, bake them very crifp; five is enough for a fide difh.

To make fine Patties.

SLICE either turkey, houfe-lamb, or chicken, with an equal quantity of the fat of lamb, loin of veal, or the infide of a firloin of beef, a little parfley, thyme, and lemon-peel fhred, put it all in a marble mortar and pound it very fine, feafon it with white pepper and falt, then make a fine puff-pafte, roll it out in thin fquare fheets, put the force-meat in the middle, cover it over, clofe them all round, and cut the pafte even: juft before they go into the oven wafh them over with the yolk of an egg, and bake them twenty minutes in a quick oven; have ready a little white gravy feafoned with pepper, falt, and a little fhalot, thickened up with a little cream or butter; as foon as the patties come out of the oven, make a hole in the top and pour in fome gravy; you muft take care not to put too much gravy in, for fear of its running out at the fides, and fpoiling the patties.

CHAP. XIV.

For LENT, *or a* FAST DINNER.

A Number of good Difhes which may be made ufe of at any other Time.

(Though Lent is not kept fo ftrictly as it was in former times, the receipts in this chapter are kept together, for the convenience of thofe perfons who may, by being near the fea-coaft, or in the country at a diftance from market towns, find it eafier to get fifh and vegetables than meat whenever they want it: at the fame time, all the difhes in the chapter are ufeful and elegant, fit for any table, and good without being too expenfive.)

A Peas Soup.

BOIL a quart of fplit-peas in a gallon of water; when they are quite foft put in half a red herring, or two anchovies, a good deal of whole pepper, black and white, two or three blades of mace, four or five cloves, a bundle of fweet herbs, a large onion, and the green tops of a bunch of celery, a good bundle of dried mint, cover them clofe, and let them boil foftly till there is about two quarts; then ftrain it off, and have ready the white part of the celery wafhed clean and cut fmall, and ſtewed tender in a quart of water, ſome ſpinage picked and waſhed clean put to the celery; let them ſtew till the water is quite waſted, and put it to your ſoup.

Take a French roll, take out the crumb, fry the cruſt brown in a little freſh butter; take ſome ſpinage, ſtew it in a little butter after it is boiled, and fill the roll; take the crumb, cut it in pieces, beat it in a mortar with a raw egg, a little ſpinage, and a little ſorrel, a little beaten mace, a little nutmeg, and an anchovy; then mix it up with your hand, and roll them into balls with a little flour, and cut ſome bread into dice, and fry them criſp; pour your ſoup into your diſh, put in the balls and bread, and the roll in the middle. Garniſh your diſh with ſpinage. If it wants ſalt, you muſt ſeaſon it to your palate: rub in ſome dried mint.

A Green Peas Soup.

Take a quart of old green peas, and boil them till they are quite tender as pap, in a quart of water; then ſtrain them through a ſieve, and boil a quart of young peas in that water. In the mean time put the old peas into a ſieve, pour half a pound of melted butter over them, and ſtrain them through the ſieve with the back of a ſpoon, till you have got all the pulp: when the young peas are boiled enough, add the pulp and butter to the young peas and liquor; ſtir them together till they are ſmooth, and ſeaſon with pepper and ſalt: you may fry a French roll, and let it ſwim in the diſh. If you like it, boil a bundle of mint in the peas.

Another Green Peas Soup.

Take a quart of green peas, boil them in a gallon of water, with a bundle of mint, and a few ſweet herbs, mace, cloves, and whole pepper, till they are tender; then ſtrain them, liquor and all, through a coarſe ſieve, till the pulp is ſtrained; put this liquor into a ſauce-pan, put to it four heads of celery clean waſhed and cut ſmall, a handful of ſpinage clean waſhed and cut ſmall, a lettuce cut ſmall, a fine leek cut ſmall, a quart of green peas, a little ſalt; cover them and let them boil very ſoftly till there is about two quarts, and that the celery is tender; then ſend it to table.

Juſt before you ſend up your ſoup, put in half a pint of ſpinage juice into it; but do not let it boil after.

Soup Meagre.

Take half a pound of butter, put it into a deep ſtew-pan, ſhake it about, and let it ſtand till it has done making a noiſe; then have ready ſix middling onions peeled and cut ſmall, throw them in and ſhake them about; take a bunch of celery clean waſhed

washed and picked, cut it in pieces half as long as your finger, a large handful of spinage clean washed and picked, a good lettuce clean washed, if you have it, and cut small, a little bundle of parsley chopped fine; shake all this well together in the pan for a quarter of an hour, then shake in a little flour, stir all together, and pour into the stew-pan two quarts of boiling water: take a handful of dry hard crust, throw in a tea-spoonful of beaten pepper, three blades of mace beat fine, stir all together, and let it boil softly for half an hour; then take it off the fire, and beat up the yolks of two eggs and stir in, and one spoonful of vinegar; pour it into the soup-dish and send it to table. If you have any green peas, boil half a-pint in the soup for change.

To make an Onion-Soup.

TAKE half a pound of butter, put it in a stew-pan on the fire, let it all melt, and boil it till it has done making any noise; then have ready ten or a dozen middling onions peeled and cut small, throw them into the butter and let them fry a quarter of an hour; then shake in a little flour, and stir them round; shake your pan, and let them do a few minutes longer; then pour in a quart or three pints of boiling water, stir them round; take a piece of upper crust, the stalest bread you have, about as big as the top of a penny-loaf cut small, and throw it in; season with salt to your palate; let it boil ten minutes, stirring it often: then take it off the fire, and have ready the yolks of two eggs beat fine, with half a spoonful of vinegar; mix some of the soup with them, then stir it into your soup and mix it well, and pour it into your dish. This is a delicious dish.

To make an Eel Soup.

TAKE eels, according to the quantity of soup you would make, (a pound will make a pint of good soup,) so, to every pound of eels put a quart of water, a crust of bread, two or three blades of mace, a little whole pepper, an onion, and a bundle of sweet herbs; cover them close and let them boil till half the liquor is wasted, then strain it, and toast some bread, cut it small, lay the bread into the dish, and pour in your soup: if you have a stew-hole, set the dish over it for a minute, and send it to table. If you find your soup not rich enough, you must let it boil till it is as strong as you would have it. You may make this soup as rich and good as if it was meat. You may add a piece of carrot to brown it.

To make a Craw-Fish Soup.

TAKE a carp, a large eel, half a thornback, cleanse and wash them clean, put them into a sauce-pan, or little pot, put to them a gallon of water, the cruſt of a penny-loaf; ſkim them well, ſeaſon it with mace, cloves, whole pepper, black and white, an onion, a bundle of ſweet herbs, ſome parſley, a piece of ginger, let them boil by themſelves cloſe covered; then take the tails of half a hundred craw-fiſh, pick out the bag, and all the woolly parts that are about them, put them into a ſauce-pan with two quarts of water, a little ſalt, a bundle of ſweet herbs; let them ſtew ſoftly, and when they are ready to boil, take out the tails, and beat all the other part of the craw-fiſh with the ſhells, and boil in the liquor the tails you took out, with a blade of mace, till it comes to about a pint, ſtrain it through a clean ſieve, and add it to the fiſh boiling; let all boil ſoftly till there is about three quarts; then ſtrain it off through a coarſe ſieve, put it into your pot again, and if it wants ſalt you muſt put ſome in, and the tails of the craw-fiſh; beat the live ſpawn of a hen lobſter very fine, and put in to give it a colour: take a French roll, and fry it criſp, and add to it; let them ſtew all together for a quarter of an hour: you may ſtew a carp with them; pour your ſoup into your diſh, the roll ſwimming in the middle.

When you have a carp, there ſhould be a roll on each ſide. Garniſh your diſh with craw-fiſh. If your craw-fiſh will not lie on the ſides of your diſh, make a little paſte, and lay round the rim, and lay the fiſh on that all round the diſh.

Take care that your ſoup be well ſeaſoned, but not too high.

To make a Muſſel-Soup.

GET a hundred of muſſels, waſh them very clean, put them into a ſtew-pan, cover them cloſe; let them ſtew till they open, then pick them out of the ſhells, ſtrain the liquor through a fine lawn ſieve to your muſſels, and pick the beard or crab out, if any.

Take a dozen craw-fiſh, beat them to maſh, with a dozen of almonds blanched and beat fine, then take a ſmall parſnip and a carrot ſcraped and cut in thin ſlices, fry them brown with a little butter: then take two pounds of any freſh fiſh, and boil in a gallon of water, with a bundle of ſweet herbs, a large onion ſtuck with cloves, whole pepper, black and white, a little parſley, a little piece of horſe-radiſh, and ſalt the muſſel-liquor, the craw-fiſh, and almonds; let them boil till half is waſted, then ſtrain them through a ſieve, put the ſoup into a ſauce-pan; put in twenty of the muſſels, a few muſhrooms, and truffles cut ſmall, and a leek waſhed and cut very ſmall; take two French rolls, take out the crumb, fry it brown, cut it into little pieces, put it into the ſoup; let it boil all together for a quarter of an hour, with the fried carrot and parſnip; in the mean while take the cruſt of the rolls fried criſp; take half a hundred of the muſſels,

muſſels, a quarter of a pound of butter, a ſpoonful of water, ſhake in a little flour, ſet them on the fire, keeping the ſauce-pan ſhaking all the time till the butter is melted; ſeaſon it with pepper and ſalt, beat the yolks of three eggs, put them in, ſtir them all the time for fear of curdling, grate a little nutmeg; when it is thick and fine, fill the rolls, pour your ſoup into the diſh, put in the rolls, and lay the reſt of the muſſels round the rim of the diſh.

To make a Scate or Thornback Soup.

TAKE two pounds of ſcate or thornback, ſkin it and boil it in ſix quarts of water; when it is enough, take it up, pick off the fleſh and lay it by; put in the bones again and about two pounds of any freſh fiſh, a very little piece of lemon-peel, a bundle of ſweet herbs, whole pepper, two or three blades of mace, a little piece of horſe-radiſh, the cruſt of a penny-loaf, a little parſley; cover it cloſe, and let it boil till there is about two quarts, then ſtrain it off, and add an ounce of vermicelli, ſet it on the fire and let it boil ſoftly; in the meantime take a French roll, cut a little hole in the top, take out the crumb, fry the cruſt brown in butter, take the fleſh of the fiſh you laid by and cut it into little pieces, put it into a ſauce-pan with two or three ſpoonfuls of the ſoup; ſhake in a little flour, put in a piece of butter, a little pepper and ſalt, ſhake them together in the ſauce-pan over the fire till it is quite thick, then fill the roll with it; pour your ſoup into your diſh, let the roll ſwim in the middle, and ſend it to table.

To make an Oyſter-Soup.

YOUR ſtock muſt be made of any ſort of fiſh the place affords; let there be about two quarts, take a pint of oyſters, beard them, put them into a ſauce-pan, ſtrain the liquor, let them ſtew two or three minutes in their own liquor, then take the hard parts of the oyſters and beat them in a mortar with the yolks of four hard eggs, mix them with ſome of the ſoup, put them with the other parts of the oyſters and liquor into a ſauce-pan, a little nutmeg, pepper, and ſalt, ſtir them well together, and let it boil a quarter of an hour: diſh it up and ſend it to table.

To make an Almond-Soup.

TAKE a quart of almonds, blanch them, and beat them in a marble mortar, with the yolks of twelve hard eggs, till they are a fine paſte; mix them by degrees with two quarts of new milk, a quart of cream, a quarter of a pound of double-refined ſugar beat fine; ſtir all well together: when it is well mixed, ſet it over a ſlow fire, and keep it ſtirring quick all the while till you find it is thick enough, then pour it into your diſh, and ſend it to table. If you be not very careful, it will curdle.

To make a Rice-Soup.

TAKE two quarts of water, a pound of rice, a little cinnamon; cover it cloſe, and let it ſimmer very ſoftly till the rice is quite tender; take out the cinnamon, then ſweeten it to your palate, grate half a nutmeg, and let it ſtand till it is cold; then beat up the yolks of three eggs with half a pint of white wine, mix them very well, then ſtir them into the rice, ſet them on a ſlow fire, and keep ſtirring all the time for fear of curdling: when it is of a good thickneſs, and boils, take it up; keep ſtirring it till you put it into your diſh.

To make a Barley-Soup.

TAKE a gallon of water, half a pound of barley, a blade or two of mace, a large cruſt of bread, a little lemon-peel; let it boil till it comes to two quarts; then add half a pint of white wine, and ſweeten to your palate.

To make a Turnip-Soup.

TAKE a gallon of water, and a bunch of turnips, pare them, ſave three or four out, put the reſt into the water, with half an ounce of whole pepper, an onion ſtuck with cloves, a blade of mace, half a nutmeg bruiſed, a little bundle of ſweet herbs, and a large cruſt of bread; let theſe boil an hour pretty faſt, then ſtrain it through a ſieve, ſqueezing the turnips through; waſh and cut a bunch of celery very ſmall, ſet it in the liquor on the fire, cover it cloſe and let it ſtew; in the mean time cut the turnips you ſaved into dice, and two or three ſmall carrots clean ſcraped, and cut in little pieces; put half theſe turnips and carrots into the pot with the celery, and the other half fry brown in freſh butter; you muſt flour them firſt, and two or three onions peeled, cut in thin ſlices, and fried brown; then put them all into the ſoup, with an ounce of vermicelli: let your ſoup boil ſoftly till the celery is quite tender, and your ſoup good: ſeaſon it with ſalt to your palate.

To make an Egg-Soup.

BEAT the yolks of two eggs in your diſh with a piece of butter as big as a hen's egg; take a tea-kettle of boiling water in one hand, and a ſpoon in the other, pour in about a quart by degrees, keep ſtirring it all the time well till the eggs are well mixed and the butter melted; then pour it into a ſauce-pan, and keep ſtirring it all the time till it begins to ſimmer; take it off the fire and pour it between two veſſels, out of one into

 another,

another, till it is quite ſmooth, and has a great froth; ſet it on the fire again, keep ſtirring it till it is quite hot; then put it into the ſoup-diſh, and ſend it to table hot.

To make Peas-Porridge.

TAKE a quart of green peas, put to them a quart of water, a bundle of dried mint, and a little ſalt; let them boil till the peas are quite tender; then put in ſome beaten pepper, a piece of butter as big as a walnut, rolled in flour, ſtir it all together, and let it boil a few minutes; then add two quarts of milk, let it boil a quarter of an hour, take out the mint, and ſerve it up.

A Spaniſh Peas-Soup.

TAKE one pound of Spaniſh peas, and lay them in water the night before you uſe them; then take a gallon of water, one quart of fine ſweet oil, a head of garlic; cover the pot cloſe, and let it boil till the peas are ſoft; then ſeaſon with pepper and ſalt; then beat the yolk of an egg, and vinegar to your palate; poach ſome eggs, lay on the diſh on ſippets, and pour the ſoup on them: ſend them to table.

To make Onion-Soup the Spaniſh Way.

TAKE two large Spaniſh onions, peel and ſlice them; let them boil very ſoftly in half a pint of ſweet oil till the onions are very ſoft, then pour on them three pints of boiling water; ſeaſon with beaten pepper, ſalt, a little beaten clove and mace, two ſpoonfuls of vinegar, a handful of parſley waſhed clean and chopped fine; let it boil faſt a quarter of an hour; in the meantime, get ſome ſippets to cover the bottom of the diſh, fried quick, not hard; lay them in the diſh, and cover each ſippet with a poached egg; beat up the yolks of two eggs and throw over them; pour in your ſoup, and ſend it to table.

Garlic and ſorrel, done the ſame way, eats well.

Milk-Soup the Dutch Way.

TAKE a quart of milk, boil it with cinnamon and moiſt ſugar; put ſippets in the diſh, pour the milk over it, and ſet it over a charcoal fire to ſimmer till the bread is ſoft; take the yolks of two eggs, beat them up, and mix it with a little of the milk, and throw it in; mix it all together, and ſend it up to table.

To make a White-Pot.

TAKE two quarts of new milk, eight eggs, and half the whites, beat up with a little roſe-water, a nutmeg, a quarter of a pound of ſugar; cut a penny-loaf in very thin ſlices, and

 pour

pour milk and eggs over; put a little bit of ſweet butter at the top. Bake it in a ſlow oven half an hour.

To make a Rice White-Pot.

Boil a pound of rice in two quarts of new milk till it is tender and thick; beat it in a mortar with a quarter of a pound of ſweet almonds blanched; then boil two quarts of cream, with a few crumbs of white bread, and two or three blades of mace; mix it all with eight eggs, a little roſe-water, and ſweeten to your taſte; cut ſome candied orange and citron peels thin, and lay it in. It muſt be put into a ſlow oven.

To make Rice-Milk.

Take half a pound of rice, boil it in a quart of water, with a little cinnamon; let it boil till the water is all waſted; take great care it does not burn; then add three pints of milk, and the yolk of an egg beat up; keep it ſtirring, and when it boils take it up; ſweeten to your palate.

To make an Orange-Fool.

Take the juice of ſix oranges, and ſix eggs well beaten, a pint of cream, a quarter of a pound of ſugar, a little cinnamon and nutmeg. Mix all together, and keep ſtirring over a ſlow fire till it is thick; then put in a little piece of butter, and keep ſtirring till cold, and diſh it up.

To make a Weſtminſter Fool.

Take a penny-loaf, cut it into thin ſlices, wet them with ſack, lay them in the bottom of a diſh; take a quart of cream, beat up ſix eggs, two ſpoonfuls of roſe-water, a blade of mace, and ſome grated nutmeg; ſweeten to your taſte; put all this into a ſauce-pan, and keep ſtirring all the time over a ſlow fire for fear of curdling: when it begins to be thick, pour it into the diſh over the bread; let it ſtand till it is cold, and ſerve it up.

To make a Gooſeberry-Fool.

Take two quarts of gooſeberries, ſet them on the fire in about a quart of water; when they begin to ſimmer, turn yellow, and begin to plump, throw them into a cullender to drain the water out, then with the back of a ſpoon carefully ſqueeze the pulp, throw the ſieve into a diſh, make them pretty ſweet, and let them ſtand till they are cold: in the meantime take two quarts of new milk, and the yolks of four eggs beat up with a little grated nutmeg; ſtir it ſoftly over a ſlow fire; when it begins to ſimmer take it off, and by degrees ſtir it into the

the gooſeberries; let it ſtand till it is cold, and ſerve it up: if you make it with cream, you need not put any eggs in; and if it is not thick enough, it is only boiling more gooſeberries: but that you muſt do as you think proper.

To make Furmity.

TAKE a quart of ready-boiled wheat, two quarts of milk, a quarter of a pound of currants clean picked and waſhed; ſtir theſe together and boil them; beat up the yolks of three or four eggs, a little nutmeg, with two or three ſpoonfuls of milk, and add to the wheat; ſtir them together for a few minutes; then ſweeten to your palate, and ſend it to table.

To make Plumb-Porridge, or Barley-Gruel.

TAKE a gallon of water, half a pound of barley, a quarter of a pound of raiſins clean waſhed, a quarter of a pound of currants clean waſhed and picked: boil theſe till above half the water is waſted, with two or three blades of mace; then ſweeten it to your palate, and add half a pint of white wine.

To make Buttered Wheat.

PUT your wheat into a ſauce-pan; when it is hot, ſtir in a good piece of butter, a little grated nutmeg, and ſweeten it to your palate.

To make Plumb-Gruel.

TAKE two quarts of water, two large ſpoonfuls of oatmeal, ſtir it together, a blade or two of mace, a little piece of lemon-peel; boil it for five or ſix minutes (take care it do not boil over), then ſtrain it off, and put it into the ſauce-pan again, with half a pound of currants clean waſhed and picked; let them boil about ten minutes, add a glaſs of white wine, a little grated nutmeg, and ſweeten to your palate.

To make a Flour Haſty-Pudding.

TAKE a quart of milk and four bay-leaves, ſet it on the fire to boil, beat up the yolks of two eggs, and ſtir in a little ſalt; take two or three ſpoonfuls of milk, and beat up with your eggs, and ſtir in your milk; then, with a wooden ſpoon in one hand and the flour in the other, ſtir it in till it is of a good thickneſs, but not too thick; let it boil, and keep it ſtirring, then pour it into a diſh, and ſtick pieces of butter here and there: you may omit the egg if you do not like it; but it is a great addition to the pudding; and a little piece of butter ſtirred in the milk makes it eat ſhort and fine; take out the bay-leaves before you put in the flour.

To make an Oatmeal Hasty-Pudding.

TAKE a quart of water, set it on to boil, put in a piece of butter and some salt; when it boils, stir in the oatmeal as you do the flour, till it is of a good thickness; let it boil a few minutes, pour it in your dish, and stick pieces of butter in it; or eat with wine and sugar, or ale and sugar, or cream, or new milk. This is best made with Scotch oatmeal.

To make a fine Hasty-Pudding.

BREAK an egg into fine flour, and with your hand work up as much as you can into as stiff paste as is possible; then mince it as small as herbs to the pot, as small as if it were to be sifted; then set a quart of milk a-boiling, and put it in the paste so cut: put in a little salt, a little beaten cinnamon and sugar, a piece of butter as big as a walnut, and keep stirring all one way; when it is as thick as you would have it, stir in such another piece of butter, then pour it into your dish, and stick pieces of butter here and there: send it to table hot.

To make an excellent Sack-Posset.

BEAT fifteen eggs, whites and yolks very well, and strain them; then put three quarters of a pound of white sugar into a pint of canary, and mix it with your eggs in a bason; set it over a chafing-dish of coals, and keep continually stirring it till it is scalding hot; in the meantime grate some nutmeg in a quart of milk and boil it; then pour it into your eggs and wine, they being scalding hot: hold your hand very high as you pour it, and somebody stirring it all the time you are pouring in the milk; then take it off the chafing-dish, set it before the fire half an hour, and serve it up.

To make another Sack-Posset.

TAKE a quart of new milk, four Naples biscuits, crumble them, and when the milk boils throw them in; just give it one boil, take it off, grate in some nutmeg, and sweeten to your palate; then pour in half a pint of sack, stirring it all the time, and serve it up. You may crumble white bread instead of biscuit.

Or make it thus:

BOIL a quart of cream or new milk, with the yolks of two eggs; first take a French roll and cut it as thin as possibly you can in little pieces; lay it in the dish you intend for the posset; when the milk boils (which you must keep stirring all the time), pour it over the bread, and stir it together; cover it close, then take a pint of canary, a quarter of a pound of sugar, and

and grate in ſome nutmeg; when it boils, pour it into the milk, ſtirring it all the time, and ſerve it up.

To make Haſty Fritters.

TAKE a ſtew-pan, put in ſome butter, and let it be hot. In the mean time take half a pint of all ale not bitter, and ſtir in ſome flour by degrees in a little of the ale; put in a few currants, or chopped apples, beat them up quick, and drop a large ſpoonful at a time all over the pan: take care they do not ſtick together, turn them with an egg-ſlice, and when they are of a fine brown, lay them in a diſh, and throw ſome ſugar over them. Garniſh them with orange cut into quarters.

To make fine Fritters.

DRY ſome of the fineſt flour well before the fire; mix it with a quart of new milk, not too thick, ſix or eight eggs, a little nutmeg, a little mace, a little ſalt, and a quarter of a pint of ſack or ale, or a glaſs of brandy: beat them well together, then make them pretty thick with pippins, and fry them dry.

To make Apple-Fritters.

BEAT the yolks of eight eggs, the whites of four, well together, and ſtrain them into a pan; then take a quart of cream, make it as hot as you can bear your finger in it; then put to it a quarter of a pint of ſack, three quarters of a pint of ale, and make a poſſet of it: when it is cool, put it to your eggs, beating it well together; then put in nutmeg, ginger, ſalt, and flour to your liking: your batter ſhould be pretty thick; then put in pippins ſliced or ſcraped, and fry them in a good deal of butter quick.

To make Curd-Fritters.

HAVING a handful of curds and a handful of flour, and ten eggs well beaten and ſtrained, ſome ſugar, cloves, mace, and nutmeg beat, a little ſaffron; ſtir all well together, and fry them quick, and of a fine light brown.

To make Fritters-Royal.

TAKE a quart of new milk, put it into a ſkillet or ſauce-pan, and, as the milk boils up, pour in a pint of ſack; let it boil up, then take it off, and let it ſtand five or ſix minutes; then ſkim off all the curd and put it into a baſon; beat it up well with ſix eggs, ſeaſon it with nutmeg; then beat it with a whiſk, add flour to make it as thick as batter uſually is, put in ſome fine ſugar, and fry them quick.

To make Skirret-Fritters.

TAKE a pint of pulp of ſkirrets, and a ſpoonful of flour, the yolks of four eggs, ſugar and ſpice, make into a thick batter, and fry them quick.

To make White Fritters.

HAVING ſome rice, waſh it in five or ſix ſeveral waters and dry it very well before the fire; then beat it in a mortar very fine, and ſift it through a lawn ſieve that it may be very fine; you muſt have at leaſt an ounce of it, then put it into a ſauce-pan, juſt wet it with milk, and when it is well incorporated with it, add to it another pint of milk; ſet the whole over a ſtove or a very ſlow fire, and take care to keep it always moving; put in a little ſugar, and ſome candied lemon-peel grated, keep it over the fire till it is almoſt come to the thickneſs of a fine paſte, flour a peel, pour it on it and ſpread it abroad with a rolling-pin: when it is quite cold, cut it into little morſels, taking care they ſtick not one to the other; flour your hands and roll up your fritters handſomely, and fry them. When you ſerve them up, pour a little orange-flower water over them, and ſugar. Theſe make a pretty ſide-diſh; or are very pretty to garniſh a fine diſh with.

To make Syringed Fritters.

TAKE about a pint of water, and a bit of butter the ſize of an egg, with ſome lemon-peel (green if you can get it), raſped preſerved lemon-peel, and criſped orange-flowers; put all together in a ſtew-pan over the fire, and when boiling throw in ſome fine flour; keep it ſtirring; put in by degrees more flour till your butter be thick enough, take it off the fire; then take an ounce of ſweet almonds, four bitter ones, pound them in a mortar, ſtir in two Naples biſcuits crumbled, two eggs beat; ſtir all together, and more eggs till your batter be thin enough to be ſyringed: fill your ſyringe, the batter being hot, ſyringe your fritters in it to make it of a true lover's knot, and, being well coloured, ſerve them up for a ſide-diſh.

At another time, you may rub a ſheet of paper with butter, over which you may ſyringe your fritters, and make them in what ſhape you pleaſe. Your butter being hot, turn the paper upſide down over it, and your fritters will eaſily drop off: when fried, ſtew them with ſugar and glaze them.

To make Vine-Leaf Fritters.

TAKE ſome of the ſmalleſt vine-leaves you can get, and having cut off the great ſtalks, put them in a diſh with ſome French

French brandy, green lemon rafped, and fome fugar; take a good handful of fine flour, mixed with white wine or ale; let your butter be hot, and with a fpoon drop in your batter; take great care they do not ftick one to the other; on each fritter lay a leaf; fry them quick, and ftrew fugar over them, and glaze them with a red-hot fhovel or falamander.

With all fritters made with milk and eggs you fhould have beaten cinnamon and fugar in a faucer, and either fqueeze an orange over it, or pour a glafs of white wine, and fo throw fugar all over the difh, and they fhould be fried in a good deal of fat; therefore they are beft fried in beef-dripping, or hog's-lard, when it can be done.

To make Clary-Fritters.

TAKE your clary-leaves, cut off the ftalks, dip them one by one in a batter made with milk and flour, your butter being hot, fry them quick. This is a pretty heartening difh for a fick or weak perfon; and comfrey-leaves do the fame way.

To make Spanifh Fritters.

TAKE the infide of a roll, and flice it in three; then foak it in milk; then pafs it through a batter of eggs, fry them in oil; when almoft done, repafs them in another batter; then let them fry till they are done, draw them off the oil, and lay them in a difh; over every pair of fritters you muft throw cinnamon, fmall coloured fugar-plumbs, and clarified fugar.

To make Plumb-Fritters with Rice.

GRATE the crumbs of a penny-loaf, pour over it a pint of boiling cream, or good milk, let it ftand four or five hours, then beat it exceeding fine, put to it the yolks of five eggs, four ounces of fugar, and a nutmeg grated; beat them well together, and fry them in hog's-lard; drain them on a fieve, and ferve them up with white wine fauce under them.

N. B. You may put currants in if you pleafe.

To make Apple Frazes.

CUT your apples in thick flices, and fry them of a fine light brown; take them up, and lay them to drain, keep them as whole as you can, and either pare them or let it alone; then make a batter as follows: take five eggs, leaving out two whites, beat them up with cream and flour, and a little fack, make it the thicknefs of a pancake-batter, pour in a little melted butter, nutmeg, and a little fugar: let your batter be hot, and drop in your fritters, and on every one lay a flice of apple, and then more batter on them: fry them of a fine light brown;

brown; take them up, and ſtrew ſome double-refined ſugar all over them.

To make an Almond Fraze.

GET a pound of Jordan almonds, blanched, ſteep them in a pint of ſweet cream, ten yolks of eggs, and four whites; take out the almonds and pound them in a mortar fine; then mix them again in the cream and eggs, put in ſugar and grated white bread, ſtir them all together, put ſome freſh butter into the pan, let it be hot and pour it in, ſtirring it in the pan till they are of a good thickneſs; and when it is enough, turn it into a diſh, throw ſugar over it, and ſerve it up.

To make German Puffs.

PUT half a pint of good milk into a toſſing-pan, and dredge it in flour till it is as thick as haſty-pudding, keep ſtirring it over a ſlow fire till it is all of a lump, then put it in a marble mortar; when it is cold put to it the yolks of eight eggs, four ounces of ſugar, a ſpoonful of roſe-water, grate a little nutmeg and the rind of half a lemon, beat them together an hour or more, when it looks light and bright, drop them into a pan of boiling lard with a tea-ſpoon, the ſize of a large nutmeg, they will riſe and look like a large yellow plumb if they are well beat; as you fry them lay them on a ſieve to drain, grate ſugar round your diſh, and ſerve them up with ſack for ſauce. It is a proper corner diſh for dinner or ſupper.

To make Pancakes.

TAKE a quart of milk, beat in ſix or eight eggs, leaving half the whites out, mix it well till your batter is of a fine thickneſs; you muſt obſerve to mix your flour firſt with a little milk, then add the reſt by degrees; put in two ſpoonfuls of beaten ginger, a glaſs of brandy, a little ſalt; ſtir all together, make your ſtew-pan very clean, put in a piece of butter as big as a walnut, then pour in a ladleful of batter, which will make a pancake, moving the pan round that the batter be all over the pan, ſhake the pan, and when you think that ſide is enough, toſs it; if you cannot, turn it cleverly; and when both ſides are done, lay it in a diſh before the fire, and ſo do the reſt; you muſt take care they are dry: when you ſend them to table ſtrew a little ſugar over them.

The brandy may be left out.

To make fine Pancakes.

TAKE half a pint of cream, half a pint of ſack, the yolks of eighteen eggs beat fine, a little ſalt, half a pound of fine ſugar, a little beaten cinnamon, mace, and nutmeg; then put in as much

much flour as will run thin over the pan, and fry them in fresh butter. This sort of pancake will not be crisp, but very good.

A second sort of fine Pancakes.

TAKE a pint of cream, and eight eggs well beat, a nutmeg grated, a little salt, half a pound of good dish-butter melted; mix all together, with as much flour as will make them into a thin batter, fry them nice, and turn them on the back of a plate.

A third Sort.

TAKE six new-laid eggs well beat, mix them with a pint of cream, a quarter of a pound of sugar, some grated nutmeg, and as much flour as will make the batter of a proper thickness; fry these fine pancakes in small pans, and let your pans be hot: you must not put above the bigness of a nutmeg of butter at a time into the pan.

A fourth Sort, called a Quire of Paper.

TAKE a pint of cream, six eggs, three spoonfuls of fine flour, three of sack, one of orange flower water, a little sugar, and half a nutmeg grated, half a pound of melted butter almost cold; mingle all well together, and butter the pan for the first pancake; let them run as thin as possible; when they are just coloured they are enough; and so do with all the fine pancakes.

To make Rice Pancakes.

TAKE a quart of cream, and three spoonfuls of flour of rice; set it on a slow fire, and keep it stirring till it is thick as pap; stir in half a pound of butter, a nutmeg grated; then pour it out into an earthen pan, and when it is cold, stir in three or four spoonfuls of flour, a little salt, some sugar, nine eggs well beaten; mix all well together, and fry them nicely. When you have no cream, use new milk, and one spoonful or more of the flour of rice.

To make Wafer Pancakes.

BEAT four eggs well with two spoonfuls of fine flour, and two of cream, one ounce of loaf-sugar, beat and sifted, half a nutmeg grated, put a little cold butter in a clean cloth, and rub your pan well with it, pour in your batter and make it as thin as a wafer, fry it only on one side, put them on a dish, and grate sugar betwixt every pancake, and send them hot to the table.

To make Tansey Pancakes.

BEAT four eggs, and put to them half a pint of cream, four spoonfuls of flour, and two of fine sugar, beat them a quarter of an an hour, then put in one ſpoonful of the juice of tanſey, and two of the juice of ſpinage, with a little grated nutmeg, beat all well together, and fry them in freſh butter: garniſh them with quarters of Seville oranges, grate double-refined ſugar over them, and ſend them up hot.

To make a pink-coloured Pancake.

BOIL a large beet-root tender, and beat it fine in a marble mortar, then add the yolks of four eggs, two ſpoonfuls of flour, and three ſpoonfuls of good cream, ſweeten it to your taſte, and grate in half a nutmeg, and put in a glaſs of brandy; beat them all together half an hour, fry them in butter, and garniſh them with green ſweet-meats, preſerved apricots, or green ſprigs of myrtle. It is a pretty corner-diſh for either dinner or ſupper.

To make a Pupton of Apples.

PARE ſome apples, take out the cores and put them into a ſkillet: to a quart mugful heaped put in a quarter of a pound of ſugar, and two ſpoonfuls of water; do them over a ſlow fire, keep them ſtirring, add a little cinnamon; when it is quite thick and like a marmalade, let it ſtand till cool; beat up the yolks of four or five eggs, and ſtir in a handful of grated bread and a quarter of a pound of freſh butter; then form it into what ſhape you pleaſe, and bake it in a ſlow oven, and then turn it upſide down on a plate, for a ſecond courſe.

To make Black-Caps.

CUT twelve large apples in halves, and take out the cores, place them on a thin patty-pan, or mazarine, as cloſe together as they can lie, with the flat ſide downwards; ſqueeze a lemon in two ſpoonfuls of orange-flower water and pour over them; ſhred ſome lemon-peel fine and throw over them, and grate fine ſugar all over; ſet them in a quick oven, and half an hour will do them. When you ſend them to table throw fine ſugar all over the diſh.

To bake Apples whole.

PUT your apples into an earthen pan with a few cloves, a little lemon-peel, ſome coarſe ſugar, a glaſs of red wine; put them in a quick oven, and they will take an hour baking.

To make a Diſh of roaſted Apples.

TAKE ſmall apples, roaſt them in a ſlow oven till they are ſoft, mind they do not fall; have ready ſome rice, cree it ſtiff with a little lemon-peel in it and a ſtick of cinnamon, when the rice is enough take out the ſeaſoning, put to it a ſpoonful of roſe-water and one of almond-water, ſweeten it to your taſte;

5 when

when cold lay apples into the dish, lay the rice neatly over them; with a knife stick them with bits of candied orange, and garnish with any thing green.

To stew Pippins whole.

TAKE twelve golden pippins, pare them, put the parings into a sauce-pan with water enough to cover them, a blade of mace, two or three cloves, a piece of lemon-peel; let them simmer till there is just enough to do the pippins in, then strain it and put it into the sauce-pan again, with sugar enough to make it like syrup; then put them in a preserving-pan, or clean stew-pan, or large sauce-pan, and pour the syrup over them; let there be enough to stew them in: when they are enough, which you will know by the pippins being soft, take them up, lay them in a hot dish with the syrup: when cold, serve them up; or hot, if you choose it.

To stew Pears.

PARE six large winter pears, and either quarter them or do them whole: they make a pretty dish with one whole, the rest cut in quarters, and the cores taken out; lay them in a deep earthen pot, with a few cloves, a piece of lemon-peel, a gill of red wine, and a quarter of a pound of fine sugar; if the pears are very large, they will take half a pound of sugar, and half a pint of red wine; cover them close with brown paper, and bake them till they are enough.

Serve them hot or cold (just as you like them), and they will be very good with water in the place of wine.

To stew Pears in a Sauce-pan.

PUT them into a sauce-pan with the ingredients as before; cover them and do them over a slow fire; when they are enough take them off, add a pennyworth of cochineal, bruised very fine.

To stew Pears purple.

PARE four pears, cut them into quarters, core them, put them into a stew-pan, with a quarter of a pint of water, a quarter of a pound of sugar; cover them with a pewter-plate then cover the pan with the lid, and do them over a slow fire; look at them often for fear of melting the plate; when they are enough, and the liquor looks of a fine purple, take them off and lay them in your dish with the liquor; when cold, serve them up for a side-dish at a second course, or just as you please.

A pretty Made-Dish.

TAKE half a pound of almonds blanched and beat fine, with a little rose or orange-flower water; then take a quart of

sweet

ſweet thick cream and boil it with a piece of cinnamon and mace; ſweeten it with ſugar to your palate, and mix it with your almonds; ſtir it well together, and ſtrain it through a ſieve; let your cream cool and thicken it with the yolks of ſix eggs; then garniſh a deep diſh and lay paſte at the bottom, then put in ſhred artichoke-bottoms (being firſt boiled), upon that a little melted butter, ſhred citron, and candied orange; ſo do till your diſh is near full, then pour in your cream, and bake it without a lid; when it is baked, ſcrape ſugar over it, and ſerve it up hot: half an hour will bake it.

To make Kickſhaws.

MAKE puff paſte, roll it thin, and if you have any moulds work it upon them; make them up with preſerved pippins: you may fill ſome with gooſeberries, ſome with raſpberries, or what you pleaſe; then cloſe them up, and either bake or fry them; throw grated ſugar over them, and ſerve them up.

Pain Perdu, or Cream Toaſts.

HAVING two French rolls, cut them into ſlices as thick as your finger, crumb and cruſt together; lay them on a diſh, put to them a pint of cream and half a pint of milk; ſtrew them over with beaten cinnamon and ſugar; turn them frequently till they are tender, but take care not to break them; then take them from the cream with the ſlice, break four or five eggs, turn your ſlices of bread in the eggs, and fry them in clarified butter: make them of a good brown colour, but not black; ſcrape a little ſugar over them. They may be ſerved for a ſecond-courſe diſh, but are fitteſt for ſupper.

Salmagundy for a Middle-Diſh at Supper.

IN the top plate in the middle, which ſhould ſtand higher than the reſt, take a fine pickled-herring, bone it, take off the head and mince the reſt fine; in the other plates round put the following things: in one pare a cucumber and cut it very thin; in another, apples pared and cut ſmall; in another, an onion peeled and cut ſmall; in another, two hard eggs chopped ſmall, the whites in one and the yolks in another; pickled girkins cut ſmall; in another celery cut ſmall; in another pickled red cabbage chopped fine; take ſome water-creſſes clean waſhed and picked, ſtick them all about and between every plate or ſaucer, and throw naſtertium-flowers about the creſſes. You muſt have oil and vinegar, and lemon, to eat with it. If it is neatly ſet out, it will make a pretty figure in the middle of the table, or you may lay them in heaps in a diſh: if you have not all theſe ingredients ſet out your plates or ſaucers with

with juſt what you fancy, and in the room of a pickled-herring you may mince anchovies.

To make a Tanſey.

TAKE ten eggs, break them into a pan, put to them a little ſalt, beat them very well; then put to them eight ounces of loaf-ſugar beat fine, and a pint of the juice of ſpinage and a little juice of tanſey; mix them well together, and ſtrain it into a quart of cream; then grate in eight ounces of Naples biſcuit or white bread, a nutmeg grated, a quarter of a pound of Jordan almonds, beat in a mortar with a little juice of tanſey to your taſte: mix theſe all together, put it into a ſtew-pan with a piece of butter as large as a pippin; ſet it over a ſlow charcoal fire, keep it ſtirring till it is hardened very well; then butter a diſh very well, put in your tanſey, bake it, and when it is enough turn it out on a pie-plate; ſqueeze the juice of an orange over it, and throw ſugar all over. Garniſh with orange cut into quarters, and ſweetmeats cut into long bits, and lay all over its ſide.

Another Way.

TAKE a pint of cream, and half a pint of blanched almonds beat fine, with roſe and orange flower water, ſtir them together over a ſlow fire; when it boils take it off, and let it ſtand till cold; then beat in ten eggs, grate in a ſmall nutmeg, four Naples biſcuits, a little grated bread; ſweeten to your taſte; and if you think it is too thick, put in ſome more cream, the juice of ſpinage to make it green; ſtir it well together, and either fry it or bake it: if you fry it, do one ſide firſt, and then with a diſh turn the other.

To make a Bean Tanſey.

TAKE two quarts of beans, blanch and beat them very fine in a mortar; ſeaſon with pepper, ſalt, and mace; then put in the yolks of ſix eggs, and a quarter of a pound of butter, a pint of cream, half a pint of ſack, and ſweeten to your palate; ſoak four Naples biſcuits in half a pint of milk, mix them with the other ingredients, half a pint of the juice of ſpinage, with two or three ſprigs of tanſey beat with it; butter a pan and bake it, then turn it on a diſh and ſtick citron and orange-peel candied, cut ſmall, and ſtuck about it. Garniſh with Seville orange.

To make a Water Tanſey.

TAKE twelve eggs, beat them very well, half a manchet grated, and ſifted through a cullender, or half a penny roll, half a pint of fair water; colour it with the juice of ſpinage and one ſmall ſprig of tanſey beat together; ſeaſon it with ſugar to your palate, a little ſalt, a ſmall nutmeg grated, two or three

three ſpoonfuls of roſe-water, put it into a ſkillet, ſtir it all one way and let it thicken like a haſty-pudding, then bake it; or you may butter a ſtew-pan and put it into; butter a diſh and lay over it; when one ſide is enough, turn it with the diſh, and ſlip the other ſide into the pan. When that is done, ſet it into a maſſereen, throw ſugar all over, and garniſh with orange.

To make a Hedge-Hog.

TAKE two pounds of ſweet almonds blanched, beat them well in a mortar, with a little canary and orange-flower water, to keep them from oiling; make them into a ſtiff paſte, then beat in the yolks of twelve eggs, leave out five of the whites, put to it a pint of cream, ſweeten it with ſugar, put in half a pound of ſweet butter melted, ſet it on a furnace or ſlow fire, and keep continually ſtirring till it is ſtiff enough to be made into the form of a hedge-hog, then ſtick it full of blanched almonds ſlit, and ſtuck up like the briſtles of a hedge-hog, then put it into a diſh. Take a pint of cream and the yolks of four eggs beat up, and mix with the cream; ſweeten to your palate, and keep them ſtirring over a ſlow fire all the time till it is hot, then pour it into your diſh round the hedge-hog; let it ſtand till it is cold, and ſerve it it up.

Or you may make a fine harſhorn-jelly, and pour into the diſh, which will look very pretty. You may eat wine and ſugar with it, or eat it without.

Or cold cream ſweetened with a glaſs of white wine in it, and the juice of a Seville orange, and pour it into the diſh. It will be pretty for change.

This is a pretty ſide-diſh at a ſecond courſe, or in the middle for ſupper, or in a grand deſert; plump two currants for the eyes.

Or make it thus for Change:

TAKE two pounds of ſweet almonds blanched, twelve bitter ones, beat them in a marble mortar well together, with canary and orange-flower water, two ſpoonfuls of the tincture of ſaffron, two ſpoonfuls of the juice of ſorrel, beat them into a fine paſte, put in half a pound of melted butter, mix it up well, a little nutmeg and beaten mace, an ounce of citron, an ounce of orange-peel, both cut fine, mix them in the yolks of twelve eggs, and half the whites beat up and mixed in half a pint of cream, half a pint of double-refined ſugar, and work it up all together; if it is not ſtiff enough to make up into the form you would have it, you muſt have a mould for it; butter it well, then put in your ingredients, and bake it. The mould muſt be made in ſuch a manner as to have the head peeping out; when it comes out of the oven have ready ſome almonds blanched

blanched and slit, and boiled up in sugar till brown; stick it all over with the almonds; and, for sauce, have red wine and sugar made hot, and the juice of an orange: send it hot to table for a first course.

You may leave out the saffron and sorrel, and make it up like chickens, or any other shape you please, or alter the sauce to your fancy. Butter, sugar, and white wine is a pretty sauce for either baked or boiled, and you may make the sauce of what colour you please; or put it into a mould, with half a pound of currants added to it, and boil it for a pudding. You may use cochineal in the room of saffron.

The following liquor you may make to mix with your sauces: beat an ounce of cochineal very fine, put in a pint of water in a skillet, and a quarter of an ounce of roche-alum; boil it till the goodness is out, strain it into a phial, with an ounce of fine sugar, and it will keep six months.

To ragoo Endive.

TAKE some fine white endive, three heads, lay them in salt and water two or three hours; take a hundred of asparagus, cut off the green heads, chop the rest small, as far as is tender; lay it in salt and water; take a bunch of celery, wash it and scrape it clean, cut it in pieces about three inches long, put it into a sauce-pan, with a pint of water, three or four blades of mace, some whole pepper tied in a rag, let it stew till it is quite tender; then put in the asparagus, shake the sauce-pan, let it simmer till the grass is enough; take the endive out of the water, drain it, lea.e one large head whole, the other leaf by leaf, put it into a stew-pan, put to it a pint of white wine; cover the pan close, let it boil till the endive is just enough, then put in a quarter of a pound of butter rolled in flour, cover it close, shaking the pan; when the endive is enough, take it up, lay the whole head in the middle, and with a spoon take out the celery and grass and lay round, the other part of the endive over that; then pour the liquor out of the sauce-pan into the stew-pan, stir it together, season it with salt, and have ready the yolks of two eggs, beat up with a quarter of a pint of cream, and half a nutmeg grated in; mix this with the sauce, keep it stirring all one way till it is thick; then pour it over your ragoo, and send it to table hot.

To ragoo French Beans.

TAKE a few beans, boil them tender; then take your stew-pan, put in a piece of butter, when it is melted shake in some flour, and peel a large onion, slice it and fry it brown in that butter; then put in the beans, shake in a little pepper and a little ſalt, grate a little nutmeg in; have ready the yolk of an egg and ſome cream; ſtir them all together for a minute or two, and diſh them up.

Another Way to ragoo French Beans.

TAKE a quarter of a peck of French beans, ſtring them, do not ſplit them, cut them in three acroſs, lay them in ſalt and water, then take them out and dry them in a coarſe cloth; fry them brown, then pour out all the fat, put in a quarter of a pint of hot water, ſtir it into the pan by degrees, let it boil; then take a quarter of a pound of freſh butter rolled in a very little flour, two ſpoonfuls of catchup, one ſpoonful of muſhroom-pickle, and four of white wine, an onion ſtuck with ſix cloves, two or three blades of mace beat, half a nutmeg grated, a little pepper and ſalt; ſtir it all together for a few minutes, then throw in the beans; ſhake the pan for a minute or two, take out the onion, and pour them into your diſh. This is a pretty ſide-diſh; and you may garniſh with what you fancy, either pickled French beans, muſhrooms, ſamphire, or any thing elſe.

A Ragoo of Beans, with a Force.

RAGOO them as above; take two large carrots, ſcrape and boil them tender, then maſh them in a pan, ſeaſon with pepper and ſalt, mix them with a little piece of butter and the yolks of two raw eggs; make it into what ſhape you pleaſe, and baking it a quarter of an hour in a quick oven will do, but a tin oven is the beſt; lay it in the middle of the diſh, and the ragoo round; ſerve it up hot for a firſt courſe.

Or this Way, Beans ragooed with Cabbage.

TAKE a nice little cabbage, about as big as a pint baſon; when the outſide leaves, top, and ſtalks are cut off, half boil it, cut a hole in the middle pretty big, take what you cut out and chop it very fine, with a few of the beans boiled, a carrot boiled and maſhed, and a turnip boiled; maſh all together, put them into a ſauce-pan, ſeaſon them with pepper, ſalt, and nutmeg, a good piece of butter, ſtew them a few minutes over the fire, ſtirring the pan often; in the meantime put the cabbage into a ſaucepan, but take great care it does not fall to pieces; put to it four ſpoonfuls of water, two of wine, and one of catchup; have a ſpoonful of muſhroom-pickle, a piece of butter rolled in a little flour, a very little pepper; cover it cloſe, and let it ſtew ſoftly till it is tender; then take it up carefully and lay it in the middle of the diſh, pour your maſhed roots in the middle to fill it up high, and your ragoo round it: you may add the liquor the cabbage was ſtewed in, and ſend it to table hot.

hot. This will do for a top, bottom, middle, or ſide diſh. When beans are not to be had, you may cut carrots and turnips into little ſlices and fry them; the carrots in little round ſlices, the turnips in pieces about two inches long, and as thick as one's finger, and toſs them up in the ragoo.

Beans ragooed with Parſnips.

TAKE two large parſnips, ſcrape them clean, and boil them in water; when tender take them up, ſcrape all the ſoft into a ſauce-pan, add to them four ſpoonfuls of cream, a piece of butter as big as an hen's egg, chop them in a ſauce-pan well; and when they are quite thick, heap them up in the middle of the diſh, and the ragoo round.

Beans ragooed with Potatoes.

BOIL two pounds of potatoes ſoft, then peel them, put them into a ſauce-pan, put to them half a pint of milk, ſtir them about, and a little ſalt; then ſtir in a quarter of a pound of butter, keep ſtirring all the time till it is ſo thick that you cannot ſtir the ſpoon in it hardly for ſtiffneſs, then put it into a halfpenny Welſh diſh, firſt buttering the diſh; heap them as high as they will lie, flour them, pour a little melted butter over it, and then a few crumbs of bread; ſet it into a tin oven before the fire; and when brown, lay it in the middle of the diſh (take great care you do not maſh it,) pour your ragoo round it, and ſend it to table hot.

To dreſs Beans in Ragoo.

YOU muſt boil your beans ſo that the ſkin will ſlip off; take about a quart, ſeaſon them with pepper, ſalt, and nutmeg, then flour them; have ready ſome butter in a ſtew-pan, throw in your beans, fry them of a fine brown, then drain them from the fat, and lay them in your diſh; have ready a quarter of a pound of butter melted, and half a pint of blanched beans boiled, and beat in a mortar, with a very little pepper, ſalt, and nutmeg; then by degrees mix them in the butter, and pour over the other beans: garniſh with boiled and fried beans, and ſo on till you fill the rim of your diſh. They are very good without frying, and only plain melted butter over them.

An Amlet of Beans.

BLANCH your beans, and fry them in ſweet butter, with a little parſley, pour out the butter, and pour in ſome cream; let it ſimmer, ſhaking your pan; ſeaſon with pepper, ſalt, and nutmeg, thicken with three or four yolks of eggs; have ready a pint of cream, thickened with the yolks of four eggs, ſeaſon

 with

with a little ſalt, pour it in your diſh, and lay your beans on the amlet, and ſerve it up hot.

The ſame way you may dreſs muſhrooms, truffles, green peas, aſparagus, and artichoke-bottoms, ſpinage, ſorrel, &c. all being firſt cut into ſmall pieces, or ſhred fine.

Carrots and French Beans dreſſed the Dutch Way.

SLICE the carrots very thin, and juſt cover them with water, ſeaſon them with pepper and ſalt, cut a good many onions and parſley ſmall, a piece of butter; let them ſimmer over a ſlow fire till done. Do French beans the ſame way.

Beans dreſſed the German Way.

TAKE a large bunch of onions, peel and ſlice them, a great quantity of parſley waſhed and cut ſmall, throw them into a ſtew-pan, with a pound of butter; ſeaſon them well with pepper and ſalt, put in two quarts of beans; cover them cloſe, and let them do till the beans are brown, ſhaking the pan often. Do peas the ſame way.

To ragoo Celery.

WASH and make a bunch of celery very clean, cut it in pieces about too inches long, put it into a ſtew-pan with juſt as much water as will cover it, tie three or four blades of mace, two or three cloves, about twenty corns of whole pepper in a muſlin rag looſe, put it into a ſtew-pan, a little onion, a little bundle of ſweet herbs; cover it cloſe, and let it ſtew ſoftly till tender; then take out the ſpice, onion, and ſweet herbs, put in half an ounce of truffles and morels, two ſpoonfuls of catchup, a gill of red wine, a piece of butter as big as an egg, rolled in flour, ſix farthing French rolls, ſeaſon with ſalt to your palate, ſtir it all together, cover it cloſe, and let it ſtew till the ſauce is thick and good; take care that the rolls do not break, ſhake your pan often; when it is enough diſh it up, and garniſh with lemon. The yolks of ſix hard eggs, or more, put in with the rolls, will make it a fine diſh. This for a firſt courſe.

If you would have it white, put in white wine inſtead of red, and ſome cream for a ſecond courſe.

To ragoo Muſhrooms.

PEEL and ſcrape the flaps, put a quart into a ſauce-pan, a very little ſalt, ſet them on a quick fire, let them boil up, then take them off, put to them a gill of red wine, a quarter of a pound of butter rolled in a little flour, a little nutmeg, a little beaten mace, ſet it on the fire, ſtir it now and then; when it is thick and fine, have ready the yolks of ſix eggs hot, and

boiled

boiled in a bladder hard, lay it in the middle of your diſh, and pour the ragoo over it: garniſh with broiled muſhrooms.

To make good Brown Gravy.

TAKE half a pint of ſmall beer, or ale that is not bitter, and half a pint of water, an onion cut ſmall, a little bit of lemon-peel cut ſmall, three cloves, a blade of mace, ſome whole pepper, a ſpoonful of muſhroom-pickle, a ſpoonful of walnut-pickle, a ſpoonful of catchup, and an anchovy; firſt put a piece of butter into a ſauce-pan, as big as a hen's egg, when it is melted ſhake in a little flour, and let it be a little brown; then by degrees ſtir in the above ingredients, and let it boil a quarter of an hour, then ſtrain it, and it is fit for fiſh or roots.

To fricaſſee Skirrets.

WASH the roots very well, and boil them till they are tender; then the ſkin of the roots muſt be taken off, cut in ſlices, and have ready a little cream, a piece of butter rolled in flour, the yolk of an egg beat, a little nutmeg grated, two or three ſpoonfuls of white wine, a very little ſalt, and ſtir all together: your roots being in the diſh, pour the ſauce over them. It is a pretty ſide-diſh. So likewiſe you may dreſs root of ſalſify and ſcorzonera.

A Fricaſſee of Artichoke-Bottoms.

TAKE them either dried or pickled; if dried, you muſt lay them in warm water for three or four hours, ſhifting the water two or three times; then have ready a little cream, and a piece of freſh butter, ſtirred together one way over the fire till it is melted; then put in the artichokes, and when they are hot, diſh them up.

A White Fricaſſee of Muſhrooms.

TAKE a quart of freſh muſhrooms, make them very clean, cut the largeſt ones in two, put them in a ſtew-pan with four ſpoonfuls of water, a blade of mace, a piece of lemon-peel; cover your pan cloſe, and ſtew them gently for half an hour; beat up the yolks of two eggs with half a pint of cream, and a little nutmeg grated in it, take out the mace and lemon-peel, put in the eggs and cream, keep it ſtirring one way all the time till it is thick, ſeaſon with ſalt to your palate; ſqueeze a little lemon-juice in, butter the cruſt of a French roll and toaſt it brown; put it in your diſh, and the muſhrooms over.

N. B. Be careful not to ſqueeze the lemon-juice in till they are finiſhed and ready to put in your diſh, then ſqueeze it in, and ſtir them about for a minute, then put them in your diſh.

Chardoons fried and buttered.

You muſt cut them about ſix inches long, and ſtring them; then boil them till tender; take them out, have ſome butter melted in your ſtew-pan, flour them and fry them brown; ſend them in a diſh, with melted butter in a cup: or you may tie them up in bundles, and boil them like aſparagus; put a toaſt under them, and pour a little melted butter over them; or cut them into dice, and boil them like peas: toſs them up in butter, and ſend them up hot.

Chardoons à la Fromage.

After they are ſtringed, cut them an inch long, ſtew them in a little red wine till they are tender; ſeaſon with pepper and ſalt, and thicken it with a piece of butter rolled in flour; then pour them into your diſh, ſqueeze the juice of orange over it, then ſcrape Parmeſan or Cheſhire cheeſe all over them; then brown it with a cheeſe-iron, and ſerve it up quick and hot.

To make a Scotch Rabbit.

Toast a piece of bread very nicely on both ſides, butter it, cut a ſlice of cheeſe about as big as the bread, toaſt it on both ſides and lay it on the bread.

To make a Welſh Rabbit.

Toast the bread on both ſides, then toaſt the cheeſe on one ſide, lay it on the toaſt, and with a hot iron brown the other ſide. You may rub it over with muſtard.

To make an Engliſh Rabbit.

Toast a ſlice of bread brown on both ſides, then lay it in a plate before the fire, pour a glaſs of red wine over it, and let it ſoak the wine up; then cut ſome cheeſe very thin, and lay it very thick over the bread, and put it in a tin oven before the fire, and it will be toaſted and browned preſently. Serve it away hot.

Or do it thus.

Toast the bread and ſoak it in the wine; ſet it before the fire, cut your cheeſe in very thin ſlices, rub butter over the bottom of a plate, lay the cheeſe on, pour in two or three ſpoonfuls of white wine, cover it with another plate, ſet it over a chafing-diſh of hot coals for two or three minutes; then ſtir it till it is done and well mixed: you may ſtir in a little muſtard; when it is enough, lay it on the bread, juſt brown it with a hot ſhovel. Serve it away hot.

To

To fry Artichokes.

First blanch them in water, then flour them, fry them in fresh butter, lay them in your dish and pour melted butter over them: or you may put a little red wine into the butter, and season with nutmeg, pepper, and salt.

Artichoke-Suckers dressed the Spanish Way.

Clean and wash them and cut them in halves; then boil them in water, drain them from the water and put them into a stew-pan, with a little oil, a little water, and a little vinegar; season them with pepper and salt; stew them a little while, and then thicken them with yolks of eggs.

They make a pretty garnish done thus: clean them, and half boil them; then dry them, flour them, and dip them in yolks of eggs, and fry them brown.

Broccoli as a Salad.

Broccoli is a pretty dish by way of salad in the middle of a table; boil it like asparagus (in the beginning of the book you have an account how to clean it); lay it in your dish, beat up with oil and vinegar and a little salt. Garnish with nastertium-buds.

Or boil it, and have plain butter in a cup: or farce French rolls with it and buttered eggs together, for change: or farce your rolls with muscles, done the same way as oysters, only no wine.

To make Potatoe Cakes.

Take potatoes, boil them, peel them, beat them in a mortar, mix them with the yolks of eggs, a little sack, sugar, a little beaten mace, a little nutmeg, a little cream, or melted butter, work it up into a paste; then make it into cakes, or just what shape you please with moulds, fry them brown in fresh butter, lay them in plates or dishes, melt butter with sack and sugar, and pour over them.

A Pudding, made thus:

Mix it as before; make it up in the shape of a pudding, and bake it; pour butter, sack, and sugar over it.

To make Potatoes like a Collar of Veal or Mutton.

Make the ingredients as before; make it up in the shape of a collar of veal, and with some of it make round balls; bake it with the balls, set the collar in the middle, lay the balls round; let your sauce be half a pint of red wine, sugar enough to sweeten it, the yolks of two eggs, beat up a little nutmeg, stir all these together for fear of curdling; when it is thick enough,

enough, pour it over the collar. This is a pretty diſh for a firſt or a ſecond courſe.

To broil Potatoes.

FIRST boil them, peel them, cut them in two, broil them till they are brown on both ſides; then lay them in the plate or diſh, pour melted butter over them.

To fry Potatoes.

CUT them into thin ſlices as big as a crown-piece, fry them brown, lay them in the plate or diſh, pour melted butter and ſack and ſugar over them. Theſe are a pretty corner-plate.

Maſhed Potatoes.

BOIL your potatoes, peel them, and put them into a ſauce-pan, maſh them well: to two pounds of potatoes put a pint of milk, a little ſalt; ſtir them well together, take care they do not ſtick to the bottom; then take a quarter of a pound of butter, ſtir it in, and ſerve it up.

To dreſs Spinage.

PICK and waſh your ſpinage well, put it into a ſauce-pan with a little ſalt; cover it cloſe, and let it ſtew till it is juſt tender, and throw it into a ſieve; drain all the liquor out, and chop it ſmall (as much as the quantity of a French roll), add half a pint of cream to it, ſeaſon with ſalt, pepper, and grated nutmeg, put in a quarter of a pound of butter, and ſet it a-ſtewing over the fire a quarter of an hour, ſtirring it often; cut a French roll into long pieces about as thick as your finger, fry them, poach ſix eggs, lay them round on the ſpinage, ſtick the pieces of roll in and about the eggs. Serve it up either for ſupper, or a ſide-diſh at a ſecond courſe.

To boil Spinage, when you have not Room on the Fire to do it by itſelf.

HAVE a tin-box, or any other thing that ſhuts very cloſe, put in your ſpinage, cover it ſo cloſe as no water can get in, and put into water, or a pot of liquor, or any thing you are boiling; It will take about an hour, if the pot or copper boils. In the ſame manner you may boil peas without water.

Aſparagus forced in French Rolls.

TAKE three French rolls, take out all the crumb, by firſt cutting a piece of the top-cruſt off; but be careful that the cruſt fits again the ſame place; fry the rolls brown in freſh butter; then take a pint of cream, the yolks of ſix eggs beat fine,

fine, a little ſalt and nutmeg, ſtir them well together over a ſlow fire till it begins to be thick; have ready a hundred of ſmall graſs boiled; then ſave tops enough to ſtick the rolls with, the reſt cut ſmall and put into the cream, fill the loaves with them: before you fry the rolls make holes thick in the top-cruſt and ſtick the graſs in; then lay on the piece of cruſt and ſtick the graſs in, that it may look as if it were growing. It makes a pretty ſide-diſh at a ſecond courſe.

Aſparagus dreſſed the Italian Way.

TAKE the aſparagus, break them in pieces, then boil them ſoft and drain the water from them; take a little oil, water, and vinegar, let it boil, ſeaſon it with pepper and ſalt, throw in the aſparagus and thicken with yolks of eggs.

Endive done this way is good; the Spaniards add ſugar, but that ſpoils them. Green peas done as above are very good; only add a lettuce cut ſmall, and two or three onions, and leave out the eggs.

To ſtew Parſnips.

BOIL them tender, ſcrape them from the duſt, cut them into ſlices, put them into a ſauce-pan with cream enough; for ſauce, a piece of butter rolled in flour, a little ſalt, and ſhake the ſauce-pan often; when the cream boils, pour them into a plate for a corner-diſh, or a ſide-diſh at ſupper.

To maſh Parſnips.

BOIL them tender, ſcrape them clean, then ſcrape all the ſoft into a ſauce-pan, put as much milk or cream as will ſtew them; keep them ſtirring, and when quite thick, ſtir in a good piece of butter, and ſend them to table.

Sorrel with Eggs.

FIRST your ſorrel muſt be quite boiled and well ſtrained, then poach three eggs ſoft, and three hard, butter your ſorrel well; fry ſome three-cornered toaſts brown, lay the ſorrel in the diſh, lay the ſoft eggs on it, and the hard between; ſtick the toaſt in and about it. Garniſh with quartered orange.

Broccoli and Eggs.

BOIL your broccoli tender, ſaving a large bunch for the middle, and ſix or eight little thick ſprigs to ſtick round; take a toaſt half an inch thick, toaſt it brown, as big as you would have it for your diſh or butter-plate; butter ſome eggs thus: take ſix eggs (more or leſs as you have occaſion), beat them well, put them into a ſauce-pan with a good piece of butter, a little ſalt, keep beating them with a ſpoon till they are thick

 enough,

enough, then pour them on the toaſt; ſet the higheſt bunch of broccoli in the middle, and the other little pieces round about; and garniſh the diſh with little ſprigs of broccoli: this is a pretty ſide-diſh or corner-plate.

Aſparagus and Eggs.

TOAST a bit of bread as big as you want, butter it and lay it on your diſh; butter ſome eggs as above, and lay over it; in the meantime boil ſome graſs tender, cut it ſmall and lay it over the eggs. This makes a pretty ſide-diſh for a ſecond courſe, or a corner-plate.

A pretty Diſh of Eggs.

BOIL ſix eggs hard, peel them, and cut them into thin ſlices, put a quarter of a pound of butter into the ſtew-pan, then put in your eggs and fry them quick: half a quarter of an hour will do them. You muſt be very careful not to break them; throw over them pepper, ſalt, and nutmeg, lay them in your diſh before the fire, pour out all the fat, ſhake in a little flour, and have ready two ſhalots cut ſmall; throw them into the pan, pour in a quarter of a pint of white wine, a little juice of lemon, and a little piece of butter rolled in flour; ſtir all together till it is thick; if you have not ſauce enough, put in a little more wine, toaſt ſome thin ſlices of bread cut three-corner ways, and lay round your diſh, pour the ſauce all over, and ſend it to table hot. You may put ſweet oil on the toaſt, if it be agreeable.

Eggs à la Tripe.

BOIL your eggs hard, take off the ſhells, and cut them longways in four quarters, put a little butter into a ſtew-pan, let it melt, ſhake in a little flour, ſtir it with a ſpoon, then put in your eggs, throw a little grated nutmeg all over, a little ſalt, a good deal of ſhred parſley; ſhake your pan round, pour in a little cream, toſs the pan round carefully, ſo that you do not break the eggs; when your ſauce is thick and fine, take up your eggs, pour the ſauce all over them; and garniſh with lemon.

A Fricaſſee of Eggs.

BOIL eight eggs hard, take off the ſhells, cut them into quarters, have ready half a pint of cream, and a quarter of a pound of freſh butter; ſtir it together over the fire till it is thick and ſmooth, lay the eggs in the diſh and pour the ſauce all over. Garniſh with the hard yolks of three eggs cut in two, and lay round the edge of the diſh.

A Ragoo of Eggs.

BOIL twelve eggs hard, take off the ſhells, and with a little knife very carefully cut the white acroſs longways, ſo that the white may be in two halves, and the yolks whole; be careful neither to break the whites nor yolks, take a quarter of a pint of pickled muſhrooms chopped very fine, half an ounce of truffles and morels boiled in three or four ſpoonfuls of water, ſave the water, and chop the truffles and morels very ſmall, boil a little parſley, chop it fine, mix them together with the truffle-water you ſaved, grate a little nutmeg in, a little beaten mace, put it into a ſauce-pan with three ſpoonfuls of water, a gill of red wine, one ſpoonful of catchup, a piece of butter as big as a large walnut, rolled in flour, ſtir all together and let it boil; in the meantime get ready your eggs, lay the yolks and whites in order in your diſh, the hollow parts of the whites uppermoſt, that they may be filled; take ſome crumbs of bread and fry them brown and criſp, as you do for larks, with which fill up the whites of the eggs as high as they will lie, then pour in your ſauce all over, and garniſh with fried crumbs of bread. This is a very genteel pretty diſh, if it be well done.

To broil Eggs.

CUT a toaſt round a quartern loaf, brown it, lay it on your diſh, butter it, and very carefully break ſix or eight eggs on the toaſt, and take a red-hot ſhovel and hold over them; when they are done, ſqueeze a Seville orange over them, grate a little nutmeg over it, and ſerve it up for a ſide-plate. Or you may poach your eggs, and lay them on a toaſt: or toaſt your bread criſp, and pour a little boiling water over it; ſeaſon with a little ſalt, and then lay your poached eggs on it.

To dreſs Eggs with Bread.

TAKE a penny-loaf, ſoak it in a quart of hot milk two hours, or till the bread is ſoft, then ſtrain it through a coarſe ſieve, put to it two ſpoonfuls of orange-flower water, or roſe-water; ſweeten it, grate in a little nutmeg, take a little diſh, butter the bottom of it, break in as many eggs as will cover the bottom of the diſh, pour in the bread and milk, ſet it in a tin oven before the fire, and half an hour will bake it; it will do on a chafing-diſh of coals; cover it cloſe before the fire, or bake it in a ſlow oven.

To farce Eggs.

GET two cabbage-lettuces, ſcald them, with a few muſh-rooms, parſley, ſorrel, and chervil; then chop them very ſmall with

with the yolks of hard eggs, seasoned with salt and nutmeg; then stew them in butter, and when they are enough, put in a little cream, then pour them into the bottom of a dish; take the whites and chop them very fine with parsley, nutmeg, and salt; lay this round the brim of the dish, and run a red-hot fire-shovel over it, to brown it.

Eggs with Lettuce.

SCALD some cabbage-lettuce in fair water, squeeze them well, then slice them and toss them up in a sauce-pan with a piece of butter; season them with pepper, salt, and a little nutmeg; let them stew half an hour, chop them well together; when they are enough, lay them in your dish, fry some eggs nicely in butter and lay on them. Garnish with Seville orange.

To fry Eggs as round as Balls.

HAVING a deep frying-pan and three pints of clarified butter, heat as hot as for fritters, and stir it with a stick till it runs round like a whirlpool; then break an egg into the middle, and turn it round with your stick till it be as hard as a poached egg; the whirling round of the butter will make it as round as a ball, then take it up with a slice, and put it in a dish before the fire: they will keep hot half an hour and yet be soft; so you may do as many as you please. You may serve these with what you please, nothing better than stewed spinage, and garnish with orange.

To make an Egg as big as Twenty.

PART the yolks from the whites, strain them both separate through a sieve, tie the yolks up in a bladder in the form of a ball; boil them hard, then put this ball into another bladder and the whites round it; tie it up oval-fashion, and boil it: these are used for grand salads. This is very pretty for a ragoo; boil five or six yolks together and lay in the middle of the ragoo of eggs; and so you may make them of any size you please.

To make a grand Dish of Eggs.

YOU must break as many eggs as the yolks will fill a pint bason, the whites by themselves, tie the yolks by themselves in a bladder round, boil them hard; then have a wooden bowl that will hold a quart, made like two butter-dishes, but in the shape of an egg, with a hole through one at the top. You are to observe when you boil the yolks, to run a packthread through, and leave a quarter of a yard hanging out. When the yolk is boiled hard, put it into the bowl-dish, but be careful to hang it so as to be in the middle; the string being drawn through

through the hole, then clap the two bowls together, and tie them tight, and with a funnel pour in the whites through the hole, then ſtop the hole cloſe and boil it hard; it will take an hour: when it is boiled enough, carefully open it, and cut the ſtring cloſe; in the meantime take twenty eggs, beat them well, the yolks by themſelves and the whites by themſelves; divide the whites into two, and boil them in bladders the ſhape of an egg; when they are boiled hard, cut one in two longways, and one croſſways, and with a fine ſharp knife cut out ſome of the white in the middle; lay the great egg in the middle, the two long halves on each ſide with the hollow part uppermoſt, and the two round flat between; take an ounce of truffles and morels, cut them very ſmall, boil them in half a pint of water till they are tender, then take a pint of freſh muſhrooms clean picked, waſhed, and chopped ſmall, and put into the truffles and morels; let them boil, add a little ſalt, a little beaten nutmeg, a little beaten mace, a gill of pickled muſhrooms chopped fine; boil ſixteen of the yolks hard in a bladder, then chop them and mix them with the other ingredients; thicken it with a lump of butter rolled in flour, ſhaking your ſauce-pan round till hot and thick, then fill the round with this, turn them down again, and fill the two long ones; what remains ſave to put into the ſauce-pan; take a pint of cream, a quarter of a pound of butter, the other four yolks beat fine, a gill of white wine, a gill of pickled muſhrooms, a little beaten mace, and a little nutmeg; put all into the ſauce-pan to the other ingredients, and ſtir all well together one way till it is thick and fine; pour it over all, and garniſh with notched lemon.

This is a grand diſh at a ſecond courſe. Or you may mix it up with red wine and butter, and it will do for a firſt courſe.

To make a pretty Diſh of Whites of Eggs.

TAKE the whites of twelve eggs, beat them up with four ſpoonfuls of roſe-water, a little grated lemon-peel, a little nutmeg, and ſweeten with ſugar; mix them well, boil them in four bladders, tie them in the ſhape of an egg, and boil them hard; they will take half an hour; lay them in your diſh; when cold, mix half a pint of thick cream, a gill of ſack, and half the juice of a Seville orange; mix all together, ſweeten with fine ſugar, and pour over the eggs. Serve it up for a ſide-diſh at ſupper, or when you pleaſe.

To ſtew Cucumbers.

PARE twelve cucumbers and ſlice them as thick as a half-crown, lay them in a coarſe cloth to drain, and when they are dry,

dry, flour them and fry them brown in fresh butter; then take them out with an egg-slice, lay them in a plate before the fire, and have ready one cucumber whole, cut a long piece out of the side, and scoop out all the pulp; have ready fried onions peeled and sliced, and fried brown with the sliced cucumbers; fill the whole cucumber with the fried onion, season with pepper and salt; put on the piece you cut out and tie it round with a packthread; fry it brown, first flouring it, then take it out of the pan and keep it hot; keep the pan on the fire, and with one hand put in a little flour, while with the other you stir it: when it is thick, put in two or three spoonfuls of water, and half a pint of white or red wine, two spoonfuls of catchup, stir it together, put in three blades of mace, four cloves, half a nutmeg, a little pepper and salt, all beat fine together; stir it into the sauce-pan, then throw in your cucumbers, give them a toss or two, then lay the whole cucumbers in the middle, the rest round, pour the sauce all over, untie the cucumbers before you lay it into the dish. Garnish the dish with fried onions, and send it to table hot. This is a pretty side-dish at a first course.

To farce Cucumbers.

TAKE six large cucumbers, cut a piece off the top, and scoop out all the pulp; take a large white cabbage boiled tender, take only the heart, chop it fine, cut a large onion fine, shred some parsley and pickled mushrooms small, two hard eggs chopped very fine, season it with pepper, salt, and nutmeg; stuff your cucumbers full, and put on the pieces, tie them with a packthread, and fry them in butter of a light brown; have the following sauce ready: take a quarter of a pint of red wine, a quarter of a pint of boiling water, a small onion chopped fine, a little pepper and salt, a piece of butter as big as a walnut, rolled in flour; when the cucumbers are enough, lay them in your dish, pour the fat out of the pan, and pour in this sauce; let it boil, and have ready the yolks of two eggs beat fine, mixed with two or three spoonfuls of the sauce, then turn them into the pan, let them boil, keeping it stirring all the time, untie the strings, and pour the sauce over. Serve it up for a side-dish. Garnish with the tops.

To stew Cucumbers.

TAKE six large cucumbers, slice them; take six large onions, peel and cut them in thin slices, fry them both brown, then drain them and pour out the fat, put them into the pan again, with three spoonfuls of hot water, a quarter of a pound of butter rolled in flour, and a tea-spoonful of mustard; season with pepper and salt, and let them stew a quarter of an hour

softly,

foftly, fhaking the pan often; when they are enough difh them up.

Fried Celery.

TAKE fix or eight heads of celery, cut off the green tops, and take off the outfide ftalks, wafh them clean and pare the roots clean; then have ready half a pint of white wine, the yolks of three eggs beat fine, and a little falt and nutmeg; mix all well together with flour into a batter, dip every head into the batter and fry them in butter; when enough, lay them in your difh, and pour melted butter over them.

Celery with Cream.

WASH and clean fix or eight heads of celery, cut them about three inches long, boil them tender, pour away all the water, and take the yolks of four eggs beat fine, half a pint of cream, a little falt and nutmeg, pour it over, keeping the pan fhaking all the while: when it begins to be thick, difh it up.

Peas Françoife.

TAKE a quart of fhelled peas, cut a large Spanifh onion, or two middling ones fmall, and two cabbage or Silefia lettuces cut fmall, put them into a fauce-pan with half a pint of water, feafon them with a little falt, a little beaten pepper, and a little beaten mace and nutmeg; cover them clofe and let them ftew a quarter of an hour, then put in a quarter of a pound of frefh butter rolled in a little flour, a fpoonful of catchup, a little piece of burnt butter as big as a nutmeg; cover them clofe and let it fimmer foftly an hour, often fhaking the pan. When it is enough, ferve it up for a fide-difh.

For an alteration, you may ftew the ingredients as above; then take a fmall cabbage-lettuce and half boil it; then drain it, cut the ftalks flat at the bottom, fo that it will ftand firm in the difh, and with a knife very carefully cut out the middle, leaving the outfide leaves whole; put what you cut out into a fauce-pan, chop it, and put a piece of butter, a little pepper, falt, and nutmeg, the yolk of a hard egg chopped, a few crumbs of bread, mix all together, and when it is hot fill your cabbage; put fome butter into a ftew-pan, tie your cabbage and fry it till you think it is enough; then take it up, untie it, and firft pour the ingredients of peas into your difh, fet the forced cabbage in the middle, and have ready four artichoke-bottoms fried and cut in two, and laid round the difh. This will do for a top-difh.

Green Peas with Cream.

TAKE a quart of fine green peas, put them into a ſtew-pan with a piece of butter as big as an egg, rolled in a little flour, ſeaſon them with a little ſalt and nutmeg, a bit of ſugar as big as a nutmeg, a little bundle of ſweet herbs, ſome parſley chopped fine, a quarter of a pint of boiling water; cover them cloſe, and let them ſtew very ſoftly half an hour, then pour in a quarter of a pint of good cream: give it one boil, and ſerve it up for a ſide-plate.

A Farce-meagre Cabbage.

TAKE a white-heart cabbage, as big as the bottom of a plate, let it boil five minutes in water, then drain it, cut the ſtalk flat to ſtand in the diſh, then carefully open the leaves and take out the inſide, leaving the outſide leaves whole; chop what you take out very fine, take the fleſh of two or three flounders or plaice clean from the bone; chop it with the cabbage, the yolks and whites of four hard eggs, a handful of picked parſley, beat all together in a mortar, with a quarter of a pound of melted butter; mix it up with the yolk of an egg and a few crumbs of bread, fill the cabbage and tie it together, put it into a deep ſtew-pan or ſauce-pan, put to it half a pint of water, a quarter of a pound of butter rolled in a little flour, the yolks of four hard eggs, an onion ſtuck with ſix cloves, whole pepper and mace tied in a muſlin rag, half an ounce of truffles and morels, a ſpoonful of catchup, a few pickled muſhrooms; cover it cloſe and let it ſimmer an hour: if you find it is not enough, you muſt do it longer. When it is done, lay it in your diſh, untie it, and pour the ſauce over it.

Red Cabbage dreſſed after the Dutch Way, good for a Cold in the Breaſt.

TAKE the cabbage, cut it ſmall and boil it ſoft, then drain it, and put it in a ſtew-pan with a ſufficient quantity of oil and butter, a little water and vinegar, and an onion cut ſmall; ſeaſon it with pepper and ſalt, and let it ſimmer on a ſlow fire till all the liquor is waſted.

Cauliflowers dreſſed the Spaniſh Way.

BOIL them, but not too much; then drain them and put them into a ſtew-pan: to a large cauliflower put a quarter of a pint of ſweet oil, and two or three cloves of garlic; let them fry till brown; then ſeaſon them with pepper and ſalt, two or three ſpoonfuls of vinegar; cover the pan very cloſe, and let them ſimmer over a very ſlow fire an hour.

Cauliflowers fried.

TAKE two fine cauliflowers, boil them in milk and water, then leave one whole, and pull the other to pieces; take half a pound of butter, with two ſpoonfuls of water, a little duſt of flour, and melt the butter in a ſtew-pan; then put in the whole cauliflower cut in two, and the other pulled to pieces, and fry it till it is of a very light brown; ſeaſon it with pepper and ſalt: when it is enough, lay the two halves in the middle, and pour the reſt all over.

To make an Oatmeal Pudding.

TAKE a pint of fine oatmeal, boil it in three pints of new milk, ſtirring it till it is as thick as a haſty-pudding; take it off, and ſtir in half a pound of freſh butter, a little beaten mace and nutmeg, and a gill of ſack; then beat up eight eggs, half the whites, ſtir all well together, lay puff-paſte all over the diſh, pour in the pudding and bake it half an hour: or you may boil it with a few currants.

To make a Potatoe Pudding.

TAKE a quart of potatoes, boil them ſoft, peel them, and maſh them with the back of a ſpoon, and rub them through a ſieve, to have them fine and ſmooth; take half a pound of freſh butter melted, half a pound of fine ſugar, beat them well together till they are very ſmooth, beat ſix eggs, whites and all, ſtir them in, and a glaſs of ſack or brandy; you may add half a pound of currants, boil it half an hour, melt butter with a glaſs of white wine, ſweeten with ſugar, and pour over it: you may bake it in a diſh, with puff-paſte all round the diſh at the bottom.

To make a ſecond Potatoe Pudding.

BOIL two pounds of potatoes, and beat them in a mortar fine, beat in half a pound of melted butter, boil it half an hour, pour melted butter over it, with a glaſs of white wine, or the juice of a Seville orange, and throw ſugar all over the pudding and diſh.

To make a third Sort of Potatoe Pudding.

TAKE two pounds of white potatoes, boil them ſoft, peel and beat them in a mortar, or ſtrain them through a ſieve till they are quite fine; then mix in half a pound of freſh butter melted, then beat up the yolks of eight eggs and three whites, ſtir them in, and half a pound of white ſugar finely pounded, half a pint of ſack, ſtir it well together, grate in half a large nutmeg, and ſtir in half a pint of cream, make a puff-paſte and lay all over the diſh and round the edges; pour it in the pudding, and bake it of a fine light brown.

For change, put in half a pound of currants; or you may ſtrew over the top half an ounce of citron and orange peel cut thin, before you put it into the oven.

To make Buttered Loaves.

BEAT up the yolks of twelve eggs, with half the whites, and a quarter of a pint of yeaſt, ſtrain them into a diſh; ſeaſon with ſalt and beaten ginger, then make it into a high paſte with flour, lay it in a warm cloth for a quarter of an hour; then make it up into little loaves, and bake them or boil them with butter, and put in a glaſs of white wine; ſweeten well with ſugar, lay the loaves in the diſh, pour the ſauce over them, and throw ſugar over the diſh.

To make an Orange Pudding.

TAKE the yolks of ſixteen eggs, beat them well with half a pound of melted butter, grate in the rind of two fine Seville oranges, beat in half a pound of fine ſugar, two ſpoonfuls of orange-flower water, two of roſe-water, a gill of ſack, half a pint of cream, two Naples biſcuits, or the crumb of a halfpenny roll ſoaked in the cream, and mix all well together; make a thin puff-paſte and lay all over the diſh and round the rim, pour in the pudding and bake it: it will take about as long baking as a cuſtard.

To make a ſecond Sort of Orange Pudding.

YOU muſt take ſixteen yolks of eggs, beat them fine, mix them with half a pound of freſh butter melted, and half a pound of white ſugar, half a pint of cream, a little roſe-water, and a little nutmeg; cut the peel of a fine large Seville orange ſo thin as none of the white appears, beat it fine in a mortar till it is like a paſte, and by degrees mix in the above ingredients all together; then lay a puff-paſte all over the diſh, pour in the ingredients and bake it.

To make a third Orange Pudding.

TAKE two large Seville oranges and grate off the rind as far as they are yellow; then put your oranges in fair water, and let them boil till they are tender; ſhift the water three or four times to take out the bitterneſs; when they are tender, cut them open and take away the ſeeds and ſtrings, and beat the other part in a mortar, with half a pound of ſugar, till it is a paſte; then put to it the yolks of ſix eggs, three or four ſpoonfuls of thick cream, half a Naples biſcuit grated; mix

theſe

these together, and melt a pound of fresh butter very thick, and stir it well in; when it is cold, put a little thin puff-paste about the bottom and rim of your dish; pour in the ingredients, and bake it about three quarters of an hour.

To make a fourth Orange Pudding.

TAKE the outside rind of three Seville oranges, boil them in several waters till they are tender, then pound them in a mortar, with three quarters of a pound of sugar; then blanch half a pound of sweet almonds, beat them very fine with rose-water to keep them from oiling, then beat sixteen eggs, but six whites, a pound of fresh butter, and beat all these together till it is light and hollow; then lay a thin puff-paste all over a dish, and put in the ingredients. Bake it with your tarts.

To make a Lemon Pudding.

TAKE three lemons, and cut the rind off very thin, boil them in three separate waters till very tender, then pound them very fine in a mortar; have ready a quarter of a pound of Naples biscuit, boiled up in a quart of milk or cream, mix them and the lemon rind with it; beat up twelve yolks and six whites of eggs very fine, melt a quarter of a pound of fresh butter, half a pound of fine sugar, a little orange-flower water; mix all well together, put it over the stove, and keep it stirring till it is thick, squeeze the juice of half a lemon in; put puff-paste round the rim of your dish, put the pudding stuff in, cut some candied sweetmeats and put over: bake it three quarters of an hour, and send it up hot.

Another Way to make a Lemon Pudding.

TAKE three lemons and grate the rinds off, beat up twelve yolks and six whites of eggs, put in half a pint of cream, half a pound of fine sugar, a little orange-flower water, a quarter of a pound of butter melted; mix all well together, squeeze in the juice of two lemons, put it over the stove, and keep stirring it till it is thick; put a puff-paste round the rim of the dish, put in your pudding stuff with some candied sweetmeats cut small over it, and bake it three quarters of an hour.

To bake an Almond Pudding.

BLANCH half a pound of sweet almonds, and four bitter ones, in warm water, take them and pound them in a marble mortar, with two spoonfuls of orange-flower water, and two of rose-water, a gill of sack; mix in four grated Naples biscuits, three quarters of a pound of melted butter; beat eight eggs, and mix them with a quart of cream boiled, grate in half a nutmeg and a quarter of a pound of ſugar; mix all well together, make a thin puff-paſte, and lay all over the diſh; pour in the ingredients, and bake it.

To boil an Almond Pudding.

BEAT a pound of ſweet almonds as ſmall as poſſible, with three ſpoonfuls of roſe-water, and a gill of ſack or white wine, and mix in half a pound of freſh butter melted, with five yolks of eggs and two whites, a quart of cream, a quarter of a pound of ſugar, half a nutmeg grated, one ſpoonful of flour, and three ſpoonfuls of crumbs of white bread; mix all well together, and boil it: it will take half an hour boiling.

To make a Sago Pudding.

LET half a pound of ſago be waſhed well in three or four hot waters, then put to it a quart of new milk, and let it boil together till it is thick; ſtir it carefully (for it is apt to burn), put in a ſtick of cinnamon when you ſet it on the fire; when it is boiled take it out; before you pour it out, ſtir in half a pound of freſh butter, then pour it into a pan, and beat up nine eggs, with five of the whites, and four ſpoonfuls of ſack; ſtir all together, and ſweeten to your taſte; put in a quarter of a pound of currants clean waſhed and rubbed, and juſt plumped in two ſpoonfuls of ſack and two of roſe-water; mix all well together, ſtir it well over a ſlow fire till it is thick, lay a puff-paſte over a diſh; pour in the ingredients, and bake it.

To make a Millet Pudding.

YOU muſt get half a pound of millet ſeed, and after it is waſhed and picked clean, put to it half a pound of ſugar, a whole nutmeg grated, and three quarts of milk; when you have mixed all well together, break in half a pound of freſh butter, and butter your diſh; pour it in, and bake it.

To make a Carrot Pudding.

YOU muſt take a raw carrot, ſcrape it very clean, and grate it; take half a pound of the grated carrot, and a pound of grated bread, beat up eight eggs, leave out half the whites, and mix the eggs with half a pint of cream; then ſtir in the bread and carrot, half a pound of freſh butter melted, half a pint of ſack, and three ſpoonfuls of orange-flower water, a nutmeg grated; ſweeten to your palate; mix all well together, and if it is not thin enough, ſtir in a little new milk or cream; let it be of a moderate thickneſs, lay a puff-paſte all over the diſh, and pour in the ingredients; bake it; it will take an hour's

 baking:

baking: or you may boil it; but then you muſt melt butter, and put in white wine and ſugar.

A ſecond Carrot Pudding.

GET two penny loaves, pare off the cruſt, ſoak them in a quart of boiling milk, let it ſtand till it is cold, then grate in two or three large carrots, then put in eight eggs well beat, and three quarters of a pound of freſh butter melted, grate in a little nutmeg, and ſweeten to your taſte; cover your diſh with puff-paſte, pour in the ingredients, and bake it an hour.

To make a Cowſlip Pudding.

HAVING got the flowers of a peck of cowſlips, cut them and pound them ſmall, with half a pound of Naples biſcuits grated, and three pints of cream; boil them a little, then take them off the fire, and beat up ſixteen eggs with a little cream and roſe-water; ſweeten to your palate; mix it all well together, butter a diſh and pour it in; bake it, and when it is enough, throw fine ſugar over and ſerve it up: or you may make half the quantity.

N. B. New milk will do in all thoſe puddings, when you have no cream.

To make a Quince, Apricot, or White-Pear Plum Pudding.

SCALD your quinces very tender, pare them very thin, ſcrape off the ſoft, mix it with ſugar very ſweet, put in a little ginger and a little cinnamon; to a pint of cream you muſt put three or four yolks of eggs, and ſtir it into your quinces till they are of a good thickneſs: it muſt be pretty thick.

So you may do apricots or white-pear plums. Butter your diſh, pour it in and bake it.

To make a Pearl-Barley Pudding.

GET a pound of pearl-barley, waſh it clean, put to it three quarts of new milk, and half a pound of double-refined ſugar, a nutmeg grated; then put it into a deep pan and bake it with brown bread: take it out of the oven, beat up ſix eggs, mix all well together, butter a diſh, pour it in, bake it again an hour, and it will be excellent.

To make a French Barley Pudding.

PUT to a quart of cream ſix eggs well beaten, half the whites, ſweeten to your palate, a little orange-flower water, or roſe-water, and a pound of melted butter; then put in ſix handfuls of French barley that has been boiled tender in milk; butter a diſh and put it in: it will take as long baking as a veniſon-paſty.

To make an Apple Pudding.

TAKE twelve large pippins, pare them, and take out the cores, put them into a ſauce-pan with four or five ſpoonfuls of water, boil them till they are ſoft and thick; then beat them well, ſtir in a pound of loaf-ſugar, the juice of three lemons, the peel of two lemons cut thin and beat fine in a mortar, the yolks of eight eggs beat; mix all well together, bake it in a ſlack oven; when it is near done, throw over a little fine ſugar. You may bake it in a puff-paſte, as you do the other puddings.

To make an Apple Pudding.

MAKE a good puff-paſte, roll it out half an inch thick, pare your apples, and core them, enough to fill the cruſt, and cloſe it up, tie it in a cloth and boil it; if a ſmall pudding, two hours; if a large one, three or four hours; when it is enough, turn it into your diſh, cut a piece of the cruſt out of the top, butter and ſugar it to your palate, lay on the cruſt again, and ſend it to table hot. A pear pudding make the ſame way. And thus you may make a damſon pudding, or any ſort of plums, apricots, cherries, or mulberries; and are very fine.

A baked Apple Pudding.—Excellent.

TAKE eight large apples, pare and core them, put them into a ſauce-pan with juſt water enough to cover them till ſoft, then pour it away and beat them very fine, ſtir in while hot a quarter of a pound of butter, loaf-ſugar to your taſte, a quarter of a pound of biſcuits finely grated, half a nutmeg, three large ſpoonfuls of brandy, two of roſe-water, the peel of a lemon grated; when cold, put in a quarter of a pint of cream, the yolks of ſix eggs well beat; put paſte at the bottom of the diſh.

To make an Italian Pudding.

TAKE a pint of cream, and ſlice in ſome French rolls, as much as you think will make it thick enough, beat ten eggs fine, grate a nutmeg, butter the bottom of the diſh, ſlice twelve pippins into it, throw ſome orange-peel and ſugar over, and half a pint of red wine, then pour your cream, bread, and eggs over it; firſt lay a puff-paſte at the bottom of the diſh and round the edges, and bake it half an hour.

To make a Rice Pudding.

TAKE a quarter of a pound of rice, put it into a ſauce-pan, with a quart of new milk, a ſtick of cinnamon, ſtir it often to keep it from ſticking to the ſauce-pan; when it has boiled thick, pour it into a pan, ſtir in a quarter of a pound of freſh butter,

butter, and ſugar to your palate; grate in half a nutmeg, add three or four ſpoonfuls of roſe-water, and ſtir it all well together; when it is cold, beat up eight eggs, with half the whites, beat it all well together, butter a diſh, pour it in and bake it. You may lay a puff-paſte firſt all over the diſh. For change, put in a few currants and ſweetmeats, if you chooſe it.

A ſecond Rice Pudding.

GET half a pound of rice, put to it three quarts of milk, ſtir in half a pound of ſugar, grate a ſmall nutmeg in, and break in half a pound of freſh butter; butter a diſh and pour it in and bake it; you may add a quarter of a pound of currants, for change. If you boil the rice and milk, and then ſtir in the ſugar, you may bake it before the fire, or in a tin oven. You may add eggs, but it will be good without.

A third Rice Pudding.

TAKE ſix ounces of the flour of rice, put it into a quart of milk and let it boil till it is pretty thick, ſtirring it all the while; then pour it into a pan, ſtir in half a pound of freſh butter and a quarter of a pound of ſugar; when it is cold, grate in a nutmeg, beat ſix eggs with a ſpoonful or two of ſack, beat and ſtir all well together, lay a thin puff-paſte on the bottom of your diſh, pour it in and bake it.

A Carolina Rice Pudding.

TAKE half a pound of rice, waſh it clean, put it into a ſauce-pan with a quart of milk, keep ſtirring it till it is very thick; take great care it does not burn; then turn it into a pan and grate ſome nutmeg into it, and two tea-ſpoonfuls of beaten cinnamon, a little lemon-peel ſhred fine, ſix apples pared and chopped ſmall; mix all together with the yolks of three eggs, and ſweeten to your palate; then tie it up cloſe in a cloth, put it into boiling water, and be ſure to keep it boiling all the time; an hour and a quarter will boil it; melt butter and pour over it, and throw ſome fine ſugar all over it: a little wine in the ſauce will be a great addition to it.

To boil a Cuſtard Pudding.

TAKE a pint of cream, out of which take two or three ſpoonfuls and mix with a ſpoonful of fine flour, ſet the reſt to boil; when it is boiled, take it off, and ſtir in the cold cream, and flour very well; when it is cool, beat up five yolks and two whites of eggs, and ſtir in a little ſalt and ſome nutmeg, and two or three ſpoonfuls of ſack; ſweeten to your palate; butter a wooden bowl, and pour it in, tie a cloth over it, and boil

boil it half an hour; when it is enough, untie the cloth, turn the pudding out into your dish, and pour melted butter over it.

To make a Flour Pudding.

TAKE a quart of milk, beat up eight eggs, but four of the whites, mix them with a quarter of a pint of milk, and stir into that four large spoonfuls of flour, beat it well together, boil six bitter almonds in two spoonfuls of water, pour the water into the eggs, blanch the almonds and beat them fine in a mortar; then mix them in with half a large nutmeg and a tea-spoonful of salt; then mix in the rest of the milk, flour your cloth well, and boil it an hour; pour melted butter over it, and sugar (if you like it) thrown all over. Observe always in boiling puddings, that the water boils before you put them into the pot; and have ready, when they are boiled, a pan of clean cold water, just give your pudding one dip in, then untie the cloth, and it will turn out without sticking to the cloth.

To make a Batter Pudding.

TAKE a quart of milk, beat up six eggs, half the whites, mix as above, six spoonfuls of flour, a tea-spoonful of salt, and one of beaten ginger; then mix all together, boil it an hour and a quarter, and pour melted butter over it: you may put in eight eggs (if you have plenty) for change, and half a pound of prunes or currants.

To make a Batter Pudding without Eggs.

TAKE a quart of milk, mix six spoonfuls of flour with a little of the milk first, a tea-spoonful of salt, two tea-spoonfuls of beaten ginger, and two of the tincture of saffron; then mix all together, and boil it an hour. You may add fruit as you think proper.

To make a grateful Pudding.

TAKE a pound of fine flour, and a pound of white bread grated, take eight eggs, but half the whites, beat them up, and mix with them a pint of new milk, then stir in the bread and flour, a pound of raisins stoned, a pound of currants, half a pound of sugar, a little beaten ginger; mix all well together, and either bake or boil it: It will take three quarters of an hour baking: put cream in instead of milk, if you have it; it will be an addition to the pudding.

To make a Bread Pudding.

CUT off all the crust of a penny white loaf, and slice it thin into a quart of milk, set it over a chafing-dish of coals till the bread has soaked up all the milk, then put in a piece of sweet butter,

butter, ſtir it round, let it ſtand till cool; or you may boil your milk and pour over your bread, and cover it up cloſe, does full as well; then take the yolks of ſix eggs, the whites of three, and beat them up with a little roſe-water and nutmeg, a little ſalt and ſugar, if you chooſe it; mix all well together, and boil it one hour.

To make a fine Bread Pudding.

TAKE all the crumb of a ſtale penny-loaf, cut it thin, a quart of cream, ſet it over a ſlow fire till it is ſcalding hot, then let it ſtand till it is cold, beat up the bread and cream well together, grate in ſome nutmeg, take twelve bitter almonds, boil them in two ſpoonfuls of water, pour the water to the cream and ſtir it in with a little ſalt, ſweeten it to your palate, blanch the almonds and beat them in a mortar with two ſpoonfuls of roſe or orange-flower water till they are a fine paſte; then mix them by degrees with the cream till they are well mixed in the cream, then take the yolks of eight eggs, the whites of four, beat them well and mix them with your cream, then mix all well together: a wooden diſh is beſt to boil it in; but if you boil it in a cloth, be ſure to dip it in the hot water, and flour it well, tie it looſe and boil it an hour; be ſure the water boils when you put it in, and keeps boiling all the time; when it is enough, turn it into your diſh, melt butter and put in two or three ſpoonfuls of white wine or ſack, give it a boil and pour it over your pudding; then ſtrew a good deal of fine ſugar all over the pudding and diſh, and ſend it to table hot. New milk will do when you cannot get cream. You may, for change, put in a few currants.

To make an ordinary Bread Pudding.

TAKE two halfpenny rolls, ſlice them thin, cruſt and all, pour over them a pint of new milk boiling hot, cover them cloſe, let it ſtand ſome hours to ſoak; then beat it well with a little melted butter, and beat up the yolks and whites of two eggs, beat all together well with a little ſalt; boil it half an hour; when it is done, turn it into your diſh, pour melted butter and ſugar over it. Some love a little vinegar in the butter. If your rolls are ſtale and grated, they will do better; add a little ginger. You may bake it with a few currants.

To make a baked Bread Pudding.

TAKE the crumb of a penny-loaf, as much flour, the yolks of four eggs, and two whites, a tea-ſpoonful of ginger, half a pound of raiſins ſtoned, half a pound of currants clean waſhed and picked, a little ſalt; mix firſt the bread and flour, ginger, ſalt, and ſugar to your palate, then the eggs, and as much milk

milk as will make it like a good batter, then the fruit, butter the dish, pour it in, and bake it.

To make a boiled Loaf.

TAKE a penny-loaf, pour over it half a pint of milk boiling hot, cover it close, let it ſtand till it has ſoaked up the milk, then tie it up in a cloth and boil it half an hour; when it is done, lay it in your diſh, pour melted butter over it, and throw ſugar all over; a ſpoonful of wine or roſe-water does as well in the butter, or juice of Seville orange. A French manchet does beſt; but there are little loaves made on purpoſe for the uſe. A French roll or oat-cake does very well boiled thus.

To make a Cheſnut Pudding.

PUT a dozen and a half of cheſnuts into a ſkillet or ſauce-pan of water, boil them a quarter of an hour, then blanch and peel them, and beat them in a marble mortar, with a little orange-flower or roſe-water and ſack, till they are a fine thin paſte; then beat up twelve eggs with half the whites, and mix them well, grate half a nutmeg, a little ſalt, mix them with three pints of cream and half a pound of melted butter; ſweeten to your palate, and mix all together; put it over the fire, and keep ſtirring it till it is thick; lay a puff-paſte all over the diſh, pour in the mixture, and bake it: when you cannot get cream, take three pints of milk, beat up the yolks of four eggs and ſtir into the milk, ſet it over the fire, ſtirring it all the time till it is ſcalding hot, then mix it in the room of the cream.

To make a fine plain baked Pudding.

YOU muſt take a quart of milk and put three bay-leaves into it; when it has boiled a little with fine flour, make it into a haſty-pudding, with a little ſalt, pretty thick; take it off the fire, and ſtir in half a pound of butter, a quarter of a pound of ſugar, beat up twelve eggs, and half the whites, ſtir all well together, lay a puff-paſte all over the diſh, and pour in your ſtuff: half an hour will bake it.

To make pretty little Cheeſe-Curd Puddings.

YOU muſt take a gallon of milk and turn it with rennet, then drain all the curd from the whey, put the curd into a mortar and beat it with half a pound of freſh butter till the butter and curd is well mixed; then beat ſix eggs, half the whites, and ſtrain them to the curd, two Naples biſcuits, or half a penny roll grated; mix all theſe together, and ſweeten to your palate; butter your patty-pans, and fill them with the ingredients; bake them, but do not let your oven be too hot; when they

they are done, turn them out into a dish, cut citron and candied orange-peel into little narrow bits, about an inch long, and blanched almonds cut in long slips, stick them here and there on the tops of the puddings, just as you fancy; pour melted butter with a little sack in it into the dish, and throw fine sugar all over the puddings and dish. They make a pretty side-dish.

To make an Apricot Pudding.

CODDLE six large apricots very tender, break them very small, sweeten them to your taste; when they are cold, add six eggs, only two whites, well beat; mix them all well together with a pint of good cream, lay a puff-paste all over your dish, and pour in your ingredients: bake it half an hour, do not let the oven be too hot; when it is enough, throw a little fine sugar all over it, and send it to table hot.

To make an Ipswich Almond Pudding.

STEEP somewhat above three ounces of the crumb of white bread sliced in a pint and a half of cream, or grate the bread; then beat half a pint of blanched almonds very fine till they are like a paste, with a little orange-flower water, beat up the yolks of eight eggs, and the whites of four: mix all well together, put in a quarter of a pound of white sugar, and stir in a little melted butter, about a quarter of pound; put it over the fire, and keep stirring it till it is thick; lay a sheet of puff-paste at the bottom of your dish, and pour in the ingredients: half an hour will bake it.

Transparent Pudding.

TAKE eight eggs and beat them well; put them in a pan with half a pound of fresh butter, half a pound of fine powdered sugar, and half a nutmeg grated; set it on the fire, and keep stirring it till it is of the thickness of buttered eggs, then put it away to cool; put a thin puff-paste round the edge of your dish; pour in the ingredients, bake it half an hour in a moderate oven, and send it up hot.

Puddings for little Dishes.

YOU must take a pint of cream and boil it, and slit a halfpenny loaf and pour the cream hot over it, and cover it close till it is cold; then beat it fine and grate in half a large nutmeg, a quarter of a pound of sugar, the yolks of four eggs, but two whites, well beat, beat it all well together: with the half of this fill four little wooden dishes; colour one yellow with saffron, one red with cochineal, green with the juice of spinage, and blue with the syrup of violets; the rest mix with an an ounce of ſweet almonds blanched and beat fine, and fill a diſh: your diſhes muſt be ſmall, and tie your covers over very cloſe with packthread; when your pot boils put them in; an hour will boil them; when enough turn them out in a diſh, the white one in the middle and the four coloured ones round; when they are enough, melt ſome freſh butter with a glaſs of ſack and pour over, and throw ſugar over the diſh. The white pudding diſh muſt be of a larger ſize than the reſt; and be ſure to butter your diſhes well before you put them in, and do not fill them too full.

To make a Sweetmeat Pudding.

PUT a thin puff-paſte all over your diſh; then have candied orange, lemon-peel, and citron, of each an ounce, ſlice them thin, and lay them all over the bottom of your diſh; then beat eight yolks of eggs and two whites, near half a pound of ſugar, and half a pound of melted butter; beat all well together; when the oven is ready, pour it on your ſweetmeats: an hour or leſs will bake it; the oven muſt not be too hot.

To make a fine plain Pudding.

GET a quart of milk, put into it ſix laurel-leaves, boil it, then take out your leaves, and ſtir in as much flour as will make it a haſty pudding pretty thick, take it off, and then ſtir in half a pound of butter, then a quarter of a pound of ſugar, a ſmall nutmeg grated, and twelve yolks and ſix whites of eggs well beaten; mix all well together, butter a diſh and put in your ſtuff: a little more than half an hour will bake it.

To make a Ratifia Pudding.

GET a quart of cream, boil it with four or five laurel-leaves, then take them out, and break in half a pound of Naples biſcuits, half a pound of butter, ſome ſack, nutmeg, and a little ſalt; take it off the fire, cover it up; when it is almoſt cold, put in two ounces of blanched almonds beat fine, and the yolks of five eggs; mix all well together, and bake it in a moderate oven half an hour; ſcrape ſugar on it as it goes into the oven.

To make a Bread and Butter Pudding.

GET a penny-loaf and cut it into thin ſlices of bread and butter as you do for tea; butter your diſh as you cut them, lay ſlices all over the diſh, then ſtrew a few currants clean waſhed and picked, then a row of bread and butter, then a few currants, and ſo on till all your bread and butter is in; then take a pint of milk, beat up four eggs, a little ſalt, half a nutmeg grated; mix all together with ſugar to your taſte; pour this over the bread,

bread, and bake it half an hour: a puff-paſte under does beſt. You may put in two ſpoonfuls of roſe-water.

To make a boiled Rice-Pudding.

HAVING got a quarter of a pound of the flour of rice, put it over the fire with a pint of milk, and keep it ſtirring conſtantly that it may not clod nor burn; when it is of a good thickneſs take it off, and pour it into an earthen pan; ſtir in half a pound of butter very ſmooth, and half a pint of cream or new milk, ſweeten to your palate, grate in half a nutmeg and the outward rind of a lemon; beat up the yolks of ſix eggs and two whites, beat all well together, boil it either in ſmall china baſons or wooden bowls: when boiled turn them into a diſh, pour melted butter over them, with a little ſack, and throw ſugar all over.

To make a cheap Rice-Pudding.

GET a quarter of a pound of rice, and half a pound of raiſins ſtoned, and tie them in a cloth; give the rice a great deal of room to ſwell; boil it two hours; when it is enough, turn it into your diſh, and pour melted butter and ſugar over it, with a little nutmeg.

To make a cheap plain Rice-Pudding.

GET a quarter of a pound of rice, tie it in a cloth, but give room for ſwelling; boil it an hour, then take it up, untie it, and with a ſpoon ſtir in a quarter of a pound of butter, grate ſome nutmeg, and ſweeten to your taſte; then tie it up cloſe and boil it another hour; then take it up, turn it into your diſh and pour your melted butter over it.

To make a cheap baked Rice-Pudding.

YOU muſt take a quarter of a pound of rice, boil it in a quart of new milk, ſtir it that it does not burn; when it begins to be thick, take it off, let it ſtand till it is a little cool, then ſtir in well a quarter of a pound of butter, and ſugar to your palate; grate a ſmall nutmeg, butter your diſh, pour it in, and bake it.

To make a Hanover Cake or Pudding.

TAKE half a pound of almonds blanched and beat fine with a little roſe-water, half a pound of fine ſugar pounded and ſifted, fifteen eggs, leaving out half the whites, and the rind of a lemon grated very fine; put a few almonds in the mortar at a time, and put in by degrees about a tea-cupful of roſe-water; keep throwing in the ſugar; when you have done the almonds and ſugar together a little at a time till they are all uſed up, then

then put it into your pan with the eggs; beat them very well together: half an hour will bake it; it muſt be a light brown.

To make a Yam Pudding.

TAKE a middling white yam and either boil or roaſt it, then pare off the ſkin and pound it very fine, with three quarters of a pound of butter, half a pound of ſugar, a little mace, cinnamon, and twelve eggs, leaving out half the whites, beat them with a little roſe-water: you may put in a little citron cut ſmall (if you like it), and bake it nicely.

A Vermicelli Pudding.

BOIL four ounces of vermicelli in a pint of new milk till it is ſoft, with a ſtick or two of cinnamon, then put in half a pint of thick cream, a quarter of a pound of butter, a quarter of a pound of ſugar, and the yolks of four beaten eggs: bake it in an earthen diſh without a paſte.

A red Sago Pudding.

TAKE two ounces of ſago, boil it in water with a ſtick of cinnamon till it be quite ſoft and thick, let it ſtand till quite cold; in the meantime grate the crumb of a halfpenny-loaf, and pour over it a large glaſs of red wine, chop four ounces of marrow, and half a pound of ſugar, and the yolks of four beaten eggs, beat them all together for a quarter of an hour, lay a puff-paſte round your diſh, and ſend it to the oven; when it comes back, ſtick it over with blanched almonds cut the long way, and bits of citron cut the ſame; ſend it to table.

To make a Spinage Pudding.

TAKE a quarter of a peck of ſpinage picked and waſhed clean, put it into a ſauce-pan with a little ſalt, cover it cloſe, and when it is boiled juſt tender, throw it into a ſieve to drain; then chop it with a knife, beat up ſix eggs, mix well with it half a pint of cream and a ſtale roll grated fine, a little nutmeg, and a quarter of a pound of melted butter; ſtir all well together, put it into the ſauce-pan you boiled the ſpinage, and keep ſtirring it all the time till it begins to thicken; then wet and flour your cloth very well, tie it up, and boil it an hour: when it is enough, turn it into your diſh, pour melted butter over it, and the juice of a Seville orange (if you like it); as to ſugar, you may add or let it alone, juſt to your taſte: you may bake it; but then you ſhould put in a quarter of a pound of ſugar. You may add biſcuit in the room of bread (if you like it better).

To make a Quaking Pudding.

TAKE a pint of good cream, ſix eggs, but half the whites, beat them well, and mix with the cream; grate a little nutmeg in, add a little ſalt, and a little roſe-water (if it be agreeable); grate in the crumb of a halfpenny-roll, or a ſpoonful of flour, firſt mixed with a little of the cream, or a ſpoonful of the flour of rice (which you pleaſe); butter a cloth well, and flour it, then put in your mixture, tie it not too cloſe, and boil it half an hour faſt: be ſure the water boils before you put it in.

To make a Cream Pudding.

TAKE a quart of cream, boil it with a blade of mace and half a nutmeg grated, let it cool; beat up eight eggs and three whites, ſtrain them well, mix a ſpoonful of flour with them, a quarter of a pound of almonds blanched and beat very fine, with a ſpoonful of orange-flower or roſe-water, mix with the eggs, then by degrees mix in the cream, beat all well together, take a thick cloth, wet it and flour it well, pour in your ſtuff, tie it cloſe, and boil it half an hour: let the water boil all the time faſt; when it is done, turn it into your diſh, pour melted butter over, with a little ſack, and throw fine ſugar all over it.

To make a Prune Pudding.

TAKE a quart of milk, beat ſix eggs, half the whites, with half a pint of the milk, and four ſpoonfuls of flour, a little ſalt, and two ſpoonfuls of beaten ginger; then by degrees mix in all the milk and a pound of prunes, tie it in a cloth, boil it an hour, melt butter and pour over it. Damſons eat well done this way in the room of prunes.

To make a Spoonful Pudding.

TAKE a ſpoonful of flour, a ſpoonful of cream or milk, an egg, a little nutmeg, ginger, and ſalt; mix all together, and boil it in a little wooden diſh half an hour. You may add a few currants.

To make a Lemon Tower or Pudding.

GRATE the outward rind of three lemons; take three quarters of a pound of ſugar, and the ſame of butter, the yolks of eight eggs, beat them in a marble mortar at leaſt an hour, then lay a thin rich cruſt in the bottom of the diſh you bake it in, as you may ſomething alſo over it: three quarters of an hour will bake it. Make an orange pudding the ſame way, but pare the rinds, and boil them firſt in ſeveral waters till the bitterneſs is boiled out.

To make Yeaſt Dumplings.

FIRST make a light dough as for bread, with flour, water, ſalt, and yeaſt, cover with a cloth, and ſet it before the fire for half an hour; then have a ſauce-pan of water on the fire, and when it boils take the dough and make it into little round balls, as big as a large hen's egg; then flat them with your hand, and put them into the boiling water; a few minutes boils them; take great care they do not fall to the bottom of the pot or ſauce-pan, for then they will be heavy; and be ſure to keep the water boiling all the time: when they are enough take them up (which they will be in ten minutes or leſs), lay them in your diſh, and have melted butter in a cup. As good a way as any to ſave trouble, is to ſend to the baker's for half a quartern of dough (which will make a great many), and then you have only the trouble of boiling it.

To make Norfolk Dumplings.

MIX a good thick batter, as for pancakes; take half a pint of milk, two eggs, a little ſalt, and make it into a batter with flour; have ready a clean ſauce-pan of water boiling, into which drop this batter; be ſure the water boils faſt, and two or three minutes will boil them; then throw them into a ſieve to drain the water away; then turn them into a diſh, and ſtir a lump of freſh butter into them; eat them hot, and they are very good.

To make Hard Dumplings.

MIX flour and water with a little ſalt, like a paſte, roll them in balls as big as a turkey's egg, roll them in a little flour, have the water boiling, throw them in the water, and half an hour will boil them: they are beſt boiled with a good piece of beef. You may add for change a few currants; have melted butter in a cup.

Another Way to make Hard Dumplings.

RUB into your flour firſt a good piece of butter, then make it like a cruſt for a pie; make them up, and boil them as above.

To make Apple Dumplings.

MAKE a good puff-paſte, pare ſome large apples, cut them in quarters, and take out the cores very nicely; take a piece of cruſt, and roll it round enough for one apple; if they are big, they will not look pretty; ſo roll the cruſt round each apple, and make them round like a ball, with a little flour in your hand; have a pot of water boiling, take a clean cloth, dip it in the water and ſhake flour over it; tie each dumpling

by

by itſelf, and put them in the water boiling, which keep boiling all the time; and if your cruſt is light and good, and the apples not too large, half an hour will boil them; but if the apples be large, they will take an hour's boiling; when they are enough, take them up and lay them in a diſh; throw fine ſugar all over them, and ſend them to table; have good freſh butter melted in a cup, and fine beaten ſugar in a ſaucer.

Another Way to make Apple Dumplings.

MAKE a good puff-paſte cruſt, roll it out a little thicker than a crown-piece, pare ſome large apples and core them with an apple-ſcoop; fill the hole with beaten cinnamon, coarſe or fine ſugar, and lemon-peel ſhred fine, and roll every apple in a piece of this paſte, tie them cloſe in a cloth ſeparate, boil them an hour, cut a little piece of the top off, pour in ſome melted butter, and lay on your piece of cruſt again; lay them in a diſh, and throw fine ſugar all over.

To make Raſpberry Dumplings.

MAKE a good cold paſte, roll it a quarter of an inch thick, and ſpread over it raſpberry-jam to your own liking, roll it up and boil it in a cloth one hour at leaſt; take it up and cut it in five ſlices, and lay one in the middle and the other four round it; pour a little good melted butter in the diſh, and grate fine ſugar round the edge of the diſh. It is proper for a corner or ſide for dinner.

Citron Puddings.

TAKE half a pint of cream, mix in it a ſpoonful of fine flour, two ounces of ſugar, a little grated nutmeg, and the yolks of three eggs beat well, put it in tea-cups, and ſtick two ounces of citron cut very thin in it; bake them in a quick oven, and turn them out on a diſh.

To make a Cheeſe-Curd Florendine.

TAKE two pounds of cheeſe-curd, break it all to pieces with your hand, a pound of blanched almonds finely pounded, with a little roſe-water, half a pound of currants clean waſhed and picked, a little ſugar to your palate, ſome ſtewed ſpinage cut ſmall; mix all well together, lay a puff-paſte in a diſh, put in your ingredients, cover it with a thin cruſt rolled and laid acroſs, and bake it in a moderate oven half an hour: as to the top-cruſt lay it in what ſhape you pleaſe, either rolled or marked with an iron on purpoſe.

A Florendine of Oranges or Apples.

GET half a dozen of Seville oranges, ſave the juice, take out the pulp, lay them in water twenty-four hours, ſhift them three or four times, then boil them in three or four waters, then drain them from the water, put them in a pound of sugar, and their juice, boil them to a syrup, take great care they do not stick to the pan you do them in, and set them by for use; when you use them lay a puff-paste all over the dish, boil ten pippins, pared, quartered, and cored, in a little water and sugar, and slice two of the oranges and mix with the pippins in the dish; bake it in a slow oven with a crust as above: or just bake the crust, and lay in the ingredients.

To make an Artichoke Pie.

BOIL twelve artichokes, take off all the leaves and chokes, take the bottoms clear from the stalk, make a good puff-paste crust, and lay a quarter of a pound of good fresh butter all over the bottom of your pie; then lay a row of artichokes, strew a little pepper, salt, and beaten mace over them; then another row, and strew the rest of your spice over them; put in a quarter of a pound more of butter in little bits, take half an ounce of truffles and morels, boil them in a quarter of a pint of water, pour the water into the pie, cut the truffles and morels very small, throw all over the pie; then have ready twelve eggs boiled hard, take only the hard yolks, lay them all over the pie, pour in a gill of white wine, cover your pie, and bake it: when the crust is done, the pie is enough: four large blades of mace and twelve pepper-corns well beat will do, with a tea-spoonful of salt.

To make a sweet Egg Pie.

MAKE a good crust, cover your dish with it, then have ready twelve eggs boiled hard, cut them in slices and lay them in your pie, throw half a pound of currants clean washed and picked all over the eggs, then beat up four eggs well mixed with half a pint of white wine, grate in a small nutmeg, and make it pretty sweet with sugar. You are to mind to lay a quarter of a pound of butter between the eggs, then pour in your wine and eggs and cover your pie; bake it half an hour, or till the crust is done.

To make a Potatoe Pie.

BOIL three pounds of potatoes, peel them, make a good crust and lay in your dish; lay at the bottom half a pound of butter, then lay in your potatoes, throw all over them first three tea-spoonfuls of salt and a small nutmeg grated, next six eggs boiled hard and chopped fine, then a tea-spoonful of pepper and half a pint of white wine; cover your pie, and bake it half an hour, or till the crust is enough.

To

To make an Onion Pie.

WASH and pare ſome potatoes and cut them in ſlices, peel ſome onions, cut them in ſlices, pare ſome apples and ſlice them, make a good cruſt, cover your diſh, lay a quarter of a pound of butter all over, take a quarter of an ounce of mace beat fine, a nutmeg grated, a tea-ſpoonful of beaten pepper, three tea-ſpoonfuls of ſalt; mix all together, ſtrew ſome over the butter, lay a layer of potatoes, a layer of onions, a layer of apples, and a layer of eggs, and ſo on till you have filled your pie, ſtrewing a little of the ſeaſoning between each layer, and a quarter of a pound of butter in bits, and ſix ſpoonfuls of water; cloſe your pie, and bake it an hour and a half. A pound of potatoes, a pound of onions, a pound of apples, and twelve eggs will do.

To make an Orangeado Pie.

MAKE a good cruſt, lay it over your diſh, take two oranges, boil them with two lemons till tender, in four or five quarts of water; in the laſt water (of which there muſt be about a pint), add a pound of loaf ſugar, boil it, take them out and ſlice them into your pie; then pare twelve pippins, core them, and give them one boil in the ſyrup; lay them all over the orange and lemon, pour in the ſyrup, and pour on them ſome orangeado ſyrup; cover your pie, and bake it in a ſlow oven half an hour.

To make a Vegetable Pie.

TAKE cauliflowers broken into neat pieces, white cabbage cut into ſmall quantities, a few heads of celery neatly cut, a few ſmall onions and potatoes peeled, and ſome endive (if white and not bitter); boil theſe ſeparately in milk and water, drain and keep them hot; raiſe the walls of your pie; fill it with ſomething to ſupport it, and lay on the lid, bake it ſufficiently to ſtand, but not quite enough; take off the lid, lay in the vegetables neatly in rows thus—a row of cauliflower, a row of onions, &c. add Cayenne, ſalt, and beaten mace as you go on, then put on your lid again; bake your pie half an hour more, take care not to burn it; have ready good fricaſſee-ſauce, take off the lid, pour over it the ſauce, and ſerve it up without the lid.

To make a Skirret Pie.

TAKE your ſkirrets and boil them tender, peel them, ſlice them, fill your pie, and take to half a pint of cream the yolk of an egg, beat fine with a little nutmeg, a little beaten mace, and a little ſalt; beat all together well, with a quarter of a pound of freſh butter melted, then pour in as much as your diſh will hold, put on the top-crust and bake it half an hour. You may put in some hard yolks of eggs; if you cannot get cream, put in milk, but cream is best: about two pounds of the root will do.

To make an Apple Pie.

MAKE a good puff-paste crust, lay some round the sides of the dish, pare and quarter your apples and take out the cores, lay a row of apples thick, throw in half the sugar you design for your pie, mince a little lemon-peel fine, throw over, and squeeze a little lemon over them, then a few cloves, here and there one, then the rest of your apples and the rest of your sugar; you must sweeten to your palate, and squeeze a little more lemon; boil the peeling of the apples and the cores in some fair water with a blade of mace, till it is very good; strain it, and boil the syrup with a little sugar till there is but very little and good, pour it into your pie, put on your upper crust and bake it. You may put in a little quince or marmalade (if you please).

Thus make a pear pie, but do not put in any quince. You may butter them when they come out of the oven: or beat up the yolks of two eggs and half a pint of cream with a little nutmeg, sweetened with sugar; put it over a slow fire and keep stirring it till it just boils up, take off the lid and pour in the cream; cut the crust in little three-corner pieces, stick about the pie, and send it to table cold.

Green Codling Pie.

TAKE some green codlings and put them in a clean pan with spring-water; lay vine or cabbage leaves over them, and wrap a cloth over and round the pan to keep in the steam; as soon as you think they are soft take the skins off, put them in the same water with the leaves over them, hang them a good distance from the fire to green; and as soon as you see them of a fine green, take them out of the water and put them in a deep dish, and sweeten them with sugar, and strew a little lemon-peel shred fine over, put a lid of puff-paste over them and bake it; when it is baked, cut the lid off, and cut it into three-corner pieces and put them round your pie, with one corner uppermost; let it stand till it is cold, and then make the following cream: boil a pint of cream or milk, beat up the yolks of four eggs, sweeten it with fine sugar, mix all well together and put it over the fire till it is thick and smooth; but be sure you do not let it boil, for that will curdle it, and put it over your codlings; or you may put clouted cream (if you like it best) and send it to table cold.

To make a Cherry Pie.

MAKE a good cruſt, lay a little round the ſides of your diſh, throw ſugar at the bottom, and lay in your fruit and ſugar at top. A few red currants do well with them; put on your lid, and bake in a ſlack oven.

Make a plum pie the ſame way, and a gooſeberry pie. If you would have it red, let it ſtand a good while in the oven after the bread is drawn. A cuſtard is very good with the gooſeberry pie.

To make a Salt Fiſh Pie.

GET a ſide of ſalt fiſh, lay it in wa er all night, next morning put it over the fire in a pan of water till it is tender, drain it and lay it on the dreſſer, take off all the ſkin, and pick the meat clean from the bones, mince it ſmall, then take the crumb of two French rolls cut in ſlices, and boil it up with a quart of new milk, break your bread very fine with a ſpoon, put to it your minced ſalt fiſh, a pound of melted butter, two ſpoonfuls of minced parſley, half a nutmeg grated, a little beaten pepper, and three tea-ſpoonfuls of muſtard; mix all well together, make a good cruſt and lay all over your diſh, and cover it up: bake it an hour.

To make a Carp Pie.

TAKE a large carp, ſcale, waſh, and gut it clean; take an eel, boil it juſt a little tender, pick off all the meat, and mince it fine with an equal quantity of crumbs of bread, a few ſweet herbs, a lemon-peel cut fine, a little pepper, ſalt, and grated nutmeg, an anchovy, half a pint of oyſters parboiled and chopped fine, the yolks of three hard eggs cut ſmall, roll it up with a quarter of a pound of butter, and fill the belly of the carp; make a good cruſt, cover the diſh, and lay in your carp; ſave the liquor you boil your eel in, put in the eel bones, boil them with a little mace, whole pepper, an onion, ſome ſweet herbs, and an anchovy; boil it till there is about half a pint, ſtrain it, add to it a quarter of a pint of white wine, and a lump of butter as big as a hen's egg, mixed in a very little flour; boil it up, and pour into your pie; put on the lid, and bake it an hour in a quick oven. If there be any force-meat left after filling the belly, make balls of it, and put into the pie; if you have not liquor enough, boil a few ſmall eels to make enough to fill your diſh.

To make a Soal Pie.

MAKE a good cruſt, cover your diſh, boil two pounds of eels tender, pick all the fleſh clean from the bones; throw the bones into the liquor you boil the eels in, with a little mace and salt, till it is very good, and about a quarter of a pint, then strain it; in the meantime cut the shell of your eel fine, with a little lemon-peel shred fine, a little salt, pepper, and nutmeg, a few crumbs of bread, chopped parsley, and an anchovy; melt a quarter of a pound of butter and mix with it, then lay it in the dish, cut the flesh off a pair of large soals, or three pair of very small ones, clean from the bones and fins, lay it on the force-meat, and pour in the broth of the eels you boiled; put the lid of the pie on, and bake it. You should boil the bones of the soals with the eel bones, to make it good; if you boil the soal bones with one or two little eels, without the force-meat, your pie will be very good. And thus you may do a turbot.

To make an Eel Pie.

MAKE a good crust; clean, gut, and wash your eels very well, then cut them in pieces half as long as your finger; season them with pepper, salt, and a little beaten mace to your palate, either high or low; fill your dish with eels, and put as much water as the dish will hold; put on your cover, and bake them well.

To make a Flounder Pie.

GUT some flounders, wash them clean, dry them in a cloth, just boil them, cut off the meat clean from the bones, lay a good crust over the dish, and lay a little fresh butter at the bottom, and on that the fish; season with pepper and salt to your mind; boil the bones in the water your fish was boiled in, with a little bit of horse-radish, a little parsley, a very little bit of lemon-peel, and a crust of bread; boil it till there is just enough of liquor for the pie, then strain it, and put it into your pie; put on the top-crust, and bake it.

To make a Herring Pie.

SCALE, gut, and wash them very clean, cut off the heads, fins, and tails; make a good crust, cover your dish, then season your herrings with beaten mace, pepper, and salt; put a little butter in the bottom of your dish, then a row of herrings, pare some apples and cut them in thin slices all over, then peel some onions and cut them in slices all over thick, lay a little butter on the top, put in a little water, lay on the lid, and bake it well.

To make a Salmon Pie.

MAKE a good crust, cleanse a piece of salmon well, season it with salt, mace, and nutmeg, lay a piece of butter at the bottom

bottom of the diſh, and lay your ſalmon in; melt buter according to your pie; take a lobſter, boil it, pick out all the fleſh, chop it ſmall, bruiſe the body, mix it well with the butter, which muſt be very good; pour it over your ſalmon, put on the lid, and bake it well.

To make a Lobſter Pie.

TAKE two or three lobſters and boil them; take the meat out of the tails whole, cut them in four pieces, longways; take out the ſpawn and the meat of the claws, beat it well in a mortar; ſeaſon it with pepper, ſalt, two ſpoonfuls of vinegar, and a little anchovy liquor; melt half a pound of freſh butter, ſtir all together with the crumbs of a halfpenny roll rubbed through a fine cullender, and the yolks of two eggs; put a fine puff-paſte over your diſh, lay in your tails, and the reſt of the meat over them; put on your cover, and bake it in a ſlow oven.

To make a Muſcle Pie.

MAKE a good cruſt, lay it all over the diſh, waſh your muſcles clean in ſeveral waters, then put them in a deep ſtew-pan, cover them and let them ſtew till they are open, pick them out, and ſee there be no crabs under the tongue; put them in a ſauce-pan with two or three blades of mace, ſtrain liquor juſt enough to cover them, a good piece of butter, and a few crumbs of bread; ſtew them a few minutes, fill your pie, put on the lid, and bake it half an hour. So you make an oyſter pie; always let your fiſh be cold before you put on the lid, or it will ſpoil the cruſt.

To make Lent Mince-Pies.

SIX eggs boiled hard and chopped fine, twelve pippins pared and chopped ſmall, a pound of raiſins of the ſun ſtoned and chopped fine, a pound of currants waſhed, picked, and rubbed clean, a large ſpoonful of ſugar beat fine, an ounce of citron, an ounce of candied orange, both cut fine, a quarter of an ounce of mace and cloves and a little nutmeg beat fine; mix all together with a gill of brandy and a gill of ſack; make your cruſt good, and bake it in a ſlack oven: when you make your pie, ſqueeze in the juice of a Seville orange.

Fiſh Paſties the Italian Way.

TAKE ſome flour and knead it with oil; take a ſlice of ſalmon, ſeaſon it with pepper and ſalt, and dip into ſweet oil; chop an onion and parſley fine and ſtrew over it; lay it in the paſte, and double it up in the ſhape of a ſlice of ſalmon; take a piece of white paper, oil it and lay under the paſty, and bake it: it is beſt cold, and will keep a month.

Mackarel done the ſame way, head and tail together folded in a paſty, eats fine.

To roaſt a Pound of Butter.

LAY it in ſalt and water two or three hours, then ſpit it and rub it all over with crumbs of bread, with a little grated nutmeg, lay it to the fire, and, as it roaſts, baſte it with the yolks of two eggs and then with crumbs of bread all the time it is roaſting; but have ready a pint of oyſters ſtewed in their own liquor, and lay in the diſh under the butter; when the bread has ſoaked up all the butter, brown the outſide, and lay it on your oyſters. Your fire muſt be very ſlow.

CHAP. XV.

DIRECTIONS FOR THE SICK.

[I do not pretend to meddle here in the Phyſical Way; but a few Directions for the Cook, or Nurſe, I preſume, will not be improper, to make ſuch a Diet, &c. as the Doctor ſhall order.]

To make Mutton Broth.

TAKE a pound of loin of mutton, take off the fat, put to it one quart of water, let it boil and ſkim it well; then put in a good piece of upper-cruſt of bread, and one large blade of mace; cover it cloſe and let it boil ſlowly an hour; do not ſtir it, but pour the broth clear off; ſeaſon it with a little ſalt, and the mutton will be fit to eat. If you boil turnips, do not boil them in the broth, but by themſelves in another ſauce-pan.

To boil a Scrag of Veal.

SET on the ſcrag in a clean ſauce-pan; to each pound of veal put a quart of water, ſkim it very clean, then put in a good piece of upper-cruſt, a blade of mace to each pound, and a little parſley tied with a thread; cover it cloſe; then let it boil very ſoftly two hours, and both broth and meat will be fit to eat.

To make Beef or Mutton Broth for very weak People, who take but little Nouriſhment.

TAKE a pound of beef or mutton, or both together; to a pound put two quarts of water, firſt ſkin the meat and take off the

the fat; then cut it into little pieces, and boil it till it comes to a quarter of a pint; feason it with a very little corn of falt, fkim off all the fat, and give a fpoonful of this broth at a time; to very weak people half a fpoonful is enough; to fome a tea-fpoonful at a time; and to others a tea-cupful: there is greater nourifhment from this than any thing elfe.

To make Beef-Drink, which is ordered for weak People.

TAKE a pound of lean beef, then take off all the fat and fkin, cut it into pieces, put it into a gallon of water with the under-cruft of a penny loaf, and a very little falt; let it boil till it comes to two quarts, then ftrain it off; and it is a very hearty drink.

To make Beef Tea.

TAKE a pound of lean beef and cut it very fine, pour a pint of boiling water over it and put it on the fire to raife the fcum; fkim it clean, ftrain it off and let it fettle; pour it clear from the fettling, and then it is fit for ufe.

To make Pork Broth.

TAKE two pounds of young pork, then take off the fkin and fat, boil it in a gallon of water with a turnip, and a very little corn of falt; let it boil till it comes to two quarts, ftrain it off and let it ftand till cold; take off the fat, then leave the fettling at the bottom of the pan, and drink half a pint in the morning fafting, an hour before breakfaft; and noon, if the ftomach will bear it.

To boil a Chicken.

LET your fauce-pan be very clean and nice; when the water boils put in your chicken, which muft be very nicely picked and clean, and laid in cold water a quarter of an hour before it is boiled; then take it out of the water boiling, and lay it in a pewter difh; fave all the liquor that runs from it in the difh; cut up your chicken all in joints in the difh; then bruife the liver very fine, add a little boiled parfley chopped fine, a very little falt, and a little grated nutmeg; mix it all well together with two fpoonfuls of the liquor of the fowl, and pour it into the difh with the reft of the liquor in the difh; if there is not liquor enough, take two or three fpoonfuls of the liquor it was boiled in, clap another difh over it; then fet it over a chafing-difh of hot coals five or fix minutes, and carry it to table hot with the cover on. This is better than butter, and lighter for the ftomach, though fome choofe it only with the liquor, and no parfley nor liver, and that is according to different palates: if it is for a very weak perfon, take off the fkin of the chicken before

before you ſet it on the chafing-diſh. If you roaſt it, make nothing but bread-ſauce, and that is lighter than any ſauce you can make for a weak ſtomach.

Thus you may dreſs a rabbit, only bruiſe but a little piece of the liver.

To boil Pigeons.

LET your pigeons be cleaned, waſhed, drawn, and ſkinned; boil them in milk and water ten minutes, and pour over them ſauce made thus: take the livers parboiled and bruiſe them fine, with as much parſley boiled and chopped fine; melt ſome butter, mix a little with the liver and parſley firſt, then mix all together, and pour over the pigeons.

To boil a Partridge, or any other Wild Fowl.

WHEN your water boils put in your partridge, let it boil ten minutes; then take it up into a pewter plate, and cut it in two, laying the inſides next the plate, and have ready ſome bread-ſauce made thus: take the crumb of a halfpenny roll, or thereabouts, and boil it in half a pint of water, with a blade of mace; let it boil two or three minutes, pour away moſt of the water; then beat it up with a little piece of nice butter, a little ſalt, and pour it over your partridge; clap a cover over it, then ſet it over a chafing-diſh of coals four or five minutes, and ſend it away hot, covered cloſe.

Thus you may dreſs any ſort of wild fowl, only boiling it more or leſs according to the bigneſs. Ducks, take off the ſkins before you pour the bread-ſauce over them; and if you roaſt them, lay bread-ſauce under them: it is lighter than gravy for weak ſtomachs.

To boil a Plaice or Flounder.

LET your water boil, throw ſome ſalt in; then put in your fiſh; boil it till you think it is enough, and take it out of the water in a ſlice to drain; take two ſpoonfuls of the liquor, with a little ſalt, a little grated nutmeg; then beat up the yolk of an egg very well with the liquor, and ſtir in the egg; beat it well together, with a knife carefully ſlice away all the little bones round the fiſh, pour the ſauce over it; then ſet it over a chafing-diſh of coals for a minute, and ſend it hot away: or in the room of this ſauce, add melted butter in a cup.

To mince Veal or Chicken for the Sick, or weak People.

MINCE a chicken, or ſome veal, very fine, take off the ſkin; juſt boil as much water as will moiſten it, and no more, with a very little ſalt, grate a very little nutmeg; then throw a little flour over it, and when the water boils put in the meat; keep

ſhaking

ſhaking it about over the fire a minute; then have ready two or three very thin ſippets, toaſted nice and brown, laid in the plate, and pour the mince-meat over it.

To pull a Chicken for the Sick.

YOU muſt take as much cold chicken as you think proper, take off the ſkin, and pull the meat into little bits as thick as a quill; then take the bones, boil them with a little ſalt till they are good, ſtrain it, then take a ſpoonful of the liquor, a ſpoonful of milk, a little bit of butter as big as a large nutmeg rolled in flour, a little chopped parſley as much as will lie on a ſixpence, and a little ſalt, if wanted, (this will be enough for half a ſmall chicken,) put all together into the ſauce-pan, then keep ſhaking it till it is thick, and pour it into a hot plate.

To make Chicken Broth.

YOU muſt take an old cock, or large fowl, flay it, then pick off all the fat, and break it all to pieces with a rolling-pin; put it into two quarts of water with a good cruſt of bread and a blade of mace, let it boil ſoftly till it is as good as you would have it; if you do it as it ſhould be done, it will take five or ſix hours doing; pour it off, then put a quart more of boiling water, cover it cloſe, let it boil ſoftly till it is good, and ſtrain it off; ſeaſon with a very little ſalt. When you boil a chicken, ſave the liquor; and when the meat is eat, take the bones, then break them, and put to the liquor you boiled the chicked in, with a blade of mace, and a cruſt of bread, let it boil till it is good, and ſtrain it off.

To make Chicken Water.

TAKE a cock or large fowl, flay it, then bruiſe it with a hammer and put it into a gallon of water with a cruſt of bread, let it boil half away, and ſtrain it off.

To make White Caudle.

YOU muſt take two quarts of water, mix in four ſpoonfuls of oatmeal, a blade or two of mace, a piece of lemon-peel, let it boil, and keep ſtirring it often: let it boil about a quarter of an hour, and take care it does not boil over; then ſtrain it through a coarſe ſieve: when you uſe it, ſweeten it to your palate, grate in a little nutmeg, and what wine is proper; and if it is not for a ſick perſon, ſqueeze in the juice of a lemon.

To make Brown Caudle.

BOIL the gruel as above, with ſix ſpoonfuls of oatmeal, and ſtrain it; then add a quart of good ale, not bitter; boil it, then ſweeten fweeten it to your palate, and add half a pint of white wine: when you do not put in white wine, let it be half ale.

To make Water-Gruel.

You muft take a pint of water and a large fpoonful of oatmeal; then ftir it together and let it boil up three or four times, ftirring it often; do not let it boil over; then ftrain it through a fieve, falt it to your palate, put in a good piece of frefh butter, brew it with a fpoon till the butter is all melted, then it will be fine and fmooth, and very good: fome love a little pepper in it.

To make Panado.

You muft take a quart of water in a nice clean fauce-pan, a blade of mace, a large piece of crumb of bread; let it boil two minutes; then take out the bread and bruife it in a bafon very fine; mix as much water as will make it as thick as you would have it; the reft pour away, and fweeten it to your palate; put in a piece of butter as big as a walnut; do not put in any wine, it fpoils it: you may grate in a little nutmeg. This is hearty and good diet for fick people.

To boil Sago.

Put a large fpoonful of fago into three quarters of a pint of water, ftir it, and boil it foftly till it is as thick as you would have it; then put in wine and fugar, with a little nutmeg to your palate.

To boil Salop.

It is a hard ftone ground to powder, and generally fold for one fhilling an ounce: take a large tea-fpoonful of the powder and put it into a pint of boiling water, keep ftirring it till it is like a fine jelly; then put in wine and fugar to your palate, and lemon, if it will agree.

To make Ifinglafs Jelly.

Take a quart of water, one ounce of ifinglafs, half an ounce of cloves; boil them to a pint, then ftrain it upon a pound of loaf-fugar, and when cold fweeten your tea with it: you may make the jelly as above, and leave out the cloves; fweeten to your palate, and add a little wine. All other jellies you have in another Chapter.

To make the Pectoral Drink.

Take a gallon of water and half a pound of pearl-barley, boil it with a quarter of a pound of figs fplit, a pennyworth of liquorice fliced to pieces, a quarter of a pound of raifins of the fun ſun ſtoned; boil all together till half is waſted, then ſtrain it off. This is ordered in the meaſles, and ſeveral other diſorders, for a drink.

To make Buttered Water, or what the Germans call Egg-Soup, who are very fond of it for Supper. You have it in the Chapter for Lent.

TAKE a pint of water, beat up the yolk of an egg with the water, put in a piece of butter as big as a ſmall walnut, two or three knobs of ſugar, and keep ſtirring it all the time it is on the fire; when it begins to boil, bruiſe it between the ſauce-pan and a mug till it is ſmooth and has a great froth; then it is fit to drink. This is ordered in a cold, or where eggs will agree with the ſtomach.

To make Seed-Water.

TAKE a ſpoonful of coriander-ſeed, half a ſpoonful of cara-way-ſeed, bruiſed and boiled in a pint of water; then ſtrain it, and bruiſe it with the yolk of an egg: mix it with ſack and double-refined ſugar, according to your palate.

To make Bread-Soup for the Sick.

TAKE a quart of water, ſet it on the fire in a clean ſauce-pan, and as much dry cruſt of bread cut to pieces as the top of a penny loaf (the drier the better) a bit of butter as big as a wal-nut; let it boil, then beat it with a ſpoon, and keep boiling it till the bread and water is well mixed; then ſeaſon it with a very little ſalt, and it is a pretty thing for a weak ſtomach.

To make artificial Aſſes Milk.

TAKE two ounces of pearl-barley, two large ſpoonfuls of hartſhorn-ſhavings, one ounce of eringo-root, one ounce of China-root, one ounce of preſerved ginger, eighteen ſnails bruiſed with the ſhells, to be boiled in three quarts of water till it comes to three pints, then boil a pint of new milk, mix it with the reſt, and put in two ounces of balſam of Tolu. Take half a pint in the morning, and half a pint at night.

Cows Milk, next to Aſſes Milk, done thus.

TAKE a quart of milk, ſet it in a pan over night, the next morning take off all the cream, then boil it and ſet it in the pan again till night; then ſkim it again, boil it, ſet it in the pan again, and the next morning ſkim it, warm it blood warm, and drink it as you do aſſes milk: it is very near as good, and with ſome conſumptive people it is better.

To

To make a good Drink.

BOIL a quart of milk and a quart of water, with the top-cruſt of a penny loaf, and one blade of mace, a quarter of an hour very ſoftly, then pour it off, and when you drink it let it be warm.

To make Barley-Water.

PUT a quarter of a pound of pearl-barley into two quarts of water, let it boil, ſkim it very clean, boil half away, and ſtrain it off; ſweeten to your palate, but not too ſweet, and put in two ſpoonfuls of white wine; drink it lukewarm.

To make Sage-Tea.

TAKE a little ſage, a little baum, put it into a pan, ſlice a lemon, peel and all, a few knobs of ſugar, one glaſs of white wine, pour on theſe two or three quarts of boiling water, cover it, and drink when thirſty; when you think it ſtrong enough of the herbs, take them out, otherwiſe it will make it bitter.

To make it for a Child.

A LITTLE ſage, baum, rue, mint, and penny-royal, pour boiling water on, and ſweeten to your palate. Syrup of cloves, &c. and black cherry-water, you have in the Chapter of Preſerves.

Liquor for a Child that has the Thruſh.

TAKE half a pint of ſpring-water, a knob of double-refined ſugar, a very little bit of alum, beat it well together with the yolk of an egg, then beat it in a large ſpoonful of the juice of ſage; tie a rag to the end of a ſtick, dip it in this liquor, and often clean the mouth. Give the child over night one drop of laudanum, and the next day proper phyſic, waſhing the mouth often with the liquor.

To boil Comfrey-Roots.

TAKE a pound of comfrey-roots, ſcrape them clean, cut them into little pieces, and put them into three pints of water, let them boil till there is about a pint, then ſtrain it, and when it is cold put it into a ſauce-pan; if there is any ſettling at the bottom, throw it away; mix it with ſugar to your palate, add half a pint of mountain wine and the juice of a lemon, let it boil, then pour it into a clean earthen pot, and ſet it by for uſe. Some boil it with milk, and it is very good where it will agree, and is reckoned a very great ſtrengthener.

To make the Knuckle Broth.

TAKE twelve ſhank-ends of a leg of mutton, break them well and ſoak them in cold ſpring-water for an hour, then take a ſmall a ſmall bruſh and ſcour them clean with warm water and ſalt, then put them into two quarts of ſpring-water and let them ſimmer till reduced to one quart; when they have been on one hour, put in one ounce of hartſhorn-ſhavings and the bottom of a halfpenny-roll; be careful to take the ſcum off as it riſes; when done, ſtrain it off, and if any fat remains, take it off with a knife when cold; drink a quarter of a pint warm when you go to bed, and one hour before you riſe: it is a certain reſtorative at the beginning of a decline, or when any weakneſs is the complaint.

N. B. If it is made right, it is the colour of calf's foot jelly, and is ſtrong enough to bear a ſpoon upright. [From the College of Phyſicians, London.]

A Medicine for a Diſorder in the Bowels.

TAKE an ounce of beef-ſuet, half a pint of milk, and half a pint of water, mix together with a table-ſpoonful of wheat-flour, put it over the fire ten minutes, and keep it ſtirring all the time; and take a coffee-cupful two or three times a-day.

CHAP. XVI.

For CAPTAINS of SHIPS.

(Many of the Receipts in this Chapter are very uſeful in Families.)

To make Catchup to keep twenty Years.

TAKE a gallon of ſtrong ſtale beer, one pound of anchovies waſhed from the pickle, a pound of ſhalots peeled, half an ounce of mace, half an ounce of cloves, a quarter of an ounce of whole pepper, three or four large races of ginger, two quarts of the large muſhroom-flaps rubbed to pieces; cover all this cloſe, and let it ſimmer till it is half waſted, then ſtrain it through a flannel bag; let it ſtand till it is quite cold, then bottle it. You may carry it to the Indies. A ſpoonful of this to a pound of freſh butter melted makes a fine fiſh-ſauce, or in the room of gravy ſauce. The ſtronger and ſtaler the beer is, the better the catchup will be.

To make Fiſh-Sauce to keep the whole Year.

YOU muſt take twenty-four anchovies, chop them, bones and all, put to them ten ſhalots cut ſmall, a handful of ſcraped horſe-radiſh, a quarter of an ounce of mace, a quart of white wine, a pint of water, one lemon cut into ſlices, half a pint of anchovy liquor, a pint of red wine, twelve cloves, twelve pepper-corns; boil them together till it comes to a quart; ſtrain it off, cover it cloſe, and keep it in a cold dry place. Two ſpoonfuls will be ſufficient for a pound of butter.

It is a pretty ſauce either for boiled fowl, veal, &c. or in the room of gravy, lowering it with hot water, and thickening it with a piece of butter rolled in flour.

To pot Dripping to fry Fiſh, Meat, Fritters, &c.

TAKE ſix pounds of good beef-dripping, boil it in ſoft water, ſtrain it into a pan, let it ſtand till cold; then take off the hard fat, and ſcrape off the gravy which ſticks to the inſide; thus do eight times; when it is cold and hard, take it off clean from the water, put it into a large ſauce-pan with ſix bay-leaves, twelve cloves, half a pound of ſalt, and a quarter of a pound of whole pepper; let the fat be all melted and juſt hot, let it ſtand till it is hot enough to ſtrain through a ſieve into the pot, and ſtand till it is quite cold, then cover it up: thus you may do what quantity you pleaſe. The beſt way to keep any ſort of dripping is to turn the pot upſide down, and then no rats can get at it. If it will keep on ſhip-board, it will make as fine puff-paſte cruſt as any butter can do, or cruſt for puddings, &c.

To pickle Muſhrooms for the Sea.

WASH them clean with a piece of flannel in ſalt and water, put them into a ſauce-pan and throw a little ſalt over them; let them boil up three times in their own liquor, then throw them into a ſieve to drain, and ſpread them on a clean cloth; let them lie till cold, then put them in wide-mouthed bottles, put in with them a good deal of whole mace, a little nutmeg ſliced, and a few cloves: boil the ſugar-vinegar of your own making with a good deal of whole pepper, ſome races of ginger, and two or three bay-leaves; let it boil a few minutes, then ſtrain it, when it is cold pour it on and fill the bottle with mutton-fat fried; cork them, tie a bladder, then a leather over them, keep it down cloſe, and in as cool a place as poſſible. As to all other pickles, you have them in the Chapter of Pickles.

To make Muſhroom Powder.

TAKE half a peck of fine large thick muſhrooms, waſh them clean from grit and dirt with a flannel rag, ſcrape out the inſide, cut out all the worms, put them into a kettle over the fire without any water, two large onions ſtuck with cloves, a large handful of ſalt, a quarter of an ounce of mace, two tea-ſpoonfuls of beaten pepper, let them ſimmer till the liquor is boiled away; take great care they do not burn; then lay them

on

on ſieves to dry in the ſun, or in tin plates, and ſet them in a ſlack oven all night to dry, till they will beat to powder: preſs the powder down hard in a pot, and keep it for uſe. You may put what quantity you pleaſe for the ſauce.

To keep Muſhrooms without Pickle.

TAKE large muſhrooms, peel them, ſcrape out the inſide, put them into a ſauce-pan, throw a little ſalt over them, and let them boil in their own liquor, then throw them into a ſieve to drain, then lay them on tin plates and ſet them in a cool oven; repeat it often till they are perfectly dry, put them into a clean ſtone jar, tie them down tight, and keep them in a dry place. They eat deliciouſly, and look as well as truffles.

To keep Artichoke-Bottoms dry.

BOIL them juſt ſo as you can pull off the leaves and the choke, cut them from the ſtalks, lay them on tin plates, ſet them in a very cool oven, and repeat it till they are quite dry; then put them in a paper bag, tie them up cloſe, and hang them up, and always keep them in a dry place; and when you uſe them lay them in warm water till they are tender; ſhift the water two or three times. They are fine in almoſt all ſauces cut in little pieces, and put in juſt before your ſauce is enough.

To fry Artichoke-Bottoms.

LAY them in water as above, then have ready ſome butter hot in a pan, flour the bottoms and fry them; lay them in your diſh and pour melted butter over them.

To ragoo Artichoke-Bottoms.

TAKE twelve bottoms, ſoften them in warm water, as in the foregoing receipts; take half a pint of water, a piece of the ſtrong ſoup, as big as a ſmall walnut, half a ſpoonful of the catchup, five or ſix of the dried muſhrooms, a tea-ſpoonful of the muſhroom powder, ſet it on the fire, ſhake all together and let it boil ſoftly two or three minutes; let the laſt water you put to the bottoms boil; take them out hot, lay them in your diſh, pour the ſauce over them, and ſend them to table hot.

To dreſs Fiſh.

As to frying fiſh, firſt waſh it very clean, then dry it well and flour it; take ſome of the beef-dripping, make it boil in the ſtew-pan, then throw in your fiſh, and fry it of a fine light brown; lay it on the bottom of a ſieve, or coarſe cloth, to drain, and make ſauce according to your fancy.

To bake Fish.

BUTTER the pan, lay in the fish, throw a little salt over it and flour; put a very little water in the dish, an onion, and a bundle of sweet herbs, stick some little bits of butter, or the fine dripping, on the fish; let it be baked of a fine light brown; when enough, lay it on a dish before the fire, and skim off all the fat in the pan; strain the liquor and mix it up either with the fish-sauce or strong soup, or the catchup.

To make a Gravy-Soup.

ONLY boil soft water, and put as much of the strong soup to it as will make it to your palate; let it boil, and if it wants salt, you must season it. The receipts for the soup you have in the Chapter for Soups.

To make Peas-Soup.

GET a quart of peas, boil them in two gallons of water till they are tender, then have ready a piece of salt pork, or beef, which has been laid in water the night before, put it into the pot, with two large onions pealed, a bundle of sweet herbs, celery (if you have it), half a quarter of an ounce of whole pepper; let it boil till the meat is enough, then take it up, and if the soup is not enough, let it boil till the soup is good; then strain it, set it on again to boil, and rub in a good deal of dry mint; keep the meat hot; when the soup is ready, put in the meat again for a few minutes and let it boil, then serve it away: if you add a piece of the portable soup, it will be very good. The onion-soup you have in the Lent Chapter.

To make a Pudding of Pork, Beef, &c.

MAKE a good crust with the dripping, or mutton-suet (if you have it) shred fine; make a thick crust, take a piece of salt pork or beef which has been twenty-four hours in soft water, season it with a little pepper, put it into this crust, roll it up close, tie it in cloth, and boil it; if of about four or five pounds, boil it five hours.

And when you kill mutton, make a pudding the same way, only cut the steaks thin; season them with pepper and salt, and boil it three hours, if large; or two hours, if small; and so according to the size.

Apple-pudding make with the same crust, only pare the apples, core them, and fill your pudding; if large, it will take five hours boiling; when it is enough, lay it in the dish, cut a hole in the top and stir in butter and sugar; lay the piece on again, and send it to table.

A prune-

A prune-pudding eats fine made the fame way, only when the cruft is ready fill it with prunes, and fweeten it according to your fancy, clofe it up, and boil it two hours.

To make a Rice-Pudding.

TAKE what rice you think proper, tie it loofe in a cloth, and boil it an hour; then take it up and untie it, grate a good deal of nutmeg in, ftir in a good piece of butter, and fweeten to your palate; tie it up clofe, boil it an hour more, then take it up and turn it into your difh; melt butter, with a little fugar, and a little white wine for fauce.

To make a Suet-Pudding.

GET a pound of fuet fhred fine, a pound of flour, a pound of currants picked clean, half a pound of raifins ftoned, two tea-fpoonfuls of beaten ginger, and a fpoonful of tincture of faffron; mix all together with falt water very thick; then either boil or bake it.

A Liver-Pudding boiled.

GET the liver of the fheep, when you kill one, and cut it as thin as you can, and chop it; mix it with as much fuet fhred fine, half as many crumbs of bread or bifcuit grated, feafon it with fome fweet herbs fhred fine, a little nutmeg grated, a little beaten pepper, and an anchovy fhred fine; mix all together with a little falt, or the anchovy liquor, with a piece of butter, fill the cruft and clofe it; boil it three hours.

To make an Oatmeal-Pudding.

GET a pint of oatmeal once cut, a pound of fuet fhred fine, a pound of currants, and half a pound of raifins ftoned; mix all together well with a little falt, tie it in a cloth, leaving room for the fwelling.

To bake an Oatmeal-Pudding.

BOIL a quart of water, feafon it with a little falt; when the water boils, ftir in the oatmeal till it is fo thick you cannot eafily ftir your fpoon: then take it off the fire, ftir in two fpoonfuls of brandy, or a gill of mountain, and fweeten it to your palate; grate in a little nutmeg, and ftir in half a pound of currants, clean wafhed and picked; then butter a pan, pour it in, and bake it half an hour.

A Rice Pudding baked.

BOIL a pound of rice juft till it is tender, then drain all the water from it as dry as you can, but do not fqueeze it; then ftir in a good piece of butter, and fweeten to your palate;

grate a ſmall nutmeg in, ſtir it all well together, butter a pan, and pour it in and bake it: you may add a few currants for change.

To make a Peas-Pudding.

Boil it till it is quite tender, then take it up, untie it, ſtir in a good piece of butter, a little ſalt, and a good deal of beaten pepper, then tie it up tight again, boil it an hour longer, and it will eat fine. All other puddings you have in the Chapter of Puddings.

To make a Harrico of French Beans.

Take a pint of the ſeeds of French beans which are ready dried for ſowing, waſh them clean and put them into a two-quart ſauce-pan, fill it with water, and let them boil two hours; if the water waſtes away too much, you muſt put in more boiling water to keep them boiling; in the meantime take almoſt half a pound of nice freſh butter, put it into a clean ſtew-pan, and when it is all melted, and done making any noiſe, have ready a pint baſon heaped up with onions peeled and ſliced thin, throw them into the pan and fry them of a fine brown, ſtirring them about that they may be all alike, then pour off the clear water from the beans into a baſon, and throw the beans all into the ſtew-pan; ſtir all together, and throw in a large tea-ſpoonful of beaten pepper, two heaped full of ſalt, and ſtir it all together for two or three minutes. You may make this diſh of what thickneſs you think proper (either to eat with a ſpoon or otherwiſe) with the liquor you poured off the beans. For change you may make it thin enough for ſoup. When it is of the proper thickneſs you like it, take it off the fire, and ſtir in a large ſpoonful of vinegar and the yolk of two eggs beat. The eggs may be left out if diſliked. Diſh it up and ſend it to table.

To make a Fowl Pie.

First make rich thick cruſt, cover the diſh with the paſte, then take ſome very fine bacon, or cold boiled ham, ſlice it, and lay a layer all over; ſeaſon with a little pepper, then put in the fowl, after it is picked and cleaned, and ſinged; ſhake a very little pepper and ſalt into the belly, put in a little water, cover it with ham ſeaſoned with a little beaten pepper, put on the lid and bake it two hours: when it comes out of the oven, take half a pint of water, boil it, and add to it as much of the ſtrong ſoup as will make the gravy quite rich, pour it boiling hot into the pie, and lay on the lid again; ſend it to table hot. Or lay a piece of beef or pork in ſoft water twenty-four hours, ſlice it in the room of the ham, and it will eat fine.

To make a Cheshire Pork Pie for Sea.

TAKE some salt pork that has been boiled, cut it into thin slices, an equal quantity of potatoes pared and sliced thin, make a good crust, cover the dish, lay a layer of meat seasoned with a little pepper, and a layer of potatoes, then a layer of meat, a layer of potatoes, and so on till your pie is full; season it with pepper when it is full, lay some butter on the top, and fill your dish above half full of soft water; close your pie up, and bake it in a gentle oven.

To make Sea Venison.

WHEN you kill a sheep, keep stirring the blood all the time till it is cold, or at least as cold as it will be, that it may not congeal; then cut up the sheep, take one side, cut the leg like a haunch, cut off the shoulder and loin, the neck and breast in two, steep them all in the blood as long as the weather will permit you, then take out the haunch and hang it out of the sun as long as you can to be sweet, and roast it as you do a haunch of venison; it will eat very fine, especially if the heat will give you leave to keep it long. Take off all the suet before you lay it in the blood, take the other joints and lay them in a large pan, pour over them a quart of red wine and a quart of rape vinegar; lay the fat side of the meat downwards in the pan, (on a hollow tray is best,) and pour the wine and vinegar over it; let it lie twelve hours, then take the neck, breast, and loin out of the pickle; let the shoulder lie a week, if the heat will let you, rub it with bay-salt, saltpetre, and coarse sugar, of each a quarter of an ounce, one handful of common salt, and let it lie a week or ten days: bone the neck, breast, and loin; season them with pepper and salt to your palate, and make a pasty as you do for venison: boil the bones for gravy to fill the pie when it comes out of the oven; and the shoulder boil fresh out of the pickle with a peas-pudding.

And when you cut up the sheep, take the heart, liver, and lights, boil them a quarter of an hour, then cut them small, and chop them very fine, season them with four large blades of mace, twelve cloves, and a large nutmeg, all beat to powder; chop a pound of suet fine, half a pound of sugar, two pounds of currants clean washed, half a pint of red wine; mix all well together and make a pie: bake it an hour: it is very rich.

To make Dumplings when you have White Bread.

TAKE the crumb of a two-penny loaf grated fine, as much beef-suet shred as fine as possible, a little salt, half a small nutmeg grated, a large spoonful of sugar, beat two eggs with two spoonfuls of sack; mix all well together, and roll them up as big

big as a turkey's egg; let the water boil and throw them in: half an hour will boil them. For ſauce, melt butter with a little ſalt, lay the dumplings in a diſh, pour the ſauce over them, and ſtrew ſugar all over the diſh.

Theſe are very pretty either at land or ſea. You muſt obſerve to rub your hands with flour when you make them up.

The portable ſoup to carry abroad, you have in the Twelfth Chapter.

To make Chouder, a Sea Diſh.

TAKE a belly-piece of pickled pork, ſlice off the fatter parts, and lay them at the bottom of the kettle, ſtrew over it onions and ſuch ſweet herbs as you can procure; take a middling large cod, bone and ſlice it as for crimping, pepper, ſalt, allſpice, and flour it a little; make a layer with part of the ſlices, upon that a ſlight layer of pork again, and on that a layer of biſcuit, and ſo on, purſuing the like rule until the kettle is filled to about four inches; cover it with nice paſte, pour in about a pint of water, lute down the cover of the kettle, and let the top be ſupplied with live wood embers: keep it over a ſlow fire about four hours. When you take it up lay it in the diſh, pour in a glaſs of hot Maderia wine, and a very little India pepper; if you have oyſters, or truffles or moreſs, it is ſtill better; thicken it with butter. Obſerve, before you put this ſauce in, to ſkim the ſtew, and then lay on the cruſt, and ſend it to table reverſe as in the kettle; cover it cloſe with the paſte, which ſhould be brown.

CHAP. XVII.

OF HOGS'-PUDDINGS, SAUSAGES, &c.

To make Almond Hogs'-Puddings.

TAKE two pounds of beef-ſuet or marrow ſhred very ſmall, a pound and a half of almonds blanched and beat very fine with roſe-water, one pound of grated bread, a pound and a quarter of fine ſugar, a little ſalt, half an ounce of mace, nutmeg, and cinnamon together, twelve yolks of eggs, four whites, a pint of ſack, a pint and a half of thick cream, ſome roſe or orange-flower water; boil the cream, tie the ſaffron in a bag and dip in the cream to colour it; firſt beat your eggs very well, then ſtir in your almonds, then the ſpice, the ſalt, and ſuet, and mix all your ingredients together; fill he guts but half full, put ſome bits of citron in the guts as you fill them, tie them up, and boil them a quarter of an hour.

Another Way.

TAKE a pound of beef-marrow chopped fine, half a pound of ſweet almonds blanched and beat fine with a little orange-flower or roſe water, half a pound of white bread grated fine, half a pound of currants clean waſhed and picked, a quarter of a pound of fine ſugar, a quarter of an ounce of mace, nutmeg, and cinnamon together, of each an equal quantity, and half a pint of ſack; mix all well together with half a pint of good cream, and the yolks of four eggs; fill the guts half full, tie them up, and boil them a quarter of an hour, and prick them as they boil to keep the guts from breaking. You may leave out the currants for change, but then you muſt add a quarter of a pound more of ſugar.

A third Way.

HALF a pint of cream, a quarter of a pound of ſugar, a quarter of a pound of currants, the crumb of a halfpenny roll grated fine, ſix large pippins pared and chopped fine, a gill of ſack, or two ſpoonfuls of roſe-water, ſix bitter almonds blanched and beat fine, the yolks of two eggs, and one white beat fine; mix all together, fill the guts better than half full, and boil them a quarter of an hour.

To make Hogs'-Puddings with Currants.

TAKE three pounds of grated bread to four pounds of beef-ſuet finely ſhred, two pounds of currants clean picked and waſhed, cloves, mace, and cinnamon, of each a quarter of an ounce finely beaten, a little ſalt, a pound and a half of ſugar, a pint of ſack, a quart of cream, a little roſe-water, twenty eggs well beaten, but half the whites; mix all theſe well together, fill the guts half full, boil them a little, and prick them as they boil to keep them from breaking the guts; take them up upon clean cloths, then lay them on your diſh; or when you uſe them, boil them a few minutes, or eat them cold.

To make Black Puddings.

FIRST, before you kill your hog, get a peck of grits, boil them half an hour in water, then drain them, and put them into a clean tub or large pan; then kill your hog, and ſave two quarts of the blood of the hog, and keep ſtirring it till the blood is quite cold, then mix it with your grits, and ſtir them well together; ſeaſon with a large ſpoonful of ſalt, a quarter of an ounce of cloves, mace, and nutmeg together, an equal quantity of each; dry it, beat it well, and mix in; take a little winter-ſavoury, ſweet-marjoram, and thyme, penny-royal ſtripped of the ſtalks, and chopped very fine; juſt enough to ſeaſon them and to give them a flavour, but no more. The next day take the leaf of the hog and cut into dice, ſcrape and waſh the guts very clean, then tie one end, and begin to fill them; mix in the fat as you fill them, be ſure put in a good deal of fat, fill the ſkins three parts full, tie the other end, and make your puddings what length you pleaſe; prick them with a pin, and put them in a kettle of boiling water; boil them very ſoftly an hour, then take them out and lay them on clean ſtraw.

In Scotland they make a pudding with the blood of a gooſe: chop off the head and ſave the blood, ſtir it till it is cold, then mix it with grits, ſpice, ſalt, and ſweet herbs, according to their fancy, and ſome beef-ſuet chopped; take the ſkin off the neck, then pull out the windpipe and fat, fill the ſkin, tie it at both ends, ſo make a pie of the giblets, and lay the pudding in the middle: or you may leave the grits out (if you pleaſe).

Savoloys.

TAKE ſix pounds of young pork, free it from bone and ſkin, and ſalt it with one ounce of ſalt-petre, and a pound of common ſalt, for two days; chop it very fine, put in three tea-ſpoonfuls of pepper, twelve ſage leaves chopped fine, and a pound of grated bread; mix it well, and fill the guts, and bake them half an hour in a ſlack oven, and eat either hot or cold.

To make fine Sauſages.

YOU muſt take ſix pounds of good pork free from ſkin, griſtles, and fat, cut it very ſmall, and beat it in a mortar till it is very fine; then ſhred ſix pounds of beef-ſuet very fine and free from all ſkin; ſhred it as fine as poſſible: take a good deal of ſage, waſh it very clean, pick off the leaves, and ſhred it very fine; ſpread your meat on a clean dreſſer or table, then ſhake the ſage all over, about three large ſpoonfuls; ſhred the thin rind of a middling lemon very fine and throw over, with as many ſweet herbs (when ſhred fine) as will fill a large ſpoon; grate two nutmegs over, throw over two tea-ſpoonfuls of pepper, a large ſpoonful of ſalt, then throw over the ſuet and mix it all well together; put it down cloſe in a pot; when you uſe them, roll them up with as much egg as will make them roll ſmooth; make them the ſize of a ſauſage, and fry them in butter, or good dripping; be ſure it be hot before you put them in, and keep rolling them about: when they are thorough hot and of a fine light brown, they are enough. You may chop this meat very fine, if you do not like it it beat. Veal eats well done thus, or veal and pork together: you may clean ſome guts and fill them.

To make common Sauſages.

TAKE three pounds of nice pork, fat and lean together, without ſkin or griſtles, chop it as fine as poſſible, ſeaſon it with a tea-ſpoonful of beaten pepper and two of ſalt, ſome ſage ſhred fine, about three tea-ſpoonfuls; mix it well together, have the guts very nicely cleaned and fill them, or put them down in a pot, ſo roll them of what ſize you pleaſe, and fry them. Beef makes very good ſauſages.

Oxford Sauſages.

TAKE a pound of lean veal, a pound of young pork, fat and lean, free from ſkin and griſtle, a pound of beef ſuet, chopped all fine together; put in half a pound of grated bread, half the peel of a lemon ſhred fine, a nutmeg grated, ſix ſage leaves waſhed and chopped very fine, a tea-ſpoonful of pepper and two of ſalt, ſome thyme, ſavoury, and marjoram ſhred fine; mix it all well together, and put it cloſe down in a pan: when you uſe it, roll it out the ſize of a common ſauſage, and fry them in freſh butter of a fine brown, or broil them over a clear fire, and ſend them to table as hot as poſſible.

To make Bologna Sauſages.

TAKE a pound of bacon, fat and lean together, a pound of beef, a pound of veal, and a pound of pork, a pound of beef-ſuet, cut them ſmall and chop them fine, take a ſmall handful of ſage, pick off the leaves, chop it fine with a few ſweet herbs; ſeaſon pretty high with pepper and ſalt. You muſt have a large gut, and fill it, then ſet on a ſauce-pan of water, when it boils put it in, and prick the gut for fear of burſting: boil it ſoftly an hour, then lay it on clean ſtraw to dry.

To make Hamburgh Sauſages.

TAKE a pound of beef, mince it very ſmall, with half a pound of the beſt ſuet; then mix three quarters of a pound of ſuet cut in large pieces; then ſeaſon it with pepper, cloves, nutmeg, a great quantity of garlic cut ſmall, ſome white wine vinegar, ſome bay-ſalt and common ſalt, a glaſs of red wine, and one of rum; mix all theſe very well together, then take the largeſt gut you can find, ſtuff it very tight; then hang it up in a chimney, and ſmoke it with ſaw-duſt for a week or ten days; hang them in the air till they are dry, and they will keep a year. They are very good boiled in peas-pottage, and roaſted with toaſted bread under it, or in an amlet.

Sausages after the German Way.

TAKE the crumb of a two-penny loaf, one pound of suet, half a lamb's lights, a handful of parsley, some thyme, marjoram, and onion, mince all very small, then season it with salt and pepper: these must be stuffed in a sheep's gut; they are fried in oil or melted suet, and are only fit for immediate use.

CHAP. XVIII.

To POT AND MAKE HAMS, &c. &c.

Observations on preserving Salt Meat, so as to keep it mellow and fine for three or four Months; and to preserve Potted Butter.

TAKE care when you salt your meat in the summer that it be quite cool after it comes from the butcher's; the way is, to lay it on cold bricks for a few hours, and when you salt it, lay it upon an inclining board to drain off the blood; then salt it afresh, add to every pound of salt half a pound of Lisbon sugar, and turn it in the pickle every day; at the month's end it will be fine. The salt which is commonly used hardens and spoils all the meat; the right sort is that called Lowndes's salt, it comes from Nantwich in Cheshire; there is a very fine sort that comes from Malden in Essex, and from Suffolk, which is the reason of that butter being finer than any other; and if every body would make use of that salt in potting butter, we should not have so much bad come to market; observing all the general rules of a dairy. If you keep your meat long in salt, half the quantity of sugar will do; and then bestow loaf sugar, it will eat much finer. This pickle cannot be called extravagant, because it will keep a great while; at three or four months end, boil it up; if you have no meat in the pickle, skim it, and when cold, only add a little more salt and sugar to the next meat you put in, and it will be good a twelvemonth longer.

Take a leg-of-mutton-piece, veiny or thick flank-piece without any bone, pickled as above, only add to every pound of salt an ounce of salt-petre; after being a month or two in the pickle, take it out and lay it in soft water a few hours, then roast it; it eats fine. A leg of mutton or shoulder of veal does the same. It is a very good thing where a market is at a great

great diſtance, and a large family obliged to provide a great deal of meat.

As to the pickling of hams and tongues, you have the receipt in the foregoing Chapters; but uſe either of theſe fine ſalts, and they will be equal to any Bayonne hams, provided your porkling is fine and well fed.

To pot Pigeons or Fowls.

CUT off their legs, draw them and wipe them with a cloth, but do not waſh them; ſeaſon them pretty well with pepper and ſalt, put them into a pot with as much butter as you think will cover them, when melted, and baked very tender; then drain them very dry from the gravy; lay them on a cloth, and that will ſuck up all the gravy; ſeaſon them again with ſalt, mace, cloves, and pepper beaten fine, and put them down cloſe into a pot; take the butter, when cold, clear from the gravy, ſet it before the fire to melt, and pour over the birds; if you have not enough, clarify ſome more, and let the butter be near an inch thick above the birds. Thus you may do all ſorts of fowl; only wild fowl ſhould be boned (but that you may do as you pleaſe).

To pot a cold Tongue, Beef, or Veniſon.

CUT it ſmall, beat it well in a marble mortar with melted butter, ſeaſon it with mace, cloves, and nutmeg, beat very fine, and ſome pepper and ſalt, till the meat is mellow and fine; then put it down cloſe in your pots, and cover it with clarified butter. Thus you may do cold wild fowl; or you may pot any ſort of cold fowl whole; ſeaſoning them with what ſpice you pleaſe.

To pot Veniſon.

TAKE a piece of veniſon, fat and lean together, lay it in a diſh, and ſtick pieces of butter all over; tie brown paper over it, and bake it; when it comes out of the oven take it out of the liquor hot, drain it, and lay it in a diſh; when cold, take off all the ſkin, and beat it in a marble mortar, fat and lean together, ſeaſon it with mace, cloves, nutmeg, black pepper, and ſalt to your mind; when the butter is cold that it was baked in, take a little of it and beat in with it to moiſten it; then put it down cloſe, and cover it with clarified butter. You muſt be ſure to beat it till it is like a paſte.

To pot a Hare.

TAKE a hare that has hung four or five days, caſe it, and cut it in quarters; put it in a pot, ſeaſon it with pepper, ſalt, and mace, and a pound of butter over it, and bake it four

hours;

hours; when it comes out, pick it from the bones, and pound it in a mortar with the butter that comes off your gravy, and a little beaten cloves and mace, till it is fine and ſmooth, then put it cloſe down in potting pots, and put clarified butter over it; tie it over with white paper.

To pot Tongues.

TAKE a neat's tongue, rub it with a pound of white ſalt, an ounce of ſalt-petre, half a pound of coarſe ſugar, rub it well, turn it every day in this pickle for a fortnight: this pickle will do ſeveral tongues, only adding a little more white ſalt; or we generally do them after our hams. Take the tongues out of the pickle, cut off the root, and boil it well till it will peel; then take your tongues and ſeaſon them with ſalt, pepper, cloves, mace, and nutmeg, all beat fine; rub it well with your hands whilſt it is hot; then put it in a pot, and melt as much butter as will cover it all over; bake it an hour in the oven, then take it out, let it ſtand to cool, rub a little freſh ſpice on it; and when it is quite cold, lay it in your pickling-pot; when the butter is cold you baked it in, take it off clean from the gravy, ſet it in an earthen pan before the fire, and when it is melted, pour it over the tongue. You may lay pigeons or chickens on each ſide; be ſure to let the butter be about an inch above the tongue.

A fine Way to pot a Tongue.

TAKE a dried tongue, boil it till it is tender, then peel it; take a large fowl, bone it; a gooſe, and bone it; take a quarter of an ounce of mace, a quarter of an ounce of cloves, a large nutmeg, a quarter of an ounce of black pepper, beat all well together; a ſpoonful of ſalt; rub the inſide of the fowl well, and the tongue; put the tongue into the fowl; then ſeaſon the gooſe, and fill the gooſe with the fowl and tongue, and the gooſe will look as if it was whole; lay it in a pan that will juſt hold it, melt freſh butter enough to cover it, ſend it to the oven, and bake it an hour and a half; then uncover the pot and take out the meat; carefully drain it from the butter, lay it on a coarſe cloth till it is cold, and when the butter is cold, take off the hard fat from the gravy, and lay it before the fire to melt, put your meat into the pot again, and pour the butter over; if there is not enough, clarify more, and let the butter be an inch above the meat; and this will keep a great while, eats fine, and looks beautiful: when you cut it, it muſt be cut croſſways down through, and looks very pretty: it makes a pretty corner-diſh at table, or ſide-diſh for ſupper: if you cut a ſlice down the middle quite through, lay it in a plate, and garniſh

garnish with green parsley and nastertium-flowers. If you will be at the expence, bone a turkey, and put over the goose. Observe, when you pot it, to save a little of the spice to throw over it, before the last butter is put on, or the meat will not be seasoned enough.

To pot Beef like Venison.

CUT the lean of a buttock of beef into pound pieces; for eight pounds of beef take four ounces of salt-petre, four ounces of petre-salt, a pint of white salt, and an ounce of sal-prunella; beat the salts all very fine, mix them well together, rub the salts into the beef; then let it lie four days, turning it twice a day, then put it into a pan, cover it with pump-water and a little of its own brine: then bake it in an oven with household bread till it is as tender as a chicken, then drain it from the gravy, and bruise it abroad, and take out all the skin and sinews; then pound it in a marble mortar, then lay it in a broad dish, mix in it an ounce of cloves and mace, three quarters of an ounce of pepper, and one nutmeg, all beat very fine; mix it all very well with the meat, then clarify a little fresh butter and mix with the meat to make it a little moist; mix it very well together, press it down into pots very hard, set it at the oven's mouth just to settle, and cover it two inches thick with clarified butter: when cold, cover it with white paper.

To pot Cheshire Cheese.

TAKE three pounds of Cheshire cheese, and put it into a mortar with half a pound of the best fresh butter you can get, pound them together, and in the beating add a gill of rich Canary wine, and half an ounce of mace finely beat, then sifted like a fine powder; when all is extremely well mixed, press it hard down into a gallipot, cover it with clarified butter, and keep it cool. A slice of this excels all the cream cheese that can be made.

To pot Ham with Chickens.

TAKE as much lean of a boiled ham as you please, and half the quantity of fat, cut it as thin as possible, beat it very fine in a mortar, with a little oiled butter, beaten mace, pepper, and salt, put part of it into a China pot, then beat the white part of a fowl with a very little seasoning; it is to qualify the ham; put a lay of chicken, then one of ham, then chicken at the top, press it hard down, and when it is cold, pour clarified butter over it; when you send it to the table, cut out a thin slice in the form of half a diamond, and lay it round the edge of your pot.

To pot Woodcocks.

PLUCK ſix woodcocks, draw out the train, ſkewer their bills through their thighs, and put the legs through each other, and their feet upon their breaſts; ſeaſon them with three or four blades of mace, and a little pepper and ſalt; then put them into a deep pot with a pound of butter over them, tie a ſtrong paper over them, and bake them in a moderate oven; when they are enough, lay them on a diſh to drain the gravy from them, then put them into potting pots, and take all the clear butter from your gravy and put it upon them, and fill up your pots with clarified butter, and keep them in a dry place.

To pot red and black Moor-Game.

PLUCK and draw them, and ſeaſon them with pepper, cloves, mace, ginger, and nutmeg, well beaten and ſifted, with a quantity of ſalt not to overcome the ſpices, roll a lump of butter in the ſeaſoning, and put it into the body of the fowls, rub the outſide with ſeaſoning, and then put them into pots with the breaſt downwards and cover them with butter, lay a paper and then a paſte over them, and bake them till they are tender; then take them out and lay them to drain, then put them into potting pots with the breaſt upwards, and take all the butter they were baked in clean from the gravy and pour upon them; fill up the pots with clarified butter, and keep them in a dry place.

To pot all Kinds of ſmall Birds.

PICK and gut your birds, dry them well with a cloth, ſeaſon them with mace, pepper, and ſalt, then put them into a pot with butter, tie your pot down with paper, and bake them in a moderate oven; when they come out, drain the gravy from them, and put them into potting pots, and cover them with clarified butter.

To ſave potted Birds that begin to be bad.

I HAVE ſeen potted birds, which have come a great way, often ſmell ſo bad that no body could bear the ſmell for the rankneſs of the butter, and by managing them in the following manner have made them as good as ever was eat:

Set a large ſauce-pan of clean water on the fire, when it boils, take off the butter at the top, then take the fowls out one by one, throw them into that ſauce-pan of water half a minute, whip it out and dry it in a clean cloth inſide and out; ſo do all till they are quite done; ſcald the pot clean; when the birds are quite cold, ſeaſon them with mace, pepper, and ſalt to your mind, pot them down cloſe in a pot, and pour clarified butter over them.

To

To pot Charrs.

AFTER having cleanfed them, cut off the fins, tails, and heads, then lay them in rows in a long baking-pan; cover them with butter, and order them as above.

To pot a Pike.

YOU muft fcale it, cut off the head, fplit it, and take out the chine-bone, then ftrew all over the infide fome bay-falt and pepper, roll it up round, and lay it in a pot; cover it, and bake it an hour; then take it out and lay it on a coarfe cloth to drain; when it is cold, put it into your pot and cover it with clarified butter.

To pot Salmon.

TAKE a piece of frefh falmon, fcale it, and wipe it clean, (let your piece or pieces be as big as will lie cleverly on your pot,) feafon it with Jamaica pepper, black pepper, mace, and cloves, beat fine, mixed with falt, a little fal-prunella beat fine, and rub the bone with; feafon with a little of the fpice, pour clarified butter over it, and bake it well; then take it out carefully, and lay it to drain; when cold, feafon it well, lay it in your pot clofe, and cover it with clarified butter as above.

Thus you may do carp, tench, trout, and feveral forts of fifh.

Another Way to pot Salmon.

SCALE and clean your falmon, cut it down the back, dry it well, and cut it as near the fhape of your pot as you can; take two nutmegs, an ounce of mace and cloves beaten, half an ounce of white pepper, and an ounce of falt; then take out all the bones, cut off the jowl below the fins, and cut off the tail; feafon the fcaly fide firft, lay that at the bottom of the pot; then rub the feafoning on the other fide, cover it with a difh, and let it ftand all night: it muft be put double, and the fcaly fide top and bottom; put butter bottom and top, and cover the pot with fome ftiff coarfe pafte: three hours will bake it, if a large fifh; if a fmall one, two hours; and when it comes out of the oven, let it ftand half an hour; then uncover it, and raife it up at one end that the gravy may run out, then put a trencher and a weight on it to prefs out the gravy: when the butter is cold, take it out clear from the gravy, add fome more to it, and put it in a pan before the fire; when it is melted, pour it over the falmon; and when it is cold, paper it up. As to the feafoning of thefe things, it muft be according to your palate, more or lefs.

N. B. Always take great care that no gravy or whey of the butter is left in the potting; if there is, it will not keep.

To pot a Lobster.

TAKE a live lobster, boil it in salt and water, and peg it that no water gets in; when it is cold, pick out all the flesh and body, take out the gut, beat it fine in a mortar, and season it with beaten mace, grated nutmeg, pepper, and salt; mix all together; melt a piece of butter as big as a large walnut, and mix it with the lobster as you are beating it; when it is beat to a paste, put it into your potting pot, and put it down as close and hard as you can; then set some fresh butter in a deep broad pan before the fire, and when it is all melted, take off the scum at the top (if any), and pour the clear butter over the meat as thick as a crown piece; the whey and churn-milk will settle at the bottom of the pan, but take care none of that goes in, and always let your butter be very good, or you will spoil all; or only put the meat whole, with the body mixed among it, laying them as close together as you can, and pour the butter over them. You must be sure to let the lobster be well boiled. A middling one will take half an hour boiling.

To pot Eels.

TAKE a large eel, skin it, cleanse it, and wash it very clean, dry it in a cloth, and cut it into pieces as long as your finger; season them with a little beaten mace and nutmeg, pepper, salt, and a little sal-prunella beat fine; lay them in a pan, then pour as much good butter over them as will cover them, and clarified as above: they must be baked half an hour in a quick oven; if a slow oven, longer, till they are enough, but that you must judge by the largeness of the eels: with a fork take them out, and lay them on a coarse cloth to drain; when they are quite cold, season them again with the same seasoning, lay them in the pot close; then take off the butter they were baked in clear from the gravy of the fish, and set it in a dish before the fire; when it is melted, pour the clear butter over the eels, and let them be covered with the butter.

In the same manner you may pot what you please. You may bone your eels, if you choose it; but then do not put in any sal-prunella.

To pot Lampreys.

SKIN them, cleanse them with salt, then wipe them dry; beat some black pepper, mace, and cloves, mix them with salt, and season them; lay them in a pan, and cover them with clarified butter; bake them an hour; order them as the eels, only let them be seasoned, and one will be enough for a pot: you must season them well; let your butter be good, and they will keep a long time.

To collar a Breaſt of Veal.

TAKE a breaſt of veal and bone it, beat it with a rolling-pin, rub it over with the yolk of an egg, beat a little mace, cloves, nutmeg, and pepper very fine, with a little ſalt, a handful of parſley, and ſome ſweet herbs, and lemon-peel ſhred fine, a few crumbs of bread; mix all together and ſtrew over; roll it up very tight, bind it with a filler, and wrap it in a cloth, then boil it two hours and a half in water made pretty ſalt, then hang it up by one end till cold: make a pickle: to a pint of ſalt and water put half a pint of vinegar, and lay it in a pan, and let the pickle cover it; and when you uſe it, cut it in ſlices, and garniſh with parſley and pickles.

To make Marble Veal.

TAKE a neat's tongue and boil it till tender; peel it and cut it in ſlices, and beat it in a mortar with a pound of butter, with a little beaten mace and pepper, till it is like a paſte; have ſome veal ſtewed and beat in the ſame manner; put ſome veal in a potting-pot, then ſome tongue in lumps over the veal, then ſome veal over that, tongue over that, and then veal again; preſs it down hard, pour ſome clarified butter over it, keep it in a cold dry place, and when you uſe it, cut it in ſlices, and garniſh with parſley.

To collar Beef.

TAKE a piece of thin flank of beef and bone it, cut the ſkin off, then ſalt it with two ounces of ſalt-petre, two ounces of ſal-prunella, two ounces of bay-ſalt, half a pound of coarſe ſugar, and two pounds of white ſalt, beat the hard ſalts fine, and mix all together; turn it every day, and rub it with the brine well, for eight days; then take it out of the pickle, waſh it and wipe it dry; then take a quarter of an ounce of cloves, and a quarter of an ounce of mace, twelve corns of all-ſpice, and a nutmeg beat very fine, with a ſpoonful of beaten pepper, a large quantity of chopped parſley, with ſome ſweet herbs chopped fine; ſprinkle it on the beef, and roll it up very tight, put a coarſe cloth round, and tie it very tight with beggar's tape; boil it in a large copper of water; if a large collar, ſix hours, a ſmall one, five hours; take it out and put it in a preſs till cold; if you have never a preſs, put it between two boards, and a large weight upon it till it is cold; then take it out of the cloth and cut it into ſlices: Garniſh with raw parſley.

To collar a Pig.

KILL your pig, dreſs off the hair, draw out the entrails, and waſh it clean, take a ſharp knife, rip it open and take out all the bones, then rub it all over with pepper and ſalt beaten fine, a few ſage leaves and ſweet herbs chopped ſmall, then roll up your pig tight, and bind it with a fillet, then fill your boiler with ſoft water, one pint of vinegar, and a handful of ſalt, eight or ten cloves, a blade or two of mace, a few pepper-corns, and a bunch of ſweet herbs; when it boils put in your pig, and boil it till it is tender, then take it up, and when it is almoſt cold, bind it over again, and put it into an earthen pot, and pour the liquor your pig was boiled in upon it, keep it covered, and it is fit for uſe.

To callar Swine's Face.

CHOP the face in many places, and waſh it in ſeveral waters, then boil it till the meat will leave the bones, take out the bones, cut open the ears, and take out the ear-roots, cut the meat in pieces, and ſeaſon it with pepper and ſalt; while it is hot put it into an earthen pot, but put the ears round the outſide of the meat, put a board on that will go on the inſide of the pot, and ſet a heavy weight upon it, and let it ſtand all night, the next day turn it out, cut it round-ways, and it will look cloſe and bright.

To collar Salmon.

TAKE a ſide of ſalmon, cut off a handful of the tail, waſh your large piece very well, dry it with a clean cloth, waſh it over with the yolks of eggs, and then make force-meat with what you cut off the tail; but take off the ſkin, and put to it a handful of parboiled oyſters, a tail or two of lobſters, the yolks of three or four eggs, boiled hard, ſix anchovies, a handful of ſweet herbs chopped ſmall, a little ſalt, cloves, mace, nutmeg, pepper beat fine, and grated bread; work all theſe together into a body, with the yolks of eggs, lay it all over the fleſhy part, and a little more pepper and ſalt over the ſalmon; ſo roll it up into a collar, and bind it with broad tape, then boil it in water, ſalt, and vinegar, but let the liquor boil firſt; then put in your collars, a bunch of ſweet herbs, ſliced ginger, and nutmeg; let it boil, but not too faſt: it will take near two hours boiling: when it is enough, take it up into your ſouſing-pan, and when the pickle is cold, put it to your ſalmon, and let it ſtand in it till uſed, or otherwiſe you may pot it. Fill it up with clarified butter, as you pot fowls: that way will keep longeſt.

To collar Eels.

TAKE your eel and ſcour it well with ſalt, wipe it clean; then cut it down the back, take out the bone, cut the head and tail off; put the yolk of an egg over it, and then take four cloves,

cloves, two blades of mace, half a nutmeg beat fine, a little pepper and falt, fome chopped parfley, and fweet herbs chopped very fine; mix them all together and fprinkle over it, roll the eel up very tight, and tie it in a cloth; put on water enough to boil it, and put in an onion, fome cloves and mace, four bay-leaves; boil it up with the bones, head, and tail for half an hour, with a little vinegar and falt; then take out the bones, &c. and put in your eels, boil them if large two hours, leffer in proportion; when done, put them away to cool; then take them out of the liquor and cloth, and cut them in flices, or fend them whole, with raw parfley under and over.

N. B. You muft take them out of the cloth, and put them in the liquor, and tie them clofe down to keep.

To collar Mackerel.

GUT and flit your mackerel down the belly, cut off the head, take out the bones, take care you do not cut it in holes, then lay it flat upon its back, feafon it with mace, nutmeg, pepper, and falt, and a handful of parfley fhred fine, ftrew it over them, roll them tight, and tie them well feparately in cloths, boil them gently twenty minutes in vinegar, falt, and water, then take them out, put them into a pot, pour the liquor on them, or the cloth will ftick to the fifh, the next day take the cloth off your fifh, put a little more vinegar to the pickle, keep them for ufe; when you fend them to the table, garnifh with fennel and parfley, and put fome of the liquor under them.

To make Dutch Beef.

TAKE the lean of a buttock of beef raw, rub it well with brown fugar all over, and let it lie in a pan or tray two or three hours, turning it two or three times, then falt it well with common falt and falt-petre, and let it lie a fortnight, turning it every day; then roll it very ftrait in a coarfe cloth, put it in a cheefe-prefs a day and a night, and hang it to dry in a chimney: when you boil it, you muft put it in a cloth; when it is cold, it will cut in flivers as Dutch beef.

To make Sham Brawn.

TAKE the belly piece and head of a young porker, rub it well with falt-petre, let it lie three or four days, wafh it clean; boil the head, and take off all the meat and cut it in pieces, have four neat's feet boiled tender, take out the bones, cut it in thin flices, mix it with the head, lay it in the belly-piece, roll it up tight, bind it round with fheeting, and boil it four hours; take it up and fet it on one end, put a trencher on it within the tin, and a large weight upon that, and let it ftand all night; in the morning take it out and bind it with a fillet; put it in ſpring-water and ſalt, and it will be fit for uſe: when you uſe it, cut it in ſlices like brawn. Garniſh with parſley. Obſerve to change the pickle every four or five days, and it will keep a long time.

To ſouce a Turkey in imitatian of Sturgeon.

YOU muſt take a fine large turkey, dreſs it very clean, dry and bone it, then tie it up as you do ſturgeon, put into the pot you boil it in one quart of white wine, one quart of water, one quart of good vinegar, a very large handful of ſalt; let it boil, ſkim it well, and then put in the turkey; when it is enough, take it out and tie it tighter; let the liquor boil a little longer; and if you think the pickle wants more vinegar or ſalt, add it when it is cold, and pour it upon the turkey; it will keep ſome months, covering it cloſe from the air, and keeping it in a dry cool place. Eat it with oil, vinegar, and ſugar (juſt as you like it); ſome admire it more than ſturgeon; it looks pretty covered with fennel for a ſide-diſh.

To pickle Pork.

BONE your pork, cut it into pieces of a ſize fit to lie in the tub or pan you deſign it to lie in, rub your pieces well with ſalt-petre, then take two parts of common ſalt, and two of bay-ſalt, and rub every piece well; lay a layer of common ſalt in the bottom of your veſſel, cover every piece over with common ſalt, lay them one upon another as cloſe as you can, filling the hollow places on the ſides with ſalt; as your ſalt melts on the top ſtrew on more, lay a coarſe cloth over the veſſel, a board over that, and a weight on the board to keep it down; keep it cloſe covered; it will, thus ordered, keep the whole year; put a pound of ſalt-petre and two pounds of bay-ſalt to a hog.

A Pickle for Pork which is to be eat ſoon.

YOU muſt take two gallons of pump-water, one pound of bay-ſalt, one pound of coarſe ſugar, ſix ounces of ſalt-petre; boil it all together, and ſkim it when cold; cut the pork in what pieces you pleaſe, lay it down cloſe, and pour the liquor over it; lay a weight on it to keep it cloſe, and cover it cloſe from the air, and it will be fit to uſe in a week: if you find the pickle begins to ſpoil, boil it again and ſkim it; when it is cold, pour it on your pork again.

The Jews' Way to pickle Beef, which will go good to the Weſt Indies, and keep a Year good in the Pickle, and with Care will go to the Eaſt Indies.

TAKE any piece of beef without bones, or take the bones out, if you intend to keep it above a month; take mace, cloves, nutmeg,

nutmeg, and pepper, and juniper-berries beat fine, and rub the beef well, mix salt and Jamaica pepper and bay-leaves; let it be well seasoned, let it lie in this seasoning a week or ten days, throw in a good deal of garlic and shalot; boil some of the best white wine vinegar, lay your meat in a pan or good vessel for the purpose with the pickle; and when the vinegar is quite cold, pour it over, cover it close; if it is for a voyage, cover it with oil, and let the cooper hoop up the barrel very well. This is a good way in a hot country where meat will not keep; then it must be put into the vinegar directly with the seasoning, then you may either roast it or stew it, but it is best stewed; and add a good deal of onion and parsley chopped fine, some white wine, a little catchup, truffles and morels, a little good gravy, a piece of butter rolled in flour, or a little oil, in which the shalot and onions ought to stew a quarter of an hour before the other ingredients are put in; then put all in, and stir it together, and let it stew till you think it is enough. This is a good pickle in a hot country to keep beef or veal, that is dressed to eat cold.

Pickled Beef for present Use.

TAKE the rib of beef, stick it with garlic and cloves, season it with salt, Jamaica pepper, mace, and some garlic pounded; cover the meat with white wine vinegar and Spanish thyme; you must take care to turn the meat every day, and add more vinegar, (if required,) for a fortnight; then put it in a stew-pan, and cover it close, and let it simmer on a slow fire for six hours, adding vinegar and white wine; (if you choose) you may stew a good quantity of onions, it will be more palatable.

To preserve Tripe to go to the East Indies.

GET a fine belly of tripe, quite fresh, take a four gallon cask well hooped, lay in your tripe, and have your pickle ready, made thus: take seven quarts of spring-water, and put as much salt into it as will make an egg swim, that the little end of the egg may be about an inch above the water (you must take care to have the fine clear salt, for the common salt will spoil it); add a quart of the best white wine vinegar, two sprigs of rosemary, an ounce of all-spice, pour it on your tripe; let the cooper fasten the cask down directly; when it comes to the Indies it must not be opened till it is just going to be dressed, for it will not keep after the cask is opened; the way to dress it is, lay it in water half an hour, then fry it or boil as we do here.

The Jews Way of preserving Salmon, and all Sorts of Fish.

TAKE either salmon, cod, or any large fish, cut off the head, wash it clean, and cut it in slices as crimped cod is, dry it it very well in a cloth, then flour it, and dip it in yolks of eggs, and fry it in a great deal of oil till it is of a fine brown and well done; take it out, and lay it to drain till it is very dry and cold. Whitings, mackarel, and flat-fish are done whole: when they are quite dry and cold lay them in your pan or vessel, throw in between them a good deal of mace, cloves, and sliced nutmeg, a few bay-leaves; have your pickle ready, made of the best white wine vinegar, in which you must boil a great many cloves of garlic and shalot, black and white pepper, Jamaica and long pepper, juniper-berries, and salt; when the garlic begins to be tender the pickle is enough; when it is quite cold pour it on your fish, and a little oil on the top: they will keep good a twelvemonth, and are to be eat cold with oil and vinegar: they will go good to the East Indies. All sorts of fish fried well in oil, eat very fine cold with shalot, or oil and vinegar. Observe in the pickling of your fish, to have the pickling ready; first put a little pickle in, then a layer of fish, then pickle, then a little fish, and so lay them down very close to be well covered; put a little saffron in the pickle. Frying fish in common oil is not so expensive with care; for present use a little does, and if the cook is careful not to burn the oil, or black it, it will fry them two or three times.

To pickle Oysters, Cockles, and Muscles.

TAKE two hundred oysters, the newest and best you can get, be careful to save the liquor in some pan as you open them, cut off the black verge, saving the rest, put them into their own liquor; then put all the liquor and oysters into a kettle, boil them about half an hour on a very gentle fire, do them very slowly, skimming them as the scum rises, then take them off the fire, take out the oysters, strain the liquor through a fine cloth, then put in the oysters again, then take out a pint of the liquor whilst it is hot, put thereto three quarters of an ounce of mace, and half an ounce of cloves; just give it one boil, then put it to the oysters, and stir up the spices well among them; then put in about a spoonful of salt, three quarters of a pint of the best white wine vinegar, and a quarter of an ounce of whole pepper; then let them stand till they are cold; then put the oysters, as many as you well can into the barrel; put in as much liquor as the barrel will hold, letting them settle a while, and they will soon be fit to eat. Or you may put them in stone-jars, cover them close with a bladder and leather, and be sure they be quite cold before you cover them up. Thus do cockles and muscles; only this, cockles are small, and to this spice you must have at least two quarts; there is nothing to pick off them: muscles you must have two quarts; take great care to pick the crab out under the tongue, and

and a little fus which grows at the root of the tongue: the two latter, cockles and mufcles, muft be wafhed in feveral waters, to clean them from the grit; put them in a ftew-pan by themfelves, cover them clofe; and when they are open, pick them out of the fhells, and ftrain the liquor.

To pickle Mackerel, called Caveach.

CUT your mackerel into round pieces, and divide one into five or fix pieces: to fix large mackerel you may take one ounce of beaten pepper, three large nutmegs, a little mace, and a handful of falt; mix your falt and beaten fpice together, then make two or three holes in each piece, and thruft the feafoning into the holes with your finger, rub the piece all over with the feafoning, fry them brown in oil, and let them ftand till they are cold; then put them into vinegar, and cover them with oil: they will keep well covered a great while, and are delicious.

To make Veal Hams.

CUT the leg of veal like a ham, then take a pint of bay-falt, two ounces of falt-petre, and a pound of common falt, mix them together with an ounce of juniper berries beat; rub the ham well, and lay it on a hollow tray, with the fkinny fide downwards; bafte it every day with the pickle for a fortnight, and then hang it in wood-fmoke for a fortnight: you may boil it, or parboil it and roaft it. In this pickle you may do two or three tongues, or a piece of pork.

To make Beef Hams.

YOU muft take the leg of a fat, but fmall beef, the fat Scotch or Welch cattle is beft, and cut it ham-fafhion; take an ounce of bay-falt, an ounce of falt-petre, a pound of common falt, and a pound of coarfe fugar (this quantity for about fourteen or fifteen pounds weight, and fo accordingly, if you pickle the whole quarter), rub it with the above ingredients, turn it every day, and bafte it well with the pickle for a month; take it out and roll it in bran or faw-duft, then hang it in wood-fmoke, where there is but little fire, and a conftant fmoke, for a month; then take it down and hang it in a dry place, not hot, and keep it for ufe; you may cut a piece off as you have occafion, and either boil it or cut it in rafhers, and broil it with poached eggs, or boil a piece, and it eats fine cold, and will fliver like Dutch beef. After this beef is done you may do a thick brifket of beef in the fame pickle: let it lie a month, rubbing it every day with the pickle, then boil it till it is tender, hang it in a dry place, and it eats finely cold, cut in flices on a plate. It is a pretty thing for a fide-difh, or for fupper. A fhoulder of mutton laid in this pickle for a week, hung in wood-fmoke two or three days, and then boiled with cabbage, is very good.

To make Mutton Hams.

You muſt take a hind-quarter of mutton, cut it like a ham, take an ounce of ſalt-petre, a pound of coarſe ſugar, a pound of common ſalt; mix them and rub your ham, lay it in a hollow tray with the ſkin downwards, baſte it every day for a fortnight, then roll it in ſaw-duſt and hang it in the wood-ſmoke a fortnight; then boil it and hang it in a dry place, and cut it out in raſhers, and broil it as you want.

To make Pork Hams.

You muſt take a fat hind-quarter of pork, and cut off a fine ham; take two ounces of ſalt-petre, a pound of coarſe ſugar, a pound of common ſalt, and two ounces of ſal-prunella, mix all together, and rub it well; let it lie a month in this pickle, turning and baſting it every day, then hang it in wood-ſmoke as you do beef, in a dry place, ſo as no heat comes to it; and if you keep them long, hang them a month or two in a damp place, and it will make them cut fine and ſhort. Never lay theſe hams in water till you boil them, and then boil them in a copper, (if you have one,) or the biggeſt pot you have; put them in the cold water, and let them be four or five hours before they boil; ſkim the pot well and often till it boils: if it is a very large one, three hours will boil it; if a ſmall one, two hours will do, provided it be a great while before the water boils; take it up half an hour before dinner, pull off the ſkin, and throw raſpings finely ſifted all over; hold a red-hot fire-ſhovel over it, and when dinner is ready, take a few raſpings in a ſieve and ſift all over the diſh; then lay in your ham, and with your finger make fine figures round the edge of the diſh; be ſure to boil your ham in as much water as you can, and to keep it ſkimming all the time till it boils: it muſt be at leaſt four hours before it boils. This pickle does finely for tongues, afterwards to lie in it a fortnight, and then hang in the wood-ſmoke a fortnight; or to boil them out of the pickle.

Yorkſhire is famous for hams; and the reaſon is this: their ſalt is much finer than ours in London; it is a large clear ſalt, and gives the meat a fine flavour. I uſed to have it from Malden in Eſſex, and that ſalt will make any ham as fine as you can deſire; it is by much the beſt ſalt for ſalting of meat; a deep hollow wooden tray is better than a pan, becauſe the pickle ſwells about it. When you broil any of theſe hams in ſlices, or bacon, have ſome boiling water ready, and let the ſlices lie a minute or two in the water, then broil them; it takes out the ſalt and makes them eat finer.

To make Bacon.

TAKE a ſide of pork, then take off all the inſide fat, lay it on a long board or dreſſer, that the blood may run away, rub it well with good ſalt on both ſides, let it lie thus a day; then take a pint of bay ſalt, a quarter of a pound of ſalt-petre, beat them fine, two pounds of coarſe ſugar, and a quarter of a peck of common ſalt; lay your pork in ſomething that will hold the pickle, and rub it well with the above ingredients; lay the ſkinny ſide downwards, and baſte it every day with the pickle for a fortnight; then hang it in wood-ſmoke as you do the beef, and afterwards hang it in a dry place, but not hot. You are to obſerve, that all hams and bacon ſhould hang clear from every thing, and not againſt a wall. Obſerve to wipe off all the old ſalt before you put it into this pickle, and never keep bacon or hams in a hot kitchen, or in a room where the ſun comes; it makes them ruſty.

CHAP. XIX.

OF PICKLING.

Rules to be obſerved in Pickling.

ALWAYS uſe ſtone jars for all ſorts of pickles that require hot pickle to them: the firſt charge is the leaſt; for theſe not only laſt longer, but keep the pickle better; for vinegar and ſalt will penetrate through all earthen veſſels; ſtone and glaſs are the only things to keep pickles in. Be ſure never to put your hands in to take pickles out, it will ſoon ſpoil it; the beſt method is, to every pot tie a wooden ſpoon, full of little holes, to take the pickles out with.

To pickle Walnuts green.

TAKE the largeſt and cleareſt you can get, pare them as thin as you can, have a tub of ſpring-water ſtand by you, and throw them in as you do them; put into the water a pound of bay-ſalt, let them lie in the water twenty-four hours, take them out, then put them into a ſtone-jar, and between every layer of walnuts lay a layer of vine-leaves at the bottom and top, and fill it up with cold vinegar; let them ſtand all night, then pour that vinegar from them into a copper, with a pound of bay-ſalt; ſet it on the fire, let it boil, then pour it hot on your nuts, tie them over with a woollen cloth, and let them ſtand a week,

 then

then pour that pickle away, rub your nuts clean with a piece of flannel, then put them again in your jar with vine-leaves, as above, and boil fresh vinegar; put into your pot to every gallon of vinegar a nutmeg sliced, cut four large races of ginger, a quarter of an ounce of mace, the same of cloves, a quarter of an ounce of whole black pepper, the like of Ordingal pepper; then pour your vinegar boiling-hot on your walnuts, and cover them with a woollen cloth; let it stand three or four days, so do two or three times; when cold, put in half a pint of mustard-seed, a large stick of horse-radish sliced, tie them down close with a bladder, and then with a leather; they will be fit to eat in a fortnight; take a large onion, stick the cloves in, and lay in the middle of the pot; if you do them for keeping, do not boil your vinegar, but then they will not be fit to eat under six months; and the next year you may boil the pickle this way: they will keep two or three years good and firm.

To pickle Walnuts white.

TAKE the largest nuts you can get, just before the shell begins to turn, pare them very thin till the white appears, and throw them into spring-water, with a handful of salt as you do them; let them stand in that water six hours, lay on them a thin board to keep them under the water, then set a stew-pan on a charcoal fire, with clean spring-water; take your nuts out of the other water, and put them into the stew-pan; let them simmer four of five minutes, but not boil; then have ready by you a pan of spring-water, with a handful of white salt in it, stir it with your hand till the salt is melted, then take your nuts out of the stew-pan with a wooden ladle, and put them into the cold water and salt; let them stand a quarter of an hour, lay the board on them as before; if they are not kept under the liquor they will turn black, then lay them on a cloth, and cover them with another to dry; then carefully wipe them with a soft cloth, put them into your jar or glass, with some blades of mace and nutmeg sliced thin; mix your spice between your nuts, and pour distilled vinegar over them; first let your glass be full of nuts, pour mutton fat over them, and tie a bladder, and then a leather.

To pickle Walnuts black.

YOU must take large full-grown nuts at their full growth, before they are hard, lay them in salt and water; let them lie two days, then shift them into fresh water; let them lie two days longer, then shift them again, and let them lie three in your pickling jar; when the jar is half full, put in a large onion stuck with cloves. To a hundred of walnuts put in half a pint of mustard-seed, a quarter of an ounce of mace, half an ounce of black

black pepper, half an ounce of all-ſpice, ſix bay-leaves, and a ſtick of horſe-radiſh; then fill your jar, and pour boiling vinegar over them; cover them with a plate, and when they are cold, tie them down with a bladder and leather, and they will be fit to eat in two or three months: the next year, if any remains, boil up your vinegar again, and ſkim it; when cold, pour it over your walnuts. This is by much the beſt pickle for uſe; therefore you may add more vinegar to it, what quantity you pleaſe: if you pickle a great many walnuts and eat them faſt, make your pickle for a hundred or two, the reſt keep in a ſtrong brine of ſalt and water, boiled till it will bear an egg, and as your pot empties fill them up with thoſe in the ſalt and water: take care they are covered with pickle.

In the ſame manner you may do a ſmaller quantity; but if you can get rape-vinegar, uſe that inſtead of ſalt and water; do them thus: put your nuts into the jar you intend to pickle them in, throw in a good handful of ſalt and fill the pot with rape vinegar; cover it cloſe, and let them ſtand a fortnight, then pour them out of the pot, wipe it clean, and juſt rub the nuts with a coarſe cloth, and then put them in the jar with the pickle, as above: if you have the beſt ſugar-vinegar of your own making, you need not boil it the firſt year, but pour it on cold; and the next year, (if any remains,) boil it up again, ſkim it, put freſh ſpice to it, and it will do again.

To pickle Gerkins.

TAKE five hundred gerkins, and have ready a large earthen pan of ſpring-water and ſalt, to every gallon of water two pounds of ſalt; mix it well together and throw in your gerkins, waſh them out in two hours, and put them to drain, let them be drained very dry, and put them in a jar; in the meantime get a bell-metal pot, with a gallon of the beſt white wine vinegar, half an ounce of cloves and mace, one ounce of all-ſpice, one ounce of muſtard-ſeed, a ſtick of horſe-radiſh cut in ſlices, ſix bay-leaves, a little dill, two or three races of ginger cut in pieces, a nutmeg cut in pieces, and a handful of ſalt; boil it up in the pot all together, and put it over the gerkins; cover them cloſe down, and let them ſtand twenty-four hours; then put them in your pot, and ſimmer them over the ſtove till they are green; be careful not to let them boil, if you do, you will ſpoil them; then put them in your jar, and cover them cloſe down till cold; then tie them over with a bladder and a leather over that; put them in a cold dry place: mind always to keep your pickles tied down cloſe, and take them out with a wooden ſpoon, or a ſpoon kept on purpoſe.

To pickle Gerkins another Way.

WIPE your ſmall gerkins with a dry cloth, then make a pickle of vinegar, ſalt, whole pepper, cloves, and mace, boil it, and pour it on hot; ſet the jar in an oven almoſt cold for three or four different days till the cucumbers are green; when cold cover them cloſe.

N. B. You muſt cover the gerkins with a linen cloth and a plate while they are doing to keep in the ſteam.

To pickle large Cucumbers in Slices.

TAKE the large cucumbers before they are too ripe, ſlice them the thickneſs of crown-pieces in a pewter diſh; to every dozen of cucumbers ſlice two large onions thin, and ſo on till you have filled your diſh, with a handful of ſalt between every row; then cover them with another pewter diſh, and let them ſtand twenty four hours, then put them into a cullendar, and let them drain very well; put them in a jar, cover them over with white-wine vinegar, and them ſtand four hours; pour the vinegar from them into a copper ſauce-pan, and boil it with a little ſalt: put to the cucumbers a little mace, a little whole pepper, a large race of ginger ſliced, and then pour the boiling vinegar on; cover them cloſe, and when they are cold tie them down. They will be fit to eat in two or three days.

To pickle Aſparagus.

TAKE the largeſt aſparagus you can get, cut off the white ends, and waſh the green ends in ſpring-water, then put them in another clean water, and let them lie two or three hours in it; then have a large broad ſtew-pan full of ſpring-water, with a good large handful of ſalt; ſet it on the fire, and when it boils put in the graſs, not tied up, but looſe, and not too many at a time, for fear you break the heads; juſt ſcald them, and no more, take them out with a broad ſkimmer, and lay them on a cloth to cool; then for your pickle take a gallon, or more according to your quantity of aſparagus, of white wine vinegar, and one ounce of bay-ſalt, boil it, and put your aſparagus in your jar; to a gallon of pickle, two nutmegs, a quarter of an ounce of mace, the ſame of whole white pepper, and pour the pickle hot over them; cover them with a linen cloth, three or four times double, let them ſtand a week, and boil the pickle; let them ſtand a week longer, boil the pickle again, and pour it on hot as before; when they are cold, cover them cloſe with a bladder and leather.

To pickle Peaches.

TAKE your peaches when they are at their full growth, juſt before they turn to be ripe; be ſure they are not bruiſed; then take

take ſpring-water, as much as you think will cover them, make it ſalt enough to bear an egg, with bay and common ſalt an equal quantity each; then put in your peaches, and lay a thin board over them to keep them under the water; let them ſtand three days, and then take them out and wipe them very carefully with a fine ſoft cloth, and lay them in your glaſs or jar, then take as much white-wine vinegar as will fill your glaſs or jar: to every gallon put one pint of the beſt well made muſtard, two or three heads of garlick, a good deal of ginger ſliced, half an ounce of cloves, mace, and nutmeg; mix your pickle well together, and pour over your peaches; tie them cloſe with a bladder and leather; they will be fit to eat in two months; you may with a fine pen-knife cut them acroſs; take out the ſtone, fill them with made muſtard and garlick, and horſe-radiſh and ginger; tie them together. You may pickle nectarines and apricots the ſame way.

To pickle Radiſh-Pods.

MAKE a ſtrong pickle, with cold ſpring-water and bay-ſalt, ſtrong enough to bear an egg, then put your pods in, and lay a thin board on them, to keep them under water; let them ſtand ten days, then drain them in a ſieve, and lay them on a cloth to dry; then take white-wine vinegar, as much as you think will cover them, boil it, and put your pods in a jar, with ginger, mace, cloves, and Jamaica pepper. Pour your vinegar boiling hot on, cover them with a coarſe cloth, three or four times double, that the ſteam may come through a little, and let them ſtand two days; repeat this two or three times; when it is cold, put in a pint of muſtard-ſeed, and ſome horſe-radiſh; cover it cloſe.

To pickle French Beans.

PICKLE your beans as you do the gerkins.

To pickle Cauliflowers.

TAKE the largeſt and cloſeſt you can get; pull them in ſprigs; put them in an earthen diſh, and ſprinkle ſalt over them; let them ſtand twenty-four hours to draw out all the water, then put them in a jar, and pour ſalt and water boiling over them; cover them cloſe, and let them ſtand till the next day; then take them out, and lay them on a coarſe cloth to drain; put them into glaſs jars, and put in a nutmeg ſliced, two or three blades of mace in each jar; cover them with diſtilled vinegar, and tie them down with a bladder, and over that a leather. They will be fit for uſe in a month.

To pickle Beet-Root.

SET a pot of ſpring-water on the fire, when it boils put in your beets, and let them boil till they are tender; take them out, and with a knife take off all the outſide, cut them in pieces according to your fancy; put them in a jar, and cover them with cold vinegar, and tie them down cloſe; when you uſe the beet take it out of the pickle, and cut it into what ſhapes you like; put it in a little diſh with ſome of the pickle over it. You may uſe it for ſallads, or garniſh.

To pickle White Plums.

TAKE the large white plums: and if they have ſtalks, let them remain on, and do them as you do your peaches.

To pickle Onions.

TAKE your onions when they are dry enough to lay up for winter, the ſmaller they are the better they look; put them into a pot, and cover them with ſpring-water, with a handful of white ſalt, let them boil up; then ſtrain them off, and take three coats off; put them on a cloth, and let two people take hold of it, one at each end, and rub them backward and forward till they are very dry; then put them in your bottles, with ſome blades of mace and cloves, a nutmeg cut in pieces; have ſome double-diſtilled white-wine vinegar; boil it up with a little ſalt; let it be cold, and put it over the onions; cork them cloſe, and tie a bladder and leather over it.

To pickle Onions another Way.

TAKE ſmall onions, lay them in water and ſalt two or three days, ſhift them once, then dry them in a cloth; boil the beſt vinegar with ſpice to your taſte, and when cold put them in it, covered with a bladder.

To pickle Lemons.

TAKE twelve lemons, ſcrape them with a piece of broken glaſs; then cut them croſs in two, four parts downright, but not quite through, but that they will hang together; put in as much ſalt as they will hold, rub them well, and ſtrew them over with ſalt; let them lie in an earthen diſh three days, and turn them every day; ſlit an ounce of ginger very thin, and ſalted for three days, twelve cloves of garlick, parboiled and ſalted three days, a ſmall handful of muſtard-ſeeds bruiſed and ſearced through a hair-ſieve, and ſome red India pepper; take your lemons out of the ſalt, ſqueeze them very gently, put them into a jar with the ſpice and ingredients, and cover them with the beſt white-wine vinegar. Stop them up very cloſe, and in a month's time they will be fit to eat.

To

To pickle Mushrooms White.

TAKE small buttons, cut the stalk, and rub off the skin with flannel dipped in salt, and throw them into milk and water; drain them out, and put them into a stew-pan, with a handful of salt over them; cover them close, and put them over a gentle stove for five minutes, to draw out all the water; then put them on a coarse cloth to drain till cold.

To make Pickle for Mushrooms.

TAKE a gallon of the best vinegar, put it into a cold still; to every gallon of vinegar put half a pound of bay-salt, a quarter of a pound of mace, a quarter of an ounce of cloves, a nutmeg cut in quarters; keep the top of the still covered with a wet cloth; as the cloth dries, put on a wet one; do not let the fire be too large, lest you burn the bottom of the still; draw it as long as you taste the acid, and no longer. When you fill your bottles, put in your mushrooms, here and there put in a few blades of mace, and a slice of nutmeg; then fill the bottle with pickle, and melt some mutton fat, strain it, and pour over it; it will keep them better than oil. You must put your nutmeg over the fire in a little vinegar, and give it a boil; while it is hot you may slice it as you please; when it is cold, it will not cut, for it will crack to pieces.

N. B. In the 24th Chapter, at the end of the receipt for making vinegar, you will see the best way of pickling mushrooms, only they will not be so white.

To pickle Codlings.

GATHER your codlings when they are the size of a large double walnut; take a pan, and put vine-leaves thick at the bottom. Put in your codlings, and cover them well with vine-leaves and spring water; put them over a slow fire till you can peel the skin off; take them carefully up in a hair-sieve, peel them very carefully with a pen-knife; put them into the same water again, with the vine-leaves as before. Cover them close, and set them at a distance from the fire, till they are of a fine green; drain them in a cullender till cold; put them in jars, with some mace and a clove or two of garlick; cover them with distilled vinegar; pour some mutton-fat over, and tie them with a bladder and leather down very tight.

To pickle Fennel.

SET spring-water on the fire, with a handful of salt; when it boils, tie your fennel in bunches, and put them into the water, just give them a scald, lay them on a cloth to dry; when cold, put it in a glass, with a little mace and nutmeg, fill it with cold vinegar, lay a bit of green fennel on the top, and over that a bladder and leather.

To pickle Grapes.

GET grapes at the full growth, but not ripe; cut them in small bunches fit for garnishing, put them in a stone jar, with vine-leaves between every layer of grapes; then take as much spring-water as you think will cover them, put in a pound of bay-salt, and as much white-salt as will make it bear an egg: Dry your bay-salt and pound it, it will melt the sooner; put it into a bell-metal, or copper-pot, boil it and skim it very well; as it boils, take all the black scum off, but not the white scum; when it has boiled a quarter of an hour, let it stand to cool and settle; when it is almost cold, pour the clear liquor on the grapes, lay vine leaves on the top, tie them down close with a linen cloth, and cover them with a dish; let them stand twenty-four hours; then take them out, and lay them on a cloth, cover them over with another, let them be dried between the cloths; then take two quarts of vinegar, one quart of spring-water, and one pound of coarse sugar. Let it boil a little while, skim it as it boils very clean, let it stand till it is quite cold, dry your jar with a cloth, put fresh vine-leaves at the bottom, and between every bunch of grapes, and on the top; then pour the clear off the pickle on the grapes, fill your jar that the pickle may be above the grapes, tie a thin bit of board in a piece of flannel, lay it on the top of the jar, to keep the grapes under the pickle; tie them down with a bladder, and then a leather; take them out with a wooden spoon. Be sure to make pickle enough to cover them.

To pickle Barberries.

TAKE white-wine vinegar; to every quart of vinegar put in half a pound of sixpenny sugar, then pick the worst of your barberries, and put into this liquor, and the best into glasses; then boil your pickle with the worst of your barberries, and skim it very clean; boil it till it looks of a fine colour, then let it stand to be cold before you strain; then strain it through a cloth, wringing it to get all the colour you can from the barberries; let it stand to cool and settle, then pour it clear into the glasses in a little of the pickle; boil a little fennel; when cold, put a little bit at the top of the pot or glass, and cover it close with a bladder and leather. To every half pound of sugar put a quarter of a pound of white salt. Red currants are done the same way. Or you may do barberries thus: pick them clean from leaves and spotted ones; put them into jars; mix spring-water and salt pretty strong, and put over them; and when you see the scum rise, change the salt and water, and they will keep a long time.

To

To pickle Red Cabbage.

SLICE the cabbage very fine crofs-ways; put it on an earthen difh, and fprinkle a handful of falt over it, cover it with another difh, and let it ftand twenty-four hours; then put it in a cullender to drain, and lay it in your jar; take white wine vinegar enough to cover it, a little cloves, mace, and all-fpice, put them in whole, with one pennyworth of cochineal bruifed fine; boil it up, and put it over hot or cold (which you like beft), and cover it clofe with a cloth till cold; then tie it over with leather.

To pickle Golden Pippins.

TAKE the fineft pippins you can get, free from fpots and bruifes, put them into a preferving-pan of cold fpring-water, and fet them on a charcoal fire; keep them turning with a wooden fpoon till they will peel; do not let them boil. When they are enough, peel them, and put them into the water again, with a quarter of a pint of the beft vinegar, and a quarter of an ounce of alum, cover them very clofe with a pewter difh, and fet them on the charcoal fire again, a flow fire, not to boil. Let them ftand, turning them now and then, till they look green; then take them out, and lay them on a cloth to cool; when cold, make your pickle as for the peaches, only inftead of made muftard, this muft be muftard-feed whole. Cover them clofe, and keep them for ufe.

To pickle Naftertium Berries and Limes; you pick them off the Lime-Trees in the Summer.

TAKE naftertium berries gathered as foon as the bloffom is off, or the limes, and put them in cold fpring-water and falt; change the water for three days fucceffively. Make a pickle of white wine vinegar, mace, nutmeg, flice fix fhalots, fix blades of garlic, fome pepper-corns, falt, and horfe-radifh cut in flices. Make your pickle very ftrong; drain your berries very dry, and put them in bottles. Mix your pickle well up together, but you muft not boil it; put it over the berries or limes, and tie them down clofe.

To pickle young Suckers, or young Artichokes, before the Leaves are hard.

TAKE young fuckers, pare them very nicely, all the hard ends of the leaves and ftalks, juft fcald them in falt and water, and when they are cold, put them into little glafs bottles, with two or three large blades of mace, and a nutmeg fliced thin; fill them either with diftilled vinegar, or the fugar-vinegar of your own making, with half fpring-water.

To pickle Artichoke-Bottoms.

BOIL artichokes till you can pull the leaves off, then take off the chokes, and cut them from the ſtalk; take great care you do not let the knife touch the top, throw them into ſalt and water for an hour, then take them out, and lay them on a cloth to drain; then put them into large wide-mouthed glaſſes; put a little mace and ſliced nutmeg between, fill them either with diſtilled vinegar, or ſugar-vinegar and ſpring-water; cover them with mutton-fat fried, and tie them down with a bladder and leather.

To pickle Samphire.

TAKE the ſamphire that is green, lay it in a clean pan, throw two or three handfuls of ſalt over, then cover it with ſpring-water; let it lie twenty-four hours, then put it into a clean braſs ſauce-pan, throw in a handful of ſalt, and cover it with good vinegar; cover the pan cloſe, and ſet it over a very ſlow fire; let it ſtand till it is juſt green and criſp; then take it off in a moment, for if it ſtands to be ſoft it is ſpoiled; put it in your pickling-pot, and cover it cloſe; when it is cold, tie it down with a bladder and leather, and keep it for uſe; or you may keep it all the year in a very ſtrong brine of ſalt and water, and throw it into vinegar juſt before you uſe it.

To pickle Mock Ginger.

TAKE the largeſt cauliflowers you can get, cut off all the flower from the ſtalks, and peel them, throw them into ſtrong ſpring water and ſalt for three days, then drain them in a ſieve pretty dry; put them in a jar, boil white wine vinegar with cloves, mace, long pepper, and all-ſpice, each half an ounce, forty blades of garlic, a ſtick of horſe-radiſh cut in ſlices, a quarter of an ounce of Cayenne pepper, and a quarter of a pound of yellow turmerick, two ounces of bay-ſalt; pour it boiling over the ſtalks; cover it down cloſe till the next day, then boil it again, and repeat it twice more; and when cold, tie it down cloſe.

To pickle Melon Mangoes.

TAKE as many green melons as you want, and ſlit them two thirds up the middle, and with a ſpoon take all the ſeeds out; put them in ſtrong ſpring-water and ſalt for twenty-four hours, then drain them in a ſieve; mix half a pound of white muſtard, two ounces of long-pepper, the ſame of all-ſpice, half an ounce of cloves and mace, a good quantity of garlic, and horſe-radiſh cut in ſlices, and a quarter of an ounce of Cayenne pepper; fill the ſeed-holes full of this mixture; put a ſmall ſkewer through the end, and tie it round with packthread cloſe

to

to the ſkewer, put them in a jar, and boil up vinegar with ſome of the mixture in it, and pour over the melons; cover them cloſe, and let them ſtand till next day, then green them the ſame as you do gerkins. You may do large cucumbers the ſame way; tie them down cloſe when cold, and keep them for uſe.

Elder-Shoots, in imitation of Bamboo.

TAKE the largeſt and youngeſt ſhoots of elder, which put out in the middle of May, the middle ſtalks are moſt tender and biggeſt; the ſmall ones are not worth doing. Peel off the outward peel or ſkin, and lay them in a ſtrong brine of ſalt and water for one night, then dry them in a cloth, piece by piece. In the mean time, make your pickle of half white wine and half beer vinegar: to each quart of pickle you muſt put an ounce of white or red pepper, an ounce of ginger ſliced, a little mace, and a few corns of Jamaica pepper; when the ſpice has boiled in the pickle, pour it hot upon the ſhoots, ſtop them cloſe immediately, and ſet the jar two hours before the fire, turning it often. It is as good a way of greening pickles as often boiling; or you may boil the pickle two or three times, and pour it on boiling hot, juſt as you pleaſe: if you make the pickle of the ſugar-vinegar, you muſt let one half be ſpring-water.

To make Paco-lilla, or Indian Pickle, the ſame the Mangoes come over in.

TAKE a pound of race-ginger, and lay it in water one night; then ſcrape it, and cut it in thin ſlices, and put to it ſome ſalt, and let it ſtand in the ſun to dry; take long-pepper two ounces, and do it as the ginger. Take a pound of garlic, and cut it in thin ſlices, and ſalt it, and let it ſtand three days; then waſh it well, and let it be ſalted again, and ſtand three days more; then waſh it well, and drain it, and put it in the ſun to dry; take a quarter of a pound of muſtard-ſeeds bruiſed, and half a quarter of ounce of turmerick, put theſe ingredients, when prepared, into a large ſtone or glaſs jar, with a gallon of very good white wine vinegar, and ſtir it very often for a fortnight, and tie it up cloſe. In this pickle you may put white cabbage, cut in quarters and put in a brine of ſalt and water for three days, and then boil freſh ſalt and water, and juſt put in the cabbage to ſcald, and preſs out the water, and put it in the ſun to dry, in the ſame manner as you do cauliflowers, cucumbers, melons, apples, French beans, plums, or any ſort of fruit. Take care they are well dried before you put them into the pickle: you need never empty the jar, but as the things come in ſeaſon, put them in, and ſupply it with vinegar

gar as often as there is occasion. If you would have your pickle look green, leave out the turmerick, and green them as usual, and put them into this pickle cold. In the above, you may do walnuts in a jar by themselves; put the walnuts in without any preparation, tied close down, and kept some time.

To pickle the fine Purple Cabbage, so much admired at the great Tables.

TAKE two cauliflowers, two red cabbages, half a peck of kidney-beans, six sticks, with six cloves of garlic on each stick; wash all well, give them one boil up, then drain them on a sieve, and lay them, leaf by leaf, upon a large table, and salt them with bay-salt; then lay them a-drying in the sun, or in a slow oven, until as dry as cork.

To make the Pickle.

TAKE a gallon of the best vinegar, with one quart of water, and a handful of salt, and an ounce of pepper; boil them, let it stand till it is cold, then take a quarter of a pound of ginger, cut in pieces, salt it, let it stand a week; take half a pound of mustard-seed, wash it, and lay it to dry; when very dry, bruise half of it; when half is ready for the jar, lay a row of cabbage, a row of cauliflowers and beans, and throw betwixt every row your mustard-seed, some black pepper, some Jamaica pepper, some ginger, mix an ounce of the root of turmerick powdered; put it in the pickle, which must go over all. It is best when it hath been made two years, though it may be used the first year.

To make India Pickle.

To a gallon of vinegar, one pound of garlic, three quarters of a pound of long-pepper, a pint of mustard-seed, one pound of ginger, and two ounces of turmerick; the garlic must be laid in salt three days, then wiped clean and dried in the sun; the long-pepper broke, and the mustard-seed bruised: mix all together in the vinegar; then take two large hard cabbages, and two cauliflowers, cut them in quarters, and salt them well; let them lie three days, and dry them well in the sun.

N. B.—The ginger must lie twenty-four hours in salt and water, then cut small, and laid in salt three days.

CHAP.

CHAP. XX.

OF MAKING CAKES, &c.

To make a rich Cake.

TAKE four pounds of flour dried and ſifted, ſeven pounds of currants waſhed and rubbed, ſix pounds of the beſt freſh butter, two pounds of Jordan almonds blanched, and beaten with orange-flower water and ſack till fine; then take four pounds of eggs, put half the whites away, three pounds of double-refined ſugar beaten and ſifted, a quarter of an ounce of mace, the ſame of cloves and cinnamon, three large nutmegs, all beaten fine, a little ginger, half a pint of ſack, half a pint of right French brandy, ſweet-meats to your liking, they muſt be orange, lemon, and citron; work your butter to a cream with your hands before any of your ingredients are in; then put in your ſugar, and mix all well together; let your eggs be well beat and ſtrained through a ſieve, work in your almonds firſt, then put in your eggs, beat them together till they look white and thick; then put in your ſack, brandy, and ſpices, ſhake your flour in by degrees, and when your oven is ready, put in your currants and ſweet-meats as you put it in your hoop: it will take four hours baking in a quick oven: you muſt keep it beating with your hand all the while you are mixing of it, and when your currants are well waſhed and cleaned, let them be kept before the fire, ſo that they may go warm into your cake. This quantity will bake beſt in two hoops.

To ice a great Cake.

TAKE the whites of twenty-four eggs, and a pound of double-refined ſugar beat and ſifted fine; mix both together in a deep earthen pan, and with a whiſk whiſk it well for two or three hours, till it looks white and thick; then with a thin broad board, or bunch of feathers, ſpread it all over the top and ſides of the cake; ſet it at a proper diſtance before a good clear fire, and keep turning it continually for fear of its changing colour; but a cool oven is beſt, and an hour will harden it: you may perfume the icing with what perfume you pleaſe.

To make a Pound Cake.

TAKE a pound of butter, beat it in an earthen pan with your hand one way till it is like a fine thick cream; then have ready twelve eggs, but half the whites, beat them well, and beat them up with the butter, a pound of flour beat in it, a pound of ſugar, and a few carraways; beat all well together for an hour with your hand, or a great wooden ſpoon, butter a pan and put it in, and then bake it an hour in a quick oven.

For change, you may put in a pound of currants, clean waſhed and picked.

To make a cheap Seed Cake.

YOU muſt take half a peck of flour, a pound and a half of butter, put it in a ſauce-pan with a pint of new milk, ſet it on the fire; take a pound of ſugar, half an ounce of all-ſpice beat fine, and mix them with the flour; when the butter is melted, pour the milk and butter in the middle of the flour, and work it up like paſte; pour in with the milk half a pint of good ale-yeaſt, ſet it before the fire to riſe, juſt before it goes to the oven: either put in ſome currants or carraway-ſeeds, and bake it in a quick oven; make it into two cakes: they will take an hour and a half baking.

To make a Butter Cake.

YOU muſt take a diſh of butter, and beat it like cream with your hands, two pounds of fine ſugar well beat, three pounds of flour well dried, and mix them in with the butter, twenty-four eggs, leave out half the whites, and then beat all together for an hour: juſt as you are going to put it into the oven, put in a quarter of an ounce of mace, a nutmeg beat, a little ſack or brandy, and ſeeds or currants, juſt as you pleaſe.

To make Gingerbread Cakes.

TAKE three pounds of flour, one pound of ſugar, one pound of butter rubbed in very fine, two ounces of ginger beat fine, a large nutmeg grated; then take a pound of treacle, a quarter of a pint of cream, make them warm together, and make up the bread ſtiff; roll it out, and make it up into thin cakes, cut them out with a tea-cup, or ſmall glaſs; or roll them round like nuts, and bake them on tin plates in a ſlack oven.

To make a fine Seed or Saffron Cake.

YOU muſt take a quarter of a peck of fine flour, a pound and a half of butter, three ounces of carraway-ſeeds, ſix eggs beat well, a quarter of an ounce of cloves and mace beat together very fine, a pennyworth of cinnamon beat, a pound of ſugar, a pennyworth of roſe-water, a pennyworth of ſaffron, a pint and a half of yeaſt, and a quart of milk; mix it all together lightly with your hands thus: firſt boil your milk and butter, then ſkim off the butter and mix with your flour, and a little of the milk; ſtir the yeaſt into the reſt and ſtrain it, mix it it with the flour, put in your ſeed and ſpice, roſe-water, tincture of ſaffron, ſugar, and eggs; beat it all up well with your hands lightly, and bake it in a hoop or pan, but be ſure to butter the pan well: it will take an hour and a half in a quick oven. You may leave out the ſeed if you chooſe it, and I think it rather better without it; but that you may do as you like.

To make a rich Seed Cake called the Nun's Cake.

YOU muſt take four pounds of the fineſt flour, and three pounds of double-refined ſugar beaten and ſifted; mix them together, and dry them by the fire till you prepare the other materials; take four pounds of butter, beat it with your hand till it is ſoft like cream; then beat thirty-five eggs, leave out ſixteen whites, ſtrain off your eggs from the treads, and beat them and the butter together till all appears like butter; put in four or five ſpoonfuls of roſe or orange-flower water, and beat again; then take your flour and ſugar, with ſix ounces of carraway-ſeeds, and ſtrew them in by degrees, beating it up all the time for two hours together; you may put in as much tincture of cinnamon or ambergris as you pleaſe; butter your hoop, and let it ſtand three hours in a moderate oven. You muſt obſerve always, in beating of butter, to do it with a cool hand, and beat it always one way in a deep earthen diſh.

To make Pepper Cakes.

TAKE half a gill of ſack, half a quarter of an ounce of whole white pepper, put it in, and boil it together a quarter of an hour; then take the pepper out, and put in as much double-refined ſugar as will make it like a paſte; then drop it in what ſhape you pleaſe on plates, and let it dry itſelf.

To make Portugal Cakes.

MIX into a pound of fine flour a pound of loaf-ſugar beat and ſifted, then rub it into a pound of pure ſweet butter till it is thick like grated white bread, then put to it two ſpoonfuls of roſe-water, two of ſack, ten eggs, whip them very well with a whiſk, then mix it into eight ounces of currants, mixed all well together; butter the tin pans, fill them but half full, and bake them; if made without currants they will keep half a year; add a pound of almonds blanched, and beat with roſe-water as above, and leave out the flour: theſe are another ſort, and better.

To make a pretty Cake.

TAKE five pounds of flour well dried, one pound of ſugar, half an ounce of mace, as much nutmeg; beat your ſpice very fine, mix the ſugar and ſpice in the flour, take twenty-two eggs, leave out six whites, beat them, put a pint of ale-yeast and the eggs in the flour, take two pounds and a half of fresh butter, a pint and a half of cream; set the cream and butter over the fire till the butter is melted; let it stand till it is blood-warm: before you put it into the flour, set it an hour by the fire to rise; then put in seven pounds of currants, which must be plumped in half a pint of brandy, and three quarters of a pound of candied peels: it must be an hour and a quarter in the oven: you must put two pounds of chopped raisins in the flour, and a quarter of a pint of sack: when you put the currants in, bake it in a hoop.

To make Gingerbread.

TAKE three quarts of fine flour, two ounces of beaten ginger, a quarter of an ounce of nutmeg, cloves, and mace beat fine, but most of the last; mix all together, three quarters of a pound of fine sugar, two pounds of treacle, set it over the fire, but do not let it boil; three quarters of a pound of butter melted in the treacle, and some candied lemon and orange peel cut fine; mix all these together well: an hour will bake it in a quick oven.

To make little fine Cakes.

ONE pound of butter beaten to cream, a pound and a quarter of flour, a pound of fine sugar beat fine, a pound of currants clean washed and picked, six eggs, two whites left out, beat them fine; mix the flour, sugar, and eggs by degrees into the batter, beat it all well with both hands; either make into little cakes, or bake it in one.

Another Sort of little Cakes.

A POUND of flour, and half a pound of sugar; beat half a pound of butter with your hand, and mix them well together: bake it in little cakes.

To make Drop-Biscuits.

TAKE eight eggs, and one pound of double-refined sugar beaten fine, twelve ounces of fine flour well dried, beat your eggs very well, then put in your sugar and beat it, and then your flour by degrees, beat it all very well together without ceasing; your oven must be as hot as for halfpenny bread; then flour some sheets of tin, and drop your biscuits of what bigness you please, put them in the oven as fast as you can, and when you see them rise, watch them; if they begin to colour, take them out, and put in more; and if the first is not enough, put them in again: if they are right done, they will have a white ice on them: you may, if you choose, put in a few carraways;

ways; when they are all baked, put them in the oven again to dry, then keep them in a very dry place.

To make common Biſcuits.

BEAT up ſix eggs, with a ſpoonful of roſe-water and a ſpoonful of ſack; then add a pound of fine powdered ſugar, and a pound of flour; mix them into the eggs by degrees, and an ounce of coriander-ſeeds; mix all well together, ſhape them on white thin paper, or tin moulds, in any form you pleaſe; beat the white of an egg, with a feather rub them over, and duſt fine ſugar over them; ſet them in an oven moderately heated, till they riſe and come to a good colour, take them out; and when you have done with the oven, if you have no ſtove to dry them in, put them in the oven again, and let them ſtand all night to dry.

To make French Biſcuits.

HAVING a pair of clean ſcales ready, in one ſcale put three new-laid eggs, in the other ſcale put as much dried flour, an equal weight with the eggs, take out the flour, and put in as much fine powdered ſugar; firſt beat the whites of the eggs up well with a whiſk till they are of a fine froth; then whip in half an ounce of candied lemon-peel cut very thin and fine, and beat well: then by degrees whip in the flour and ſugar, then ſlip in the yolks, and with a ſpoon temper it well together; then ſhape your biſcuits on fine white paper with your ſpoon, and throw powdered ſugar over them: bake them in a moderate oven, not too hot, giving them a fine colour on the top: when they are baked, with a fine knife cut them off from the paper, and lay them in boxes for uſe.

To make Mackeroons.

TAKE a pound of almonds, let them be ſcalded, blanched, and thrown into cold water, then dry them in a cloth, and pound them in a mortar, moiſten them with orange-flower water, or the white of an egg, leſt they turn to oil; afterwards take an equal quantity of fine powder ſugar, with three or four whites of eggs, and a little muſk, beat all well together, and ſhape them on a wafer-paper, with a ſpoon round: bake them in a gentle oven on tin plates.

To make Shrewſbury Cakes.

TAKE two pounds of flour, a pound of ſugar finely ſearced, mix them together (take out a quarter of a pound to roll them in); take four eggs beat, four ſpoonfuls of cream, and two ſpoonfuls of roſe-water; beat them well together, and mix them

them with the flour into a paſte, roll them into thin cakes, and bake them in a quick oven.

To make Madling Cakes.

To a quarter of a peck of flour, well dried at the fire, add two pounds of mutton-ſuet tried and ſtrained clear off; when it is a little cool, mix it well with the flour, ſome ſalt, and a very little all-ſpice beat fine; take half a pint of good yeaſt, and put in half a pint of water, ſtir it well together, ſtrain it, and mix up your flour into a paſte of moderate ſtiffneſs: you muſt add as much cold water as will make the paſte of a right order; make it into cakes about the thickneſs and bigneſs of an oat-cake: have ready ſome currants clean waſhed and picked, ſtrew ſome juſt in the middle of your cakes between your dough, ſo that none can be ſeen till the cake is broke. You may leave the currants out, if you do not chooſe them.

Wiggs.

TAKE three pounds of well dried flour, one nutmeg, a little mace and ſalt, and almoſt half a pound of carraway-comfits; mix theſe well together, and melt half a pound of butter in a pint of ſweet thick cream, ſix ſpoonfuls of good ſack, four yolks and three whites of eggs, and near a pint of good light yeaſt; work theſe well together, cover it, and ſet it down to the fire to riſe; then let them reſt, and lay the remainder, the half pound of carraways on the top of the wiggs, and put them upon papers well floured and dried, and let them have as quick an oven as for tarts.

To make light Wiggs.

TAKE a pound and a half of flour, and half a pint of milk made warm, mix theſe together, cover it up, and let it lie by the fire half an hour; then take half a pound of ſugar, and half a pound of butter, then work theſe into a paſte, and make it into wiggs, with as little flour as poſſible; let the oven be pretty quick, and they will riſe very much: mind to mix a quarter of a pint of good ale-yeaſt in the milk.

To make very good Wiggs.

TAKE a quarter of a peck of the fineſt flour, rub it into three quarters of a pound of freſh butter till it is like grated bread, ſomething more than half a pound of ſugar, half a nutmeg, half a race of ginger grated, three eggs (yolks and whites) beat very well, and put to them half a pint of thick ale-yeaſt, three or four ſpoonfuls of ſack, make a hole in the flour, and pour in your yeaſt and eggs, as much milk, juſt warm, as will

make

make it into a light paſte; let it ſtand before the fire to riſe half an hour, then make it into a dozen and a half of wiggs, waſh them over with egg juſt as they go into the oven: in a quick oven half an hour will bake them.

To make Buns.

TAKE two pounds of fine flour, a pint of good ale-yeaſt, put a little ſack in the yeaſt, and three eggs beaten, knead all theſe together with a little warm milk, a little nutmeg, and a little ſalt; and lay it before the fire till it riſes very light, then knead in a pound of freſh butter, a pound of rough carraway-comfits, and bake them in a quick oven, in what ſhape you pleaſe, on floured paper.

A Cake the Spaniſh Way.

TAKE twelve eggs, three quarters of a pound of the beſt moiſt ſugar, mill them in a chocolate-mill till they are all of a lather; then mix in one pound of flour, half a pound of pounded almonds, two ounces of candied orange-peel, two ounces of citron, four large ſpoonfuls of orange-water, half an ounce of cinnamon, and a glaſs of ſack: it is better when baked in a ſlow oven.

Another Way.

TAKE one pound of flour, one pound of butter, eight eggs, one pint of boiling milk, two or three ſpoonfuls of ale-yeaſt, or a glaſs of French brandy; beat all well together; then ſet it before the fire in a pan, where there is room for it to riſe; cover it cloſe with a cloth and flannel, that no air comes to it; when you think it is raiſed ſufficiently, mix half a pound of the beſt moiſt ſugar, an ounce of cinnamon beat fine, four ſpoonfuls of orange-flower water, one ounce of candied orange-peel, one ounce of citron; mix all well together, and bake it.

How to make Uxbridge Cakes.

TAKE a pound of wheat-flour, ſeven pounds of currants, half a nutmeg, four pounds of butter, rub your butter cold very well amongſt the meal; dreſs your currants very well in the flour, butter, and ſeaſoning; and knead it with ſo much good new yeaſt as will make it into a pretty high paſte, (uſually two pennyworth of yeaſt to that quantity); after it is kneaded well together let it ſtand an hour to riſe: you may put half a pound of paſte in a cake.

To make Biſcuit Bread.

TAKE half a pound of very fine wheat-flour, and as much ſugar finely ſearced, and dry them very well before the fire, dry the flour more than the ſugar; then take four new-laid eggs,

eggs, take out the ftrains, then fwing them very well, then put the fugar in, and fwing it well with the eggs, then put the flour in it, and beat all together half an hour at the leaft; put in fome anife-feeds, or carraway-feeds, and rub the plates with butter, and fet them into the oven.

To make Carraway Cakes.

TAKE two pounds of white flour, and two pounds of coarfe loaf-fugar well dried and fine fifted; after the flour and fugar are fifted and weighed, mingle them together, fift the flour and fugar together, through a hair fieve, into the bowl you ufe it in; to them you muft have two pounds of good butter, eighteen eggs, leaving out eight of the whites; to thefe you muft add four ounces of candied orange, five or fix ounces of carraway-comfits; you muft firft work the butter with rofe-water till you can fee none of the water, and your butter muft be very foft; then put in flour and fugar, a little at a time, and likewife your eggs; but you muft beat your eggs very well, with ten fpoonfuls of fack, fo you muft put in each as you think fit, keeping it conftantly beating with your hand till you have put it into the hoop for the oven; do not put in your fweet-meats and feeds till you are ready to put it into your hoops; you muft have three or four doubles of cap-paper under the cakes, and butter the paper and hoop: you muft fift fome fine fugar upon your cake when it goes into the oven.

To make a Bride Cake.

TAKE four pounds of fine flour well dried, four pounds of frefh butter, two pounds of loaf-fugar, pound and fift fine a quarter of an ounce of mace, the fame of nutmegs, to every pound of flour put eight eggs, wafh four pounds of currants, pick them well, and dry them before the fire, blanch a pound of fweet almonds, and cut them lengthways very thin, a pound of citron, one pound of candied orange, the fame of candied lemon, half a pint of brandy; firft work the butter with your hand to a cream, then beat in your fugar a quarter of an hour, beat the whites of your eggs to a very ftrong froth, mix them with your fugar and butter, beat your yolks half an hour at leaft, and mix them with your cake, then put in your flour, mace, and nutmeg, keep beating it well till your oven is ready, put in your brandy, and beat your currants and almonds lightly in, tie three fheets of paper round the bottom of your hoop to keep it from running out, rub it well with butter, put in your cake, and lay your fweet-meats in three lays, with cake betwixt every lay; after it is rifen and coloured, cover it with paper before your oven is ftopped up: it will take three hours baking.

To

To make Bath Cakes.

RUB half a pound of butter into a pound of flour, and one ſpoonful of good barm, warm ſome cream, and make it into a light paſte, ſet it to the fire to riſe; when you make them up, take four ounces of carraway-comfits, work part of them in, and ſtrew the reſt on the top, make them into a round cake, the ſize of a French roll, bake them on ſheet-tins, and ſend them in hot for breakfaſt.

To make Queen Cakes.

TAKE a pound of loaf-ſugar, beat and ſift it, a pound of flour well dried, a pound of butter, eight eggs, half a pound of currants waſhed and picked, grate a nutmeg, the ſame quantity of mace and cinnamon, work your butter to a cream, then put in your ſugar, beat the whites of your eggs near half an hour, mix them with your ſugar and butter, then beat your yolks near half an hour, and put them to your butter, beat them exceedingly well together, then put in your flour, ſpices, and the currants; when it is ready for the oven, bake them in tins, and duſt a little ſugar over them.

To make Ratafia Cakes.

TAKE half a pound of ſweet almonds, the ſame quantity of bitter, blanch and beat them fine in orange, roſe, or clear water, to keep them from oiling, pound and ſift a pound of fine ſugar, mix it with your almonds; have ready, very well beat, the whites of four eggs, mix them lightly with the almonds and ſugar, put it in a preſerving-pan, and ſet it over a moderate fire, keep ſtirring it quick one way until it is pretty hot; when it is a little cool, roll it in ſmall rolls, and cut it in thin cakes, dip your hands in flour and ſhake them on it, give them each a light tap with your finger, put them on ſugar papers, and ſift a little fine ſugar over them juſt as you are putting them into a ſlow oven.

To make little Plum Cakes.

TAKE two pounds of flour dried in the oven, or at a great fire, and half a pound of ſugar finely powdered, four yolks of eggs, two whites, half a pound of butter waſhed with roſe-water, ſix ſpoonfuls of cream warmed, a pound and a half of currants unwaſhed, but picked and rubbed very clean in a cloth; mix all well together, then make them up in cakes, bake them in an oven almoſt as hot as for a manchet, and let them ſtand half an hour till they are coloured on both ſides, then take down the oven-lid, and let them ſtand to ſoak: you muſt rub the butter into the flour very well, then the egg and cream, and then the currants.

CHAP. XXI.

Of CHEESECAKES, CREAMS, JELLIES, WHIP-SYLLABUBS, &c.

To make fine Cheesecakes.

TAKE a pint of cream, warm it, and put to it five quarts of milk warm from the cow, then put runnet to it, and give it a stir about; and when it is come, put the curd in a linen bag or cloth, let it drain well away from the whey, but do not squeeze it much; then put it in a mortar, and break the curd as fine as butter; put to your curd half a pound of sweet almonds blanched and beat exceeding fine, and half a pound of mackeroons beat very fine: if you have no mackeroons, get Naples biscuits; then add to it the yolks of nine eggs beaten, a whole nutmeg grated, two perfumed plums, dissolved in rose or orange flower water, half a pound of fine sugar; mix all well together, then melt a pound and a quarter of butter and stir it well in it, and half a pound of currants plumped, to let stand to cool till you use it; then make your puff-paste thus: take a pound of fine flour, wet it with cold water, roll it out, put into it by degrees a pound of fresh butter, and shake a little flour on each coat as you roll it: make it just as you use it.

You may leave out the currants, for change; nor need you put in the perfumed plums, if you dislike them; and for variety, when you make them of mackeroons, put in as much tincture of saffron as will give them a high colour, but no currants: this we call saffron cheesecakes; the other without currants, almond cheesecakes: with currants, fine cheesecakes; with mackeroons, mackeroon cheesecakes.

To make Lemon Cheesecakes.

TAKE the peel of two large lemons, boil it very tender, then pound it well in a mortar, with a quarter of a pound or more of loaf-sugar, the yolks of six eggs, and half a pound of fresh butter, and a little curd beat fine; pound and mix all together, lay a puff-paste in your patty-pans, fill them half full and bake them. Orange cheesecakes are done the same way, only you boil the peel in two or three waters, to take out the bitterness.

A second Sort of Lemon Cheesecakes.

TAKE two large lemons, grate off the peel of both, and squeeze out the juice of one, and add to it half a pound of double-refined sugar, twelve yolks of eggs, eight whites well beaten, then melt half a pound of butter in four or five spoonfuls of cream, then ſtir it all together and ſet it over the fire, ſtirring it till it begins to be pretty thick; then take it off, and when it is cold fill your patty-pans little more than half full; put a paſte very thin at the bottom of your patty-pans; half an hour, with a quick oven, will bake them.

To make Almond Cheeſecakes.

TAKE half a pound of Jordan almonds and lay them in cold water all night, the next morning blanch them into cold water, then take them out and dry them in a clean cloth, beat them very fine in a little orange-flower water, then take ſix eggs, leave out four whites, beat them and ſtrain them, then half a pound of white ſugar with a little beaten mace; beat them well together in a marble mortar, take ten ounces of good freſh butter, melt it, a little grated lemon-peel, and put them in the mortar with the other ingredients; mix all well together, and fill your patty-pans.

Cheeſecakes without Currants.

TAKE two quarts of new milk, ſet it as it comes from the cow, with as little runnet as you can; when it is come, break it as gently as you can, and whey it well; then paſs it through a hair-ſieve, put it into a marble mortar, and beat into it a pound of new butter waſhed in roſe-water; when that is well mingled in the curd, take the yolks of ſix eggs, and the whites of three, beat them very well with a little thick cream and ſalt; and after you have made the coffins, juſt as you put them into the cruſt (which muſt not be till you are ready to ſet them into the oven), then put in your eggs and ſugar and a whole nutmeg finely grated; ſtir them all well together, and ſo fill your cruſts; and if you put a little fine ſugar ſearced into the cruſt, it will roll the thinner and cleaner; three ſpoonfuls of thick ſweet cream will be enough to beat up your eggs with.

To make Citron Cheeſecakes.

BOIL a quart of cream, beat the yolks of four eggs, mix them with your cream when it is cold, then ſet it on the fire, let it boil till it curds, blanch ſome almonds, beat them with orange-flower water, put them into the cream with a few Naples biſcuits, and green citron ſhred fine, ſweeten it to your taſte, and bake them in tea-cups.

To make Lemon Cuſtards.

TAKE a pint of white wine, half a pound of double-refined ſugar, the juice of two lemons, the out-rind of one pared very thin, the inner-rind of one boiled tender and rubbed through a ſieve, a ſieve, let them boil a good while, then take out the peel and a little of the liquor, ſet it to cool, pour the reſt into the diſh you intend for it; beat four yolks and two whites of eggs, mix them with your cool liquor, ſtrain them into your diſh, ſtir them well up together, ſet them on a ſlow fire, or boiling water to bake as a cuſtard; when it is enough, grate the rind of a lemon all over the top; you may brown it over with a hot ſalamander. It may be eat either hot or cold.

To make Orange Cuſtards.

Boil the rind of half a Seville orange very tender, beat it in a marble mortar till it is very fine, put to it one ſpoonful of the beſt brandy, the juice of a Seville orange, four ounces of loaf-ſugar, and the yolks of four eggs, beat them all together ten minutes, then pour in by degrees a pint of boiling cream; keep beating them till they are cold, put them in cuſtard-cups, and ſet them in an earthen diſh of hot water; let them ſtand till they are ſet, then take them out and ſtick preſerved orange on the top, and ſerve them up either hot or cold. It is a pretty corner-diſh for dinner, or a ſide-diſh for ſupper.

To make a Beeſt Cuſtard.

Take a pint of beeſt, ſet it over the fire, with a little cinnamon, or three bay-leaves, let it be boiling hot, then take it off, and have ready mixed one ſpoonful of flour and a ſpoonful of thick cream; pour your hot beeſt upon it by degrees, mix it exceeding well together, and ſweeten it to your taſte: you may either put it in cruſts or cups, or bake it.

To make Almond Cuſtards.

Take a pint of cream, blanch and beat a quarter of a pound of almonds fine, with two ſpoonfuls of roſe-water; ſweeten it to your palate, beat up the yolks of four eggs, ſtir all together one way over the fire till it is thick, then pour it out into cups: or you may bake it in little china cups.

To make baked Cuſtards.

One pint of cream boiled with mace and cinnamon; when cold take four eggs, two whites left out, a little roſe and orange-flower water and ſack, nutmeg and ſugar to your palate; mix them well together, and bake them in china cups.

To make plain Cuſtards.

Take a quart of new milk, ſweeten it to your taſte, grate in a little nutmeg, beat up eight eggs, leave out half the whites, beat them up well, ſtir them into the milk, and bake it in

 china

china basons, or put them in a deep china dish; have a kettle of water boiling, set the cup in, let the water come above half way, but do not let it boil too fast for fear of its getting into the cups, and take a hot iron and colour them at the top: you may add a little rose-water.

To make Orange Butter.

TAKE the yolks of ten eggs beat very well, half a pint of Rhenish, six ounces of sugar, and the juice of three sweet oranges; set them over a gentle fire, stirring them one way till it is thick: when you take it off, stir in a piece of butter as big as a large walnut.

To make Fairy Butter.

TAKE the yolks of two hard eggs, and beat them in a marble mortar, with a large spoonful of orange-flower water, and two tea-spoonfuls of fine sugar beat to powder; beat this all together till it is a fine paste, then mix it up with about as much fresh butter out of the churn, and force it through a fine strainer full of little holes into a plate. This is a pretty thing to set off a table at supper.

Almond Butter.

TAKE a quart of cream, put in some mace whole, and a quartered nutmeg, the yolks of eight eggs well beaten, and three quarters of a pound of almonds well blanched, and beaten extremely small, with a little rose-water and sugar; and put all these together, set them on the fire, and stir them till they begin to boil; then take it off, and you will find it a little cracked; so lay a strainer in a cullender and pour it into it, and let it drain a day or two, till you see it is firm like butter; then run it through a cullender, and it will be like little comfits, and so serve it up.

To make Steeple Cream.

TAKE five ounces of hartshorn, and two ounces of ivory, and put them in a stone-bottle, fill it up with fair water to the neck, put in a small quantity of gum-arabic, and gum-dragon; then tie up the bottle very close, and set it into a pot of water, with hay at the bottom; let it stand six hours, then take it out and let it stand an hour before you open it, lest it fly in your face; then strain it, and it will be a strong jelly; then take a pound of blanched almonds, beat them very fine, mix it with a pint of thick cream, and let it stand a little; then strain it out, and mix it with a pound of jelly, set it over the fire till it is scalding hot, sweeten it to your taste with double-refined sugar, then

then take it off, put in a little amber, and pour it into ſmall high gallipots, like a ſugar-loaf at top; when it is cold, turn them, and lay cold whipt-cream about them in heaps: be ſure it does not boil when the cream is in.

Lemon Cream.

TAKE five large lemons, pare them as thin as poſſible, ſteep them all night in twenty ſpoonfuls of ſpring-water, with the juice of the lemons, then ſtrain it through a jelly-bag into a ſilver ſauce-pan (if you have one), the whites of ſix eggs beat well, ten ounces of double-refined ſugar, ſet it over a very ſlow charcoal fire, ſtir all the time one way, ſkim it, and when it is as hot as you can bear your fingers in, pour it into glaſſes.

A ſecond Lemon Cream.

TAKE the juice of four large lemons, half a pint of water, a pound of double-refined ſugar beaten fine, the whites of ſeven eggs, and the yolk of one beaten very well, mix all together, ſtrain it, and ſet it on a gentle fire, ſtirring it all the while, and ſkim it clean, put into it the peel of one lemon; when it is very hot, but does not boil, take out the lemon-peel, and pour it into china diſhes. You muſt obſerve to keep it ſtirring one way all the time it is over the fire.

Jelly of Cream.

TAKE four ounces of hartſhorn, put it on in three pints of water, let it boil till it is a ſtiff jelly, which you will know by taking a little in a ſpoon to cool; then ſtrain it off, and add to it half a pint of cream, two ſpoonfuls of roſe-water, two ſpoonfuls of ſack, and ſweeten it to your taſte; then give it a gentle boil, but keep ſtirring it all the time or it will curdle; then take it off and ſtir it till it is cold; then put it into broad bottomed cups, let them ſtand all night, and turn them out into a diſh; take half a pint of cream, two ſpoonfuls of roſe-water, and as much ſack, ſweeten it to your palate, and pour over them.

To make Orange Cream.

TAKE and pare the rind of a Seville orange very fine, and ſqueeze the juice of four oranges; put them into a ſtew-pan, with half a pint of water, and half a pound of fine ſugar, beat the whites of five eggs and mix into it, and ſet them on a ſlow fire; ſtir it one way till it grows thick and white, ſtrain it through a gauze, and ſtir it till cold; then beat the yolks of five eggs very fine, and put into your pan with the cream; ſtir it over a gentle fire till it is ready to boil; then put it in a baſon and ſtir it till it is cold, and put it in your glaſſes.

To

To make Goofeberry Cream.

TAKE two quarts of goofeberries, put to them as much water as will cover them, fcald them, and then run them through a fieve with a fpoon; to a quart of the pulp you muft have fix eggs well beaten; and when the pulp is hot, put in an ounce of frefh butter, fweeten it to your tafte, put in your eggs, and ftir them over a gentle fire till they grow thick, then fet it by; and when it is almoft cold, put into it two fpoonfuls of juice of fpinage, and a fpoonful of orange-flower water or fack; ftir it well together, and put it into your bafon: when it is cold, ferve it to table.

To make Barley Cream.

TAKE a fmall quantity of pearl-barley, boil it in milk and water till it is tender, then ftrain the liquor from it, put your barley into a quart of cream and let it boil a little, then take the whites of five eggs and the yolk of one, beaten with a fpoonful of fine flour, and two fpoonfuls of orange-flower water; then take the cream off the fire, and mix in the eggs by degrees, and fet it over the fire again to thicken; fweeten to your tafte, pour it into bafons, and, when it is cold, ferve it up.

Another Way.

TAKE a quart of French barley, boil it in three or four waters till it be pretty tender; then fet a quart of cream on the fire with fome mace and nutmeg; when the water begins to boil, drain out the barley from it, put in the cream, and let it boil till it be pretty thick and tender; then feafon it with fugar and falt: when it is cold ferve it up.

To make Ice Cream.

PARE and ftone twelve apricots, and fcald them, beat them fine in a mortar, add to them fix ounces of double-refined fugar, and a pint of fcalding cream, and work it through a fieve; put it in a tin with a clofe cover, and fet it in a tub of ice broken fmall, with four handfuls of falt mixed among the ice; when you fee your cream grows thick round the edges of your tin, ftir it well, and put it in again till it is quite thick; when the cream is all froze up, take it out of the tin, and put it into the mould you intend to turn it out of; put on the lid, and have another tub of falt and ice ready as before; put the mould in the middle, and lay the ice under and over it; let it ftand four hours, and never turn it out till the moment you want it, then dip the mould in cold fpring-water, and turn it into a plate. You may do any fort of fruit the fame way.

To make Pistachio Cream.

TAKE half a pound of pistachio-nuts, break them, and take out the kernels; beat them in a mortar with a spoonful of brandy, put them in a stew-pan with a pint of good cream, and the yolks of two eggs beat very fine; stir it gently over a slow fire till it is thick, but be sure it does not boil, then put it into a soup-plate; when it is cold, stick some kernels cut longways all over it, and send it to table.

Hartshorn Cream.

TAKE four ounces of hartshorn shavings, and boil it in three pints of water till it is reduced to half a pint, and run it through a jelly-bag; put to it a pint of cream and four ounces of fine sugar, and just boil it up; put it into cups or glasses, and let it stand till quite cold; dip your cups or glasses in scalding water and turn them out into your dish; stick sliced almonds on them: it is generally eat with white wine and sugar.

To make Almond Cream.

TAKE a quart of cream, boil it with a nutmeg grated, a blade or two of mace, a bit of lemon-peel, and sweeten to your taste; then blanch a quarter of a pound of almonds, beat them very fine, with a spoonful of rose or orange flower water; take the whites of nine eggs well beat and strain them to your almonds, beat them together, rub them very well through a coarse hair sieve; mix all together with your cream, set it on the fire, stir it all one way all the time till it almost boils; pour it into a bowl, and stir it till cold, and then put it in cups or glasses, and send it to table.

To make a fine Cream.

TAKE a quart of cream, sweeten it to your palate, grate a little nutmeg, put in a spoonful of orange-flower water and rose-water, and two spoonfuls of sack, beat up four eggs, but two whites; stir it all together one way over the fire till it is thick; have cups ready, and pour it in.

To make Ratafia Cream.

TAKE six large laurel-leaves, boil them in a quart of thick cream; when it is boiled, throw away the leaves; beat the yolks of five eggs with a little cold cream, and sugar to your taste, then thicken the cream with your eggs, set it over the fire again, but do not let it boil; keep it stirring all the while one way, and pour it into china dishes: when it is cold it is fit for use.

To make whipt Cream.

TAKE a quart of thick cream and the whites of eight eggs beat well, with half a pint of ſack; mix it together, and ſweeten it to your taſte with double-refined ſugar. You may perfume it (if you pleaſe) with a little muſk or ambergris tied in a rag, and ſteeped a little in the cream; whip it up with a whiſk, and ſome lemon-peel tied in the middle of the whiſk; take the froth up with a ſpoon, and lay it in your glaſſes or baſons. This does well over a fine tart.

How to make the clear Lemon Cream.

TAKE a gill of clear water, infuſe in it the rind of a lemon till it taſtes of it; then take the whites of ſix eggs, the juice of four lemons; beat all well together, and run them through a hair ſieve, ſweeten them with double-refined ſugar, and ſet them on the fire, not too hot, keep ſtirring; and when it is thick enough, take it off.

Sack Cream like Butter.

TAKE a quart of cream, boil it with mace, put to it ſix egg yolks well beaten, ſo let it boil up; then take it off the fire and put in a little ſack, and turn it; then put it in a cloth, and let the whey run from it; then take it out of the cloth and ſeaſon it with roſe-water and ſugar, being very well broken with a ſpoon; ſerve it up in the diſh, and pink it as you would do a diſh of butter, and ſend it in with cream and ſugar.

Clouted Cream.

TAKE four quarts of new milk from the cow, and put it in a broad earthen pan and let it ſtand till the next day, then put it over a very ſlow fire for half an hour; make it nearly hot to ſet the cream, then put it away till it is cold, and take the cream off, and beat it ſmooth with a ſpoon. It is accounted in the weſt of England very fine for tea or coffee, or to put over fruit tarts or pies.

Quince Cream.

TAKE your quinces and put them in boiling water unpared, boil them apace uncovered leſt they diſcolour when they are boiled, pare them, beat them very tender with ſugar, then take cream and mix it till it be pretty thick; if you boil your cream with a little cinnamon it will be better, but let it be cold before you put it to your quince.

Citron Cream.

TAKE a quart of cream and boil it with three pennyworth of good clear iſinglaſs, which muſt be tied up in a piece of thin tiffany; put in a blade or two of mace ſtrongly boiled in your cream and isinglass till the cream be pretty thick; sweeten it to your taste with perfumed hard sugar; when it is taken off the fire, put in a little rose-water to your taste; then take a piece of your green freshest citron and cut it in little bits, the breadth of point-dales, and about half as long; and the cream being first put into dishes, when it is half cold put in your citron, so as it may sink from the top that it may not be seen, and may lie before it be at the bottom; if you wash your citron before in rose-water, it will make the colour better and fresher; so let it stand till the next day, where it may get no water, and where it may not be shaken.

Cream of Apples, Quinces, Gooseberries, Prunes, or Raspberries.

TAKE to every quart of cream four eggs, being first well beat and strained, and mix them with a little cold cream, and put it to your cream, being first boiled with whole mace; keep it stirring till you find it begins to thicken at the bottom and sides; your apples, quinces, and berries must be tenderly boiled, so as they will crush in the pulp; then season it with rose-water and sugar to your taste, putting it into dishes; and when they are cold, if there be any rose-water and sugar which lies waterish at the top, let it be drained out with a spoon: this pulp must be made ready before you boil the cream, and when it is boiled, cover over your pulp a pretty thickness with your egg-cream, which must have a little rose-water and sugar put to it.

Sugar Loaf Cream.

TAKE a quarter of a pound of hartshorn, and put to it a pottle of water, and set it on the fire in a pipkin covered till it be ready to seeth; then pour off the water and put a pottle of water more to it, and let it stand simmering on the fire till it be consumed to a pint, and with it two ounces of isinglass washed in rose-water, which must be put in with the second water; then strain it and let it cool; then take three pints of cream and boil it very well with a bag of nutmeg, cloves, cinnamon, and mace; then take a quarter of a pound of Jordan almonds, and lay them one night in cold water to blanch, and when they are blanched, let them lie two hours in cold water, then take them out, and dry them in a clean linen cloth, and beat them in a marble mortar, with fair water or rose-water; beat them to a very fine pulp, then take some of the aforesaid cream well warmed, and put the pulp by degrees into it, straining it through a cloth with the back of a spoon, till all the goodness of the almonds be strained out into the cream; then season the cream with rose-water and sugar; then take the aforesaid jelly, warm it till it dissolves, and season it with rose-water and sugar, and a grain

grain of ambergris or musk (if you please); then mix your cream and jelly together very well, and put it into glasses well warmed (like sugar-loaves), and let it stand all night; then put them out upon a plate or two, or a white china dish, and stick the cream with piony kernels, or serve them in glasses, one on every trencher.

To make Whipt Syllabubs.

TAKE a quart of thick cream, and half a pint of sack, the juice of two Seville oranges or lemons, grate in the peel of two lemons, half a pound of double-refined sugar, pour it into a bread earthen pan, and whisk it well; but first sweeten some red wine or sack, and fill your glasses as full as you choose, then as the froth rises take it off with a spoon, and lay it on a sieve to drain; then lay it carefully into your glasses till they are as full as they will hold: do not make these long before you use them. Many use cyder sweetened, or any wine you please, or lemon, or orange whey made thus: squeeze the juice of a lemon, or orange into a quarter of a pint of milk; when the curd is hard, pour the whey clear off, and sweeten it to your palate; you may colour some with the juice of spinage, some with saffron, and some with cochineal (just as you fancy).

To make Everlasting Syllabub.

TAKE five half pints of thick cream, half a pint of Rhenish, half a pint of sack, and the juice of two large Seville oranges; grate in just the yellow rind of three lemons, and a pound of double-refined sugar well beat and sifted; mix all together with a spoonful of orange-flower water; beat it well together with a whisk half an hour, then with a spoon take it off, and lay it on a sieve to drain, then fill your glasses: these will keep above a week, and are better made the day before. The best way to whip syllabub is, have a fine large chocolate-mill, which you must keep on purpose, and a large deep bowl to mill them in: it is both quicker done, and the froth stronger; for the thin that is left at the bottom, have ready some calf's-foot jelly boiled and clarified, there must be nothing but the calf's-foot boiled to a hard jelly; when cold take off the fat, clear it with the whites of eggs, run it through a flannel bag, and mix it with the clear which you saved of the syllabubs; sweeten it to your palate, and give it a boil, then pour it into basons, or what you please: when cold, turn it out, and it is a fine flummery.

To make Solid Syllabubs.

To a quart of rich cream put a pint of white-wine, the juice of two lemons, the rind of one grated, sweeten it to your taste;

mill it with a chocolate-mill till it is all of a thickness; then put it in glasses, or a bowl, and set it in a cool place till next day.

To make a Syllabub from the Cow.

MAKE your syllabub of either cyder or wine, sweeten it pretty sweet, and grate nutmeg in; then milk the milk into the liquor: when this is done, pour over the top half a pint or a pint of cream, according to the quantity of syllabub you make. You may make this syllabub at home, only have new milk; make it as hot as milk from the cow, and out of a tea-pot, or any such thing, pour it in, holding your hand very high, and strew over some currants well washed and picked, and plumped before the fire.

To make a Trifle.

COVER the bottom of your dish or bowl with Naples biscuits broke in pieces, mackeroons broke in halves, and ratafia cakes; just wet them all through with sack, then make a good boiled custard, not too thick, and when cold pour it over it, then put a syllabub over that. You may garnish it with ratifia cakes, currant jelly, and flowers, and strew different coloured nonpareils over it.

N. B.—These are bought at the confectioners.

To make Hartshorn Jelly.

BOIL half a pound of hartshorn in three quarts of water over a gentle fire, till it becomes a jelly. If you take out a little to cool, and it hangs on the spoon, it is enough. Strain it while it is hot, put it in a well-tinned sauce-pan, put to it a pint of Rhenish wine, and a quarter of a pound of loaf-sugar; beat the whites of four eggs or more to a froth; stir it all together that the whites mix well with the jelly, and pour it in, as if you were cooling it. Let it boil two or three minutes; then put in the juice of three or four lemons; let it boil a minute or two longer; when it is finely curdled, and a pure white colour, have ready a swan-skin jelly-bag over a china bason, pour in your jelly, and pour it back again till it is as clear as rock water; then set a very clean china bason under, have your glasses as clean as possible, and with a clean spoon fill your glasses. Have ready some thin rind of the lemons, and when you have filled half your glasses, throw your peel into the bason; and when the jelly is all run out of the bag, with a clean spoon, fill the rest of the glasses, and they will look of a fine amber colour. Now in putting in the ingredients there is no certain rule. You must put in lemon and sugar to your palate; most people love them sweet; and indeed they are good for nothing unless they are.

To make Orange Jelly.

TAKE half a pound of hartſhorn ſhavings, or four ounces of iſinglaſs, and boil it in ſpring-water till it is of a ſtrong jelly; take the juice of three Seville oranges, three lemons, and ſix China oranges, and the rind of one Seville orange, and one lemon pared very thin; put them to your jelly, ſweeten it with loaf-ſugar to your palate; beat up the whites of eight eggs to a froth, and mix well in, then boil it for ten minutes, then run it through a jelly-bag till it is very clear, and put it in moulds till cold, then dip your mould in warm water, and turn it out into a china diſh, or a flat glaſs, and garniſh with flowers.

To make Ribband Jelly.

TAKE out the great bones of four calves feet, put the feet into a pot with ten quarts of water, three ounces of hartſhorn, three ounces of iſinglaſs, a nutmeg quartered, and four blades of mace; then boil this till it comes to two quarts, ſtrain it through a flannel bag, let it ſtand twenty-four hours, then ſcrape off all the fat from the top very clean, then ſlice it, put to it the whites of ſix eggs beaten to a froth, boil it a little, and ſtrain it through a flannel bag, then run the jelly into little high glaſſes, run every colour as thick as your finger, one colour muſt be thorough cold before you put another on, and that you put on muſt be but blood-warm, for fear it mix together. You muſt colour red with cochineal, green with ſpinage, yellow with ſaffron, blue with ſyrup of violets, white with thick cream, and ſometimes the jelly by itſelf. You may add orange-flower water, or wine and ſugar, and lemon if you pleaſe; but this is all fancy.

To make Calves Feet Jelly.

BOIL two calves feet in a gallon of water till it comes to a quart, then ſtrain it, let it ſtand till cold, ſkim off all the fat clean, and take the jelly up clean. If there is any ſettling in the bottom, leave it; put the jelly into a ſauce-pan, with a pint of mountain wine, half a pound of loaf-ſugar, the juice of four large lemons; beat up ſix or eight whites of eggs with a whiſk, then put them into a ſauce-pan, and ſtir all together well till it boils; let it boil a few minutes; have ready a large flannel bag, pour it in, it will run through quick; pour it in again till it runs clear, then have ready a large china baſon, with the lemon-peels cut as thin as poſſible, let the jelly run into that baſon; and the peels both give it a fine amber-colour, and alſo a flavour; with a clean ſilver ſpoon fill your glaſſes.

To make Currant Jelly.

STRIP the currants from the ſtalks, put them in a ſtone jar, ſtop it cloſe, ſet it in a kettle of boiling water half way the jar, let it boil half an hour, take it out and ſtrain the juice through a coarſe hair ſieve; to a pint of juice put a pound of ſugar, ſet it over a fine quick clear fire in your preſerving-pan or bell-metal ſkillet; keep ſtirring it all the time till the ſugar is melted, then ſkim the ſcum off as faſt as it riſes. When your jelly is very clear and fine, pour it into gallipots; when cold, cut white paper, juſt the bigneſs of the top of the pot, and lay on the jelly, dip thoſe papers in brandy; then cover them cloſe with white paper, and prick it full of holes; ſet it in a dry place, put ſome into glaſſes and paper them.

To make Pippin Jelly.

PARE and core your pippins; juſt cover them with ſpring-water, ſet them on to boil quick till it is a kind of jelly, then put them in a jelly-bag, and let them drop; put in one ſmall lump of ſugar to preſerve the colour.

To make China Orange Jelly.

To two ounces of iſinglaſs, boiled down very ſtrong by itſelf, put one quart of orange-juice, with a little cinnamon, mace, as much ſugar as you find requiſite, the whites of eight eggs, boil all together about ten minutes pretty faſt, run it through a bag; and after it is cleared, take ſome of the ſkin of the orange, cut ſmall like ſtraws, and put into it.

N. B.—It is a great improvement to add the juice of two Seville oranges.

To make Raſpberry Jam.

TAKE a pint of this currant jelly and a quart of raſpberries, bruiſe them well together, ſet them over a ſlow fire, keeping them ſtirring all the time till it boils. Let it boil gently half an hour, and ſtir it round very often to keep it from ſticking, and rub it through a cullender; pour it into your gallipots, paper as you do the currant jelly, and keep it for uſe. They will keep for two or three years, and have the full flavour of the raſpberry.

To make a Hedge-Hog.

TAKE two pounds of blanched almonds, beat them well in a mortar, with a little canary and orange-flower water, to keep them from oiling. Make them into ſtiff paſte, then beat in the yolks of twelve eggs, leave out five of the whites, put to it a pint of cream ſweetened with ſugar, put in half a pound of ſweet

ſweet butter melted, ſet it on a furnace or ſlow fire, and keep it conſtantly ſtirring, till it is ſtiff enough to be made in the form of a hedge-hog; then ſtick it full of blanched almonds, ſlit and ſtuck up like the briſtles of a hedge-hog, then put it into a diſh; take a pint of cream, and the yolks of four eggs beat up, ſweetened with ſugar to your palate; ſtir them together over a ſlow fire till it is quite hot; then pour it round the hedge-hog in a diſh, and let it ſtand till it is cold, and ſerve it up; or a rich calf's foot jelly, made clear and good, poured into the diſh round the hedge-hog; when it is cold, it looks pretty, and makes a neat diſh; or it looks pretty in the middle of a table for ſupper.

To make Moon-Shine.

FIRST have a piece of tin made in the ſhape of a half-moon, as deep as a half-pint baſon, and one in the ſhape of a large ſtar, and two or three leſſer ones; boil two calves feet in a gallon of water till it comes to a quart, then ſtrain it off, and when cold ſkim off the fat, take half the jelly and ſweeten it with ſugar to your palate, beat up the whites of four eggs, ſtir all together over a ſlow fire till it boils; then run it through a flannel bag till clear, put it in a clean ſauce-pan, and take an ounce of ſweet almonds blanched and beat very fine in a marble mortar, with two ſpoonfuls of roſe-water, and two of orange-flower water; then ſtrain it through a coarſe cloth, mix it with the jelly; ſtir in four large ſpoonfuls of thick cream, ſtir it all together till it boils; then have ready the diſh you intend it for, lay the tin in the ſhape of a half-moon in the middle, and the ſtars round it; lay little weights on the tin to keep them in the places you would have them lie; then pour in the above blanc-mange into the diſh, and when it is quite cold take out the tin things, and mix the other half of the jelly with half a pint of good white wine, and the juice of two or three lemons, with loaf-ſugar enough to make it ſweet, and the whites of eight eggs beat fine; ſtir it all together over a ſlow fire till it boils, then run it through a flannel bag till it is quite clear into a china baſon, and very carefully fill up the places where you took the tin out; let it ſtand till cold, and ſend it to table.

N. B.—You may for change fill the diſh with a fine thick almond cuſtard; and when it is cold, fill up the half-moon and ſtars with a clear jelly.

The Floating-Iſland, a pretty Diſh for the Middle of a Table at a Second Courſe, or for Supper.

YOU may take a ſoup-diſh, according to the ſize and quantity you would make, but a pretty deep glaſs is beſt, and ſet it it on a china dish; first take a quart of the thickest cream you can get, make it pretty sweet with fine sugar, pour in a gill of sack, grate the yellow rind of a lemon in, and mill the cream till it is all of a thick froth; then carefully pour the thin from the froth into a dish; take a French roll (or as many as you want), cut it as thin as you can, lay a layer of that as light as possible on the cream, then a layer of currant jelly, then a very thin layer of roll, and then hartshorn jelly, then French roll, and over that whip your froth which you saved off the cream very well milled up, and lay at top as high as you can heap it; and as for the rim of the dish, set it round with fruit or sweet-meats, according to your fancy. This looks very pretty in the middle of a table with candles round it; and you may make it of as many different colours as you fancy, and according to what jellies and jams, or sweet-meats you have; or at the bottom of your dish you may put the thickest cream you can get; but that is as you fancy.

To make a Fish-Pond.

FILL four large fish-moulds with flummery, and six small ones, take a china bowl, and put in a half a pint of stiff clear calf's foot jelly, let it stand till cold, then lay two of the small fishes on the jelly, the right side down, put in half a pint more jelly, let it stand till cold, then lay in the four small fishes across one another, that when you turn the bowl upside down the heads and tails may be seen, then almost fill your bowl with jelly, and let it stand till cold, then lay in the jelly four large fishes, and fill the bason quite full with jelly, and let it stand till the next day; when you want to use it, set your bowl to the brim in hot water for one minute, take care that you do not let the water go into the bason, lay your plate on the top of the bason, and turn it upside down; if you want it for the middle, turn it out upon a salver; be sure you make your jelly very stiff and clear.

To make a Hen's Nest.

TAKE three or five of the smallest pullet eggs you can get, fill them with flummery; and when they are stiff and cold, peel off the shells, pare off the rinds of two lemons very thin, and boil them in sugar and water to take off the bitterness, when they are cold, cut them in long shreds to imitate straws, then fill a bason one-third full of stiff calf's foot jelly, and let it stand till cold, then lay in the shred of the lemons in a ring about two inches high in the middle of your bason, strew a few corns of sago to look like barley, fill the bason to the height of the peel and let it stand till cold, then lay your eggs of flummery in the middle of the ring that the straw may be seen round,

round, fill the bason quite full of jelly, and let it stand, and turn it out the same way as the fish-pond.

To make a Mouse Trap.

TAKE a pint of cream and eggs, prepared as if for custards to put into cups, fill your dish, and have ready some fine jar raisins stoned, or dried cherries, stick these into the custard, have ready some clear barley-sugar (as none else will do), set it by the fire till it dissolves, so draw it out into lengths and cross it, draw some of it as small as a thread, let the custard be cold in the dish before this is put on: garnish as you please.

To make the Moon and Stars in Jelly.

TAKE the dish you intend for the table, have ready some white jelly, the same as for flummery; likewise a mould the shape of half a moon and two or three the shape of stars, fix them on your dish before you put in your white jelly, which is to represent the sky; have ready some clear jelly such as is for glasses, when your white jelly is cold on the dish, take out the moulds of the moon and stars carefully, and fill up the places with the clear jelly, but not hot, least it dissolves the white: it is a pretty dish by candle-light.

Hen and Chickens in Jelly.

MAKE some flummery with a deal of sweet almonds in it, colour a little of it brown with chocolate, and put it in a mould the shape of a hen; then colour some more flummery with the yolk of a hard egg beat as fine as possible, leave part of your flummery white, then fill the moulds of seven chickens, three with white flummery, and three with yellow, and one the colour of the hen; when cold, turn them into a deep dish; put under and round them lemon-peel boiled tender and cut like straw; then put a little clear calf's-foot jelly under them to keep them in their places, and let it stand till it is stiff, then fill up your dish with more jelly. They are a pretty decoration for a grand table.

To make a Desert Island.

TAKE a lump of paste and form it into a rock three inches broad at the top, colour it, and set it in the middle of a deep china dish, and set a cast figure on it, with a crow on its head, and a knot of rock-candy at the feet; then make a roll of paste an inch thick, and stick it on the inner edge of the dish, two parts round, and cut eight pieces of eringo roots, about three inches long, and fix them upright to the roll of paste on the edge; make gravel-walks of shot-comfits, from the middle of the end of the diſh, and ſet ſmall figures in them, roll out ſome paſte, and cut it open like Chineſe rails; bake it, and fix it on either ſide of one of the gravel-walks with gum, have ready a web of ſpun ſugar, and ſet it on the pillars of eringo root, and cut part of the webb off, to form an entrance where the Chineſe rails are. It is a pretty middle diſh for a ſecond courſe at a grand table, or a wedding ſupper, only ſet two crowned figures on the mount inſtead of one.

Gilded Fiſh in Jelly.

MAKE a little clear blanc-mange, then fill two large fiſh-moulds with it, and when it is cold turn it out, and gild them with gold leaf, or ſtrew them over with gold and ſilver bran mixed, then lay them on a ſoup diſh, and fill it with clear thin calf's-foot jelly, it muſt be ſo thin as they will ſwim in it: if you have no jelly, Liſbon wine or any kind of pale made wines will do.

To make Hartſhorn Flummery.

BOIL half a pound of the ſhavings of hartſhorn in three pints of water till it comes to a pint, then ſtrain it through a ſieve into a baſon, and ſet it by to cool; then ſet it over the fire, let it juſt melt, and put to it half a pint of thick cream ſcalded and grown cold again, a quarter of a pint of white wine, and two ſpoonfuls of orange-flower water; ſweeten it with ſugar, and beat it for an hour and a half, or it will not mix well nor look well; dip your cups in water before you put in the flummery, or elſe it will not turn out well: it is beſt when it ſtands a day or two before you turn it out. When you ſerve it up, turn it out of the cups, and ſtick blanched almonds cut into long narrow bits on the top. You may eat them with wine or cream.

A ſecond Way to make Hartſhorn Flummery.

TAKE three ounces of hartſhorn, and put to it two quarts of ſpring-water, let it ſimmer over the fire ſix or ſeven hours till half the water is conſumed, or elſe put it into a jug, and ſet it in the oven with houſehold-bread, then ſtrain it through a ſieve, and beat half a pound of almonds very fine, with ſome orange-flower water in the beating; when they are beat, mix a little of your jelly with it, and ſome fine ſugar; ſtrain it out and mix it with your other jelly, ſtir it together till it is little more than blood-warm; then pour it into half pint baſons or diſhes for the purpoſe, and fill them up half full: when you uſe them, turn them out of the diſh as you do flummery; if it does not come out clean, ſet your baſon a minute or two in warm water. You may ſtick almonds in or not, juſt as you pleaſe. Eat it with wine and ſugar. Or make your jelly this way: put

put six ounces of hartshorn in a glazed jug with a long neck, and put to it three pints of soft water, cover the top of the jug close, and put a weight on it to keep it steady; set it in a pot or kettle of water twenty-four hours, let it not boil, but be scalding hot; then strain it out, and make your jelly.

To make Oatmeal Flummery.

GET some oatmeal, put it into a broad deep pan, then cover it with water, stir it together and let it stand twelve hours, then pour off that water clear, and put on a good deal of fresh water, shift it again in twelve hours, and so on in twelve more; then pour off the water clear, and strain the oatmeal through a coarse hair sieve, and pour it into a sauce-pan, keeping it stirring all the time with a stick till it boils and is very thick; then pour it into dishes; when cold, turn it into plates, and eat it with what you please, either wine and sugar, or beer and sugar, or milk. It eats very pretty with cyder and sugar. You must observe to put a great deal of water to the oatmeal, and when you pour off the last water, pour on just enough fresh as to strain the oatmeal well. Some let it stand forty-eight hours, some three days, shifting the water every twelve hours; but that is as you love it for sweetness or tartness. Grits once cut does better than oatmeal. Mind to stir it together when you put in fresh water.

Blanc-mange.

TAKE a quart of cream, and half an ounce of isinglass, beat it fine, and stir it into the cream; let it boil softly over a slow fire a quarter of an hour, keep it stirring all the time; then take it off, sweeten it to your palate, and put in a spoonful of rose-water, and a spoonful of orange-flower water; strain it, and pour it into a glass or bason, or what you please, and when it is cold turn it out. It makes a fine side-dish. You may eat it with cream, wine, or what you please. Lay round it baked pears. It both looks very pretty, and eats fine.

Dutch Blanc-mange.—Excellent.

To an ounce of isinglass put half a pint of boiling water; boil it till dissolved, if much wasted, add more water to make it half a pint, boil a piece of lemon-peel in it, then take half a pint of white wine, yolks of three eggs well beat, and mix with the wine, then put it to the isinglass, add the juice of lemon and sugar to your taste, mix it well and boil it a little, strain it through a lawn sieve, stir it till near cold, then put it in your shapes.

A but-

A buttered Tort.

TAKE eight or ten large codlings and ſcald them, when cold ſkin them, take the pulp and beat it as fine as you can with a ſilver ſpoon; then mix in the yolks of ſix eggs and the whites of four, beat all well together; ſqueeze in the juice of a Seville orange, and ſhred the rind as fine as poſſible, with ſome grated nutmeg and ſugar to your taſte; melt ſome fine freſh butter, and beat up with it according as it wants, till it is all like a fine thick cream, and then make a fine puff-paſte, have a large tin patty that will juſt hold it, cover the patty with the paſte, and pour in the ingredients; do not put any cover on, bake it a quarter of an hour, then ſlip it out of the patty on a diſh, and throw fine ſugar well beat all over it. It is a very pretty ſide diſh for a ſecond courſe. You may make this of any large apples you pleaſe.

To make Fruit Wafers, of Codlings, Plumbs, &c.

TAKE the pulp of any fruit rubbed through a hair ſieve, and to every three ounces of fruit take ſix ounces of ſugar finely ſifted; dry the ſugar very well till it be very hot; heat the pulp alſo till it be very hot; then mix it, and ſet over a ſlow charcoal fire till it be almoſt a-boiling, then pour it into glaſſes or trenchers, and ſet it on the ſtove till you ſee it will leave the glaſſes; but before it begins to candy, take them off, and turn them upon papers in what form you pleaſe: you may colour them red with clove-gilliflowers ſteeped in the juice of lemon.

To make White Wafers.

BEAT the yolk of an egg, and mix it with a quarter of a pint of fair water; then mix half a pound of beſt flour, and thin it with damaſk-roſe-water till you think it of a proper thickneſs to bake; ſweeten it to your palate with fine ſugar finely ſifted.

To make Brown Wafers.

TAKE a quart of ordinary cream, then take the yolks of three or four eggs, and as much fine flour as will make it into a thin batter; ſweeten it with three quarters of a pound of fine ſugar finely ſearced, and as much pounded cinnamon as will make it taſte; do not mix them till the cream be cold; butter your pans, and make them very hot before you bake them.

How to make Gooſeberry Wafers.

TAKE gooſeberries before they are ready for preſerving, cut off the black heads, and boil them with as much water as will cover them all, to maſh; then paſs the liquor and all, as it will

run,

run, through a hair ſieve, and put ſome pulp through with a ſpoon, but not too near: it is to be pulped neither too thick nor too thin; meaſure it, and to a gill of it take half a pound of double-refined ſugar, dry it, put it to your pulp, and let it ſcald on a ſlow fire, not to boil at all; ſtir it very well, and then will riſe a frothy white ſcum, which take clear off as it riſes; you muſt ſcald and ſkim it till no ſcum riſes and it comes clean from the pan-ſide, then take it off, and let it cool a little; have ready ſheets of glaſs very ſmooth, about the thickneſs of parchment, which is not very thick; you muſt ſpread it on the glaſſes with a knife, very thin, even, and ſmooth, then ſet it in the ſtove with a ſlow fire; if you do it in the morning, at night you muſt cut it into long pieces with a broad caſe-knife, and put your knife clear under it, and fold it two or three times over, and lay them in a ſtove, turning them ſometimes till they are pretty dry; but do not keep them too long, for they will loſe their colour: if they do not come clean off your glaſſes at night, keep them till next morning.

How to make Orange Wafers.

TAKE the beſt oranges and boil them in three or four waters till they be tender, then take out the kernels and the juice, and beat them to pulp in a clean marble mortar, and rub them through a hair ſieve; to a pound of this pulp take a pound and a half of double-refined ſugar, beaten and ſearced; take half of your ſugar and put it into your oranges, and boil it till it ropes; then take it from the fire, and when it is cold make it up in paſte with the other half of your ſugar; make but a little at a time, for it will dry too faſt; then with a little rolling-pin roll them out as thin as tiffany upon papers; cut them round with a little drinking glaſs, and let them dry, and they will look very clear.

How to make Orange Cakes.

TAKE the peels of four oranges, being firſt pared, and the meat taken out, boil them tender, and beat them ſmall in a marble mortar; then take the meat of them, and two more oranges, your ſeeds and ſkins being picked out, and mix it with the peelings that are beaten; ſet them on the fire with a ſpoonful or two of orange-flower water, keeping it ſtirring till that moiſture be pretty well dried up; then have ready to every pound of that pulp, four pounds and a quarter of double-refined ſugar, finely ſearced; make your ſugar very hot, and dry it upon the fire, then mix it and the pulp together, and ſet it on the fire again till the ſugar be very well melted, but be ſure it does not boil: you may put in a little peel, ſmall, ſhred, or grated, and when it is cold, draw it up in double papers; dry them before the fire, and when you turn them, put two together; or you may keep them in deep glaſſes or pots, and dry them as you have occaſion.

To make Orange Loaves.

TAKE your orange and cut a round hole in the top, take out all the meat, and as much of the white as you can, without breaking the ſkin; then boil them in water till tender, ſhifting the water till it is not bitter, then take them up and wipe them dry; then take a pound of fine ſugar, a quart of water (or in proportion to the oranges), boil it, and take off the ſcum as it riſes; then put in your oranges, and let them boil a little, and let them lie a day or two in the ſyrup; then take the yolks of two eggs, a quarter of a pint of cream (or more), beat them well together, then grate in two Naples biſcuits, or white bread, a quarter of a pound of butter, and four ſpoonfuls of ſack; mix it all together till your butter is melted, then fill the oranges with it, and bake them in a ſlow oven as long as you would a cuſtard, then ſtick in ſome cut citron, and fill them up with ſack, butter, and ſugar grated over.

How to make Orange Biſcuits.

PARE your oranges, not very thick, put them into water, but firſt weigh your peels, let it ſtand over the fire, and let it boil till it be very tender; then beat it in a marble mortar, till it be very fine ſmooth paſte; to every ounce of peels put two ounces and a half of double-refined ſugar well ſearced, mix them well together with a ſpoon in the mortar, then ſpread it with a knife upon pie-plates, and ſet it in an oven a little warm, or before the fire; when it feels dry upon the top, cut it into what faſhion you pleaſe, and turn them into another plate, and ſet them in a ſtove till they are dry; where the edges look rough, when it is dry, they muſt be cut with a pair of ſciſſars.

To make White Cakes like China Diſhes.

TAKE the yolks of two eggs, and two ſpoonfuls of ſack, and as much roſe-water, ſome carraway-ſeeds, and as much flour as will make it a paſte ſtiff enough to roll very thin: if you would have them like diſhes, you muſt bake them upon diſhes buttered: cut them out into what work you pleaſe to candy them; take a pound of fine ſearced ſugar perfumed, and the white of an egg, and three or four ſpoonfuls of roſe-water, ſtir it till it looks white; and when that paſte is cold, do it with a feather on one ſide: this candied, let it dry, and do the other ſide ſo, and dry it alſo.

To make a Lemon Honeycomb.

TAKE the juice of one lemon, and ſweeten it with fine ſugar to your palate; then take a pint of cream, and the white of an egg, and put in ſome ſugar, and beat it up; and as the froth riſes, take it off and put it on the juice of the lemon, till you have taken all the cream off upon the lemon: make it the day before you want it, in a diſh that is proper.

To make Sugar of Pearl.

TAKE damaſk roſe-water half a pint, one pound of fine ſugar, half an ounce of prepared pearl beat to powder, eight leaves of beaten gold; boil them together according to art; add the pearl and gold leaves when juſt done; then caſt them on a marble.

Almond Rice.

BLANCH the almonds, and pound them in a marble or wooden mortar, and mix them in a little boiling water; preſs them as long as there is any milk in the almonds, adding freſh water every time; to every quart of almond juice, a quarter of a pound of rice, and two or three ſpoonfuls of orange-flower water; mix them all together, and ſimmer it over a very ſlow charcoal fire, keep ſtirring it often; when done, ſweeten it to your palate; put it into plates, and throw beaten cinnamon over it.

Almond Knots.

TAKE two pounds of almonds and blanch them in hot water, beat them in a mortar to a very fine paſte, with roſe-water; do what you can to keep them from oiling; take a pound of double-refined ſugar, ſifted through a lawn ſieve, leave out ſome to make up your knots, put the reſt into a pan upon the fire till it is ſcalding hot, and at the ſame time have your almonds ſcalding hot in another pan; then mix them together with the whites of three eggs beaten to froth, and let it ſtand till it is cold, then roll it with ſome of the ſugar you left out, and lay them in platters of paper: they will not roll into any ſhape, but lay them as well as you can, and bake them in a cool oven; it muſt not be hot, neither muſt they be coloured.

How to make fine Almond Cakes.

TAKE a pound of Jordan almonds, blanch them, beat them very fine with a little orange-flower water to keep them from oiling; then take a pound and a quarter of fine ſugar, boil it to a candy height; then put in your almonds; then take two freſh lemons, grate off the rind very thin, and put as much juice as to make it of a quick taſte; then put it into your glaſſes, and ſet it into your ſtove, ſtirring them often that they do not candy: ſo when it is a little dry, put it into little cakes upon ſheets of glaſs.

Sugar Cakes.

TAKE a pound and a half of very fine flour, one pound of cold butter, half a pound of ſugar, work all theſe well together into a paſte, then roll it with the palms of your hands into balls, and cut them with a glaſs into cakes; lay them in a ſheet of paper, with ſome flour under them: to bake them you may make tumblets, only blanch in almonds, and beat them ſmall; lay them in the midſt of a long piece of paſte, and roll it round with your fingers, and caſt them into knots in what faſhion you pleaſe: prick them and bake them.

Sugar Cakes another Way.

TAKE half a pound of fine ſugar ſearced, and as much flour, two eggs beaten with a little roſe-water, a piece of butter about the bigneſs of an egg, work them well together till they be a ſmooth paſte; then make them into cakes, working every one with the palms of your hands; then lay them in plates, rubbed over with a little butter; ſo bake them in an oven little more than warm. You may make knots of the ſame the cakes are made of; but in the mingling you muſt put in a few carraway-ſeeds; when they are wrought to a paſte, roll them with the ends of your fingers into ſmall rolls, and make it into knots; lay them upon pie-plates rubbed with butter, and bake them.

Cracknels.

TAKE half a pound of the whiteſt flour, and a pound of ſugar beaten ſmall, two ounces of butter cold, one ſpoonful of carraway-ſeeds ſteeped all night in vinegar; then put in three yolks of eggs, and a little roſe-water, work your paſte all together; and after that beat it with a rolling-pin till it be light; then roll it out thin, and cut it with a glaſs, lay it thin on plates buttered, and prick them with a pin; then take the yolks of two eggs, beaten with roſe-water, and rub them over with it; then ſet them into a pretty quick oven, and when they are brown, take them out and lay them in a dry place.

To make German Puffs.

TAKE two ſpoonfuls of fine flour, two eggs beat well, half a pint of cream or milk, two ounces of melted butter, ſtir all well together, and add a little ſalt and nutmeg; put them in tea-cups, or little deep tin moulds, half full, and bake them a quarter of an hour in a quick oven; but let it be hot enough

so

to colour them at top and bottom: turn them into a diſh, and ſtrew powder-ſugar over them.

To make Carolina Snow Balls.

TAKE half a pound of rice, waſh it clean, divide it into ſix parts; take ſix apples, pare them and ſcoop out the cores, in which place put a little lemon-peel ſhred very fine; then have ready ſome thin cloths to tie the balls in; put the rice in the cloth, and lay the apple on it; tie them up cloſe, put them into cold water, and when the water boils they will take an hour and a quarter boiling: be very careful how you turn them into the diſh that you do not break the rice, and they will look as white as ſnow, and make a very pretty diſh. The ſauce is, to this quantity, a quarter of a pound of freſh butter melted thick, a glaſs of white wine, a little nutmeg, and beaten cinnamon, made very ſweet with ſugar; boil all up together, and pour it into a baſon, and ſend it to table.

Ginger Tablet.

MELT a pound of loaf-ſugar with a little bit of butter over the fire, and put in an ounce of pounded ginger; keep it ſtirring till it begins to riſe into a froth, then pour it into pewter plates, and let it ſtand to cool: the platter muſt be rubbed with a little oil, and then put them in a china diſh, and ſend them to table. Garniſh with flowers of any kind.

How to make the thin Apricot Chips.

TAKE your apricots or peaches, pare them and cut them very thin into chips, and take three quarters of their weight in ſugar, it being finely ſearced; then put the ſugar and the apricots into a pewter diſh, and ſet them upon coals; and when the ſugar is all diſſolved, turn them upon the edge of the diſh out of the ſyrup, and ſo ſet them by: keep them turning till they have drank up the ſyrup; be ſure they never boil. They muſt be warmed in the ſyrup once every day, and ſo laid out upon the edge of the diſh till the ſyrup be drank.

Sham Chocolate.

TAKE a pint of milk, boil it over a ſlow fire, with ſome whole cinnamon, and ſweeten it with Liſbon ſugar; beat up the yolks of three eggs, throw all together into a chocolate-pot, and mill it one way, or it will turn: ſerve it up in chocolate-cups.

To make Chocolate.

SIX pounds of cocoa-nuts, one of aniſe-ſeeds, four ounces of long pepper, one of cinnamon, a quarter of a pound of al-

 monds,

monds, one ounce of piſtachios, as much achiote as will make it the colour of brick, three grains of muſk, and as much ambergris, ſix pounds of loaf-ſugar, one ounce of nutmegs, dry and beat them, and ſearce them through a fine ſieve; your almonds muſt be beat to a paſte and mixed with the other ingredients; then dip your ſugar in orange-flower or roſe water, and put it in a ſkillet on a very gentle charcoal fire; then put in the ſpice and ſtew it well together, then the muſk and ambergris, then put in the cocoa-nuts laſt of all, then achiote, wetting it with the water the ſugar was dipt in; ſtew all theſe very well together over a hotter fire than before; then take it up and put it into boxes, or what form you like, and ſet it to dry in a warm place: the piſtachios and almonds muſt be a little beat in a mortar, then ground upon a ſtone.

Another Way to make Chocolate.

TAKE ſix pounds of the beſt Spaniſh nuts, when parched and cleaned from the hulls, take three pounds of ſugar, two ounces of the beſt cinnamon, beaten and ſifted very fine; to every two pounds of nuts put in three good vanillas, or more or leſs as you pleaſe; to every pound of nuts half a drachm of cardamum-ſeeds, very finely beaten and ſearced.

CHAP. XXII.

OF MADE-WINES; BREWING; BAKING FRENCH BREAD AND MUFFINS; CHEESE, &c.

To make Raiſin Wine.

TAKE two hundred of raiſins (ſtalks and all), and put them into a large hogſhead, fill it with water, let them ſteep a fortnight, ſtirring them every day; then pour off all the liquor and preſs the raiſins; put both liquors together in a nice clean veſſel that will juſt hold it, for it muſt be full; let it ſtand till it has done hiſſing, or making the leaſt noiſe, then ſtop it cloſe and let it ſtand ſix months; peg it, and if you find it quite clear, rack it off in another veſſel; ſtop it cloſe and let it ſtand three months longer; then bottle it, and when you uſe it, rack it off into a decanter.

The beſt Way to make Raiſin Wine.

TAKE a clean wine or brandy hogſhead, take great care it is very ſweet and clean, put in two hundred of raiſins (ſtalks and

and all), and then fill the veſſel with fine clear ſpring-water; let it ſtand till you think it has done hiſſing, then throw in two quarts of fine French brandy; put in the bung ſlightly, and, in about three weeks or a month (if you are ſure it has done fretting), ſtop it down cloſe; let it ſtand ſix months, peg it near the top, and if you find it very fine and good, fit for drinking, bottle it off, or elſe ſtop it up again, and let it ſtand ſix months longer: it ſhould ſtand ſix months in the bottle. This is by much the beſt way of making it, as I have ſeen by experience, as the wine will be much ſtronger, but leſs of it: the different ſorts of raiſins make quite a different wine; and after you have drawn off all the wine, throw on ten gallons of ſpring-water; take off the head of the barrel and ſtir it well twice a day, preſſing the raiſins as well as you can; let it ſtand a fortnight or three weeks, then draw it off into a proper veſſel to hold it, and ſqueeze the raiſins well; add two quarts of brandy, and two quarts of ſyrup of alder-berries, ſtop it cloſe when it has done working, and in about three months it will be fit for drinking. If you do not chooſe to make this ſecond wine, fill your hogſhead with ſpring-water, and ſet it in the ſun for three or four months, and it will make excellent vinegar.

How to make Blackberry Wine.

TAKE your berries when full ripe, put them into a large veſſel of wood or ſtone, with a ſpicket in it, and pour upon them as much boiling water as will juſt appear at the top of them; as ſoon as you can endure your hand in them, bruiſe them very well, till all the berries be broke: then let them ſtand cloſe covered till the berries be well wrought up to the top, which uſually is three or four days, then draw off the clear juice into another veſſel; and add to every ten quarts of this liquor one pound of ſugar, ſtir it well in, and let it ſtand to work in another veſſel like the firſt, a week or ten days; then draw it off at the ſpicket through a jelly-bag into a large veſſel; take four ounces of iſinglaſs, lay it in ſteep twelve hours in a pint of white wine; the next morning boil it till it be all diſſolved upon a ſlow fire; then take a gallon of your blackberry-juice, put in the diſſolved iſinglaſs, give it a boil together, and put it in hot.

To make Alder Wine.

PICK the alder-berries when full ripe, put them into a ſtone-jar and ſet them in the oven, or a kettle of boiling water till the jar is hot through; then take them out and ſtrain them through a coarſe-cloth, wringing the berries, and put the juice into a clean kettle: to every quart of juice put a pound of fine Liſbon ſugar, let it boil, and ſkim it well; when it is clear and fine,

 pour

pour it into a jar; when cold, cover it close, and keep it till you make raisin wine; then when you tun your wine, to every gallon of wine put half a pint of the elder-syrup.

To make Orange Wine.

TAKE twelve pounds of the best powder sugar, with the whites of eight or ten eggs well beaten, into six gallons of spring-water, and boil three quarters of an hour; when cold, put into it six spoonfuls of yeast, and the juice of twelve lemons, which, being pared, must stand with two pounds of white sugar in a tankard, and in the morning skim off the top, and then put it into the water; then add the juice and rinds of fifty oranges, but not the white parts of the rinds, and so let it work all together two days and two nights; then add two quarts of Rhenish or white wine, and put it into your vessel.

To make Orange Wine with Raisins.

TAKE thirty pounds of new Malaga raisins picked clean, chop them small, take twenty large Seville oranges, ten of them you must pare as thin as for preserving; boil about eight gallons of soft water till a third be consumed, let it cool a little; then put five gallons of it hot upon your raisins and orange-peel, still it well together, cover it up, and when it is cold let it stand five days, stirring it once or twice a day; then pass it through a hair sieve, and with a spoon press it as dry as you can, put it in a runlet fit for it, and put to it the rind of the other ten oranges, cut as thin as the first; then make a syrup of the juice of twenty oranges, with a pound of white sugar. It must be made the day before you tun it up; stir it well together, and stop it close; let it stand two months to clear, then bottle it up. It will keep three years, and is better for keeping.

To make Alder-Flower Wine, very like Frontiniac.

TAKE six gallons of spring-water, twelve pounds of white sugar, six pounds of raisins of the sun chopped; boil these together one hour, then take the flowers of alder, when they are falling, and rub them off to the quantity of half a peck; when the liquor is cold, put them in; the next day put in the juice of three lemons, and four spoonfuls of good ale yeast; let it stand covered up two days, then strain it off and put it in a vessel fit for it. To every gallon of wine put a quart of Rhenish, and put your bung lightly on a fortnight, then stop it down close: let it stand six months; and if you find it is fine, bottle it off.

To make Goofeberry Wine.

GATHER your goofeberries in dry weather, when they are half ripe, pick them, and bruife a peck in a tub, with a wooden mallet; then take a horfe-hair cloth and prefs them as much as poffible, without breaking the feeds; when you have preffed out all the juice, to every gallon of goofeberries put three pounds of fine dry powder fugar, ftir it all together till the fugar is diffolved, then put it in a veffel or cafk, which muft be quite full: if ten or twelve gallons, let it ftand a fortnight; if a twenty gallon cafk, five weeks. Set it in a cool place, then draw it off from the lees, clear the veffel of the lees, and pour in the clear liquor again: if it be a ten gallon cafk, let it ftand three months; if a twenty gallon, four months; then bottle it off.

To make Currant Wine.

GATHER your currants on a fine dry day, when the fruit is full ripe; ftrip them, put them in a large pan, and bruife them with a wooden peftle. Let them ftand in a pan or tub twenty-four hours to ferment; then run it through a hair fieve, and do not let your hand touch the liquor. To every gallon of this liquor put two pounds and a half of white fugar, ftir it well together, and put it into your veffel. To every fix gallons put in a quart of brandy, and let it ftand fix weeks. If it is fine, bottle it; if it is not, draw it off as clear as you can into another veffel or large bottles; and in a fortnight, bottle it in fmall bottles.

White Currant Wine.

SQUEEZE your currants through a cullender, then wring them through a cloth; to each gallon of juice, three gallons of water, three pounds and a half of fugar; boil the fugar and water together, take off the fcum clear, put it to cool, put the juice to it, then put it in a barrel; let it ftand a month or fix weeks, then draw it off and put it in the fame barrel again, with a quart of brandy; if you choofe, you may add a handful of clary.

To make Cherry Wine.

PULL your cherries when full ripe off the ftalks, and prefs them through a hair fieve; to every gallon of liquor put two pounds of lump fugar beat fine, ftir it together, and put it into a veffel; it muft be full: when it has done working and making any noife, ftop it clofe for three months, and bottle it off.

To

To make Birch Wine.

THE ſeaſon for procuring the liquor from the birch-trees is the beginning of March, while the ſap is riſing, and before the leaves ſhoot out; for when the ſap is come forward, and the leaves appear, the juice, by being long digeſted in the bark, grows thick and coloured, which before was thin and clear. The method of procuring the juice is, by boring holes in the body of the tree, and putting in foſſets, which are commonly made of the branches of elder, the pith being taken out. You may without hurting the tree, if large, tap it in ſeveral places, four or five at a time, and by that means ſave from a good many trees ſeveral gallons every day; if you have not enough in one day, the bottles in which it drops muſt be corked cloſe, and roſined or waxed; however, make uſe of it as ſoon as you can. Take the ſap and boil it as long as any ſcum riſes, ſkimming it all the time: to every gallon of liquor put four pounds of good ſugar, the thin peel of a lemon, boil it afterwards half an hour, ſkimming it very well, pour it into a clean tub, and when it is almoſt cold, ſet it to work with yeaſt ſpread upon a toaſt, let it ſtand five or ſix days, ſtirring it often; then take ſuch a caſk as will hold the liquor, fire a large match dipped in brimſtone, and throw it into the caſk, ſtop it cloſe till the match is extinguiſhed, tun your wine, lay the bung on light till you find it has done working; ſtop it cloſe and keep it three months, then bottle it off.

To make Quince Wine.

GATHER the quinces when dry and full ripe; take twenty large quinces, wipe them clean with a coarſe cloth, and grate them with a large grate or raſp as near the core as you can, but none of the core; boil a gallon of ſpring-water, throw in your quinces, let it boil ſoftly about a quarter of an hour; then ſtrain them well into an earthen pan on two pounds of double-refined ſugar, pare the peel of two large lemons, throw in and ſqueeze the juice through a ſieve, ſtir it about till it is very cool, then toaſt a little bit of bread very thin and brown, rub a little yeaſt on it, let it ſtand cloſe covered twenty-four hours, then take out the toaſt and lemon, put it up in a keg, keep it three months, and then bottle it. If you make a twenty gallon caſk, let it ſtand ſix months before you bottle it; when you ſtrain your quinces, you are to wring them hard in a coarſe cloth.

To make Cowſlip or Clary Wine.

TAKE ſix gallons of water, twelve pounds of ſugar, the juice of ſix lemons, the whites of four eggs beat very well, put all together

together in a kettle, let it boil half an hour, ſkim it very well: take a peck of cowſlips (if dry ones, half a peck), put them into a tub, with the thin peeling of ſix lemons, then pour on the boiling liquor, and ſtir them about; when almoſt cold, put in a thin toaſt baked dry and rubbed with yeaſt: let it ſtand two or three days to work. If you put in (before you tun it) ſix ounces of ſyrup of citron or lemons, with a quart of Rheniſh wine, it will be a great addition; the third day ſtrain it off, and ſqueeze the cowſlips through a coarſe cloth; then ſtrain it through a flannel bag, and tun it up; lay the bung looſe for two or three days to ſee if it works, and if it does not, bung it down tight; let it ſtand three months, then bottle it.

To make Turnip Wine.

TAKE a good many turnips, pare, ſlice, and put them in a cyder-preſs, and preſs out all the juice very well; to every gallon of juice have three pounds of lump-ſugar, have a veſſel ready juſt big enough to hold the juice, put your ſugar into a veſſel, and alſo to every gallon of juice half a pint of brandy; pour in the juice, and lay ſomething over the bung for a week, to ſee if it works; if it does, you muſt not bung it down till it has done working: then ſtop it cloſe for three months, and draw it off in another veſſel. When it is fine, bottle it off.

To make Raſpberry Wine.

TAKE ſome fine raſpberries, bruiſe them with the back of a ſpoon, then ſtrain them through a flannel bag into a ſtone jar. to each quart of juice put a pound of double-refined ſugar, ſtir it well together, and cover it cloſe; let it ſtand three days, then pour it off clear. To a quart of juice put two quarts of white wine, bottle it off; it will be fit to drink in a week. Brandy made thus is a very fine dram, and a much better way than ſteeping the raſpberries.

How to make Mead.

TAKE ten gallons of water, and two gallons of honey, a handful of raced ginger; then take two lemons, cut them in pieces, and put them into it, boil it very well, keep it ſkimming; let it ſtand all night in the ſame veſſel you boil it in, the next morning barrel it up, with two or three ſpoonfuls of good yeaſt. About three weeks or a month after, you may bottle it.

To make White Mead.

TAKE five gallons of water, add to that one gallon of the beſt honey; then ſet it on the fire, boil it together well, and ſkim it very clean; then take it off the fire, and ſet it by; then

take

take two or three races of ginger, the like quantity of cinnamon and nutmegs, bruise all these grossly, and put them in a little Holland bag in the hot liquor, and so let it stand close covered till it be cold; then put as much ale-yeast to it as will make it work. Keep it in a warm place, as they do ale; and when it hath wrought well, tun it up; at two months you may drink it, having been bottled a month. If you keep it four months, it will be the better.

RULES for BREWING.

CARE must be taken, in the first place, to have the malt clean; and after it is ground, it ought to stand four or five days.

For strong October, five quarters of malt to three hogsheads, and twenty-four pounds of hops. This will afterwards make two hogsheads of good keeping small beer, allowing five pounds of hops to it.

For middling beer, a quarter of malt makes a hogshead of ale, and one of small beer; or it will make three hogsheads of good small beer, allowing eight pounds of hops. This will keep all the year. Or it will make twenty gallons of strong ale, and two hogsheads of small beer that will keep all the year.

If you intend your ale to keep a great while, allow a pound of hops to every bushel; if to keep six months, five pounds to a hogshead; if for present drinking, three pounds to a hogshead, and the softest and clearest water you can get.

Observe the day before to have all your vessels very clean, and never use your tubs for any other use except to make wines.

Let your cask be very clean the day before with boiling water; and if your bung is big enough, scrub them well with a little birch-broom or brush; but if they be very bad, take out the heads, and let them be scrubbed clean with a hand-brush, sand, and fullers-earth. Put on the head again, and scald them well, throw into the barrel a piece of unslacked lime, and stop the bung close.

The first copper of water, when it boils, pour into your mash-tub, and let it be cool enough to see your face in; then put in your malt, and let it be well mashed; have a copper of water boiling in the mean time, and when your malt is well mashed, fill your mashing-tub, stir it well again, and cover it over with the sacks. Let it stand three hours, set a broad shallow tub under the cock, let it run very softly; and if it is thick, throw it up again till it runs fine, then throw a handful of hops in the under tub, let the mash run into it, and fill your tubs

tubs till all is run off. Have water boiling in the copper, and lay as much more as you have occaſion for, allowing one third for boiling and waſte. Let that ſtand an hour, boiling more water to fill the maſh-tub for ſmall beer; let the fire down a little, and put it into tubs enough to fill your maſh. Let the ſecond maſh be run off, and fill your copper with the firſt wort; put in part of your hops, and make it boil quick. About an hour is long enough; when it has half boiled, throw in a handful of ſalt. Have a clean white wand, and dip it into the copper; and if the wort feels clammy, it is boiled enough; then ſlacken your fire, and take off your wort. Have ready a large tub, put two ſticks acroſs, and ſet your ſtraining baſket over the tub on the ſticks, and ſtrain your wort through it. Put other wort on to boil with the reſt of the hops; let your maſh be covered again with water, and thin your wort that is cooled in as many things as you can; for the thinner it lies, and the quicker it cools, the better. When quite cool, put it into the tunning-tub. Throw a handful of ſalt into every boil. When the maſh has ſtood an hour, draw it off; then fill your maſh with cold water, take off the wort in the copper, and order it as before. When cool, add to it the firſt in the tub; ſo ſoon as you empty one copper, fill the other, ſo boil your ſmall beer well. Let the laſt maſh run off, and when both are boiled with freſh hops, order them as the two firſt boilings; when cool, empty the maſh-tub, and put the ſmall beer to work there. When cool enough, work it; ſet a wooden bowl of yeaſt in the beer, and it will work over with a little of the beer in the boil. Stir your tun up every twelve hours, let it ſtand two days, then tun it, taking off the yeaſt. Fill your veſſels full, and ſave ſome to fill your barrels; let it ſtand till it has done working; then lay your bung lightly for a fortnight, after that ſtop it as cloſe as you can. Mind you have a vent-peg at the top of the veſſel; in warm weather open it; and if your drink hiſſes, as it often will, looſen it till it has done, then ſtop it cloſe again. If you can boil your ale in one boiling it is beſt, if your copper will allow of it; if not, boil it as conveniency ſerves.

When you come to draw your beer, and find it is not fine, draw off a gallon, and ſet it on the fire, with two ounces of iſinglaſs cut ſmall and beat; diſſolve it in the beer over the fire: when it is all melted, let it ſtand till it is cold, and pour it in at the bung, which muſt lay looſe on till it has done fermenting, then ſtop it cloſe for a month. Take great care your caſks are not muſty, or have any ill taſte; if they have, it is a hard thing to ſweeten them. You are to waſh your caſks with cold water before you ſcald them, and they ſhould lie

lie a day or two soaking, and clean them well, then scald them.

The best Thing for Rope.

MIX two handfuls of bean flour and one handful of salt, throw this into a kilderkin of beer, do not stop it close till it has done fermenting, then let it stand a month, and draw it off; but sometimes nothing will do with it.

When a Barrel of Beer has turned Sour.

TO a kilderkin of beer throw in at the bung a quart of oatmeal, lay the bung on loose two or three days, then stop it down close, and let it stand a month. Some throw in a piece of chalk as big as a turkey's egg, and when it has done working, stop it close for a month, then tap it.

How to make Cyder.

AFTER all your apples are bruised, take half of your quantity and squeeze them; and the juice you press from them, pour upon the others half bruised, but not squeezed, in a tub for the purpose, having a tap at the bottom; let the juice remain upon the apples three or four days; then pull out your tap, and let your juice run into some other vessel set under the tub to receive it; and if it runs thick, as at the first it will, pour it upon the apples again, till you see it run clear; and as you have a quantity, put it into your vessel, but do not force the cyder, but let it drop as long as it will of its own accord; having done this, after you perceive that the sides begin to work, take a quantity of isinglass (an ounce will serve forty gallons), infuse this in some of the cyder till it be dissolved; put to an ounce of isinglass a quart of cyder, and when it is so dissolved, pour it into the vessel, and stop it close for two days, or something more; then draw off the cyder into another vessel: this do so often till you perceive your cyder to be free from all manner of sediment that may make it ferment and fret itself: after Christmas you may boil it. You may, by pouring water on the apples and pressing them, make a pretty small cyder: if it be thick and muddy, by using isinglass, you may make it as clear as the rest; you must dissolve the isinglass over the fire till it be jelly.

For fining Cyder.

TAKE two quarts of skim-milk, four ounces of isinglass, cut the isinglass in pieces, and work it lukewarm in the milk over the fire; and when it is dissolved, then put it cold into the hogshead of cyder, and take a long stick and stir it well from top to bottom for half a quarter of an hour.

After it has fined.

TAKE ten pounds of raiſins of the ſun, two ounces of turmerick, half an ounce of ginger beaten; then take a quantity of raiſins, and grind them as you do muſtard-ſeed in a bowl, with a little cyder, and ſo the reſt of the raiſins; then ſprinkle the turmerick and ginger amongſt it; then put all into a fine canvaſs bag, and hang it in the middle of the hogſhead cloſe, and let it lie. After the cyder has ſtood thus a fortnight or a month, then you may bottle it at your pleaſure.

B A K I N G.

To make White Bread, after the London Way.

TAKE a buſhel of the fineſt flour well dreſſed, put it in the kneading-trough at one end, take a gallon of water (which we call liquor) and ſome yeaſt; ſtir it into the liquor till it looks of a good brown colour and begins to curdle, ſtrain and mix it with your flour till it is about the thickneſs of a ſeed-cake; then cover it with the lid of the trough, and let it ſtand three hours; and as ſoon as you ſee it begin to fall, take a gallon more of liquor; weigh three quarters of a pound of ſalt, and with your hand mix it well with the water: ſtrain it, and with this liquor make your dough of a moderate thickneſs, fit to make up into loaves; then cover it again with the lid, and let it ſtand three hours more. In the mean time, put the wood into the oven and heat it. It will take two hours heating. When your ſpunge has ſtood its proper time, clear the oven, and begin to make your bread. Set it in the oven, and cloſe it up, and three hours will bake it. When once it is in, you muſt not open the oven till the bread is baked; and obſerve in ſummer that your water be milk-warm, and in winter as hot as you can bear your finger in it.

N. B. As to the quantity of liquor your dough will take, experience will teach you in two or three times making; for all flour does not want the ſame quantity of liquor; and if you make any quantity, it will raiſe up the lid and run over.

To make French Bread.

TAKE three quarts of water, and one of milk; in winter ſcalding hot, in ſummer a little more than milk warm; ſeaſon it well with ſalt, then take a pint and a half of good ale yeaſt not bitter, lay it in a gallon of water the night before, pour it off the water, ſtir in your yeaſt into the milk and water, then with your hand break in a little more than a quarter of a pound of butter, work it well till it is diſſolved, then beat up two eggs in a baſon, and ſtir them in; have about a peck and a half of flour, mix it with your liquor; in winter make your dough pretty ſtiff, in ſummer more ſlack: ſo that you may uſe a little more or leſs flour, according to the ſtiffneſs of your dough: mix it well, but the leſs you work the better: make it into rolls, and have a very quick oven. When they have lain about a quarter of an hour, turn them on the other ſide, let them lie about a quarter longer, and then take them out and chip all your French bread with a knife, which is better than raſping it, and make it look ſpungy and of a fine yellow, whereas the raſping takes off all that fine colour, and makes it look too ſmooth. You muſt ſtir your liquor into the flour as you do for the pie-cruſt. After your dough is made, cover it with a cloth, and let it lie to riſe while the oven is heating.

To make Muffins and Oat-Cakes.

To a buſhel of Hertfordſhire white flour, take a pint and a half of good ale yeaſt, from pale malt, if you can get it, becauſe it is whiteſt; let the yeaſt lie in water all night, the next day pour off the water clear, make two gallons of water juſt milk-warm, not to ſcald your yeaſt, and two ounces of ſalt; mix your water, yeaſt, and ſalt well together for about a quarter of an hour; then ſtrain it and mix up your dough as light as poſſible, and let it lie in your trough an hour to riſe; then with your hand roll it, and pull it into little pieces about as big as a large walnut, roll them with your hand like a ball, lay them on your table, and as faſt as you do them, lay a piece of flannel over them, and be ſure to keep your dough covered with flannel; when you have rolled out all your dough, begin to bake the firſt, and by that time they will be ſpread out in the right form; lay them on your iron; as one ſide begins to change colour, turn the other; take great care, they do not burn, or be too much diſcoloured, but that you will be a judge of in two or three makings. Take care the middle of the iron is not too hot, as it will be; but then you may put a brick-bat or two in the middle of the fire to ſlacken the heat. The thing you bake on muſt be made thus:

Build a place as if you were going to ſet a copper; and, in the ſtead of a copper, a piece of iron all over the top, fixed in form juſt the ſame as the bottom of an iron pot, and make your fire underneath with coal, as in a copper. Obſerve, muffins are made the ſame way; only this, when you pull them to pieces, roll them in a good deal of flour, and with a rolling-pin roll them thin, cover them with a piece of flannel, and they will riſe

rise to a proper thickness; and if you find them too big or too little, you must roll dough accordingly. These must not be the least discoloured. When you eat them, toast them crisp on both sides, then with your hand pull them open, and they will be like a honeycomb; lay in as much butter as you intend to use, then clap them together again, and set it by the fire. When you think the butter is melted, turn them, that both sides may be buttered alike, but do not touch them with a knife, either to spread, or cut them open; if you do, they will be as heavy as lead, only when they are buttered and done, you may cut them across with a knife.

N. B. Some flour will soak up a quart or three pints more water than other flour; then you must add more water, or shake in more flour in making up, for the dough must be as light as possible.

A Receipt for making Bread without Barm by the Help of a Leaven.

TAKE a lump of dough, about two pounds of your last making, which has been raised by barm, keep it by you in a wooden vessel, and cover it well with flour; (this is your leaven); then the night before you intend to bake, put the said leaven to a peck of flour, and work them well together with warm water; let it lie in a dry wooden vessel, well covered with a linen cloth and a blanket, and keep it in a warm place: this dough kept warm will rise again next morning, and will be sufficient to mix with two or three bushels of flour, being worked up with warm water and a little salt; when it is well worked up, and thoroughly mixed with all the flour, let it be well covered with the linen and blanket until you find it rise; then knead it well, and work it up into bricks or loaves, making the loaves broad, and not so thick and high as is frequently done, by which means the bread will be better baked; then bake your bread.

Always keep by you two or more pounds of the dough of your last baking, well covered with flour, to make leaven to serve from one baking-day to another; the more leaven is put to the flour, the lighter and spungier the bread will be: the fresher the leaven, the bread will be the less sour.

[From the Dublin Society.]

A Method to preserve a large Stock of Yeast, which will keep and be of Use for several Months, either to make Bread or Cakes.

WHEN you have yeast in plenty, take a quantity of it, stir and work it well with a whisk until it becomes liquid and thin, then get a large wooden platter, cooler, or tub, clean and dry, and with a soft brush lay a thin layer of the yeast on the tub, and turn the mouth downwards that no dust may fall upon it,

 but

but so that the air may get under to dry it; when that coat is very dry, then lay on another till you have a sufficient quantity, even two or three inches thick, to serve for several months, always taking care the yeast in the tub be very dry before you lay more on: when you have occasion to use this yeast, cut a piece off and lay it in warm water; stir it together, and it will be fit for use. If it is for brewing, take a large handful of birch tied together, and dip it into the yeast and hang it up to dry; take great care no dust comes to it, and so you may do as many as you please. When your beer is fit to set to work, throw in one of these, and it will make it work as well as if you had fresh yeast.

You must whip it about in the wort, and then let it lie; when the vat works well, take out the broom and dry it again, and it will do for the next brewing.

N. B. In the building of your oven for baking, observe that you make it round, low roofed, and a little mouth; then it will take less fire, and keep in the heat better than a long oven and high roofed, and will bake the bread better.

CHEESE.

To make Slip-coat Cheese.

TAKE six quarts of new milk hot from the cow, the stroakings, and put to it two spoonfuls of rennet; and when it is hard coming, lay it into the fat with a spoon, not breaking it all; then press it with a four-pound weight, turning of it with a dry cloth once an hour, and every day shifting it into fresh grass. It will be ready to cut, if the weather be hot, in fourteen days.

To make a Brick-Bat Cheese. It must be made in September.

TAKE two gallons of new milk, and a quart of good cream, heat the cream, put in two spoonfuls of rennet, and when it is come, break it a little, then put it into a wooden mould, in the shape of a brick. It must be half a year old before you eat it: you must press it a little, and so dry it.

To make Cream Cheese.

PUT one large spoonful of steep to five quarts of afterings, break it down light, put it upon a cloth in a sieve bottom, and let it run till dry, break it, cut and turn it in a clean cloth, then put it into the sieve again, and put on it a two-pound weight, sprinkle a little salt on it and let it stand all night, then lay it on a board to dry; when dry, lay a few strawberry leaves on it, and ripen it between two pewter diſhes in a warm place, turn it, and put on freſh leaves every day.

To make Bullace Cheeſe.

TAKE your bullace when they are full ripe, put them into a pot, and to every quart of bullace put a quarter of a pound of loaf-ſugar beat ſmall; bake them in a moderate oven till they are ſoft, then rub them through a hair ſieve; to every pound of pulp add half a pound of loaf-ſugar beat fine, then boil it an hour and a half over a ſlow fire, and keep ſtirring it all the time, then pour it into potting pots, and tie brandy papers over them, and keep them in a dry place; when it has ſtood a few months, it will cut out very bright and fine.

N. B. You may make ſloe cheeſe the ſame way.

To make Stilton Cheeſe.

TAKE the night's cream and put it to the morning's new milk with the rennet, when the curd is come, it is not to be broken, as is done with other cheeſes, but take it out with a ſoil-diſh all together, and place it on a ſieve to drain gradually, and as it drains, keep gradually preſſing it till it becomes firm and dry, then place it in a wooden hoop; afterwards to be kept dry on boards, turned frequently, with cloth binders round it, which are to be tightened as occaſion requires. In ſome dairies the cheeſes, after being taken out of the wooden hoop, are bound tight round with a cloth, which is changed every day till the cheeſe is firm enough to ſupport itſelf; after the cloth is taken off they are rubbed all over daily with a bruſh for two or three months, and if the weather is damp, twice a day; and even before the cloth is taken off, the top and bottom are well rubbed every day.

N. B. The dairy-maid muſt not be diſheartened if ſhe does not perfectly ſucceed the firſt time.

CHAP. XXIII.

JARRING CHERRIES, PRESERVES, &c.

To jar Cherries, Lady North's Way.

TAKE twelve pounds of cherries, ſtone them, put them in your preſerving-pan, with three pounds of double-refined ſugar and a quart of water; then ſet them on the fire till they are ſcalding hot, take them off a little while, and ſet on the fire

fire again; boil them till they are tender, then ſprinkle them with half a pound of double-refined ſugar pounded, and ſkim them clean; put them all together in a china bowl, let them ſtand in the ſyrup three days; drain them through a ſieve, take them out one by one, with the holes downwards on a wicker ſieve, then ſet them in a ſtove to dry, and as they dry turn them upon clean ſieves: when they are dry enough, put a clean white ſheet of paper in a preſerving-pan, then put all the cherries in, with another clean white ſheet of paper on the top of them; cover them cloſe with a cloth, and ſet them over a cool fire till they ſweat: take them off the fire, then let them ſtand till they are cold, and put them in boxes or jars to keep.

To dry Cherries.

To four pounds of cherries put one pound of ſugar, and juſt put as much water to the ſugar as will wet it; when it is melted, make it boil; ſtone your cherries, put them in, and make them boil; ſkim them two or three times, take them off, and let them ſtand in the ſyrup two or three days, then boil your ſyrup and put to them again, but do not boil your cherries any more; let them ſtand three or four days longer, then take them out, lay them in ſieves to dry, and lay them in the ſun, or in a ſlow oven to dry; when dry, lay them in rows in papers, and ſo a row of cherries, and a row of white paper in boxes.

Another Way.

Take eight pounds of cherries, one pound of the beſt powdered ſugar, ſtone the cherries over a great deep baſon or glaſs, and lay them one by one in rows, and ſtrew a little ſugar; thus do till your baſon is full to the top, and let them ſtand till the next day; then pour them out into a great poſnip, ſet them on the fire, let them boil very faſt a quarter of an hour, or more; then pour them again into your baſon, and let them ſtand two or three days; then take them out, and lay them one by one on hair ſieves, and ſet them in the ſun, or an oven, till they are dry, turning them every day upon dry ſieves: if in the oven, it muſt be as little warm as you can juſt feel it, when you hold your hand in it.

To preſerve Cherries with the Leaves and Stalks green.

First dip the ſtalks and leaves in the beſt vinegar boiling hot, ſtick the ſprig upright in a ſieve till they are dry; in the meantime boil ſome double-refined ſugar to ſyrup, and dip the cherries, ſtalks, and leaves in the ſyrup, and juſt let them ſcald; lay them on a ſieve, and boil them to a candy height, then dip the cherries, ſtalks, leaves, and all; then ſtick the branches

branches in ſieves, and dry them as you do other ſweet-meats. They look very pretty at candle-light in a deſert.

To preſerve Cherries in Brandy.

CUT the ſtalks half off, put them in a jar, and fill them up with brandy ſweetened to your taſte with ſugar-candy, pour in a little currant jelly, diſſolved, at the top, and tie them down for uſe.

To preſerve Cherries.

TAKE two pounds of cherries, one pound and an half of ſugar, half a pint of fair water, melt your ſugar in it; when it is melted, put in your other ſugar and your cherries, then boil them ſoftly till all the ſugar be melted; then boil them faſt, and ſkim them; take them off two or three times and ſhake them, and put them on again, and let them boil faſt; and when they are of a good colour, and the ſyrup will ſtand, they are enough.

Another Way.

TAKE their weight in ſugar before you ſtone them; when ſtoned, make your ſyrup, then put in your cherries, let them boil ſlowly at the firſt till they be thorougly warmed, then boil them as faſt as you can; when they are boiled clear, put in the jelly, with almoſt the weight in ſugar, ſtrew the ſugar on the cherries; for the colouring you muſt be ruled by your eye; to a pound of ſugar put a jack of water, ſtrew the ſugar on them before they boil, and put in the juice of currants ſoon after they boil.

To barrel Morello Cherries.

TO one pound of full ripe cherries, picked from the ſtems, and wiped with a cloth, take half a pound of double refined ſugar, and boil it to a candy height, but not a high one; put the cherries into a ſmall barrel, then put in the ſugar by a ſpoonful at a time till it is all in, and roll them about every day till they have done fermenting; then bung it up cloſe, and they will be fit for uſe in a month: it muſt be an iron-hooped barrel.

To make Orange Marmalade.

TAKE the cleareſt Seville oranges and cut them in two; take out all the pulp and juice into a pan, and pick all the ſkins and ſeeds out; boil the rinds in hard water till they are very tender, and change the water three times while they are boiling, and then pound them in a mortar, and put in the juice and pulp; put them in a preſerving-pan, with double their weight of loaf-ſugar, ſet it over a ſlow fire, boil it gently

 forty

forty minutes, put it into pots; cover it with brandy-paper, and tie it down close.

Marmalade of Eggs the Jews Way.

TAKE the yolks of twenty-four eggs, beat them for an hour; clarify one pound of the best moist sugar, four spoonfuls of orange-flower water, one ounce of blanched and pounded almonds; stir all together over a very slow charcoal fire, keeping stirring it all the while one way till it comes to a consistence; then put it into coffee-cups, and throw a little beaten cinnamon on the top of the cups.

This marmalade, mixed with pounded almonds, with orange-peel, and citron, are made in cakes of all shapes, such as birds, fish, and fruit.

Marmalade of Cherries.

TAKE five pounds of cherries, stoned, and two pounds of hard sugar; shred your cherries, wet your sugar with the juice that runneth from them; then put the cherries into the sugar, and boil them pretty fast till it be a marmalade; when it is cold, put it up in glasses for use.

To make white Marmalade of Quinces.

PARE and core the quinces as fast as you can, then take to a pound of quinces (being cut in pieces, less than half quarters,) three quarters of a pound of double-refined sugar beat small, then throw half the sugar on the raw quinces, set it on a slow fire till the sugar is melted and the quinces tender; then put in the rest of the sugar, and boil it up as fast as you can; when it is almost enough, put in some jelly and boil it apace; then put it up, and when it is quite cold, cover it with white paper.

Marmalade of Quince White. Another way.

TAKE the quinces, pare them and core them, put them into water as you pare them, to be kept from blacking; then boil them so tender that a quarter of straw will go through them; then take their weight of sugar, and beat them, break the quinces with the back of a spoon; and then put in the sugar, and let them boil fast uncovered, till they slide from the bottom of the pan: you may make paste of the same, only dry it in a stove, drawing it out into what form you please.

To make Red Marmalade.

TAKE full ripe quinces, pare and cut them in quarters, and core them; put them in a sauce-pan, cover them with the parings. fill the sauce-pan nearly full of spring-water, cover it close,

close, and ſtew them gently till they are quite ſoft, and a deep pink colour; then pick out the quince from the parings, and beat them to a pulp in a mortar; take their weight in loaf-ſugar, put in as much of the water they were boiled in as will diſſolve it, and boil and ſkim it well; put in your quinces, and boil them gently three quarters of an hour; keep ſtirring them all the time, or it will ſtick to the pan and burn; put it into flat pots, and when cold tie it down cloſe.

To preſerve Oranges whole.

TAKE the beſt Bermudas or Seville oranges you can get, and pare them with a pen-knife very thin, and lay your oranges in water three or four days, ſhifting them every day; then put them in a kettle with fair water, and put a board on them to keep them down in the water, and have a ſkillet on the fire with water that may be ready to ſupply the kettle with boiling water; as it waſtes, it muſt be filled up three or four times while the oranges are doing, for they will take ſeven or eight hours boiling; they muſt be boiled till a white ſtraw will run through them, then take them out and ſcoop the ſeeds out of them very carefully, by making a little hole in the top, and weigh them: to every pound of oranges put a pound and three quarters of double-refined ſugar, beat well and ſifted through a clean lawn ſieve, fill your oranges with ſugar, and ſtrew ſome on them; let them lie a little while, and make your jelly thus:

Take two dozen of pippins or John apples and ſlice them into water, and when they are boiled tender ſtrain the liquor from the pulp, and to every pound of oranges you muſt have a pint and a half of this liquor, and put to it three quarters of the ſugar you left in filling the oranges, ſet it on the fire, and let it boil, ſkim it well, and put it in a clean earthen pan till it is cold, then put it in your ſkillet; put in your oranges; with a ſmall bodkin job your oranges as they are boiling to let the ſyrup into them, ſtrew on the reſt of your ſugar whilſt they are boiling, and when they look clear take them up and put them in your glaſſes, put one in a glaſs juſt fit for them, and boil the ſyrup till it is almoſt a jelly, then fill up your glaſſes: when they are cold, paper them up, and keep them in a dry place.

Or thus: Cut a hole out of the ſtalk end of your orange as big as a ſixpence, ſcoop out all the pulp very clean, tie them ſingly in muſlin, and lay them two days in ſpring water; change the water twice a day, and boil them in the muſlin till tender; be careful you keep them covered with water, weigh the oranges before you ſcoop them; to every pound add two pounds of double-refined ſugar and a pint of water; boil the fugar and water with the orange juice to a fyrup, fkim it well, let it ftand till it is cold, take the oranges out of the muflin, and put them in and boil them till they are quite clear, and put them by till cold; then pare and core fome green pippins, and boil them in water till it is very ftrong of the pippin; do not ftir them, put them down gently with the back of a fpoon, and ftrain the liquor through a jelly-bag till it is clear; put to every pint of liquor a pound of double-refined fugar, and the juice of a lemon ftrained as clear as you can; boil it to a ftrong jelly; drain the oranges out of your fyrup, and put them in glafs or white ftone jars of the fize of the orange, and pour the jelly on them; cover them with brandy-papers, and tie them over with a bladder. You may do lemons in the fame manner.

Quinces whole.

TAKE your quinces and pare them; cut them in quarters, or leave them whole, which you pleafe; put them into a fauce-pan and cover them with hard water; lay your parings over them to keep them under water; cover your fauce-pan clofe, that no fteam can come out; fet them over a flow fire till they are foft, and a fine pink colour; then let them ftand till cold: make a fyrup of double-refined fugar, with as much water as will wet it; boil and fkim it well; put in your quinces, let them boil ten minutes; take them off, and let them ftand three hours; then boil them till the fyrup is thick and the quinces clear; then put them in deep jars, and when cold put brandy-paper over them, and tie them down clofe.

How to preferve White Quinces whole.

TAKE the weight of your quinces in fugar, and put a pint of water to a pound of fugar, make it into a fyrup, and clarify it; then core your quince and pare it, put it into your fyrup and let it boil till it be all clear, then put in three fpoonfuls of jelly, which muft be made thus: over night, lay your quince-kernels in water, then ftrain them and put them into your quinces, and let them have but one boil afterwards.

To make Quince Cakes.

YOU muft let a pint of the fyrup of quinces, with a quart or two of rafpberries, be boiled and clarified over a clear gentle fire, taking care that it be well fkimmed from time to time; then add a pound and a half of fugar, caufe as much more to be brought to a candy height, and poured in hot: let the whole be continually ftirred about till it is almoft cold, then fpread it on plates, and cut it out into cakes.

To

To preserve Apricots.

TAKE your apricots, ſtone and pare them thin, and take their weight in double-refined ſugar, beaten and ſifted; put your apricots in a ſilver cup or tankard, cover them over with ſugar, and let them ſtand ſo all night; the next day put them in a preſerving-pan, ſet them on a gentle fire, and let them ſimmer a little while, then let them boil till tender and clear, taking them off ſometimes to turn and ſkim: keep them under the liquor as they are doing, and with a ſmall clean bodkin, or great needle, job them, that the ſyrup may penetrate into them; when they are enough, take them up, and put them in glaſſes: boil and ſkim your ſyrup; and when it is cold, put it on your apricots: put brandy-paper over, and tie them cloſe.

Another Way.

TAKE your apricots and pare them, then ſtone what you can whole, then give them a light boil in a pint of water, or to your quantity of fruit; then take the weight of your fruit in ſugar, and take the liquor in which you boil them and your ſugar, and boil it till it comes to a ſyrup, and give them a light boil, taking off the ſcum as it riſes; when the ſyrup jellies it is enough; then take up the apricots and cover them with the jelly, and cut paper over them, and lay them down when cold.

To preserve Damſons whole.

YOU muſt take ſome damſons and cut them in pieces, put them in a ſkillet over the fire, with as much water as will cover them; when they are boiled, and the liquor pretty ſtrong, ſtrain it out; add for every pound of the damſons (wiped clean) a pound of ſingle-refined ſugar, put the third part of your ſugar into the liquor, ſet it over the fire, and when it ſimmers, put in the damſons; let them have one good boil, and take them off for half an hour, covered up cloſe; then ſet them on again, and let them ſimmer over the fire after turning them; then take them out and put them in a baſon, ſtrew all the ſugar that was left on them, and pour the hot liquor over them; cover them up and let them ſtand till next day, then boil them up again till they are enough: take them up, and put them in pots; boil the liquor till it jellies, and pour it on them when it is almoſt cold; ſo paper them up.

To preserve Gooſeberries whole without ſtoning.

TAKE the largeſt preſerving gooſeberries, and pick off the black eye, but not the ſtalk; then ſet them over the fire in a pot of water to ſcald, cover them very cloſe, but not boil or break, and when they are tender take them up into cold water; then take a pound and a half of double-refined ſugar to a pound

 of

of goofeberries, and clarify the fugar with water, a pint to a pound of fugar, and when your fyrup is cold, put the goofeberries fingle in your preferving-pan, put the fyrup to them, and fet them on a gentle fire; let them boil, but not too faft, left they break; and when they have boiled, and you perceive that the fugar has entered them, take them off, cover them with white paper, and fet them by till the next day; then take them out of the fyrup, and boil the fyrup till it begins to be ropy; fkim it and put it to them again, then fet them on a gentle fire, and let them fimmer gently till you perceive the fyrup will rope; then take them off, fet them by till they are cold, cover them with paper, then boil fome goofeberries in fair water, and when the liquor is ftrong enough, ftrain it out; let it ftand to fettle, and to every pint take a pound of double-refined fugar, then make a jelly of it, put the goofeberries in glaffes when they are cold; cover them with the jelly the next day, paper them wet, and then half dry the paper that goes in the infide, it clofes down the better, and then white paper over the glafs: fet in your ftove, or a dry place.

To preferve White Walnuts.

FIRST pare your walnuts till the white appears, and nothing elfe; you muft be very careful in the doing of them that they do not turn black, and as faft as you do them throw them into falt and water, and let them lie till your fugar is ready; take three pounds of good loaf-fugar, put it into your preferving-pan, fet it over a charcoal fire, and put as much water as will juft wet the fugar; let it boil, then have ready ten or a dozen whites of eggs ftrained and beat up to froth; cover your fugar with a froth as it boils, and fkim it; then boil it, and fkim it till it is as clear as cryftal, then throw in your walnuts; juft give them a boil till they are tender, then take them out and lay them in a difh to cool; when cool, put them in your preferving-pan, and when the fugar is as warm as milk, pour it over them; when quite cold, paper them down.

Thus clear your fugar for all preferves, apricots, peaches, goofeberries, currants, &c.

To preferve Walnuts green.

WIPE them very clean, and lay them in ftrong falt and water twenty-four hours; then take them out and wipe them very clean, have ready a fkillet of water boiling, throw them in, let them boil a minute and take them out; lay them on a coarfe cloth, and boil your fugar as above; then juft give your walnuts a fcald in the fugar, take them up and lay them to cool; put them in your preferving-pot, and pour on your fyrup as above.

To

To preserve the large Green Plums.

FIRST dip the ſtalks and leaves in boiling vinegar; when they are dry, have your ſyrup ready, and firſt give them a ſcald, and very carefully with a pin take off the ſkin; boil your ſugar to a candy height, and dip in your plums, hang them by the ſtalk to dry, and they will look finely tranſparent, and by hanging that way to dry will have a clear drop at the top: you muſt take great care to clear your ſugar nicely.

To preserve Peaches.

TAKE the largeſt peaches you can get, not over ripe, rub off the lint with a cloth, and run them down the ſeam with a pin, ſkin deep; cover them with French brandy, tie a bladder over them, and let them ſtand a week; make a ſtrong ſyrup, and boil and ſkim it well; take the peaches out of the brandy, and put them in and boil them till they look clear; then take them out, put them in glaſſes, mix the ſyrup with the brandy, and when cold pour it over your peaches: tie them cloſe down with a bladder, and leather over it.

To preserve Golden Pippins.

TAKE the rind of an orange and boil it very tender, lay it in cold water for three days; take two dozen of golden pippins, pare, core, quarter them, and boil them to a ſtrong jelly, and run it through a jelly-bag till it is clear; take the ſame quantity of pippins, pare them, and take out the cores, put three pounds of loaf-ſugar in a preſerving-pan, with three half pints of ſpring-water; when it boils, ſkim it well, and put in your pippins, with the orange-rind cut in long thin ſlips, let them boil faſt till the ſugar is thick, and will almoſt candy, then put in three half-pints of pippin jelly, and boil it faſt till the jelly is clear; then ſqueeze in the juice of a lemon, give it a boil, and put them in pots or glaſſes, with the orange-peel: you may uſe lemon-peel inſtead of orange, but then you muſt only boil it, not ſoak it.

To preserve Grapes.

GET ſome fine grapes, not over ripe, either red or white, but very cloſe, and pick all the ſpecked ones; put them in a jar, with a quarter of a pound of ſugar-candy, and fill the jar with common brandy; tie them down cloſe, and keep them in a dry cold place. You may do morello cherries the ſame way.

To preserve Green Codlings.

GATHER your codlings when they are the ſize of a walnut, with the ſtalks, and a leaf or two on; put a handful of vine-leaves

leaves into a preferving-pan, then a layer of codlings, then vine-leaves, and then codlings, till it is full, and vine-leaves pretty thick at top, and fill it with fpring-water, cover it clofe to keep in the fteam, and fet it on a flow fire till they grow foft; then take them out, and take off the fkins with a pen-knife, and put them in the fame water again with the vine-leaves, which muft be quite cold, or it will make them crack; put in a little roche-allum, and fet them over a flow fire till they are green, then take them out and lay them on a fieve to drain: make a good fyrup, and give them a gentle boil for three days, then put them in fmall jars, with brandy-paper over them, and tie them down tight.

To preferve Apricots or Plums green.

TAKE your plums before they have ftones in them, which you may know by putting a pin through them; then coddle them in many waters till they are as green as grafs; peel them and coddle them again; you muft take the weight of them in fugar, and make a fyrup; put to your fugar a jack of water, then put them in, fet them on the fire to boil flowly till they be clear, fkimming them often, and they will be very green: put them up in glaffes, and keep them for ufe.

To preferve Barberries.

TAKE the ripeft and beft barberries you can find; take the weight of them in fugar; then pick out the feeds and tops, wet your fugar with the juice of them, and make a fyrup; then put in your barberries, and when they boil take them off and fhake them, then fet them on again and let them boil, and repeat the fame till they are clean enough to put into glaffes.

White Pear Plums.

TAKE the fineft and cleareft from fpecks you can get; to a pound of plum take a pound and a quarter of fugar, the fineft you can get, a pint and a quarter of water; flit the plums and ftone them, and prick them full of holes, faving fome fugar beat fine, laid in a bafon; as you do them, lay them in, and ftrew fugar over them; when you have thus done, have half a pound of fugar, and your water, ready made into a thin fyrup, and a little cold; put in your plums with the flit fide downwards, fet them on the fire, keep them continually boiling, neither too flow nor too faft; take them often off, fhake them round, and fkim them well, keep them down into the fyrup continually for fear they lofe their colour; when they are thoroughly fcalded, ftrew on the reft of your fugar, and keep doing fo till they are enough, which you may know by their glafing; towards the latter end, boil them them up quickly.

To

To preferve Currants.

TAKE the weight of the currants in fugar, p[illegible]e feeds; take to a pound of fugar half a jack or w[illegible] it melt, then put in your berries, and let them do very [illegible]y, fkim them and take them up, let the fyrup boil; then put [illegible]m on again, and when they are clear, and the fyrup thick enough, take them off, and when they are cold put them up in glaffes.

To preferve Rafpberries.

TAKE of the rafpberries that are not too ripe, and take the weight of them in fugar, wet your fugar with a little water, and put in your berries, and let them boil foftly, take heed of breaking them; when they are clear, take them up, and boil the fyrup till it be thick enough, then put them in again, and when they are cold, put them in glaffes.

Pippins in Slices.

WHEN your pippins are prepared, but not cored, cut them in flices, and take the weight of them in fugar, put to your fugar a pretty quantity of water, let it melt, and fkim it, let it boil again very high, then put them into the fyrup when they are clear; lay them in fhallow glaffes, in which you mean to ferve them up; then put into the fyrup a candied orange-peel cut in little flices very thin, and lay about the pippin; cover them with fyrup, and keep them about the pippin.

To preferve Cucumbers equal with any Italian Sweet meats.

TAKE fine young gerkins, of two or three different fizes, put them into a ftone jar, cover them well with vine-leaves, fill the jar with fpring-water, cover it clofe; let it ftand near the fire, fo as to be quite warm, for ten days or a fortnight; then take them out and throw them into fpring-water; they will look quite yellow, and ftink, but you muft not mind that; have ready your preferving-pan, take them out of that water and put them into the pan, cover them well with vine leaves, fill it with fpring-water, fet it over a charcoal fire, cover them clofe, and let them fimmer very flow; look at them often, and when you fee them turned quite of a fine green, take off the leaves, and throw them into a large fieve; then into a coarfe cloth, four or five times doubled; when they are cold, put them into the jar, and have ready your fyrup made of double-refined fugar, in which boil a great deal of lemon-peel and whole ginger, pour it hot over them, and cover them down clofe; do it three times; pare your lemon-peel very thin, and cut them in long thin bits, about two inches long: the ginger

muft

muſt be well boiled in water before it is put in the ſyrup. Take long cucumbers, cut them in halfs, ſcoop out the inſide; do them the ſame way: they eat very fine in minced pies or puddings; or boil the ſyrup to a candy, and dry them on ſieves.

To make Conſerve of red Roſes, or any other Flowers.

TAKE roſe-buds, or any other flowers, and pick them; cut off the white part from the red, and ſift the red part of the flowers through a ſieve to take out the ſeeds; then weigh them, and to every pound of flowers take two pounds and a half of loaf-ſugar; beat the flowers pretty fine in a ſtone mortar, then by degrees put the ſugar to them, and beat it very well, till it is well incorporated together; then put it into gallipots, tie it over with paper, over that a leather, and it will keep ſeven years.

To make Conſerve of Hips.

GATHER hips before they grow ſoft, cut off the heads and ſtalks, ſlit them in halves, take out all the ſeeds and white that is in them very clean, then put them into an earthen pan, and ſtir them every day, or they will grow mouldy: let them ſtand till they are ſoft enough to rub them through a coarſe hair ſieve; as the pulp comes, take it off the ſieve: they are a dry berry, and will require pains to rub them through; then add its weight in ſugar, mix them well together without boiling, and keep it in deep gallipots for uſe.

Conſerve of Roſes boiled.

TAKE red roſes, take off all the whites at the bottom, or elſewhere, take three times the weight of them in ſugar, put to a pint of roſes a pint of water, ſkim it well, ſhred your roſes a little before you put them into water, cover them, and boil the leaves tender in the water, and when they are tender put in your ſugar; keep them ſtirring, leſt they burn when they are tender, and the ſyrup be conſumed: put them up, and ſo keep them for your uſe.

To make Syrup of Roſes.

INFUSE three pounds of damaſk roſe-leaves in a gallon of warm water, in a well-glazed earthen pot, with a narrow mouth, for eight hours, which ſtop ſo cloſe that none of the virtue may exhale; when they have infuſed ſo long, heat the water again, ſqueeze them out, and put in three pounds more of roſe-leaves, to infuſe for eight hours more; then preſs them out very hard; then to every quart of this infuſion add four pounds of fine ſugar, and boil it up to a ſyrup.

To make Syrup of Citron.

PARE and ſlice your citrons thin, lay them in a baſon, with layers of fine ſugar; the next day pour off the liquor into a glaſs, ſkim it, and clarify it over a gentle fire.

To make Syrup of Clove-Gilliflowers.

CLIP your gilliflowers, ſprinkle them with fair water, put them into an earthen pot, ſtop it up very cloſe, ſet it in a kettle of water, and let it boil for two hours; then ſtrain out the juice, put a pound and a half of ſugar to a pint of juice, put it into a ſkillet, ſet it on the fire, keep it ſtirring till the ſugar is all melted, do not let it boil; then ſet it by to cool, and put it into bottles.

To make Syrup of Peach-Bloſſoms.

INFUSE peach-bloſſoms in hot water, as much as will handſomely cover them; let them ſtand in balneo, or in ſand, for twenty-four hours covered cloſe; then ſtrain out the flowers from the liquor, and put in freſh flowers; let them ſtand to infuſe as before, then ſtrain them out, and to the liquor put freſh peach-bloſſoms the third time, and (if you pleaſe) a fourth time; then to every pound of your infuſion add two pounds of double-refined ſugar; and, ſetting it in ſand, or balneo, make a ſyrup, which keep for uſe.

To make Syrup of Quinces.

GRATE quinces, paſs their pulp through a cloth to extract the juice, ſet their juices in the ſun to ſettle, or before the fire, and by that means clarify it; for every four ounces of this juice take a pound of ſugar boiled brown: if the putting in the juice of the quinces ſhould check the boiling of the ſugar too much, give the ſyrup ſome boiling till it becomes pearled; then take it off the fire, and when cold, put it into the bottles.

To candy any Sort of Flowers.

TAKE the beſt treble-refined ſugar, break it into lumps, and dip it piece by piece into water, put them into a veſſel of ſilver, and melt them over the fire; when it juſt boils, ſtrain it and ſet it on the fire again, and let it boil till it draws in hairs, which you may perceive by holding up your ſpoon; then put in the flowers, and ſet them in cups or glaſſes; when it is of a hard candy, break it in lumps, and lay it as high as you pleaſe: dry it in a ſtove, or in the ſun, and it will look like ſugar-candy.

To make Citron.

QUARTER your melon, and take out all the inſide, then put into the ſyrup as much as will cover the coat; let it boil in the ſyrup till the coat is as tender as the inward part, then put them in the pot with as much ſyrup as will cover them; let them ſtand for two or three days that the ſyrup may penetrate through them, and boil your ſyrup to a candy height, with as much mountain wine as will wet your ſyrup, clarify it, and then boil it to a candy height; then dip in the quarters, and lay them on a ſieve to dry, and ſet them before a ſlow fire, or put them in a ſlow oven till dry. Obſerve that your melon is but half ripe, and when they are dry, put them in deal boxes in paper.

To candy Cherries or Green Gages.

DIP the ſtalks and leaves in white wine vinegar boiling, then ſcald them in ſyrup; take them out and boil the ſyrup to a candy height; dip in the cherries, and hang them to dry with the cherries downwards; dry them before the fire, or in the ſun; then take the plums, after boiling them in a thin ſyrup, peel off the ſkin and candy them, and ſo hang them up to dry.

To candy Angelica.

TAKE it in April, boil it in water till it be tender; then take it up and drain it from the water very well, then ſcrape the outſide of it, and dry it in a clean cloth, and lay it in the ſyrup, and let it lie in three or four days, and cover it cloſe; the ſyrup muſt be ſtrong of ſugar, and keep it hot a good while, and let it not boil; after it is heated a good while, lay it upon a pie-plate, and ſo let it dry; keep it near the fire leſt it diſſolve.

To candy Caſſia.

TAKE as much of the powder of brown caſſia as will lie upon two broad ſhillings, with what muſk and ambergris you think fitting; the caſſia and perfume muſt be powdered together, then take a quarter of a pound of ſugar, and boil it to a candy height; then put in your powder, and mix it well together, and pour it in pewter ſaucers or plates, which muſt be buttered very thin, and when it is cold it will ſlip out. The caſſia is to be bought at London; ſometimes it is in powder, and ſometimes in a hard lump.

To dry Pears without Sugar.

TAKE the Norwich pears, pare them with a knife, and put them in an earthen pot, and bake them, not too ſoft; put them

into

into a white plate pan, and put dry ſtraw under them, and lay them in an oven after bread is drawn, and every day warm the oven to the degree of heat as when bread is newly drawn. Within one week they muſt be dry.

To dry Plums.

TAKE pear-plums, fair and clear coloured, weigh them, and ſlit them up the ſides; put them into a broad pan, and fill it full of water, ſet them over a very ſlow fire; take care that the ſkin does not come off; when they are tender take them up, and to every pound of plums put a pound of ſugar, ſtrew a little on the bottom of a large ſilver baſon; then lay your plums in, one by one, and ſtrew the remainder of your ſugar over them; ſet them into your ſtove all night, with a good warm fire the next day; heat them and ſet them into your ſtove again, and let them ſtand two days more, turning them every day; then take them out of the ſyrup, and lay them on glaſs plates to dry.

How to dry Peaches.

TAKE the faireſt and ripeſt peaches, pare them into fair water; take their weight in double-refined ſugar; of one half make a very thin ſyrup, then put in your peaches, boiling them till they look clear, then ſplit and ſtone them; boil them till they are very tender, lay them a-draining; take the other half of the ſugar and boil it almoſt to a candy; then put in your peaches, and let them lie all night; then lay them on a glaſs, and ſet them in a ſtove till they are dry. If they are ſugared too much, wipe them with a wet cloth a little; let the firſt ſyrup be very thin, a quart of water to a pound of ſugar.

To dry Damſins.

TAKE four pounds of damſins; take one pound of fine ſugar, make a ſyrup of it, with about a pint of fair water; then put in your damſins, ſtir it into your hot ſyrup, ſo let them ſtand on a little fire to keep them warm for half an hour; then put all into a baſon and cover them, let them ſtand till the next day; then put the ſyrup from them, and ſet it on the fire; and when it is very hot, put it on your damſins: this do twice a day for three days together; then draw the ſyrup from the damſins, and lay them in an earthen diſh, and ſet them in an oven after bread is drawn; when the oven is cold, take them and turn them, and lay them upon clean diſhes; ſet them in the ſun, or in another oven, till they are dry.

To dry Pear-Plums.

TAKE two pounds of pear-plums to one pound of ſugar; ſtone them, and fill them every one with ſugar; lay them in an earthen pot, put to them as much water as will prevent burning them; then ſet them in an oven after bread is drawn, let them ſtand till they be tender, then put them into a ſieve to drain well from the ſyrup, then ſet them in an oven again until they be a little dry; then ſmooth the ſkins as well as you can, and ſo fill them; then ſet them in the oven again to harden; then waſh them in water ſcalding hot, and dry them very well; then put them in the oven again very cool, to blue them; put them between two pewter diſhes, and ſet them in the oven.

The Filling for the aforeſaid Plums.

TAKE the plums, wipe them, prick them in the ſeams, put them in a pitcher, and ſet them in a little boiling water, let them boil very tender, then pour moſt of the liquor from them, then take off the ſkins and the ſtones; to a pint of the pulp put a pound of ſugar well dried in the oven; then let it boil till the ſcum riſes, which take off very clean, and put into earthen plates, and dry it in an oven, and ſo fill the plums.

To clarify Sugar after the Spaniſh Way.

TAKE one pound of the beſt Liſbon ſugar, nineteen pounds of water, mix the white and ſhell of an egg, then beat it up to a lather; then let it boil, and ſtrain it off: you muſt let it ſimmer over a charcoal fire till it diminiſh to half a pint; then put in a large ſpoonful of orange-flower water.

CHAP. XXIV.

To make Anchovies, Vermicelli, Catchup, Vinegar; and to keep Artichokes, French Beans, &c.

To make Anchovies.

TO a peck of ſprats, two pounds of common ſalt, a quarter of a pound of bay-ſalt, four pounds of ſalt-petre, two ounces of ſal-prunella, two pennyworth of cochineal; pound all in a mortar, put them into a ſtone pot, a row of ſprats, a layer of your compound, and ſo on to the top alternately. Preſs them hard down, cover them cloſe, let them ſtand ſix months, and they will be fit for uſe. Obſerve that your ſprats be very freſh, and do not waſh or wipe them, but juſt take them as they come out of the water.

To pickle Smelts, where you have Plenty.

TAKE a quarter of a peck of ſmelts, half an ounce of pepper, half an ounce of nutmeg, a quarter of an ounce of mace, half an ounce of ſalt-petre, a quarter of a pound of common ſalt, beat all very fine, waſh and clean the ſmelts, gut them, then lay them in rows in a jar, and between every layer of ſmelts ſtrew the ſeaſoning with four or five bay-leaves, then boil red wine, and pour over enough to cover them. Cover them with a plate, and when cold tie them down cloſe. They exceed anchovies.

To make Vermicelli.

MIX yolks of eggs and flour together in a pretty ſtiff paſte, ſo as you can work it up cleverly, and roll it as thin as it is poſſible to roll the paſte. Let it dry in the ſun; when it is quite dry, with a very ſharp knife cut it as thin as poſſible, and keep it in a dry place. It will run up like little worms, as vermicelli does; though the beſt way is to run it through a coarſe ſieve whilſt the paſte is ſoft. If you want ſome to be made in haſte, dry it by the fire, and cut it ſmall. It will dry by the fire in a quarter of an hour. This far exceeds what comes from abroad, being freſher.

To make Catchup.

TAKE the large flaps of muſhrooms gathered dry, and bruiſe them; put ſome at the bottom of an earthen pan; ſtrew ſome ſalt over, then muſhrooms, then ſalt, till you have done. Put in half an ounce of cloves and mace, and the like of all-ſpice. Let them ſtand ſix days, ſtir them up every day, then ſend them to the oven, and bake them gently for four hours. Take them out, and ſtrain the liquor through a cloth or fine ſieve. To every gallon of liquor add a quart of red wine. If not ſalt enough, add a little more, a race or two of ginger cut ſmall; boil it till one quart is waſted; ſtrain it into a pan, and let it be cold. Pour it from the ſettlings; bottle it, and cork it tight.

Another Way to make Catchup.

TAKE the large flaps and ſalt them as above; boil the liquor, ſtrain it through a thick flannel bag; to a quart of that liquor put a quart of ſtale beer, a large ſtick of horſe-radiſh cut in little ſlips, five or ſix bay-leaves, an onion ſtuck with twenty or thirty cloves, a quarter of an ounce of mace, a quarter of an ounce of nutmegs beat, a quarter of an ounce of black and white pepper, a quarter of an ounce of all-ſpice, and four or five races of ginger. Cover it cloſe, and let it ſimmer very ſoftly till about one-third is waſted; then ſtrain it through a flannel bag: when it is cold, bottle it in pint bottles, cork it

 cloſe,

close, and it will keep a great while. The other receipt you have in the Chapter for the Sea.

Artichokes to keep all the Year.

BOIL as many artichokes as you intend to keep; boil them so as just the leaves will come out; then pull off all the leaves and choke, cut them from the strings, lay them on a tin plate, and put them in an oven where tarts are drawn; let them stand till the oven is heated again, take them out before the wood is put in, and set them in again after the tarts are drawn; so do till they are as dry as a board, then put them in a paper bag, and hang them in a dry place. You should lay them in warm water three or four hours before you use them, shifting the water often. Let the last water be boiling hot. They will be very tender, and eat as fine as fresh ones. You need not dry all your bottoms at once, as the leaves are good to eat; so boil a dozen at a time, and save the bottoms for this use.

Artichokes preserved the Spanish Way.

TAKE the largest you can get, cut the tops of the leaves off, wash them well and drain them; to every artichoke, pour in a large spoonful of oil; season with pepper and salt. Send them to the oven, and bake them, they will keep a year.

N. B. The Italians, French, Portuguese, and Spaniards have variety of ways of dressing fish, which we have not, *viz.* As making fish-soups, ragoos, pies, &c. For their soups they use no gravy, nor in their sauces, thinking it improper to mix flesh and fish together; but make their fish-soups with fish, viz. either of craw-fish, lobsters, &c. taking only the juice of them. For example: take your craw-fish, tie them up in a muslin rag, and boil them; then press out their juice for the above-said use.

To keep French Beans all the Year.

TAKE fine young beans, gather them on a very fine day, have a large stone jar ready, clean and dry, lay a layer of salt at the bottom, and then a layer of beans, then salt, and then beans, and so on till the jar is full; cover them with salt, tie a coarse cloth over them, and a board on that, and then a weight to keep it close from all air; set them in a dry cellar; and when you use them, cover them close again; wash them you took out very clean, and let them lie in soft water twenty-four hours, shifting the water often; when you boil them, do not put any salt in the water. The best way of dressing them is, boil them with just the white heart of a small cabbage, then drain them, chop the cabbage, and put both into a sauce-pan with a piece of butter as big as an egg, rolled in flour; shake a little pepper,

pepper, put in a quarter of a pint of good gravy, let them stew ten minutes, and then dish them up for a side-dish. A pint of beans to the cabbage. You may do more or less, just as you please.

To keep Green Peas till Christmas.

TAKE fine young peas, shell them, throw them into boiling water with some salt in, let them boil five or six minutes, throw them into a cullender to drain; then lay a cloth four or five times double on a table, and spread them on; dry them very well, and have your bottles ready, fill them and cover them with mutton-fat tried; when it is a little cool, fill the necks almost to the top, cork them, tie a bladder and a lath over them, and set them in a cool dry place. When you use them, boil your water, put in a little salt, some sugar, and a piece of butter; when they are boiled enough, throw them into a sieve to drain; then put them into a sauce-pan with a good piece of butter, keep shaking it round all the time till the butter is melted, then turn them into a dish, and send them to table.

Another Way to preserve Green Peas.

GATHER your peas on a very dry day, when they are neither old, nor too young, shell them, and have ready some well dried quart bottles with little mouths; fill the bottles and cork them well, have ready a pipkin of rosin melted, into which dip the necks of the bottles, and set them in a very dry place that is cool.

To keep Green Peas, Beans, &c. and Fruit, fresh and good till Christmas.

OBSERVE to gather all your things on a fine clear day, in the increase or full moon; take well-glazed earthen or stone pots quite new, that have not been laid in water, wipe them clean, lay in your fruit very carefully, and take great care none is bruised or damaged in the least, nor too ripe, but just in their prime; stop down the jar close, and pitch it, and tie a leather over. Do kidney-beans the same; bury two feet deep in the earth, and keep them there till you have occasion for them. Do peas and beans the same way, only keep them in the pods, and do not let your peas be either too young or too old; the one will run to water, and the other the worm will eat; as to the two latter, lay a layer of fine writing-sand, and a layer of pods, and so on till full; the rest as above. Flowers you may keep the same way.

To keep Green Gooseberries till Christmas.

PICK your large green gooseberries on a dry day, have ready your bottles clean and dry, fill the bottles, and cork them, set them in a kettle of water up to the neck, let the water boil very ſoftly till you find the gooſeberries are coddled, take them out, and put in the reſt of the bottles till all are done; then have ready ſome roſin melted in a pipkin, dip the necks of the bottles in, and that will keep all air from coming at the cork, keep them in a cold dry place where no damp is, and they will bake as red as a cherry. You may keep them without ſcalding, but then the ſkins will not be ſo tender, nor bake ſo fine.

To keep Red Gooſeberries.

PICK them when full ripe; to each quart of gooſeberries put a quarter of a pound of Liſbon ſugar, and to each quarter of a pound of ſugar put a quarter of a pint of water; let it boil, then put in your gooſeberries, and let them boil ſoftly two or three minutes, then pour them into little ſtone jars; when cold, cover them up, and keep them for uſe; they make fine pies with little trouble. You may preſs them through a cullender; to a quart of pulp put half a pound of fine Liſbon ſugar, keep ſtirring over the fire till both be well mixed and boiled, and pour it into a ſtone jar; when cold, cover it with white paper, and it makes very pretty tarts or puffs.

To keep Walnuts all the Year.

TAKE a large jar, a layer of ſea-ſand at the bottom, then a layer of walnuts, then ſand, then the nuts, and ſo on till the jar is full; and be ſure they do not touch each other in any of the layers. When you would uſe them, lay them in warm water for an hour, ſhift the water as it cools; then rub them dry, and they will peel well and eat ſweet. Lemons will keep thus covered better than any other way.

Another Way to keep Lemons.

TAKE the fine large fruit that are quite ſound and good, and take a fine packthread about a quarter of a yard long, run it through the hard nib at the end of the lemon; then tie the ſtring together, and hang it on a little hook in an airy dry place; ſo do as many as you pleaſe; but be ſure they do not touch one another, nor any thing elſe, but hang as high as you can. Thus you may keep pears, &c. only tying the ſtring to the ſtalk.

To keep White Bullice, Pear Plums, or Damſins, &c. for Tarts or Pies.

GATHER them when full grown, and juſt as they begin to turn. Pick all the largeſt out, ſave about two-thirds of the fruit, the other third put as much water to as you think will cover the reſt. Let them boil, and ſkim them; when the fruit is is boiled very ſoft, then ſtrain it through a coarſe hair ſieve; and to every quart of this liquor put a pound and a half of ſugar, boil it, and ſkim it very well; then throw in your fruit, juſt give them a ſcald; take them off the fire, and when cold, put them into bottles with wide mouths; pour your ſyrup over them, lay a piece of white paper over them, and cover them with oil. Be ſure to take the oil well off when you uſe them, and do not put them in larger bottles than you think you ſhall make uſe of at a time, becauſe all theſe ſorts of fruits ſpoil with the air.

To make Sour Crout.

TAKE your fine hard white cabbage, cut them very ſmall, have a tub on purpoſe with the head out, according to the quantity you intend to make; put them in the tub; to every four or five cabbages throw in a large handful of ſalt; when you have done as many as you intend, lay a very heavy weight on them to preſs them down as flat as poſſible, throw a cloth on them, and lay on the cover; let them ſtand a month, then you may begin to uſe it. It will keep twelve months; but be ſure to keep it always cloſe covered, and the weight on it; if you throw a few carraway-ſeeds pounded fine amongſt it, they give it a fine flavour. The way to dreſs it is with a fine fat piece of beef ſtewed together. It is a diſh much made uſe of amongſt the Germans, and in the North Countries, where the froſt kills all the cabbages; therefore they preſerve them in this manner before the froſt takes them. Cabbage-ſtalks, caulliflower-ſtalks, and artichoke-ſtalks, peeled, and cut fine down in the ſame manner, are very good.

To raiſe Muſhrooms.

COVER an old hot-bed three or four inches thick with fine garden mould, and cover that three or four inches thick with mouldy long muck, of a horſe muck-hill, or old rotten ſtubble; when the bed has lain ſome time thus prepared, boil any muſhrooms that are not fit for uſe, in water, and throw the water on your prepared bed; in a day or two after, you will have the beſt ſmall button muſhrooms.

To make Vinegar.

TO every gallon of water put a pound of coarſe Liſbon ſugar, let it boil, and keep ſkimming it as long as the ſcum riſes; then pour it into tubs, and when it is as cold as beer to work, toaſt a good toaſt, and rub it over with yeaſt. Let it work twenty-four hours; then have ready a veſſel iron-hooped, and well painted, fixed in a place where the ſun has full power, and fix it ſo as not to have any occaſion to move it. When you draw it off, then fill your veſſels, lay a tile on the bung to keep the duſt out. Make it in March, and it will be fit to uſe in

 June

June or July. Draw it off into little ftone bottles the latter end of June or beginning of July, let it ftand till you want to ufe it, and it will never foul any more; but when you go to draw it off, and you find it is not four enough, let it ftand a month longer before you draw it off. For pickles to go abroad ufe this vinegar alone; but in England you will be obliged, when you pickle, to put one half cold fpring-water to it, and then it will be full four with this vinegar. You need not boil it, unlefs you pleafe, for almoft any fort of pickles; it will keep them quite good. It will keep walnuts very fine without boiling, even to go to the Indies; but then do not put water to it. For green pickles, you may pour it fcalding hot on two or three times. All other fort of pickles you need not boil it. Mufhrooms only wafh them clean, dry them, put them into little bottles, with a nutmeg juft fcalded in vinegar, and fliced (whilft it is hot) very thin, and a few blades of mace; then fill up the bottle with the cold vinegar and fpring-water, pour the mutton fat tried over it, and tie a bladder and leather over the top. Thefe mufhrooms will not be fo white, but as finely tafted as if they were juft gathered; and a fpoonful of this pickle will give fauce a very fine flavour. White walnuts, fuckers, and onions, and all white pickles, do in the fame manner, after they are ready for the pickle.

CHAP. XXV.

DISTILLING.

To diftil Walnut-Water.

TAKE a peck of fine green walnuts, bruife them well in a large mortar, put them in a pan, with a handful of baum bruifed, put two quarts of good French brandy to them, cover them clofe, and let them lie three days; the next day diftil them in cold ftill; from this quantity draw three quarts, which you may do in a day.

To diftil Red Rofe Buds.

WET your rofes in fair water; four gallons of rofes will take near two gallons of water; then ftill them in a cold ftill; take the fame ftilled water, and put into it as many frefh rofes as it will wet, then ftill them again.

Mint, baum, parfley, and penny-royal water, diftil the fame way.

How

How to use this Ordinary Still.

YOU muſt lay the plate, then wood aſhes thick at the bottom, then the iron pan, which you are to fill with your walnuts and liquor; then put on the head of the ſtill; make a pretty briſk fire till the ſtill begins to drop, then ſlacken it ſo as juſt to have enough to keep the ſtill at work. Mind to keep a wet cloth all over the head of the ſtill all the time it is at work, and always obſerve not to let the ſtill work longer than the liquor is good, and take great care you do not burn the ſtill; and thus you may diſtil what you pleaſe. If you draw the ſtill too far it will burn, and give your liquor a bad taſte.

To make Treacle-Water.

TAKE the juice of green walnuts, four pounds of rue, carduus, marigold, and baum, of each three pounds, roots of butter-bur half a pound, roots of burdock one pound, angelica and maſter-wort, of each half a pound, leaves of ſcordium ſix handfuls, Venice treacle and mithridate, of each half a pound, old Canary wine two pounds, white wine vinegar ſix pounds, juice of lemon ſix pounds; and diſtil this in an alembic.

To diſtil Treacle-Water Lady Monmouth's Way.

TAKE three ounces of hartſhorn, ſhaved and boiled in borage-water, or ſuccory, wood-ſorrel or reſpice-water, or three pints of any of theſe waters boiled to a jelly; and put the jelly and hartſhorn both into the ſtill, and add a pint more of theſe waters when you put it into the ſtill; take the roots of elecampane, gentian, cypreſs tuninſil, of each an ounce; bleſſed thiſtle, called carduus, and angelica, of each an ounce; ſorrel-roots two ounces; baum, ſweet-marjoram, and burnet, of each half a handful; lily-comvally flowers, borage, bugloſs, roſemary, and marigold-flowers, of each two ounces; citron-rinds, carduus-ſeeds, and citron-ſeeds, alkermes berries, and cochineal, each of theſe an ounce.

Prepare all theſe Simples thus:

GATHER the flowers as they come in ſeaſon, and put them in glaſſes with a large mouth, and put with them as much good ſack as will cover them, and tie up the glaſſes cloſe with bladders wet in the ſack, with a cork and leather tied upon it cloſe, adding more flowers and ſack as occaſion is; and when one glaſs is full, take another, till you have your quantity of flowers to diſtil; put cochineal into a pint bottle, with half a pint of ſack, and tie it up cloſe with a bladder under the cork, and another on the top, wet with ſack, tied up cloſe with brown thread;

and then cover it up close with leather, and bury it standing upright in a bed of hot horse-dung for nine or ten days; look at it, and if dissolved, take it out of the dung, but do not open it till you distil; slice all the roses, beat the seeds and the alkermes berries, and put them into another glass; amongst all, put no more sack than needs; and when you intend to distil, take a pound of the best Venice treacle and dissolve it in six pints of the best white wine, and three of red rose-water; and put all the ingredients into a bason, and stir them all together, and distil them in a glass still, balneum Mariæ; open not the ingredients till the same day you distil.

To make Black Cherry Water.

TAKE six pounds of black cherries and bruise them small; then put to them the tops of rosemary, sweet marjoram, spearmint, angelica, baum, marigold flowers, of each a handful, dried violets one ounce, anise-seeds and sweet fennel-seeds, of each half an ounce bruised; cut the herbs small, mix all together, and distil them off in a cold still.

To make Hysterical Water.

TAKE betony, roots of lovage, seeds of wild parsnips, of each two ounces; roots of single-piony four ounces, of misletoe of the oak three ounces, myrrh a quarter of an ounce, castor half an ounce; beat all these together, and add to them a quarter of a pound of dried millepedes: pour on these, three quarts of mugwort-water, and two quarts of brandy; let them stand in a close vessel eight days, then distil it in a cold still pasted up. You may draw nine pints of water, and sweeten it to your taste. Mix all together, and bottle it up.

To make Plague-Water.

Roots.	Flowers.	Seeds.
Angelica,	Wormwood,	Hart's tongue,
Dragon,	Succory,	Horehound,
Maywort,	Hysop,	Fennel,
Mint,	Agrimony,	Melilot,
Rue,	Fennel,	St. John's wort,
Carduus,	Cowslips,	Comfrey,
Origany,	Poppies,	Feverfew,
Winter-savoury,	Plaintain,	Red rose leaves,
Broad thyme,	Setfoyl,	Wood-sorrel,
Rosemary,	Vocvain,	Pellitory of the wall,
Pimpernell,	Maidenhair,	Heart's ease,
Sage,	Motherwort,	Centaury,
Fumitory,	Cowage,	Sea-drink, a good handful of
Coltsfoot,	Golden-rod,	each of the aforesaid things.

Scabeous,

Roots.	Flowers.	Seeds.
Scabeous,	Gromwell,	Gentian-root,
Borrage,	Dill.	Dock-root,
Saxafrage,		Butterbur-root,
Betony,		Piony-root,
Liverwort,		Bay-berries,
Germander.		Juniper-berries, of each of these a pound.

One ounce of nutmegs, one ounce of cloves, and half an ounce of mace; pick the herbs and flowers, and ſhred them a little. Cut the roots, bruiſe the berries, and pound the ſpices fine; take a peck of green walnuts and chop them ſmall; mix all theſe together, and lay them to ſteep in ſack lees, or any white wine lees, if not in good ſpirits; but wine lees are beſt. Let them lie a week, or better; be ſure to ſtir them once a day with a ſtick, and keep them cloſe covered, then ſtill them in an alembic with a ſlow fire, and take care your ſtill does not burn. The firſt, ſecond, and third running is good, and ſome of the fourth. Let them ſtand till cold, and then put them together.

To make Surfeit-Water.

YOU muſt take ſcurvy-graſs, brook-lime, water-creſſes, Roman wormwood, rue, mint, baum, ſage, clivers, of each one handful; green merery two handfuls; poppies, if freſh half a peck, if dry a quarter of a peck; cochineal, ſix pennyworth, ſaffron, ſix pennyworth; aniſe-ſeeds, carraway-ſeeds, coriander-ſeeds, cardamom-ſeeds, of each an ounce; liquorice two ounces ſcraped, figs ſplit a pound, raiſins of the ſun ſtoned a pound, juniper-berries an ounce bruiſed, nutmeg an ounce beat, mace an ounce bruiſed, ſweet fennel-ſeeds an ounce bruiſed, a few flowers of roſemary, marigold and ſage-flowers; put all theſe into a large ſtone-jar, and put to them three gallons of French brandy; cover it cloſe, and let it ſtand near the fire for three weeks. Stir it three times a week, and be ſure to keep it cloſe ſtopped, and then ſtrain it off; bottle your liquor, and pour on the ingredients a gallon more of French brandy. Let it ſtand a week, ſtirring it once a day, then diſtil it in a cold ſtill, and this will make a fine white ſurfeit-water. You may make this water at any time of the year, if you live at London, becauſe the ingredients are always to be had either green or dry; but it is the beſt made in ſummer.

To make Milk-Water.

TAKE two good handfuls of wormwood, as much carduus, as much rue, four handfuls of mint, as much baum, half as much

much angelica; cut these a little, put them into a cold ſtill, and put to them three quarts of milk. Let your fire be quick till your ſtill drops, and then ſlacken your fire. You may draw off two quarts. The firſt quart will keep all the year.

Another Way.

TAKE the herbs agrimony, endive, fumitory, baum, elder-flowers, white-nettles, water-creſſes, bank-creſſes, ſage, each three handfuls; eye-bright, brook-lime, and celandine, each two handfuls; the roſes of yellow dock, red madder, fennel, horſe-radiſh, and liquorice, each three ounces; raiſins ſtoned, one pound; nutmegs ſliced, Winter's bark, turmerick, galangal, each two drachms; carraway and fennel ſeeds three ounces, one gallon of milk. Diſtil all with a gentle fire in one day. You may add a handful of May wormwood.

The Stag's Hart Water.

TAKE baum four handfuls, ſweet-marjoram one handful, roſemary flowers, clove giliflowers dried, dried roſe-buds, borage flowers, of each an ounce; marigold flowers half an ounce, lemon-peel two ounces, mace and cardamum, of each thirty grains; of cinnamon ſixty grains, or yellow and white ſanders, of each a quarter of an ounce, ſhavings of hartſhorn, an ounce; take nine oranges, and put in the peel, then cut them in ſmall pieces; pour upon theſe two quarts of the beſt Rheniſh, or the beſt white wine; let it infuſe three or four days, being very cloſe ſtopped in a cellar or cool place: if it infuſe nine or ten days, it is the better. Take a ſtag's heart and cut off all the fat, and cut it very ſmall, and pour in ſo much Rheniſh or white wine as will cover it; let it ſtand all night cloſe covered in a cool place; the next day add the aforeſaid things to it, mixing it very well together; adding to it a pint of the beſt roſe-water, and a pint of the juice of celandine: if you pleaſe, you may put in ten grains of ſaffron, and ſo put it in a glaſs ſtill, diſtilling in water, raiſing it well to keep in the ſteam, both of the ſtill and receiver.

To make Angelica Water.

TAKE eight handfuls of the leaves, waſh and cut them, and lay them on a table to dry; when they are dry, put them into an earthen pot, and put to them four quarts of ſtrong wine lees; let it ſtay for twenty-four hours, but ſtir it twice in the time; then put it into a warm ſtill or an alembic, and draw it off; cover your bottles with a paper, and prick holes in it; let it ſtand two or three days, then mingle it all together, and ſweeten it; and when it is ſettled, bottle it up and ſtop it cloſe.

To

To make Cordial Poppy Water.

TAKE two gallons of very good brandy, and a peck of poppies, and put them together in a wide-mouthed glaſs, and let them ſtand forty-eight hours, and then ſtrain the poppies out; take a pound of raiſins of the ſun, ſtone them, and an ounce of coriander-ſeeds, an ounce of ſweet-fennel ſeeds, and an ounce of liquorice ſliced, bruiſe them all together, and put them into the brandy, with a pound of good powder-ſugar, and let them ſtand four or eight weeks, ſhaking it every day; and then ſtrain it off, and bottle it cloſe up for uſe.

[How to diſtil Vinegar is in the Chapter of Pickles.]

CHAP. XXVI.

Neceſſary Directions whereby the Reader may eaſily attain the polite and uſeful ART of CARVING.

To cut up a Turkey.

RAISE the leg, open the joint, but be ſure not to take off the leg; lace down both ſides of the breaſt, and open the pinion of the breaſt, but do not take it off; raiſe the merry-thought between the breaſt-bone and the top; raiſe the brawn, and turn it outward on both ſides, but be careful not to cut it off, nor break it; divide the wing pinions from the joint next the body, and ſtick each pinion where the brawn was turned out; cut off the ſharp end of the pinion, and the middle-piece will fit the place exactly. A buſtard, capon, or pheaſant, is cut up in the ſame manner.

To rear a Gooſe.

CUT off both legs in the manner of ſhoulders of lamb; take off the belly-piece cloſe to the extremity of the breaſt; lace the gooſe down both ſides of the breaſt, about half an inch from the ſharp bone: divide the pinions and the fleſh firſt laced with your knife, which muſt be raiſed from the bone, and taken off with the pinion from the body; then cut off the merry-thought, and cut another ſlice from the breaſt-bone, quite through; laſtly, turn up the carcaſe, cutting it aſunder, the back above the loin-bones.

To unbrace a Mallard or Duck.

FIRST, raiſe the pinions and legs, but cut them not off; then raiſe the merry-thought from the breaſt, and lace it down both ſides with your knife.

To

To unlace a Coney.

THE back muſt be turned downward, and the apron divided from the belly; this done, ſlip in your knife between the kidneys, looſening the fleſh on each ſide; then turn the belly, cut the back croſs-ways between the wings, draw your knife down both ſides of the back-bone, dividing the ſides and leg from the back. Obſerve not to pull the leg too violently from the bone when you open the ſide, but with great exactneſs lay open the ſides from the ſcut to the ſhoulder; and then put the legs together.

To wing a Partridge or Quail.

AFTER having raiſed the legs and wings, uſe ſalt and powdered ginger for ſauce.

To allay a Pheaſant or Teal.

THIS differs in nothing from the foregoing, but that you muſt uſe ſalt only for ſauce.

To diſmember a Hern.

CUT off the legs, lace the breaſt down each ſide, and open the breaſt-pinion, without cutting it off; raiſe the merry-thought between the breaſt-bone and the top of it; then raiſe the brawn, turning it outward on both ſides; but break it not, nor cut it off; ſever the wing-pinion from the joint neareſt the body, ſticking the pinions in the place where the brawn was; remember to cut off the ſharp end of the pinion, and ſupply the place with the middle-piece.

In this manner ſome people cut up a capon or pheaſant, and likewiſe a bittern, uſing no ſauce but ſalt.

To thigh a Woodcock.

THE legs and wings muſt be raiſed in the manner of a fowl, only open the head for the brains. And ſo you thigh curlews, plover, or ſnipe, uſing no ſauce but ſalt.

To diſplay a Crane.

AFTER his legs are unfolded, cut off the wings; take them up, and ſauce them with powdered ginger, vinegar, ſalt, and muſtard.

To lift a Swan.

SLIT it fairly down the middle of the breaſt, clean through the back, from the neck to the rump; divide it in two parts, neither breaking nor tearing the fleſh; then lay the halves in a charger, the ſlit ſides downwards; throw ſalt upon it, and ſet it again on the table. The ſauce muſt be chaldron ſerved up in ſaucers.

CHAP.

CHAP. XXVII.

MISCELLANEOUS.

Containing many uſeful MEDICAL and other FAMILY RECEIPTS.

A certain Cure for the Bite of a Mad Dog.

LET the patient be blooded at the arm nine or ten ounces. Take of the herb called in Latin *lichen cinereus terreſtris*, in Engliſh, aſh-coloured, ground liverwort, cleaned, dried, and powdered, half an ounce. Of black pepper, powdered, two drachms. Mix theſe well together, and divide the powder into four doſes, one of which muſt be taken every morning faſting, for four mornings ſucceſſively, in half a pint of cow's milk warm. After theſe four doſes are taken, the patient muſt go into the cold bath, or a cold ſpring or river every morning faſting for a month. He muſt be dipped all over, but not to ſtay in (with his head above water) longer than half a minute, if the water be very cold. After this he muſt go in three times a week for a fortnight longer.

N. B.—The lichen is a very common herb, and grows generally in ſandy and barren ſoils all over England. The right time to gather it is in the months of October and November. [*D. Mead.*]

Another Cure for the Bite of a Mad Dog.

FOR the bite of a mad dog, for either man or beaſt, take ſix ounces of rue clean picked and bruiſed, four ounces of garlic peeled and bruiſed, four ounces of Venice treacle, and four ounces of filed pewter, or ſcraped tin. Boil theſe in two quarts of the beſt ale, in a pan covered cloſe, over a gentle fire, for the ſpace of an hour; then ſtrain the ingredients from the liquor. Give eight or nine ſpoonfuls of it warm to a man, or a woman, three mornings faſting. Eight or nine ſpoonfuls is ſufficient for the ſtrongeſt; a leſſer quantity to thoſe younger, or of a weaker conſtitution, as you may judge of their ſtrength. Ten or twelve ſpoonfuls for a horſe or a bullock; three, four, or five to a ſheep, hog, or dog. This muſt be given within nine days after the bite: it ſeldom fails in man or beaſt. If you bind ſome of the ingredients on the wound, it will be ſo much the better.

Receipt againſt the Plague.

TAKE of rue, ſage, mint, roſemary, wormwood, and lavender, a handful of each; infuſe them together in a gallon of white wine vinegar, put the whole into a ſtone pot, cloſely covered up, upon warm wood-aſhes for four days, after which draw off (or ſtrain through fine flannel) the liquid, and put it into bottles well corked; and into every quart bottle put a quarter of an ounce of camphor: with this preparation waſh your mouth, and rub your loins and your temples every day; ſnuff a little up your noſtrils when you go into the air, and carry about you a bit of ſpunge dipped in the ſame, in order to ſmell to upon all occaſions, eſpecially when you are near any place or perſon that is infected. They write, that four malefactors, (who had robbed the infected houſes, and murdered the people during the courſe of the plague,) owned, when they came to the gallows, that they had preſerved themſelves from the contagion by uſing the above medicine only: and that they went the whole time from houſe to houſe without any fear of the diſtemper.

To make a fine Bitter.

TAKE an ounce of the fineſt Jeſuit powder, half a quarter of an ounce of ſnake-root powder, half a quarter of an ounce of ſalt of wormwood, half a quarter of ſaffron, half a quarter of cochineal; put it into a quart of the beſt brandy, and let it ſtand twenty-four hours; every now and then ſhaking the bottle.

For a Conſumption; an approved Receipt, by a Lady at Paddington.

TAKE the yolk of a new laid egg, beat it up well with three large ſpoonfuls of roſe water; mix it well in half a pint of new milk from the cow, ſweeten it well with ſirup de capillaire, and grate ſome nutmeg in it. Drink it every morning faſting for a month, and refrain from ſpirituous liquors of any kind.

N. B. Mr. Powel, who kept the Crown, a public houſe in Swallow-ſtreet, St. James's, was in ſo deep a decline as to be ſcarce able to walk; when he coughed, the phlegm he brought from his ſtomach was green and yellow; and he was given over by his phyſician, who, as the laſt reſource, adviſed him to go into the country to try what the air would do. He happily went to lodge at Paddington: the woman of the houſe underſtanding his condition, recollected that an old lady, who had lodged in the ſame houſe, had left a book with a collection of receipts in it for various diſorders, inſtantly fetched it, and found the foregoing, which he having ſtrictly followed, found himſelf much better in a fortnight; and, by continuing the ſame, in leſs than a month he began to have an appetite, and with the bleſſing of God, in a ſhort time, by degrees he recovered his health, to the aſtoniſhment and ſurpriſe of all who knew him, and declared to me he was as well and hearty as ever he was in his life, and did not ſcruple to tell every perſon the means and method of his recovery.

N. B. This receipt I had from his own mouth.

To

To stop a violent Purging, or the Flux.

TAKE a third part of a gill of the very best double distilled anise-seeds; grate a third part of a large nutmeg into it. To be taken the same quantity an hour after breakfast, one hour after dinner, and, if occasion, an hour before going to bed. *Probatum est.*

For Obstructions in Females.

SUCCOTORINE aloes, one ounce; cardamum-seed, a quarter of an ounce; snake-root, a quarter of an ounce; gum-myrrh, a quarter of an ounce; saffron, a quarter of an ounce; cochineal, two scruples; zedoary, two scruples; rhubarb, two scruples: let these drugs be well beaten in a mortar, and put them into a large bottle; add thereto a pint and a half of mountain wine; place it near the fire for the space of three days and nights, shaking it often. Let the patient take a small tea-cup-full twice a week in the morning, an hour before rising.

Another for Obstructions.

THREE pennyworth of alkermes, two pennyworth of Venice treacle, and a quarter of an ounce of spermaceti; to be made into four boluses, one to be taken every evening going to bed.

Half a pint of pennyroyal-water, a quarter of a pint of hysteric-water, and a quarter of a pint of pepper-mint-water; to be taken every morning and evening, a tea-cup full.

For a Hoarseness.

TWO ounces of pennyroyal-water, the yolk of a new laid egg beaten, thirty drops of cochineal, twenty drops of oil of anise-seed, mixed well and sweetened with white sugar candy. A large spoonful to be taken night and morning.

Lozenges for the Heart-burn.

TAKE one pound of chalk, beat it to a powder in a mortar, with one pound and a half of white loaf-sugar, and one ounce of bole-ammoniac; mix them well together, and put in something to moisten them, to make it of a proper consistency or paste; make them into small lozenges, and let them lie in a band-box on the top of an oven a week or more to dry, shaking the box sometimes.

Lozenges for a Cold.

TAKE two pounds of common white loaf-sugar, beat it well in a mortar, dissolve six ounces of Spanish liquorice in a little warm water; one ounce of gum-arabic dissolved likewise; add thereto a little oil of anise-seed; mix them well to a proper consistency, and cut them into small lozenges; let them lie in a band box on the top of an oven a considerable time to dry, shaking the box sometimes.

The genuine Receipt to make Turlington's Balsam.

BALSAM of Peru, one ounce; best storax, two ounces; benjamin, impregnated with sweet almonds, three ounces; aloes Succotorine, myrrh elect, purest frankincense, roots of angelica, flowers of St. John's wort, of each of these half an ounce; beat the drugs well in a mortar, and put them into a large glass bottle; add thereto a pint, or rather more, of the best spirits of wine, and let the bottle stand by the kitchen fire, or in the chimney-corner, two days and two nights; then decant it off in small bottles for use, and let them be well corked and sealed.

N. B. The same quantity of spirits of wine poured on the ingredients, letting them stand by the fire, or in some warm place for the space of six days and nights, will serve for common use; pour off the same in small bottles, and let them be well corked and sealed.

How to keep clear from Bugs.

FIRST take out of your room all silver and gold lace, then set the chairs about the room, shut up your windows and doors, tack a blanket over each window, and before the chimney, and over the doors of the room, set open all closets and cupboard doors, all your drawers and boxes, hang the rest of your bedding on the chair-backs, lay the feather-bed on a table, then set a large broad earthen pan in the middle of the room, and in that set a chafing-dish that stands on feet, full of charcoal well lighted; if your room is very bad, a pound of rolled brimstone; if only a few, half a pound; lay it on the charcoal, and get out of the room as quick as possibly you can, or it will take away your breath: shut your door close, with the blanket over it, and be sure to set it so as nothing can catch fire: if you have any India pepper, throw it in with the brimstone. You must take great care to have the door open whilst you lay in the brimstone, that you may get out as soon as possible. Do not open the door under six hours, and then you must be very careful how you go in to open the windows: then brush and sweep your room very clean; wash it well with boiling lee, or boiling water with a little unslacked lime in it; get a pint of spirits of wine, a pint of spirits of turpentine, and an ounce of camphire, shake all well together, and with a bunch of feathers wash your bedstead very well, and sprinkle the rest over the feather-bed and about the room.

If

If you find great ſwarms about the room, and ſome not dead, do this over again, and you will be quite clear. Every ſpring and fall waſh your bedſtead with half a pint, and you will never have a bug; but if you find any come in with new goods or boxes, &c. only waſh your bedſtead, and ſprinkle all over your bedding and bed, and you will be clear; but be ſure to do it as ſoon as you find one. If your room is very bad, it will be well to paint the room after the brimſtone is burnt in it.

This never fails, if rightly done.

An effectual Way to clear your Bedſtead of Bugs.

TAKE quickſilver and mix it well in a mortar with the white of an egg till the quickſilver is all well mixed, and there are no bubbles; then beat up ſome white of an egg very fine, and mix with the quickſilver till it is like a fine ointment, then with a feather anoint the bedſtead all over in every creek and corner, and about the lacing and binding, where you think there is any. Do this two or three times: it is a certain cure, and will not ſpoil any thing.

DIRECTIONS *to the* HOUSEMAID.

ALWAYS when you ſweep a room, throw a little wet ſand all over it, and that will gather up all the flew and duſt, prevent it from riſing, clean the boards, and ſave the bedding, pictures, and all other furniture from duſt or dirt.

How to make Yellow Varniſh.

TAKE a quart of ſpirit of wine, and put to it eight ounces of ſandarach, ſhake it half an hour; next day it will be fit for uſe, but ſtrain it firſt: take lamp-black, and put in your varniſh about the thickneſs of a pancake; mix it well, but ſtir it not too faſt; then do it eight times over, and let it ſtand ſtill the next day; then take ſome burnt ivory, and oil of turpentine as fine as butter; then mix it with ſome of your varniſh, till you have varniſhed it fit for poliſhing; then poliſh it with tripoly in fine flour; then lay it on the wood ſmooth, with one of the bruſhes, then let it dry, and do it ſo eight times at the leaſt; when it is very dry, lay on your varniſh that is mixed, and when it is dry, poliſh it with a wet cloth dipped in tripoly, and rub it as hard as you would do platters.

How to make a pretty Varniſh to colour little Baſkets, Bowls, or any Board where nothing hot is ſet on.

TAKE either red, black, or white wax, which colour you want to make; to every two ounces of ſealing-wax one ounce of ſpirit of wine, pound the wax fine, then ſift it through a fine lawn ſieve till you have made it extremely fine; put it into a

 large

large phial with the ſpirits of wine, ſhake it, let it ſtand within the air of the fire forty-eight hours, ſhaking it often; then with a little bruſh rub your baſkets all over with it; let it dry, and do it over a ſecond time, and it makes them look very pretty.

How to clean Gold and Silver Lace.

TAKE alabaſter finely beaten and ſearced, and put it into an earthen pipkin, and ſet it upon a chafing-diſh of coals, and let it boil for ſome time, ſtirring it often with a ſtick firſt; when it begins to boil, it will be very heavy; when it is enough, you will find it in the ſtirring very light; then take it off the fire, lay your lace upon a piece of flannel, and ſtrew your powder upon it; knock it well in with a hard cloth bruſh; when you think it is enough, bruſh the powder out with a clean bruſh.

To clean White Sattins, Flowered Silks with Gold and Silver in them.

TAKE ſtale bread crumbled very fine, mixed with powder-blue, rub it very well over the ſilk or ſattin; then ſhake it well, and with clean ſoft cloths duſt it well: if any gold or ſilver flowers, afterwards take a piece of crimſon in grain velvet, and rub the flowers with it.

To keep Arms, Iron, or Steel, from ruſting.

TAKE the filings of lead, or duſt of lead, finely beaten in an iron mortar, putting to it oil of ſpike, which will make the iron ſmell well; and if you oil your arms, or any thing that is made of iron or ſteel, you may keep them in moiſt airs from ruſting.

To take Iron-molds out of Linen.

TAKE ſorrel, bruiſe it well in a mortar, ſqueeze it through a cloth, bottle it, and keep it for uſe: take a little of the above juice, in a ſilver or tin ſauce-pan, boil it over a lamp; as it boils dip in the iron-mold, do not rub it, but only ſqueeze it; as ſoon as the iron-mold is out, throw it into cold water.

To take Iron-molds out of Linen, and Greaſe out of Woollen or Silk.—One Shilling a Bottle.

TAKE four ounces of ſpirits of turpentine, and one ounce of eſſence of lemon; mix them well together, and put it into bottles for uſe.

To prevent the Infection among Horned Cattle.

MAKE an iſſue in the dewlap, put in a peg of black hellebore, and rub all the vents both behind and before with tar.

RECEIPTS

FOR

PERFUMERY, &c.

ADVERTISEMENT.

THE following Collection of approved Receipts in Perfumery has been added to this Edition of the Art of Cookery, in order to render the Work of more extensive Utility than the former; and which, it is presumed, will be considered by the Reader as a valuable Acquisition.

RECEIPTS

FOR

PERFUMERY, &c.

To make Red, Light, or Purple Wash-Balls.

GET ſome white ſoap, beat it in a mortar; then put it into a pan, and cover it down cloſe; let the ſame be put into a copper, ſo that the water does not come to the top of the pan; then cover your copper as cloſe as you can, to ſtop the ſteam; make the water boil ſome time; take the pan out, and beat it well with a wooden ſtirrer till it is all melted with the heat of the water; then pour it out into drops, and cut them into ſquare pieces as ſmall as a walnut; let it lie three days on an oven in a band-box; afterwards put them into a pan, and damp them with roſe-water, maſh it well with your hands, and mould them according to your fancy, viz. ſqueeze them as hard and as cloſe as you poſſibly can; make them very round, and put them into a band-box or a ſieve two or three days; then ſcrape them a little with a waſh-ball ſcraper (which are made for that purpoſe), and let them lie eight or nine days; afterwards ſcrape them very ſmooth and to your mind.

N. B. If you would have them red, when you firſt maſh them, put in a little vermilion; if light, ſome hair-powder; and if purple, ſome roſe-pink.

To make Blue, Red, or Purple Waſh-Balls, or to marble Ditto.

GET ſome white ſoap and cut it into ſquare pieces about the bigneſs of dice; let it lie in a band-box or a ſieve on the top of an oven to dry; beat it in a mortar to a powder, and put it into a pan; damp it with roſe-water, mix it well with your hands, put in ſome hair-powder to make it ſtiff; then ſcent it with oil of thyme, and oil of carraways.

If you would have them blue, put in ſome powder-blue; if red, ſome vermilion; if purple, ſome roſe-pink; mix them well together with your hands, and ſqueeze them as cloſe as poſſible; make them very round, of a ſize agreeable to your mind; put them into a ſieve two or three days; then ſcrape

 them

them a little with a wash-ball scraper, and let them lie in the sieve eight or nine days; afterwards scrape them very smooth, and agreeable to your mind.

If you would have them marbled, after being scented with oil of thyme and oil of carraways (as in the first process), cut them into pieces, about as much as will make a ball each, make it into a flat square piece, then take a very thin knife, and dip it into the powder-blue, vermilion, or rose pink, (according to the colour you would fancy,) and chop it in according to your mind; double it up, make it into a hard and round ball, and use the same process as beforementioned.

White Almond Wash Balls.

TAKE some white soap and slice it thin, put it into a band-box on the top of an oven to dry, three weeks or more; when it is dry, beat it in a mortar till it is a powder; to every four ounces of soap add one ounce of hair-powder, half an ounce of white-lead; put them into a pan, and damp them with rose-water to make it of a proper consistency; make them into balls as hard and close as possible, scrape them with a ball-scraper, and use the same process as beforementioned, letting them lie three weeks in a sieve to dry; then finish them with a ball-scraper to your mind.

Brown Almond Wash-Balls.

TAKE some common brown hard soap, slice it thin, and put it into a band-box on the top of an oven to dry, for the space of three weeks, or more; when quite dry, beat it in a mortar to a powder; to every three ounces of soap add one ounce of brown almond-powder; put it in a mortar, and damp it with rose-water, to make it of a proper consistency; beat it very well, then make them into balls according to a process before-mentioned, letting them lie three weeks in a sieve to dry; then finish them with a ball-scraper, agreeable to your mind.

Windsor Soap.—Two shillings per Pound.

GET some of the whitest soap, shave it into thin slices; melt it in a stew-pan over a slow fire, and scent it very strong with oil of carraways; pour it into a drawer made for that purpose; let it stand three days or more, and cut it into square pieces to your fancy.

To make Lip Salve.

TAKE half a pound of hog's lard, put it into a pan, with one ounce and a half of virgin-wax; let it stand on a slow fire till it is melted; then take a small tin-pot, and fill it with water, and put therein some alkanet-root; let it boil till it is of a fine red

red colour; then ſtrain ſome of it, and mix it with the ingredients according to your fancy, and ſcent it with eſſence of lemon; pour it into ſmall boxes, and ſmooth the top with your finger.

N. B.—You may pour a little out firſt, to ſee if it is of a proper colour to your fancy.

To make White Lip Salve, and for chopped Hands and Face.—Six Shilings and Threepence per Pot.

MELT ſome ſpermaceti in ſweet oil; add thereto a ſmall bit of white wax; when it is melted, put in a ſmall quantity of white ſugar-candy, and ſtir it well therein; then pour it into pots for uſe.

French Rouge.—Five Shillings per Pot.

TAKE ſome carmine, and mix it with hair-powder to make it as pale as you pleaſe, according to your fancy.

Opiate for the Teeth.—Two Shillings and Sixpence per Pot.

TAKE one pound of honey, let it be very well boiled and ſkimmed, a quarter of a pound of bole-ammoniac, one ounce of dragon's-blood, one ounce of oil of ſweet almonds, half an ounce of oil of cloves, eight drops of eſſence of bergamot, one gill of honey-water; mix all well together, and pour it into pots for uſe.

Deleſcot's Opiate.

HALF an ounce of bole-ammoniac, one ounce of powder of myrrh, one ounce of dragon's-blood, half an ounce of orrice-root, half an ounce of roch-alum, half an ounce of ground ginger, two ounces of honey; mix all well together, and put it in pots for uſe.

Tooth-Powder.—One Shilling per Bottle.

BURN ſome roch-alum, and beat it in a mortar, ſift it fine; then take ſome roſe-pink, and mix them well together to make it of a pale red colour; add thereto a little powder of myrrh, and put it into bottles for uſe.

To make Shaving-Oil.—One Shilling per Bottle.

DISSOLVE a quantity of oil-ſoap, cut it into thin ſlices, in ſpirits of wine; let it ſtand a week, then put in as much ſoft-ſoap till the liquor becomes of a clammy ſubſtance: ſcent as you pleaſe, and bottle it for uſe.

To make Shaving-Powder.

TAKE ſome white-ſoap, and ſhave it in very thin ſlices; let it be well dried on the top of an oven in a band box; beat it in a mortar a mortar till it is very fine, fift it through a fine fieve, and fcent it as you pleafe.

Soap to fill Shaving-Boxes.

TAKE fome of the whiteft foap, beat it in a mortar, and fcent it with oil of carraways, make it flat; then chop in fome vermilion, or powder blue, to marble it, with a very thin knife dipt in the fame; double it up, and fqueeze it hard into the boxes; then fcrape it fmooth with a knife.

Wafh for the Face.

TAKE one quart of milk, a quarter of a pound of falt-petre beaten to a powder; put in two pennyworth of oil of anife-feed, one pennyworth of oil of cloves, about four thimbles full of the beft white wine vinegar; put it into a bottle, and let it ftand in fand half-way up, in the fun, or in fome warm place for a fortnight without the cork; afterwards cork and feal it up.

How to make Almond Milk for a Wafh.

TAKE five ounces of bitter almonds, blanch them and beat them in a marble mortar very fine; you may put in a fpoonful of fack when you beat them; then take the whites of three new-laid eggs, three pints of fpring-water, and one pint of fack. Mix them all very well together; then ftrain it through a fine cloth, and put it into a bottle, and keep it for ufe. You may put in lemon, or powder of pearl, when you make ufe of it.

An approved Method practifed by Mrs. Dukely, the Queen's Tire-Woman, to preferve Hair, and make it grow thick.

TAKE one quart of white wine, put in one handful of rofemary flowers, half a pound of honey, diftil them together; then add a quarter of a pint of oil of fweet almonds, fhake it very well together, put a little of it into a cup, warm it blood-warm, rub it well on your head, and comb it dry.

A Stick to take Hair out.

TAKE two ounces and a half of rofin, and one ounce of bees-wax; melt them together, and make them into fticks for ufe.

Liquid for the Hair.—Two Shillings a Quarter of a Pint.

To three quarts of fweet-oil, put a quarter of a pound of alkanet-root, cut in fmall pieces; let it be boiled fome time over a fteam; add thereto three ounces of oil of jeffamine, and one ounce of oil of lavender; ftrain it through a coarfe cloth, but do not fqueeze it.

To make White Almond-Paste.

TAKE one pound of bitter-almonds, blanch and beat them very fine in a mortar; put in the whites of four eggs, one ounce of French white of Trois; add some rose-water and spirits of wine, a little at a time, until it is of a consistency for paste.

To make Brown Almond-Paste.

TAKE one pound of bitter-almonds; beat them well in a mortar; add to them one pound of raisins of the sun stoned; beat and mix them very well together, and put in a little brandy.

Sweet-scented Bags to lay with Linen—At one Shilling and Sixpence, Two Shillings and Sixpence, &c. &c. &c. each Bag.

EIGHT ounces of coriander-seeds, eight ounces of sweet orrice root, eight ounces of damask-rose leaves, eight ounces of calamus-aromaticus, one ounce of mace, one ounce of cinnamon, half an ounce of cloves, four drachms of musk powder, two drachms of white loaf-sugar, three ounces of lavender-flowers, and some Roduam wood, beat them well together, and sew them up in small silk bags.

Orange-Butter.

MELT a small quantity of spermaceti in sweet-oil, and put in a little fine Dutch pink to colour it; then add a little oil of orange to scent it; and lastly, while it is very hot, put in some spirits of wine to curdle it.

Lemon-Butter.

Is made the same as orange butter, only put in no Dutch pink, and scent it with essence of lemons, instead of oil of orange.

Marecballe Powder. Sixteen Shillings per Pound.

ONE ounce of cloves, one ounce of mace, one ounce of cinnamon, beat them very well to a fine powder, add to them four pounds of hair-powder, and half a pound of Spanish burnt amber beaten very fine, a quarter of an ounce of oil of lavender, half an ounce of oil of thyme, a quarter of an ounce of essence of amber, five drops of oil of laurel, a quarter of an ounce of oil of sassafras; mix them all well together.

Virgin's Milk.—Two Shillings per Bottle.

PUT one ounce of tincture of benjamin into a pint of cold water: mix it well, and let it stand one day; then run it through a flannel-bag with some tow in it; put it in bottles for use.

Honey-Water.—One Shilling per Bottle.

ONE quart of rectified ſpirits of wine, two drachms of tincture of ambergreaſe, two drachms of tincture of muſk, half a pint of water; filter it according to your fancy, and put it into ſmall bottles.

Pearl-Water.

MIX pearl-powder with honey and lavender-water; and then the pearl-powder will never be diſcoloured.

Milk Flude Water.

ONE quart of ſpirits of wine, half an ounce of oil of cloves, one drachm of eſſence of lemons, fifteen drops of oil of Rhodium, a little cochineal in powder, to colour it of a fine pink; let it ſtand one day, then filter it, but with no water.

Beautifying-Water,

Is *balſamum coſmeticum* put into a ſmall quantity of elder-flower water.

Miſs in her Teens.

ONE quart of ſpirits of wine; eſſence of bergamot, one ounce; oil of Rhodium, two drachms; tincture of muſk, half a drachm, and half a pint of water; mix them well together, and put them into bottles for uſe.

Lady Lilley's Ball.

TAKE twelve ounces of oil-ſoap ſhaved very fine, ſpermaceti three ounces, melt them together; two ounces of bizmuth diſſolved in roſe-water for the ſpace of three hours, one ounce of oil of thyme, one ounce of the oil of carraways, one ounce of eſſence of lemons; mix all well together.

Nun's Cream.

One ounce of pearl-powder, twenty drops of oil of Rhodium, and two ounces of fine pomatum; mix all well together.

Cold Cream.

TAKE one pint of trotter-oil, a quarter of a pound of hog's-lard, one ounce of ſpermaceti, a bit of virgin-wax; warm them together with a little roſe-water, and beat it up with a whiſk.

The Ambroſia Noſegay.

TAKE one pint of ſpirits of wine, one drachm of oil of cloves, one ounce of oil of nutmegs; mix them, and filter it as you pleaſe.

Eau

Eau de Bouquet.

TAKE one quart of ſpirits of wine, half an ounce of muſk, two drachms of tincture of ſaffron, mix them well together, and let them ſtand one day; then filter it with any water.

Eau de Luce.

Two ounces of the beſt rectified ſpirits of wine, one drachm of oil of amber, two drachms of ſalt of tartar, prepared powder of amber two drachms, twenty drops of oil of nutmegs; put them all into a bottle, and ſhake it well; let it ſtand five hours, then filter it, and always keep it by you, and when you would make *eau de luce*, put it into the ſtrongeſt ſpirits of ſal-ammoniac.

Eau ſans Pareil.

ONE quart of ſpirits of wine, one ounce of eſſence of bergamot, two drachms of tincture of muſk, add to them half a pint of water, and bottle them for uſe.

Hard Pomatum.

TAKE three pounds of mutton-ſuet, boil and ſkim it well till it is quite clear, pour it off from the droſs which remains at the bottom; then add thereto eight ounces of virgin-wax, melt them together, and ſcent it with eſſence of lemon; make it into rolls according to fancy.

Soft Pomatum.

TAKE a quantity of hog's lard, boil and ſkim it very well, put in a ſmall quantity of hair-powder, when it is cool, to make it agreeable to your mind; and ſcent it with eſſence of lemons.

N. B.—You may take a ſmall quantity out firſt, and let it cool; if it is too ſoft, add a little hair-powder to make it ſtiffer.

To make Sirop de Capillaire.

PUT ſeven pounds of common lump-ſugar into a pan, and thereto add ſeven pints of water; boil it well, and keep ſkimming it; then take the white of an egg, put it in ſome water, and beat it up well with a whiſk; take the froth off and ſcatter it therein, and keep it ſkimming until it is quite clear; then add thereto half a pint of orange-flower-water; mix it well together, let it ſtand till cold, and put it into a ſtone bottle, or in bottles for uſe, let them be quite clean and dry before it is put into them, otherwiſe it will make it mothery and ſpoil it.

N. B.—If you chuſe to have it of a high colour, burn a little ſugar in a pan, of a brown colour; afterwards put a little capillaire thereto, ſtir it about with a wooden ſpoon, and mix it well with the capillaire according to your fancy.

To make Dragon-Roots.

TAKE ſome mallow-roots, ſkin them, and pick one end with a pin or needle till you have made it like a bruſh; then take ſome powder of braſil, and ſome cochineal, boil them together, and put in the roots till you think they are thoroughly dyed; then take them out, and lay them by the fire to dry.

INDEX.

INDEX.

A.

B.

Balm,

C.

F.

I.

K.

L.

M.

Moonshine,

N.

O.

P.

Q.

R.

S.

To

T.

V. U.

15

W.

Currant,

THE END.

ERRATA.

Page 150. line 11. *for* beu *read* bleu.
290. — 11. *for* callar *read* collar.
381. — 4 *from the bottom, for* mullard *read* mallard.

The Two Babylons **QTY**
Alexander Hislop

You may be surprised to learn that many traditions of Roman Catholicism in fact don't come from Christ's teachings but from an ancient Babylonian "Mystery" religion that was centered on Nimrod, his wife Semiramis, and a child Tammuz. This book shows how this ancient religion transformed itself as it incorporated Christ into its teachings....

Religion/History **Pages:358**

ISBN: ***1-59462-010-5*** *MSRP* ***$22.95***

The Power Of Concentration
Theron Q. Dumont

It is of the utmost value to learn how to concentrate. To make the greatest success of anything you must be able to concentrate your entire thought upon the idea you are working on. The person that is able to concentrate utilizes all constructive thoughts and shuts out all destructive ones...

Self Help/Inspirational **Pages:196**

ISBN: ***1-59462-141-1*** *MSRP* ***$14.95***

Rightly Dividing The Word
Clarence Larkin

The "Fundamental Doctrines" of the Christian Faith are clearly outlined in numerous books on Theology, but they are not available to the average reader and were mainly written for students. The Author has made it the work of his ministry to preach the "Fundamental Doctrines." To this end he has aimed to express them in the simplest and clearest manner..

Religion **Pages:352**

ISBN: ***1-59462-334-1*** *MSRP* ***$23.45***

The Law of Psychic Phenomena
Thomson Jay Hudson

"I do not expect this book to stand upon its literary merits; for if it is unsound in principle, felicity of diction cannot save it, and if sound, homeliness of expression cannot destroy it. My primary object in offering it to the public is to assist in bringing Psychology within the domain of the exact sciences. That this has never been accomplished..."

New Age **Pages:420**

ISBN: ***1-59462-124-1*** *MSRP* ***$29.95***

Beautiful Joe
Marshall Saunders

When Marshall visited the Moore family in 1892, she discovered Joe, a dog they had nursed back to health from his previous abusive home to live a happy life. So moved was she, that she wrote this classic masterpiece which won accolades and was recognized as a heartwarming symbol for humane animal treatment...

Fiction **Pages:256**

ISBN: ***1-59462-261-2*** *MSRP* ***$18.45***

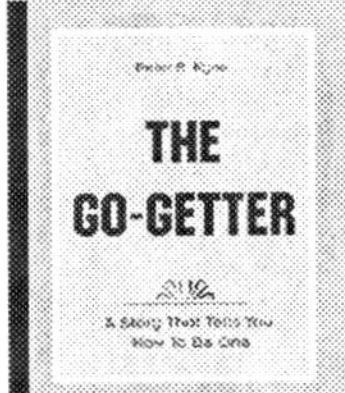

The Go-Getter
Kyne B. Peter

QTY

The Go Getter is the story of William Peck.He was a war veteran and amputee who will not be refused what he wants. Peck not only fights to find employment but continually proves himself more than competent at the many difficult test that are throw his way in the course of his early days with the Ricks Lumber Company...

Business/Self Help/Inspirational **Pages:68**

ISBN: ***1-59462-186-1*** *MSRP* ***$8.95***

Self Mastery
Emile Coue

Emile Coue came up with novel way to improve the lives of people. He was a pharmacist by trade and often saw ailing people. This lead him to develop autosuggestion, a form of self-hypnosis. At the time his theories weren't popular but over the years evidence is mounting that he was indeed right all along...

New Age/Self Help **Pages:98**

ISBN: ***1-59462-189-6*** *MSRP* ***$7.95***

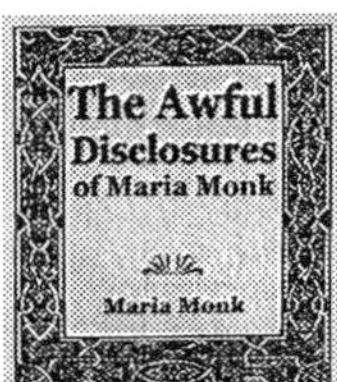

The Awful Disclosures Of Maria Monk

"I cannot banish the scenes and characters of this book from my memory. To me it can never appear like an amusing fable, or lose its interest and importance. The story is one which is continually before me, and must return fresh to my mind with painful emotions as long as I live..."

Religion **Pages:232**

ISBN: ***1-59462-160-8*** *MSRP* ***$17.95***

As a Man Thinketh
James Allen

"This little volume (the result of meditation and experience) is not intended as an exhaustive treatise on the much-written-upon subject of the power of thought. It is suggestive rather than explanatory, its object being to stimulate men and women to the discovery and perception of the truth that by virtue of the thoughts which they choose and encourage..."

Inspirational/Self Help **Pages:80**

ISBN: ***1-59462-231-0*** *MSRP* ***$9.45***

The Enchanted April
Elizabeth Von Arnim

It began in a woman's club in London on a February afternoon, an uncomfortable club, and a miserable afternoon when Mrs. Wilkins, who had come down from Hampstead to shop and had lunched at her club, took up The Times from the table in the smoking-room...

Fiction **Pages:368**

ISBN: ***1-59462-150-0*** *MSRP* ***$23.45***

Lightning Source UK Ltd.
Milton Keynes UK
10 September 2009

143532UK00001B/128/A